37th Congress, 2d Session. } SENATE.

PRELIMINARY REPORT

ON

THE EIGHTH CENSUS.

1860.

By JOS. C. G. KENNEDY,
SUPERINTENDENT.

WASHINGTON:
GOVERNMENT PRINTING OFFICE.
1862.

IN THE SENATE OF THE UNITED STATES, *May* 24, 1862.

Resolved, That there be printed and bound for the use of the Senate forty-seven thousand five hundred copies of the Preliminary Report on the Eighth Census, and two thousand five hundred copies for the use of the Department of the Interior; and that the same be printed at the government printing establishment under the supervision of the Superintendent of the Census.

Attest:

J. W. FORNEY, *Secretary*.

LETTER

OF

THE SECRETARY OF THE INTERIOR,

COMMUNICATING

A preliminary report on the Eighth Census.

MAY 21, 1862.—Referred to the Joint Committee on Printing and ordered to be printed.

DEPARTMENT OF THE INTERIOR,
Washington, May 19, 1862.

SIR: I have the honor to communicate a preliminary report on the Eighth Census, by the Superintendent of that work.

Very respectfully, your obedient servant,

CALEB B. SMITH,
Secretary.

The PRESIDENT *of the Senate.*

INDEX.

	Page.
AFRICAN RACE, future increase of, in the United States	7
AGRICULTURAL IMPLEMENTS—	
Total value of	61
Increase of value in different sections	61
Decrease of, in some Southern States	61
Tabular statement of	169
AGRICULTURE—	
Army worm destructive to	82
Associations, beneficial influence of farmers	100
Connexion of, with branches of industry	81
Cotton crop increased 110 per cent. in 10 years	84
tabular statement of	201
Dairy products	84
Great increase of	80
Butter, quantity produced	84
Cheese, quantity produced	84
nutritious and rich in flesh-forming constituents	84
exportation of	84
should be used in the army	84
Tabular statement of agricultural products in United States	196
Diseases of animals	100
Veterinary surgeons and schools needed	100, 101
Domestic animals, numbers of, estimated	84
Draining, great progress in estimation and practice	90
tile factories established	90
effects of underground	90
instance of success in	90
implement for making furrow and laying pipe	90
Exhibitions, beneficial influence of	100
Grain, aphis destructive to	82
Hay, quantity of	89
crop may be increased by introduction of best varieties of	89
Illinois the great cattle-raising State	80
Immense saving in Great Britain by new implements of	81
Implements, tables of value of	169
Improvements, progress in	80–89
animal force available through machinery	89
employment of steam	90
Indian corn, amount of crop and increase	84
indispensable to Great Britain	80
Influence of London Exhibition of 1851 on	80
Influence of, on Europe	80
Insects injurious to	83
Instruments adapted to tillage and harvesting	81
Introduction of new plants and animals	80
Irrigation necessary in Utah, New Mexico, and California	90
Meteorological observations, importance of, to farmer	101
Molasses, number of gallons imported	87
derived from Chinese sugar-cane	87
number of gallons made	88
New domestic animals	100
Orchards, product principally of apples and peaches	89
improved varieties of fruit introduced	89
pear affected by blight	89
Periodicals, forty, devoted to farming and gardening published	100
Products of, abundant at this important crisis	81

Page.

AGRICULTURE—
Ratio of increase greater than of population 80
Schools and colleges, but few now established 100
Sheep, number of, to square mile 85, 86
a necessity to good husbandry 86
fine wool varieties of 86
coarse mutton-breeds of 86
importation of foreign breeds 86
Randall's treatise on fine wool sheep-husbandry 87
Silk, production of 89
value of silks imported 89
Sugar, amount paid for imported 87
supplied by Chinese sugar-cane 87
maple, amount of product 88
Sorghum saccharatum or Chinese sugar-cane 80
Supply of staples adequate to any contingency 80
Threshing, winnowing, and cleaning machines 82
Threshing instruments, progress of invention of 90
primitive modes employed 91
ancient and modern forms of 91
use of machines proposed in Virginia in 1650 92
history of adoption of, in Great Britain 92
first inventor, Jethro Tull 92
Sterling's improvements 92
Evers's machine 93
Meikle's improved machine 93
description of Lee's 94
steam applied to 94
Sylvester, of Maryland, roller introduced by 95
first patent issued in this country, 1791 96
Mulliken's inventions 96
machines of Anderson, Wardrop, Prentiss, &c 96
patents from 1803–1810, and subsequently 97
Allen's threshing-machine 97
machines exhibited at World's Fair in New York, 1853 98
trial of machines at Paris 99
success of Pitt's American thresher 99
portable steam-engines for farms 99, 100
Tobacco, amount of crop 88
effect in impoverishing the soil 88
increase of product 88
raised in Northern States 88
Value of animals slaughtered 85
manufactures depending on 85
Various applications of invention to 81
View of condition and progress of 80
Wheat, quantity grown 82
increase of 82
Dr. Fitch on depredatory insects 82
Wine, very large increase in product 88
domestic wines increased 88
amount paid for imported 89
Wool, quantity of, produced 85
Wool, imports of 85
exports of 85
prices of 85
Randall's treatise on 87
general tables of productions of 196
ALCOHOL, manufacture of 65
APHIS, grain, Dr. Fitch's account of 82
ASSISTANT MARSHALS, number of (4,417) 1
AUSTRALIA, compared with United States, as adapted to production of wool 86

Page.

BANKS—
Increase of, an evidence of prosperity 75
Action of, the index of production and trade 76
Great expansion of 76
Comparison of condition of, with imports, exports, and population 76
Influence of failure of foreign harvests on 79
Prosperity of, in 1850 76
Great accumulation of capital 77
Number of, in New York city 77
Clearing system 77
Tables of 192
BEER, manufacture of 65
BENZINE OR BENZOLE 74
BLIND—
Taught in deaf and dumb institutions 36
First establishment for, in Paris, 1260 41
Haüy's experiments for instructing 41
First school for, in Great Britain, 1791 41
List of institutions for, in Great Britain and Ireland, when founded, and number of inmates 41
Associations for the relief of, in Great Britain 42
Institutions for, on the continent of Europe 42
Institutions for, in the United States, when founded, and number of inmates 43
Proportion of, in several States, and to whole population 44
Comparison of proportions of, in United States and Europe 45
Influence of climate on number of 46
Causes of blindness 46
Systems of printin· for 46
Books for, now published 47
Employment of, worthy of consideration 48
BOOK AND NEWSPAPER PRINTING 63
BOOTS AND SHOES—
Great number of operatives in manufacture of 68
Number of establishments for making 68
Capital employed in manufacture of 68
Value of manufactured 69
Machinery used for manufacture 69
Table of 185
BREWERIES, number and value of 65
BRITISH CENSUS FOR 1861, facts from 112
BUREAU OF STATISTICS—
Establishment of, recommended 110
Importance of, to Congress and the country 111
CANALS AND RIVER IMPROVEMENTS, tabular statement of 238
CABINET FURNITURE, manufacture of 69
CANDLES, tables of 189
CENSUS OF GREAT BRITAIN FOR 1861, facts from 112
CENSUS OF IRELAND 113
CENSUS, EIGHTH, OF UNITED STATES, number of persons employed in taking, &c 1
CHEMICAL MANUFACTURES, increase of 70
CHEMISTRY, improvements in products of 70
CHOLERA, ravages of, in 1849 23
CITIES, population of 117
CLIMATE, effect of, on mortality 23,22
CLOCKS, manufacture of 69
CLOTHING—
Labor employed in manufacture of 64
Table of 175
COAL—
Value of product of 63
Great increase in product of 63
Anthracite, statistics of product 63
Bituminous, statistics of product 63

Page.

COAL, table of ... 173
COLONIZATION OF FREE COLORED, average 400 per annum ... 8
COLORED EMIGRANTS, number of, sent to Liberia ... 8
COLORED RACE, future increase of, in the United States ... 7
COLUMBIA INSTITUTION FOR DEAF, DUMB, AND BLIND, account of ... 35
COMMERCE more easily appreciated than manufactures ... 60
CONCLUSION OF REPORT and general summary of results ... 118
CONGRESS, number of members of ... 20
COPPER, table of ... 173
COTTON, used in woollen manufactures ... 67
COTTON GOODS—
- Value of, manufactured ... 65
- Ratio of increase of manufacture of ... 66, 65
- Rate *per capita* of production and consumption ... 66
- Number of hands employed in manufacture ... 66
- Average product of labor of operatives ... 66
- Number of spindles ... 66
- Quantity of cotton used, per spindle ... 66
- Table of ... 180

CRASH, manufacture of ... 67
DEAF AND DUMB—
- Historical references to ... 32
- Instruction of, in England and Germany ... 33
- Peculiarities of different systems of instructing ... 34
- Number of schools for ... 35, 36
- Grant by Congress to American asylum for ... 35
- Numbers of, in Europe ... 36
- Number of, regulated by general laws ... 37
- Proportion of, to population ... 37
- color ... 39
- Effect of emigration on number of ... 39
- Influence of climate and topography on number of ... 40
- Tables of ... 168

DEATHS—
- In United States for the year ending June 1, 1860 ... 22
- Ratio of, to living population, by States ... 22
- Of foreigners in 1850 and 1860 ... 23
- Census of, deficient in numbers ... 24
- In the United States by months and sexes ... 27
- Reported by Surgeon General ... 28
- Corrections in number of, estimate of ... 28
- Influence of climate on ... 28
- Classified by ages and by sex ... 29
- Ratio of, in Europe ... 30
- Annual, in United States ... 30
- Corrections for deficient returns of ... 30
- From different diseases ... 115, 116
- Caused by violence or accident ... 116
- From suicide ... 117
- General tables of ... 138, 142, 162

DISEASES AND CAUSES OF DEATH—
- Statistics of ... 114
- Rule for estimating the number of sick ... 114
- Epidemics and endemics ... 114
- Zymotic diseases ... 115, 114
- Prevailing during the year 1850 ... 115

DISEASES—
- Peculiarities of some forms of ... 116
- The most fatal in United States ... 116

DURATION OF LIFE among colored persons ... 6
EDUCATION, general facts relative to ... 19

	Page.
DEATHS, aid by government to promote	20
ELECTRO-METALLURGY, improvements in, applied to cheap jewelry	69
EMPLOYEES IN CENSUS OFFICE	1
EMANCIPATION, gradual, provided for by different States	10
ESTATE, REAL AND PERSONAL, increase in value, absolute and relative	79
EXPECTATION OF LIFE among colored persons	6
EXPENDITURES for the Census	1
FEMALES AND MALES, relative number of	9
FIRE-ARMS—	
Improvements in	75
Reputation of American	75
Machinery for	75
Enfield rifle	75
Armstrong gun	75
Additional facts relative to	118
FISHERIES—	
Decrease in value of product of	70
Value of oyster	70
Value of whale	70
Whale and fish oils supplied by lard and coal oils	70
Table of	188
FLAX—	
Machinery for spinning perfected	68
A substitute for cotton	68
FLAX COTTON, manufacture of, commenced	68
FLOUR AND GRIST MILLS—	
Product of	64
Table of	177
FOREIGNERS, deaths of, in 1850 and 1860	23
FOSSIL FUEL	63
FOUNDERIES, value of productions of	63
FREE COLORED POPULATION—	
Increase of	6
Mortality of, in New England, &c	6
FRUIT	89
FUGITIVE SLAVES	11, 12, 137
FURNITURE—	
Value of, made in 1860	69
Growth of manufacture	69
Employment to skilled labor given	69
Tabular statement of	186
GAS, ILLUMINATING—	
Quantity and value of, manufactured	70
First mention of, production of	92
Table of	187
GOLD MINES, decrease in product of, in Atlantic States	63
GRIST AND FLOUR MILLS, product of	64
GROUPING OF STATES by situation, productions, &c.	8
IDIOCY, causes of	57
IDIOTIC—	
Number of, decreased in ratio to population	57
Incapable of mental improvement	57
Number of in United States in 1860	58
Proportion of, to population	58
IMMIGRANTS—	
Allowances and addition to be made in considering number of	14
Number of, in decades	14
Ages and sexes of, on arrival	15
Ages of, by decades	15
Residences selected by	16
Deaths of, on voyage	16

Page.

IMMIGRANTS—
Occupations of ... 16,17
Number of ... 17
Nativities of ... 18
IMMIGRATION—
Prior to 1800 ... 12
Influence of, on value of lands ... 12
INDIANS, table of population of tribes of ... 136
INDIAN SLAVERY, west of Arkansas ... 10,11
INDUSTRIAL PRODUCTS ... 59,190
INSANE—
Great and beneficial change in treatment of ... 48
First institution for, in America ... 48
Pennsylvania hospital for, opened 1752 ... 48
Virginia hospital for, opened 1773 ... 48
New York hospital for, opened 1791 ... 48
Friends' Asylum, in Philadelphia, 1817 ... 49
McLean Asylum, Massachusetts, 1818 ... 50
Asylums for, established from 1815 to 1840 ... 50
Association of medical superintendents of institutions for ... 51
American Journal of ... 51
Asylums established, 1850 to 1860 ... 51
Government hospital for, in Washington, account of ... 52
Private establishments for ... 53
Table showing number of, in United States, in 1860, (free and slave) ... 57
INSANITY, intemperance the most productive cause of ... 56
INSECTS, injury from, to crops, and means of prevention ... 82
INSTRUMENTS, MUSICAL, manufacture of ... 69
INSURANCE—
Progress of, accompanies commerce and trade ... 78
Reasons for ... 78
Number of companies and amounts of risks in Massachusetts ... 78
Number of companies and amounts of risks in other States ... 79
Amount at risk in all the companies ... 79
Amount of losses in 1860 ... 79
INTERNAL IMPROVEMENTS, influence of ... 80
INTERNATIONAL STATISTICAL CONGRESS ... 110
IRON—
Large productions of, an indication of progress ... 61,62
Manufacture of, related to other interests ... 61,62
Pig, quantity, value, and increase of ... 61
table of ... 170
Bar and other rolled, quantity, value, and increase of ... 61
table of ... 170
Materials for manufacture of, abundant ... 62
Independence of foreign supplies of ... 62
Founderies, value of productions of ... 63
table of ... 172
JEWELRY—
Manufacture of ... 69
Table of ... 187
KEROSENE OIL ... 73
LEATHER—
Manufacture of ... 68
Importance of, to agriculturists and stock-raisers ... 68
Tanning and currying establishments ... 68
Great number of operatives employed in manufacture of ... 68
Table of ... 184
LIFE TABLES, Halley & Carlisle's ... 31,32
LINEN GOODS—
Manufacture of ... 67

Page.

LINEN GOODS—
Twine, shoe, and other thread mills 68
Flax cotton, improved manufacture of 68
LIQUORS, MALT—
Manufacture of 65
Table of 179
LIQUORS, SPIRITUOUS—
Manufacture of 65
Table of 178
LUMBER, SAWED AND PLANED—
Manufacture of 64
Increase of, and value 64
Improvements in manufactures of 64
Table of 176
MACHINERY—
Manufactures of 62
Value of product of general machinists and millwrights 62
Ratio of increase of, in different sections 62
Tables of 171
MALES AND FEMALES, comparison of relative number 9
MALT LIQUORS—
Increase in manufacture of 65
Value and amount of product 65
Number and location of breweries 65
MANUFACTURES—
Increase exhibited 59
Value of, in 1850 and 1860 59
Increase in value in 10 years 59
Product *per capita* 59
Number of persons supported by 59
Value of, only recognized from Census 60
Influence of, on civilization and wealth 60
Agricultural implements 61
Iron, abundant supply of materials for 62
Machinery 62
Water power abundant for, in United States 62
Sewing-machines 64
Intimate relation of, to agriculture and landed interests 64
Of flour and meal surpass all others in value of products and of raw material consumed 64
Progress of, in Europe 81
Books and newspapers 63
Boots and shoes 68
Cabinet furniture 69
Chemicals 70
Clothing 64
Cotton goods 65
Flour and meal 64
Furnishing goods, ladies' and gentlemen's 64
Furniture 69
Gas 70
Jewelry 69
Leather 68
Linen goods 67
Liquors, malt and spirituous 65
Lumber, sawed and planed 64
Musical instruments 69
New England rum from imported molasses 65
Salt 70
Sewing silks 68
Woollen goods 67
Table of 191
MANUMISSION OF SLAVES, statistics of 11

Page.
MANUMISSION OF SLAVES, tables of ... 137
MARSHALS—
Number of, (64) ... 1
Payments to ... 1
MECHANIC ARTS, importance and influence of ... 60
MILLS, FLOUR AND GRIST—
Product of ... 64
Increase and value of, in different sections of United States ... 65
Largest ... 65
MINES—
Coal, iron, lead, copper, zinc, gold, silver, &c ... 63
Tables of ... 173
MINING, large amount of capital and labor employed in ... 63
MISSISSIPPI RIVER, climatic effects of ... 26
MORTALITY—
Excessive among free colored in New England, &c ... 6
Statistics of ... 22
Importance and interest of statistics of ... 22
Rate of ... 22
In 1849, caused by cholera ... 23
Relative, in different sections ... 25
Effect of temperature and climate on ... 25
In the great Atlantic plain ... 26
In the alluvial tract of the Mississippi ... 26
In the Alleghany region ... 26
On the Pacific coast ... 27
In the northeastern and northwestern States ... 27
According to seasons, months, and sexes ... 27
According to *age* and *sex* ... 29
Ratio of, in Europe ... 30
Among different classes and occupations ... 31
Compared with topography ... 31
Comparison of, in cities and country ... 31
Importance to sanitary improvements in cities ... 31
Halley and Carlisle's life tables ... 31
Tables of ... 139–142–162
MUSICAL INSTRUMENTS—
Manufacture of ... 69
Table of ... 186
NEWSPAPERS—
Influence and statistics of ... 63–101
Table of ... 211
NORTHWEST, great resources of ... 5
NOTES ... 117
OIL, scarcity of whale and fish ... 70
Increased production of lard ... 70
Artificial and natural sources of ... 70
OIL, COAL—
Made, in 1846, by Dr. Gesner, of Nova Scotia ... 73
First company on Long Island ... 73
Breckinridge works on the Ohio ... 73
Candles manufactured from ... 74
Number of refineries or factories ... 74
OIL, PETROLEUM—
Rock or mineral ... 71
Found in foreign countries ... 71
History of discovery of ... 71
Bowditch and Drake's operations, Titusville, Pa., 1857 ... 72
Wells and borings for, in 1859 and 1860 ... 72
Statistics of trade in, and export of ... 73–72
Number of establishments for refining ... 74–73

Page.

Oil, Petroleum—
- Manufacture of benzine, benzole, and candles from........ 74
- Adapted to manufacture of gas........ 74
- New and beautiful dyes produced from........ 74

Paper, manufacture of........ 63

Payments—
- Amount of, to marshals, &c........ 1
- Suspension of, to some officers........ 1

Periodicals—
- Statistics of........ 100, 101
- Table of........ 211

Personal Estate—
- Increase in value of........ 79
- Table of........ 194, 195

Petroleum Oil........ 71

Piano Fortes, manufacture of........ 69

Plated Wares, manufactures of........ 69

Popular Representation fixed by law in 1850........ 20

Population in 1860, general table, by States........ 2

Population—
- Influx of foreign........ 3
- General rate of increase, in decades........ 3
- Table of decennial increase........ 133
- Density of, in New England States........ 4
- Effect of manufactures and commerce on........ 4
- Limit to increase of, in rural districts........ 3
- Gain of Indiana, Michigan, Wisconsin, and Iowa........ 5
- Of slaveholding States........ 5
- Actual gain of, in slaveholding States........ 5
- Of free States, and increase........ 5
- Disproportion in rate of gain of, between North and South........ 5
- Progress of, from 1790 to 1860........ 5
- Progress of free colored........ 6, 7
- Progress of slave........ 6, 7
- Estimate of, in the years 1870, 1880, 1890, and 1900........ 7, 8
- Of States by groups or sections........ 8
- Table of, by sexes........ 134
- Relation of, to wealth........ 80
- Table of, by States and Territories........ 129
- Table of, by counties........ 245
- Of cities and towns........ 117
- Table of........ 242
- Table of Indian........ 136

Press—
- The public........ 63, 101
- Origin and gradual development........ 102
- Earliest English newspaper........ 102
- Number and increase of different classes of papers........ 103
- Circulation of newspapers........ 103

Printing—
- Influence of diffusion of........ 63
- Value of book........ 63
- Table of........ 174

Printing Press—
- Influence of, on character of our army........ 63
- Used by soldiers in the field, emigrants, &c........ 63
- Effects of unprecedented increase of........ 63

Printing Paper, increase in manufacture of........ 63

Products of Industry........ 59–190

Progress, causes of our national........ 9

Property, value of and increase........ 79

Page.

RAILROADS—

Great expenditures in construction of ... 77
Progress of, during decade, 1850–'60 ... 103
Number of miles in operation ... 103
History of different principal roads ... 104
Tonnage of railroads in New York for 1860 ... 105
Massachusetts ... 105
Estimate of tonnage of all the roads in United States ... 105
Length of interior roads and tons transported ... 106
In the United States ... 214
In Alabama ... 223
In Arkansas ... 224
In California ... 229
In Connecticut ... 217
In Delaware ... 220
In Florida ... 223
In Georgia ... 222
In Illinois ... 227
In Indiana ... 226
In Iowa ... 226
In Kentucky ... 225
In Louisiana ... 224
In Maine ... 214
In Maryland ... 221
In Massachusetts ... 215
In Michigan ... 227
In Mississippi ... 223
In Missouri ... 229
In New Hampshire ... 214
In New Jersey ... 218
In New York ... 217
In North Carolina ... 222
In Ohio ... 225
In Oregon ... 229
In Pennsylvania ... 219
In Rhode Island ... 217
In South Carolina ... 222
In Tennessee ... 224
In Texas ... 224
In Vermont ... 215
In Virginia ... 221
In Wisconsin ... 228
Total in the United States ... 230
City passenger ... 231
In Boston ... 231
In Brooklyn ... 232
In Cincinnati ... 233
In Hoboken ... 232
In New York ... 232
In Philadelphia ... 232
In St. Louis ... 233
Recapitulation of ... 233
Number of miles in operation ... 234
In Gulf States ... 235
In Interior States North ... 235
In Interior States South ... 235
In Middle Atlantic States ... 234
In New England States ... 234
In Pacific States ... 235
In Southern Atlantic States ... 234
Total United States ... 235

Page.

RAILROADS—
Number of miles brought into use during each year from 1851 to 1860, inclusive ... 236
In Gulf States ... 237
In Interior States North ... 237
In Interior States South ... 237
In Middle Atlantic States ... 236
In New England States ... 236
In Pacific States ... 237
In Southern Atlantic States ... 236
Total United States ... 237
REAL ESTATE—
Increase in value of ... 79
Table of ... 194
REBELLION, the influence of, on our prosperity ... 118, 119
RELATIVE POSITION OF STATES IN AREA, POPULATION, &c., diagram and table ... 117
REPRESENTATION—
Preponderance of, advancing westward ... 21
Comparison of, in old and new States ... 21
REPRESENTATIVES—
Apportionment of ... 20
Decrease in number of ... 20
Number fixed by law in 1850 ... 20
Number of, in 38th Congress ... 20
Increase in number of ... 20
RIBBONS, manufacture of ... 68
RUM, manufacture of ... 65
SALT—
Number of establishments for making ... 70
Value of production of ... 70
States where produced ... 70
Sixty per cent. made in New York State ... 70
Table of ... 188
SANITARY improvement ... 31
SCHOOLS—
Scholars in, during 1860 ... 19
Appropriation of land for ... 20
SEWING MACHINES—
Export of ... 64
Table of ... 174
SHEEP RAISING, greatly extended since 1850 ... 67
SHIPS, number and class of, built in each State in 1860 ... 107
SILK, chief manufactures of, consist of dress trimmings, coach lace, &c ... 68
SILKS, SEWING, manufacture of ... 68
SILVER WARE, manufacture of ... 69
SLAVERY—
Origin of ... 9
Abolition of, in Northern States ... 10
Indian tribes maintaining ... 11, 10
When and where abolished ... 10
SLAVES—
Number of, and rate of increase ... 6
Tables of manumitted and fugitive ... 137
Introduction of Indian, in West Indies ... 9
Introduction of Africans into Brazil, &c ... 9
Introduction of Africans into United States ... 9
Not to be introduced from abroad into Virginia after 1778 ... 10
Not to be introduced from abroad into Maryland after 1783 ... 10
Fugitive ... 12, 11
Manumission of ... 11
SLAVE-TRADE of different nations ... 10
SOAP AND CANDLES, tables of ... 189

Page.

South America compared with United States as adapted to production of wool 86
Spirits, manufacture of, from domestic materials 95 per cent........ 65
State Registry of births, marriages, and deaths........ 24
Steam Engines, tables of value of........ 171
Stove Founderies, extensive, in New York........ 63
Tanning and Currying Establishments........ 68
Taxation, assessment of property for........ 79
Territories, increase in number of........ 3
Tonnage of the United States—
Decrease by decay, wreck, &c........ 106
Amount built in each decade since 1815........ 106
Number and class of vessels built in each State........ 107
Statistics of, showing a loss of 2½ per cent. per annum........ 108
Tonnage of the United States—
Tonnage owned in New York and built in 1859–'61........ 109
Amount built in different States........ 109
Value of, in United States in 1861........ 109
Vaccination........ 31
Value of Real and Personal Estate........ 79
Vessels, number and class of, built in each State in 1860........ 107
Warfare, implements of, improvements in........ 75
Watches, manufacture of........ 69
Wealth—
Increase of, in real and personal estate........ 79
Estimate of, to be modified by residence........ 80
Relation of population to........ 80
Effect of internal improvements on........ 80
Wheat........ 82
Whiskey, manufacture of........ 65
Wool—
Quantity of, produced........ 67
Large quantities of, still imported........ 67
Woollen Goods—
Increase in, and value of manufacture........ 67
Number of establishments........ 67
Capital invested in........ 67
Hands, spindles, and looms employed........ 67
Quantity of wool consumed in........ 67
Proportion of, made in different States........ 67
Shipment of wool to Europe........ 97
Importance of extension of........ 67
Essential for clothing in our climate........ 67
Importation of wool still necessary for........ 67
Tabular statement of........ 182

PRELIMINARY REPORT

ON

THE EIGHTH CENSUS.

CENSUS OFFICE, DEPARTMENT OF THE INTERIOR,
Washington, May 20, 1862.

SIR: It seems proper, in view of the general desire expressed for information relating to the Eighth Census, that a synopsis of the results should be made public at as early a moment and to such an extent as the condition of the work will justify. The unusual interest manifested on this subject induces me to present a preliminary report which, while it may want completeness, and in some of its details fail of that minute accuracy wherein the work when completed, it is hoped, will not be deficient, may be relied on as being substantially correct and entitled to confidence.

It is a subject of congratulation that the unhappy state of affairs which has interposed to impede the ordinary course of events has not interfered with the rendition of complete returns from all sections of the country, and that we are enabled to represent the condition of all the great elements of a nation's prosperity as they existed in the year 1860—a circumstance, probably, of no trifling significance in facilitating the early and happy settlement of our domestic troubles.

In the collection of the details to be embodied in the Eighth Census there have been employed sixty-four marshals, comprising those of all the United States judicial districts, under whose direction, and that of those special agents appointed for unorganized territory, there have been employed 4,417 assistants, upon whom devolved the duty of enumerating the people and collecting the other statistics required by law. To these officers there has been paid the sum of $1,045,206 75; the sum of $247,000 remaining suspended on account of the presumed or known disloyalty of officers, or the existence of some good reason for suspending payments. There are employed in this office at the present time 168 clerks and 16 messengers, laborers, and watchmen. The wants of the War Department have made it seem proper to allow that branch of the government the services of several clerks, who were for a considerable time engaged in the office of the Quartermaster General, while the demands of other government departments, committees in Congress, and State legislatures, for information only to be had from the census records, and which could not be disregarded, have seriously impeded the progress of this work, and thrown charges upon our fund which it has appeared impossible to avoid. Nevertheless, we have not transcended, and it is my hope that our expenditures will not exceed the appropriations heretofore made for this service.

While in the prosecution of their duties the marshals were generally faithful to their trusts, and manifested an anxious desire for the proper completion of their duties, it is stated, with regret, that there were one or two exceptions, wherein the cupidity of the officer not only involved a violation of law, but wrought injustice to his assistants and retarded the progress of the work.

In my review of the condition and progress of the various interests which comprise the census, my statements are not limited to the exhibition of facts as they are presented in the returns of the Eighth Census. It seemed a duty to make the report one of the past as well as the present, and the more so while in doing this the opportunity is afforded of presenting statistical facts in a more popular form and agreeable dress.

By a liberality unprecedented in the history of the world, our federal and State governments having munificently provided for the care of the children of affliction by the endowment of hospitals for the insane and idiotic, and institutions for the education of the deaf and dumb, and the blind; and as a record of these unfortunates is now made in every census, and there exists no official history of their numbers at different periods, or of the care which has been devoted to them, it has been my endeavor to give a correct narrative on these subjects, and one which it is believed will prove acceptable to Congress and contribute to the diffusion of useful information throughout the country. Having indulged in no theories, with no prejudices to sustain, it will be my aim to present facts impartially, in the hope of enjoying your approval, and administering to the gratification and information of the country.

Having had the exclusive superintendence of the taking of two censuses under the law of May 23, 1850, and compiled the principal details, my opinions are confirmed in the general excellence of the plan, and in the belief that with each enumeration the statistics are collected with increased accuracy and greater ease.

POPULATION.

(Appendix—Table No. 1.)

The subjoined table exhibits the population returns of the Eighth Census, and presents a complete view of the number of inhabitants of the United States and Territories in 1860, according to the enumeration then taken in pursuance of the Constitution:

Alabama	964,201	New Jersey	672,035
Arkansas	435,450	New York	3,880,735
California	379,994	North Carolina	992,622
Connecticut	460,147	Ohio	2,339,502
Delaware	112,216	Oregon	52,465
Florida	140,425	Pennsylvania	2,906,115
Georgia	1,057,286	Rhode Island	174,620
Illinois	1,711,951	South Carolina	703,708
Indiana	1,350,428	Tennessee	1,109,801
Iowa	674,948	Texas	604,215
Kansas	107,206	Vermont	315,098
Kentucky	1,155,684	Virginia	1,596,318
Louisiana	708,002	Wisconsin	775,881
Maine	628,279	Colorado Territory	34,277
Maryland	687,049	Dakota Territory	4,837
Massachusetts	1,231,066	Nebraska Territory	28,841
Michigan	749,113	Nevada Territory	6,857
Minnesota	173,855	New Mexico Territory	93,516
Mississippi	791,305	Utah Territory	40,273
Missouri	1,182,012	Washington Territory	11,594
New Hampshire	326,073	District of Columbia	75,080

Though the number of States has increased during the last decennial period from thirty-one to thirty-four, and five new Territories have been organized, the United States has received no accessions of territory within that term, except a narrow strip to the southward of the Colorado river, along the Mexican line, not yet inhabited. As general good health prevailed, and peace reigned throughout the country, there was no apparent cause of disturbance or interruption to the natural progress of population. It is true that the very large immigration from Europe, together with an influx of considerable magnitude from Asia to California, has added largely to the augmentation which the returns show to have taken place during the decade.

In comparing the gain of any class of the population, or of the whole of it, one decade with another, the rate per cent. is not a full test of advancement. The *rate* of gain necessarily diminishes with the density of population, while the absolute increase continues unabated. The actual increase of the entire free and slave population from 1850 to 1860, omitting the Indian tribes, was 8,225,464, and the rate per cent. is set down at 35.46; while from 1840 to 1850 the positive increment of all classes was 6,122,423, yet the ratio of gain was 35.87 per cent. The two decades from 1800 to 1810, and from 1840 to 1850, were marked by the great historical facts of the annexation of Louisiana, and the acquisition of Texas, New Mexico, and California. Each of these regions contributed considerably to the population of the country, and we accordingly find that during those terms there was a ratio of increase in the whole body of the people greater by a small fraction than shown by the table annexed for the decade preceding the Eighth Census. The preponderance of gain, however, for that decennial term above all the others since 1790, is signally large. No more striking evidence can be given of the rapid advancement of our country in the first element of national progress than that the increase of its inhabitants during the last ten years is greater by more than 1,000,000 of souls than the whole population in 1810, and nearly as great as the entire number of people in 1820. That the whole of this gain is not from natural increase, but is, in part, derived from the influx of foreigners seeking here homes for themselves and their children, is a fact which may justly enhance rather than detract from the satisfaction wherewith we should regard this augmentation of our numbers.

Thus far in our history no State has declined in population. Vermont has remained nearly stationary, and is saved from a positive loss of inhabitants by only one-third of one per cent. New Hampshire, likewise, has gained but slowly, her increment being only 8,097, or two and one-half per cent. on that of 1850. Maine has made the satisfactory increase of 45,110, or 7.74 per cent. The old agricultural States may be said to be filled up, so far as regards the resources adapted to a rural population in the present condition of agricultural science. The conditions of their increase undergo a change upon the general occupation and allotment of their areas. Manufactures and commerce, then, come in to supply the means of subsistence to an excess of inhabitants beyond what the ordinary cultivation of the soil can sustain. This point in the progress of population has been reached, and, perhaps, passed in most, if not all, of the New England States. But while statistical science may demonstrate within narrow limits the number of persons who may extract a subsistence from each square mile of arable land, it cannot compute with any reasonable approach to certainty the additional population, resident on the same soil, which may obtain its living by the thousand branches of artificial industry which the demands of society and civilization have created. This is forcibly illustrated by the returns relative to the three other New England States—Massachusetts, Rhode Island,

and Connecticut—which contain 13,780 square miles. The following table shows their population in 1850 and 1860, and its density at each period.

States.	1850.		1860.	
	Population.	Number of inhabitants to the square mile.	Population.	Number of inhabitants to the square mile.
Massachusetts	994,514	127.49	1,231,066	157.83
Connecticut	370,792	79.33	460,147	98.42
Rhode Island	147,545	112.97	174,620	133.63
	1,412,851	....	1,865,833	....

The aggregate territorial extent of Maine, New Hampshire, and Vermont, is 48,336 square miles; the number of their inhabitants 1,269,450, or 26.26 to the square mile. The stated point of density was passed by the three States named in the table more than fifty years ago, and yet they go on increasing in population with a rapidity as great as at any former period of their history.

South Carolina has gained during the decade 35,201 inhabitants of all conditions, equal to 5.27 per cent. Of this increase 16,825 are whites, and the remainder free colored and slaves. It is perhaps a little remarkable that the relative increase of the free colored class in this State was more considerable than that of any other. As their number, 9,914, is so small as to excite neither apprehension or jealousy among the white race, the increase is probably due both to manumission and natural causes. This State has made slower progress during the last term than any other in the south, having advanced only from 27.28 to 28.72 inhabitants to the square mile.

Tennessee, it will be observed, has made but the moderate gain of 10.68 per cent. for all classes. Of this aggregate increase the whites have gained at the rate of 9.24 per cent. upon 1850, the free colored 13.67, and slaves 15.14.

The next lowest in the rate of increase in the list of southern States is Virginia, whose gain upon her aggregate population, in 1850, was 174,657, equal to 12.29 per cent. The white class gained 152,611, or 17.06 per cent., the slaves 18,337, or 3.88 per cent.

These are examples of the States wherein the population has advanced with slowest progress the past ten years. Turning now to the States which have made the most rapid advance, we find that New York has increased from 3,097,394 to 3,880,735, exhibiting an augmentation of 783,341 inhabitants, being at the rate of 25.29 per cent. The free colored population has fallen off 64 since 1850, a diminution to be accounted for probably by the operation of the fugitive slave law, which induced many colored persons to migrate further north.

The gain of Pennsylvania has been in round numbers 595,000. In that State the free colored have increased about 3,000. The greater mildness of the climate and a milder type of the prejudices connected with this class of population, the result of benevolent influences and its proximity to the slaveholding States, may account for the fact that this race holds its own in Pennsylvania, while undergoing a diminution in the State next adjoining on the north.

Minnesota was chiefly unsettled territory at the date of the Seventh Census; its large present population, as shown by the returns, is therefore nearly clear gain.

The vast region of Texas ten years since was comparatively a wilderness. It has now a population of over 600,000, and the rate of its increase is given as 184 per cent.

Illinois presents the most wonderful example of great, continuous, and healthful increase. In 1830 Illinois contained 157,445 inhabitants; in 1840, 476,183; in 1850, 851,470; in 1860, 1,711,951. The gain during the last decade was, therefore, 860,481, or 101.06 per cent. So large a population, more than doubling itself in ten years, by the regular course of settlement and natural increase, is without a parallel. The condition to which Illinois has attained under the progress of the last thirty years is a monument of the blessings of industry, enterprise, peace, and free institutions.

The growth of Indiana in population, though less extraordinary than that of her neighboring State, has been most satisfactory, her gain during the decade having been 362,000, or more than thirty-six per cent. upon her number in 1850.

Michigan, Wisconsin, and Iowa have participated to the full extent in the surprising development of the northwest. The remarkable healthfulness of the climate of that region seems to more than compensate for its rigors, and the fertility of the new soil leads men eagerly to contend with and overcome the harshness of the elements. The energies thus called into action have, in a few years, made the States of the northwest the granary of Europe, and that section of our Union which, within the recollection of living men, was a wilderness, is now the chief source of supply in seasons of scarcity for the suffering millions of another continent.

Looking cursorily over the returns, it appears that the fifteen slaveholding States contain 12,240,000 inhabitants, of whom 8,039,000 are whites, 251,000 free colored persons, and 3,950,000 are slaves. The actual gain of the whole population in those States from 1850 to 1860, was 2,627,000, equal to 27.33 per cent. The slaves advanced in numbers 749,931, or 23.44 per cent. This does not include the slaves of the District of Columbia, who decreased 502 in the course of the ten years. The nineteen free States and seven Territories, together with the federal District, contained, according to the Eighth Census, 19,201,546 persons, including 27,749 Indians; of whom 18,936,579 were white, and 237,218 free colored. The increase of both classes was 5,598,603, or 41.24 per cent. No more satisfactory indication of the advancing prosperity of the country could be desired than this general and remarkable progress in population. North and south we find instances of unprecedented gains, as in the case of Illinois, just adverted to. In the southwest the great State of Missouri has increased by the number of 500,000 inhabitants, which is within a fraction of 74 per cent. It is due to candor to state that the marked disproportion between the rate of gain in the north and south respectively, is manifestly to some extent caused by the larger number of immigrants who settle in the former section, on account of congeniality of climate, the variety of occupation, the dignity wherewith respectable employment is invested, and the freedom of labor.

Having thus briefly and imperfectly noticed the manner in which the general gain of population during the last ten years has been distributed among the States, we may with advantage examine the progress of the country as a whole, in this respect, from 1790 to 1860. In order to show the progress of the entire population, and of each class for this period, table No. 1 has been prepared, which is hereunto appended.

The figures in that table show considerable uniformity in the rate of progression of the whole population. It has varied in the different decades from $32\frac{6}{10}$ per cent. increase to $36\frac{1}{2}$. The whites, constituting the great bulk of the inhabitants, have governed the ratio of augmentation for the mass. The lowest rate of increase shown for that class was by the census of 1830, namely, a fraction less than 34 per cent. In 1850 it has risen above 38 per cent., and continued to be about the same from 1850 to 1860. The number of free colored persons was small in 1790, and as a condition or class in society it holds about the same position as then. We possess very insufficient means for estimating the natural increase of this division of our population. Their aggregate number has been so continually affected by manumissions, by legislation changing their condition, and to a small extent by emigration, that from these causes, rather than by the ordinary progress of increase, they have reached a total of nearly half a million, and the rate per cent. of their advancement in seventy years, has been equal to that of the whole population, and not very far below that of the whites; and that at the same time they have gained in a ratio nearly one-half greater than the slaves.

In the interval from 1850 to 1860, the total free colored population of the United States increased from 434,449 to 488,005, or at the rate of 12.33 per cent. in ten years, showing an annual increase of one per cent. This result includes the number of slaves liberated and those who have escaped from their owners, together with the natural increase. In the same decade the slave population, omitting those of the Indian tribes west of Arkansas, increased 23.39 per cent., and the white population 37.97 per cent., which rates exceed that of the free colored by twofold, and three or fourfold, respectively. Inversely, these comparisons imply an excessive mortality among the free colored, which is particularly evident in the large cities. Thus, in Boston during the five years ending with 1859, the city registrar observes: "The number of colored births was one less than the number of marriages, and the deaths exceeded the births in the proportion of nearly two to one." In Providence, where a very correct registry has been in operation under the superintendence of Dr. Snow, the deaths are one in twenty-four of the colored; and in Philadelphia during the last six months of the census year, the new city registration gives 148 births against 306 deaths among the free colored. Taking town and country together, however, the results are more favorable. In the State registries of Rhode Island and Connecticut, where the distinction of color has been specified, the yearly deaths of the blacks and mulattoes have generally, though not uniformly, exceeded the yearly births—a high rate of mortality chiefly ascribed to consumption and other diseases of the respiratory system.

Owing, among other causes, to the extremes of climate in the more northern States, and in other States to expulsive enactments of the legislatures, the free colored show a decrease of numbers during the past ten years according to the census, in the following ten States: Arkansas, Florida, Indiana, Maine, Mississippi, New Hampshire, New York, Oregon, Texas, and Vermont.

The free colored have gained eleven thousand in Ohio, three thousand in North Carolina, and nine thousand in Maryland. In the latter State the prejudice against this class appears to exist only to a limited extent, and constituting as it does 12¼ per cent. of the whole population, it forms an important element in the free labor of Maryland.

With regard to the mean duration or expectation of life among colored persons in different localities of the country, reference may be made to some comparative tables published in the census report to Congress in 1852, page 13. The returns of 1860, when cast into the same form, would, doubtless, exhibit similar results. In a simple statement, when viewed apart from the liberations or manumission in the southern States, the aggregate free colored in this country must represent *nearly* what is termed "a stationary population," characterized by an equality of the current of births and deaths.

There are now in the United States about 4,000,000 slaves. They have advanced to that vast number from about 700,000 in 1790. The rate of progress of this class of population has been somewhat more fluctuating than can be easily accounted for. Why, for example, they should have increased over 30 per cent. from 1820 to 1830, and only $23\frac{8}{10}$ per cent. during the next decade, does not appear from any facts bearing upon their condition during this period. It may, perhaps, be attributed to the large emigration to Texas, prior to 1840, which, doubtless, exerted no small influence upon the ordinary progress of the slave population in the United States during that decade. There is no importation nor emigration of slaves into or from the country, and it would seem that they should be subject to no cause of increase or decadence except what nature decrees. This law is that of gradual and steady increase, and under it the total number of slaves in 1860 should have been 4,130,000, had they gained at the same ratio as during the preceding ten years.

It is important to observe the growing disparity between the pace at which the white and colored races are advancing in this country. While the whites, from 1850 to 1860, gained 38 per cent., the slaves and free colored increased somewhat less than 22 per cent., and the total increase of the free colored and slaves for 70 years was but 485 per cent. against 757 per cent. for the whites.

With regard to the future increase of the African race in this country, various extravagant speculations have been recently promulgated. An attentive survey of the statistics of the census will guide to a more satisfactory approximation. The following summary exhibits the numbers of the colored race and their rates of increase during the last seventy years:

Census of slaves and free colored.

Census of—	Free colored.	Increase, per cent.	Slaves.	Increase, per cent.	Free colored and slaves.	Increase, per cent.
1790	59,466	....	697,897	....	757,363	....
1800	108,395	82.28	893,041	27.97	1,001,436	32.23
1810	186,446	72.00	1,191,364	33.40	1,337,810	37.58
1820	233,524	25.23	1,538,038	28.79	1,771,562	28.58
1830	319,599	36.87	2,009,043	30.61	2,328,642	31.44
1840	386,303	20.87	2,487,455	23.81	2,873,758	23.41
1850	434,449	12.46	3,204,313	28.82	3,638,762	26.62
1860	482,122	10.97	3,953,587	23.38	4,435,709	21.90

Here the rate of increase will be seen at a glance to have been gradually diminishing, especially during the last thirty years. The greater apparent increase among slaves from 1840 to 1850 is connected with the admission of Texas in 1845. For the future, the rate will probably continue to diminish; and to apply unchanged the rate of the last ten years, must give results exceeding, rather than falling short of the truth. The following estimates, therefore, have been computed on the assumption that the rate of the last ten years, 21.9, shall continue twenty years longer, or until 1880, after which the rate is diminished to 20.0 until the close of the present century, for the colored population. And, to facilitate comparison, the next column exhibits the aggregate of whites, free colored, and slaves, based on the well-known and very correct assumption of a mean annual increase of three per cent.:

Probable future population of the United States.

Year.	Free colored and slaves.	Aggregate of whites and colored.	Percentage of colored.
1870	5,407,130	42,328,432	12.77
1880	6,591,292	56,450,241	11.68
1890	7,909,550	77,263,989	10.24
1900	9,491,459	100,355,802	9.46

Thus, according to the best estimates, the total population of the United States at the close of the present century will be about a hundred millions. All observing persons will perceive that the relative increase of the whites exceeds that of the colored, and that the disparity is gradually becoming more and more favorable to this part of our population. Leaving the issue of the present civil war for time to determine, it should be observed, if large numbers of slaves shall be hereafter emancipated, so many will be transferred from a faster to a slower rate of increase. In this case, nine millions of the colored, in the year 1900, appears a large estimate. Of these a great portion will be of mixed descent, since in 1850 one-ninth part of the whole colored class were returned as mulattoes. In regard to emigration, the number colonized by the American Colonization Society and its auxiliaries during the past ten years, has averaged about 400 per annum, besides the Africans captured on several slave-ships. The total number of colored emigrants sent to Liberia from 1820 to 1856 inclusive, is stated at 9,502, of whom 3,676 were free born.

In the report on the Seventh Census, for 1851, a table was published in which the States were arranged into sections or groups according to geographical situation, productions, climate, the pursuits of their inhabitants, and other prominent characteristics. The progress of these groups combined is that of the entire republic, and the opportunity of observing the growth of each of them separately, enables us the more satisfactorily to ascertain the advancement of the whole country. The table is therefore here repeated, being extended so as to embrace the results of the census of 1860.

States.	Area in square miles.	1850.		1860.	
		Population.	No. of inhabitants to square mile.	Population.	No. of inhabitants to square mile.
New England States, (6)	63,272	2,728,106	43.11	3,135,283	49.55
Middle States, including Maryland, Delaware, and Ohio, (6)	151,760	8,553,713	56.36	10,597,661	69.83
Coast planting States, including South Carolina, Georgia, Florida, Alabama, Mississippi, and Louisiana, (6)	286,077	3,557,872	12.43	4,364,927	15.25
Central slave States, Virginia, North Carolina, Tennessee, Kentucky, Missouri, and Arkansas, (6)	309,210	5,167,276	16.71	6,471,887	20.93
Northwestern States, Indiana, Illinois, Michigan, Wisconsin, Iowa, Minnesota, and Kansas, (7)	250,295	2,734,945	10.92	5,543,382	22.14
Texas	237,321	212,592	0.89	604,215	2 55
California	188,982	165,000	0.87	379,994	2.01

Without going into the minutiæ of decimal computations, an inspection of the above table will show that the great middle States have gained in density 25 per cent., and the northwestern group 100. The growth of those States, as of California and Texas, represents the settlement of new lands and the development of agricultural, mining, and pastoral pursuits. The production of grain, cotton, and wool, the rearing of sheep, horned stock, and swine, and the abundance of gold and other valuable minerals, give employment to the population, add to its numbers, and augment the wealth of the State. But it cannot be overlooked that there are other portions of the earth of equal extent which possess similar natural advantages, but exhibit no such proofs of prosperity as the divisions of our country referred to. The causes of the noble and beneficent result in our case are attributable to the attraction of our institutions, the freedom of industry, the cheapness and fertility of our lands, and, above all, the long enjoyment of, and, as we believed, perfect guarantees of peace. Let us hope that the experience of the now passing decade will not cause us to look back with regret upon that which we are reviewing as the culmination of our national progress.

SEXES.

(Appendix—Table No. 2.)

The excess of male population in the United States, compared with that of the other sex, presents a marked difference with respect to other countries. While in the United States and Territories there is an excess of about 730,000 males in more than 31,000,000 of people, the females of the United Kingdom of Great Britain and Ireland outnumber the males some 877,000 in a population of little more than 29,000,000. This disparity is the result of many causes. The emigration from the mother country of men in the prime of life, and the large demands of their military, naval, and marine service, seem to account for some proportion of the excess of females; while immigration from all parts of Europe, our small military and naval service, and the few losses we have sustained from the contingencies incident to a state of war, have served to exhibit a larger male population, in proportion, than can be shown in any country on the globe.

The great excess of males in newly-settled territories illustrates the influence of emigration in affecting a disparity in the sexes. The males of California outnumber the females near 67,000, or about one-fifth of the population. In Illinois the excess of males amounts to about 92,000, or one-twelfth of the entire population. In Massachusetts the females outnumber the males some 37,600. Michigan shows near 40,000 excess of males; Texas, 36,000; Wisconsin, 43,000. In Colorado the males are as twenty to one female. In Utah the numbers are nearly equal; and while in New York there is a small preponderance of females, the males are more numerous in Pennsylvania.

SLAVERY.

For more than three and a half centuries slavery has existed in the West Indies. Indians from the American coast were conveyed to St. Domingo and Cuba in large numbers. The plea for the capture and employment of the aborigines was their conversion to Christianity, which but few lived long to enjoy, as, under the effects of labor and the climate, they died with a rapidity too shocking to contemplate.

This circumstance directed the attention of the Spaniards to Africa, from which country slaves were imported about the year 1503, the licenses for that object greatly enriching the Spanish exchequer for a long period after. The introduction of Africans into Brazil and Peru dates almost simultaneously with the conquest of the countries by Cortez and Pizarro, early in the sixteenth century. By the middle of that century the aborigines of the West Indies had disappeared, and their places were occupied by Africans, who were introduced about this period in very large numbers throughout the Spanish and Portuguese possessions in South America. It was but shortly subsequent that English adventurers embarked successfully in the slave trade, which they pursued under charters from Elizabeth and James I.

The first negro slaves were imported into Virginia in 1619, where they numbered about 2,000 in 1670. It is believed that the first slave ship fitted out in the English colonies sailed from Boston in 1646. In 1624 the French introduced slaves into their island of St. Christopher, and soon after into Martinique and Guadeloupe, and shortly established slavery in all their American colonies. The Dutch embarked in the traffic with other civilized nations; so that the conclusion is inevitable that all the enlightened nations of the world who enjoyed any extended commerce simultaneously participated in a trade now deemed contraband, and towards which the world is now as equally united in hostility. Had slavery continued to expand in numbers in other parts of America as it has grown in the United States, there would at the present time be more than 21,000,000 of this class of persons in the United States and the British, French, Spanish, and Brazilian possessions. It is believed, however, that in all American countries and islands of our seas, except in the United States, the number of slaves was only maintained from time to time by the prosecution of the slave trade. While slavery in North América extended, in 1775, from and including the Canadian provinces to Florida, its northern limit has been gradually contracting, while indications clearly point to its western termini, which have doubtless been already attained. The importation of slaves to the United States was interdicted by law in 1808. In 1774 the legislature of Rhode Island interdicted the importation of slaves into that colony, and the next year enacted a law of emancipation by declaring the children of all slave mothers to be born, free. Massachusetts abolished slavery by her bill of rights in 1780. In 1784 Connecticut barred the introduction of slaves, and declared all born after the 1st of March of that year free at the age of 26. Pennsylvania, in 1780, by law prohibited the introduction of slaves, and declared free all children of slave mothers born thereafter. Virginia prohibited the introduction of slaves from abroad in 1778; Maryland in 1783. New Hampshire abolished slavery in 1792; New York in 1799; New Jersey in 1820. Such has been the progress and decline of African slavery in our country, where its severities have been humanity compared with other countries, and where, although among the last to cling to the institution, the traffic in this class of persons was first seriously, as it has been persistently, opposed. It may not be out of place to state that the American States, which in the past century abolished slavery, permitted the free colored population to enjoy every right consistent with their condition as a class, and allowed bond and free to remain during their natural lives in the State or colony where they lived. This fact, although sometimes questioned, can be demonstrated beyond cavil; and the contrary can only be urged by such as are unfamiliar with the subject or have an object in the misrepresentation. The plan of gradual emancipation probably tended to this result, as those who were living in bondage continued to be slaves, while their descendants were generally to become free at such period as they were qualified to maintain their own existence by labor.

An examination of the relative number at different successive periods, until slavery become extinct, must lead to conclusions that no material deportation of slaves occurred shortly before or after the passage of emancipation acts—a fact which cannot be controverted; and while it must be conceded that the northern people prosecuted the slave trade at an early period with energy and thrift, they are entitled to the award of sincerity and honesty in giving the earliest examples of the abolition of the institution of slavery within their own borders.

INDIAN SLAVERY.

(Appendix—Table No. 3.)

A new element has been developed by the present census, viz: that of the statistics of negro slavery among the Indian tribes west of Arkansas, comprising the Choctaw, Cherokee, Creek, and Chickasaw nations; also the number of white and free colored population scattered throughout these tribes; all of which, with an estimate from the most reliable sources of the whole number of aborigines, will be found appended to the population tables. By reference to this table it will appear that the Choctaws held 2,297 negro slaves, distributed among 385 owners; the Cherokees, 2,504, held by 384 owners; the Creeks, 1,651, owned by 267 Indians; and the Chickasaws, 917 to 118 owners. As, under all the circumstances of slavery everywhere, the servile race is very unequally distributed, so will appear to be the case with the Indian tribes. While one Choctaw is the owner of 227 slaves, and ten of the largest proprietors own 638, averaging nearly 64, the slaves average about six to each owner of slaves in that tribe, while the Indians number about as eight to one slave.

Among the Cherokees the largest proprietor holds 57 slaves; the ten largest own 353, averaging a little over 35, and the number to each holder averages a little more than a half per cent. more than with the Choctows, while the population of Indians in the tribe to slaves as about nine to one. Among the Creeks two hold 75 slaves each; ten own 433, while the ratio of slaves to the whole number of Indians varies but little from that with the Cherokees. The largest proprietor among the Chickasaws holds 61 slaves; ten own 275, or an average of 27½, while the average is nearly eight to each owner in the tribe, and one to each five and a half Indians in the tribe. It thus appears that in those tribes there are nearly eight Indians to each negro slave, and that the slaves form about 12½ per cent. of the population, omitting the whites and free colored. The small tribe of Seminoles, although like the tribes above mentioned, transplanted from slaveholding States, holds no slaves, but intermarry with the colored population. These tribes, while they present an advanced state of civilization, and some of them have attained to a condition of comfort, wealth, and refinement, form but a small portion of the Indian tribes within the territory of the United States, and are alluded to on account of their relation to a civil condition recognized by a portion of the States, and which exercises a significant influence with the country at large.

MANUMISSION OF SLAVES.

(Appendix—Table No. 4.)

With regard to manumission it appears from the returns that during the census year they numbered a little more than 3,000, being more than double the number who were liberated in 1850, or at the rate of one each to 1,309; whereas, during 1850, the manumissions were as one to every 2,181 slaves. Great irregularity, as might naturally be expected, appears to exist for the two periods whereof we have returns on this subject. By the Eighth Census it appears that manumissions have greatly increased in number in Alabama, Georgia, Louisiana, Maryland, Mississippi, North Carolina, and Tennessee, while they have decreased in Delaware and Florida, and varied but little in Kentucky, Missouri, South Carolina, and Virginia, and other slaveholding States not mentioned.

FUGITIVE SLAVES.

(Appendix—Table No. 5.)

The number of slaves who escaped from their masters in 1860 is not only much less in proportion than in 1850, but greatly reduced numerically. The greatest increase of escapes appears to have occurred in Mississippi, Missouri, and Virginia, while the decrease is most marked in Delaware, Georgia, Louisiana, Maryland, and Tennessee.

That the complaint of insecurity to slave property by the escape of this class of persons into the free States, and their recovery impeded, whereby its value has been lessened, is the result of misapprehension is evident, not only from the small number who have been lost to their owners, but from the fact that up to the present time the number of escapes has been gradually diminishing to such an extent that the whole annual loss to the southern States from this cause bears less proportion to the amount of capital involved than the daily variations which in ordinary times occur in the fluctuations of State or government securities in the city of New York alone.

From the tables annexed, it appears that while there escaped from their masters 1,011 slaves in 1850, or one in each 3,165 held in bondage, (being about $\frac{1}{30}$ of one per cent.,) during the census year ending June 1, 1860, out of 3,949,557 slaves, there escaped only 803, being one to about 5,000, or at the rate of $\frac{1}{50}$ of one per cent. Small and inconsiderable as this number appears, it is not pretended that all missing in the border states, much less any considerable number escaping from their owners in the more southern regions, escaped into the free States; and when we consider that in the border States not 500 escaped out of more than 1,000,000 slaves in 1860, while near 600 escaped in 1850 out of 910,000, and that at the two periods near 800 are reported to have escaped from the more southern slaveholding States, the fact becomes evident that the escape of this class of persons, while rapidly decreasing in ratio in the border slave States, occurs independent of proximity to a free population, being in the nature of things incident to the relation of master and slave.

It will scarcely be alledged that these returns are not reliable, being, as they are, made by the persons directly interested, who would be no more likely to err in the number lost than in those retained. Fortunately, however, other means exist of proving the correctness of the results ascertained, by noting the increase of the free colored population, which, with all its artificial accretions, is proven by the census to be less than 13 per cent., in the last ten years, in the free States, whereas the slaves have increased 23½ per cent., presenting a natural augmentation altogether conclusive against much loss by escapes; the natural increase being equal to that of the most favored nations, irrespective of immigration, and greater than that of any country in Europe for the same period, and this in spite of the 20,000 manumissions which are believed to have occurred in the past ten years. An additional evidence of the slave population having been attended from year to year, up to the present time, with fewer vicissitudes, is further furnished by the fact that the free colored population, which from 1820 to 1830 increased at the rate of 36⅕ per cent., in 1840 exhibited but 20⅘ per cent. increase, gradually declining to 1860, when the increase throughout the United States was but one per cent. per annum.

IMMIGRATION.

One of the commissioners sent by the Continental Congress to Europe, Silas Deane, expressed the expectation that if the colonies established their independence, the immigration from the Old World would be prodigiously increased; and as a consequence, the cultivated lands would rise in value, and new lands would be brought into market. This anticipation has been strikingly and abundantly realized. And in connexion with the census of nativities, the records of immigration have a special importance as indicating the progressive augmentation of the immigrants who have sought to improve their fortunes in the New World.

From a survey of the irregular data previous to 1819, by Dr. Seybert, Prof. Tucker, and other statists, it appears that from 1790 to 1800, about 50,000 Europeans, or "aliens," arrived in this country; in the next ten years the foreign arrivals were about 70,000, and in the ten years following, 114,000, ending with 1820. To determine the actual settlers, a deduction of 14.5 per cent. from these numbers should probably be made for transient passengers, as hereafter described.

Louisiana was purchased from France in 1803. The portion of this territory south of the thirty-third parallel, according to the historian Hildreth, comprised a population of about 50,000, more than half of whom were slaves. With these should be counted about 10,000 in the settlements north of that parallel, augmented by a recent immigration, with a predominance of whites. The foreign population acquired with the whole Louisiana territory may thus be reckoned at 60,000; about one-half or 30,000 being whites of French, Spanish, and British extraction; and the other 30,000 being slaves and free colored. This number of whites should evidently be added to the current immigration by sea already mentioned, in order to obtain the foreign accession to the white population of the United States during that period.

Instead of scattered notices from shipping lists, the arrival of passengers has been officially recorded at the custom-houses, since 1819, by act of Congress. There are some deficiences perhaps in the returns of the first ten or twelve years, but the subsequent reports are considered reliable. While the classified lists exhibit the whole number of foreign passengers, the great majority of whom are emigrants, they also furnish valuable information not otherwise obtainable respecting the statistical history of immigration.

The following numbers, registered under the act of 1819, are copied from the authentic summary of Bromwell, to which the numbers for the last five years have been added from the annual reports of the State Department, thus bringing the continuation down to the year of the present census.

Statement of the number of Alien passengers arriving in the United States by sea from foreign countries from September 30, 1819, *to December* 31, 1860.

Year.	Males.	Females.	Sex not stated.	Total.
Year ending September 30, 1820	4,871	2,393	1,121	8,385
1821	4,651	1,636	2,840	9,127
1822	3,816	1,013	2,082	6,911
1823	3,598	848	1,908	6,354
1824	4,706	1,393	1,813	7,912
1825	6,917	2,959	323	10,199
1826	7,702	3,078	57	10,837
1827	11,803	5,939	1,133	18,875
1828	17,261	10,060	61	27,382
1829	11,303	5,112	6,105	22,520
1830	6,439	3,135	13,748	23,322
1831	14,909	7,724	....	22,633
1832	34,596	18,583	....	53,179
Quarter ending December 31, 1832	4,691	2,512	100	7,303
Year ending December 31, 1833	41,546	17,094	....	58,640
1834	38,796	22,540	4,029	65,365
1835	28,196	17,027	151	45,374
1836	47,865	27,553	824	76,242
1837	48,837	27,653	2,850	79,340
1838	23,474	13,685	1,755	38,914
1839	42,932	25,125	12	68,069
1840	52,883	31,132	51	84,066
1841	48,082	32,031	176	80,289
1842	62,277	41,907	381	104,565
First three quarters of 1843	30,069	22,424	3	52,496
Year ending September 30, 1844	44,431	34,184	....	78,615
1845	65,015	48,115	1,241	114,371
1846	87,777	65,742	897	154,416
1847	136,086	97,917	965	234,968
1848	133,906	92,149	472	226,527
1849	177,232	119,280	512	297,024

Statement of the number of Alien passengers, &c—Continued.

Year.	Males.	Females.	Sex not stated.	Total.
Year ending September 30, 1850	196,331	112,635	1,038	310,004
Quarter ending December 31, 1850	32,990	26,805	181	59,976
Year ending December 31, 1851	217,181	162,219	66	379,466
1852	212,469	157,696	1,438	371,603
1853	207,958	160,615	72	368,645
1854	256,177	171,656	....	427,833
1855	115,307	85,567	3	200,877
1856	115,846	84,590	....	200,436
1857	146,215	105,091	....	251,306
1858	72,824	50,002	300	123,126
1859	69,161	51,640	481	121,282
1860	88,477	65,077	86	153,640
Total	2,977,603	2,035,536	49,275	5,062,414

The following aggregates also exhibit the number of arrivals of passengers from foreign countries during periods of nearly ten years each, and thus indicate the accelerated progress of immigration:

Periods.	Passengers of Foreign birth.	American and Foreign.
In the 10 years ending September 30, 1829	128,502	151,636
In the 10¼ years ending December 31, 1839	538,381	572,716
In the 9¾ years ending September 30, 1849	1,427,337	1,479,478
In the 11¼ years ending December 31, 1860	2,968,194	3,255,591
In the 41¼ years ending December 31, 1860	5,062,414	5,459,421

Adjusting the returns to the periods of the decennial census, by the aid of the quarterly reports, we find very nearly the following numbers:

Three census periods.	Passengers of Foreign birth.
In the 10 years previous to June 1, 1840	552,000
Do.............do.......1850	1,558,300
Do.............do.......1860	2,707,624

To arrive at the true immigration, these numbers should be largely increased for those who have come by way of Canada. On the other hand, they should be diminished for return emigrants, and for the merchants, factors, and visitors who go and come repeatedly, and are thus enumerated twice or more in the returns.

For an example of the former class, according to British registry, 17,798 emigrants returned from the United States to Great Britain in the year 1860. How numerous has been the latter class who have been counted twice or more, is not definitely known; to make note of these would constitute a desirable improvement in the future official reports.

The preceding summaries embrace passengers of foreign birth, together with 397,007 native born Americans, who were also registered as arriving from foreign ports. In the record of ages following, both classes are united; but since the foreigners are far more numerous, the result will exhibit very nearly the relative number at each age of the foreign passengers. A careful reduction of the whole number whose ages were specified, has just been completed in connexion with the census, as follows:

Distribution of Ages on arrival.

Ages.	Number of ages stated from 1820 to 1860.			Proportions.		
	Males.	Females.	Total.	Males.	Females.	Total.
Under 5	218,417	200,676	419,093	4.143	3.806	7.949
5 and under 10	199,704	180,606	380,310	3.788	3.425	7.213
10 and under 15	194,580	166,833	361,413	3.691	3.164	6.855
15 and under 20	404,338	349,755	754,093	7.669	6.633	14.302
20 and under 25	669,853	428,974	1,098,827	12.706	8.136	20.842
25 and under 30	576,822	269,554	846,376	10.940	5.112	16.052
30 and under 35	352,619	163,778	516,397	6.688	3.106	9.794
35 and under 40	239,468	114,165	353,633	4.542	2.165	6.707
40 and upwards	342,022	200,322	542,344	6.487	3.799	10.286
Total	3,197,823	2,074,663	5,272,486	60.654	39.346	100.000

From the foregoing table it will be seen that the distribution is materially different from that of a settled population; the females are less than the males in the ratio of two to three; almost precisely one-half of the total passengers are between fifteen and thirty years of age. It will further be noted that the sexes approach nearest to equality in children and the youthful ages, as would naturally be expected in the migration of families; while from twenty-five years of age to forty the male passengers are double the number of females. The total distribution of ages has never varied very materially from the average, as appears from the following table:

Total Proportions for different periods.

Ages.	1820 to 1830.	1830 to 1840.	1840 to 1850.	1850 to 1860.	1820 to 1860.
Under 5	6.904	8.511	8.284	7.674	7.949
5 and under 10	5.763	7.552	7.434	7.077	7.213
10 and under 15	4.568	7.817	7.564	6.328	6.855
15 and under 20	11.652	11.830	13.059	15.762	14.302
20 and under 25	22.070	19.705	21.518	20.617	20.842
25 and under 30	19.574	16.661	15.722	15.944	16.052
30 and under 35	10.194	10.215	9.914	9.609	9.794
35 and under 40	8.171	7.875	6.563	6.466	6.707
40 and upwards	11.704	9.834	9.942	10.523	10.286
Total	100.000	100.000	100.000	100.000	100.000

The passengers from foreign ports arrive at all seasons of the year; the greatest number, however, make the passage in the second and third quarters, or in the summer months, and a smaller number in the winter months.

The deaths on the voyage during the last five years have been only about one-sixth of one per cent.; the time of passage being generally some thirty days. With regard to the question, how many of the passengers are emigrants, the reports of the State Department during the past five years—1855 to 1860—have specified the places of residence as follows:

Country where the passengers from foreign ports mean to reside; also the country where born.

Country.	Mean to reside in—			Born in—
	Males.	Females.	Total.	Males & females.
United States	551,095	357,395	908,490	126,794
British America	7,682	4,044	11,726	25,443
Great Britain and Ireland	2,207	1,037	3,244	407,429
Azores	544	133	677	1,954
Spain	389	65	454	4,097
West Indies	271	72	343	5,170
France	130	47	177	19,338
Germany	140	36	176	279,957
Other countries specified	329	67	396	82,185
Not stated	....	....	50,901	23,317
Total of 5 years, 1855 to 1860	....	....	976,584	976,584

Deducting the number at the head of the last column who were born in the United States, it will be seen that in these five years 781,696 out of a total of 849,790 alien passengers, designed to make their permanent home in the United States. Further statistics of 24,848 second passages, and about 30,000 emigrants, to Canada, *via* New York, indicate that *the alien passengers should be diminished* 14.5 *per cent. to determine the number of actual settlers.*

From the first of the two following tables it will be seen that the most numerous class among the passengers is that of *laborers;* the next in order are *farmers,* mechanics, and merchants. The "seamstresses and milliners," and nearly all of the "servants," are females; the other female passengers, with few exceptions, have been entered under the category of "not stated," and comprise about five-sevenths of that division.

It will be proper to mention that the ten trades and professions marked with a star in the table were always enumerated during the whole period. The other occupations were not reported during the four years 1856–'59, except that their aggregate only was embraced under the single title of "other occupations." But the omission could be roughly supplied by assuming the number in each trade during the four years to be the same fraction of the yearly passengers as it was in the other six years.

In 1856–'59, the deaths on the passage also were omitted in the official total of passengers, though retained in all previous years and in 1860; for the sake of uniformity this temporary omission of deaths is restored in the present collection of tables, which have been verified throughout with the greatest care.

The next following table, stating the birthplace or "country where born," will form a valuable supplement to the decennial census of nativities. Excepting the first numeric column, which commenced with small numbers October 1, 1819, the remaining columns correspond as nearly with the census periods as the official yearly reports allow without interpolation.

The total number arriving from the United Kingdom of Great Britain and Ireland on our shores is thus stated to be 2,750,874. But a recent statement from British official sources† gives the number emigrating to the United States in the forty-six years, 1815–'60, as 3,048,206. The difference of the two returns will be explained partly by those who emigrated in the interval, 1815—19, before our registry commenced, being about 55,000; and chiefly by the more numerous class who entered the United States by way of Canada, and so were not included in our custom-house returns.

In the same period of forty-six years it is also stated that 1,196,521 persons emigrated from the United Kingdom to the British colonies in North America. A large portion of these are known to have eventually settled in the United States. Thus it appears safe to assume that since the close of the last war with that country, in 1814, about three and a quarter millions of the natives of Great Britain and Ireland, "a population for a kingdom," have emigrated to this country.

Next in magnitude is the migration from Germany, amounting to 1,486,044 by our custom-house returns; the next is that from France, 208,063; and from the other countries, as shown in the table. A large share of the German emigrants have embarked from the port of Havre; others from Bremen, Hamburg, Antwerp; many have also crossed over and taken passage from British ports.

As our own people, following "the star of empire," have migrated to the west in vast numbers, their places have been supplied by Europeans, which has modified the character of the population, yet the great mass of the immigrants are found to cherish true patriotism for the land of their adoption.

Occupation of passengers arriving in the United States from foreign countries during the forty-one years ending with 1860.

Occupation.	1820 to 1830.	1831 to 1840.	1841 to 1850.	1851 to 1860.	1820 to 1860.
*Merchants	19,434	41,881	46,388	124,149	231,852
*Farmers	15,005	88,240	256,880	404,712	764,837
*Mechanics	6,805	56,582	164,411	179,726	407,524
*Mariners	4,995	8,004	6,398	10,087	29,484
*Miners	341	368	1,735	37,523	39,967
*Laborers	10,280	53,169	281,229	527,639	872,317
Shoemakers	1,109	1,966	63	336	3,474
Tailors	983	2,252	65	334	3,634
Seamstresses and milliners	413	1,672	2,096	1,065	5,246
Actors	183	87	233	85	588
Weavers and spinners	2,937	6,600	1,303	717	11,557
*Clergymen	415	932	1,559	1,420	4,326
Clerks	882	1,143	1,065	792	3,882
*Lawyers	244	461	831	1,140	2,676
*Physicians	805	1,959	2,116	2,229	7,109
Engineers	226	311	654	825	2,016
Artists	139	513	1,223	615	2,490
Teachers	275	267	832	154	1,528
Musicians	140	165	236	188	729
Printers	179	472	14	40	705

† British Almanac, 1862.

* See page 16.

Occupation of passengers arriving in the United States, &c.—Continued.

Occupation.	1820 to 1830.	1831 to 1840.	1841 to 1850.	1851 to 1860.	1820 to 1860.
Painters	232	369	8	38	647
Masons	793	1,435	24	58	2,310
Hatters	137	114	1	4	256
Manufacturers	175	107	1,833	1,005	3,120
Millers	199	189	33	210	631
Butchers	329	432	76	108	945
Bakers	583	569	28	92	1,272
*Servants	1,327	2,571	24,538	21,058	49,494
Other occupations	5,466	4,004	2,892	13,844	26,206
Not stated	101,442	363,252	969,411	1,544,494	2,978,599
Total	176,473	640,086	1,768,175	2,874,687	5,459,421

Country where born.

Countries.	1820 to 1830.	1831 to 1840.	1841 to 1850.	1851 to 1860.	1820 to 1860.
England	15,837	7,611	32,092	247,125	302,665
Ireland	27,106	29,188	162,332	748,740	967,366
Scotland	3,180	2,667	3,712	38,331	47,890
Wales	170	185	1,261	6,319	7,935
Great Britain and Ireland	35,534	243,540	848,366	297,578	1,425,018
Total United Kingdom	81,827	283,191	1,047,763	1,338,093	2,750,874
France	8,868	45,575	77,262	76,358	208,063
Spain	2,616	2,125	2,209	9,298	16,248
Portugal	180	829	550	1,055	2,614
Belgium	28	22	5,074	4,738	9,862
Prussia	146	4,250	12,149	43,887	60,432
Germany	7,583	148,204	422,477	907,780	1,486,044
Holland	1,127	1,412	8,251	10,789	21,579
Denmark	189	1,063	539	3,749	5,540
Norway and Sweden	94	1,201	13,903	20,931	36,129
Poland	21	369	105	1,164	1,659
Russia	89	277	551	457	1,374
Turkey	21	7	59	83	170
Switzerland	3,257	4,821	4,644	25,011	37,733
Italy	389	2,211	1,590	7,012	11,202
Greece	20	49	16	31	116
Sicily	17	35	79	429	560
Sardinia	32	7	201	1,790	2,030
Corsica	2	5	2	....	9
Malta	1	35	78	5	119
Iceland	....	....	....	10	10
Europe	2	....	51	473	526
British America	2,486	13,624	41,723	59,309	117,142
South America	542	856	3,579	1,224	6,201
Central America	107	44	368	449	968
Mexico	4,818	6,599	3,271	3,078	17,766
West Indies	3,998	12,301	13,528	10,660	40,487

Country where born—Continued.

Countries.	1820 to 1830.	1831 to 1840.	1841 to 1850.	1851 to 1860.	1820 to 1860.
China	3	8	35	41,397	41,443
East Indies	9	39	36	43	127
Persia	....	....	7	15	22
Asia	3	1	4	19	27
Liberia	1	8	5	5	19
Egypt	....	4	....	....	4
Morocco	....	4	1	....	5
Algiers	....	....	2	....	2
Barbary States	4	....	....	....	4
Cape of Good Hope	2	....	....	....	2
Africa	10	36	47	186	279
Azores	13	29	327	2,873	3,242
Canary Islands	271	6	1	8	286
Madeira Islands	70	52	3	189	314
Cape Verd Islands	4	15	3	7	29
Sandwich Islands	1	6	28	44	79
Society Islands	....	....	1	6	7
Australia	2	3	....	104	109
St. Helena	....	1	3	13	17
Isle of France	....	2	1	....	3
South Sea Islands	79	....	....	....	79
New Zealand	....	....	....	4	4
Not stated	32,892	69,799	52,725	25,438	180,854
Total Aliens	151,824	599,125	1,713,251	2,598,214	5,062,414
United States	24,649	40,961	54,924	276,473	397,007
Total	176,473	640,086	1,768,175	2,874,687	5,459,421

EDUCATION.

The returns of the marshals present the statistics of education and educational institutions under the same general heads as in 1850, viz: the number of persons who attended school any time in the year preceding the 1st day of June, 1860, the number of schools, with their pupils and teachers, together with the amounts received for their support from taxes, permanent funds, tuition, and other sources, for the year previous. Although these returns have not yet been reduced to a tabulated form, enough is ascertained to authorize the statement that not far from 5,000,000 persons received instruction in the various educational institutions of the different States in the year ending June, 1860, or about one-fifth of the entire free population of the country. And it is gratifying to know, from the official reports of State and municipal authorities, that in a majority of the States these institutions, in number, material outfit of buildings, furniture, and apparatus, and in the professional knowledge and zeal of their teachers, have kept pace with the growth of their respective communities in population, wealth, and industrial prosperity generally.

As the plan heretofore adopted of presenting the returns under the general heads of colleges, academies, and private schools does not exhibit the peculiarities of the system and means of instruction in each State, nor the prodigious magnitude and comprehensive character of the educational interests of the whole country, an attempt will be made, in addition to the tables heretofore given, to arrange the institutions in a manner which will throw much light upon the nature of our institutions, and exhibit the action of the general government in relation to schools and education, as in its appropriation of over 50,000,000 acres of public lands to educational purposes in the several States, and of the policy of the different States in the disposition of the same, and of the history of the military and naval academies of the government.

POPULAR REPRESENTATION.

By the law of May, 1850, the principle was first established of permanently limiting the number of representatives, and relieving the country and Congress from the necessity of fixing every ten years the number of members whereof the House should be composed. The law establishes the number of representatives under each census at two hundred and thirty-three, who are apportioned among the several States respectively, by dividing the number of the free population of the States, to which, in slaveholding States, three-fifths of the slaves is added, by the number two hundred and thirty-three, and the product of such division (rejecting all fractions of a unit) being the ratio of representation of the several States. But as the number and amount of the fractions among so many dividends would, of course, in the aggregate be sufficient to reduce the number of representatives below the number specified, it was provided that the whole number should be supplied by assigning to so many States having the largest fractions an additional member each for its fraction, until the total number of two hundred and thirty-three members should be assigned to the several States. It is also provided that new States being admitted subsequently to any one of the decennial enumerations shall have representatives on the same basis, while it is at the same time provided that such excess in the number of members of the House of Representatives shall only continue until the apportionment of representatives under the next succeeding census.

In pursuance with law, the apportionment was made and proclaimed on the 5th day of July, 1861, distributing the representation in the thirty-eighth Congress among the several States, according to their federal population, as follows:

State		State	
Alabama	6	Minnesota	1
Arkansas	3	Mississippi	5
California	3	Missouri	9
Connecticut	4	New Hampshire	3
Delaware	1	New Jersey	5
Florida	1	New York	31
Georgia	7	North Carolina	7
Illinois	13	Ohio	18
Indiana	11	Oregon	1
Iowa	5	Pennsylvania	23
Kansas	1	Rhode Island	1
Kentucky	8	South Carolina	4
Louisiana	5	Tennessee	8
Maine	5	Texas	4
Maryland	5	Vermont	2
Massachusetts	10	Virginia	11
Michigan	6	Wisconsin	6

According to the apportionment, the States which have their representation increased are: Arkansas *one*, California *one*, Illinois *four*, Iowa *three*, Louisiana *one*, Michigan *two*, Missouri *two*, Texas *two*, Wisconsin *three*.

The States where representation is diminished by the new apportionment are: Alabama *one*, Georgia *one*, Kentucky *two*, Maine, Maryland, Massachusetts, Minnesota, each *one*, New York *two*, North Carolina *one*, Ohio *three*, Pennsylvania *two*, Rhode Island *one*, South Carolina *two*, Tennessee *two*, Vermont *one*, Virginia *two*. The arrangement of representatives for the 38th Congress under the law of May 23, 1850, was changed subsequent to the apportionment by the law of March 4, 1862, which increased the number of representatives to 241, by giving one additional to the States of Illinois, Iowa, Kentucky, Minnesota, Ohio, Pennsylvania, Rhode Island, and Vermont. This act makes the number of representatives 241 from and after the 3d of March, 1863. It is understood that the bill as originally passed by the House added 6 to the 233 representatives theretofore provided, and added these to States having unrepresented fractions on the apportionment of July 5, 1861, whenever the addition of a representative to any State would bring the representative constituencies of that State *nearer* to the ratio of representation, ascertained according to the act of May 23, 1850, than they would be on the apportionment; and the effect was to make the constituencies in every State approximate *nearest to the ratio*. As the ratio is the law of absolute equality, it was claimed that this rule of apportionment approaches in the nearest practicable degree to equality among the States according to their respective representative populations. It appeared subsequently that, by assuming 239 as the number from which to deduce the ratio of representation, two States only would be entitled to an additional representative on the above rule, and the bill was amended accordingly by the Senate and concurred in by the House; so, in fact, the ratio for the next decade is on the basis of 239 representatives, with two (2) added to equalize representation among the several States.

It will be perceived that the preponderance of representation is rapidly but steadily advancing westward, and that regions unorganized and with scarcely a civilized inhabitant in 1790 now form populous States, with a larger representation than was enjoyed by all the States at that time. The increase of population and, as a consequence, of representation in the new States of the west is prominently illustrated by a comparison of the representation of Illinois, Indiana, Iowa, Michigan, Ohio, and Wisconsin, under the census of 1860, with that of Virginia, Massachusetts, Pennsylvania, New York, North Carolina, Maryland, and Connecticut, the six States having the largest representation, respectively. Under the census of 1790 Virginia had nineteen representatives, the largest number of any of the original States under the first census. Her representation is reduced under the census of 1860 to eleven, while Ohio, which was admitted into the Union in 1802, has nineteen representatives. Indiana, admitted into the Union in 1816, has the same number of representatives as Virginia; and Illinois, admitted into the Union in 1818, has fourteen representatives under the new apportionment. Massachusetts, with a representation of fourteen under the census of 1790, is reduced to ten under the new census. Pennsylvania and New York, the one with thirteen representatives and the other with ten under the first census, notwithstanding the immense resources of those two great States, have, under the census of 1860, the one thirty-one and the other twenty-three representatives. The ratio of increase in population in those two States since the census of 1850 was 25.51 per cent. in New York, and 25.71 per cent. in Pennsylvania, while in Illinois the ratio of increase during the same period was 101.04, and in Indiana 86.83 per cent. The probability is, therefore, should the ratio of increase of population continue in the States of the west as indicated by the census of 1860, that in the course of three or four decades New York and Pennsylvania, now the two most powerful States, may yield to some of their younger sisters, as Virginia, sometimes, not inappropriately, termed the mother of States, first yielded to them, and has now yielded to two new States carved out of territory originally her own.

North Carolina, under the census of 1790, had ten representatives; Maryland eight, and Connecticut seven. These three States have, under the census of 1860, (the first, seven; the second, five; and the third, four representatives,) an average representation of sixteen instead of twenty-five, as under the first apportionment. Thus the power of the old States declines, while that of the new States west of the Alleghanies increases more rapidly than they lose. Iowa, admitted into the Union in 1846, Michigan in 1837, and Wisconsin in 1848, have six representatives each under the last apportionment—two more than Connecticut or Maryland, and only one less than North Carolina. And here it must be borne in mind that the ratio of representation under the census of 1790 was one representative to every thirty-three thousand of representative population, while it is fixed by the last census at one representative for every 127,000.

STATISTICS OF MORTALITY.

(APPENDIX—TABLE No. 6.)

The present returns constitute the second general enumeration of annual deaths in the United States. The accumulated materials are the more valuable since they furnish instructive comparisons with the former returns of 1850, as well as with those of the nations of Europe which are favored with a permanent registration.

The rate of mortality has ever been a leading object of statistical inquiry, and in connexion with the number of births and migrations indicates the annual loss and gain of population. Besides the numerical proportion, expressively termed "the death figure" by a German statist, the records of mortality have a physical significance in our own land for elucidating the relative prevalence of diseases, and the comparative salubrity of the climate on the Atlantic coast contrasted with the elevated interior and the valley of the Mississippi. It is an interesting inquiry, whether the record of deaths over so large an extent of the New World shall disprove or confirm, and enlarge the conclusions drawn from vital statistics in other lands, and shall point to similar means of promoting health and longevity.

Adopting, in a first view, the civil divisions of the United States, the *number of deaths returned* to the Census office, and their *ratio to the living population*, are as follows. In making the present comparison, the population was changed according to the mean rate of increase from the end to the middle of the year in which the deaths occurred.

Deaths in the United States for the year ending June 1, 1860.

States and Territories.	Annual deaths.	Population to one death.	Deaths per cent.	Per cent. in 1850.	States and Territories.	Annual deaths.	Population to one death.	Deaths per cent.	Per cent. in 1850.
Alabama	12,759	74	1.34	1.20	Maryland.	7,370	92	1.09	1.68
Arkansas	8,855	48	2.06	1.46	Massachusetts	21,303	57	1.76	1.98
California	3,704	101	0.99	1.00	Michigan	7,390	100	1.00	1.16
Connecticut	6,138	74	1.35	1.59	Minnesota	1,108	153	0.65	0.50
Delaware	1,246	89	1.13	1.34	Mississippi	12,213	64	1.57	1 46
Florida	1,764	78	1.28	1.08	Missouri	17,652	66	1.52	1.83
Georgia	12,816	81	1.23	1.11	New Hampshire	4,469	72	1.39	1.35
Illinois	19,299	87	1.14	1.38	New Jersey	7,525	88	1.14	1.34
Indiana	15,325	87	1.15	1.32	New York	46,881	82	1.22	1.49
Iowa	7,259	92	1.09	1.08	North Carolina	11,602	84	1.19	1.21
Kansas	1,443	73	1.37	......	Ohio	24,724	93	1.07	1.48
Kentucky	16,466	69	1.45	1.56	Oregon	237	218	0.46	0.36
Louisiana	12,324	57	1.76	2.35	Pennsylvania	30,214	95	1.06	1.26
Maine	7,614	81	1.23	1.32	Rhode Island	2,479	69	1.44	1.55

Deaths in the United States—Continued.

States and Territories.	Annual deaths.	Population to one death.	Deaths per cent.	Per cent. in 1850.	States and Territories.	Annual deaths.	Population to one death.	Deaths per cent.	Per cent. in 1850.
South Carolina........	9,745	71	1.41	1.22	Nebraska............	381	75	1.34	......
Tennessee...........	15,153	72	1.39	1.20	Nevada	....	......	......	......
Texas...............	9,377	63	1.58	1.48	New Mexico.......	1,305	71	1.42	1.91
Vermont	3,355	92	1.08	1.02	Utah	374	106	0.94	2.13
Virginia	22,472	70	1.43	1.36	Washington	50	228	0.44	......
Wisconsin......	7,141	107	0.93	0.97	District of Columbia ..	1,285	58	1.74	1.66
Colorado	....	......	......	.....					
Dakota...............	4	......	......	......	Total, United States.	392,821	79	1.27	1.41

It will be seen that the total return of deaths of all classes and ages, white and colored, for 1860, amounts to 392,821. In 1850 the returns gave 323,272; whence it appears that the number of annual deaths, after an interval of ten years, has been augmented by 69,549, that is, an increase of 21.51 per cent. In the same interval the total increase of the whole population, according to the census, has been 35.58 per cent. Thus the mortality has not increased in proportion to the increase of population.

Under equal conditions this fact would favor a progressive salubrity in our climate, and undoubtedly there has been a sanitary improvement in many places. But the principal part of the difference in the rate of mortality is to be ascribed to the *prevalence of cholera in* 1849, swelling the deaths to an unusual amount. A previous visitation of Asiatic cholera in 1832 with alarming reports of its ravages in Europe, and the consequent excitement of the public here, will long be remembered. Near the beginning of the year 1849 the pestilential scourge reappeared almost simultaneously in New York and New Orleans, and thence gradually spread over the whole country. Along the chain of the lakes, and in the Mississippi valley, it raged with peculiar violence, and chiefly in the summer months, which are embraced in the census year, commencing on the first of June. Therefore, to render the circumstances of the two enumerations more equal, let the deaths by cholera, 31,506 in number, be first taken out of the total mortality of 1850, the remaining deaths are 291,766. Comparing this number with the whole enumeration in 1860, which was a healthy year, we find an increase of 34.64 per cent., which differs but slightly, as will be seen, from the current increase of the living population. Thus, with proper and obvious corrections, the one class of returns has advanced in nearly equal proportion with the other.

Among persons of foreign birth the outbreak of this disease in 1849 appears to have been more violent than among the native residents. In the foreign portion of the population 11,056 deaths by cholera were reported in the census of 1850, besides an increase from the other zymotic diseases. It was in the midst of the vast emigration which has continued to arrive on our shores, and being attracted to the commercial centres where the disease chiefly prevailed, the mortality of emigrants then rose to nearly as large an amount as it has now reached ten years after. Including persons of unknown birth-place, the returns have been as follows:

Deaths of foreigners in 1850................................ 32,970
Deaths of foreigners in 1860................................ 34,705

Another feature worthy of mention is the small mortality in the new States of Minnesota and Oregon, and in Washington Territory. On examining the returns we find here the least mortality; but early explorations in this territory had determined "the skiey influences" to be favorable, and the climate healthy. Besides, it appears a general characteristic of the pioneer States that the more hardy and enterprising class predominate among the first settlers; with a comparative absence of young and aged persons the deaths are less frequent. As immigration progresses, entire families with members of all ages become residents. The soil is broken by the plough, exposing vegetable matter to decomposition, and the deaths gradually occur in a greater ratio, as exhibited in the returns of the census.

A State registry of the annual deaths, births, and marriages has been for several years in operation in Massachusetts, Connecticut, Rhode Island, New Jersey, Pennsylvania, Vermont, South Carolina, and Kentucky. The deaths in nearly all of the principal cities are annually registered and reported chiefly in connexion with the boards of health. Whenever the deaths could be more correctly ascertained from these local records the census marshals were authorized to copy them. But on examination they appear to have rarely availed themselves of the privilege, with one large exception, mentioned below. The records were generally obtained by inquiry from house to house, in the same manner as the facts embraced in the other schedules. It is evident that the population in all varieties of young and old, male and female, was a present and visible fact to the enumerator, with scarce a chance of omission. But the deaths of the past twelve months were matters of recollection of which a portion would naturally be forgotten, and in the occasional removal and breaking up of families another portion would be lost. A precise enumeration was therefore impracticable, and the census of deaths is admitted to be deficient in numbers; nevertheless, being taken in the same manner over extensive sections of country, the returns stand on the same footing, and though not the whole, will be regarded as very large examples or representative numbers of the whole, and relatively reliable.

A full registration of the social statistics is a work of time and experience, proceeding yearly from deficient to more and more complete returns. In Massachusetts such an organization is in successful operation, and our marshals appear in this instance to have resorted to the State registry. The resulting proportion of deaths exhibited in the foregoing summary is noticed to be relatively greater in Massachusetts, but the disparity will be rightly ascribed to the better conditions under which the permanent registry operates, rather than to any marked difference of climate compared with that of the adjoining States.

Having thus far considered the civil divisions, let us now combine the returns under a new form, having reference to the physical aspects of the country.

The relative mortality in the great natural divisions is found to be as follows:

Natural Divisions.	Rate of Mortality.		
	Annual deaths, 1860.	Per cent. of population.	Per cent. in 1850.
I. LOWLANDS OF THE ATLANTIC COAST, Comprising a general breadth of two counties along the Atlantic from Delaware to Florida, inclusive	15,292	1.34	1.45
II. THE LOWER MISSISSIPPI VALLEY, Comprising Louisiana and a breadth of two counties along each bank of the river northward to Cape Girardeau, in Missouri	30,154	1.81	2.38
III. THE ALLEGHANY REGION, From Pennsylvania, through Virginia, Eastern Tennessee, &c., to Northern Alabama	26,346	1.08	0.96
IV. THE INTERMEDIATE REGION Surrounding the Alleghanies, and extending to the lowlands of the Atlantic and to the Mississippi valley	79,615	1.32	1.19
V. THE PACIFIC COAST, California, Oregon, and Washington	3,991	0.95	0.92
VI. THE NORTHEASTERN STATES, Maine, New Hampshire, and Vermont	15,438	1.24	1.25
VII. THE NORTHWESTERN STATES, Wisconsin, Iowa, and Minnesota	15,508	0.98	1.01
The whole United States		1.27	1.41

For reasons before stated, the percentages in the last two columns will be understood as expressing not the absolute, but the *relative*, mortality of one section compared with another section, or with the whole United States. The third, fifth, and seventh divisions will be seen to exhibit the smallest proportions of mortality, nearly equal or differing but little from 0.98, the mean value. The second division shows by far the greatest mortality; the relative mean of two different years being 2.09 per cent. of the population, while the first, fourth, and sixth divisions, together with the remaining States not included above, conform nearly to the general average of the whole United States.

The conclusions from the census, thus briefly stated, appear entirely accordant with the topography of the country, and illustrate how far the human system has power to withstand the influence of diverse temperatures and climates. Leaving out the Alleghany region, and its extension through the Catskill and White mountains to Maine, the surface of the populated States nowhere rises more than a few hundred feet above the sea level. The extent from north to south, through twenty degrees of latitude, presents an agreeable "interchange of hill and valley, rivers, woods, and plains," most happily situated between the rigors of the polar and the flaming heat of the tropic regions. Hence, with the exceptions indicated, a considerable uniformity might be expected in the prevailing rate of mortality; and such is, in fact, the result of the census. There appear no marked deviations on a large scale from the common standard, or mean of the two enumerations in 1850 and 1860, except in the divisions already specified, where climatic causes of a diverse nature are plainly in operation.

The first division, comprising *the great Atlantic plain,* was remarked by the early explorers in America on account of its uniform level over a length of a thousand miles along the coast, and extending from fifty to one hundred miles inland. The sea and shore meet, for the most part, in a mingled series of bays, estuaries, and small islands rising just above the tide. The low grounds in summer abound in miasm, and a single night's exposure in the rice-fields of Carolina is said to be very dangerous, and carefully avoided. But, away from the cypress swamps and marshes, there is generally a sandy soil; and the aggregate mortality is found by the census to rise above, though not much above, the general average of the whole country. In every few years, however, it is well known that the low portions from Norfolk, southward and extending around the Gulf of Mexico, are visited by epidemic disease, when the mortality rises much higher than the ordinary amount.

In respect to the second division it may be observed that while the low valley or trough of the Missouri river, for example, is five miles in width, *the alluvial tract of the Mississippi* is often from forty to fifty miles in breadth. On each side of this river plain are the line of bluffs, which are very steep, and in some places rise two or three hundred feet in height. The river is described as coursing its way between these bluffs, so called, here veering to one side; there, to the other, and occasionally leaving the whole alluvial tract on one side. The annual flood commences in March, continuing two or three months. During this time the river plain is submerged to the not unusual depth of fifty feet below the junction of the Ohio river, the additional depth decreasing to ten or twelve feet at New Orleans. The lateral overflow is principally on the western side, and covers an area from ten to fifty miles wide. A periodic inundation of such vast dimensions will rank among the grandest features of the western continent. Towards the last of May the water subsides, leaving the broad alluvial plain interspersed with lakes, stagnant pools, and swamps, abounding in cottonwood, cypress, and coarse grass. The flood leaves also a new layer of vegetable and animal matter exposed to fermentation and decay under the augmenting heat of the summer sun. When, in addition to this, the air becomes unusually damp during the hot season, the conditions of epidemic disease, according to medical authority, are fully present. What the Roman poet expressively termed the "cohort of fevers" then advances upon the human race as it were in destructive conflict; the abundant alluvial matter decomposing under a high temperature, with occasionally a more humid and stagnant atmosphere. These are stated to be the conditions by which the mortality of the lower Mississippi valley has reached the high rate indicated by the census. The portion embraced in the foregoing classification was terminated on the north with the county of Cape Girardeau, for the reason that the hilly country in that vicinity is connected with a rocky stratum traversing the beds of both the Mississippi and Ohio rivers. From this great chain southward to the Gulf of Mexico is an extent of between six and seven hundred miles. The entire valley, according to geologists, may have been once an arm or estuary of the ocean extending inland from the Gulf of Mexico. The present influence of so large an area of alluvial matter must pervade the adjacent borders to a certain undefined extent.

The third division, or *Alleghany country,* is exhibited by the statistics as a region of great salubrity. It consists of high ridges running nearly parallel with the sea-coast through an extent of nine hundred miles, with a breadth varying from fifty to two hundred miles. The ridges are generally well watered and wooded to the summit, and between are extensive and fertile valleys; they are known as the Blue ridge, Alleghany ridge, North mountain, Cumberland ridge, and others. The region has been termed an elevated plateau or water-shed, whence the rivers flow eastward to the Atlantic and westward to the Mississippi and Ohio valleys. The ridges being for the most part about half a mile high, appear to exercise no other influence on the climate than what is due to mere elevation, thus securing a pure atmosphere and other conditions favorable to the growth of a healthy and vigorous population.

On the *Pacific coast* the seasons of the year have an entirely different type from that of the eastern United States. A cold sea current apparently cools down the temperature of summer, so that July is only 8° or 9° Fahrenheit warmer than January, and September is the hottest month. From this cause, Indian corn fails to come to maturity, although wheat and other cereals, as well as orchard fruits flourish in fine perfection. The elastic atmosphere and bracing effect of the climate have been remarked by settlers from all quarters of the globe.

In the northwestern States a continental, as distinguished from a sea, climate prevails with wide extremes of temperature. In the northeastern States, also, the thermometer ranges through more than a hundred degrees from winter to summer, yet the year appears generally healthy. Without entering into further details on this or the other divisions, enough evidence has been offered to show a certain correspondence between the physical features of the country and the mortality returns of the census.

Let us next examine the record of mortality with reference to changes in the different months and *seasons* of the year. The annual course of the sun through equinox and solstice brings on the vicissitudes of the seasons, with the attendant train of periodic phenomena, among which is the varying distribution of mortality. During the twelve months ending June 1, 1860, the deaths are stated to have occurred as follows:

Deaths in the United States, by Months and by Sex, 1860.

Months.	Number recorded.			Proportions.			State registry.
	Males.	Females.	Total.	Males.	Females.	Total.	
January	17,537	15,156	32,693	4.42	3.82	8.24	7.60
February	17,791	16,208	33,999	4.79	4.37	9.16	7.75
March	20,569	18,473	39,042	5.18	4.65	9.83	8.11
April	19,336	17,593	36,929	5.03	4.58	9.61	7.88
May	21,365	19,376	40,741	5.38	4.88	10.26	7.25
June	14,323	13,223	27,546	3.73	3.44	7.17	6.81
July	16,181	14,351	30,532	4.08	3.62	7.70	8.01
August	18,287	16,558	34,845	4.61	4.17	8.78	10.99
September	17,243	15,852	33,095	4.49	4.13	8.62	11.40
October	15,457	13,692	29,149	3.89	3.45	7.34	8.81
November	13,194	11,365	24,559	3.44	2.96	6.40	7.45
December	14,614	12,753	27,367	3.68	3.21	6.89	7.94
Unknown	1,338	986	2,324	....	....	....	....
Total	207,235	185,586	392,821	52.72	47.28	100.00	100.00

To facilitate a perception of the relations, the numbers in the last four colums are represented by proportional parts of 100, that is, by percentages whereof the sum is 100. A correction in this part of the table has been made for unequal months, by first adding one-thirtieth part to the deaths in April, June, September, November, and two twenty-ninths to the deaths in February; thus changing all to the majority standard of 31 days before casting the proportions. The mean monthly proportion is 8.33, and those which are below this value of course indicate months having less than the average mortality.

The year of the census ends with the last of May, and the deaths in that month are the most numerous in the returns. This circumstance, however, is very unusual, and after extensive scrutiny the most natural interpretation appears to be, not that May is the most fatal month, but that such deaths being the more recent, were better recollected and more fully reported to the marshals. Many facts concur to indorse this explanation, especially the results of the permanent State registry of Massachusetts during the nine years ending with 1859; these having been corrected to equality of months are subjoined in the last column for comparison; and the less numerous returns in Rhode Island furnish like results. It is at once evident, from the nature of the case, that the few State registries in which the deaths are noted at the time of occurrence are adapted to show the monthly proportions of mortality more correctly than this part of the census, where the deaths are set down only at the end of the year. In the latter case an unknown portion of the earlier deaths must be indistinctly remembered or often totally forgotten.

Without disguising this unexpected peculiarity, or concealing any defects of the census, it is better to exhibit it in its true light as shown by comparison in the preceding table. The inquiry will naturally arise, must the distinction of months therefore be omitted and the mortality statistics be considered only from other points of view? Without fully answering this question at present, it will be proper to observe that even as the eye perceives the nearer objects of a landscape more fully and distinctly than the remote, so the recollection of past events has a similar recession which is subject to laws. On this ground, passing back from May, the monthly returns might be successively augmented, with some variations, in an ascending scale, to correct for forgetfulness. Approximate corrections of this nature can be obtained from the army statistics of mortality at more than eighty different posts scattered over the whole United States. During the twenty-one years ending with 1859 the official number of deaths returned to the Surgeon General's office in the four quarters of the year commencing with January were:

	First quarter.	Second quarter.	Third quarter.	Fourth quarter.	Year.
Deaths	904	956	1,227	1,096	4,183
Proportions	21.61	22.86	29.33	26.20	100.00

These proportions do not essentially differ from those of the two State registries before mentioned. Without presuming on entire accuracy, the *relative* deficiencies of the United States census of 1860 would be corrected to the same standard by taking the returns of the first quarter, or first three months, in the former table, unchanged, adding 6, 46, and 58 per cent. to the deaths in the second, third, and fourth quarters, respectively.

In the United States the greatest number of deaths occurs during the third quarter, comprising the months of August and September. In England the climate is less subject to extremes of winter and summer temperature than ours, and the deaths are much more evenly distributed through the year. With but a small average difference, the least number of deaths there occurs in the third quarter, and the greatest number in the first quarter, or winter season.

Generally speaking, the *normal* course of temperature and moisture through the year, in any place, is the most favorable to agricultural productions and the most conducive to public health; while great and sudden extremes of heat and cold are alike injurious to organic life and to the human constitution. In the promotion of public hygiene it has further been observed that the influence of the weather upon mortality is exerted more immediately upon infants and the aged, whose vital force is less than that of persons in middle life.

Once more let us glance at the statistics of mortality with reference to the *Ages at death.* The whole number, including white and colored, are exhibited in the following table. The right hand columns on the scale of 100 are designed to serve, in some degree, the purpose of a diagram for illustrating the relative numbers deceased at different periods of life:

Deaths classified by Ages and by Sex, 1860.

Ages.	Number enumerated.			Proportions.			
	Males.	Females.	Total.	Males.	Females.	Total, '60.	Total, '50.
0— 1	44,480	36,794	81,274	11.35	9.39	20.74	16.90
1— 2	20,588	17,648	38,236	5.25	4.51	9.76	
2— 3	12,493	11,153	23,646	3.19	2.85	6.04	21.41
3— 4	7,567	7,083	14,650	1.93	1.81	3.74	
4— 5	5,332	5,147	10,479	1.36	1.31	2.67	
5—10	13,822	13,637	27,459	3.53	3.48	7.01	6.68
10—15	6,369	6,768	13,137	1.63	1.73	3.36	4.12
15—20	8,111	9,265	17,376	2.07	2.36	4.43	4.79
20—25	10,398	10,551	20,949	2.65	2.69	5.34	11.74
25—30	9,452	9,560	19,012	2.41	2.44	4.85	
30—40	16,224	15,343	31,567	4.14	3.92	8.06	9.07
40—50	13,470	10,522	23,992	3.44	2.68	6.12	7.14
50—60	11,902	8,514	20,416	3.04	2.17	5.21	5.56
60—70	11,284	8,823	20,107	2.88	2.25	5.13	5.12
70—80	8,995	8,009	17,004	2.30	2.05	4.35	4.17
80—90	4,776	4,808	9,584	1.22	1.23	2.45	2.54
90—..................	1,284	1,590	2,874	0.33	0.41	0.74	0.76
Unknown	688	371	1,059	....	....	....	....
Total	207,235	185,586	392,821	52.72	47.28	100.00	100.00

In the last column but one the sum of the four percentages between one and five years of age is 22.21, which does not essentially differ from 21.41, the corresponding percentage in 1850. By comparison throughout the last two columns, it will further appear that the only marked difference in the distribution of ages at death, in 1850 and 1860, is in early infancy, or under one year of age. From some misapprehension, occasionally an assistant marshal, not regarding infants as a part of the active population, has been less careful of their enumeration; and the greater proportion of infants in 1860 should doubtless be ascribed to a more complete enumeration. Upon the middle ages of life, in 1850, the cholera has traced a perceptible effect, as was to be expected from the immigration. With proper allowance for this feature, the return of deaths in 1860, for all ages above the first, appears similar and conformable to that of 1850.

As before shown, the total deaths returned in 1860 were 1 in 79 of the population; and in the less healthy year of 1850 the stated deaths were 1 in 71 of the population, a few still-births being included. In Europe the corresponding ratios, exclusive of still-births, have been recently collected by Professor Wappäus* from ten years official statistics, and are shown in the middle column following:

* Bevölkerungsstatistik, I, p. 160.

Ratio of Deaths in Europe.

Countries.	Population to one death.	The same adjusted to the scale of population in the U. States in 1850.*
Norway	56	....
Sweden	49	....
Denmark	49	....
England	44	47
France	44	44
Belgium	42	46
Netherlands	39	....
Prussia	36	....

The wide deviation of the stated ratio in the United States from these values is partly due to the more youthful character of the American population, sustained by a constant immigration. However, by the aid of the rates of mortality at different ages in England and France,* with those of Belgium, applied to the United States census of 1850, the unequal distribution of ages is here corrected in the three values of the last column. A large deficiency in our return of deaths is still indicated.

With regard to the question frequently asked, How much ought to be added to the census return of deaths, in order to approximate to the true numbers? the way for an answer, as definite as the subject admits, has been opened by a recent investigation. From a combination of statistical data, it has been demonstrated by Mr. L. W. Meech that the rate of mortality in the United States during the last half century has continued between limits, whereof the higher is represented by the English life table, and the lower by those of continental Europe. From this proposition, compared with the last column above, the conclusion is derived, that *the annual deaths in the United States have been one in* 45 *or* 46 *of the population.* There are localities where the "length of days" among the people is considerably above this standard, and others where it is below it; the value just stated, in the long average, cannot be far from the truth.

The question of supplying the deficient number of deaths can now be answered by an approximate correction. To avoid irregularities in the registry of infants, the returns "under five" are at present omitted. Applying the foregoing method, and regarding the deaths of 1850 as excesssive from cholera, it finally appears that the census of deaths above five years of age should be increased by about five-twelfths. The same rule may possibly apply to the deaths noted as "one and under five;" but "under one," the number should be increased in a greater ratio, not here determined. Thus in the aggregate of the whole country, so far as can now be ascertained, where seventeen deaths actually occurred, only twelve were reported in the census, exclusive of early infancy.

According to the preceding determination of one annual death in 45.5 living at the middle of the year, the 323,272 deaths returned in 1850, by supplying the omissions, become 501,000; and the 392,821 deaths enumerated in 1860 should similarly be increased to 680,000. At this rate, nearly six millions (5,905,000) of our population have deceased in the past ten years, and their places have been supplied by the advancing numbers of a new generation.

* Eighteenth Report of the Registrar General, (England), p. 32.

In concluding this discussion, it may be observed that the census of mortality compared with the topography of the United States will tend to illustrate the advantages of intercommunication. Our magnificent railroads and steamboat lines traversing immense distances, while promoting an exchange of products, and accommodating alike the tourist and the man of business, constitute an important agency for relieving the mind and improving the health of the people. To those persons who find the sea-coast air injurious, to the sedentary professions and city residents wearied with the dust and heat of summer and the cares of business, a change of air, and the shifting panorama of new scenes open renewed sources of enjoyment, in which all members of the family should participate. A few mineral springs and "watering places" at the sea-side or among the mountains are liberally patronized. Yet the adaptation of our country to a more general system of travel and periodic resort, for sanitary objects, presents a most useful field of inquiry.

The mortality of cities still exceeds that of the country, especially among children. And in both town and country a vast amount of needless sickness exists, which is proved to be preventible by ordinary means. The sanitary improvement of cities must be chiefly intrusted to health officers on the spot, who are conversant with the localities. Yet many of the topics have a popular interest; such as the introduction of the water-supply, of which the Fairmount, the Cochituate, and the Croton water-works are examples, the difficult art of complete sewerage and drainage, the opening of public parks and gardens, and the construction of improved tenement buildings. The vaccination of children before admission to the large public schools has been proposed, on account of the loss and annoyance from irruptions of the small-pox, a requisite which parental duty should have anticipated. The universal practice of this safeguard is strenuously urged, for, besides frequent cases of unavoidable exposure, of loathsome sickness and entailed suffering, many lives are annually lost by the culpable neglect of vaccination.

A great improvement in the registration of deaths, beyond the bare enumeration of the old "bills of mortality," consists in noting the principal circumstances of decease. This prepares the way, in skilful hands, for special and instructive researches. The classification of deaths with reference to intemperance, to different occupations and trades, will determine *among what classes the mortality is the most excessive,* and aid to disclose the causes. The value of this statistical method is illustrated by several remarkable sanitary investigations which have appeared within the last half century in Europe and America. After the facts comes the demand for new improvements and inventions. Some are required in the line of Davy's safety lamp for diminishing casualties, and others for adapting the operations and processes of the work-room to the health of the operatives. The subject is one of special interest, and worthy of sustained examination by our physicians and inventors. In numerous ways the information is so important that an official registration of deaths, notwithstanding the first deficiencies, is gaining adoption among all civilized nations.

On a general Life Table.—Were the enumeration of deaths entirely correct, and were the record combined with that of population, and cast into the systematic form of a life table, the value of this part of the census would be very greatly augmented. The plainest and most advantageous mode of expressing the relations of mortality to the population is conceded to be the life table, devised by Dr. Halley. In its elementary form it shows at a glance the proportion of persons surviving from one age to any other given age; in another form it exhibits the average duration or "expectation of life."

The Carlisle table, which has chiefly been used in England and America, was constructed by Milne from the returns during nine years, 1779–'87, of two healthy parishes in the city and suburbs of Carlisle, in the north of England. That this table should represent life insurance risks with accuracy during half a century is singular and remarkable. The coincidence is ascribed to what is termed "the selection of lives," since all the offices have required a medical examination of the assured.

The standard of longevity in the Carlisle table may thus be well adapted to life insurance, while it is too high for the whole population. Mr. Baily, a distinguished authority in London, forcibly remarks: "It must appear extremely incorrect to take the mortality in one particular town as a criterion for that of the whole country. The observations ought to be made on the kingdom at large, in the same manner as in Sweden; more particularly as, in the real business of life, the calculations are general and uniform, and adapted to persons in every situation. But till the legislature thinks proper to admit some efficient plan for furnishing these data, we must rest contented with the laudable exertions of public spirited individuals, and avail ourselves of the best light which they afford on this subject." (See continuation of chapter on mortality, p. 114.)

DEAF AND DUMB.

(Appendix—Table No. 7.)

Though the deaf and dumb, from the peculiar mental and moral phenomena which they display, have been objects of the curious attention of philosophers from the earliest dawn of science, it is only within three centuries that any successful efforts have been made to alleviate their misfortune by education, and only within the last forty years that an enumeration has been made of the deaf and dumb of any country. That deaf-mutes were quite numerous in ancient times is evident from the mention of them in the writings of that period. From the frequent mention of the restoration of the deaf to hearing and of the dumb to speech, in the history of our Saviour, the afflictions in question must have been common in Judea. And then, as now, congenital deaf-mutes were found in the highest as well as in the lower classes of society. The story of the deaf and dumb son of King Crœsus is well known; and Pliny speaks of a painter* at Rome, deaf-mute from birth, who was a relative of the Emperor Augustus.

We have, however, no means of estimating what might have been the numbers of deaf-mutes in ancient times. We only know that the infirmity appeared often to force itself on the attention of the philosopher and of the lawgiver. The wisest of the ancient philosophers could find no remedy for the closing of the customary channel of communication among men, and abandoned the unfortunate deaf and dumb as utterly incapable of instruction in letters. The celebrated code of Justinian, the foundation of modern European jurisprudence, classed the deaf and dumb with those persons who, by defect or alienation of mind, were rendered incapable of the legal management of their affairs. In the middle ages deaf-mutes were held to be incapable of feudal succession; otherwise there might possibly have been deaf-mute sovereigns on record, for we are told that an uncle of one of the kings of Sardinia was one of the earliest examples of a well-educated deaf-mute.

The first recorded attempts to instruct this class of unfortunates were made in Spain, about three centuries ago, by Pedro Ponce, a Benedictine monk, who conducted, and, as we are assured on the testimony of several cotemporary writers, with remarkable success, the education of several deaf-mutes of noble families, including the brothers and sister of the constable of Castile. Ponce died in 1504. Spain also presents the name of Bonet, who, half a century later, taught a brother of another constable of Castile, probably a nephew of the pupils of Ponce, and who published, in 1620, the earliest known treatise on the art of deaf-mute instruction. Both Ponce and Bonet instructed their pupils in

* Quintus Pedius.

articulation. A highly-colored account of the success of the latter was brought to England by Sir Kenelm Digby, one of the companions of Prince Charles in his romantic journey into Spain, and probably prompted the efforts of the earliest English teachers of deaf-mutes.

The Germans, jealous of the honor of their fatherland, claim that Rodolph Agricola records the case of a deaf-mute who had been taught to read and write a full century before the time of Ponce, without, however, giving any information as to the mode of instruction; and that about the same time that Ponce began his labors, Pasch, a clergyman of Brandenburg, instructed his deaf-mute daughter by the aid of pictures. In the next century (the seventeenth) we find a few instances recorded in England, in which more or less success was attained in teaching deaf-mutes to write, and even to speak. Dr. John Wallis, the most distinguished of the early English teachers, left on record in the philosophical transactions an account of his methods, which served as a guide to later teachers; and engaged, towards the end of the century, with a younger teacher of deaf-mutes on the continent, John Conrad Amman, of Amsterdam, who is noted for the wild extravagance of his views respecting articulation. Amman ascribed to speech a mysterious efficacy in the operations of the intellect, holding it to be not merely the most convenient, but the only instrument of thought and reasoning; a theory which, carried out to its logical results, would make the instruction of the deaf and dumb from birth utterly hopeless; since speech, properly so called, is to them incommunicable, all they can acquire of it being limited to the visible and felt movements of the organs of speech. Nevertheless these absurd views of Amman on the exclusive fitness of speech as an instrument of thought still influence the practice of the German teachers of our own times.

During the two centuries that succeeded the first labors of Ponce we only find here and there, at long intervals, a teacher who, moved in some cases by philosophical curiosity, in others by the hope of gain, and in others by parental affection, undertook, with more or less success, the education of one or two deaf-mutes. In many cases these early teachers were ignorant of the labors of their predecessors; the teacher had to grope his own way, and the processes were invented over and over again. Thus the art made little progress till the time of the Abbé de l'Epée.

This justly celebrated man, while living in Paris a life of literary ease, had his sympathies interested in the case of two sisters, twins, whose privation of speech and hearing seemed to cut them off from the hope of religious instruction. He gave himself to their instruction with the zeal of a missionary, who believes the eternal welfare of immortal souls at stake. Succeeding beyond his hopes in this new vocation, he devoted his fortune and his life to the cause of the deaf and dumb; and in the school which he founded was seen a spectacle which the world had never seen before—a large community of deaf-mutes restored to the full enjoyment of social intercourse through a language of their own. Having collected more than sixty into his own school, and finding that numbers more existed beyond his reach, De l'Epée labored with success to impart some of his own zeal to others, and (while other early teachers made a secret monopoly of their art) freely communicated his method to the world. Teachers formed by his lessons founded schools in Germany, Italy, Switzerland, Holland, and even Spain. Flattered by the frequent presence at his lessons of eminent visitors, up to the rank of emperor, De l'Epée labored with success to make the institution of the deaf and dumb popular. The impulse given by his zeal and labors opened a new era for the deaf and dumb. It is only from his time that the duty of educating them began to take hold of the public conscience. The school which he founded, and long supported from his own means, was taken under the patronage of the government after his death.

De l'Epée began his labors in behalf of the deaf and dumb between the years 1755 and 1760. Just about the same time began the labors of two other remarkable instructors—Thomas Braidwood in Scotland, and Samuel Heinicke in Saxony. Each of these distinguished men founded institutions which were the parents of many others. Nearly all the schools in the British isles sprang from that of Braidwood, and most of those in Germany originated, directly or indirectly, from that of Heinicke. On the other hand, the school of De l'Epée was the parent of nearly all the existing schools for deaf-mutes in the other countries of Europe and in America.

This is not the place to describe the different methods of those schools. We may, however, observe generally that the great object of the German schools is the teaching of an articulation which, in most cases, is both a very uncertain and an unpleasant means of communication with the deaf. Articulation was also a prominent part of the method of Braidwood, more because the idea of restoring the dumb to speak is so attractive to their friends and to the public, than from any real advantages which the pupils taught to articulate derive in the intercourse of society from any attainments in speaking possible to the deaf and dumb. For many years past the tendency of the more correct public opinion in England has been to the disuse of the efforts to teach articulation, as producing, in most cases, results of very trifling value at an unreasonable expense of time and labor.

The main peculiarity of the French system, or that of De l'Epée as improved by his able successors, Sicard and Bebian, was the cultivation and expansion of the language of gestures—the natural language of the deaf and dumb—as the means of mental and moral development, and the principal medium of instruction, by which the meaning of written language is imparted, enabling the pupil to communicate with all who can read and write, and opening to him that world of knowledge found in books.

This system prevails in all the schools for the deaf and dumb in the United States, having been brought to this country in 1816 by the late venerated founder of the American Asylum, Thomas H. Gallaudet, father of the present worthy principal of the institution in the federal capital. Mr. Gallaudet having become interested in the case of a deaf-mute, daughter of Dr. Cogswell, of Hartford, went to Europe to acquire the method of instruction, and being providentially repelled from the British schools, whose teachers then made a secret and a monopoly of their art, proceeded to Paris, studied the methods of Sicard, the celebrated pupil of De l'Epée, and returning, brought with him Laurent Clerc, himself a deaf-mute, already distinguished as the best teacher in the school of Paris, from which he brought a more thorough knowledge of the art of deaf-mute instruction, in the best state it had then reached, than probably any other man at that time possessed. The American teachers had thus, at the beginning, the advantage of a long cultivated and improved system. Nor has the art been suffered to remain stationary in this country. It has been diligently cultivated among us by many men of eminent ability during half a century; and the results attained in our schools for the deaf and dumb are certainly not inferior, in point of practical utility, to those attained in any of the European schools.

NUMBER OF SCHOOLS.

The number of schools for the deaf and dumb has been rapidly increasing during the current century. At the beginning of the century there were hardly a dozen such schools. Thirty years ago the number of European institutions for the deaf and dumb was about 118, containing, at most, 3,300 pupils. Ten years ago the number of institutions was estimated at 180, and the number of pupils at 6,000. Of the European institutions there are about 80, mostly small ones, in Germany, 45 in France, and 22 in the British isles. There are also two or three schools in British America. The three largest European schools are those of London, with about 300 pupils, Paris with about 170, and Groningen in Holland, with about 150.

The number of American institutions has also steadily increased. The American Asylum at Hartford is the oldest, having been opened in 1817. The New York institution is next in age, dating from 1817, and the Pennsylvania institution was opened in 1820. The Kentucky institution was opened in 1823, that of Ohio in 1829, and that of Virginia in 1839. The progress of the cause may be seen by the annexed table:

Date.	No. of institutions.	No. of teachers.	No. of pupils.
1834	6	34	466
1851	13	75	1,162
1857	20	118	1,760
1860	22	130	2,000

The New York institution is the largest in the country, and probably in the world, having 310 pupils. The asylum at Hartford has about 225, the institution at Philadelphia 206, and the schools of Ohio, Indiana, and Illinois from 140 to 170. The southern institutions are comparatively small, but their present condition cannot be ascertained. Of the 130 teachers, including the principals, about half are men of liberal education, about 15 are females, and about 50 are educated deaf-mutes.

The support of these twenty-two institutions costs not far from $350,000 annually, of which as much as $300,000 is appropriated by the legislatures of twenty-nine States. Provision for the education of the deaf and dumb, in some cases restricted to the indigent, in others made free to all, is made by law in all the States, except the sparsely settled ones of Florida, Arkansas, Minnesota, Kansas, and Oregon. All the New England States send their beneficiaries to Hartford, New Jersey sends hers to New York and Philadelphia, and Maryland and Delaware send theirs to Philadelphia, or to the institution at Washington, under the patronage of the President and Congress.

In the buildings and grounds of these several institutions, up to the date of our last information, over a million and a half of dollars had been invested. Except the necessary buildings and appurtenances, the institutions generally possess no permanent funds, being dependent on annual appropriations from the States; but there are three or four exceptions. The only considerable permanent fund is that of the American Asylum, derived from a grant of a township of land, made by Congress, through the generous aid of Henry Clay, as early as 1819. This fund now amounts to $200,000. The Texas institution has been munificently endowed by the legislature of that State with a grant of 100,000 acres of land.

Some prominent notice is due to the Columbia Institution for the instruction of the deaf and dumb, and the blind, at the national capital, which commenced its operations in June, 1857, under the provisions of an act of Congress, approved on the 16th of February in the same year.

The objects of the institution as contemplated in its organization were twofold: First, to provide suitable instruction for the deaf and dumb and the blind of the District of Columbia, and for children thus afflicted whose parents are in the military or naval service of the United States; secondly, to establish at the national capitol an institution for the instruction of the deaf and dumb, which should carry their education to a higher point than has yet been attained in other institutions. In other words to afford deaf-mutes in America an opportunity of obtaining a collegiate education, to qualify them as instructors, to enable them to engage in pursuits and occupations which are now (for lack only of the necessary training) beyond their reach.

The success of the institution has fully equalled the expectations of its founders. The first object has been entirely realized. The last annual report of the institution showed an attendance of forty-one pupils. The deaf-mutes are being carried forward in their education according to the French system, improved and introduced into this country by Doctor Gallaudet.

The blind are pursuing their studies in the manner adopted at the Boston institution.

A collegiate department will be organized as soon as the pupils of the institution are sufficiently advanced to enter upon the prescribed course of study. This stage will probably be reached in the year 1864.

The appropriations granted by Congress to the institution have amounted to $38,509 51; and there has been received from private sources the sum of $18,025.

The buildings of the institution, which will accommodate sixty pupils with the necessary officers and teachers, are healthfully located on an eminence commanding a view of the city, about a mile and a quarter northeast of the Capitol.

Mr. Kendall is the president of the board of directors, and has contributed liberally to the endowment of the institution, the immediate management whereof has been from the beginning in the hands of the principal, Edward M. Gallaudet, M. A., formerly instructor in the institution at Hartford.

The corps of instruction consists of the principal, two assistant instructors of the deaf and dumb, one instructress of the blind, and a teacher of drawing and the arts of design. Instruction is also given in mechanical labor.

In estimating the cost of instructing the deaf and dumb of the United States, it must be remembered that seven of the twenty-two institutions, those of Virginia, North Carolina, South Carolina, Louisiana, Michigan, California, and the Columbian Institution in Washington are also institutions for the blind as well as for the deaf and dumb, and that the support of their 136 blind pupils is included in the sum already given as the total annual expense of the twenty-two institutions. Allowing for these, the actual expense of educating the 2,000 deaf-mutes now in school may be estimated at $330,000. The number now under instruction ought to be considerably larger, especially in the southern States, to give all the deaf and dumb that education which alone can raise them to the rank of intelligent and useful citizens. It is restricted less from the difficulty of obtaining appropriations from the State legislatures than from the apathy of unenlightened parents, and their unwillingness to part with their children.

STATISTICS OF THE DEAF AND DUMB.

The earliest known attempt to estimate the number of deaf-mutes in a given country was made by the benevolent De l'Epée, who states that there were, about the year 1773, two hundred of these afflicted persons in the city of Paris, whence he calculated that there must have been 3,000 in the whole kingdom. If this last number is not an error of the press, the calculation seems very erroneous, for we know that the population of Paris at that day little exceeded half a million of souls, while that of France exceeded twenty millions. If there were then two hundred deaf-mutes in Paris, a like proportion for the whole kingdom would give 8,000 instead of 3,000. It was not till 1853 that an enumeration of the deaf-mutes of France was actually made, and the result gave a proportion for Paris and its vicinity just about that estimated by De l'Apée eighty years before—one in about 2,500 inhabitants; while the ascertained proportion for all France was one deaf-mute in 1,212 souls, more than twice as great as that for Paris.

The two earliest censuses known to us made by governmental authority, in which the number of deaf-mutes was noted, were that of the State of New York for 1825, and that of Prussia for the same year. The deaf and dumb of the United States were first enumerated at the national census of 1830, and at each census since. Enumerations of this class of the population have been made at different times within the last thirty years in several countries of Europe. In Great Britain they were first noted in the returns for the census of 1851.

The general result of these enumerations is that, except in a few extreme cases, the number of deaf-mutes in a given country is seldom more than about eight hundred in a million, or less than about four hundred. The later enumerations show a somewhat larger proportion than the earlier; but this may be owing to greater care in making the enumeration. The Prussian census for 1828 gave one deaf-mute in 1,548 souls; that of 1849 one deaf-mute to 1,364 souls. Thirty years ago the general average of all the European enumerations then made was about one deaf-mute in 1,500 souls. Ten years ago, according to a table prepared by Dr. Peet, of the New York Institution, there had been found 70,700 deaf-mutes, in those countries of Europe in which enumerations had been made, in a population of 92,710,000 inhabitants; a proportion of one deaf-mute to 1,311 souls. This proportion would have been reduced to about one in 1,360, had the result in England, which returned only one deaf-mute to 1,754 souls, then been known.

In this, as in other departments of vital statistics, we find, in any large district, a remarkable degree of uniformity from one period to another, showing that the prevalence of deaf-dumbness, as of other afflictions of mortality, is regulated by general laws. The proportion in the population of Prussia, as we have seen, varied less than a sixth part in twenty-one years; and that in the United States, according to our census returns, has only varied about one-tenth part in thirty years. The amount of variation will be seen from the annexed table, calculated for the white population alone for 1830, 1840, and 1850, and for the whole free population for 1860:

Years.	No. of deaf and dumb.	Population, 1 to—
1830	5,363	1,964
1840	6,682	2,123
1850	9,085	2,152
1860	14,269	1,925

The increased proportion for 1860 is probably owing, in part, to the fact that a considerable number of persons returned as "deaf" were counted with the deaf and dumb in making the abstract of the last census. This class of persons was carefully excluded in making the abstract from the census schedules of 1850, as it will be in the revision of the tables of the Eighth Census, which for want of time has not yet been effected.

The deaf and dumb, properly so called, are those who were born deaf, and in consequence grew up dumb, together with those who lost hearing by disease or accident at so early an age as to lose also the faculty of speech more or less completely. Besides these, there are many persons who lost hearing in childhood or youth, after acquiring the permanent power of speech, but who, incapable of being taught in ordinary schools, are entitled to the privileges of a special institution for deaf-mutes. These are sometimes returned as deaf and dumb, especially if they are or have been pupils of an institution for deaf-mutes; sometimes they are returned as "deaf," and often, especially when their misfortune is recent, they are not distinguished at all. If none but this second class of persons (technically known as semi-mutes) were returned as deaf, there could be no hesitation in including them all with the deaf and dumb. But there are many people who become deaf in mature life, or with advancing age, and these are gratuitously marked as "deaf" on the census schedules, in so many cases as to materially affect, in some districts, the general accuracy of our calculations. None who become deaf after the age of ten or twelve should be included in tables of the deaf and dumb; but this distinction was not generally understood by the census-takers.

Another source of error of a different kind is the frequent return as "dumb" of persons who are dumb, not as a consequence of deafness, but from defect of intellect. If all who are thus returned were known to be idiots, all should be excluded from our tables of the deaf and dumb; but the same word appears to be used in many cases to designate the proper deaf and dumb, and we have no means of discriminating between those who are *dumb* because *deaf*, and those who are *dumb* from deficient intellect. To insure more perfect accuracy for the general report, the list of the deaf and dumb in the United States, made out in this office from the original schedules, will, as far as practicable, be submitted to the inspection of the conductors of the several institutions that their extensive knowledge of individual cases may be availed of to correct the returns in a sufficient number of cases to give a general average of corrections, and thus enable us to approximate much more nearly to accuracy in this branch of our statistics. A small expenditure for the printing of this list may be necessary to this end.

Though by including many returned as "deaf" only, and others returned as "dumb" only, the returned number of the deaf and dumb may be considerably increased; there is reason to believe this increase is not more than equal to the number of omissions. Dr. Peet has made it appear probable, for instance, that owing to the reluctance of parents to describe their children as dumb a large number of deaf-mute children under the age of ten or twelve were omitted;* that the returns of deaf-mutes from most of our larger towns are also deficient; and that, from the greater difficulty of obtaining information in the case of our foreign population, their deaf and dumb are not as fully returned as in the case of the native population. To these we should add many omitted by accident or through the hurry or carelessness of the marshals. Allowing for all these causes of omission, it is not improbable that the proportion of deaf-mutes in the white population of the United States is as great as that found in England and Germany.

Taking the returns as they are, we find the sources of error so uniform in their influence that the results will serve for the purpose of comparison between different classes of the population and between different sections of the Union. We may thus, in time, be aided in forming accurate conclusions as to the causes of deafness; a prospect that gives a higher interest to the returns, since a knowledge of the causes may lead to the knowledge of preventions, whereby the prevalence of this distressing infirmity may be diminished.

The particulars, however, to be gathered from our census, relating to the deaf and dumb, are not nearly as full as would be desirable in this point of view. They do not show, for instance, how many are deaf and dumb from birth, and

* In 1850 the proportion of deaf-mutes returned under 10 years was to the population of the same age (whites) only as 1 : 3,570 for males, and 1 : 4,200 for the females; while between the ages of 10 and 30 the proportion was 1 : 1,550 males, and 1 : 1,930 females.—(*Statistics of Deaf and Dumb, by H. P. Peet, LL.D.*)

how many from disease or accident, (the latter supposed to be nearly half the whole in this country, though only one-fifth of the whole in Europe;)* nor in how many cases there are two or more deaf and dumb children in the same family; nor in how many cases the parents were blood relatives; nor in how many cases the infirmity is transmitted from parents to children. The general laws to be gathered from our census returns are of another kind, and relate to the influence of race, of emigration, of climate, or of geological formation on the prevalence of deaf-dumbness, although they present facilities for the prosecution of inquiries which, if followed up, will enable us to throw much light on the subject generally.

We note *first*, that the white race appears from our census returns to be much more liable to deaf-dumbness than the black, and of course the free colored, which has a larger admixture of white blood, is more liable to that infirmity than the slave population; on the other hand, it is supposed that the colored population is more liable to blindness than the whites. This greater prevalence of deaf-mutes, (after allowing for errors in the two enumerations of 1830 and 1840, which appear to have risen from accidentally placing figures in the wrong columns,) is manifested in every one of the four enumerations from 1830 to 1860, and in the returns from every State. The general average of the census of 1860 gives only one slave deaf-mute to every 4,900 slaves, whereas there is one to every 1,925 among the free population. In 1850, excluding, as already observed, the "deaf," there was returned one deaf-mute to 2,152 whites, one to 3,151 free colored persons, and one to 6,034 slaves. The small proportion returned among the slaves may indeed be due, in part, to less care and particularity in making the enumeration; but it is difficult to believe in a carelessnes so general as to account for so great a discrepancy as is here shown. It seems, therefore, safe to assume that the colored race is less liable to deaf-dumbness than the white race; and such, according to the testimony of missionaries, seems also the case with the Mongolian population of China as compared with Europeans.

The next fact to be noted is that there is a larger proportion of deaf-mutes among a population from which emigration has been large than among a population which is gaining largely by emigration. This fact is patent from the returns of every census, as will appear from the annexed table, calculated as before for the white population in 1830, 1840, and 1850, and for the whole free population in 1860:

	The Atlantic States, from Maine to Georgia, inclusive.	All the remaining States and Territor's.
Number of deaf mutes in 1830	4,031	1,332
Proportion to population	1 to 1,864	1 to 2,265
Number of deaf mutes in 1840	4,475	2,207
Proportion to population	1 to 1,993	1 to 2,388
Number of deaf mutes in 1850	5,737	3,732
Proportion to population	1 to 1,961	1 to 2,245
Number of deaf mutes in 1860	7,819	6,450
Proportion to population	1 to 1,796	1 to 2,080

* Dr. Peet estimates that in Europe there are in a population of a million 615 deaf-mutes who are so from birth, and only 154 by disease or accident; while in the United States the former class number 278 in a million, and the latter 222.—(See *the Thirty-fifth New York Report.*)

This law is more strikingly exemplified by the returns from the extreme west. California and Oregon, for instance, returned in 1850 only 7 deaf-mutes in a population of 105,000, and in 1860 only 84 in a population of 432,000. Though it may be that the returns from sparsely settled districts are apt to be less accurate than the average, still there can be no doubt that a comparatively small proportion of deaf-mutes go along with the stream of emigration. Families with deaf-mute children have an inducement to remain in the older States, at least till their children can be educated; and it may be that such families, as a general rule, do not belong to the more energetic and restless part of the population. It may be owing in part to a similar cause that the proportion of deaf-mutes is smaller in America than in Europe.

The proportion of deaf-mutes among the slaves of the border States and that found in the extreme southern States offers a contrast even more marked, which is no doubt due, at least in part, to a like cause, the deportation of so many slaves southward, since we may assume that a deaf and dumb slave would be less desirable for a trader than one who can hear. In 1860 there were returned from the slave States north of the parallel of 35°, including North Carolina, but excluding Arkansas, 458 deaf and dumb slaves, one to 3,340 slaves; and from the more southern slave States only 350, but one deaf-mute to 6,920 slaves. This difference can hardly be due to climate, for the proportion of deaf-mutes among the white population of South Carolina was greater in 1830 than in any other State, except Connecticut and New Jersey; and at the last census the greatest proportion in the whole Union, allowing for the large number from other States collected into the school in Connecticut, was returned from the comparatively southern States of Virginia and Kentucky. We cannot, therefore, assume from the census returns that coldness of climate has any marked influence on the prevalence of deaf-mutes.

It has been supposed that mountainous and sterile countries have a larger proportion of deaf-mutes than those that are level and well cultivated. In Europe the greatest known proportion is found among the mountains of Switzerland, the smallest on the fertile plains of Belgium. But we have no such deep, dark humid valleys as those of some parts of Switzerland, where the population seems to deteriorate from generation to generation, and where cretinism, often allied to deaf-dumbness, prevails to a painful extent. Whether in our mountainous districts deaf-mutism is more prevalent than in more level regions can hardly be determined till our population becomes more stationary. We observe that, by the British census of 1851, the proportion of deaf-mutes was, indeed, smaller in level and fertile England than in the more mountainous and sterile countries of Wales and Scotland; but on the other hand, Ireland, a comparatively level country, presents a larger proportion than Wales, and about as large as Scotland. In our own country the proportion in Vermont and New Hampshire, though greater than in most of the other northern States, is less than in the fertile regions of Kentucky.

If we assume as a probable theory that congenital deafness is, in most cases, an arrest of development, owing in some cases to deficient vital power in one or both parents, and in other cases to a physiological unfitness of the parents for each other, and that the loss of hearing by disease or accident is more prevalent among children whose constitutional vigor is impaired, it is difficult to see why mountainous regions, that are found favorable to general health and to longevity, as many mountainous regions are known to be, should present more cases of deaf-mutes than other regions.

The inquiry as to the influence of the geological formation of a country on the prevalence of deaf-mutism is an interesting one, but partly from the difficulty of determining the geological character of a given district, partly from the labor requisite for the investigation, very little has yet been done to elucidate this point. Kentucky has returned at each census a large proportion of deaf-mutes, and Kentucky is a limestone country. This statement embraces about all that may at present be hazarded on this point.

BLIND.

The first regularly organized establishment for the charitable relief of the blind is known as "*The Hospital Imperiale des Quinze Vingts.*" It was founded in Paris by St. Louis in 1260, and still exists. It contains, as its name implies, fifteen score, or 300 blind. It is an asylum only for adults, and does not attempt to instruct its inmates.

Although much had been done by celebrated blind persons and others in overcoming the privations of sight by ingenious contrivances for the touch, the first successful effort in systematic instruction was made by *Valentin Haüy.* Inspired by the success of the Abbé de l'Epée in the education of the deaf and dumb, M. Haüy conceived that equal results could be effected for the blind, who were deemed more helpless. He reflected upon the fact that the touch of the blind is so exceedingly sensitive as rarely to be deceived in distinguishing the different coins. Why might they not distinguish letters if made tangible? Letters were printed in relief; maps with raised lines were made; a class of blind children was collected and instructed, and the experiment was successful. Such was the simple basis of the system which has been followed over the civilized world.

A house was procured in 1784, in Paris, under the patronage of the Philanthropic Society, which may be regarded as the cradle of the present Imperial Institution for the young blind.

In 1791 "the Liverpool school for the blind" was founded, which was the first in Great Britain.

The following table exhibits the institutions and asylums for the blind in Great Britain and Ireland, the dates of their foundation, and the number of inmates in each:

No.	Location.	Founded.	Inmates.
1	Liverpool	1791	80
2	Edinburg	1792	115
3	Bristol	1793	66
4	London	1799	154
5	Norwich	1805	36
6	Dublin, ("Richmond," for males)	1809	20
7	Dublin, ("Molyneaux," for females)	1815	35
8	Glasgow	1828	106
9	Belfast	1831	13
10	Yorkshire	1835	60
11	Limerick, (for females)	1835	12
12	Manchester	1837	75
13	Newcastle	1838	41
14	London, ("Society for teaching the blind to read")	1838	56
15	Liverpool, (Catholic, for females)	....	17
16	Exeter	1838	26
17	Aberdeen	....	30
18	Bath	1840	24
19	Brighton	1841	21
20	Nottingham	1842	30
21	Birmingham	1846	59
22	*Plymouth	....	....

TABLE—Continued.

No.	Location.	Founded.	Inmates.
23	*Bath, (blind school-house)	....	....
24	*Edinburg, (Abbey Hill)	....	....
25	*Dublin, (Catholic)	....	....
26	*Cork	....	....
27	*London, (Milton Institution)	....	....
28	*Midland Institution	....	....
	Total in twenty-one institutions	....	1,076

* Schools and asylums more recently established, and of smaller size; the dates and numbers not ascertained.

Associations and societies for the relief of the blind in Great Britain.

1. London.—"Association for Promoting the General Welfare of the Blind." The object is to supply the adult blind with employment. It has six branches in other parts of the kingdom, viz: in Bradford, Davenport, Leicester, Liverpool, Sheffield, and Surry.
2. London.—Society for Printing and Distributing Books for the Blind, 1854.
3. London.—Indigent Blind Visiting Society, 1837.
4. London.—Christian Blind Relief Society, 1843.
5. London.—Society for Supplying Home Teachers.
6. London.—"The Blind Man's Friend, or Day's Charity." (Founded by the late Mr. Day, who left £100,000 for the benefit of persons suffering under loss of sight.)
7. London.—Rev. Wm. Hetherington's charity (1774) appropriates £10, yearly, each to 50 blind persons over 60 years of age.
8. London.—The Painters and Stainers' Company (1780) for the relief of blind persons above 61 years of age.
9. London.—The Cordwainers' Company (1782) distributes £5, annually, to 105 blind persons.
10. London.—Society for Improving the Social Position of the Blind.
11. London.—The Cloth-workers' Company.
12. London.—The Drapers' Company.
13. London.—The Goldsmiths' Company.
14. London.—The Society for Granting Annuities to the Blind.

The last six grant small annuities for the relief of blind persons.

Institutions for the blind on the Continent of Europe.

No.	Location.	Founded.
1	Paris, Hospital Imperiale des Quinze Vingts	1260
2	Paris, Imperial Institution for the young blind	1784
3	Vienna, Austria	....
4	Prague, Bohemia	1804
5	Amsterdam, Holland	1804
6	St. Petersburg, Russia	1806
7	Berlin, Prussia	1806
8	Milan, Sardinia	....
9	Dresden, Saxony	1809
10	Zurich, Switzerland	1809
11	Copenhagen, Denmark	1811
12	Brussels, Belgium	....
13	Lausanne, Switzerland	....

Institutions for the blind on the Continent of Europe—Continued.

No.	Location.	Founded.
14	Breslau, Prussia	1816
15	Konigsburg, Prussia	1816
16	Stockholm, Sweden	1817
17	Barcelona, Spain	1820
18	Naples, Italy	1822
19	Germund, Wurtemberg	1823
20	Lintz, Austria	1824
21	Pesth, Hungary	1825
22	Friesingen	1828
23	Bruchsal, Baden	1828
24	Hamburg, Holland	1830
25	Antwerp, Belgium	
26	Bruges, Belgium	
27	Brunswick, Brunswick	
28	Frankfort-on-the-Mayn	
29	Friedberg, Hesse	
30	Lille, France	
31	Berne, Switzerland	
32	Stuttgardt, Wurtemberg	
33	Friedberg, Switzerland	
34	Liege, Belgium	
35	Christiana, Norway	

Institutions for the blind in the United States, with the number of pupils and blind persons employed by them.

No.	Location.	State.	Founded.	No. of pupils and blind employed.
1	Boston	Massachusetts	1833	111
2	New York	New York	1833	167
3	Philadelphia	Pennsylvania	1833	177
4	Columbus	Ohio	1837	120
5	Staunton	Virginia	1838	44
6	Louisville	Kentucky	1842	54
7	Nashville	Tennessee	1844	36
8	Raleigh	North Carolina	1845	18
9	Indianapolis	Indiana	1846	72
10	Jacksonville	Illinois	1847	50
11	Cedar Springs	South Carolina	1848	17
12	Janesville	Wisconsin	1850	40
13	St. Louis	Missouri	1851	29
14	Macon	Georgia	1851	31
15	Baton Rouge	Louisiana	1852	14
16	Jackson	Mississippi	1852	10
17	Iowa City	Iowa	1853	40
18	Baltimore	Maryland	1853	25
19	Flint	Michigan	1853	35
20	Austin	Texas	1856	12
21	Washington	District of Columbia	1857	6
22	Little Rock	Arkansas	1859	10
23	San Francisco	California	1860	8
	Total pupils and inmates			1,126

Proportion of blind persons in the several States, and to the whole population in the United States.

States.	Free, blind.	Slaves, blind.	Free, one in—	Slaves, one in—
Alabama	204	114	2,594	3,816
Arkansas	118	26	2,749	4,273
California	63	....	6,032	....
Connecticut	152	....	3,027	....
Delaware	42	....	2,629	....
Florida	15	21	5,245	2,940
Georgia	297	188	2,003	2,458
Illinois	476	....	3,617	....
Indiana	530	....	2,548	....
Iowa	192	....	3,515	....
Kansas	10	....	10,711	....
Kentucky	530	144	1,755	1,565
Louisiana	112	118	3,365	2,811
Maine	233	....	2,696	....
Maryland	264	34	2,272	2,564
Massachusetts	498	....	2,472	....
Michigan	254	....	2,595	....
Minnesota	23	....	7,044	....
Mississippi	147	116	2,413	3,764
Missouri	388	60	2,727	1,915
New Hampshire	142	....	2,296	....
New Jersey	208	....	3,230	....
New York	1,768	....	2,199	....
North Carolina	392	189	1,687	1,751
Ohio	899	....	2,602	....
Oregon	9	....	5,829	....
Pennsylvania	1,187	....	2,448	....
Rhode Island	85	....	2,054	....
South Carolina	171	120	1,761	3,353
Tennessee	437	117	1,908	2,356
Texas	119	31	3,535	5,889
Vermont	165	....	1,903	....
Virginia	557	232	1,984	2,115
Wisconsin	220	....	3,526	....
Dakota Territory	....	....	....	....
District of Columbia	47	....	....	....
Nebraska Territory	3	....	....	....
New Mexico Territory	149	....	....	....
Utah Territory	17	....	....	....
Washington Territory	2	....	....	....
Total	11,125	1,510	....	....

Proportion of blind slaves to all slaves, one in........ 2,616
Proportion of blind to the whole population, one in........ 2,470

For the advantage of comparisons the following statistics of the blind in Europe are given:

According to the census of 1851 the whole number of blind persons in Great Britain and Ireland was 29,074, viz:

In England and Wales	18,306;	1 in 979
In Scotland	3,010;	1 in 960
In islands in the British sea	171	
Total in Great Britain	21,487;	1 in 975
In Ireland	7,587;	1 in 878
Total in Great Britain and Ireland	29,074;	1 in 950

A larger proportion of blind persons is found to exist in the agricultural districts of Great Britain than in the manufacturing and mining districts and large cities. There is—

In London	1 blind to every 1,025 persons
In Birmingham	1 blind to every 1,181 persons
In Leeds	1 blind to every 1,203 persons.
In Sheffield	1 blind to every 1,141 persons.
In the whole kingdom	1 blind to every 950 persons.

The British census of 1851 gives some remarkable facts in regard to the *ages* of blind persons, widely different from estimates hitherto received. Of the 21,487 blind persons in England, Scotland, and Wales, there were—

Under 20 years of age, only	2,929, or 14 per cent.
Between 20 and 60	8,456, or 39 per cent.
Above 60	10,102, or 47 per cent.

While less than one-seventh were under 20, nearly *one-half* were at the advanced age of 60 and upwards; showing the small proportion blind in infancy, the large number blinded by old age, and also the longevity of the blind.

In Prussia (1831) it was estimated that, out of 9,212 blind persons, 846, or nearly $\frac{1}{11}$, were between the ages of 1 and 15. In Brunswick, out of 286 blind, $\frac{1}{20}$ were under 7.

We have no authentic information of the blind in France. But if the proportion is the same as that of adjoining countries, there were in 1836 24,675 blind, or 1 to every 1,360 inhabitants.

Comparative portion of blind persons to the whole number of inhabitants in Europe and in the United States.

Great Britain and Ireland, (1851,)	1 in 950
France, (census of 1836,)	1 in 1,360
Belgium, (1831,)	1 in 1,316
Level portions of the German States	1 in 950
More elevated portions of Germany	1 in 1,340
Prussia, (average of census in 1831, 1834, and 1837,)	1 in 1,401
Alpine regions, (1831,)	1 in 1,500
Sweden	1 in 1,091
Norway	1 in 482
United States, (1850,)	1 in 2,470

The remarkable fact is given by this table that the blind in the United States but little exceeds *two-fifths* of the number in Great Britain and Ireland, and are less than *three-fifths* of the number in France, in proportion to the populations of those countries.

The proportion of the blind in each of the United States to the population, considered in relation to geographical position, shows that whatever causes may have modified these proportions, *climate* has had little or no influence; and that the tables of Dr. Zenue, of Berlin, so much referred to as showing the proportions of the blind according to *latitude*, are entirely inapplicable to the United States.

According to those tables the proportion is—

In latitude 20 to 30	1 in 100	In latitude 50 to 60.....	1 in 1,400
In latitude 30 to 40	1 in 300	In latitude 60 to 70.....	1 in 1,000
In latitude 40 to 50	1 in 800		

The following contrary results appear in certain geographical districts of the United States:

Southern States.

Louisiana, latitude 29 to 33	1 to 3,365
Mississippi, latitude 30 to 35	1 to 2,413
Alabama, latitude 30 to 35	1 to 2,594

Northern States.

Maine, latitude 43 to 47	1 to 2,696
Massachusetts, latitude 42 to 43	1 to 2,472
Michigan, latitude 42 to 46	1 to 2,595

In other respects, and from other causes, large differences occur in the proportions of blind persons in some of the States. In Texas (latitude between 26 and 30) there is 1 blind to 3,535; Oregon, 1 to 5,829; California, 1 to 6,032; Minnesota, 1 to 7,044; Kansas, 1 to 10,711. These are distant and thinly-populated States, to which blind persons would rarely emigrate, and contain comparatively few aged persons, among whom a larger portion of the blind are found.

The extraordinary exemption from blindness in the United States compared with Great Britain, according to the census returns, which give the latter about two and a half times more blind than the former country, is a fact of great importance, and suggests inquiries into the causes. We have too little data to warrant any certain conclusions. Sufficient exists, however, to show that *small-pox* has been a prolific cause of blindness in Great Britain, but not in the United States.

Of 1,456 blind persons received into the Liverpool School for the Blind, from 1791 to 1860, 250, or more than *one-sixth*, were blinded by *small-pox*.

Of the pupils in the Glasgow Asylum nearly *one-fifth* were blinded by small-pox.

In the Pennsylvania Institution, of 476 pupils received, only 21, or about $\frac{1}{22}$ part of the whole were blinded by small-pox. Of 118 pupils in the Ohio Institution, to a certain date, only *one* was blinded by small-pox. Dr. Crampton, of Manchester, England, estimated that between 4,000 and 5,000 were blinded by small-pox in Great Britain.

SYSTEM OF PRINTING FOR THE BLIND.

The blind of necessity read by the touch. The method of printing in raised letters originated, as stated, with *Valentin Haüy*, in Paris, in 1784. Since then various kinds of embossed letters and characters have been adopted. The alphabetical systems are known as the *Roman capitals*, as in the books printed at the Glasgow and Pennsylvania institutions; the combined *capital* and *lower case*, as in books from the Bristol, Paris, and some of the German institutions; and the *angular lower case*, of the Massachusetts institution.

The arbitrary systems are known as Braille's in France; Carton's in Belgium; *Lucas's*, *Frere's*, and *Moore's* in England. Both systems have their peculiar advantages. While some institutions adopt the principle that the alphabets and all tangible apparatus should conform as nearly as possible to those universally in use by the seeing, it must be conceded that the simple arbitrary characters of Braille, Lucas, and others, are more readily learned by the adult blind and those whose touch has become less sensitive by work.

Books for the blind are quite limited in number and dear. Of the principal works of this character may be named: the whole Bible, printed at the Glasgow Asylum, in 19 volumes, quarto, price $48; the whole Bible, in 8 large volumes, price $20; A cyclopedia, 8 large volumes, (unfinished;) Milton's Poetical Works, 2 volumes; Paley's Evidences, 1 volume; Combe on the Constitution of Man, 1 volume; Philosophy of Natural History, 1 volume; Rudiments of Natural Philosophy, 1 volume; Lardner's Universal History, 3 volumes; Common Prayer, 1 volume; Pope's and Diderot's Essays, 1 volume, and other works from the Boston Institution. A dictionary of the English language, 3 large volumes; Select Library, 5 volumes; Church Music, 3 volumes; Student's Magazine, 6 volumes, and other works from the Philadelphia Institution. History of the United States, 3 volumes, and several other works from the Virginia Institution. These and some volumes of moderate extent from the Bristol and London presses are all in the alphabetical type. The New Testament, and portions of it and part of the Old, have been printed and duplicated several times in the three arbitrary characters of Lucas, Frere, and Moore, used in England.

While these various arbitrary systems do credit to the ingenuity of the inventors, two of whom are blind, it is unfortunate, considering the paucity of embossed books, that the efforts of the friends of the blind have not been concentrated upon some one or two kinds of print.

GENERAL VIEW AND OBJECTS OF THE INSTITUTIONS FOR THE BLIND.

The great object of all institutions for the education of the blind is to remove the disabilities under which they labor, as far as possible, by substituting the sense of touch for the lost sight; by a correct system of moral, and mental, and physical training, and by giving them a knowledge of music or some useful mechanic art to prepare them for the active duties and enjoyments of life. Without deciding how their mental and physical condition will compare with the general standard, it is demonstrated that they have capacities for receiving a good education in the various departments of useful knowledge, and of becoming church organists and piano instructors. The largest number become practical workmen in several branches of plain handicraft. While the cultivation of music is to them a source of the greatest delight, and is almost universally taught to the younger blind as affording a benevolent compensation for the loss of all that is beautiful in nature, the exercise of the industrial powers supplies to the mass of the blind the great necessity of their condition. Occupation of mind and body in all these respects gives to the blind in the public institutions that tone of cheerfulness which is considered so remarkable in their condition.

But the great result is the preparation of the blind for *self-support* when they return to become members of the community. It is for this end that private bounty and legislative aid have been so generously granted in the United States. While the young blind are admitted for a term of years to receive an education in the school and music departments, in connexion with handicraft, adults at all ages under 50 are received in some of the institutions for a period of one or two years to acquire a simple trade, when they go on their way rejoicing in their ability to support themselves, or at least to remove the necessity of an entire and hopeless dependence on their friends or the public.

In Europe thousands of blind persons are paupers in the poor-houses or burdens upon friends who would be able, if instructed in simple trades, to earn a large part of their support. Many adult blind in the United States are in the same dependent condition. This number is being partially provided for by those institutions which receive adults.

The employment of the graduate blind by existing institutions is a subject of interest in the United States as in Europe. It is certain that many worthy and industrious blind persons fail to support themselves fully. How far and in what way they may be aided by existing institutions or by others organized for their welfare is an important question claiming and receiving serious attention by those prepared to judge practically upon the subject.

INSANE.

Among the many evidences of progressive science and enlightened philanthropy furnished by the history of the last three-quarters of a century, none are more characteristic, and perhaps no one appears in bolder relief, than the system of treatment of the insane which, adopted within that period, now widely prevails among civilized nations. In a civil, social, and moral point of view, the space is broad which separates the gloomiest cell of a prison, with its bolts, bars, and chains, from spacious apartments furnished with the conveniences and comforts as well as many of the luxuries of life. Yet this space has been traversed by the insane within the seventy years next preceding the present time. It is proposed to give in this place a brief sketch of the history, more especially in respect to the United States, of this important amelioration of the condition of a large class of our fellow-men.

About the middle of the eighteenth century some philanthropists of Philadelphia took preliminary measures for the foundation of a general curative institution in that city; and in 1751 the provincial assembly of Pennsylvania passed an act of incorporation under the title: "The Contributors of the Pennsylvania Hospital." This charter provided not only for the relief of persons suffering from general diseases, but also for the "reception and cure of lunatics."

It is believed that this was the first legislative provision in the American colonies for the restorative treatment, in a public hospital, of persons afflicted with mental alienation. The hospital was opened on February 11, 1752, and thenceforward one of its departments was specially appropriated to that class of patients.

The next practical movement in a similar direction was in Virginia; and to her belongs the honor of being the pioneer of all the colonies in the establishment of an institution exclusively devoted to the insane. An act providing for the lunatics and idiots of the colony passed her legislature on November 10, 1769. A hospital was erected at Williamsburg at the expense of £1, 070, and opened on or about September 14, 1773. In the course of the war of independence the building was evacuated and used as barracks for the colonial troops. Subsequently, but at what precise period we are not informed, it was re-opened, and has since been conducted in accordance with its original purpose.

In 1771 the Earl of Dunmore, then governor of the colony of New York, granted a charter for the institution now known as the "New York Hospital," in the city of New York. The intervention of the war with England prevented the opening of this hospital until January 3, 1791. Insane patients, so far as appears by the records, were not admitted until 1797.

Such, and such alone, according to present knowledge, were the completed provisions for the care and treatment of the insane in the hospitals of the United States prior to the close of the eighteenth century. But the character of the treatment was more custodial than curative; and the means employed, including as they did, the severest forms of bodily restraint, were better adapted to felons than to persons laboring under disease.

We have now arrived at the period of initiation in another country of an enterprise which, whether we regard the boldness of its beginning, the rapidity of its progress, the extent of territory over which it has spread, the success which it has achieved, or the amount of good to mankind of which it has been the minister, challenges the admiration of every advocate of human improvement and every lover of his race.

In the midst of all the horrors of the French revolution, Dr. Pinel walked the reddened streets of Paris a minister of benevolence, a physician with a heart. He was connected with the Bicêtre Hospital, in which many of the insane were confined in cells and loaded with manacles and chains. After repeated solicitations he at length, in the latter part of the year 1791, obtained permission from the public authorities to remove these torturing implements of bodily restraint. The first person upon whom the experiment was tried was an English captain, who, being subject to paroxysms of extreme violence, had been chained there forty years. A promise of good behavior having been obtained from him the chains were loosed, and the man, returning as it were to the joys of life, kept his promise, rendered himself useful, and had no recurrence of maniacal fury during the two additional years of his residence in the hospital. Twelve inmates of the hospital were thus relieved from their irons on the first day of the experiment, and in the course of a few days forty-one more were similarly released. History furnishes few sketches of more touching interest than the account of these proceedings given by M. Scipion Pinel, son of the chief actor in them.

Nearly simultaneously with the early measures of Pinel, and, as is believed, without any knowledge of them, William Tuke, of York, England, conceived the plan of founding a hospital for the treatment of the insane upon principles more enlightened and humane than had theretofore prevailed in Great Britain. His plan was carried into execution by the construction of the Friend's Retreat for the Insane at York, which was opened in the year 1796.

Such was the twofold source of the movement which, though compelled to contend with the precedents and the prejudices of ages, and though for this and other reasons its progress was slow for many years, was destined fully to triumph over established usage in the countries of its origin.

Before the close of the eighteenth century German students in the medical school of Paris had carried home the new theory and practice of Pinel, and had begun that work of reformatory regeneration of the institutions for the insane in their native land, which, though small at its beginning and repressed by hindrances similar to those already alluded to, has since been prosecuted with perhaps no less vigor or success than in France or England.

The spirit of the enterprise crossed the Atlantic more slowly than it traversed the boundaries of the German States. The first decennium of the current century furnishes no new movement on behalf of the insane in the United States, except the erection for their accommodation of a separate though nearly adjacent building at the New York hospital. This occurred in 1808.

As early as 1797 Mr. Jeremiah Yellot, of Baltimore, gave seven acres of land to the State of Maryland, on condition that the government should found a hospital for the treatment of insanity and general diseases. In 1798 an appropriation for the purpose was made, and increased by private contributions as well as by an appropriation by the municipal government of Baltimore, applied to the construction of a suitable building. But the hospital was not opened until 1816.

The success of the retreat at York having become known upon this side of the Atlantic, some members of the Society of Friends, in Pennsylvania, desiring to provide hospital accommodations for the insane, formed an association in 1812, obtained a charter, erected a building near the village of Frankford, but now within the limits of the city of Philadelphia, and under the title "Asylum for the Relief of Persons deprived of the use of their Reason;" the institution was opened in May, 1817.

In the course of these proceedings in Pennsylvania measures for the attainment of a similar end were taken by the trustees of the Massachusetts general hospital, in Boston. A distinct establishment, though a branch of that institution, was constructed near Charlestown, now in Somerville, and designated as the "McLean Asylum for the Insane," was opened on the 6th of October, 1818.

Five institutions for the care and curative treatment of the insane in the United States went into operation in the course of the decennium, terminating with the close of 1830. In 1815 preliminary measures were prosecuted by the board of governors of the New York hospital for the foundation, at Bloomingdale, of a branch of that institution. A grant from the State legislature of an annuity of ten thousand dollars for forty years was obtained, an edifice erected and opened for patients in 1821, under the title of "Bloomingdale Asylum for the Insane." The retreat for the insane at Hartford, Connecticut, and the Kentucky Eastern Lunatic Asylum, at Lexington, first received patients in 1824; and the Western Lunatic Asylum of Virginia, at Staunton, as well as the State Lunatic Asylum of South Carolina, at Columbia, in 1828.

Earliest in the next succeeding period of ten years was the State Lunatic Hospital, at Worcester, Massachusetts, which was opened in 1833. The Vermont Asylum for the Insane, at Brattleboro', followed in 1836; the Central Ohio Lunatic Asylum, at Columbus, in 1838; the City Lunatic Asylum, at South Boston, Massachusetts, and the New York City Lunatic Asylum, on Blackwell's Island, both pauper institutions, in 1839; and the Maine Insane Hospital, at Augusta, and the Tennessee Hospital for the Insane, at Nashville, in 1840.

It was during this decennium that the greatest impulse was given to the scheme for ameliorating the condition of the insane in the United States. In the production of this impulse no man exerted greater influence than the late Doctor Samuel B. Woodward, who was at that time superintendent of the State Lunatic Hospital, at Worcester, Massachusetts. The zeal and hopefulness with which he illuminated a sphere thitherto almost universally regarded in the popular mind as shrouded with clouds and involved in darkness, and the elaborate and interesting reports which, emanating from his pen, were scattered broadly through the country, all contributed to the awaking of an interest in the subject which had never previously been manifested.

In the course of this period, also, that eminent philanthropist, Miss Dorothea L. Dix, began a series of benevolent and beneficent labors to which female biography, throughout the history of the world, probably exhibits no equal. Beginning in Massachusetts, and subsequently proceeding to other States, she traversed the counties and townships within their several jurisdictions, visited all the public receptacles for the insane, together with all the private hovels, dens, garrets, and cellars for solitary maniacs to which access could be gained. She stimulated individuals to exertions and contributions in the cause, and in memorials to legislatures and by appeals to Congress called upon the governments to extend the assistance of the commonwealth to this class of its suffering people.

In 1839 a pamphlet entitled "A visit to Thirteen Asylums for the Insane in Europe," by Dr. Pliny Earle, was published in Philadelphia and extensively circulated among physicians and others interested, or likely to become interested, in the subject. As the first somewhat comprehensive account of the European establishments which appeared in this country, it had no small influence in the promotion of the cause.

The Pennsylvania Hospital for the Insane, situated about two miles west of the old State House in Philadelphia, and a branch of the Pennsylvania Hospital. was opened in 1841. The New Hampshire Asylum for the Insane, at Concord; the Mount Hope Institution, at Baltimore, Maryland; and the Lunatic Asylum of the State of Georgia, at Milledgeville, commenced operations in 1842; the New York State Lunatic Asylum, at Utica, in 1843; the first hospital disconnected from the almshouse for the insane poor of Kings county, New York, at Flatbush, in 1845; the Butler Hospital for the Insane, a corporate institution, at Providence, Rhode Island, in 1847; and the New Jersey State Lunatic Asylum, at Trenton; the Indiana Hospital for the Insane, at Indianapolis, and the Insane Asylum of the State of Louisiana, at Jackson, in 1848. About the middle of the decennium the patients with general diseases were removed from the Maryland Hospital, at Baltimore, and that institution was thenceforth devoted to the treatment of insanity alone.

Such were the completed results of the increased activity of the enterprise in the fourth decade of the century. Among the most important agencies in the promotion of the cause, in the course of this period, was the "Association of Medical Superintendents of American Institutions for the Insane," which held its first meeting in Philadelphia, in 1845.

The propositions relative to the construction, arrangements, and organization of hospitals for the insane, drawn up by Dr. Thomas S. Kirkbride, of the Pennsylvania Hospital for the Insane, and adopted by this association, have generally been received as the highest authority upon the subjects. Although the idea may have occurred to others, yet Dr. Francis T. Stribling, superintendent of the Western Lunatic Asylum of Virginia, was the first to take the active measures which led to the promotion of this useful association, which has greatly contributed to a uniformity of views and practice among the superintendents of American institutions for the insane.

The first number of the American Journal of Insanity was issued in July, 1844. It was edited by its originator, the late Dr. Amariah Brigham, at that time superintendent of the New York State Lunatic Asylum at Utica. Intended not for the benefit of professional readers alone, but also for the dissemination of more accurate views of insanity among the people, its editor endeavored to adapt its contents to the attainment of this twofold object. The Journal is still continued under the editorship of Dr. John P. Gray and the officers of the asylum at Utica. It has assumed a more purely scientific and professional character, and has done great service in the cause to which it is devoted.

In the course of this decade Dr. Luther V. Bell, of the McLean Asylum, Dr. Isaac Ray, of the Butler Hospital, Dr. H. A. Buttotph, of the New Jersey State Lunatic Asylum, and Dr. Pliny Earle, for several years connected with the Bloomingdale Asylum, visited the rapidly improving institutions of Europe. Among the fruits of their observations we have the design of the Butler Hospital, by Dr. Bell; an elaborate résumé entitled "Observations on the Principal Hospitals for the Insane in Great Britain and Germany," by Dr. Ray; some articles in the Journal of Insanity, by Dr. Buttotph; and a descriptive work entitled "Institutions for the Insane in Prussia, Austria, and Germany," by Dr. Earle.

No less than eighteen new institutions were put in operation during the decennium from 1851 to 1860, inclusive. The State Lunatic Hospital of Pennsylvania, at Harrisburg; the State Lunatic Asylum of Missouri, at Fulton, and the Illinois State Hospital for the Insane, at Jacksonville, were organized and first received patients in 1851. The new building of the Tennessee Hospital, a few miles from Nashville, was so far completed as to be occupied in 1852. The State Insane Asylum of California, at Stockton, and the Hamilton County Lunatic Asylum, a pauper institution, now at Mill Creek, near Cincinnati, Ohio, and called the Longview Asylum, were opened in 1853; the Massachusetts State Lunatic Hospital, at Taunton, and the Western Lunatic Asylum of the State of Kentucky, (since destroyed by fire,) at Hopkinsville, in 1854; the United States Government Hospital for the Insane, near Washington, District of Columbia; the new building of the Kings County Lunatic Asylum, at Flatbush,

New York; the Mississippi State Lunatic Asylum, at Jackson; the Northern Ohio Lunatic Asylum, at Newburg; the Southern Ohio Lunatic Asylum, at Dayton, and Brigham Hall, a corporate institute at Canandaigua, New York, in 1855; the Insane Asylum of North Carolina, at Raleigh, and a department of the Western Pennsylvania Hospital, at Pittsburg, (soon to be transferred to an extensive establishment, and called the Dixmont Hospital for the Insane,) in 1856; the Massachusetts State Lunatic Hospital, at Northampton, and the New York State Asylum for Insane Convicts, at Auburn, in 1858; the Michigan Asylum for the Insane, at Kalamazoo, and a department of the Marshall Infirmary, at Troy, New York, in 1859; the Alabama Hospital for the Insane, at Tuscaloosa, and the Wisconsin State Lunatic Asylum, at Madison, in 1860.

In January, 1860, the Pennsylvania Hospital for the Insane separated the sexes, by placing them in two distinct establishments, about one quarter of a mile apart, but on the same grounds and under the same general medical superintendence. The buildings of the department for males are as large as the original buildings which now constitute the department for females, and were erected and furnished wholly by the contributions of private citizens, most of Philadelphia. This is the first example, in America, of a system for the treatment of the sexes in separate, independent, but united establishments.

A valuable work entitled "A Manual for Attendants in Hospitals for the Insane," by Dr. John Curwen, of the State Lunatic Hospital of Pennsylvania, appeared in 1851; and in 1854 Dr. Thomas S. Kirkbride published a treatise "On the Construction, Organization, and General Arrangements of Hospitals for the Insane," which has become a standard authority."

So far as our knowledge extends, the only hospital which has gone into operation since the commencement of the current decennium is the Iowa State Hospital for the Insane, at Mount Pleasant, which was opened in 1861. A State hospital at Austin, Texas, was begun several years since, and a superintendent appointed, but no intelligence of its opening has reached us.

Inasmuch as the people of all the States have a community of interest in one of the public hospitals above mentioned, it is proper that we should give a more particular account of that institution than of those of a more local character.

The Government Hospital for the Insane was specially intended for the insane of the army, the navy, the revenue cutter service, and the indigent of the District of Columbia. It is situated on the eastern shore of the Potomac river, within the limits of the District of Columbia, and about two miles south of the Capitol, in Washington. The principal building, constructed of brick, is seven hundred and twenty feet in length. Its architectural plan and internal arrangements are among the best which have resulted from the experience and the studies of many able men employed in the specialty. A farm of one hundred and ninety-five acres belongs to the establishment.

The first appropriation by Congress for this institution was made in August, 1852. Dr. Charles H. Nichols was soon afterwards appointed as superintendent, and under his direction and supervision the building was begun in May, 1853. A section of it was completed and opened for the reception of patients in January, 1855. It is now (1862) complete, with the exception of the internal finish of a small section. The aggregate amount of appropriations for the purchase of the farm and the construction of the buildings is $473,040.

The number of patients on the first of July, in each year since the hospital was opened, was as follows: in 1855, 63; in 1856, 92; in 1857, 110; in 1858, 117; in 1859, 138; in 1860, 167; and in 1861, 180. The number of *persons* treated, prior to the 1st of July, 1861, was 439. Of these 261 were natives of the United States; 169 of foreign countries, and the place of birth of 9 is unknown.

The hospital is under the general supervision of the Department of the Interior. Since it was commenced four different men, representing as many shades of political opinions, have held the office of secretary, and all of them have manifested an intelligent, liberal, and benevolent interest in the success of the enterprise. In no instance has the department sought to control the patronage of the institution, or in any degree to cripple its usefulness by making it contribute to the especial advantage of the political party in power. Congress has been liberal in its appropriations; and among its members the hospital, in every stage of its progress, has found warm and earnest supporters, whose aid was honorable to themselves and a cause of gratitude in the heart of every American philanthropist. The hospital remains in the charge of Dr. Nichols, under whose supervision it has been wholly created.

Aside from the public institutions, a few private establishments for the treatment of the insane have been opened in the United States in the course of the last forty years. Although some of them which have been discontinued were directed by able and humane men, and several others still in operation are considerably patronized and well conducted by men of high character, yet a consciousness of the undeniable tendency to abuse involved in a purely private pecuniary enterprise of this kind as shown in the history of similar establishments in Europe, has operated to discourage their multiplication and prosperity in this country.

Since the opening of the public institutions nearly all of them have been enlarged, some to the extent of doubling or trebling their original capacity. With few exceptions, chiefly among those most recently founded, the buildings have been undergoing changes of internal architecture and arrangement in conformity with progressive knowledge. They differ very materially in plan, extent, structure, and means and facilities for the prosecution of curative treatment. A large proportion of them will not suffer in comparison with the better class of similar institutions in Great Britain, France, and Germany. It is believed that in executive administration they are governed with prudence, benevolence, and kindness; that their officers are generally earnest laborers, emulous of improvement; and that the unfortunate insane may be committed to them in full confidence of immunity from cruelty or abuse.

Inasmuch as mind can be perceived and studied in its manfestations alone, its essential nature cannot be understood. It is consequently impossible to reduce to a positive demonstration any answer to the proposition whether insanity is really a disease of the mind itself, or merely the effect of corporeal disorder. Much has been written upon the subject, especially by the psychologists of Germany. Among the physicians making insanity a speciality in the United States we know of no one who believes it to be a disease of the spiritual part of our nature. They are unanimous in the opinion that it is the result of corporeal impediments to the free evolutions of the operations of the mind, as irregularity in the movements of a watch may be the effect of some small substance placed among the internal works, and thus preventing the gradual but continual development of the elasticity of the main spring. The watch indicates false time, but the spring is unimpaired. The insane man talks incoherently and fantastically, but his spiritual being is in its normal condition. The fact that a single portion of appropriate medicine has more than once entirely cured a paroxysm of violent mania is, perhaps, of itself a sufficient proof of the truth of this theory; for is it not absurd to suppose that the essential structure or nature of the spirit can be reached and modified by a cathartic?

The causes of mental alienation are various. They have been divided into classes, as the predisposing and the exciting, the remote and the immediate. Some causes are difficult of classification, and the subject in this brief sketch is of but trifling importance.

Among the manifestly remote causes are hereditary predisposition, constitutional organization, and descent from parents nearly allied by consanguinity. Like many other maladies, insanity is disposed to propagate and perpetuate itself in the line of family descent, and instances are not unfrequent in which several children of an insane parent have become insane. The peculiar organization, whatsoever it may be, which favors an attack of mental alienation, often arises, *de novo*, in one person or more of a family theretofore exempt from the disorder.

The disposition to degeneracy, in some form, in the offspring of marriages of cousins, or others near of kin, has long been known, but comparatively recent investigations in both Europe and the United States, and particularly those of M. Devay, in France, and Dr. Bemiss, of Kentucky, have more fully illustrated the subject and more satisfactorily demonstrated the fact. It is very clearly proven that sterility attends, and that bodily malformation, tubercular consumption, spasmodic diseases, epilepsy, blindness, deafness, idiocy, and insanity follow in the offspring of such marriages much more frequently than in matrimonial alliances between the parties to which there is no traceable affinity by blood. Researches have not hitherto been sufficiently extensive to demonstrate the comparative proportion, but it is sufficient for the purpose of the philosopher, the philanthropist, or the statesman that the predominance of those unfortunate results in the marriages of cousins and other near relatives is placed beyond a reasonable doubt.

The subject has already commanded the attention of the legislatures of some of the States, but no law, so far as we are informed, has as yet been enacted in regard to it.

The prevailing system of education acts, perhaps, as both a remote and an immediate cause of insanity. The early age at which children are placed in school, their confinement often to ill-constructed seats, in imperfectly ventilated rooms, and the burdens which, in the multiplicity of lessons, are thrown upon them, tend to an undue development of the brain, enfeeblement of all the other vital organs, and exhaustion of the nervous power, which is the essence or basis of vitality.

Immunity from these results can be secured only by making general physical development and energy keep pace with mental education. As a general rule, whatever exhausts the power of the brain and nerves, depresses vitality, or debilitates the body, may, through these effects, become the causative agent of insanity. Hence ill health, the intemperate use of spiritous liquors, debauchery, self-abuse, excessive and prolonged labor, either manual or mental, night-watching, or great loss of sleep from any cause, excitement upon religious subjects, domestic and pecuniary difficulties, disappointment and grief, are among the most prolific causes of the disorder. It is a disease of debility, and not of a superabundance of strength, as was in former times generally, and is still, to a wide extent, believed. It is almost unknown among aboriginal races, whose habits and customs promote corporeal development, strength, and vigor, and make no detrimental strain upon the nervous system. It increases with advancing civilization, and abounds to the greatest extent wherever man is most enlightened, because there the artificial habits and customs which call the brain most powerfully into action are the most prevalent.

The treatment of insanity, as pursued at the present day, is properly divided into two parts or systems. One of these might be termed the *direct*, the other the *indirect*, but they are generally called the *medical* and the *moral* treatment. The medical treatment consists in the use of such medicines as in each particular case will be likely to restore the body to a healthy condition. This treatment, as a system, has undergone a radical change within the last fifty—mostly within the last thirty—years. Formerly, based upon the theory that insanity is a disease of strength, or of active inflammation, it chiefly consisted in the liberal employment of blisters, purgatives, cupping, and blood-letting. Now, founded upon the well-supported theory that the disorder originates in debility, its principal remedies are stimulants and tonics. The success of the present method demonstrates not only the excellence of the practice but the truth of the theory.

The moral treatment includes the exercise of a mild but firm directive and disciplinary power over the actions of the patient, by which he is gradually restored to healthful habits and wholesome self-restraint, and the attempt to win him from the vagaries of his delusions to those mental and manual pursuits which give solidity, strength, and activity to the normal mind. The means adopted for the attainment of these ends, the regular hours of hospital life, appropriate manual labor, walking, riding, athletic and other games, attendance upon religious services, reading and other literary pursuits, lectures upon scientific and miscellaneous subjects, dramas, concerts, balls, and other recreations, entertainments, and amusements. In the method of moral treatment the change has been no less than in that of medical treatment. This change may be comprehended in two brief, generic statements: first, the almost absolute disuse of mechanical appliances for bodily restraint; and, secondly, the introduction of the conveniences, comforts, and to some extent the luxuries that appertain to civilized life, into the apartments of the patients, and to all parts of the hospital establishments where such means will benefit them. This change has been gradual, and the detailed history of its progress would occupy more space than is compatible with our present purpose.

In 1838 Mr. Hill, house surgeon of the Lincoln Lunatic Asylum, England, published a work in which he advanced the following proposition as a principle: "In a properly constructed building, with a sufficient number of suitable attendants, restraint is *never necessary*, *never justifiable*, and always injurious, in *all cases* of lunacy whatever." This proposition appears to have been founded upon Mr. Hill's experience at the asylum mentioned. At that institution, in 1830, of 92 patients, 54 were placed under mechanical restraint a total of 2,364 times, during an aggregate time of 27,113 hours. The sum of this restraint was diminished in succeeding years until, in 1836, with 115 patients, 12 were thus restrained a total of 39 times, and during an aggregate time of 334 hours; and in March, 1837, all mechanical restraint was abandoned.

The doctrine of Mr. Hill found many advocates and followers in England, but in France, Germany, and the United States it has been almost universally rejected. All men of experience in the specialty are well aware that there are occasional instances in which the true interest and welfare of the patient are best promoted by restraint, *of some kind*, upon the limbs. Even Mr. Hill admits this as a truth; and the great defect, as appeared to us, in the practical working of his principle is that, in order to secure this restraint, the hands of an attendant are substituted for some mechanical appliance. What man, sane or insane, would not be more restive and violent if held by another man than if confined by a leathern muff upon his hands?

While, therefore, the superintendents of American hospitals reject the arbitrary rule of Mr. Hill, they adopt the safer one of employing mechanical restraints only when they are required by the best interests or true welfare of the patient.

If subjected to proper treatment in its early stages, insanity, in a very large proportion of cases, may be cured. Many statistics upon the subject have been published, but in some instances they were collected under conditions so restrictive that they conveyed an erroneous impression.

It may perhaps be safely asserted that, in cases placed under proper treatment within even one year from their origin, from sixty to seventy per cent. are cured. But the earlier the treatment is adopted the greater is the probability of restoration, and a delay of three months is a misfortune, as it is a detriment to the patient.

Of all the cases, both recent and chronic, received at our public institutions, the average of cures is not far from forty per cent. At thirty hospitals in the

United States, in 1859, the number of cases admitted was 4,140, and the number discharged as cured 1,728, equal to 41.7 per cent. Of 57,978 cases received, in a series of years anterior to 1860, at twenty-nine of our hospitals, 24,573 had been discharged cured; this is equal to 42.38 per cent. It must be remembered, however, that in mental alienation, as in other diseases, many patients suffer from relapse, or recurrence of the disorder, and hence, in the reported number of cures last given, there are many instances of two or more cures of the same person. The statistics of our hospitals are still crude, the only thorough analysis hitherto published being that of the cases at the Bloomingdale asylum prior to 1845. By those it appears that, although the *admissions* or *cases* had been 2,308, the number of *persons* was but 1,841. The number admitted twice, each, was 280; thrice, each, 81; four times, each, 33; five times, each, 18; and thus the number diminished until it ends with one patient who was admitted twenty-two times, and discharged cured every time. Of the 1,841 persons, 742, or 40.3 per cent., were cured.

In cases where the disease has existed more than one year, the average of cures varies at different hospitals and in different periods. Some reports state it as below *fifteen*, others as somewhat above *twenty*, per cent. At many institutions no distinction between old and recent cases is made in the reports.

The foregoing facts appeal strongly to the friends of the insane to permit no delay in placing them under curative treatment. They address themselves also, in connexion with the subject of pauper insanity, to the political economist and the legislature. The indigent man becoming insane may, if soon restored, preserve his pecuniary independence; if not restored he becomes a charge for life to his friends or to the public, generally to the latter.

Of twenty *recent* cases treated and cured at the Western Lunatic Asylum of Virginia, the average period during which they were at the asylum at public cost was 17 weeks and 3 days; the total, $1,265, and the average cost, $63 25. Of twenty *chronic* cases at the same institution the average time during which they had been supported from the public treasury was 13 years, 4 months, and 24 days; their total cost, $41,653, and their average cost, $2,082 65.

The disparity in expense is great; but the actual sum of pecuniary difference does not wholly appear in the figures. The twenty persons cured had again become producers instead of mere consumers, the twenty persons with chronic insanity still lived at the public expense, and so would continue through life. Similar comparative statements showing like results have been made in the reports of several of our hospitals.

Intemperance has been mentioned as one of the most prolific causes of insanity. It is probably the most productive of all. Hence, whatsoever diminishes intemperance reduces, indirectly, the number of the insane. In connexion with this subject it may be stated that delirium tremens, often a somewhat immediate effect of excessive potations, is not generally included under the term "insanity;" yet persons laboring under that disease are treated in many of our institutions for the insane. But they are out of place, and almost invariably are a detriment to the other patients, and notorious infringers of the rules of the hospital.

For these reasons, among many others, special institutions for inebriates are among the greatest of public needs. The subject has been discussed to some extent for thirty years, and yet but one institution of the kind has been founded. This is near Binghamton, New York.

Insane convicts constitute another class of patients who, for many and mostly obvious reasons, ought not to be received at the ordinary public institutions. The superintendents of many of the hospitals have earnestly protested against the practice, but hitherto with comparatively little effect. New York is the only State which has a hospital specially intended for the class in question.

The laws, both civil and criminal, relating to insanity and the insane are still imperfect in all the States, perhaps less so in Maine than in any other part of the Union.

So far as relates to the treatment of patients in the public institutions, those of Ohio are well adapted to the attainment of the great ends of the restoration of curable cases and the reduction of the amount of insanity. Still, a general code embracing all the rights, privileges, immunities, necessities, and responsibilities of both the insane and sane, in relation to the disease, is a thing of the future and not of the present.

Table showing the number of insane in the United States and Territories according to the Eighth Census, 1860.

States and Territories.	Insane.		States and Territories.	Insane.	
	Free.	Slave.		Free.	Slave.
Alabama	225	32	North Carolina	597	63
Arkansas	82	5	Ohio	2,293	....
California	456	....	Oregon	23	....
Connecticut	281	....	Pennsylvania	2,766	....
Delaware	60	....	Rhode Island	288	....
Florida	20	5	South Carolina	299	18
Georgia	447	44	Tennessee	612	28
Illinois	683	....	Texas	112	13
Indiana	1,035	....	Vermont	693	....
Iowa	201	....	Virginia	1,121	58
Kansas	10	....	Wisconsin	283	....
Kentucky	590	33	District of Columbia	204	....
Louisiana	132	37	Dakota	....	....
Maine	704	....	Nebraska	5	....
Maryland	546	14	New Mexico	28	....
Massachusetts	2,105	....	Utah	15	....
Michigan	251	....	Washington	3	....
Minnesota	25	....			
Mississippi	236	36		23,593	406
Missouri	750	20			
New Hampshire	506	....		....	23,593
New Jersey	589	....			
New York	4,317	....	Total	....	23,999

IDIOTIC.

The number of those unfortunate beings who constitute this class, while numerically greater, has decreased slightly in ratio to the population. As but little has been effected for the elevation of these imbeciles, and as it is conceded that their condition has rendered them, for the most part, incapable of mental improvement, the efforts of humanity have been mainly directed to their personal comfort and physical requirements.

Among the numerous attributed causes of idiocy, none is more generally conceded by those who have investigated the subject, than the intermarriage of near relatives.

The following table represents their number, and their proportion to the free and slave population:

Table showing the number of idiotic in the United States and Territories.

States and Territories.	Idiotic.		Free, one in—	Slave, one in—
	Free.	Slave.		
Alabama	403	134	1,312	3,246
Arkansas	152	24	2,133	4,629
California	42	....	9,047	....
Connecticut	226	....	2,036	....
Delaware	67	....	1,648	....
Florida	52	16	1,513	3,859
Georgia	541	183	1,099	2,525
Illinois	588	....	2,911	....
Indiana	907	....	1,488	....
Iowa	289	....	2,335	....
Kansas	17	....	6,306	....
Kentucky	903	155	1,030	1,454
Louisiana	143	104	2,631	3,189
Maine	658	....	954	....
Maryland	243	62	2,468	1,406
Massachusetts	712	....	1,729	....
Michigan	333	....	2,249	....
Minnesota	31	....	5,608	....
Mississippi	193	76	1,837	5,745
Missouri	447	63	2,387	1,824
New Hampshire	336	....	970	....
New Jersey	365	....	1,841	....
New York	2,314	....	1,677	....
North Carolina	739	241	895	1,373
Ohio	1,788	....	1,308	....
Oregon	15	....	3,497	....
Pennsylvania	1,842	....	1,577	....
Rhode Island	101	....	1,728	....
South Carolina	282	121	1,068	3,325
Tennessee	732	149	1,139	1,850
Texas	164	37	2,571	4,933
Vermont	263	....	1,198	....
Virginia	1,065	214	1,037	2,293
Wisconsin	257	....	3,018	....
District of Columbia	27	....	2,662	....
Dakota	1	....	4,837	....
Nebraska	3	....	9,608	....
New Mexico	40	....	2,337	....
Utah	5	....	8,048	....
Washington	....	....	....	....
Totals	17,286	1,579 17,286	1,590	2,503
Total	....	18,865		

In 1850 there were of the free population	14,666	idiotic, or one in 1,366.
In 1850 there were of the slave population	1,040	idiotic, or one in 3,081.
Total free and slave	15,706	idiotic, or one in 1,476.
In 1860 there were total free and slave	18,865	idiotic, or one in 1,666.

PRODUCTS OF INDUSTRY.

The returns of MANUFACTURES exhibit a most gratifying increase, and present at the same time an imposing view of the magnitude to which this branch of the national industry has attained within the last decennium.

The total value of domestic manufactures, (including fisheries and the products of the mines,) according to the Census of 1850, was $1,019,106,616. The product of the same branches for the year ending June 1, 1860, as already ascertained in part and carefully estimated for the remainder, will reach an aggregate value of *nineteen hundred millions of dollars* (1,900,000,000.) This result exhibits *an increase of more than eighty-six* (86) *per centum in ten years!* The growth of this branch of American labor appears, therefore, to have been in much greater ratio than that of the population. Its increase has been 123 per cent. greater than that even of the white population by which it was principally produced. Assuming the total value of manufactures in 1860 to have been as already stated, the product *per capita* was in the proportion of sixty dollars and sixty-one hundredths ($60 61) for every man, woman, and child in the Union. If to this amount were added the very large aggregate of mechanical productions below the annual value of five hundred dollars—of which no official cognizance is taken—the result would be one of startling magnitude.

The production of the immense aggregate above stated gave employment to about 1,100,000 men and 285,000 women, or one million and three hundred and eighty-five thousand persons. Each of these, on an average, maintained two and a half other individuals, making the whole number of persons supported by manufactures four millions eight hundred and forty-seven thousand and five hundred, (4,847,500,) or nearly one-sixth of the whole population. This was exclusive of the number engaged in the production of many of the raw materials, and of food for the manufacturers; in the distribution of their products, such as merchants, clerks, draymen, mariners, the employés of railroads, expresses, and steamboats; of capitalists, various artistic and professional classes, as well as carpenters, bricklayers, painters, and the members of other mechanical trades not classed as manufacturers. It is safe to assume, then, that one-third of the whole population is supported, directly and indirectly, by manufacturing industry.

These general facts, therefore, plainly indicate that, in point of productive value, and far-reaching industrial influences alone, our manufactures are entitled to a front rank among the great interests of the country. Indeed, the collection and classification of facts relating to the material progress of the people periodically intrusted to the Census Office, furnish in general, valuable milestones in the pathway of the nation's greatness. But among the facts so collected, none are more instructive—none have more numerous or intimate relations to every department of the public economy, to the general welfare of the people, domestic, social, industrial, or moral—than these records of their productive capacities in the automatic and handicraft arts. However uninteresting to many, the details are full of instruction to the statist. As the mountain rill, minute and inappreciable in its source, is constantly swelled by other streams, and goes on widening and deepening in its course until it is swallowed up and loses its identity in the ocean, so these streams of knowledge, pouring in towards a common reservoir from every factory, hamlet, town, and State, appear at length to be merged in one vast and useless aggregate, devoid of either individual, local, or general interest. But the great collection of truths which they serve to swell may bear up the ark of a nation's hopes and confidence. The result may form a subject of national pride and gratulation, and may, like the ocean itself, become impressive to all nations from its grandeur. The mental eye may also follow back each separate stream to its source, and dwell with pleasure and instruction upon the scenes fertilized, refreshed, and gladdened in its progress. Such emotions of pride and pleasure cannot fail to be generally awakened by the evidences which a just appreciation of the wisdom of Congress has enabled the proper department to accumulate and classify, with greater accuracy and completeness than heretofore, of the progressive development and present stature of this important interest. The subject is grand in its outlines; but contemplated in its pervasive influence upon the welfare of the whole people, the dry and repulsive skeleton of mere facts and figures, presented in the official tables, gradually takes on the form, substance, and habilaments, and becomes animated with something of the life, activity, and beauty of a living economy. The statistics of looms, spindles, and factories, of furnaces and forges, of steam-engines and sewing-machines, and of a thousand other instruments of creative industry, become the representatives of almost every form of national and individual happiness, exertion, aspiration, and power.

The mechanic arts—particularly in our country, where they are most diffused, and all but universal—appear to contribute more directly than any others to the general comfort and improvement of the people. All others are dependent upon them for the principal agents and instruments of their success. They are scarcely more subservient to the primary wants of mankind than to the higher ministrations of taste and refinement. The acquisition and diffusion of knowledge, the means of intercommunication and transportation, the comforts, enjoyments, and security of the fireside, and even the honor and integrity of the nation itself, are dependent upon the skill and enterprise of the manufacturer and the mechanician; but the results of their labors are, from their nature, less obtrusive or obvious to the general apprehension than some others. The annual movements of our immense crops of grain, cotton, and other bulky staples, are easily appreciated. The pulsations of commerce may be counted by a superficial observer, in the arrival and departure of ships, and upon the records of the custom-house and the Exchange; but in the hands of the manufacturer a modicum of crude material undergoes a process of division, transformation, and elaboration, and then silently and unobtrusively disappears—diminished in bulk, but augmented, it may be, many hundredfold in value—in the ordinary channels of distribution, where it is often undistinguished from its foreign rival. It is only when the nation decennially takes its account of stock that any approximate idea is obtained of the value of this item in the general account.

And who can justly estimate the influence upon the general happiness and prosperity—upon the progress in civilization of the sum total of effective labor, capital, and skill represented by such an aggregate as we have stated? What an amount of fixed capital—of labor, enterprise, ingenuity—of resources, material and immaterial—involved in the creation of nearly two thousand millions worth of manufactures in a single year! The addition of nearly one thousand millions to the annual product of domestic manufactures—an amount almost equal to the total home consumption thereof in 1850—implies also vast additions to the permanent wealth of the Union and to the elements of a progressive civilization. The increased support given to agriculture, commerce, and the mining interests by the consumption of hundreds of millions of dollars worth of raw material, and to hundreds of thousands of men, women, and children, who would have been otherwise unemployed, or forced into competition with the farmer and planter, instead of being consumers of their produce, form but a part of the benefits conferred upon the community at large. The independence and security contributed by the large body of intelligent manufacturers and mechanics capable of ministering to every want, whether of supply or defence, cannot be overestimated. As might have been expected from the revelations of the Census, the country has been able to lean with confidence upon this arm of its strength in the trying emergency which has put the nation in armor for the defence of its dearest interests.

It is a gratifying fact, shown by the official statistics, that while our older communities have greatly extended their manufactures, the younger and more purely agricultural States, and even the newest Territories, have also made rapid progress. Nor has this department of American industry been cultivated at the expense of any other. There is much reason to believe that it affords the safest guarantee of the permanency and success of every other branch. Evidence bearing upon this point is found in the manufacture of agricultural machines and implements, which is one of the branches that shows the largest increase in the period under review. There is little doubt that the province of manufactures and invention in this case has been rather to create than to follow the demand. The promptness of Americans to adopt labor-saving appliances, and the vast areas devoted to grain and other staples in the United States, have developed the mechanics of agriculture to an extent and perfection elsewhere unequalled. The adoption of machinery to the extent now common in farm and plantation labor furnishes the best assurance that the development of agriculture or manufactures to their utmost, can never again justify the old charge of antagonism between them in regard to labor, or injuriously affect either by materially modifying its cost or supply.

The total value of AGRICULTURAL IMPLEMENTS made in 1860 (Table No. 8) was $17,802,514, being an increase of 160.1 per cent. upon the total value of the same branch in 1850, when it amounted to the sum of $6,842,611. This manufacture amounted in New England to over two and three-quarter millions of dollars—an increase of 65.8 per cent. In the middle States the value was nearly five and a half millions, having increased at the rate of 122.2 per centum. In the western States, where the increase was most extraordinary, the value of implements produced was augmented from $1,923,927 to $7,955,545. The increment alone in those States was, therefore, only a fraction less than the product of the whole northern section of the Union in 1850, and was greater by 313 per cent. than their own manufacture in that year. In each of the States of Ohio and Illinois, which are the largest manufacturers in the west, the value of the product exceeded two and a half millions dollars, being an increase in the former of 382, and in the latter of 235 per cent. in ten years. Michigan, Indiana, and Wisconsin increased their production of agricultural implements 1,250, 386 and 201 per cent., respectively. While in some of the southern States there has been a decrease, in Virginia, Alabama, and Louisiana the increase in this branch has been large, and in Texas, which reported none in 1850, agricultural implements of the value of $140,000 were manufactured in 1860. The whole value produced in the southern States in the latter year (including cotton gins) was $1,582,483, exhibiting an increase of over 101 per cent. in the last decade.

The quantity of PIG IRON returned by the census of 1860 (Table No. 9) was 884,474 tons, valued at $19,487,790, an increase of 44.4 per cent upon the value returned in 1850. Bar and other ROLLED IRON (Table No. 10) amounted to 406,298 tons, of the value of $22,248,796, an increase of 39.5 per cent. over the united products of the rolling mills and forges, which in 1850 were of the value of $15,938,786. This large production of over one and a quarter million of tons of iron, equivalent to 92 pounds for each inhabitant, speaks volumes for the progress of the nation in all its industrial and material interests. The manufacture holds relations of the most beneficial character to a wide circle of important interests intimately affecting the entire population; the proprietors and miners of ore, coal, and limestone lands; the owners and improvers of woodlands, of railroads, canals, steamboats, ships, and of every other form of transportation; the producers of food, clothing, and other supplies, in addition to thousands of workmen, merchants, and capitalists and their families, who have directly participated in the benefits resulting from this great industry. It has supplied the material for an immense number of founderies, and for thousands of blacksmiths, machinists, millwrights, and manufacturers of nails, hardware, cutlery, edged tools, and other workers in metals, whose products are of immense aggregate value and of the first necessity. The production of so large a quantity of iron, and particularly of bar iron, and the demand for additional quantities from abroad, tell of the progress of the country in civil and naval architecture and all the engineering arts; of the construction of railroads and telegraphs, which have spread like a net over the whole country; of steam-engines and locomotives; of spinning, weaving, wood, and metal working, milling, mining, and other machinery; and of all the multiform instruments of science, agriculture, and the arts, both of peace and of war; of the manufacture of every conceivable article of convenience or luxury of the household, the field, or the factory. The aggregate statistics of iron exhibit the extent to which the general condition of the people has been improved by this great agent of civilization during the ten years embraced in this retrospect.

The materials for the manufacture of iron—ore, coal and other fuel, water power, &c.—are so diffused, abundant, and cheap that entire independence of foreign supplies appears to be alike desirable and attainable at no distant period.

Probably no class of statistics possesses more general interest, as illustrating the recent progress of the country in all the operative branches, and in mechanical engineering, than those relating to MACHINERY, (Table No. 11.) Nearly every section of the country, particularly the Atlantic slope, possesses a great affluence of water power, which has been extensively appropriated for various manufacturing purposes. The construction of hydraulic machinery, of stationary and locomotive steam-engines, and all the machinery used in mines, mills, furnaces, forges, and factories; in the building of roads, bridges, canals, railways, &c.; and for all other purposes of the engineer and manufacturer, has become a pursuit of great magnitude. The annual product of the general machinists' and millwrights' establishments, as returned in the census of 1850, was valued at $27,998,344. The value of the same branch, exclusive of sewing-machines, amounted in 1860 to $47,118,550, an increase of over eighteen millions in ten years. The middle States were the largest producers, having made over 48 per cent. of the whole, but the southern and western States exhibit the largest relative increase. The ratio of increase in the several sections was as follows: New England, 16.4 per cent.; middle States, 55.2; southern, 387; and western, 127 per cent. The Pacific States produced machinery of the value of $1,686,510, of which California made $1,600,510. In Rhode Island the business was slightly diminished, but in Connecticut it had increased 165 per centum. The great facilities possessed by New York and Pennsylvania in iron, coal, and transportation, made them the largest manufacturers of machinery, which in the former was made to the value of $10,484,863, and in the latter, $7,243,453—an increase of 24.4 and 75 per cent., respectively. New Jersey raised her product to $3,215,673, an increase of 261 per cent., while Delaware and Maryland and the District of Columbia exhibited an increase of 82, 41, and 667 per cent., respectively. In all the southern States the value of the manufacture, though small, was largely increased; the ratio in Virginia, the largest producer, being 236 per cent., while in Mississippi, Alabama, and South Carolina, the next in amount of production, it was 1,626, 270, and 525 per centum, respectively. This was exclusive of cotton-gins, which were included with agricultural machinery. Ohio was the largest producer in the west, and the fourth in the Union, having made to the value of $4,855,005, an increase of 125 per cent. on the product of 1850. Kentucky ranked next among the western States, having produced over one million dollars' worth, and increased her product 213 per cent. The ratio of increase in the other western States was, in Indiana, 98; in Illinois, 24; Wisconsin, 208; Missouri, 214; and Iowa, 2,910 per cent, respectively; but in Michigan there was a small decrease in the amount manufactured.

Besides a large amount of machinery and other castings included in the returns of machine shops, the value of the production of IRON FOUNDERIES, returned by the census of 1860, (Table No. 12,) reached the sum of $27,970,193, an increase of 42 per cent. on the value of that branch in 1850, which was $20,111,517. New York, whose extensive stove founderies swell the amount of production in that State, made to the value of $8,216,124, and Pennsylvania, $4,977,793, an increase of 39 and 60.9 per cent., respectively.

With the subject of iron and its various manufactures that of FOSSIL FUEL (Table No. 13) naturally associates itself. The unequalled wealth and rapid development of the coal fields of the United States as a dynamic element in our industrial progress affords one of the most striking evidences of our recent advance. The product of all the coal mines of the United States, in 1850, was valued at $7,173,750. The annual value of the anthracite and bituminous coal, according to the Eighth Census, was *over nineteen millions* of dollars. The in-increase was over twelve millions of dollars, and was at the rate of 169.9 per cent. on the product of 1850. It was chiefly produced in Pennsylvania, Ohio, and Virginia. The coal mined in Pennsylvania, in 1850, was valued at $5,268,351. In the year ending June 1, 1860, the State produced 9,397,332 tons of anthracite, worth $11,869,574, and of bitumious coal, 66,994,295 bushels, valued at $2,833,859, making a total value of $14,703,433, or an excess of $7,529,683 over the total product of the Union in 1850. Of bituminous coal, Ohio raised 28,339,900 bushels, the value of which was $1,539,713; and Virginia, 9,542,627 bushels, worth $690,188. The increase in Ohio was $819,587, and in Virginia, $222,780, in the value of mineral fuel, being at the rate of 113 per cent. in the former, and 47.6 per cent. in the latter. The increase in Pennsylvania was 179 per centum on the yield of 1850.

The development of our several valuable mines of coal, iron, lead, copper, zinc, gold, silver, quicksilver, chrome, &c., (Table No. 14,) is a subject of the highest satisfaction, constituting, as they do, the repository and fountainhead of crude materials for an immense and varied industry in the metallurgic and chemical arts. Mining in its several branches employs a very large amount of capital and great numbers of our laborious population, and shows a steady increase in the last ten years. The product of the gold mines in the Atlantic States has, however, fallen off since the discoveries of gold in California.

The increase of PRINTING PRESSES in the book and newspaper manufacture (Table No. 15) has been great beyond all precedent, and has exerted the most beneficent influence by cheapening and multiplying the vehicles of instruction. Its effects are everywhere apparent. Never did an army before possess so much of cultivated intellect, or demand such contributions for its mental food as that now marshalled in its country's defence. Many of these reading soldiers ripened their intellectual tastes during the last ten years. In fact, many divisions of our army carry the printing press and type, and the soldiers issue publications and print the forms for official papers. The press is, indeed, the great prompter of enterprise. It constantly travels with the emigrant to diffuse light and intelligence from our remotest frontiers, where it speedily calls into existence the paper-mill and all the accessories which it supports in older communities

In New England, the Middle, and Western States the value of book, job, and newspaper printing is returned as $39,428,043, of which eleven millions' worth consisted of books, the value of the latter being nearly equal to the whole product of the same branch in 1850, which was returned at $11,586,549. The manufacture of PAPER, especially of printing paper, has increased in an equal ratio, the State of Massachusetts alone producing paper of the value of $5,968,469, being over 58 per cent. of the product of the Union in 1850. New York returned paper of the value of $3,516,276; Connecticut, $2,528,758; and Pennsylvania, $1,785,900.

The SEWING MACHINE (table No. 16) has also been improved and introduced, in the last ten years, to an extent which has made it altogether a revolutionary instrument. It has opened avenues to profitable and healthful industry for thousands of industrious females to whom the labors of the needle had become wholly unremunerative and injurious in their effects. Like all automatic powers, it has enhanced the comforts of every class by cheapening the process of manufacture of numerous articles of prime necessity, without permanently subtracting from the average means of support of any portion of the community. It has added a positive increment to the permanent wealth of the country by creating larger and more varied applications of capital and skill in the several branches to which it is auxiliary. The manufacture of the machines has itself become one of considerable magnitude, and has received a remarkable impulse since 1850. The returns show an aggregate of 116,330 machines made in nine States in 1860, the value of which was $5,605,345. A single establishment in Connecticut manufactured machines to the value of over $2,700,000, or nearly one-half of the whole production in that year. During the year 1861 sewing-machines to the value of over $61,000 were exported to foreign countries. It is already employed in a great variety of operations and upon different materials, and is rapidly becoming an indispensable and general appendage to the household.

Among the branches of industry which have been signally promoted by the introduction of the sewing-machine is the manufacture of men's and women's CLOTHING (Table No. 17) for sale, which has heretofore ranked with the cotton manufactures in the number of hands—two-thirds of them females—and the cost of labor employed. The increase of this manufacture has been general throughout the Union, and in the four cities of New York, Philadelphia, Cincinnati, and Boston, amounted in value to nearly forty and one-quarter millions of dollars, or over 83 per cent. of the product of the whole Union in 1850. The manufacture of shirts and collars, of ladies' cloaks and mantillas—a new branch which has received its principal impulse within the last ten years—and of ladies' and gentlemen's furnishing goods generally, form very large items in the general aggregate of this branch. They severally employ extensive and numerous establishments, many of them in our large cities with heavy capital. In Troy, New York, the value of shirt collars alone annually manufactured is nearly $800,000, approximating in value to the product of the numerous and extensive iron founderies which have been a source of wealth to that city.

The influence of improved machinery is also conspicuously exhibited in the manufacture of SAWED and PLANED LUMBER, (Table No. 18,) in which the United States stands altogether unrivalled, as well for the extent and perfection of the mechanism employed as the amount of the product. This reached, in 1850, the value of $58,521,976, and, in 1860, $95,912,286, an increase of 64 per cent. in the last decade. The western States alone, in the latter year, produced lumber to the value of $33,274,793, an increase of $18,697,543, or 128 per cent. over their manufacture in 1850. The Pacific States and Territories produced to the value of $6,171,431, and the southern $17,941,162, a respective increase of $3,841,826 and $9,094,686 in those sections, being a ratio of 162.7 and 102.3 per centum.

Several branches of manufacture have an intimate relation to agriculture and the landed interests, and by their extension powerfully promote those interests as well as that of commerce. Surpassing all others of this or any other class in the value of products and of the raw material consumed, is the manufacture of flour and meal. The product of FLOUR and GRIST MILLS in 1850 (Table No. 19) reached a value of nearly one hundred and thirty-six millions of dollars, while in 1860 the returns exhibit a value of $223,144,369—an increase of

$87,246,563, or 64.2 per cent. in the last ten years. The production and increase of the several sections were as follows:

	Value of flour and meal.	Increase.	Per cent. increase.
New England States	$11,155,445	$4,834,959	76.5
Middle States	79,086,411	10,653,232	15.5
Western States	96,038,794	53,364,802	125.0
Southern States	30,767,457	14,185,640	85.5
Pacific States	6,096,262	4,207,930	222.8

The largest mill is in Oswego, New York, which in 1860 produced 300,000 barrels of flour; the next two, in Richmond, Virginia, made 190,000 and 160,000, respectively; and the fourth, in New York city, returned 146,000 barrels. The value of annual production of each ranged from one million and a half to one million dollars.

The manufacture of SPIRITUOUS LIQUORS in the United States (Table No. 20) employed 1,138 distilleries, independent of a large number of rectifying establishments, the product of the former being over eighty-eight millions of gallons, of the value of $24,253,176. The middle and western States were the largest producers, the latter yielding nearly forty-five and the former thirty-seven millions of gallons of whisky, high wines, and alcohol, the aggregate value in each section being almost eleven millions of dollars. It is satisfactory to observe, that more than ninety-five per cent. of all the spirits made, was from materials of domestic production, a little over four million gallons of New England rum having been the product of imported molasses.

The manufacture of MALT LIQUORS, (Table No. 21,) though of less magnitude, and far less pernicious in its effects, shows a still larger increase. It derives its material wholly from agriculture, and its extension promises more substantial benefits to the country than the last.

The northern States returned 969 breweries, or more than double the number in the Union in 1850. The quantity of all kinds of malt liquors made, including 855,803 barrels of lager beer, was 3,235,545 barrels—an increase of 175 per cent. upon the total product of 1850, while its value was returned at $17,977,135, being more than three times the amount produced by breweries in that year. Nearly one-half of the whole quantity was made in New York and Pennsylvania. The former had 175 establishments—45 of them in the city of New York—and the latter State 172, of which Philadelphia contained 68. The manufacture of lager beer was much increased in all the middle and western States, about 41 per cent. of the whole being the product of the two States last named. Among the eastern States, Massachusetts, and among the western States, Ohio, Illinois, and Missouri, were the largest producers of malt liquors. There were 71 breweries in California and 8 in Oregon, producing together about 7 per cent. of the total value of the manufacture.

Among the great branches of pure manufacture in the United States, that of COTTON GOODS holds the first rank in respect to the value of the product and the amount of capital employed. Aided by the possession of the raw material as a product of our own soil, and by the enterprise and ingenuity of our people, this valuable industry has grown with a rapidity almost unrivalled.

The total value of cotton goods (Table No. 22) manufactured in New England was $80,301,535, and in the middle States $26,272, 111—an increase of 83.4 per cent. in the former, and 77.7 in the latter. The remaining States produced to the value of $8,564,280, making the whole production during that year

$115,137,926, against $65,501,687, the value of this branch in 1850, or an increase in the general business of nearly 76 per centum in ten years. In the States of Maine and New Jersey the manufacture increased in the same time 152 per cent.; in Pennsylvania, over 102 per cent.; in New Hampshire and Connecticut, over 87 per cent.; in Massachusetts nearly 69 per cent., and in Rhode Island 88.7 per cent. The total production in this branch was at the rate *per capita* of $3 69 for every individual in the Union, equivalent to 46⅛ yards of cloth for each, at the medium price of 8 cents per yard. The average product per head in 1850 was 32¼ yards. The increase alone has, therefore, been at the rate of 11 yards for each person, or nearly equal to the average annual consumption *per capita* in 1830, when it was estimated to amount to twelve yards. The number of hands employed in the manufacture in 1860 was 45,315 males, and 73,605 females, an increase in the male operatives of 10,020, and in the female of 10,944 since 1850. The average product of the labor of each operative was $969. The number of spindles was returned at 5,035,798, being an increase of 1,402,105, or 38.5 per cent. over the aggregate in 1850, which was estimated at 3,633,693. The New England States possess 3,959,297, or 78.6 per cent. of the whole, while Massachusetts alone employs 1,739,700, or 29.3 per cent. of the number returned in the Union. The increase of spindles in the last decade was, in New England, 1,208,219, or 30 per cent. In the State of Maine, 186,100, or 163.3 per cent.; in the State of New Hampshire, 229,484, or 52.1 per cent.; in the State of Massachusetts, 451,609, or 35 per cent; in the State of Rhode Island, 141,862, or 22.7 per cent.; in the State of Connecticut, 211,188, or 83.1 per cent.; while in Vermont it exhibited a decrease.

The product per spindle varies in the different States, partly accounted for by the fact that many manufacturers purchase yarns which have been spun in other States.

The product of cotton goods per spindle is as follows: In Maine, $22 12; Massachusetts, $21 12; New Hampshire, $24 87; Vermont, $18 13; Rhode Island, $16; Connecticut, $16 46. The average in the New England States is $20 30; in the middle States, $30 48, and in the whole Union, $22 86.

The quantity of cotton used in the fabrication of the above goods was 364,036,123 pounds, or 910,090 bales of 400 pounds each. Of this amount the New England States consumed 611,738 bales, and Massachusetts alone 316,665. The consumption per spindle in that year in the various States and sections was as follows:

	No. of spindles.	Pounds of cotton.	Pounds per spindle.
Maine	300,000	23,438,723	78
New Hampshire	669,885	39,212,644	58.5
Vermont	19,712	1,057,250	53
Massachusetts	1,739,700	126,666,089	72.8
Rhode Island	766,000	38,521,608	50.2
Connecticut	464,000	15,799,140	34
In New England	3,959,297	237,844,854	61.8
In the Middle States	861,661	76,055,666	88.26
In the United States	5,035,798	364,036,123	72 2

When we consider the large number of hands, and especially of women and children, who find employment in this business, the quantity of raw material, of machinery and of fuel, exclusively of American production, employed in this branch, and the amount of comfortable clothing and household stuffs supplied at cheap rates, or the amount it contributes to the internal and foreign commerce of the Union—its progressive increase is a subject of the highest satisfaction, and its growth both here and abroad is one of the marvels of the nineteenth century.

The returns of WOOLLEN MANUFACTURES (Table No. 23) show an increase of over fifty-one per cent. in ten years. The value of woollen and mixed goods made in 1850 was $45,281,764. In 1860 it amounted to $68,865,963. The establishments numbered 1,909, of which 453 were in New England, 748 in the middle, 479 in the western, 2 in the Pacific, and 227 in the southern States. The aggregate capital invested in the business was $35,520,527, and it employed 28,780 male and 20,120 female hands, 639,700 spindles, and 16,075 looms, which worked up more than eighty million pounds of wool, the value of which, with other raw materials, was $40,360,300. The foregoing figures include satinets, Kentucky jeans, and other fabrics of which the warp is cotton, though usually classed with woollens. In the manufacture of these mixed goods the amount of cotton consumed is 16,008,625 pounds, which, with 364,036,123 pounds used in making cotton goods, as previously stated, amounts to 380,044,748 pounds, or 950,112 bales, exclusive of a considerable quantity used, annually, in household manufactures, and for various other purposes.

The largest amount of woollens was made in New England, where the capital was nearly twenty millions of dollars, and the value of the product $38,509,080, but little less than the total value in 1850. More than half the capital, and nearly one-half of the product of New England belonged to Massachusetts, which had 131 factories of large size. Rhode Island ranked next, and had increased its manufacture 163 per cent. in ten years, that of Massachusetts being 48 per cent. The value of woollens produced in the middle States was $24,100,488, in the western $3,718,092, and in the Pacific and southern $2,538,303. The sectional increase was, in New England 52.1, in the middle States 54, and in the south 107—the last showing the greatest relative increase. Pennsylvania, next to Massachusetts, was the largest producer, having 447 factories, which made $12,744,373 worth of woollen and mixed fabrics, an increase of 120 per cent. A value of $8,919,019 was the product of 222 establishments in the city of Philadelphia.

The State of New York holds the third rank in relation to this industry, its manufactures amounting to more than nine millions of dollars. The woollen manufactures of Maryland exhibit an increase of 86 per cent. In Ohio, which produced in 1850 a greater value of woollens than all the other western States, there was a decrease on the product of 1850, owing, probably, to the shipments of wool to Europe, which, in 1857, was found to be the most profitable disposition of the rapidly increasing wool crops of that State. In Kentucky, now the largest manufacturer of wool in the west, the product was $1,128,882, and the increase in ten years 40.4 per cent.; while in Indiana, which ranks next, it was 31 per cent., and in Missouri 18.8, on the product of 1850.

The extension of this important manufacture is a subject of great interest to the country, inasmuch as our climate renders woollen clothing necessary throughout a large part of the Union during much of the year; and because it would supply the best market to the wool-grower.

The quantity of wool returned for the whole Union in 1850 was upwards of fifty-two and a half millions of pounds. Sheep raising has been greatly extended and improved since that date in Ohio, Texas, California, and other States, and the clip in 1860 amounted to 60,511,343 pounds, an increase of 15.2 per cent. in ten years. The yield still falls far short of the consumption, and large quantities continue to be imported, notwithstanding the amount of territory adapted to sheep husbandry.

The manufacture of LINEN GOODS has made but little progress in this country. A few mills, chiefly in Massachusetts, make crash and other coarse fabrics;

the largest two in that State produced six million yards in 1860. Others are extensively engaged in making twines, shoe and other threads. It is to be regretted that the manufacture of flax has not attained greater magnitude in a country where the raw material is so easily and cheaply grown. Farmers throughout the west have raised the crop simply for the seed, and thrown out the fibre as valueless.

The manufacture of fabrics from FLAX COTTON has been commenced, and success in a new branch of industry is confidently expected. The inventive genius of our countrymen has perfected machinery for the preparation of flax for spinning, which can be furnished, it is alleged, at as low a rate as the product of southern cotton fields.

The manufacture of SEWING SILKS is extensively carried on in this country. Including tram, organzine, &c., the production exceeded five million dollars in the States of Connecticut, New Jersey, Massachusetts, Pennsylvania, and New York—their relative values being in the order mentioned. Ribbons are made to a small extent, but the chief manufactures of silk consist of ladies dress trimmings, coach lace, &c., of which the cities of Philadelphia and New York produce to the value of $1,260,725 and $796,682, respectively.

The production of LEATHER (Table No. 24) is also a leading industry of much importance to the agriculturist and stock raiser, as well as to the commercial interest, inasmuch as it consumes all the material supplied by the former, and feeds an active branch of our foreign import trade. The tanning and currying establishments of the United States produced in 1850 leather, exclusive of Morocco and patent leather, to the value of $37,702,333. The product of the same branch in 1860 reached $63,090,751, an increase of nearly 67 per centum. In the New England States it was $16, 333, 871, in the Middle States, $36,344,548, and in the Western States, $5,986,457; being an increase 66.6 per cent., 90.7 and 13.3 in those sections, respectively. The Pacific States and Territories, (including Utah,) which returned no leather in 1850, produced in 1860 to the value of $351,469. The largest producers of leather are New York, $20,758,017; Pennsylvania, $12,491,631; and Massachusetts, $10,354,056; an increase in those States of 111.7, 98.4, and 82.3 per cent., respectively. Including Morocco and patent leather the aggregate value produced in the Union in 1860 exceeded sixty-seven millions of dollars.

If we add to the sum total of this manufacture the aggregate value of all the allied branches into which it enters as a raw material, or take an account of the capital, the number of hands, and the cost of labor and material employed in the creation and distribution of its ultimate products, it is doubtful if any other department of industry is entitled to precedence over that of leather.

The manufacture of BOOTS and SHOES (Table No. 25) employs a larger number of operatives than any other single branch of American industry. The census of 1850 showed that there were 11,305 establishments, with a capital of nearly thirteen millions of dollars, engaged in making boots and shoes to the value of $53,967,408, and employing 72,305 male and 32,948 female hands. The returns of 1860 show that 2,554 establishments in the New England States employed a capital only $2,516 less than that of the whole Union at the former date; and with 56,039 male and 24,978 female employés produced boots and shoes of the value of $54,767,077 or eight hundred thousand dollars more than the entire value of the business in 1850, and 82.8 per centum in excess of their own production in that year. Massachusetts increased 92.6 per cent., having made boots and shoes of the value of $46,440,209, equal to 86.6 per cent. of the general business in 1850. The State of New York returned 2,276 factories, with an aggregate production of $10,878,797; and New England, New York, Pennsylvania, and New Jersey together produced $75,674,946 worth of these articles, being 40.4 per cent. more than the product of all the States in 1850, and 67.9 per cent. more than their own manufacture in that year. The three counties of Essex, Worcester, and Plymouth, in Massachusetts, produced boots and shoes to the value severally of about 14½, 9½, and 9¼ millions of dollars. The largest production of any one town was that of Philadelphia, in which it amounted to $5,329,887; the next that of Lynn, Massachusetts, was $4,867,399; the third, Haverhill, $4,130,500; the fourth, New York city, $3,869,068. The largest production of a single establishment was of one in North Brookfield, Massachusetts, and amounted to over $750,000. This establishment was the largest of five the same proprietors had in operation that year, the total production whereof was over one million pairs of boots and shoes, valued at more than thirteen hundred thousand dollars! Machinery propelled by steam power is now used in many large manufactories with highly satisfactory results.

INDIA RUBBER GOODS were made chiefly in Connecticut, New York, New Jersey, and Massachusetts to the value of $5,729,900, an increase of 90 per cent. in the last decade.

The value of CABINET FURNITURE (Table No. 26) made in 1860 in the New England, Middle and Western States reached the sum of $22,701,304, an increase of 39.8 per cent. over the product of those States in 1850, and exceeding the production of the whole Union in 1850. New York returned in 1860 furniture of the value of $7,175,060, (or 40.6 per cent. of the whole amount made in 1850.) Massachusetts, $3,365,415, and Pennsylvania, $2,938,503. The growth of this branch keeps pace with the increase of population and wealth, and serves to swell the amount of our exports. It gives employment at remunerative prices to skilled labor, which it attracts from the crowded labor-markets of Europe.

Our advance in wealth and refinement is attested by the rapid increase in the manufacture of piano fortes and other MUSICAL INSTRUMENTS, (Table No. 27.) New England, New York, and Pennsylvania produced musical instruments to the value of $5,791,807; an increase of 150 per cent. over their own production in 1850, and 124 over the whole value of that branch in the Union in the same year. New York alone made $3,392,577 worth, being $811,862 more than the whole amount returned in 1850. In this branch, our manufacturers have achieved marked success. Without claiming for them superiority over their brethren in France and Germany, it is admitted that church organs and other instruments made in this country are better suited to the climate, and in other respects fully equal to those which come from the most celebrated establishments in Europe.

The increased amount of the precious metals and the greater ability of all classes to indulge the promptings of taste or luxury, have added greatly to the manufacture of JEWELRY, (Table No. 28,) and of all kinds of gold, silver, and plated wares. In the New England and Middle States, the production of jewelry and watches reaches over eleven millions in value; of silver, silver-plated wares, &c., over six and one-half millions; making nearly eighteen millions of dollars, exclusive of gold leaf and foil, and the assaying and refining the precious metals, exceeding the product of the whole Union, in 1850, by $7,016,908 in value; an increase of over sixty-four per cent., and of seventy per cent. on the production of those States in that year. The production of cheap jewelry has been greatly augmented by recent improvements in electro-metallurgy.

The manufacture of American WATCHES, commenced within the last ten years in Boston as an experiment, has proved eminently successful. Unable, heretofore to compete with the low-priced labor of European workmen, our ingenious countrymen have perfected machinery, by the aid of which watch movements are fabricated equal, if not superior, to the hand-made. The continued growth of this branch will diminish the importation of foreign watches, and may, at no distant period, earn for our country a reputation in this manufacture equal to that she enjoys in the kindred branch of clock-making. Gold and silver watch cases are now produced to a very large extent, chiefly in the cities of Philadelphia, New York, and Newark.

Improvements in technical CHEMISTRY have added largely to the number and value of its products. The manufacture of articles strictly classed as chemical, exclusive of white lead, ochres, paints, varnish, glue, perfumes, cements, pot and pearl ashes, &c., amounted, in 1850, to the value of nearly five millions of dollars. The production, in 1860, exhibited a considerable increase. This branch is susceptible of almost unlimited extension and application in the creation of commercial and useful articles from the refuse of every other manufacture, and the diversified products, vegetable, animal, and mineral, of our own or other lands. Many of the chemical branches, apart from the money value of their manufactures, are of the highest economical importance to our country, as auxiliaries to almost every other industry of the people. Chemistry has as yet revealed but a tithe of the vast wealth of its resources.

The manufacture and consumption of GAS, (Table No. 29,) for illumination and other purposes, which is one of the remarkable fruits of chemical science, has been greatly increased, not only in our northern cities, but in the large towns and villages throughout the Union. The quantity returned is but four thousand million feet of the value of eleven million dollars, but the whole quantity made exceeded 5,000,000,000 cubic feet, the value of which was about thirteen millions of dollars.

The making and refining of SALT (Table No. 30) in the United States in 1850 employed 340 establishments, and the value of their production was $2,177,945. The four States of New York, Virginia, Ohio, and Pennsylvania, which, in the order named, are the principal salt-producing States, made, according to the Eighth Census, nearly twelve million bushels, the cost of which was $2,200,000, an average of about 18½ cents per bushel. Texas, Kentucky, Massachusetts, and California are also salt-producing States. About sixty per cent. of the whole was made in New York, at an average cost of 17 cents per bushel.

In the aggregate product of the FISHERIES (Table No. 31) there was an increase of 28.5 per cent. over their value in 1850. The total value of the lake, river, shore, and deep-sea fisheries, including oysters to the value of $382,170, and $7,521,588 as the product of the whaling business, amounted in 1860 to $12,924,092. Of this amount $6,526,238 in the whale and $2,774,204 in the cod, mackerel, halibut, and other shore fisheries, belonged to the maritime industry of Massachusetts, and constituted nearly seventy-two per cent. of the whole. This favorite occupation of her enterprising sons has made Boston, which has been over two and a quarter centuries engaged in the business, the principal distributing fish market of the Union, and has raised the port of Gloucester to the third rank among New England seaports in the amount of its foreign commerce. The latter has become the largest seat of the domestic fisheries in the United States, if not in the world, and distributes the products to all the large cities of the Union and to foreign countries.

The State of Maine holds the second place in respect to the value of its fishing interests, and returned $1,050,755 as the value of the cod, mackerel, herring, &c., taken by its fishermen. North Carolina had the largest shad fishery, amounting in value to $99,768. New Jersey, New York, and Virginia took the largest amount of oysters, and Michigan returned the largest value in white fish, amounting to $250,467.

A slight decline in the value of the whale fishery arose from the increasing scarcity of the whale in its former haunts. The consequent deficiency of bone, teeth, and oil, as raw materials, proved embarrassing to some branches of manufacture, particularly those employing whalebone. The scarcity of whale and other fish oils in the arts has been supplied by an increased production of lard oil, and especially by that beneficent law of compensation which pervades the economy of nature, and when one provision fails her children, opens to them another in the exhaustless storehouse of her material resources, or leads out their mental energies upon new paths of discovery for the supply of their own wants. Thus, when mankind was about to emerge from the simplicity of the primitive and pastoral ages, the more soft and fusible metals no longer sufficed for the artificer, and veins of iron ore revealed their wealth and use in the supply of his more artificial wants, and became potent agents of his future progress. When the elaboration of the metals and other igneous arts were fast sweeping the forests from the earth, the exhaustless treasures of fossil fuel, stored for his future use, were disclosed to man, and when the artificial sources of oil seemed about to fail, a substitute was discovered flowing in almost perennial fountains from the depths of these same carboniferous strata. A decline of the cod and whale fisheries is, nevertheless, to be regretted, as they have been from the earliest period of our history the nurseries of seamen and of our naval and commercial marine, and therefore contributing to the national defence, to foreign commerce, ship-building, agriculture, and other important interests.

Petroleum.—An important development of the natural resources of the country, and a valuable addition to its exports, have been made by the discovery, within two or three years, that certain indications, known to the aboriginal and early European inhabitants of the western country, of natural reservoirs of inflammable oil existing upon the headwaters of the Alleghany river in New York and Pennsylvania, were but the clue to apparently inexhaustible supplies of native oil, accessible at no great depth throughout an extended belt of country, embracing the bituminous coal measures of several States.

Petroleum, rock, or mineral oil, a natural product of the decomposition of organic matter, emitted from the soil in various formations, particularly those of rock salt, was known and employed to some extent by the ancients, having been mentioned by the father of history twenty-three hundred years ago, and by Greek and Roman writers of later date. In its more fluid form, as found on the shores of the Caspian Sea, near the Irawaddy of Burmah, in Italy, and some parts of our country, it has borne the name of naptha, while the more solid elements of the same substance predominated in the articles known as asphaltum and bitumen, found abundantly in the Great Pitch Lake of the Island of Trinidad, near the Dead Sea in Judea, and elsewhere. Petroleum is nearly identical in properties with the artificial oils, which have been long derived from the destructive distillation of different minerals, as cannel coal and brown coal, or lignite, bituminous shales, sands, clays, peat, &c., which have been the subject of numerous patents in Europe and America, and within the last eight years have been manufactured to a considerable extent in the United States and the neighboring provinces, until the native petroleum springs opened a source of cheaper supply.

As a product of our own country this remarkable substance was brought to the notice of the white population, as early as the middle of the last century, by the Seneca Indians, who found it upon Oil creek, a branch of the Alleghany, in Venango county, Pennsylvania, and near the head of the Genesee river, in New York, whence it received the name of "Seneca oil" and "Genesee oil." It was used by the natives in their religious ceremonies, and as medicament for wounds, &c. For the last-named purpose it has been long collected and sold in small quantities at a high price. A perennial flow of oil has been known to exist on Oil creek, above referred to, for a century. For the last forty years the spring has been enclosed in a vat, or structure of wood and stones, which was daily skimmed by the proprietor and made the source of considerable revenue. We have seen extensive diggings in this region made by the French more than a century since, while that nation held the valley of the Mississippi, which were evidently made with a view to ascertain the basis or source of what, no doubt, impressed the French officers as a most interesting and curious development of the bounty of nature. Petroleum, doubtless, formed an article of considerable traffic between the Indians and traders of that region; as we have seen, in some old account books of the last century, "gallons" and "kegs" of Seneca oil credited to Indians.

Its existence in any vast amount appears to have been unknown until 1845, when a spring was "struck," while boring for salt, near Tarentum, thirty-five miles above Pittsburg, on the Alleghany. Experiments having proved its constituents to be nearly the same as those of the artificial carbon oil, a company was organized in New York to attempt its purification by the same process applied to the latter. But little was effected, however, and in 1857 Messrs. Bowditch and Drake, of New Haven, commenced operations at Titusville, on Oil creek, where traces of early explorations were found, and in August, 1859, a fountain was reached by boring, at the depth of seventy-one feet, which yielded 400 gallons daily. Before the close of the year 1860, the number of wells and borings was estimated to be about two thousand, of which seventy-four of the larger ones were producing daily, by the aid of pumps, an aggregate of eleven hundred and sixty-five barrels of crude oil, worth, at twenty cents a gallon, about ten thousand dollars. Wells were soon after sunk to the depth of five or six hundred feet, and the flow of petroleum became so profuse that no less than 3,000 barrels were obtained in a day from a single well, the less productive ones yielding from fifteen to twenty barrels per diem. In several instances extraordinary means were found necessary to check and control the flow, which is now regulated in such wells according to the state of the market, by strong tubing and stop-cocks. The quantity sent to market by the Sunbury and Erie railroad from the Pennsylvania oil region, which has thus far been the principal source, increased from 325 barrels in 1859 to 134,927 barrels in 1861. The whole quantity shipped in the last-mentioned year was nearly 500,000 barrels. Since August, 1861, the product has rapidly increased. The present capacity of the wells is estimated at 250,000 to 300,000 barrels per week. So important, however, have the operations in this article become that a railroad, we understand, has been chartered in Pennsylvania exclusively for the transportation of the oil to market. From a recent number of the "Register," a newspaper published at Oil City, Pennsylvania, we copy the following statement respecting the product of petroleum in that vicinity: "We learn that the number of wells now flowing is seventy-five, the number of wells that formerly flowed and pumped is sixty-two; the number of wells sunk and commenced is three hundred and fifty-eight; total, four hundred and ninety-five. The amount of oil shipped is set down at 1,000,000 barrels; amount on hand to date, 92,450 barrels; present amount of daily flow, 5,717 barrels. The average value of the oil, at $1 per barrel, is $1,092,000; average cost of wells, at $1,000 each, is $495,000; machinery, building, &c., from $500 to $700 each, $500,000. The total number of refiners is twenty-five. The detailed report of the condition of the wells shows that production is on the increase. Holders are firm at fifty cents per barrel at the wells, and don't seem to care about selling any great amount at that price." With increased facilities for getting it to the seaboard at a cheap rate for transportation, the operations will doubtless become much more extended than at present.

The exportation of crude and refined petroleum from the principal Atlantic cities to Europe, South America, and the West Indies, has already become considerable, the larger proportion being shipped to England. Much of it is sent to Europe in this crude state, in which form it is said to be preferred for the sake of the collateral products obtained in the process of refining. It is probable, however, that the highly inflammable character of the unrefined article, owing to the presence of certain gaseous or exceedingly volatile compounds may prove an objection to its shipment in that state.

The quantity exported from the cities of Philadelphia, New York, Boston, Baltimore, and San Francisco, from the 1st of January to the 1st of April, 1862, amounted to 2,342,042 gallons, valued at $633,949. The receipts at Cincinnati, during the same period, of carbon and petroleum oils, were 519,960 gallons, or 13,000 barrels, nearly one-half of which was petroleum oil. The exports from the three cities first mentioned, from the first of January to the 16th of May of the present year, were 3,651,130 gallons, worth $889,886, and the shipments in the last week of that period from the same places, were 255,600 gallons, valued at $42,160.

A large reduction has taken place in the price since the commencement of the trade, and particularly during the last few months. The price of crude petroleum in Philadelphia on the 4th January, 1862, was from 22½ to 23 cents a gallon, and of refined oil 37½ to 45 cents. On the 29th March the prices had declined at the same place to 10 and 12 cents for crude, and 25 to 32 cents for refined oil, while the most recent price current lists place it at 9 and 19 cents. Although the capacity of the existing wells already exceeds a profitable demand, there appears to be no assignable limit to the flow, or to the localities which may be found to yield it, whenever an augmented demand shall warrant farther search or increased production. The bituminous coal areas of the United States are estimated to cover upward of 62,000 square miles in eight of the middle, southern, and western States. Springs and reservoirs of petroleum have been discovered throughout nearly their whole extent. They have also been noticed by Captain Stansbury on a branch of the Yellow creek, 83 miles from Salt Lake City, in Utah, on the route to Fort Leavenworth. They exist also in some of the neighboring British provinces. It is probable that the saliferous strata of our western country may be generally found to yield this interesting mineral product.

The importance of this article is not limited to its value as an item in the export trade of our cities. Attention appears to have been first directed to it on account of the demand for a safe and cheap material for illumination, in place of the dangerous compounds of turpentine and other explosive hydro-carbons, as well as for lubricating purposes in which it has proved to be a valuable substitute for animal oils. There is no doubt that the various other uses of crude petroleum, or its constituents, will render it a valuable acquisition to the arts. The business of refining the raw product, in order to remove from it all corrosive and volatile elements, already employs a number of establishments, and will become one of some magnitude. Practical chemistry is daily adding to the number and variety of uses which the substances eliminated in the process of rectification may be made to subserve in the arts.

Although the extraction of oil, pitch, and tar from bituminous shale was the subject of a patent in England as early as 1695, and the manufacture and purification of oil, gas, and other hydro-carbons from coal received several improvements by the Earl of Dundonald and others at a later period, the patent of Mr. Young, of Manchester, secured in England in 1850, and in the United States in 1852, "for the obtaining of paraffine oil, or an oil containing paraffine, and paraffine from bituminous coal," appears to have given the first great impulse to the manufacturing of these oils as a source of artificial light. The patent, which covered a very successful process, has given rise to suits at law, one of which was recently brought, without success, to restrain the sale in England of petroleum oils, by the name of American paraffine oil, as damaging to the sale of his "paraffine oil," on account of the highly inflammable character of the former.

Illuminating oil from coal appears to have been made as early as 1846 by Dr. Gesner, of Nova Scotia, and in 1854 the Kerosene Oil Company, on Long Island, commenced the first manufacture of carbo-hydrogen oil under patents secured by Dr. Gesner, using cannel coal from England, New York, and other parts of the United States. The Breckenridge coal-oil works on the Ohio, at Cloverport, Kentucky, were commenced in 1856, and were soon followed by others, to the number of twenty-five in operation in 1860 in Ohio alone, with a working capacity of three hundred gallons of light oil each, per diem. There were then about fifty-six factories in the United States, exclusive of some fifteen engaged altogether on petroleum, and several small private coal-oil works. The capital expended in coal-oil works and cannel coal mines was estimated at nearly four million dollars. The manufacture of coal-oil lamps, resulting from the use of the oil, formed the principal business of sixteen companies, who employed 2,150 men and 400 women and boys, and work for 125 looms in making the lamp-wick.

The cannel coal employed by them, as well as wood, peat, and other substances of vegetable origin, when subjected to destructive distillation in close vessels, at a heat below that at which they yield gas in abundance, affords a large quantity of a light supernatant oil, amounting to about one-fifth of the product, which, having been purified and re-distilled, yields a very volatile and napthalous fluid, of light specific gravity, containing some paraffine oil, and highly inflammable, owing to the presence of benzoin or benzole. There is also obtained a heavier oil, which is a safe and valuable burning oil, a denser lubricating oil, and solid paraffine, a peculiar white crystalline substance, beautifully adapted for candles, and now manufactured to some extent for that and other practical uses. The petroleum of our country has been found to be a more economical source for these several compounds of carbon and hydrogen, and enables the manufacturer to dispense with the first stage of the process referred to. The cheapness of crude petroleum, and the simple and comparatively unexpensive process by which a safe and economical illuminating oil may be obtained, give an unusual interest to this subject, as affording the means of preventing the great loss of life shown by the recent census to result from the dangerous compounds so extensively used for that purpose. Although the petroleum oils, when imperfectly rectified, so that all the benzole has not been expelled, are exceedingly explosive, owing to the heat generated by the combustion of the solid paraffine readily vaporizing and igniting the more ethereal portion, it may with great facility be freed from all volatile substances, and a very simple and practical test enables the purchaser to ascertain its fitness for use. The precautions required in the treatment of petroleum, as well as the expense of thoroughly purifying it, being somewhat greater than with coal oils, many are tempted to neglect it or even to add a portion of the lighter and cheaper oil to make the heavy oil burn more readily.

All these oils possess an advantage over other kinds in the fact, that when once properly deodorized, they do not become rancid or ferment by keeping, but rather lose by age any odor they may have retained.

Of eight several products obtained from petroleum by chemical analysis, two or three only were solidified by cold of fifteen degrees below zero, the first three or four remaining perfectly fluid, and none possessed corrosive qualities, showing their fitness as lubricators. Experiments have shown that crude petroleum is admirably adapted to the manufacture of gas, and have led to the expectation that its use will greatly reduce the cost of its manufacture, if it does not entirely supersede the use of coal for that purpose. The "carburation of gas," by attaching to the gas-burner a reservoir of oil, through which the gas is made to pass before combustion, has been found greatly to increase the economy and illuminating power of coal-gas.

The various collateral and residuary products of the distillation, which have been generally wasted heretofore, will all doubtless be utilized as the progress in analytical and technical chemistry throws more light upon their nature and relations. Several of them are already employed in Europe, if not in this country, in the manufacture of some of the new and beautiful dyes which practical science has recently introduced in the arts. Benzine, which it is the object of the rectifier to eliminate, is used, to some extent, as a flavoring material, though some recent facts make it doubtful if it is wholly innoxious to the health.

The acids, caustic alkalies, and other materials used in the purification of the crude qualities of petroleum may all be restored to use or employed as fertilizers, and the dense, pitchy liquids obtained in the manufacture are available in the composition of water-proof cements, roofing, varnish, and fuel. The absence of fatty acids may possibly prevent the saponification of these oils with alkalies for the manufacture of soap, but the more extended use of petroleum for the purposes we have named, which will be effected by time and improved manipu lations of the article, will suffice to render it a most valuable acquisition to the raw materials and manufactures of the country.

Having partially reviewed the progressive industry of our country during the last decade, and seen the advancement in all that relates to the peaceful arts, the numerous improvements made in the implements and enginery of warfare, which are patent and undeniable, deserve consideration. Our improved fire-arms, especially rifles and pistols, have obtained a reputation not alone in Europe, but in Africa, Asia, and the islands of the sea, the traveller finds that his revolvers of American invention and manufacture exert a salutary influence on the Bedouin and the robber.

The machinery for making the various parts of rifles and other fire-arms, which, in its automatic exercise, seems almost endowed with reasoning faculties, owes its origin to the inventive genius of New England. The Enfield rifle was transplanted to England by a son of Vermont, under whose superintendence the arms were made. And even the Armstrong gun, which obtained for its reputed inventor the honor of knighthood, was invented in this country, for a model was submitted and the principle demonstrated to scientific gentlemen at Harvard College anterior to its appearance in Great Britain. (See notes.)

In the year preceding June 1, 1860, a year devoted to peaceful pursuits, the manufacture of fire-arms was limited, and yet two establishments in a single city of Connecticut produced to the value of over one million of dollars. Had the national inventory been taken two years later, the magnitude of this and kindred branches of manufacture, stimulated by the necessities of the country, would have excited astonishment. (See note on fire-arms, p. 118.)

Without any special stimulus to growth—depressed, indeed, during the years 1857 and 1858, in common with other public interests, by the general financial embarrassments of those years—and with a powerful competition in the amazing growth of manufactures in Great Britain and nearly every other nation of Europe, the manufactories of the United States had nevertheless been augmented, diversified, and perfected in nearly every branch, and almost uniformly throughout the Union. Domestic materials, whether animal, vegetable, or mineral, found ready sales at remunerative prices, and were increased in amount with the demand, while commerce and internal trade were invigorated by the distribution of both raw and manufactured products. Invention was stimulated and rewarded. Labor and capital found ample and profitable employment, and new and unexpected fields were opened for each. Agriculture furnished food and materials at moderate cost, and the skill of our artizans cheapened and multiplied all artificial instruments of comfort and happiness for the people. Even the more purely agricultural States of the south were rapidly creating manufactories for the improvement of their great staples and their abundant natural resources. The nation seemed speedily approaching a period of complete independence in respect to the products of skilled labor, and national security and happiness seemed about to be insured by the harmonious development of all the great interests of the people. Peace reigned within our borders and waited upon our name abroad. But in an evil hour the tide of prosperity has been stayed, whether to be rolled back or not, the ninth census will reveal.

BANKS AND INSURANCE.

(Appendix—Table No. 34.)

Among the evidences of prosperity and general accumulation of wealth in the United States, the multiplication of banks with increased aggregate capital is one of the most significant. When, as in this country has been generally the case, individual promises representing produce and merchandize, and made available through the instrumentality of banks, are almost the sole means by which commodities pass from the producers to the consumers, the increased action of the banks becomes the index of larger production and more active trade. Where crops and the products of manufacturing industry are more abundant, the aggregate amount of paper created by their interchange is larger, and the negotiations of this paper require greater banking facilities. This want usually manifests itself in a more lucrative banking business, which draws more capital into that employment. Such a state of affairs presented itself during the decade which closed with 1860. The bank movement in the United States during that period underwent great expansion without becoming less sound. In that respect it presented a strong contrast to the expansion that occurred in the decade which ended with 1840. In that period a season of speculation in bank stocks and wild lands manifested itself, and the paper created for bank negotiation represented imaginary or speculative values rather than commodities produced. Those values were never realized, and the whole paper system based on them collapsed. If we compare the aggregate features of the banks at each decade with the population and the sum of the imports and exports for corresponding dates, the results are as follows:

Years.	No. of banks.	Capital.	Loans.	Specie.	Circulation.	Import & export.	Population.
1830..	330	$145,192,268	$230,451,214	$22,114,917	$61,323,898	$144,726,428	12,866,020
1840....	901	358,442,692	462,896,523	33,105,155	106,968,572	239,227,465	17,069,453
1843....	691	228,861,948	251,544,937	33,505,806	58,563,608	149,090,279	....
1850....	872	227,469,074	412,607,653	48,677,138	155,012,911	330,037,038	23,191,876
1860....	1,562	421,880,095	691,945,580	83,594,537	207,102,477	762,288,550	31,445,080

The year 1843 was that of the lowest depression after the extensive liquidation that followed the expansions of 1837–'39. In that year the bank credits were, however, large, as measured by the foreign trade or the sum of the imports and exports, but an internal trade had been developed through the settlements of the western country which required more credits. The operation of the general bankrupt law aided in clearing away the wreck of over two hundred banks that had failed, and which failures involved that of several sovereign States that had loaned their credits for bank capital.

The elements of prosperity were now again active, and banking facilities were required to a greater extent. The severe losses the public had suffered made some more comprehensive guarantee necessary to a full restoration of confidence in bank paper. In New York, in 1838, a new principle had been adopted—that of requiring the banks to deposite security for their circulating notes and holding stockholders liable to an amount equal to the value of their shares. On this basis the banking of New York was thenceforth to operate; and the principle, as its value became recognized, was gradually adopted in other States.

The failure of the Irish harvests of 1846–'47, followed by those of England in 1848–'49 by creating a great demand for American breadstuffs, stimulated business and gave a new impulse to banking. The year 1850 showed an amount of foreign trade more than double that of 1843. With the increase of business the banks were very prosperous, as is manifest in the fact, that although the capital of the banks was no more in that year than in 1843, their discounts were one hundred and fifty millions, or 60 per cent. greater. Thus the decade opened with a very lucrative banking business, and amid the greatest excitement in relation to the gold discoveries of California. The spirit of enterprise abroad was very strong, and the impression that prices were to rise by reason of the depreciation of gold was prevalent; hence the general desire to operate, in order to avail of the anticipated profits. Industry of all descriptions was very active and productive, and there never was a period when the national capital accumulated so fast, a remarkable evidence of which was afforded in the vast amount expended in the construction of railroads; while, of the large capital accumulated, a considerable portion was employed in banking. The incorporated bank capital increased nearly two hundred millions, and the private bank capital half as much. The report of the Treasury Department gave the latter amount at $118,036,080. The distribution of the incorporated banks among the several States is given in the Appendix, (Table No. 33.)

The increase of bank capital was large in the Atlantic cities, particularly in Boston and New York, of which the number and capital were respectively as follows:

	1850.		1860.		Increase.	
	No.	Capital.	No.	Capital.	No.	Capital
Boston	30	$21,760,000	42	$36,581,700	12	$14,821,700
New York	31	33,600,602	55	69,758,777	24	36,158,175
Total of two cities	61	55,360,602	97	106,340,477	36	50,979,875

This increase of banks, following the general expansion of business, brought with it the necessity of some improved means of adjusting the daily mutual balances. The fifty-five banks in New York city, for example, were each compelled to settle as many accounts daily. To obviate that great labor the clearing system was devised. Each bank sends every morning to the clearing-house all the checks and demands it may have received the day previous, in the course of business, upon all others. These in a short time are interchanged, and a balance struck and paid. This system was established in 1853, and the amount of the exchanges and balances annually were as follows:

Year.	Amount exchanged.	Balances.
1854	$5,750,455,987 06	$297,411,493
1855	5,362,912,098 33	289,694,137
1856	6,906,213,328 47	334,714,489
1857	8,333,226,718 06	365,313,901
1858	4,756,664,386 09	314,238,910
1859	6,448,005,956 01	363,984,682
1860	7,231,143,056 69	308,693,438
1861	5,915,742,758 05	353,383,944
Total for eight years	50,704,365,288 81	2,627,434,997

With the development of business the transactions grew immensely up to to 1858, when they fell off nearly one-half under the panic of that year. They recovered gradually up to the breaking out of the rebellion. The banks of Boston and Philadelphia adopted the same system with similar results. The figures indicate to what an extent the credits of individuals, created in the operations of business, are cancelled through the intervention of the banks of the cities where the commerce of the whole country centralizes.

In the States of Illinois, Mississippi, Arkansas and Florida, after the collapse of 1837, no banks were again created up to 1850, and the three last named are still without them, with the exception of two small ones in Florida. Texas has a small bank at Galveston, and Utah, Oregon, and New Mexico have none. In the District of Columbia four old banks expired by limitation of charter in the hands of trustees, and Congress refused to recharter them; but they continue to transact business.

It is probable that a large portion of the increase in banking, particularly at the west, has been due to the introduction of the security system of New York, the idea of which seemed to popularize that which had previously been in bad odor. The following table shows the States which have adopted the free banking principle in whole or in part:

States.	Year adopted.	1860.	
		Stocks held.	Circulation.
New York	1838	$26,897,874	$29,959,506
Michigan	1849	192,831	222,197
New Jersey	1850	962,911	4,811,832
Virginia	1851	3,584,078	9,812,197
Illinois	1851	9,826,691	8,981,723
Ohio	1851	2,153,552	7,983,889
Indiana	1852	1,349,466	5,390,246
Wisconsin	1854	5,031,504	4,429,855
Missouri	1856	725,670	7,884,885
Tennessee	1852	1,233,432	5,538,378
Louisiana	1853	5,842,096	11,579,313
Iowa	1858	101,849	568,806
Minnesota	1858	50,000	50,000
Massachusetts	1859	....	....
Total	....	57,951,954	97,212,827

The principle cannot be said to have worked well except in New York, where it required constant alterations for many years to bring it to perfection. In Illinois it was an entire failure, and the new constitutional convention adopted a clause looking to the prohibition of any more banks and to the suppression of the existing circulation.

INSURANCE.

The progress of insurance in the United States has been rapidly following the development of commerce and trade, of which it is the necessary accompaniment, since the system of buying and selling goods on credit necessitates the resort to every possible means of making those credits safe. None is more obvious than that of requiring all goods to be insured. It follows that as commodities increase in quantity and value, the amount to be covered by insurance must expand in the same proportion. Unfortunately, however, there have been no regular statistics collated from year to year, as in the case of banks, by which that interesting index to the growth of the national wealth might be compared. The State of Massachusetts has paid most attention to this matter, and the annual reports are very valuable. The number of companies and amounts at risk have been as follows in that State:

Year.	Number of companies.	Capital stock.	Fire risks.	Marine risks.
1840	41	$7,475,000	$51,998,596	$50,631,877
1850	30	6,106,875	63,943,273	76,082,529
1860	117	6,353,100	348,923,289	101,972,974

The total property at risk has increased in the ten years $310,870,461. Under the present laws of New York the insurance returns are well organized. Taking the figures in connexion with those of the leading ones of other States, the results are as follows:

	Number of companies.	Capital and assets.	At risk.
New York	135	$53,287,547	$916,474,956
Massachusetts	117	6,353,100	450,896,263
Connecticut	12	5,364,686	279,322,184
Rhode Island	6	2,419,688	32,187,104
Philadelphia	10	6,510,601	139,229,374
New Orleans	9	6,738,031	221,100,000
Charleston	2	....	47,291,000
Augusta, Georgia	1	952,858	7,000,000
Jersey City	1	179,713	5,231,061
Peoria, Illinois	1	363,995	6,806,377
Total	....	....	2,105,538,319

The amount at risk by all the companies in the Union may approach three thousand millions, and the losses were reported as follows for 1860:

Vessels and freights	$13,525,000
Cargoes	15,050,700
Total marine	28,575,700
By fire	22,020,000
Total losses	50,595,700

The number of United States life insurance companies is about 47; number of lives insured, 60,000; total amount insured, $180,000,000; annual premiums, $7,000,000.

VALUE OF REAL AND PERSONAL ESTATE.

(APPENDIX—TABLE NO. 35.)

The marshals of the United States were directed to obtain from the records of the States and Territories respectively, an account of the value of real and personal estate as assessed for taxation. Instructions were given these officers to add the proper amount to the assessment, so that the return should represent as well the true or intrinsic value as the inadequate sum generally attached to property for taxable purposes. The result of this return by all the census takers will be found in table No. 34, whereby it will appear that the value of individual property in the States and territories exceeds the sum of sixteen thousand millions of dollars, representing an increase of one hundred and twenty-six and a half per centum in ten years in value in the aggregate, and an increase of sixty-eight per cent. per capita of the free population. The rate of increase has been immense in the western States, while the absolute gain in the older States has been no less remarkable. For example, the rate of increase in Iowa has been more than nine hundred per cent., while the absolute increase of wealth has been two hundred and forty-seven millions of dollars; while Pennsylvania has increased at the rate of ninety-six per cent., with an an absolute gain in wealth of near seven thousand millions of dollars. The wealth per capita for Iowa in 1850 was $123, while in 1860 it amounted to $366, a rate of increase of one hundred and ninety-seven and a half per cent. The wealth of Pennsylvania in 1850 per capita was $312; in 1860 per capita was $487; the rate of increase fifty-six per cent.

It must be borne in mind that the value of all taxable property was returned, including that of foreigners as well as natives, while all was omitted belonging to the States or United States. In considering the relation of population to wealth, the fact must be borne in mind that a much larger proportion of the property of the western than eastern States is held by non-residents, and that this circumstance is not without its influence in exaggerating the wealth of individuals in States where large investments have been made by persons resident elsewhere.

The effect of internal improvements upon the prosperity and wealth of the country can not be better illustrated than by the rapid enhancement in value of all property brought within their influence.

To trace the causes of our great progress in wealth, and to pursue the investigation in detail, would be profitable and interesting, but the want of time makes it incumbent to postpone further review of this table to another time.

AGRICULTURE.

(Appendix—Table No. 36.)

View of the condition and progress of agriculture in the United States.

It appears from the returns of the last census, that the ratio of increase of the principal agricultural products of the United States has more than kept pace with the increase of population. Indeed, there appears no reason to doubt the continuance of an abundant supply of all the great staple articles, equal to the necessities of any possible increase of population or national contingency for ages to come. It is also gratifying to note the evidences of improvement in some of the most important agricultural operations, proving that our farmers are fully in sympathy with the progressive spirit of the age, and not behind their fellow-citizens engaged in other industrial occupations. The products of the great west are giving a tone to the markets of Great Britain and the continent. Chicago has become one of the first grain markets in the world, and as the boundless region still further west is being developed, every channel of communication with the Atlantic coast will teem with the products of the soil. Illinois alone sends now to the great market at New York an average of two thousand head of cattle weekly, and other States, comprising regions almost unknown at the former census, and still more distant from the seaboard, are adding and increasing their contributions.

New plants and animals have been introduced in the past decade. From the products of the sugar cane—*sorghum saccharatum*—transplanted from the Chinese empire, the west is furnished with a new article of domestic luxury and utility, and rendered comparatively independent of the sugar cane of more southern States.

The great dairy interest in our country during this period has increased the production of cheese and butter, and already American cheese is as well known in English markets as the best English dairy cheese.

Indian corn is now an indispensable article for Great Britain, and each succeeding year is increasing the demand for this important product of our country, which is raised in every State and Territory of our Union.

While it is admitted that very much remains to be accomplished by the agricultural interest of our country, it cannot be doubted that the past ten years has shown to the world that the United States has within its own territory the resources which will enable us to compete with the older nations of the world in every department of domestic industry.

The London exhibition in 1851 made known that the United States had the means of supplying the implements and machinery needed in every country in Europe. Since that time our reapers and mowers, ploughs, steam-engines, and railroad cars have found their way to the Old World, and an American in taking the tour of the continent will, in the great empire of Russia, find himself on board of an American railroad car drawn by an American locomotive on a railroad built by an American engineer. We point to these advances as evidence that the enterprise of our countrymen, with so wide a scope for its development at home, manifests itself wherever a profitable field opens for its exercise abroad.

At a period like the present, when, for the preservation of the national life and character, the resources of the country are subjected to a greater strain than they have ever yet borne, when a large portion of its effective labor is diverted to the same sacred duty, and all the productive forces of the Union are controlled to an unprecedented extent by causes more pervading and subversive in their effects than any which could possibly arise from extraneous sources, it is a subject of the highest gratification that we are blessed with the amplest returns from the labors of the husbandman. The crops of hay and grain, as the result of a favorable season and a broader cultivation of land, are believed especially to have afforded abundant and timely harvests. Regarded either as a source of cheap and ample supply for a vast commissariat with the least possible drain upon the public chest, of cheap and plenary subsistence to the numerous unemployed and dependent classes, or as a source of exports and employment for the commercial and shipping interests, the bounty of our land is at the present time a subject of national congratulation and thankfulness.

The increasing annual products of agriculture in our highly-favored country, and the hay and grain crops in particular, furnish striking illustrations of the close interdependence and connexion of all branches of the national industry. The dependence of agriculture upon the results of mechanical skill, as well as the astonishing progress of the latter within the last half century, is strongly exemplified in the application of labor-saving appliances, which become still more valuable, in emergencies like the present, in all the operations of the farm. The saving effected by new and improved implements in Great Britain within a dozen years preceding 1851 was stated by a competent authority to be not less than one-half on all the main branches of farm labor. Our own progress in this respect is believed to have been more rapid than that of any other agricultural people, and to be in advance of our application of the fruits of purely scientific research in the improvement of agriculture. In nearly every department of rural industry mechanical power has wrought a revolution. The inventive genius of the country has not only contrived to make it prepare the crop for market and to sew or knit the family apparel of the farmer, but to rock and "tend" the infant as well as to rend from the embrace of earth the century-rooted oak which our fathers were forced to leave to the slow eradication of time. Whether the superior agricultural advantages and the demand for improved implements and machinery in the United States have stimulated the facile ingenuity of our mechanics, or have only been seconded by its ready contributions to industry, we shall not stop to inquire. The greatest triumphs of mechanical skill in its application to agriculture are witnessed in the instruments adapted to the tillage, harvesting, and subsequent handling of the immense grain crops of the country, and particularly upon the western prairies. Without the improvements in ploughs and other implements of tillage which have been multiplied to an incredible extent, and are now apparently about to culminate in the steam plough, the vast wheat and corn crops of those fertile plains could not probably be raised. But were it possible to produce wheat upon the scale that it is now raised, much of the profit and not a little of the product would be lost were the farmer compelled to wait upon the slow process of the sickle, the cradle, and the hand-rake for securing it when ripe. The reaping-machine, the harvester, and machines for threshing, winnowing, and cleaning his wheat for the market have become quite indispensable to every large grain grower. The commercial importance of the wheat crop and its various relations to the subject of domestic and foreign supply, to markets, the means of transportation, storage, &c., make it highly important that the producer shall have the means of putting his crop in the market at the earliest or most favorable time and with the greatest precision.

Wheat.—The quantity of wheat grown in all the States and Territories in the year 1849 was 100,485,944 bushels. The quantity grown in 1859 was 171,183,381 bushels, an increase of nearly seventy per centum, or about double the increase of population in the same period. Some of the older wheat-growing States—Pennsylvania, Virginia, New York, and Ohio—do not show a proportionate increase, owing to the destructive agency of the wheat midge, and the consequent unwillingness of farmers to subject themselves to repeated losses from this cause. Fortunately, the midge is diminishing where it was formerly most destructive, and wheat-growing will soon be resumed in many localities in these States where for a time it was almost abandoned. To the introduction and greatly extended cultivation of spring wheat in the northwestern States, is the country mainly indebted for the increase in the amount of wheat produced. In Illinois this crop has increased in ten years from 9,414,577 bushels to 24,159,500 bushels; in Wisconsin, from 4,286,131 to 15,812,625 bushels in the same period. In many cases in these States the quantity grown has exceeded the means of ready transportation, or the demands of the market, and has therefore been too great to be profitable.

There appears among the contributions of the New York State Agricultural Society a statement of Dr. Asa Fitch, entomologist for that useful association, relating to depredatory insects, of so much general interest as to claim insertion in this report. It is a matter of no small import that this association have introduced into this country from abroad certain parasites which Providence has created to counteract the destructive powers of some of these depredators, by limiting their efficiency and destroying their numbers. We have heretofore been suffering from the destructive agency of some of these enemies to the grain crop, which have been introduced from abroad, without enjoying the influence of their natural enemies which remained at home. It is gratifying to realize that the New York State Agricultural Society has manifested a spirit so philanthropic in conception, with the prospect of results so important.

Dr. Fitch remarks:

"The grain aphis made its advent in a most remarkable manner. That an insect never seen before and not known to be present in our country should suddenly be found everywhere in New England, and most of the State of New York, in profuse numbers in every grain field of this wide extent of territory, and literally swarming upon and smothering the crop in many fields, was a phenomenon which probably has no parallel in the annals of science. How it was possible for this insect so suddenly to become thus astonishingly numerous was a mystery which seemed to most persons to be inexplicable. It is the most prolific of any insect which has ever been observed. I find it commences bearing when it is but three days old, and produces four young daily. Thus the descendants of a single aphis will in twenty days amount to upwards of two millions, each day increasing their number to almost double what they were the day before. This serves to account for the surprising numbers which we had of this insect.

"The aphis was everywhere supposed to be a new insect, and one writer went so far as to name and describe it scientifically, in full confidence that the world had never before known anything like it. My examinations, however, fully assured me that it was identical with a species which has long been known in the grain fields of Europe. And on my announcing this, the erroneous views which one and another were adopting were speedily abandoned.

"Our best European accounts of this insect are very imperfect. They only speak of it as occurring in June and July, whereas I find it is present on the grain the whole year round. And when the grain is but a few inches high, if half a dozen of these insects happen to locate themselves on the same plant they suck out its juice to such an extent that the plant withers and dies.

"As yet I have never been able to find a male of this species. They are all females. This is proved by placing any one supposed to be a male in a vial; next morning two or three young lice are always found in the vial with it. The general habits of insects of this kind are well known. The aphis on the apple tree and other fruit trees, when cold weather arrives, give birth to males. The sexes then pair, and the female thereupon deposits eggs, which remain through the winter to start these insects again the following year. I had supposed it would be the same with this aphis on the grain. I thought, when autumn arrived, I should meet with males and find eggs dropped on the blades of the grain. But there were none. The females and their young continued to appear on the grain till the end of the season. They are everywhere on the grain now, buried under the snow, ready to warm into life and activity again when the spring opens. And on grain growing in flower pots, on which I am keeping these insects in full activity through the winter to notice what I can of their habits, no males have yet appeared. When, and under what circumstances this sex will be produced, is a most curious subject, still remaining to be ascertained. It at present looks as though the female and their descendants were prolific permanently, without any intercourse of the sexes.

"Last summer such multitudes of parasites, ladybugs, and other destroyers of this aphis, had become gathered in the grain fields at harvest time that it seemed as though it would be exterminated by them. But at the end of the season this insect appeared as common on the young rye as I had noticed it at the opening of spring. The present indications, therefore, are that this aphis will be as numerous on the grain the coming summer as it was the past, if the season proves favorable to its increase.

"As to the *army worm*, it may be remarked that for almost a century it had been known that in this country was a kind of worm whose habit it was to suddenly appear in particular spots in such immense numbers as to wholly consume the herbage over an extent frequently of several miles, and then abruptly vanish, nothing being seen of it afterwards. Thus it was one of the most singular and also one of the most formidable and alarming creatures of this class that was known to be in our world. Yet, what kind of worm this was, and what insect produced it, remained wholly unknown down to the present day. Appearing here and there all over the country the past season, this army worm became an object of the deepest interest; and from Illinois on the one hand, and Massachusetts on the other, specimens of the moths bred from these worms were sent to me for information as to what the name of this insect really was.

"With regard to the *wheat midge*, I would observe that in this country injurious insects are much more numerous than in Europe, occasioning us far greater losses than are there experienced. A year ago I received from France a vial filled with insects as they were promiscuously gathered by the net in the wheat fields of a district where the midge was doing much injury. It then occurred to me that by gathering the insects of our wheat fields here in the same manner, it would furnish materials for a very accurate comparison of the wheat insects of this country with those of Europe. As the result of a comparison thus made, I find that in our wheat fields here the midge formed 59 per cent. of all the insects on this grain the past summer; whilst in France, the preceding summer, only seven per cent. of the insects on wheat were of this species. In France, the parasitic destroyers of the midge amounted to 85 per cent; while, in this country, our parasites form only 10 per cent. And after the full investigation of the subject which I have now made, I can state this fact with confidence—*we have no parasites in this country that destroy the wheat midge.* The insect so common on wheat, and which resembles the European parasites of the midge so closely that, in the New York Natural History, it is described as being one of that species, and in the Ohio Agricultural Reports it is confidently set down as another of them, I find has nothing to do with the wheat midge, but is the parasite of an ash gray bug which is common on grain and grass, laying its eggs in the eggs of this bug, and thus destroying them.

"I stated to the society, a year since, that the wheat midge had wholly vanished the previous summer; not one of its larvæ could I find, on a careful search over an extensive district around me. But the past season this insect appeared in the wheat again, as numerous as usual. This has led us into important changes in our views of the habits of this insect. How was it possible for it to utterly disappear from the wheat one year and be back in it in swarms the next year? Obviously it must have other places of breeding than in the wheat. And, therefore, if no wheat was grown in this country for a few years, as has so often been proposed, it would not starve and kill out this insect. The insect would resort to other situations, and would sustain itself there, returning into the wheat again as numerous as before, when its cultivation was recommenced. And what could it be that banished this insect from the wheat in 1860, and brought it back again in 1861? The remarkable difference in the weather of these two years furnishes an answer to this question. When the midge fly came out to deposit its eggs in June, 1860, the weather was excessively dry; in 1861 it was very wet and showery. And thus we learn the fact that these flies cannot breathe a dry, warm atmosphere; they are forced to retreat to places where the air is damp and moist. When the uplands, the ploughed fields, are parched with drought, the midge cannot abide in them; it must go to the lowlands along the margins of streams, where it must remain so long as the drought continues. Here it must lay its eggs and rear its young, depositing them, probably, in the grass growing in these situations. And hence we also learn that if the last half of June is unusually dry, our wheat that year will escape injury from the midge; but if the last half of June is very wet and showery, this crop will be severely devastated."

Indian corn.—This crop in 1849 was 592,071,104 bushels; in 1859 it was 830,451,707 bushels, which is an increase of more than forty per cent. In a majority of the States this is undoubtedly the most popular crop; it is less liable to failure than any other, and is applied to so great a variety of useful purposes. No important changes have been made either in the varieties cultivated or in the modes of cultivation, except in the gradual substitution of animal for human labor.

Cotton.—The rapidity with which the cultivation of cotton has increased in the United States is truly wonderful. In the beginning of the present century the annual exportation was less than 5,000 bales; in 1849 the quantity grown had reached 2,445,793 bales of ginned cotton of 400 pounds each; in 1859 it had further increased to 5,196,944 bales, or more than 110 per cent. in ten years. The whole crop is the product of thirteen States, but is chiefly obtained from eight of them. Immense as is the quantity of cotton produced, the demand is equal to the supply. Prior to the production of cotton in such vast quantities in the more southern States, it was extensively cultivated for domestic purposes in North Carolina, Virginia, Maryland, Delaware, and southern Illinois, and it is not improbable that its cultivation may be re-established in some of these States with profit to the producer and advantage to the consumer.

Dairy products.—The quantity of butter produced in the census year 1859–'60 is set down at 460,509,854 pounds, which is an increase of 46 per cent. on the product of 1849–'50. The amount of cheese returned is 105,875,135 pounds, or 339,242 pounds more than the product of 1849–'50. Cheese is especially rich in flesh-forming constituents, and is therefore regarded as a highly nutritious article of diet, well adapted to the use of the laboring man, and capable of doing more to repair the waste of muscular exertion than many times its weight of butter or of fat meat. Still it appears that cheese does not enter largely into the daily food of the working classes of this country, as it does in Germany and Great Britain. Were it produced more abundantly, and sold at a lower price, it is probable that an article of food so convenient and economical would be more fully used. The cheese exported from the United States to other countries is about 15,000,000 pounds annually. In fact, were cheese-making as well understood in our country generally as it is in Europe, the demand would be greatly increased. It is believed that our people suffer immensely by not thoroughly understanding the most approved processes of cheese-making. Comparatively little of the prodigious quantity produced can be termed a first rate article. While many of our most enterprising dairymen supply an article creditable to the country, in Europe what is termed American cheese is not purchased with that confidence with which we receive theirs, and for the reason that the processes have not reached that perfection which alone contributes to uniformity of excellence and distinctiveness of character.

When this point is attained a taste is cultivated, and increasing demand follows, and profits enlarge. An article so nutritious and easy of transportation should form some portion of our army rations.

Domestic animals.—The tables of agriculture will show a satisfactory increase in the live stock of the country. In addition to returns of animals employed in agriculture and possessed by farmers, we have prepared a table from the returns of the census-takers which represent an *estimate* of the different varieties of live stock which, being owned by persons not engaged in agricultural pursuits, were not included in the agricultural schedule. These returns we believe entitled to confidence, and they swell considerably the numbers contained in the official statements. As all live stock thus circumstanced was omitted in the previous census, we have, in all our comparisons and calculations, ignored it, because, being omitted in previous censuses, its introduction into the figures at this time would interfere with the apparent rate of increase.

The horses included in the table referred to comprise carriage, team, and other horses which were previously, and in this census, omitted, but which will be seen to make a vast increase to the number returned in the agricultural schedule. The addition to all varieties of live stock thus made to appear, and which exists, is a matter of no inconsiderable importance.

Value of animals slaughtered.—The value of slaughtered animals for 1849 was $111,703,142, in 1859 it had reached $212,871,653, the largest part of the increase being in the western States. The manufacturers of soap, candles, leather, glue, bone-black and others depending on this source for their material have received a proportionate development.

Sheep and wool.—The number of sheep returned by the census of 1850 was 21,723,220, and the amount of wool 52,516,959 pounds. In 1860 the number of sheep returned was 23,317,756, and the amount of wool 60,511,343 pounds.

In addition to the number of sheep above mentioned as returned by the census, the assistant marshals reported 1,505,810 as their estimate of the number of sheep not included because owned by others than farmers, so that the entire number of sheep in the United States on the 1st day of June may safely be placed at 62,017,153, and a proportionate amount may be added with propriety to the clip of wool for the same period.

While the sheep of the United States increased but 1,594,536 between 1850 and 1860, the imports of wool and woollens during that period were as follows:

Year.	Value of imports of unmanufactured wool.	Value of imports of manufact'ed wool.	Year.	Value of imports of unmanufactured wool.	Value of imports of manufact'ed wool.
1850	$1,681,691	$17,151,509	1856	$1,665,064	$31,961,793
1851	3,833,157	19,507,309	1857	2,125,744	31,286,118
1852	1,930,711	17,573,964	1858	4,022,635	26,486,091
1853	2,669,718	27,621,911	1859	4,444,954	33,521,956
1854	2,822,185	32,382,594	1860	4,842,152	37,937,190
1855	2,072,139	24,404,149			

The aggregate exports of domestic wool during the whole of the same period only reached the value of $1,562,502; and there were no exports of domestic manufactures of wool.

The average price of fine wool in one of our principal wool markets, (Boston,) for the last thirty-five years has been $50\frac{3}{10}$ cents per pound; of medium, $42\frac{8}{10}$ cents; of coarse, $35\frac{1}{2}$ cents. The consumption of mutton has rapidly increased. The supply now as rarely exceeds the demand as with any other meat, and the best qualities out-sell beef in our markets.

No country is better adapted by natural, and on the whole, by artificial conditions to the production of wool than the United States. It appears to be conceded that Australia and South America contain the only very extensive regions of the earth now capable of competing with equal areas of our country in this production. That narrow rim of vegetation which encloses the vast inland deserts of Australia presents not a circumstance of superiority, for this object, over the immense natural pastures of our western and southwestern States and Territories, and it is manifestly inferior to them in important conditions. Portions of it are destitute of running streams for hundreds of miles, and it is subject to the periodical recurrence of droughts, which in some cases have extended through years, drying up all minor vegetation, and proving most destructive to flocks and herds. The government price of lands is higher than in the United States. Its distance from its wool market equals nearly half the circumference of the globe. Yet its exports of wool rose between 1810 and 1850 from 167 pounds to 40,000,000 pounds! South America is also becoming an extensive producer and exporter of this staple. Here, too, no natural conditions of superiority over those of the United States present themselves, while there are political and moral ones which undeniably are hostile to the security and permanence of so exposed a branch of industry.

Apart from the mere question of the cheap production of wool, the experience of the most advanced agricultural nations, like England, Germany, and France, goes to show that sheep are a necessity of a good general system of husbandry on even the highest priced lands and amidst the densest population. They afford as much food to man, in proportion to their own consumption, as any other domestic animals. They are believed to return more fertilizing matter to the soil. In addition to these things, they alone furnish wool. England proper has about five hundred and ninety sheep to the square mile. The United States proper (exclusive of Territories) have about forty-eight to the square mile.

Our people have not lacked the necessary breeds to embark vigorously and advantageously in every department of sheep husbandry. In fine-wool varieties we have selections from the best flocks of Germany. In varieties ranging from fine to medium we have the American merino, yielding fifty per centum more wool than his Spanish ancestor, without a deterioration in its quality. In coarse varieties, we have the choicest mutton-breeds of England, and also hardy and productive sub-varieties between these and what are termed our native sheep. No country has ever been so liberal in importing the most highly-esteemed foreign breeds of sheep, and none has been more successful in acclimating them. Some have been greatly improved among us, and none, it is believed, have degenerated where the systems adapted to their culture have been found profitable.

In view of all the preceding facts, it would seem most anomalous that a people so intelligent and enterprising as our own should have advanced so slowly in one of the most important departments of industry, should have consented so long and so largely to import a prime necessary of life which they could actually produce and market at a less cost than the exporter.

American wool-growers attribute this state of things mainly to two causes: tariff regulations, which give protection to the woollen manufacturer and not to the producer, and to the unsteadiness which has marked our tariff policies. Though the monetary state of the country and other incidental causes have undoubtedly contributed their influences, it is not to be denied that a comparison of wool prices under the different tariffs gives color to the first conclusion, because, contrary to all the earlier anticipations of the growers, they show that there has been no coincidence whatever between high and low wool prices and what are termed high and low tariffs, but quite as often precisely the reverse. If the above position of the producer is well taken—if he is not equally protected with the manufacturer—it is not a sufficient answer to his complaint to say that he needs no protection because he can already produce the staple as cheaply as his foreign competitor. The ordinary wool-growers of the United States can no more live as he now lives, on the same profits which content the wealthy Anglo-Australian or South American grower, than can our ordinary manufacturers live as they now live on the profits which content the manufacturers of Europe. Much the greater number of our producers are comparatively small land-holders and capitalists, yet they have the duties of intelligent freemen to discharge and the expenses of liberal members of society to incur. Their expenditures in directions which tend to comfort and self-respect, and which promote civilization and the public interests, are ten times greater than those of persons of the same wealth in the foreign countries from which the competition comes. Is not our government as much bound, both by justice and expediency, to assist this class of men to preserve their respectable status as to render like assistance to any other class? Is the production of a great staple of less consequence to our country than its manufacture?

It is complained that the rapid and almost radical changes which have taken place in our tariff legislation, now stimulating both the producer and manufacturer of wool beyond the boundaries of prudence, and now suddenly withdrawing much of the protection on which their anticipations and arrangements for the future were founded, have necessarily led to ruinous disappointments, and finally impaired the confidence of the community in the safety of investments in a husbandry subject to such interferences.

The present would seem an auspicious period to establish permanent policies in these particulars. One of the principal causes which has rendered it difficult to estimate the public receipts in advance—the fluctuations between large and small sales of the public lands—is now probably removed. These sales, always advancing at the same time with imports and duties, that is, in periods of pecuniary inflation, were sometimes sufficient at such periods, with the aid of only a moderate tariff, to lead to the accumulation of large surpluses of revenue. These produced clamorous and successful calls for a reduction of duties. But in periods of pecuniary depression the sales of the public lands fell off; the reduced tariff was found insufficient to raise the necessary revenue, and another change in the opposite direction became necessary.

While it is not probable that surplus revenues will accrue, from any cause, for many years to come, the most intelligent and experienced wool-growers of our country ask for no extreme or disproportioned legislation in their behalf. They only ask that in establishing a system of revenue adequate to the public wants, the interest they represent receive a share of protection fairly proportioned to its importance and requirements. If this is accorded, and the policy established is allowed to acquire a permanent character, it is not doubted by our agriculturists that this important branch of industry will rapidly attain a development which will no longer leave us tributary to foreign nations for one of the most important necessaries of life.

In view of the limited number of American publications devoted to sheep husbandry which have appeared, we feel it a duty to refer to a valuable repertory of useful information, being a treatise on fine-wool sheep husbandry, by Henry S. Randall, LL.D., of New York, read before the New York State Agricultural Society, February 12, 1862. 127 pages, 8vo.

Sugar and molasses.—Notwithstanding the large quantities of sugar and molasses produced in the United States, a large amount is obtained from abroad. The sum paid for imported sugars, in 1859, exceeded $31,000,000, and in the same season 30,000,000 of gallons of molasses were imported.

The rapidly increasing culture of the Chinese sugar-cane is supplying a great want. The introduction of such a crop to the notice of the American farmer is a prominent feature of the past decade. While, in the present state of knowledge, much difficulty and uncertainty seems to attend the manufacture of sugar from this plant, it has proved its value as very productive in sirup or molasses. The plants introduced into this country are from Asia and Africa, and vary considerably in character. They are liable to hybridization with each other, and with the broom corn, and much care is required to preserve the varieties distinct. So far as we have information, Mr. J. H. Smith, of Quincy, Illinois, has been the most successful cultivator of the imphee, and his efforts have been attended with much success. While, with our knowledge of the disappointments which have been experienced in Europe and this country as to results, we would not recommend a heedless expenditure of time and means in the culture of the imphee, we are sufficiently confident in its value, under many circumstances, as to hope that farmers generally of the north and west will devote some attention to the culture of the plant, and fairly test its utility for the production of sugar.

The product of cane sugar, as returned by the Seventh Census, was 237,133 hogsheads of 1,000 pounds each; in 1859 it was 302,205 hogsheads. The product of molasses for the former year was 12,700,991 gallons; for the latter 16,337,080 gallons. From the sorghum and imphee, 7,235,025 gallons of molasses were made in 1859.

The amount of maple sugar made in 1850 was 34,253,436 pounds; in 1860 the product was 38,863,884 pounds. This increase is not large, but sufficient to afford gratifying evidence that our beautiful maple groves and forests are not becoming extinct, while many are preserved with commendable care. We wish it could, with truth, be added that the cultivation of this noble tree was extending in a ratio equal that wherein the old trees in the forest are diminishing under bad treatment and the demands for new land for tillage. The landholder who appropriates a few rods of land to the preservation or cultivation of the sugar tree not only increases the value of his estate but confers a benefit upon future generations.

Tobacco.—The tobacco crop, in 1849, amounted to 199,752,655 pounds, being a decrease of more than 19,000,000 pounds according to the previous census; in 1859 it reached 429,390,771 pounds.

To the production of this amount every State and Territory contributed, although Virginia and Kentucky furnished much more than any other. It would seem surprising that a crop which is said to impoverish the soil more than any other, and to injure to some extent every one who uses it, should be found so desirable as to increase 106 per cent. in ten years; but such is the effect of a ready market with remunerative prices. Several of the northern States present a very large increase in the production of this article. Among these, Ohio, New York, Connecticut, Massachusetts, and Pennsylvania exhibit both the largest product and the greatest increase. Ohio raised, in 1859, over 25½ million pounds, and New York increased her production from 83,189 pounds to 5,764,582 pounds; Massachusetts from 138,246 to 3,233,198, and Connecticut from 1,267,624 to 6,000,133 pounds. Virginia, North Carolina, Maryland, Kentucky, and other of the more southern States show a greatly augmented growth of the staple.

There has been a commensurate increase in the manufacture of snuff, cigars, and other ultimate products of the tobacco crop, while the consumption of the article in various forms doubtless keeps pace with the production.

Wine.—The returns upon the subject of wine-making show a very large increase in an article which promises to become one of great commercial value. The wine culture has increased in a considerable number of States, but more particularly in Ohio, California, and Kentucky. The quantity of domestic wines was increased from 221,249 gallons in all the States and Territories in 1850, to 1,860,008 gallons in twenty-two States in 1860, or at the rate of 740 per cent. Of this quantity the three States above named made nearly one million gallons, and Ohio alone more than half a million gallons. The return was probably far short of the real amount.

The culture of the grape and the manufacture of wine are rapidly increasing. So soon as cultivators become assured that they possess varieties of the grape of sufficiently good quality, thoroughly hardy and adapted to our climate, the development of this form of industry is likely to be still more rapid. More than $4,000,000 was paid by citizens of the United States in 1859 for imported wines; the amount paid by consumers for a factitious home-made article it is perhaps impossible to ascertain. A good native wine may and should at once take the place of the spurious article, and in a few years of a large part of the imported. This is the more desirable, inasmuch as the disease which so seriously affects the vineyards of Europe greatly diminishes the quantity and increases the price of good wine, and at the same time tempts producers there to practice extensive adulterations. Nothing will effect a substantial temperance reform so certainly and speedily as the production of good wines in such quantity as to place them within the means of the poor as well as the rich; and every man who plants a vine will be a useful co-operator in the beneficent work of relieving the country from the evils of intemperance by the substitution of a healthy beverage for the various forms of poisons which take the name of spirits and concentrate and diffuse misery over the land.

Hay and clover.—The hay crop of 1849 was 13,838,642 tons; in 1859 the quantity reported is 19,129,128 tons. This increase is not proportionate to the increase of live stock in the country, but it appears that, with better farming, more roots and cut straw and other rough fodder are used, and therefore less hay is required. Without adding to the present extent of meadow lands, the hay crop might probably be greatly increased by the careful introduction of the best varieties of grass.

The quantity of clover-seed grown in 1849 was 468,978 bushels; in 1859 the amount was 929,010 bushels. This increase is important not only in a commercial point of view, but still more so as indicative of improvement in our agricultural system.

Orchard products.—These consist principally of apples and peaches, dried and undried. Their value in 1849 was $7,723,186; in 1859 it had reached $19,759,361. This large increase is principally due to the fact that for several years great attention has been paid to the introduction and cultivation of improved varieties of fruit, and to processes for the preservation of fruits by artificial means, which now occupy a great amount of capital. The pear, which for several years was almost left out of general cultivation on account of what was termed the "blight," has of late been less affected by this injury than formerly, and is now extending rapidly in public estimation, being justly regarded as one of the most delicious and profitable of fruits.

Silk.—The production of raw silk in the United States still remains inconsiderable in comparison with what was at one time expected. It has, however, been demonstrated that many parts of the country are well adapted to the growth of the mulberry, and that the production of silk is profitable. Were silk-raising pursued steadily wherever the climate is suitable, very profitable employment would be afforded to thousands of persons, especially females, who are now almost without such employment during a considerable portion of their time. The best way to make silk-growing profitable to individuals and the country, is to encourage its production in small quantities by many families, rather than for a few persons to undertake its production on a large scale; at least, such is the lesson taught by all silk-producing countries. By such means the cost would prove trifling, but the aggregate product would be immense. The value of silks of all kinds imported in the year ending June, 1860, exceeded $33,000,000.

Improvements.—No better evidence of the progressive improvement of American agriculture need be adduced than the great amount of animal forces employed to assist the labor of man. The number of horses, mules, and oxen engaged in agricultural labor is probably greater than the number of men, a proportion that has no parallel in any other country. All of this animal force is, of course, made available through some form of machinery. Since the preceding census the use of the reaper and mower has become not merely general but almost universal. Some of the most important crops are now seeded, cultivated, gathered, and prepared for use or market with little or no labor from man except where he is aided by mechanical appliances and animal force. The employment of steam in agricultural operations is much less common in the United States than in Great Britain, but is gradually increasing.

Draining.—This important improvement has made great progress in the estimation and practice of our farmers. Tile factories have been established extensively in many parts of the country, and consequently the material for making permanent drains is much cheapened.

Should the next ten years witness an equal advance in this direction, under-draining will be regarded as among the most indispensable operations of the farm, and its benefits will soon be fully realized.

Underground draining involves an amount of wealth not yet appreciated, though rapidly becoming realized by the American farmer. It is an undoubted fact that the most productive portions of our farms, and which are fertile in fevers, lie neglected and worse than useless for the want of knowledge or the absence of enterprise. An assistant marshal in the State of New York made report of one farmer near Geneva, who has laid on a moderate-sized farm some fifty miles of tiles, and acquired wealth as the result. A single year's crop from land before useless, has sometimes paid all the expense of the improvement, and the drains made twenty years since are as efficient as when first constructed. For health and wealth nothing contributes more where circumstances admit of it—and where do they not, to a greater or less extent?—than underground drainage. An implement of great value has recently been patented, which opens and covers a furrow of considerable depth, and lays at the same time pipe for introducing or carrying off water.

Irrigation.—This is already found to be necessary or highly beneficial in Utah, New Mexico, and California, and is there extensively practiced. To systematic irrigation we may look for covering with luxuriant vegetation millions of acres now commonly regarded as unfit for cultivation. It will doubtless be found to prove remunerative in many of the older States where it has not yet been adopted.

Progress of invention in threshing instruments.—As next in point of importance to the production of grain consists the facility for its early and economical preparation for market, the value of implements and machinery tending to this end cannot be overestimated; and as the progress whereby perfection is attained in any improvement so valuable as that which has, through a long process of years, attended the construction of threshing implements, is interesting to the political economist as well as the farmer and statesman, we have endeavored to group together all the essential facts connected with their history. The plough, hay and grain cutters, and some other implements of husbandry, have attained to such perfection within a short period, and their history is so generally known to the present generation, that special allusion to them may with propriety be deferred to a future period.

It appears that the number of patents granted in the United States for threshing-machines, exclusive of a considerable number for threshing clover, and those combining threshing apparatus with cider or grist mills, straw-cutters, &c., was *three hundred and fifty-four*—a larger number than had been given for any other instrument or process, except the plough and the water-wheel.

Some kind of mechanical means for separating grain from the ear appears to have been early contrived. A complete history of the successive changes in the means and instruments for effecting this would be a curious and interesting chapter in the record of the world's progress. Such a retrospect, could it be made, would show a remarkable uniformity in the methods adopted throughout the world in ancient and modern times. It would show that, until within a recent period, mankind has been altogether unsuccessful in originating or transmitting any essential improvement upon the most ancient plan of which we have any record.

The primitive mode of "treading out the corn" upon a smooth circular "threshing floor" in the open air, beneath the feet of the unmuzzled ox, or other animals, has prevailed among eastern nations from remote antiquity. This triturating process, however, appears from very early times to have been facilitated by certain instruments. Thus, "threshing instruments of iron" are mentioned by the prophet Amos; and "a new sharp threshing instrument having teeth," at a later period, by Isaiah. Smaller grains, having a less adhesive envelope, appear to have been separated by implements analogous to the flail, as elsewhere mentioned by the same prophet: "For the fitches are not threshed with a threshing instrument, neither is a cart-wheel turned about upon the cummin; but the fitches are beaten out with a staff, and the cummin with a rod." Cummin is threshed by the same mode in Malta at the present day, and in Syria may still be seen in common use the representative of the new, sharp threshing instrument with teeth. It is described as a thick plank or sledge drawn by oxen, and having inserted upon its under surface pieces of stone, flint, or iron, projecting from three-quarters to half an inch, by which the ears of corn are torn asunder. Its more ancient form among the Hebrews was frequently that of a square frame with rollers, encircled by three rings or wheels serrated in the manner of a saw. It sometimes resembled in form a cart, by which name it is called in the passage quoted. The threshing floor of level, hard-rolled earth was sometimes covered so as to afford shelter to the laborers during harvest; as that of the wealthy Boaz, which has furnished so interesting an illustration of the simplicity of ancient manners and customs. It was usually constructed upon an elevation exposed to currents of wind, to carry off the chaff; as that of Ornan, the Jebusite, occupied the rocky eminence of Mount Moriah, and, with the threshing instruments and oxen, was purchased by David to be forever honored as the site of the holy temple. Hesiod, who soon after wedded the muse to agriculture, directs the threshing floor to be so placed:

> "Smooth be the level floor on gusty ground,
> Where winnowing gales may sweep in eddies round."

That the threshing instruments employed had great mechanical effect upon the sheaves over which they were drawn may be inferred from their frequent use in the imagery of the prophets as descriptive of violence and ruin. The *tribula*, as the same implement was called by the Romans, has furnished our language with a synonym for the worst forms of affliction.

It is uncertain at what time the flail was first introduced. But it was in common use among the Romans, and throughout the greater part of the empire, as well as among most nations of modern Europe, for several centuries superseded nearly every other implement. This highly efficient but tedious and laborious instrument still holds its place upon small farms, and for certain kinds of crops upon large ones, in Great Britain and America. There are few, whose privilege it is to have been born in the country, who are not familiar with an article pleasantly associated with the rural literature and experience of ancient and modern times.

The earliest attempt on record to produce an implement of the character of the modern threshing-machine was made toward the middle of the last century.

The genius of mechanics appears about that time to have suddenly invaded the domain of rural economy. The horse-hoe, the drill-plough, and many other valuable contributions were made by it to the labor of the farm and the fireside.

In place of the spinning-wheel and the distaff, it supplied the spinning mill and the jenney. The threshing floor of clay, the trampling of oxen, and the flail of the thresher—

> "Sweating over his bread
> Before he eats it; the primal curse;
> But softened into mercy, made the pledge
> Of cheerful days and nights without a groan,"

it sought to replace by the threshing-machine. For the dash of the water-wheel and the moil of men and brutes it substituted the Briarean arms and tireless energy of the steam-engine. These and a thousand other subtitutions in agricultural and general mechanics, if less picturesque than the objects they have supplanted, have made ample amends by their pre-eminent service to mankind; and if mowing, reaping, and threshing machines shall ever have their protean forms arrested and fixed in a definite and recognizable shape, they may in time gather about them as many agreeable associations as their earlier and simple representatives—the scythe, the sickle, and the flail.

It is an interesting fact that as the first specific mention of the production of artificial light from coal gas was made nearly two hundred years ago in an historical account of Virginia, given to the Royal Society of England, by the Rev. John Clayton, of Yorkshire, so the earliest proposition on record, probably, to apply machinery, and perhaps water-power to the threshing of grain, occurs in a work upon that colony of still earlier date. It is found in a tract published in London, in 1650, by Ed. Williams. He urges a vigorous prosecution of the plan of colonization in that quarter, and states, among other reasons, that it would stimulate the invention of labor-saving engines, which were necessary to half-peopled plantations, but were regarded as oppressive monopolizers of labor in over-populous countries. He gives an "explication of the saw-mill, an engine wherewith, by force of a wheel in the water, to cut timber with great speed." This mechanism he proposed to introduce into Virginia, and finishes his description of it by saying that the artificer might "easily convert the same to an instrument of threshing wheat, breaking of hemp or flax, and other as profitable uses." It does not appear that the machine was at that early period ever applied to any of those "profitable uses." A number of the first attempts, however, to construct threshing mills in this country were made in the Old Dominion.

We propose to glance at some of the early attempts to introduce this class of machinery upon American farms and at some of the results of later invention to show that our people have not been slow to appreciate the advantages of such mechanism nor unsuccessful in supplying it. It is proper, however, before speaking of American machines to look a little at what has been done in Great Britain, where they were first invented. Our own progress may thus be better understood.

The first person who ever projected a threshing-machine is said to have been the celebrated Jethro Tull, of Shelborne, in Berkshire, the inventor of the drill-plough, and the father of the horse-hoeing husbandry and of systematic agriculture in England, who died in 1740. In constructing an effective threshing-machine he was far from successful. His attempt was immediately followed by that of Michael Menzies, a Scotchman, belonging to the fertile grain district of East Lothian. His more successful machine, patented in 1732, is considered the initial instrument of its class. It consisted of a system of flails attached to a revolving cylinder, driven by a water-wheel, and was pronounced by a committee of the Society of Improvers, in Scotland, "of great use to farmers both in threshing the grain clean from the straw and in saving a great deal of labor, for one man would be sufficient to manage a machine which would do the work of six." The next attempt appears to have been made about twenty years after by Michael Sterling, who made a machine on a very different principle, that of the flax-hulling machine, in common use. It was found to break off the heads, and to be only well adapted for threshing oats. In 1766 a machine, which could be moved either by horse or water power, and was said to thresh great quantities of corn in a short time, was presented to the London Society of Arts, by Mr. Evers, of Swillington, in Yorkshire, the inventor of a winnowing-machine deposited with the society.

Messrs. Alderton and Stewart, of Northumberland, in 1772, devised a machine, with an indented drum six feet in diameter and a number of fluted rollers, between which the grain was rubbed from the ear. "A mill for separating grain from straw," patented in 1785 by William Winlan, of Marylebone, was constructed upon the principle of the coffee-mill, and performed more than it promised by grinding as well as threshing the grain. The price of this machine was about £15, as appears from a letter of General Washington, dated November 1, 1787, to Arthur Young, in the sixth volume of whose Annals of Agriculture he had seen a cut and description of it. He requested Mr. Young to procure one, if he was able to recommend it and thought it sufficiently simple to be kept in order by common laborers. In a subsequent letter the general says he is convinced that a Scotch machine, described by his correspondent, was superior to Winlan's, and he concluded to wait a little before he procured one. Some other machines, constructed upon the rubbing principle, were found to damage the grain—an objection thought by some to lie against all machines when used for seed-wheat, and were laid aside.

In 1792 Mr. Willoughby, of Bedford, in Notts, returned to the system of flails introduced by Menzies, and constructed a machine with loose beaters attached to a horizontal axis or cylinder, turned rapidly by means of a horse-wheel and made to act upon a grated flooring. A Mr. Jubb, of Lewes, in 1795, also made a threshing-machine in which the straw was carried by feeding rollers between two rapidly revolving beaters, whence the corn fell into a winnowing-machine.

During the next year the model of a threshing-machine was presented to the Society of Arts of which we have no description. About the same time the description of a curious machine, worked by one horse, walking in a circle of forty feet and moving a cylinder upon which were placed thirty-two flails, making twenty revolutions to one of the horse-wheel was given to the same society. It did not prove to be an efficient agency.

In October of that year John Steedman, of Trentham, patented a machine having a number of flails fixed upon a rotary cylinder, while a circular table, revolving horizontally, brought the straw beneath their strokes. All the foregoing machines and a machine with flails, invented by J. Wardrop, of Virginia, introduced the same year in England, have long been regarded as nearly impracticable in principle.

The machine which was more properly the basis of those now in use in Scotland and elsewhere, was brought out in 1785, by Andrew Meikle, of Tyrringham, in East Lothian, through a gentleman named Stein, who had long seen the defect of the rubbing process and agreed with the son of Mr. Meikle to build him a perfect instrument. The machine was completed in 1786.

It introduced the corn between two rollers and threshed it by four beaters fixed upon a revolving drum. Previous to obtaining a patent, an improvement was made upon the original form of the beaters by substituting for a flat surface a comparatively sharp edge, thus "scutching out the grain," as he termed it, by acting in the direction of the ear, a modification not easily explained without a cut. The inventor, according to Sir John Sinclair, received substantial evidence of the gratitude of his countrymen, whose "voluntary donations" made a comfortable provision for his old age and for his family after him. Professor Low remarks, that "to Andrew Meikle, beyond a question, belongs the honor of having perfected the threshing-machine," although many changes have since been made in many parts. It was probably the instrument referred to in the letter of General Washington.

In 1789 the first machine with a rake and fan attached, to perfect the cleaning of the grain, was invented, it is believed, by J. Bailey, of Chillingham. In 1795 Mr. Wigfall, of Lynn, patented some improvements, in which he attempted to combine the stroke of the flail with revolving beaters. The latter were loosely attached by short bits of chain instead of being fixed, as in Meikle's scutchers. The grain was carried to the fan by a shaking screen and rolling cloth on an endless arch.

About the year 1800 or 1801 the Society of Arts first offered a premium of thirty guineas or a gold medal for a threshing-machine. The medal was accordingly adjudged by the society, in 1810, to H. P. Lee, esq., of Maidenhead Thicket, who, finding the machines then in use so complicated, inefficient, and liable to get out of order, had one constructed under his own directions, which was highly commended for its simplicity and effectiveness. In it rollers were first dispensed with for feeding the straw to be threshed. It was three feet in diameter and two and a half feet in length, and, with two horses, would thresh about twelve bushels in an hour. It consisted of four vanes or beaters, fixed to an axis revolving within a drum or cylinder, formed of iron plates grooved or ribbed parallel to the axis, and connected by wooden curbs so as to admit of being placed nearer or further from the beaters, according to the kind of grain to be threshed. It was made at a cost, including the horse-wheel by which it was carried, of £40. It was subsequently improved by Mr. William Lester, of Paddington. Another invention called the bolting-machine, afterward much improved by R. Garrett & Son, of Leicester, was highly spoken of at a later period. A patent was taken out in England over twenty years ago by Joseph Atkinson, of Braham Hall, Yorkshire, for a machine said to have been previously patented in this country by S. Turner, of New York.

Many other threshing-machines of various degrees of merit were introduced in Great Britain during the first half of this century. Hand threshing-machines were quite common, and received several improvements by Ransom and other large manufacturers. The machines in use in Scotland twenty years ago were generally on the principle of Meikle's, and combined all the later improvements. Those in use in the eastern part of England were generally portable threshers, without rakes or fanners attached.

There was much difference in the performance of different machines. A machine erected for J. Hanning, esq., of Dorset, about 1801, would thresh, clean, and sack, it was said, in twelve hours, with the assistance of five men, four hundred bushels of grain. A report on the Scotch machines in 1796 states that those carried by water, or four horses, would generally thresh from one hundred and fifty to one hundred and eighty bushels per diem. Arthur Young states in a report of Norfolk, in 1804, that machines built by Wigfall cost from £120 to £210, and worked by six or seven men and four to six horses, would thresh in a day, of wheat, from eighty to one hundred and sixty bushels; of barley, one hundred and twenty to two hundred and fifty-six; and of oats or peas, from one hundred and sixty to three hundred and twenty bushels. The only threshing mill in use in Kent, in 1805, R. Boy's, had by many improvements and alterations been brought to work extremely well. Operated by four horses and twelve men it would thresh, of wheat one hundred and ninety-two bushels, of barley two hundred and fifty-six, and of oats three hundred and twenty bushels daily. A machine of R. Kerr's, described by Sir John Sinclair in 1812 would, with six horses, four men, and four women, thresh about three hundred bushels of wheat in a day, at a saving of one-half the expense of the ordinary mode of threshing. Steam was applied to the business of threshing upon the example farm of Lord Ducie, at Whitfield, where a machine with some valuable modifications was constructed under the directions of his manager, John Morton, and was driven by an engine of six-horse power.

Thus it is apparent that considerable skill and enterprise had been expended upon this class of machines at an early period in the present century. Although tolerably successful, the inventors do not appear to have as yet produced instruments devoid of considerable complication and expense, both in the construction and working of them, which would preclude their general use on farms of moderate size. The early attempt to introduce from abroad into the United States did not, on these accounts, meet with much success. Their high cost, complexity, and liability to get out of order, as well as the amount of horse power and manual assistance required, were objections which led many to doubt the utility of such machines upon American farms.

The flail, therefore, and the primitive system of treading out grain by cattle, continued in use as the favorite modes during many years of the present century. The former prevailed in most of the northern States, while in parts of Pennsylvania, in Delaware, the eastern shores of Maryland and Virginia, and, we believe, in Rhode Island, grain was generally trodden out by oxen or horses as the more expeditious method. Horses were preferred for this work. A crop of 3,000 bushels could thus be threshéd and secured from "the best laid schemes of mice and men" in ten days, which would employ five threshers with the flail for one hundred days. The treading floors were from forty to one hundred and thirty feet, more commonly sixty to one hundred feet in diameter, with a path twelve to fourteen feet wide near the periphery upon which the grain was laid. The horses were led round at a slow trot, in platoons equidistant from each other, so that four ranks could preserve the distance of one-fourth of a circle and represent the four cardinal points. The floors were sometimes removed from field to field, but permanent floors made hard and smooth, and kept so by careful use, were preferred. They were commonly fenced round, sometimes with an outer and inner fence.

Toward the end of the last century Mr. Benjamin Sylvester, of Caroline county, Maryland, introduced the use of a roller to be attached to the horses upon the treading floor. It consisted of a good piece of white oak six and one-half feet long by twelve to fifteen inches square, which was reduced to an octagon or eight square, and encircled at each end with an iron ring, and had an iron axis in each end. Each of the eight planes were bored with about a dozen two-inch holes, in which were inserted stout pegs of oak, alternating with those in the next row, and made shorter at one end of the roller than the other to fit them for running in a circle. This appendage to the threshing floor cost about twelve dollars, and drawn by three horses, with four men to turn the straw, would thresh a floor of thirty bushels in favorable weather in two hours, or from sixty to eighty bushels in a day. It was introduced into Kent county, Delaware, by Judge John Clayton, who, after an experience of over twenty years in preparing for market an annual crop of five hundred to eight hundred bushels of wheat, and as many of oats, considered it superior to any other known mode of threshing. George Cummins, esq., a senator from that county and a large farmer, continued its use for the same length of time, and with Mr. Nicholas Ridgely, of Dover, whose account of it was published in the memoirs of the Philadelphia Society for Promoting Agriculture in 1816, and other experienced farmers, concurred in the opinion of Mr. Clayton. Although a Scottish threshing-machine was about that time introduced into some parts of the State, the wheat from Kent county was all threshed in the manner above described, and was said to be more sought after and to bring a better price at Wilmington than any other.

A good threshing machine of moderate cost was a desideratum, however, with the mass of farmers, and as the Scotch machines were expensive, the attention of American farmers and mechanics had been long turned to the construction of an instrument adapted to the circumstances of the country. An effort in this direction appears to have been made before the revolution. In the Pennsylvania Magazine or American Monthly Museum, vol. 1, for 1775, is a plate and description of a threshing-machine constructed with some improvements after a model shown by Mr. Ferguson in his lectures in London. In the account of it the maker is said to have heard of machines for threshing grain erected in America, but had never seen or heard a description of them. We have met with no other reference to such inventions in this country during the colonial period. We find our mechanics, however, immediately upon the organization of the Patent Office, prepared to put on record their inventions in this line, and it is probable some of them may have been made much earlier.

The first patent issued by the Secretary of State for a threshing-machine, was dated March 11, 1791, being the seventh on the records of the office. It was to Samuel Mulliken, of Philadelphia, who on the same day received letters patent for machines for breaking and swingling hemp, for cutting and polishing marble, and for raising a nap on cloth, &c., all of which could scarcely have fallen ready armed and equipped for use from his fertile brain. On the second of August of the same year another patent was recorded for a threshing-machine by William Thompson, of Virginia. In the following year Colonel Alexander Anderson, of Philadelphia, an extensive distiller who made some important improvements in the application of steam to his own branch of manufacture, endeavored to supply the desideratum of a threshing-machine. His machine, a model of which was deposited with the American Philosophical Society, was not patented. But one erected upon its plan in Maryland was found to answer well. After a time the wheel warped so as to impede its action, and from want of confidence or energy in the owner, and the absence of the inventor, it was laid aside.

In 1794 two patents for threshing-machines were taken out by Virginians—one dated April 28, by William Hodgson, and the other November 5, by James Wardrop, of Ampthill, in that State. Wardrop's machine, as already mentioned, was introduced in England in 1796. It was made with flails or elastic rods twelve feet in length, of which twelve were attached in a series having each a spring requiring a power of twenty pounds to raise it three feet high at the point. A wallower shaft with catches or teeth, in its revolution successively lifted each flail in alternate movements, so that three of the flails were operated upon by the whole power, viz, twenty pounds. The whole weight to be overcome was one hundred and twenty pounds, and the machine was worked by two men. The flails beat upon a grating, to which the corn to be threshed was fed by hand. We cannot say what success it met with in England.

Patents were taken out in March, 1797, by William Booker, also of Virginia, and in November by Richard B. Elliott, of Massachusetts, who were followed in June, 1798, by Thomas C. Montin, who patented a threshing-machine, making nine inventions of that kind in eight years. The next machine brought before the public was that of Christopher Hoxie, of Hudson, New York, patented August 20, 1801. It was considered more promising than any of its predecessors, but did not come into general use.

During the year 1802 a Mr. Prentiss, from Edinburg, erected in Pennsylvania, New Jersey, and Delaware, six or seven machines upon the Scotch principle, which were found to answer well. But on account of the extreme care required in feeding them and the inability of common workmen to keep them in repair, the builder being engaged in another business at a distance, prevented their general adoption. The increased demand for American breadstuffs in Europe during the continental wars, and the impulse given to American agriculture about this time, produced frequent attempts to project a threshing-machine adapted to general use. In July of this year two patents were issued for threshing and cleaning grain—one to Ezekiel Miller, of New York, and one to Joseph Pope, of Boston, afterwards of Hallowell, Maine, a very ingenious mechanic and the inventor of an orrery which was purchased by Harvard College. Twenty years after, and four years before his death, Pope received another patent for a machine for the same purpose. In October, 1803, J. F. Turner, of Delaware, followed with a threshing-machine, and during the following year patents were issued to Thomas Barnatt, of Philadelphia, for threshing and cleaning grain; to Samuel Houston, of Virginia, for the Columbian threshing, break, and cleaning fan; and to James Deneale, of Dumfries, in the same State, for an improvement in threshing-machines. B. B. Bernard, of Virginia, and Simon Willard, jr., of Hudson, New York, took patents in 1807, the former for a simple thresher, and the latter for threshing and cleaning. But one patent was given in 1808, four in 1809, and six in 1810, for threshing and cleaning grain, including one by Isaiah Jennings, of Brookfield, New York, the inventor of the patent burning fluid so extensively used in late years.

The number of threshing-machines patented during the next twenty-five years, including those which combined other operations and horse power, was over 240, or nearly ten annually upon an average.

In 1815 the trustees of the Massachusetts Society for Promoting Agriculture offered, among others, a premium of one hundred dollars for the most approved machine for threshing and separating grain, adapted to a farm of medium size, to be claimed before the first of June, 1816. In the summer of the last-mentioned year a Mr. Dumbleton, from England, introduced in the middle States a threshing-machine which was thought at the time to supply all that was desirable. He erected one at Port Penn, Delaware, which gave complete satisfaction. It was speedy, clean in its threshing, easy of management, and portable. We have not seen a full description of it.

A machine patented by Seth Ballou, of Livermore, in Maine, in 1821, was the subject of patented improvements by Messrs. Boyd and Ketchum, of Pennsylvania, in 1825, by the inventor in 1826, and by George Jessup, of Troy, New York, in 1830. During the latter year the large number of thirty-four patented inventions connected with the threshing of grain were recorded, and in the following year thirty-eight—the largest number in any year of the period before mentioned. Many of our most ingenious mechanics exercised their skill upon these machines, including Moses Pennock, of Kennett square, Pennsylvania, the inventor of the revolving horse-rake; Jacob Perkins, the inventor of the machine for cut-nails, and numerous others. Pennock patented a vibrating thresher in May, 1827. A machine patented in January, 1831, by Samuel Turner, of Aurelius, New York, was, a few years after, patented in England by a Mr. Atkinson, of Yorkshire. It appears to have been upon the principle of those now in use, having a drum surrounded by a series of pegs so arranged as to pass a similar row of pegs placed on a concave, surrounding nearly one-half the circumference of the drum.

In the year 1831 two patents were issued for horse power for threshing-machines to N. P. Stanton, of Syracuse, New York, and to John Lammon, of Macedonia, in that State. These, which now form an important branch of the business of the manufactures of agricultural machinery, have been the subject of 147 patents up to 1857.

The great exhibition in London, in 1851, gave an immense impulse to the use and construction of agricultural machines in England and America. Europe was on that occasion first made acquainted with the extent and excellence of American inventions in this department, in which our greatest triumphs were achieved. A great variety of threshing-machines were there exhibited, adapted to steam and horse power. All the English horse-power machines required from four to eight horses to work them. Only one, which was exhibited by the Messrs. Allen, of New York, was operated by a single horse.

New York manufacturers have shown much enterprise in the department of rural mechanics. In July, 1852, under the direction of the executive committee of the New York State Agricultural Society, an extended and thorough trial of agricultural implements, lasting eight days, was made at Geneva before a select committee. Trials were, on that occasion, made of simple threshers entered by Messrs. Emory & Co., of Albany; George Westinghouse, of Central Bridge; Eddy & Co., Union Village; Ezra W. Badger, of Fly Creek, and George F. Jerome, of Hempstead. The Messrs. J. A. Pitts, of Buffalo; Harris Scovill, of Tompkins county; Daniel Woodbury, of Palmyra; J. Rapalje & Co., of Rochester, and Hall & Thompson, of Rochester, exhibited threshers and separators combined. Nearly all of this large number from a single State were found to be highly efficient machines. One of the largest of them was found to be capable of threshing and cleaning, with eight horses and seven men, 250 bushels of grain in a day, at a cost of four cents and seven mills per bushel. A less efficient machine, requiring double the time to perform the same work, would thresh, without cleaning, 135 bushels, with the aid of five men and two horses, at a cost of four cents and four mills per bushel. The balance of economy generally was found to be in favor of the large machines. The price of the larger machine was $150, and of the smaller but $35. Of nine competing machines the price of three was $150; of one, $145; of two, $40; and of three, $35 each.

The horse power exhibited by the same manufacturers was also subjected to careful tests. They were both upon the chain or railroad principle and upon that of the sweep or lever, and cost about $100 each.

We thus perceive what an immense gain had been effected in the economy of threshing over the most approved methods and instruments in use in England and America only forty or fifty years before.

The World's Fair in New York, in 1853, brought together also splendid illustrations of the progress of the United States in the application of mechanics to the business of the farm. There was a good representation of threshing-machines, of which the following were the principal, which may be supposed to exhibit the highest perfection which the instrument had then attained:

The "Farmer's Labor-saving Machine," for threshing, separating, cleaning, and bagging grain, ready measured for the market at one operation, was designed for two horses, and was said to be capable of threshing and cleaning 100 bushels per day. It was patented in June, 1848, by E. S. Snyder, of Charlestown, Virginia, who also exhibited the model of another thresher with an upright cylinder.

The rotary seed and grain thresher, with revolving flails, invented by R. W. Palmer, of North Carolina, possessed some new features; and a machine on the old spiked cylinder plan, exhibited by the same manufacturer, contained several improvements. Mr. Palmer took out a patent in England in 1853, and in the United States the next year.

Hathaway's combined threshing, hulling, and cleaning machine for all kinds of grain and seeds patented in 1848 by Bradford G. H. Hathaway, of Yates county, New York, was said by the inventor to be capable of threshing and cleaning 600 to 800 bushels of wheat in a day.

Gilbert's excelsior thresher and cleaner, patented by Joseph C. Gilbert, of New York, possessed some peculiarities in the construction of the cylinder, for which superiority to all others was claimed; A No. 3 machine of this patent, costing $110, would thresh and clean, it was said, with two horses, 10 to 1,200 bushels of wheat in a day.

The improved threshing and separating machine, patented by J. R. Moffit, of Piqua, Ohio, differed in many respects from any other. It was a powerful machine with much complicated but ingenious mechanism.

Moffit's machine was introduced in England soon after the New York exhibition. It was put in operation upon the farm of Mr. Mechi, at Tiptree Hall, in Essex, and driven by a steam power of four horses, and threshed 256 bushels of wheat in four hours, cleaning it in perfect readiness for the market. Of barley it afterwards threshed 56 quarters or 448 bushels in six hours, turning out the grain clean and ready for malting or sale; it turned out 10 quarters in 73 minutes, and outstripped all the exertions of the feeders. Its weight was 12½ hundred-weight without wheels and driving gear, and cost in America $115.

During the Paris exhibition, a trial of mowing, reaping, and threshing machines was made about thirty miles from Paris, which attracted a great concourse from the capital. A correspondent of the New York Tribune says: "Six men were set to threshing with flails at the same moment that the different machines commenced operations, and the following were the results of half an hour's work:

"Six threshers with flails	60	litres of wheat.	
Pitt's American thresher	740	"	"
Clayton's English thresher	410	"	"
Dunoir's French thresher	250	"	"
Pinet's Belgium thrasher	150	"	""

In regard to Pitt's machine the "Moniteur" says: "Pitt's machine has, therefore, gained the honors of the day; this machine literally devours the sheaves of wheat; the eye cannot follow the work which is effected between the entrance of the sheaves and the end of the operation.

"It is one of the greatest results which it is possible to obtain.

"The impression which this spectacle produced upon the Arab chiefs was profound."

The "Moniteur" might have added that the effect was no less wonderful to the Prince Napoleon, who returned twice to the machine and declared that it was "frightful to look at,!" as it must have been to all those who never before saw a genuine, fast American thresher.

The machine of Dunoir is used almost exclusively in France, but already the demand for the Buffalo machine is so great that without doubt it will supersede all others.

A machine by G. F. S. Zimmerman, of Virginia, the patentee combined operations for threshing, separating, cleaning twice, screening and bagging all kinds of small grain at one and the same time. For this machine it was claimed that with six or eight horses it would prepare for the mill 300 to 500 bushels of wheat, and with twelve horses and as many men 800 to 1,000 bushels in a day.

Mr. R. L. Allen, of New York, and perhaps other manufacturers also, exhibited threshing-machines, and the Messrs. Von Brocklin, Winter & Co., of Branford, Canada East, sent a machine of their invention and manufacture, having some resemblance to Moffit's, and which had the appearance of being simple, strong, and efficient.

The portable steam-engines for farm purposes began, about twenty years ago, to be advocated by the Royal Agricultural Society of England, and are now in very general use. They travel, with or without threshers attached, from farm to farm to do the threshing and other work. They are from three to eight or ten horse power, and consume about one hundred weight of coals per diem for each horse power. One of the smallest size named will thresh 20 quarters or more daily.

Most of the large farms in England and Scotland have also fixed steam-engines of four to ten horse power for threshing and other uses. Their average cost in 1844 was about $600 each, but is now much reduced.

By the use of steam and improved threshing-machines the crop is now threshed in the field in about the same time it would take to remove it to the barn.

Steam-engines and steam-threshers have within a few years been introduced in Ohio and other parts of the west.

A machine of about ten-horse power was several years ago built at Chilicothe, Ohio, and was employed in threshing grain in the fields of the farmers. With three men accompanying it, and some assistance from the farm hands, it did the work of seventy flails, threshing about 100 bushels an hour, or 700 bushels in a day.

It was estimated that the counties of Ross and Pickaway, in Ohio, would require thirty steam-threshers to prepare for market an average wheat crop, the united savings of which would be equal to the labor of forty thousand men.

The immense importance of the threshing-machine with steam as a motive power, as well to the grain-grower as to the manufacturer, when they shall have been more generally introduced throughout our extended country, may be readily inferred. To the farmer, in enabling him to take advantage of any sudden rise in the price of grain, and to secure it from mischances by fire, weather, or otherwise, its value is very apparent.

Messrs. Hoard & Brodferd, of Watertown, New York, were among the first in this country to manufacture steam-engines for farm use. The specimens exhibited by them at the World's Fair in London were, perhaps, not inferior in merit to the best of a large collection.

New domestic animals.—Camels and Cashmere goats have been successfully introduced, and strong hopes are entertained of their perfect acclimation and permanent utility. Italian bees have also been brought into the country, and are believed to possess many advantages over the common black variety.

Associations and exhibitions.—Among the means and incentives to improvement enjoyed by the farming community we cannot overlook the influence of associations and annual exhibitions. These are not new, but they prove none the less useful, are now established in most of the States, and in almost every county of some of them. A somewhat new and important application of the association principle has been made in many towns and neighborhoods by the organization of local societies or *farmers' clubs.* The great advantage of these township associations consists in their adaptation to bring agricultural improvement home to all the people.

Agricultural schools and colleges.—But few agricultural schools are in successful operation, although several have been established. New York, Pennsylvania, Maryland, Michigan, and Iowa, have each one, and one or more are about to be established in other States. It does not argue well for the agricultural taste of our people, that while we are in advance of most European countries in the number of our common schools and colleges, we are greatly behind some of them in institutions designed to teach the innumerable applications of science to agriculture, and to elevate and throw a charm around this noble employment.

Periodicals.—The number and excellence of agricultural and horticultural periodicals leave little to be desired except that some of them were in the hands of every farmer. Forty papers and magazines, devoted almost exclusively to topics pertinent to farming and gardening, are published in the country.

Diseases of animals.—Among the embarrassments which still interfere seriously with farming operations are the diseases of domestic animals. Two forms of disease have more especially attracted attention—the pleuro-pneumonia of neat cattle in Massachusetts, and what is known as hog-cholera in the western States. In reference to the former, the people of the whole Union have incurred a heavy debt of gratitude to the State in which it first appeared, for the prompt and energetic measures adopted to prevent its diffusion. The disease which prevailed among swine caused great destruction, and unfortunately but small success attended any efforts devised to arrest its progress.

These visitations, with others of more common occurrence, cannot fail to suggest the necessity of a class of well-educated veterinary surgeons. In this particular most European countries are greatly in advance of the United States. It is believed there is nothing about the rural economy of the Old World from which we may so profitably learn a lesson as in securing skilful, medical, and surgical treatment for domestic animals. This necessity has been made still more apparent by recent losses of army horses. We are of the opinion that the country, in the purchase and loss of horses during the insurrection, has incurred expenses already which, under other, circumstances, could have been avoided, to an amount greater than would have been required to maintain a national veterinary school or college on an extended scale for half a century. In truth, we are not sure that the interest on the amount lost would not permanently support such an institution. The multiplication and cost of insurances on live stock furnishes proof of the little reliance placed on the skill of the professed cattle and horse doctor.

Destructive insects.—In many instances whole armies of destructive insects have rendered the labors of the husbandman unprofitable or fruitless. The wheat midge, the chinch bug, and the army worm, besides those that have for years preyed on the products of the orchard and garden, occasion the loss of millions of dollars annually. By the labors of entomologists we have been taught to know these enemies more fully, and led to cherish the hope that we shall yet learn how to protect our crops from their ravages.

Meteorological observations.—The want of meteorological knowledge, and consequent want of adaptation of our industry to the laws of climate, both general and local, is a frequent source of loss to the farmer.

Through the system of meteorology inaugurated by the Surgeon General of the United States army, and that now efficiently carried on by the Smithsonian Institution, the climate of the United States will soon be as well understood as its geology or geography. When the knowledge thus obtained is thoroughly popularized we may expect to see it beneficially applied.

For information respecting agricultural products, not referred to in the foregoing notes, the reader is referred to the tables of agriculture appended to the report. The great labor required in the preparation of tables involving such vast interests and varied details has precluded their completion prior to the moment when it becomes necessary to submit them to the printer, a circumstance which is sufficiently explanatory of what some may be disposed to consider a meagre commentary upon a matter of so great importance.

It is not improbable that some inconsiderable errors may be detected in the foregoing notes, attributable to the tables having, in some cases, been slightly varied after their adoption as the text for comment. It is confidently believed, however, that no material error or discrepancy will be found to exist in any part of the report.

THE PUBLIC PRESS.

(APPENDIX, TABLE NO. 37.)

Among the elements which determine the characteristics of a people no branch of social statistics occupies a more important place than that which exhibits the number, variety, and diffusion of newspapers and other periodicals. Composing, as they do, a part of the reading of all, they furnish nearly the whole of the reading which the greater number, whether from inclination or necessity, permit themselves to enjoy, and it was in virtue of this fact that the most philosophical of British statesmen signalized "newspaper circulations" as a more important instrument of the popular intelligence than was generally imagined in his day. The writers of these papers, he added, "are indeed, for the greater part, either unknown or in contempt, but they are like a battery in which the stroke of any one ball produces no effect, but the amount of continued repetition is decisive. Let us only suffer any person to tell us his story, morning and evening, but for a twelvemonth, and he will become our master."

And if such was the idea of Burke respecting the influence of the public press, it is equally true that the quality and the dissemination of its fugitive sheets may be said to stand as an exponent at once of the intelligence and the domestic economy of any people.

It was in this view that Lord John Russell, in his great speech on Parliamentary reform, delivered in the year 1822, cited the multiplication and improvement in newspapers as gratifying evidences of the augmented wealth and expanding culture of the middle classes in Great Britain. And it was in this view, also, that a great Greek scholar was accustomed to say that a single newspaper published in the age of Pericles (had that age produced any such phenomenon) would, if handed down to us, be a better index of Athenian life and manners than can now be found in any existing memorials of the Grecian civilization.

The newspaper and periodical press, now covering so wide a field of activity in every department of thought, has won its way to the commanding position it occupies from very small beginnings. Taking its origin in Italy, and under a form bearing some resemblance to that of modern times, capable of being traced to the sixteenth century, the newspaper has in our day enlarged equally the area of its diffusion and the character of its contents, while the celerity with which it is disseminated equalizes throughout large tracts of country the conditions of that popular intelligence which make up an enlightened public opinion. The earliest English newspaper, entitled the "Murcurie," was little more than the present "Court Circular" in respect of its matter, while its periodical visits from London to York were, in the time of Cromwell, accomplished "in the brief space of a fortnight or three weeks,"

At the present day the newspaper and the periodical have become "popular educators."

Instead of mere chronicles of formal proceedings or passing events they are vast depositories of discussion and information on all topics which engage the thoughts or enlist the activity of men in the figure of society. A free press has thus become the representative and, for the masses, the organ of that free speech which is found indispensable to the development of truth, either in the religious, the political, the literary, or the scientific world. In each and all of these domains the newspaper and the periodical have accordingly become most efficient agents.

And in no country has their influence been more sensibly witnessed, or more widely extended, than in the United States. The universal diffusion of education, combining with the moderate prices at which the daily visits of the public press may be secured, has given to the newspaper a very great currency among us. And where so large a share of the popular activity is, from the very nature of our civil institutions, engrossed in social and political discussions, it is easy to predict that the public press must here ever exert a power which renders it mighty for good or for evil, according to the intelligence and the virtue of those who preside over its conduct.

The tabular statement appended to this report, relating to this subject, strikingly illustrates the fact that the people of the United States are peculiarly "a newspaper-reading nation," and serves to show how large a portion of their reading is political. Of 4,051 papers and periodicals published in the United

States, at the date of the census of 1860, three thousand two hundred and forty-two, or 80.02 per cent., were political in their character. Two hundred and ninety-eight, or 7.38 per cent., are devoted to literature. Religion and theology compose the province of two hundred and seventy-seven, or 6.83 per cent., while two hundred and thirty-four, or 5.77 per cent., are classed as miscellaneous.

The last decade in our civil history has been one of extraordinary political agitation. Accordingly we find that there has been a very large increase in the number of political papers and periodicals, as compared with corresponding publications at the date of the preceding census. In 1850 their number was 1,630. In 1860 it was 3,242, being an increase of nearly 100 per cent. In 1850 the number of religious papers and periodicals was 191. In 1860 it was stated at 277, being an increase of 45 per cent. In 1850 the number of papers and periodicals of every class in the United States was 2,526. In 1860 the aggregate under this head reaches, as before stated, 4,051, showing a rate of increase of 60.37. The total circulation of all kinds amounted in 1850 to 426,409,978 copies. In 1860 the annual circulation is stated at 927,951,548 copies, showing a ratio of increase of 117.61.

The total white population of the United States was stated at the date of the census of 1850 to be 19,553,114. In 1860 the census returns report it at 27,008,081, the ratio of increase being 38.12. These figures show how largely the increment of the newspaper and periodical circulation has exceeded the increase of population during the last ten years.

In 1850 the annual circulation of all kinds afforded 21.81 copies to each white person in the Union. In 1860 the total circulation was at the rate of 34.36 per person.

New Hampshire and South Carolina are the only States which, as compared with the data of 1850, show any considerable decline in the number of copies of papers and periodicals published within their limits. In the States of Maryland and Vermont, and in the District of Columbia, the emissions of the public press at the two dates are nearly uniform. The largest increase, as might have been expected, occurs in the State of California. Of the total circulation in the country, three States, New York, Pennsylvania, and Massachusetts, furnish 539,026,124 copies, or considerably more than half of the aggregate amount.

PROGRESS OF RAILROADS IN THE UNITED STATES FOR THE DECADE OF 1850–'60.

(APPENDIX, TABLE No. 38.)

The decade which terminated in 1860 was particularly distinguished by the progress of railroads in the United States. At its commencement the total extent in operation was 8,588.79 miles, costing $296,260,128; at its close, 30,598.77 miles, costing $1,134,452,909; the increase in mileage having been 22,004.08 miles, and in cost of construction $838,192,781.

While the increase in mileage was nearly 300 per cent., and the amount invested still greater, the consequences that have resulted from these works have been augmented in vastly greater ratio. Up to the commencement of the decade our railroads sustained only an unimportant relation to the internal commerce of the country. Nearly all the lines then in operation were local or isolated works, and neither in extent nor design had begun to be formed into that vast and connected system which, like a web, now covers every portion of our wide domain, enabling each work to contribute to the traffic and value of all, and supplying means of locomotion and a market, almost at his own door, for nearly every citizen of the United States.

Previous to the commencement of the last decade only one line of railroad had been completed between tide-water and the great interior basins of the country, the products of which now perform so important a part in our internal and foreign commerce. Even this line, formed by the several links that now compose the New York Central road, was restricted in the carriage of freight except on the payment of canal tolls, in addition to other charges for transportation, which restriction amounted to a virtual prohibition. The commerce resulting from our railroads consequently has been, with comparatively slight exceptions, a creation of the last decade.

The line next opened, and connecting the western system of lakes and rivers with tide-water, was that extending from Boston to Ogdensburg, composed of distinct links, the last of which was completed during 1850. The third was the New York and Erie, which was opened on the 22d of April, 1851. The fourth, in geographical order, was the Pennsylvania, which was completed in 1852, although its mountain division was not opened till 1854. Previous to this time its summit was overcome by a series of inclined planes, with stationary engines, constructed by the State. The fifth great line, the Baltimore and Ohio, was opened, in 1853, still further south. The Tennessee river, a tributary of the Mississippi, was reached, in 1850, by the Western and Atlantic railroad of Georgia, and the Mississippi itself, by the Memphis and Charleston railroad, in 1859. In the extreme north the Atlantic and St. Lawrence, now known as the Grand Trunk, was completed early in 1853. In 1858, the Virginia system was extended to a connexion with the Memphis and Charleston and with the Nashville and Chattanooga railroads.

The eight great works named, connecting the interior with the seaboard, are the trunks or base lines upon which is erected the vast system that now overspreads the whole country. They serve as outlets to the interior for its products, which would have little or no commercial value without improved highways, the cost of transportation over which does not equal one-tenth that over ordinary roads. The works named, assisted by the Erie canal, now afford ample means for the expeditious and cheap transportation of produce seeking eastern markets, and could, without being overtaxed, transport the entire surplus products of the interior.

Previous to 1850 by far the greater portion of railroads constructed were in the States bordering the Atlantic, and, as before remarked, were for the most part isolated lines, whose limited traffics were altogether local. Up to the date named, the internal commerce of the country was conducted almost entirely through *water* lines, natural and artificial, and over ordinary highways. The period of the settlement of California marks really the commencement of the new era in the physical progress of the United States. The vast quantities of gold it produced imparted new life and activity to every portion of the Union, particularly the western States, the people of which, at the commencement of 1850, were thoroughly aroused as to the value and importance of railroads. Each presented great facilities for the construction of such works, which promised to be almost equally productive. Enterprises were undertaken and speedily executed which have literally converted them into a net-work of lines, and secured their advantages to almost every farmer and producer.

The progress of these works in the aggregate, year by year, will be seen by the tabular statements at the close of the report. The only important line opened in the west, previous to 1850, was the one from Sandusky to Cincinnati, formed by the Mad River and Little Miami roads. But these pioneer works were rude, unsubstantial structures compared with the finished works of the present day, and were employed almost wholly in the transportation of passengers. Within the decade, in place of this one line, railroads have been constructed radiating from lakes Erie and Michigan, striking the Mississippi at *ten* and the Ohio at *eight* different points, and serve as trunk lines between the two great hydrographic systems of the west. These trunk lines are cut every few miles by cross lines, which, in the States east of the Mississippi, are sufficiently numerous to meet every public and private want, and to afford every needful encouragement to the development of the resources of this country.

The southern States have been behind the northern in their public enterprises, though, at the date of the census, they were prosecuting them with great energy and vigor. The progress inland of the great trunk lines of the south has been already noted. The opening of the Mobile & Ohio, and of the Mississippi Central, which will soon take place, will give completeness to the system of the southwestern States, and leave little to be done to make it all that is wanted for that section of the country.

West of the Mississippi less has been done, for the reason that the settlements there are of a more recent date, and the people less able to provide the means for their construction than those of the older States. But even upon our western frontier extensive systems have been undertaken and very considerable progress made in their execution.

A more interesting subject than the progress of our public works would be their results, as shown in the increased commerce and wealth of the country. But such inquiries do not come within the scope of this report. It is well ascertained, however, that our railroads transport in the aggregate at least 850 tons of merchandise per annum to the mile of road in operation. Such a rate would give 26,000,000 tons as the total annual tonnage of railroads for the whole country. If we estimate the value of this tonnage at $150 per ton, the aggregate value of the whole would be $3,900,000,000. Vast as this commerce is, more than three-quarters of it has been created since 1850.

To illustrate the correctness of the estimate made, the following statement is added of the tonnage transported by the railroads of the State of New York for 1860, with the estimated value of the same. The classifications are made by the companies:

Kinds of freight.	Tons carried.	Value per ton.	Total value.
Products of the forest	373,424	$20 00	$7,468,480
Products of animals	895,519	200 00	179,103,800
Vegetable food	1,103,640	50 00	55,182,000
Other agricultural products	143,219	15 00	2,148,055
Manufactures	511,916	250 00	127,979,000
Merchandise	783,811	500 00	391,905,500
Other articles	930,244	10 00	9,302,440
Totals	4,741,773	163 00	773,089,275

If we make a deduction of one-quarter for duplications—a portion of the tonnage passing over more than one road—the aggregate would be 3,556,330 tons, having a value of $579,681,790.

The railroads of Massachusetts transported, for the same year, 4,094,369 tons; or, making the deductions for duplications, 3,070,027 tons, and having a value of $500,524,201. The number of miles of railroad employed in the transportation of freight being 2,569 in the State of New York and 1,317 in the State of Massachusetts, with the deductions named, the amount of freight transported in these States average 1,700 tons per mile. We have estimated the tonnage of all the railroads of the United States to average one-half the amount of the roads in these States. That this is not an overestimate is shown by the following statement of the tonnage of several interior lines:

Roads.	Length of miles.	Tons transported.
Cleveland, Columbus, and Cincinnati	141	295,835
Little Miami	120	343,961
Cleveland and Toledo	147	250,483
Michigan Central	282	378,570
Michigan Southern	525	398,679
Illinois Central	700	496,390
Chicago, Burlington, and Quincy	310	538,670
Chicago and Rock Island	228	301,668
Galena and Chicago	259	381,188
Total	2,712	3,386,393

Average per mile, 1,250 tons.

TONNAGE OF THE UNITED STATES.

	Tons.
The total tonnage of the United States in the year 1814 was	1, 368, 127
Since which period have been built (to June, 1861, inclusive)	8, 307, 397
Total owned and built since 1814	9, 675, 524
The total tonnage owned at the close of the last fiscal year (June 30, 1861) was	5, 539, 812
Showing the total decrease in forty-seven years, by decay, wreck, and other loss, to have been	4, 135, 712

It would appear that the loss by wear and tear, decay, wreck, fire, and other causes, was in forty-seven years 42.75 per cent., while in the past ten years alone it has been about twenty-five per cent.

The rapid advance in the ship-building interest during the last forty-seven years, in which the northern States have largely participated, is shown in the following tabular statement of the tonnage built in each decade since 1821, and in the seven years previous:

	Tonnage built in United States.	Annual average.
	Tons.	*Tons.*
Seven years, 1815—1821	638,563	91,223
Ten years, 1822—1831	901,598	90,159
Ten years, 1832—1841	1,178,693	117,867
Ten years, 1842—1851	1,999,263	199,926
Ten years, 1852—1861	3,589,300	358,930
Total forty-seven years	8,307,417	176,753

Recapitulation of the number and class of vessels built in each State of the Union during the fiscal year ending June 30, 1860.

States and Territories.	Class of vessels.					Total built.	Total tonnage.
	Ships and barks.	Brigs.	Schooners.	Sloops and canal boats.	Steamers.		
Maine	43	20	95	2	2	172	57,867
New Hampshire	4	....	....	1	....	5	3,808
Vermont	....	....	....	2	....	2	110
Massachusetts	30	2	91	2	7	132	33,460
Rhode Island	2	1	....	....	1	4	1,395
Connecticut	6	1	15	9	4	35	7,758
New York	4	3	31	125	38	201	31,936
New Jersey	....	....	20	17	1	38	4,264
Pennsylvania	1	2	16	68	65	152	21,615
Delaware	....	....	7	1	6	14	5,826
Maryland	8	6	24	2	3	43	7,798
District of Columbia	....	....	....	36	....	36	2,458
Virginia	1	1	3	4	17	26	4,372
North Carolina	....	....	9	5	3	17	864
South Carolina	....	....	1	....	1	2	72
Georgia	....	....	....	....	4	4	667
Florida	....	....	2	....	1	3	255
Alabama	....	....	3	....	5	8	1,189
Mississippi	....	....	5	1	1	7	326
Louisiana	....	....	4	....	8	12	1,500
Tennessee	....	....	....	....	5	5	433
Kentucky	....	....	....	....	29	29	8,631
Missouri	....	....	....	....	13	13	4,081
Illinois	....	....	....	....	....	....	....
Ohio	....	....	5	3	32	40	6,192
Wisconsin	....	....	1	....	1	2	96
Michigan	1	....	6	8	8	23	2,903
Texas	....	....	14	1	1	16	1,006
California	....	....	20	2	3	30	2,023
Oregon	....	....	....	....	....	....	....
Washington Territory	....	....	....	....	....	....	....
Total 1859—'60	110	36	372	289	264	1,071	212,892
1858—'59	89	28	297	284	172	870	156,602
1857—'58	122	46	431	400	226	1,225	242,286
1856—'57	251	58	504	358	263	1,434	378,804
1855—'56	306	103	594	479	221	1,703	469,393
1854—'55	381	126	605	669	243	2,024	583,450
Total six years	....	....	....	....	....	....	2,043,427
Average	....	....	....	....	....	....	340,571

The total tonnage of the United States at the end of the fiscal year 1851 was 3,772,439 tons. If to this we add the tonnage since built and officially reported as 3,589,200 tons, it will show a total of 7,361,639 tons.

	Tonnage own'd in the United States.	Year built.	Tons.	At the end of the year—	
				Presumed tonnage.	Actual tonnage.
June 30, 1851	3,772,439	1851-'2	351,493	4,123,932	4,138,440
1852	4,138,440	1852-'3	425,471	4,563,911	4,407,010
1853	4,407,010	1853-'4	535,616	4,942,626	4,802,902
1854	4,802,902	1854-'5	583,450	5,386,352	5,212,001
1855	5,212,001	1855-'6	469,393	5,681,394	4,871,652
1856	4,871,652	1856-'7	378,804	5,250,456	4,940,843
1857	4,940,843	1857-'8	242,286	5,183,129	5,049,808
1858	5,049,808	1858-'9	156,601	5,206,409	5,145,037
1859	5,145,037	1859-'60	212,892	5,357,929	5,353,868
1860	5,353,868	1860-'1	233,194	5,587,062	5,539,812
Tons			3,589,200	51,283,200	49,461,373
Presumed loss in ten years					1,821,827
					51,283,200

This is equivalent to a total loss in ten years, from July 1, 1851, to June 30, 1861, of 1,821,827 tons, viz:

	Tons.
Existing June 30, 1851	3, 772, 439
Built since, (ten years, to June 30, 1861)	3, 589, 200
Total owned and built in ten years	7, 361, 639
Actually reported June 30, 1861	5, 539, 812
Loss in ten years by decay, wreck, and other causes	1, 821, 827

According to the United States treasury report, the loss in ten years has been 1,821,827 tons, or nearly twenty-five per cent., or about 2½ per cent. per annum. What portion of this loss is by wreck, and what portion by actual decay, are not shown. Unfortunately the statistics of wrecks and of total and partial losses are not preserved by authority of law, but, in view of their importance, it seems proper that they should be carefully ascertained by private enterprise or public authority.

The total tonnage of the United States, at the close of the fiscal year June 30, 1861, was 5,539,812 tons, of which the State of New York owned 1,740,940 tons, or nearly thirty per cent. of the whole. During the same fiscal year the tonnage built was 233,194 tons, of which New York built 46,359 tons, or nearly twenty per cent. The tonnage owned in each district of the State, and built during the two years 1859–1861, was as follows:

Tonnage owned in New York and built in 1859–'61.

	Tonnage built 1859—1860.	Tonnage built 1860—1861.	Tonnage owned June 30, 1861.
New York	23,484	33,122	1,539,355
Buffalo	3,786	8,292	108,224
Oswego	....	4,718	55,552
Greenport	381	....	7,080
Sag Harbor	150	166	5,621
Dunkirk	....	....	4,274
Oswegatchie	....	....	7,332
Genesee	....	....	2,982
Champlain	....	....	1,791
Cape Vincent	....	61	5,228
Cold Spring	....	....	1,839
Sackett's Harbor	3,988	....	888
Niagara	116	....	774
State of New York	31,905	46,359	1,740,940
All other States	180,986	186,835	3,798,872
Total tons	212,891	233,194	5,539,812
1859—1860	....	212,891	5,353,868
1858—1859	....	156,602	5,145,037
1857—1858	....	242,286	5,049,808
1856—1857	....	378,804	4,940,843

Maine takes the lead as a ship-building State; New York is the second. The other prominent ones are as follows for the past three years, showing a more rapid advance in New York than in other States:

States.	1860—1861.	1859—1860.	1858—1859.	Total tons, three years.
	Tons.	Tons.	Tons.	
Maine	57,343	57,867	40,905	156,115
New York	46,359	31,936	16,313	94,608
Massachusetts	37,206	33,461	31,270	101,937
Pennsylvania	24,754	21,615	14,476	60,845
All other States	67,532	68,013	53,638	189,183
Tons built, years 1859—1861	233,194	212,892	156,602	602,688

Thus New York, which in 1858–'9 built but little over ten per cent., has, in the last year, built about twenty per cent. of the whole, and is the second instead of the fourth State in this industrial work. The immense value of this large property in tonnage, owned by our people in 1861, both as a source of temporary profit to the owners, and as an active and permanent means of extending abroad and at home the commerce and manufactures of the country, can scarcely be overestimated. Assuming the average value per ton at forty dollars, the value of this tonnage may be stated at $221,592,480, viz:

State of New York	1,740,940 tons =	$69,637,600,	or 31.41 per cent.
Other States	3,798,872 tons =	151,954,880,	or 68.59 per cent.
Total, U. S., June, 1861	5,539,812 tons =	221,592,480	

INTERNATIONAL STATISTICAL CONGRESS.

During my superintendency of the seventh census, the Secretary of the Interior, upon the recommendation of the Census Board, directed me to proceed to Europe to investigate the manner of conducting statistical operations in other countries, that we might avail ourselves of all useful information attainable as to the best plan of arranging the details of our census, and my instructions enjoined it upon me to effect, if possible, some arrangement whereby the results of periodical censuses should be ascertained as nearly uniform in time and details as practicable, and the facts classified upon like principles as far as circumstances would admit, in order to allow of the more ready comparison of their details. In my report of December, 1851, representation was made of the course pursued for accomplishing the objects of my mission, and it now gives me pleasure to state that the views of my superior officers here, being at the same time cordially advocated by Baron Quetelet, of Belgium, Doctor Farr, of London, and other distinguished men of science, an important general movement occurred throughout Europe resulting in arrangements for an international congress to elevate the science and improve the administration of statistics, to be held at Brussels the succeeding year, which, however, on account of the unsettled state of Europe, was postponed to the latter days of August, 1853, when the first statistical congress convened at that city, and closed on the 2d of September. In the opening address Baron Quetelet referred complimentarily to my efforts as those of one of the originators of this great movement, and expressed his regret that a political change had severed my connexion with the administration of the census and occasioned my absence. Encouraged by the success attending the convention at Brussels, congresses have since been held at Paris in the month of September, 1855, at Vienna, in September, 1857, and lastly in London, in July, 1860; and arrangements have been made for a fifth congress to be held in Berlin in 1863. I was present at the congress of Paris, and presented a paper which was read and is published at length in its proceedings. As at the first congress held at Brussels, so in the last convened in London, an unequivocal tribute was paid to the agency of this country in directing public attention to the importance of this movement. All these congresses have been attended by many of the most distinguished scientific men of Europe, and their proceedings, which form several quarto volumes, in three languages, contain perhaps the most valuable contributions to statistical science which have ever been published.

BUREAU OF STATISTICS.

It may not be improper in this connexion to express the opinion that the establishment of a permanent bureau of statistics would prove of inestimable advantage to the country. Such a bureau is maintained by every enlightened government of Europe, and the want of one here has been seriously felt by Congress and the people. Such a bureau has been frequently recommended by Presidents and heads of departments. Eighteen years since the subject was referred to a select committee of the House of Representatives, which made an able report, from which the following extracts are made:

"The *importance* of statistical knowledge is proved by the circumstance that scarcely any civilized government exists in the world where a *department* or *bureau* has not been established for the purpose of collecting, recording, and arranging statistical facts, and for the dissemination of correct information upon the fiscal, commercial, agricultural, and manufacturing interests of the respective countries wherein such institutions are established. England, France, Austria, Prussia, Russia, Sweden, Belgium, &c., and several of the smaller powers of Germany and Italy, have, in some shape or other, and under various desiginations, long possessed the advantages of correct official information upon their several national statistics."

"Correct and extensive statistical information is no less necessary to the mass of the people, in order that they may desire, appreciate, and understand correct legislation, than it is for the legislator to enable him to comprehend and to promote the best interests of his constituents. The want of such of a bureau, or rather the want of the information which it would be the means of collecting and disseminating, has long been felt and acknowledged, and by none more than by those members of the national legislature who have been anxious to legislate correctly and impartially, and thereby best advance the true interests of the nation. In many cases the information which has been necessary, owing to the want of a systematic and regular arrangement of materials, cannot be procured but after very great delay; and, in some cases, no diligence or exertion of the department upon which the call has been made can furnish the necessary replies. There are now calls on some of the departments remaining unanswered which were made *two years ago;* and such is the quantity of extra labor thrown upon the departments by these calls for information that, in one office, the number of *extra clerks* employed is greater than that of the *regular clerks* of the department."

"Such a bureau would furnish correct information respecting the commercial, the financial, the navigating and shipping, the manufacturing, and the agricultural interests of the country; a digested body of facts relative to the revenue, the custom-house, the post office, the land office, and the Indian department; correct statements respecting the population, the expenses and details of the army and navy, the progress of internal improvements, the state of banks and other institutions, and of monetary affairs and exchanges; and, in short, a regular, connected, and methodized arrangement of every subject to which facts and figures bear any relation, and which are in any way connected with the history, the progress and the condition of the nation at large, and those of the various States and Territories. And here it may be remarked, that, by a full and complete arrangement of the prices of stocks, the rates of exchanges, the quantity of unemployed capital, as exhibited by the amount of deposits in banks and other variations in the money market, the best opportunities for the execution of government financial operations would be ascertained, and the public interest materially promoted."

"The duties of the bureau would extend to the arrangement, condensation, and elucidation of the *statistics of foreign nations*, and to all the various branches of *international commercial intercourse*, materials for which are daily accumulating, especially from consuls and other public agents abroad."

The labors of a statistical bureau would most essentially contribute to the increase of sound knowledge upon all subjects connected with national and international affairs among the people. The theories, often conflicting, of political economists would give place to the practical results of experience, the sober truths of figures, and the unerring demonstrations of facts.

The true interests of the people of the country, as a people *one and indivisible,* would be perceived and understood. Knowledge of the most important kind would be given to the community; additional power, the result of knowledge, be placed in the hands of the legislature; the welfare of the country advanced by its interests being better understood; and legislation would be consistent and onwards, uniformly conducing to individual happiness and national honor and prosperity. It is hoped that nations will no longer seek to conquer by war or physical force, but by an honorable rivalry in the cultivation of the arts of peace, of commerce, of agriculture, of manufactures, and of science. Practical and useful information must be furnished to our people, to enable them to compete with other nations in their laudable career. The object of this bureau would be to furnish this information, and thus place the materials for sound thought, and the foundation for correct action, within the grasp of every American citizen. The committee above referred to closed their report with these words:

"It is, therefore, respectfully submitted *that the establishment of a statistical bureau* would be a measure *highly advantageous to the public interests,* one of very *easy and ready practicability,* and productive of not only a saving of *time* and *labor,* but an *absolute diminution of the annual expenses of the general government.*"

No words of mine could add force to such representations, which are doubly applicable in the present condition of the country.

It may not inappropriately be added that the census has become so cumbersome on account of the vast area embraced within its operations, and the increasing numbers of population, and enlargement of our material interests, that its successful management demands administrative talent only to be acquired by experience, and must require most of the years of a decade for its completion. With the facilities this office possesses, it would add but little comparatively to its labors to prepare an annual report on population, agriculture, manufactures, commerce, internal improvements, &c., &c., while its permanent establishment would insure the maintenance of a valuable repository of statistical information important to the legislator and statesman. In my opinion, a permanent bureau of statistics, having charge of the census, would add but little to the expenses of the government, as its effect would be to obviate the necessity of employing the vast clerical force now requisite because of their inexperience, and for the reason that the great statistical facts of the country are collected by the census but once in ten years.

THE BRITISH CENSUS FOR 1861.

The population returns of the British census for 1861 have been courteously furnished to this office in advance of the publication of the full results. They show the number of inhabitants, the division of the sexes, the amount of emigration during the preceding ten years, and, as to Ireland, the religious profession of the people, together with a few other particulars.

The census was taken on the 8th of April, and on that day the population of England and Wales, and of the islands in the British seas, was 20,205,504. It was estimated that the portion of the army, navy, and merchant seamen out of the country belonging to England and Wales, not enumerated, was 162,021. The actual increase of population in these divisions of the kingdom was 2,169,576, which was greater than in any previous decade, though the *rate of increase* has somewhat diminished, owing, it was supposed, to emigration to the United States and elsewhere. The islands in the British seas had a population of 143,779.

In respect to the sexes, there were 9,825,246 males and 10,380,258 females, showing an excess of 555,012 females. The disparity is in part accounted for by the absence of men in the army, navy, and merchant service, and from the greater number of males than females who emigrate.

The number of inhabited houses enumerated was 3,745,463, of uninhabited 153,494, total 3,898,957; being an increase of 467,424 since 1851. This gives 5.33 inmates for each inhabited house, and would appear to afford a very comfortable amount of aggregate accommodation in regard to shelter to the inhabitants.

The progress of population in England and Wales for sixty years has been surprisingly regular. In 1801, the whole number of inhabitants was 9,156,171; in 1811, 10,454,529; in 1821, 12,172,664; in 1831, 14,051,986; in 1841, 16,035,198; in 1851, 18,054,170; in 1861, 20,223,746. The rates of increase per cent. during these several decades, beginning with the end of 1801, was 14, 16, 15, 14, 15, 12. As has been observed, the falling off in the rate per cent. of increase from 1851 to 1861 was accidental, emigration having carried out of the kingdom during the ten years no less than 2,287,205 persons.

In eleven districts there was an excess of registered births over registered deaths of 2,260,576, and in the same districts there was an ascertained increase of 2,134,116 persons.

The census of Scotland, taken on the same day, exhibits a total population of 3,061,251, of whom 1,446,982 were males and 1,614,269 females. There were 679,025 separate families, and 393,289 inhabited houses. The number of children attending school between the ages of five and fifteen was 456,699. The increase in the whole population since 1851 was 172,509, or a trifle over six per cent. The females outnumbered the males in Scotland by 167,287.

In the returns for Scotland a list of seventy-six cities and towns is given, containing 1,244,578 inhabitants. Whether this comprises the entire urban, as distinguished from the rural population, does not appear; but such is probably the fact, since a few of the places named are mere villages or hamlets of less than five hundred inhabitants. The number of inhabited houses in these cities and towns was 89,520, showing 13.90 inmates to each house. The number of separate families is stated to be 286,585, giving 4.28 individuals to each family. Edinburg, the capital, contains 9,820 inhabited houses, and a population of 168,000; each house, therefore, contains 17.12 inhabitants. Glasgow is the principal commercial city. Its population is 394,857, and it has 13,873 houses which are inhabited, showing that each house accommodates 28.45 persons.

Ireland.—It was found that on the 8th of April, 1861, Ireland contained 5,764,543 inhabitants, of whom 2,804,961 were males and 2,959,582 females. The decrease of the whole population from 1851, as shown by this return, was 787,842, being at the rate of 12.02 per cent. during the ten years. In 1841 the population of Ireland was 8,175,124, and in 1851 6,552,385. The falling off during that decade was 1,622,739, or 19.85 per cent. The only localities in which an increase of population was shown by the last census, were Dublin and the towns of Carrickfergus and Belfast, where there is a gain of 18.88 per cent. on the returns of 1851. In explanation of the general decrease of population in Ireland, it is stated that of 2,249,255 emigrants leaving the ports of the United Kingdom from the 31st March, 1851, to the 8th April, 1861, 1,230,986 were Irish, of whom 1,174,179 persons were set down as permanent emigrants. It is remarked that the whole of the last decade was remarkably free from famine, pestilence, riots, and civil commotions, so that the condition of the country was such as ordinarily produces an increase rather than a decline of population But the effects of the great calamities of 1846 and subsequent years extended over the first few years of the last decade, precluding the restorative energies of the country from coming into force and action.

As to religion, the Irish people are divided as follows: 4,490,583 are Roman Catholics; 678,661 belong to the established church of England, and 586,563 are Protestant Dissenters. The last-named class includes 528,992 Presbyterians and 44,532 Methodists. The Protestant population are chiefly found in the province of Ulster, where they are about equal in numbers to the Catholics. The commissioners, in their report, note it as a fact worthy of remark, that no objections were made to the inquiries directed to be put on the subject of religion, and that fifteen complaints were made to them of the inaccuracy of the results.

The total number of inhabited houses in Ireland in 1861 was 993,233; in 1851, 1,046,223; and in 1841, 1,328,839. This shows a falling off corresponding with the decrease of population. The diminution of inhabited houses from 1841 to 1851 was at the rate of 21.27 per cent., and the decrease since 1851 was 5.08 per cent. It was found that there were 1.14 families in each house.

The number of families returned was 1,129,218, showing a decrease of 75,101, or 6.24 per cent. on the returns for 1851. The decrease from 1841 to 1851 was 268,468 families, being at the rate of 18.23 per cent.; (the average number of persons to a family in 1861 was 5.10; in 1851, 5.44; in 1841, 5.54;) results showing a gradual thinning out of the households, attributable to emigration and the other causes leading to a decline in the population. From these statements it will be perceived that the people of Great Britain and Ireland but little exceeds twenty-nine millions, and that the population of the United States has not only, for the first time, reached that of the mother country, but has run beyond her near two and a half millions of people.

DISEASES, AND CAUSES OF DEATH.

(Appendix, Table No. 6.)

[Continuation of the chapter on mortality, ending page 32.]

In the previous discussion of mortality statistics from other points of view, the conclusion was reached (p. 30) that the actual deaths in the United States occur at the rate of one in forty-five or forty-six of the whole population, and that they amounted to about 680,000 during the year 1860. It will further be admitted, in respect to the corresponding prevalence of sickness and invaliding, that twice the number of annual deaths in a large community will exhibit very nearly the number that are constantly sick. This rule is practically confirmed by numerous statistical comparisons, and though applicable more directly to manhood than to infancy and old age, yet on the whole it is found to furnish a near and convenient approximation. Accordingly, doubling the number of deaths, we readily obtain 1,360,000 for the number constantly sick during the year of the census.

The number of sick will be seen to constitute about one twenty-third part of the whole population. Besides watch-care, maintenance, and other attendant charges, so much is the efficiency of our population in respect to labor diminished, and so much is lost to industry and production. It is true that a certain prevalence of disease must be deemed, in the course of nature, "the inevitable lot," yet a large portion is needless, being clearly traceable to the neglect of temperance and the laws of health. The diminution of the current rate of sickness and mortality evidently pertains to the general prosperity and happiness, and may well constitute the leading idea in examining the statistics of disease.

What diseases are most influenced by the vicissitudes of climate, and what by the conditions of place? The former depending on the condition of the atmosphere, and attacking many persons at the same time, have long since been designated epidemic diseases; of which fever, dysentery, influenza, smallpox, and scarlatina or scarlet fever, are examples. The diseases arising from some peculiarity of the soil and surface have been similarly termed endemic; thus, ague is endemic in some marshy districts. More recently it has been proposed to include both epidemic and endemic, together with contagious diseases under the single title of *zymotic diseases*. The *zymotic*, from a Greek word signifying leaven or fermentation, are the first division in the general classification of diseases by Dr. Farr, whose researches now constitute a fundamental portion of the system of vital statistics.

Among *zymotics* are arranged four diseases which are contagious, and which can visit the same individual, as a general rule, but once in the lifetime; these are *smallpox*, *measles*, *scarlatina*, and *whooping-cough*. The last three prevail among children more especially. Other maladies under this head, such as dysentery, fevers, and cholera, are noted for wide fluctuations in different periods. Such peculiarities give to this category the greatest interest, and the question whether one particular year or locality is more healthy than another chiefly depends on the relative mortality from zymotic diseases. All other diseases may be regarded as isolated disorders, such as apoplexy, consumption, dropsy, which bear off nearly the same proportion of the living in every year.

Zymotic diseases.

	Deaths, 1860.	Deaths, 1850.	Proportions, 1860.	Proportions 1850.
Cholera	985	33,074	0.28	11.87
Cholera infantum	4,804	3,960	1.35	1.45
Croup	15,188	10,706	4.25	3.84
Diarrhœa	7,847	6,366	2.20	2.28
Dysentery	10,461	20,556	2.93	7.38
Erysipelas	2,756	2,786	0.77	1.00
Fever, intermittent	4,447	964	1.25	0.35
Fever, remittent	11,102	18,496	3.11	6.63
Fever, typhoid, typhus	19,207	13,099	5.38	4.69
Fever, yellow	657	785	0.18	0.28
Influenza	387	252	0.11	0.09
Measles	3,900	2,983	1.09	1.07
Scarlatina	26,393	9,584	7.39	3.44
Smallpox	1,263	2,352	0.35	0.84
Syphilis	231	146	0.07	0.05
Thrush	554	424	0.16	0.15
Whooping-cough	8,400	5,280	2.35	1.90
Total zymotic	118,582	131,813	33.22	47.28
Other specified diseases	218,261	134,803	61.14	48.36
Violent deaths	20,115	12,174	5.64	4.36
Unknown	36,648	44,233	....	....
Grand total	393,606	323,023	100.00	100.00

Here the wide and striking difference between the proportions of zymotic disease, 33 and 47 per cent., at once indicates the year ending June 1, 1850, to have been one of unusual mortality. The prevalence of Asiatic cholera has already been mentioned.—(Page 23.) It will be seen that *dysentery* and *remittent or common fever* also prevailed in excess during the same year with the Asiatic or epidemic cholera. But deaths from *intermittent fever* (fever and ague) and from *scarlatina* (scarlet fever) were more frequent in the year of 1860 than from the same diseases in the former year.

Cholera, meaning primarily a vomiting or purging of bile, has the three varieties of cholera morbus, Asiatic cholera, and cholera infantum. The first two have been classed under the single head of cholera, since both have similar characteristics. It is usually after long intervals that some contagion in the air gives the disease a malignant type, as above noted. Of the deaths returned in 1850 there were 1,568 from cholera morbus, although there appears no very definite line of distinction between this and epidemic cholera.

Cholera infantum, allied to diarrhœa, is one of the summer diseases of children, which proves most fatal with those from three to eighteen months old, and during the process of teething. The deaths from this disease appear to have been almost equally distributed in 1850 and 1860, and very many of them have probably occurred in the large cities.

Yellow fever appears not to have prevailed extensively in either year. Only 785 deaths from this cause were reported in 1850, and only 657 in the year 1860. At intervals of years this disease takes a malignant type and prevails a dreaded scourge in tropical climates along the sea-coast.

The whole population increased in the last ten years about 35 per cent. Therefore, by adding a little more than one-third to the deaths by each disease in 1850 the results can then be compared with those of 1860 on an equal basis of population. By this method it will be found that *measles* and *thrush* (cancerous sore mouth) occurred with equal rates of mortality in both years; *croup* and some other diseases nearly so, as will be seen by inspection of the preceding statistics.

The inquiry, What maladies have been the most fatal in the United States? is answered by the table given in the Appendix. A slight inspection will show that the number of deaths by *consumption* is the greatest of all. Next to this is the family of *fevers*, of which the mortality has just been stated. The deaths from consumption and some other noted diseases have been as follows:

Diseases.	Deaths in 1860.	Deaths in 1850.
Consumption	48,971	33,516
Pneumonia	27,076	12,130
Pleurisy	1,262	2,167
Scrofula	2,683	1,860
Delirium tremens, intemperance	1,504	951
Dropsy	12,034	11,217
Diphtheria	1,663	....

Consumption, according to medical authority, "begins with a change in the constitution, followed by the deposit of a cheese-like matter, forming tubercles in the lungs and other parts, ending in ulceration. When this tuberculous matter is deposited in the glands of the neck and in the bones and joints it constitutes *scrofula;* in the glands of the abdomen, mesenteric disease; neither of which affections differs from consumption in its essential anatomical cause." Consumption is believed to prevail more extensively in the northern States, as fevers predominate in the southern States. *Pneumonia* is characterized by inflammation of the lungs, and *pleurisy* by inflammation of the lining membrane of the lungs. The total deaths in 1860 from consumption, pneumonia, and pleurisy were 77,309.

Delirium tremens, or *mania à potu*, "a disease caused by the abuse of spirituous liquors, is characterized by tremor, sleeplessness, and delirium." Under the same head are brought the deaths returned from intemperance, making a total of 1,504, and showing the large increase of 58 per cent. during the past ten years.

Diphtheria is the most recent name of a disease characterized by a thick membranous exudation in the throat. It is allied to *croup* and to *scarlet fever*, with which it is sometimes confounded. It is asserted to be not contagious, but curable in a large majority of cases. In 1850 the name had attracted little or no attention; and in 1860 the number of deaths from this cause were but 1,663, a number much less than the notoriety of the disease would imply. It belongs to the zymotic class.

Lastly, the statistics of *Violent Deaths* will be found interesting, as the causes of demise are more intelligible or less shrouded in mystery than those of disease. It appears that only 5,669 "accidental deaths" of females were reported, against 12,399 deaths of males by accident. A still greater disparity of the same kind is shown in the subdivisions of "drowning, fall, fire-arms, freezing," and "railroad" accidents. The deaths by "suffocation," however, are quite evenly distributed among the two sexes. But among the deaths by "burns and scalds" the predominant loss ranges decidedly to the side of females, a result of fire naturally following from domestic avocations and difference in attire. On the whole, taking the accidental deaths as the measures of risk during that year contrasted with the present, the implied inference may be expressed that the male class are fully twice as much exposed to dangers as the female class, in their usual habits of life.

Under the head of *suicides* are counted 794 deaths of males and 208 of females, or nearly as four to one. Among these desertions from life, "hanging" is the principal resort. To complete the dark picture in which has been given to the "unproportioned thought, its act," 458 deaths by justifiable and unjustifiable "homicide" are also reported, together with 526 "murders" and 61 "executions." So many distinct cases have been gathered, and a considerable number more have doubtless escaped registration.

For further details, until the full returns of the census are published, reference may be made to the table of diseases and violent deaths in the Appendix. As to arrangement, the alphabetical list of diseases extends across four successive pages for the first group of States from Alabama to Illinois, inclusive; then a second group of States from Indiana to Michigan is inserted in the same manner; and so on, making five groups in all, with a final aggregate for the whole United States.

NOTES.

THE RELATIVE POSITION OF STATES, IN AREA, POPULATION, DENSITY OF POPULATION, RATIO OF INCREASE, AND INCREASE ACCORDING TO AREA.

The diagram and table which precede the population tables in the Appendix are designed to illustrate the relative rank and position of the several States from different points of view.

The diagram exhibits the numerical position according to gross population. The light lines indicate the slaveholding States, the black lines the free States. Virginia, for example, having the largest population in 1790, maintained that position until 1810, after which she successively sunk to the second, third, fourth, and, in 1860, to the fifth place. Ohio, which was first included in the census in 1800, then standing eighteen, stood thirteen in 1810, five in 1820, four in 1830, three in 1840, 1850, and 1860. The upper figures, with the circles, give the decennial ratios of increase. The detached column of circles contains the *mean* ratios of increase.

The table gives the numerical position in 1860 of the several States in point of area, population, population per square mile, average ratios of increase for the time during which each State has been represented in the census, and actual numerical increase of population per square mile from 1850 to 1860, and also from 1790 to 1860 for those States which were included in the first census Were we to continue the erroneous estimate of the area of Iowa entertained in 1850, that State would occupy an improper position in this table. The correct area is 55,045 miles, population per square mile 12.26, absolute increase per square mile, 1850 to 1860, 8.77.

POPULATION OF CITIES.

(APPENDIX, TABLE No. 40.)

The table above referred to shows the population of some of the more prominent cities of the United States, as returned by the census of 1850 and of 1860, respectively; also the increase and decrease, and rate per cent. of increase and decrease in population from 1850 to 1860.

The average increase in the population of the cities above enumerated is 78.62 per cent.; the increase of the whole population of the United States during the same period (as is shown in another table) is 35.59 per cent.

The average decrease of the ten cities in the table, whose population has diminished since the returns of the census of 1850, is 14.66 per cent.

INCREASE IN POPULATION.

Cities.	From 1840 to 1850.	From 1850 to 1860.
	Per cent.	*Per cent.*
New York	64.86	56.27
Philadelphia*	54.27	65.43
Boston	19.68	29.90
Baltimore	65 23	25.65
Cincinnati	149.11	39.51
Saint Louis	372.26	106.49
New Orleans	13.87	44.94
Chicago	570.31	264.65

* The bounds of Philadelphia were extended in the year 1852 so as to embrace the entire county, which accounts to some extent, for the great and unusual increase of population during the last decade.

CONCLUSION.

It has been my endeavor in the foregoing statement, to represent impartially the condition of the material interests of the country for the year ending June 1, 1860; that previous to the one in which the unhappy rebellion, at present existing against the integrity of the government, assumed shape and form. However imperfect in detail and deficient in completeness, it has been my aim to impart all the information available, in a form acceptable to the general reader.

The figures which we have given, make it appear that during the decade from 1850 to 1860 our population, in the aggregate, has increased more than thirty-five per cent. More than fifty millions of acres of land were brought into cultivation. The productions of agriculture multiplied in ratio greater than the population. The products of manufacture increased nine hundred millions of dollars, or at the rate of eighty-six per cent. The banking capital ran up from $227,469,074 in 1850, to $421,880,095 in 1860, while the circulating currency was augmented $52,089,560. The amount of insurances increased about $311,000,000. More than 22,000 miles of railroad were completed, and the capital involved increased from $296,640,148 in 1850, to $1,151,560,829 in 1860; while to indicate on the map of our country the lines of telegraph would be to represent the web of the spider over its entire surface. Our internal and foreign trade kept pace with our advance in production and increase of capital. Education, free to a great extent, has been made more accessible, and crime has rather diminished. We experienced no effects of wide-spread pestilence, and our country seemed the chosen abode of prosperity and peace.

Admitting that the insurrection has tended to depress commerce, to paralyze many branches of industry, and plunged the nation into a debt of surpassing magnitude, and while the ordinary internal trade, so vast in its amount, has been suspended between the North and West and the South, there may be found abundant causes for thankfulness that the mass of our population has thus far experienced but gently, the sufferings and desolation usually attendant upon a revolution of so wide-spread and serious a nature as this has proved. The na-

---

CHANGES OF AREA.

By such as desire to institute a very minute consideration of the progress of particular States, and the District of Columbia, for all periods, the fact should not be lost sight of, that for a period of near half a century a portion of Virginia, including the city of Alexandria, was enumerated as part of the District of Columbia, but for the last two censuses has been included in Virginia—a circumstance which affected the ratio of progress from the sixth census of Virginia and the District. In this connexion it may be mentioned for the benefit of future inquirers, that since the taking of the eighth census, two towns (Seekonk and Pawtucket) of Massachusetts have been assigned to and have become part of Rhode Island, and Fall River, of the latter State, has become a part of the city of Fall River, Massachusetts. By the eighth census the population of these places was as follows, viz: Seekonk, 2,662; Pawtucket, 4,200; Fall River, 3,377. This arrangement gives to Rhode Island 6,862 of the population of Massachusetts, and to the latter State the population of Fall River, resulting in the gain to the former State of 3,485 on the number returned by the census, and the loss of that number to the State of Massachusetts.

FIRE-ARMS.

[Continued from page 75.]

The first rifles made by machinery to use the Minie ball, or its equivalent, were made at Hartford, Connecticut, and Windsor, Vermont, for the English government. The machinery and tools for the armory at Enfield, England, were made at Windsor, Vermont; Hartford, Connecticut; and Chicopee, Massachusetts. Robbins & Lawrence did most of the work on such machinery and tools, and James T. Ames, agent of the Chicopee Works, got out the stocking machinery, and some other parts.

tion may seem to bend with its present burdens, but the American people possess a buoyancy and energy equal to the emergency. The truth is, the mass of our people feel some of the calamitous effects of the insurrection less than those of other governments experience them, and the singular and anomalous fact is apparent to all, that, while the people of the United States beyond the direct influence of the rebellion, and who constitute a large proportion of its inhabitants, are prospering in every branch of industry, and while our government securities are being eagerly absorbed, and the stocks of the Northern States are coveted at a premium, many of the powerful nations of Europe witness the prostration of their manufactures and decline of commerce with serious apprehensions lest the pressure on their people may lead to deplorable sufferings.

The manufactures of the North and the agriculture of the vast West have progressed with a vigor altogether beyond expectation, and while the influx of gold and the unexampled exports of breadstuffs, and the demand for army supplies, in provisions, forage, horses, and various fabrics of our own production, have protected the North and West from financial convulsions and pecuniary suffering, the spirit of self-dependence which the comparatively helpless condition of many of the Southern States, cut off from foreign supplies, has compelled them to encourage in the promotion of manufactures, will doubtless exercise a wholesome effect upon their future prosperity.

That, amid the immense and unexampled exportations of grain and provisions, the large withdrawal of labor from agriculture and manufacturing pursuits, the country should possess, as it does, an immense surplus of provisions, and that the means of subsistence should have scarcely appreciated in value, or the cost of labor should not have greatly risen, affords the strongest proofs of the energies of our people and the inexhaustible nature of the resources of the land; and it is hoped that the truth as presented by the census, will teach us the importance of union and harmony, and stimulate a proper pride in the country and people as one and indivisible. A people who have in twenty-five years doubled their numbers and much more than quadrupled their wealth need not apprehend with misgiving any inability to pay all the national debt which has been incurred.

That we have suffered and lost materially, and temporarily in national dignity, notwithstanding what we continue to enjoy, must be evident to all; but, as in the convulsions of nature and the physical sufferings of communities or desolations of cities, the evil is generally but transitory, often resulting in accelerated prosperity, by the sweeping off of the feebler elements and bringing new energies and resources into action, we may not unreasonably hope that a few years will obliterate most of the painful reminiscences resulting from our present unhappy condition, and that while history will point to this period as one of dire calamity in our experience as a nation, we will, before the taking of the ninth census, be restored to harmony, and, profiting by the past, realize the importance of peace and the blessings of prosperity, with a good assurance of the long continuance of both.

I have the honor to be your obedient servant,

JOS. C. G. KENNEDY,
Superintendent.

Hon. CALEB B. SMITH,
Secretary of the Interior.

DIAGRAM

Illustrating the relative course and position of each State, with ratio of increase, from 1790 to 1860.

1790.	1800.	1810.	1820.	1830.	1840.	1850.	1860.		MEAN RATIO.
Va. 1	17.63 1	10.73 1	43.14 1	39.76 1	26.60 1	27.52 1	25.29 1	N. Y.	42.61
Pa. 2	38.67 2	63.45 2	9.51 2	28.47 2	27.87 2	34.09 2	25.71 2	PA.	31.26
N. C. 3	72.57 3	34.49 3	29.55 3	13.71 3	62.01 3	30.33 3	18.14 3	O.	122.07
Mass. 4	21.42 4	16.19 4	15.00 4	61.31 4	2.34 4	14.60 4	101.06 4	ILL.	183.40
N. Y. 5	11.76 5	11.53 5	151.96 5	15.52 5	21.06 5	20.92 5	12.29 5	VA.	11.54
Md. 6	38.75 6	20.12 6	38.52 6	21.09 6	13.36 6	34.81 6	36.63 6	IND.	202.83
S. C. 7	6.82 7	88.98 7	10.68 7	61.28 7	2.09 7	44.11 7	23.79 7	MASS.	18.61
Conn. 8	5.40 8	11.42 8	21.11 8	16.65 8	20.85 8	25.98 8	73.30 8	MO.	180.92
N. J. 9	202.36 9	4.48 9	61.55 9	22.02 9	33.78 9	31.07 9	17.64 9	KY.	57.60
N. H. 10	15.10 10	147.84 10	7.04 10	61.57 10	99.94 10	15.36 10	10.68 10	TENN.	79.77
Me. 11	29.50 11	55.73 11	35.08 11	9.74 11	2.27 11	78.81 11	16.67 11	GA.	45.75
Vt. 12	96.37 12	15.86 12	30.45 12	33.89 12	90.86 12	30.62 12	14.20 12	N. C.	14.25
Ga. 13	80.84 13	408.67 13	13.04 13	133.07 13	25.62 13	77.75 13	24.96 13	ALA.	72.11
Ky. 14	57.16 14	50.74 14	5.02 14	15.58 14	202.44 14	12.47 14	30.47 14	MISS.	131.81
R. I. 15	195.05 15	40.95 15	13.90 15	142.01 15	5.14 15	61.46 15	154.06 15	WIS.	520.47
Del. 16	.02 16	16.65 16	8.29 16	8.17 16	173.18 16	16.22 16	88.38 16	MICH.	217.05
Ten. 17	8.76 17	11.44 17	100.35 17	19.04 17	174.96 17	24.04 17	36.74 17	LA.	58.50
	Ohio 18	La. 18	600.24 18	10.31 18	16.36 18	46.92 18	5.27 18	S. C.	17.43
	Miss. 19	13.07 19	Ala. 19	40.09 19	63.3? 19	31.14 19	17.81 19	MD.	11.72
	Ind. 20	355.95 20	7.83 20	185.17 20	4.13 20	87.34 20	251.14 20	IOWA	298.99
		402.97 21	86.97 21	110.94 21	4.02 21	10.62 21	37.27 21	N. J.	20.62
		Mo. 22	0.10 22	81.08 22	5.66 22	11.74 22	7.74 22	Me.	31.69
		Ill. 23	219.43 23	17.02 23	570.09 23	7.59 23	184.22 23	Tex.	184.22
		Mich. 24	349.53 24	5.05 24	11.97 24	868.88 24	24.10 24	Conn.	10.12
			Ark. 25	Fla. 25	221.09 25	Tex. 25	107.46 25	Ark.	130.14
			86.81 26	255.65 26	1.74 26	115.12 26	310.37 26	Cal.	310.37
				112.91 27	56.86 27	345.85 27	11.74 27	N. H.	12.91
					Iowa 28	35.57 28	0.31 28	Vt.	23.01
					Wis. 29	Cal. 29	18.37 29	R. I.	18.60
						17.22 30	2760.87 30	Minn.	2760.87
						60.52 31	60.59 31	Fla.	59.37
						Ore. 32	22.60 32	Del.	9.79
						Min. 33	33	Kan.	
							294.65 34	Ore.	294.65

States in the order of their area and population.

ARRANGEMENT OF STATES ACCORDING TO—

Area in sq. miles.	Population.	Population per square mile.	Mean ratio.	Absolute increase of population per square mile.	
				1790 to 1860.	1850 to 1860.
1. Tex.. 237,321	1. N. Y.. 3,880,735	1. Mass. 157.83	1. Minn. 2,760.87	1. Mass. 109.28	1. Mass. 30.33
2. Cal... 188,982	2. Pa... 2,906,115	2. R. I.. 133.71	2. Wis.. 520.47	2. R. I.. 80.79	2. N. J. 21.93
3. Ore.. 95,274	3. Ohio. 2,339,502	3. Conn. 98.45	3. Cal.. 310.37	3. N. Y. 76.97	3. R. I.. 20.74
4. Minn. 83,531	4. Ill... 1,711,951	4. N. Y. 84.36	4. Iowa. 298.99	4. N. J. 58.64	4. Conn. 19.12
5. Mo... 67,380	5. Va... 1,596,318	5. N. J.. 80.77	5. Ore.. 294.65	5. Pa... 53.74	5. N. Y. 17.03
6. Va... 61,352	6. Ind.. 1,350,428	6. Md... 73.43	6. Mich. 217.65	6. Conn. 47.50	6. Ill... 15.54
7. Fla.. 59,268	7. Mass. 1,231,066	7. Pa... 63.18	7. Ind.. 202.83	7. Mo.. 39.26	7. Pa... 12.93
8. Ga... 58,000	8. Mo.. 1,182,012	8. Ohio. 58.54	8. Tex. 184.22	8. Ky.. 28.73	8. Md.. 11.06
9. Mich. 56,243	9. Ky... 1,155,684	9. Del.. 52.93	9. Ill... 183.40	9. Del.. 25.05	9. Ind.. 10.72
10. Ill... 55,405	10. Tenn. 1,109,801	10. Ind.. 39.93	10. Ark.. 139.14	10. Vt... 24.26	10. Del.. 9.76
11. Iowa. 55,045	11. Ga... 1,057,286	11. N. H. 35.14	11. Miss. 131.81	11. Tenn. 23.55	11. Ohio. 8.99
12. Wis.. 53,924	12. N. C. 992,622	12. Vt... 34.79	12. Mo... 130.92	12. N. H. 19.85	12. Wis.. 8.99
13. Ark.. 52,198	13. Ala.. 964,201	13. Ill... 30.90	13. Ohio. 122.07	13. S. C. 18.55	13. Iowa. 8.77
14. Ala.. 50,722	14. Miss. 791,305	14. Ky... 30.67	14. Tenn. 79.77	14. Me.. 17.72	14. Mo.. 7.43
15. Miss. 47,156	15. Wis.. 775,881	15. S. C.. 28.72	15. Ala.. 72.11	15. Ga.. 16.81	15. Mich. 6.25
16. La... 46,431	16. Mich. 749,113	16. Va... 26.02	16. Fla.. 59.32	16. Va.. 13.83	16. La... 4.65
17. N. Y. 46,000	17. La... 708,002	17. Tenn. 24.34	17. La... 58.20	17. N. C. 13.31	17. Ky.. 4.60
18. Pa... 46,000	18. S. C.. 703,708	18. N. C. 22.06	18. Ky.. 57.60	....	18. Ark. 4.32
19. Tenn. 45,600	19. Md.. 687,049	19. Me.. 20.94	19. Ga... 45.75	....	19. Miss. 3.93
20. N. C. 45,000	20. Iowa. 674,948	20. Ala... 19.01	20. N. Y. 42.61	....	20. Ala.. 3.80
21. Ohio. 39,964	21. N. J.. 672,035	21. Ga... 18.23	21. Me.. 31.69	....	21. Va.. 2.85
22. Ky.. 37,680	22. Me... 628,279	22. Mo... 17.54	22. Pa... 31.26	....	22. N. C. 2.76
23. Ind.. 33,809	23. Tex.. 604,215	23. Miss. 16.78	23. Vt... 23.01	....	23. Ga... 2.61
24. Me... 30,000	24. Conn. 460,147	24. La... 15.25	24. N. J.. 20.62	....	24. Tenn. 2.35
25. S. C.. 24,500	25. Ark.. 435,450	25. Wis.. 14.39	25. Mass. 18.61	....	25. Minn. 1.98
26. Md.. 9,356	26. Cal.. 379,994	26. Mich. 13.32	26. R. I. 18.60	....	26. Tex.. 1.66
27. N. H. 9,280	27. N. H. 326,073	27. Iowa. 12.26	27. S. C. 17.43	....	27. Cal.. 1.53
28. Vt... 9,056	28. Vt... 315,098	28. Ark.. 8.34	28. N. C. 14.25	....	28. Me.. 1.50
29. N. J.. 8,320	29. R. I.. 174,620	29. Tex.. 2.55	29. N. H. 12.91	....	29. S. C. 1.44
30. Mass. 7,800	30. Minn. 173,855	30. Fla.. 2.37	30. Md... 11.72	....	30. Fla.. .89
31. Conn. 4,674	31. Fla.. 140,425	31. Minn. 2.08	31. Va... 11.54	....	31. N. H. .88
32. Del.. 2,120	32. Del... 112,216	32. Cal.. 2.01	32. Conn. 10.12	....	32. Vt... .11
33. R. I.. 1,306	33. Kan. 107,206	33. Ore.. .55	33. Del.. 9.79	....	....
	34. Ore.. 52,465	....	....	....	....

APPENDIX,

COMPRISING

TABLES REFERRED TO IN THE REPORT.

TABLE No. 1.—*Population of the States and Territories from*

NOTES.—(*) Indicates all persons, excepi indians, not taxed. (†) Added or deducted to make the aggregates,

STATES.	CENSUS OF 1790.			
	White.	Free colored.	Slave.	Total.
Alabama	....	....	....	....
Arkansas	....	....	....	....
California	....	....	....	....
Connecticut	232,581	2,801	2,759	238,141
Delaware	46,310	3,899	8,887	59,096
Florida	....	....	....	....
Georgia	52,886	398	29,264	82,548
Illinois	....	....	....	....
Indiana	....	....	....	....
Iowa	....	....	....	....
Kansas	....	....	....	....
Kentucky	61,133	114	11,830	73,077
Louisiana	....	....	....	....
Maine	96,002	538	....	96,540
Maryland	208,649	8,043	103,036	319,728
Massachusetts	373,254	5,463	....	378,717
Michigan	....	....	....	....
Minnesota	....	....	....	....
Mississippi	....	....	....	....
Missouri	....	....	....	....
New Hampshire	141,111	630	158	141,899
New Jersey	169,954	2,762	11,423	184,139
New York	314,142	4,654	21,324	340,120
North Carolina	288,204	4,975	100,572	393,751
Ohio	....	....	....	....
Oregon	....	....	....	....
Pennsylvania	424,099	6,537	3,737	434,373
Rhode Island	64,689	3,469	952	69,110
South Carolina	140,178	1,801	107,094	249,073
Tennessee	32,013	361	3,417	35,791
Texas	....	....	....	....
Vermont	85,144	255	17	85,416
Virginia	442,115	12,766	293,427	748,308
Wisconsin	....	....	....	....
	3,172,464	59,466	697,897	3,929,827
TERRITORIES.				
Colorado	....	....	....	....
Dakota	....	....	....	....
Nebraska	....	....	....	....
Nevada	....	....	....	....
New Mexico	....	....	....	....
Utah	....	....	....	....
Washington	....	....	....	....
District of Columbia	....	....	....	....
	3,172,464	59,466	697,897	3,929,827

1790 to 1860, respectively, with the rate of increase and decrease.

published incorrectly in those years. (‡) Persons on board vessels-of-war in the U. S. naval service. (*l*) Loss.

CENSUS OF 1800.				RATIO OF INCREASE FROM 1790 TO 1800.			
White.	Free colored.	Slave.	Total.	White.	Free colored.	Slave.	Total.
....	....	....	....	....	....	....	....
....	....	....	....	....	....	....	....
....	....	....	....	....	....	....	....
244,721	5,330	951	251,002	5.21	90.28	65.53 *l*	5.40
49,852	8,268	6,153	64,273	7.64	112.05	30.76 *l*	8.76
....	....	....	....	....	....	....	....
101,678	1,019	59,404	162,101	92.25	156.03	102.99	96.37
....	....	....	....	....	....	....	....
4,577	163	135	4,875	....	....	....	....
....	....	....	....	....	....	....	....
....	....	....	....	....	....	....	....
179,871	741	40,343	220,955	194.22	550.00	241.02	202.36
....	....	....	....	....	....	....	....
150,901	818	....	151,719	57.18	52.04	....	57.16
216,326	19,587	105,635	341,548	3.67	143.52	2.52	6.82
416,793	6,452	....	423,245	11.66	18.01	....	11.76
....	....	....	....	....	....	....	....
....	....	....	....	....	....	....	....
5,179	182	3,489	8,850	....	....	....	....
....	....	....	....	....	....	....	....
182,898	856	8	183,762	29.61	35.87	94.93 *l*	29.50
195,125	4,402	12,422	211,949	14.81	59.37	8.74	15.10
556,039	10,374	20,343	586,756	77.00	122.09	4.06 *l*	72.51
337,764	7,043	133,296	478,103	17.19	41.56	32.53	21.42
45,028	337	....	45,365	....	....	....	....
....	....	....	....	....	....	....	....
586,094	14,561	1,706	602,361	38.19	122.74	54.34 *l*	38.67
65,437	3,304	381	69,122	1.15	4.75 *l*	59.97 *l*	.02
196,255	3,185	146,151	345,591	40.00	76.84	36.46	38.75
91,709	309	13,584	105,602	186.47	14.04 *l*	297.54	195.05
....	....	....	....	....	....	....	....
153,908	557	....	154,465	80.76	118.43	....	80.84
514,280	20,124	345,796	880,200	16.32	57.63	17.84	17.63
....	....	....	....	....	....	....	....
4,294,435	107,612	889,797	5,291,844	35.37	80.96	27.50	34.66
....	....	....	....	....	....	....	....
....	....	....	....	....	....	....	....
....	....	....	....	....	....	....	....
....	....	....	....	....	....	....	....
....	....	....	....	....	....	....	....
....	....	....	....	....	....	....	....
....	....	....	....	....	....	....	....
10,066	783	3,244	14,093	....	....	....	....
4,304,501 † less 12	108,395	893,041	5,305,937 † less 12	35.68	82.28	27.97	35.02

TABLE No. 1.—*Population of the States and Territories, &c.*—1810.

STATES.	CENSUS OF 1810.				RATIO OF INCREASE FROM 1800 TO 1810.			
	White.	Free colored.	Slave.	Total.	White.	Free colored.	Slave.	Total.
Alabama	...	...	...	...	...	...	...	...
Arkansas	...	...	...	...	...	...	...	...
California	...	...	...	...	...	...	...	...
Connecticut	255,279	6,453	310	262,042	4.31	21.06	67.04 l	4.40
Delaware	55,361	13,136	4,177	72,674	11.05	58.87	32.11 l	13.07
Florida	...	...	...	...	...	...	...	...
Georgia	145,414	1,801	105,218	252,433	43.01	76.74	77.12	55.73
Illinois	11,501	613	168	12,282	...	...	...	...
Indiana	23,890	393	237	24,520	421.95	141.01	75.55	402.97
Iowa	...	...	...	...	...	...	...	...
Kansas	...	...	...	...	...	...	...	...
Kentucky	324,237	1,713	80,561	406,511	80.26	131.17	99.69	83.98
Louisiana	34,311	7,585	34,660	76,556	...	...	...	...
Maine	227,736	969	...	228,705	50.91	18.45	...	50.74
Maryland	235,117	33,927	111,502	380,546	8.68	73.21	5.55	11.42
Massachusetts	465,303	6,737	...	472,040	11.63	4.41	...	11.53
Michigan	4,618	120	24	4,762	...	...	...	...
Minnesota	...	...	...	...	...	...	...	...
Mississippi	23,024	240	17,088	40,352	344.56	31.86	389.76	355.95
Missouri	17,227	607	3,011	20,845	...	...	...	...
New Hampshire	213,390	970	...	214,360	16.67	13.31	...	16.65
New Jersey	226,861	7,843	10,851	245,555	16.26	78.16	12.64 l	15.86
New York	918,699	25,333	15,017	959,049	65.22	144.19	26.18 l	63.45
North Carolina	376,410	10,266	168,824	555,500	11.44	45.76	26.65	16.19
Ohio	228,861	1,899	...	230,760	408.26	463.05	...	408.67
Oregon	...	...	...	...	...	...	...	...
Pennsylvania	786,804	22,492	795	810,091	34.24	54.46	53.39 l	34.49
Rhode Island	73,314	3,609	108	77,031	12.03	9.23	71.65 l	11.44
South Carolina	214,196	4,554	196,365	415,115	9.14	42.98	34.35	20.12
Tennessee	215,875	1,317	44,535	261,727	135.39	326.21	227.84	147.84
Texas	...	...	...	...	...	...	...	...
Vermont	216,963	750	...	217,713	40.96	34.64	...	40.95
Virginia	551,534	30,570	392,518	974,622	7.24	59.09	13.51	10.73
Wisconsin	...	...	...	...	...	...	...	...
	5,845,925	183,897	1,185,969	7,215,791	36.13	70.89	33.28	36.36
TERRITORIES.								
Colorado	...	...	...	...	...	...	...	...
Dakota	...	...	...	...	...	...	...	...
Nebraska	...	...	...	...	...	...	...	...
Nevada	...	...	...	...	...	...	...	...
New Mexico	...	...	...	...	...	...	...	...
Utah	...	...	...	...	...	...	...	...
Washington	...	...	...	...	...	...	...	...
District of Columbia	16,079	2,549	5,395	24,023	59.73	225.54	66.30	70.46
	5,862,004	186,446	1,191,364	7,239,814	36.18	72.00	33.40	36.45

TABLE No. 1.—*Population of the States and Territories, &c.*—1820.

STATES.	CENSUS OF 1820.				RATIO OF INCREASE FROM 1810 TO 1820.			
	White.	Free colored.	Slave.	Total.	White.	Free colored.	Slave.	Total.
Alabama	85,451	571	41,879	127,901	....	....	....	....
Arkansas	12,579	59	1,617	*18 14,255	....	....	....	....
California	....	....	....	....	....	....	....	....
Connecticut	267,161	7,844	97	*100 275,102	4.65	21.55	l68.07	5.02
Delaware	55,282	12,958	4,509	72,749	l0.14	l1.35	7.94	0.10
Florida	....	....	....	....	....	....	....	....
Georgia	189,566	1,763	149,654	*4 340,983	30.36	*2.01l	42.23	35.08
Illinois	53,788	457	917	*49 55,162	367.68	l25.44	445.83	349.53
Indiana	145,758	1,230	190	147,178	510.12	212.97	l19.83	500.24
Iowa	....	....	....	....	....	....	....	....
Kansas	....	....	....	....	....	....	....	....
Kentucky	434,644	2,759	126,732	*182 564,135	34.05	61.06	57.31	38.82
Louisiana	73,383	10,476	69,064	*484 152,923	113.87	38.11	99.26	100.39
Maine	297,340	929	....	*66 298,269	30.56	l4.12	....	30.45
Maryland	260,223	39,730	107,397	407,350	10.67	17.01	l3.68	7.04
Massachusetts	516,419	6,740	....	*128 523,159	10.98	0.04	....	10.86
Michigan	8,591	174	....	*131 8,765	86.03	45.00	....	86 81
Minnesota	....	....	....	....	....	....	....	....
Mississippi	42,176	458	32,814	75,448	83.18	90.83	92.02	86.97
Missouri	55,988	347	10,222	*29 66,557	225.00	l42.83	239.48	219.43
New Hampshire	243,236	786	....	*139 244,022	13.98	l18.96	....	13.90
New Jersey	257,409	12,460	7,557	*149 277,426	13.46	58.86	l30.35	13.04
New York	1,332,744	29,279	10,088	*701 1,372,111	45.06	15.57	l32.82	43.14
North Carolina	419,200	14,612	205,017	638,829	11.36	42.33	21.43	15.00
Ohio	576,572	4,723	....	*139 581,295	151.93	148.07	....	151.96
Oregon	....	....	....	....	....	....	....	....
Pennsylvania	1,017,094	30,202	211	*1,951 1,047,507	29.26	34.27	l73.45	29.55
Rhode Island	79,413	3,554	48	*44 83,015	8.31	l1.52	l55.55	7.83
South Carolina	237,440	6,826	258,475	502,741	10.85	49.89	31.62	21.11
Tennessee	339,927	2,727	80,107	*52 422,761	57.46	107.06	79.87	61.55
Texas	....	....	....	....	....	....	....	....
Vermont	234,846	903	....	*15 235,749	8.24	20.04	....	8.29
Virginia	603,087	36,889	425,153	*250 1,065,129	9.34	20.67	8.31	9.31
Wisconsin	....	....	....	....	....	....	....	....
	7,839,317	229,456	1,531,748	9,605,152	34.10	24.77	28.85	33.11
TERRITORIES.								
Colorado	....	....	....	....	....	....	....	....
Dakota	....	....	....	....	....	....	....	....
Nebraska	....	....	....	....	....	....	....	....
Nevada	....	....	....	....	....	....	....	....
New Mexico	....	....	....	....	....	....	....	....
Utah	....	....	....	....	....	....	....	....
Washington	....	....	....	....	....	....	....	....
District of Columbia	22,614	4,048	6,377	33,039	40.64	58.08	18.02	37.53
	7,861,931 † Add 6	233,504 † Add 20	1,538,125 † Less 87	9,638,191 † Less 60	34.11	25.23	28.79	33.13

TABLE No. 1.—*Population of the States and Territories, &c.*—1830.

STATES.	CENSUS OF 1830.				RATIO OF INCREASE FROM 1820 TO 1830.			
	White.	Free colored.	Slave.	Total.	White.	Free colored.	Slave.	Total.
Alabama	190,406	1,572	117,549	309,527	122.82	175.03	180.68	142.01
Arkansas	25,671	141	4,576	30,388	104.07	138.98	182.99	112.91
California	....	....	....	....	....	....	....	....
Connecticut	289,603	8,047	25	297,675	8.04	2.58	74.22l	8.17
Delaware	57,601	15,855	3,292	76,748	4.19	22.35	26.99l	5.05
Florida	18,385	844	15,501	34,730	....	....	....	....
Georgia	296,806	2,486	217,531	516,823	56.57	41.00	45.35	51.57
Illinois	155,061	1,637	747	157,445	188.28	258.02	18.53l	185.17
Indiana	339,399	3,629	3	343,031	132.85	195.04	98.42l	133.07
Iowa	....	....	....	....	....	....	....	....
Kansas	....	....	....	....	....	....	....	....
Kentucky	517,787	4,917	165,213	687,917	19.12	78.21	30.36	21.09
Louisiana	89,441	1,190	109,588	215,739	21.88	59.05	58.67	40.63
Maine	398,263	16,710	2	399,455	33.94	28.09	....	33.89
Maryland	291,108	52,938	102,994	447,040	11.86	33.24	4.09l	9.74
Massachusetts	603,359	7,048	1	610,408	16.83	4.56	....	16.65
Michigan	31,346	261	32	31,639	264.87	50.00	....	255.65
Minnesota	....	....	....	....	....	....	....	....
Mississippi	70,443	519	65,659	136,621	67.02	13.31	100.09	81.08
Missouri	114,795	569	25,091	140,455	105.03	63.97	145.46	110.94
New Hampshire	268,721	604	3	269,328	10.47	23.15l	....	10.31
New Jersey	300,266	18,303	2,254	320,823	16.64	46.89	70.17l	15.58
New York	1,873,663	44,870	75	1,918,608	40.58	53.24	99.25l	39.76
North Carolina	472,843	19,543	245,601	737,987	12.79	33.74	19.79	15.52
Ohio	928,329	9,568	6	937,903	61.00	102.58	....	61.31
Oregon	....	....	....	....	....	....	....	....
Pennsylvania	1,309,900	37,930	403	1,348,233	28.78	25.58	90.99	28.47
Rhode Island	93,621	3,561	17	97,199	17.89	0.19	64.58l	17.02
South Carolina	257,863	7,921	315,401	581,185	8.06	16.04	22.02	15.06
Tennessee	535,746	4,555	141,603	681,904	57.06	67.03	76.76	61.28
Texas	....	....	....	....	....	....	....	....
Vermont	279,771	881	....	280,652	19.12	2.43	....	19.04
Virginia	694,300	47,348	469,757	1,211,405	15.12	28.35	10.49	13.71
Wisconsin	....	....	....	....	....	....	....	....
	‡5,318	....	....	‡5,318	....	....	....	....
	10,509,815	313,447	2,002,924	12,826,186	34.07	36.60	30.76	33.53
TERRITORIES.								
Colorado	....	....	....	....	....	....	....	....
Dakota	....	....	....	....	....	....	....	....
Nebraska	....	....	....	....	....	....	....	....
Nevada	....	....	....	....	....	....	....	....
New Mexico	....	....	....	....	....	....	....	....
Utah	....	....	....	....	....	....	....	....
Washington	....	....	....	....	....	....	....	....
District of Columbia	27,563	6,152	6,119	39,834	21.28	51.97	4.04l	20.57
	10,537,378	319,599	2,009,043	12,866,020	34.03	36.87	30.61	33.49

TABLE No. 1.—*Population of the States and Territories, &c.*—1840.

STATES.	CENSUS OF 1840.				RATIO OF INCREASE FROM 1830 TO 1840.			
	White.	Free colored.	Slave.	Total.	White.	Free colored.	Slave.	Total.
Alabama	335,185	2,039	253,532	590,756	76.03	29.07	115.68	90.86
Arkansas	77,174	465	19,935	97,574	200.62	229.78	335.64	221.09
California	....	....	....	....	....	....	....	....
Connecticut	301,856	8,105	17	309,978	4.23	0.72	32.00*l*	4.13
Delaware	58,561	16,919	2,605	78,085	1.66	6.71	20.86*l*	1.74
Florida	27,943	817	25,717	54,477	51.98	3.19*l*	65.09	56.86
Georgia	407,695	2,753	280,944	691,392	37.36	10.74	29.15	33.78
Illinois	472,254	3,598	331	476,183	204.56	119.79	55.68*l*	202.44
Indiana	678,698	7,165	3	685,866	99.97	97.43	....	99.94
Iowa	42,924	172	16	43,112	....	....	....	....
Kansas	....	....	....	....	....	....	....	....
Kentucky	590,253	7,317	182,258	779,828	13.99	48.81	10.31	13.36
Louisiana	158,457	25,502	168,452	352,411	77.16	52.61	53.71	63.35
Maine	500,438	1,355	....	501,793	25.65	13.86	....	25.62
Maryland	318,204	62,078	89,737	470,019	9.03	17.26	12.87*l*	5.14
Massachusetts	729,030	8,669	....	737,699	20.82	22.99	....	20.85
Michigan	211,560	707	....	212,267	574.91	170.88	....	570.09
Minnesota	....	....	....	....	....	....	....	....
Mississippi	179,074	1,366	195,211	375,651	154.21	163.19	197.31	174.96
Missouri	323,888	1,574	58,240	383,702	182.14	176.62	132.11	173.18
New Hampshire	284,036	537	1	284,574	5.69	11.09*l*	66.66*l*	5.66
New Jersey	351.588	21,044	674	373,306	17.09	14.97	70.09*l*	16.36
New York	2,378,890	50,027	4	2,428,921	26.96	11.49	94.66*l*	26.60
North Carolina	484,870	22,732	245,817	753,419	2.54	16.31	0.08	2.09
Ohio	1,502,122	17,342	3	1,519,467	61.08	81.25	50.00*l*	62.01
Oregon	....	....	....	....	....	....	....	....
Pennsylvania	1,676,115	47,854	64	1,724,033	27.95	26.16	84.11*l*	27.87
Rhode Island	105,587	3,238	5	108,830	12.78	9.07*l*	70.58*l*	11.97
South Carolina	259,084	8,276	327,038	594,398	0.47	4.48	3.68	2.27
Tennessee	640,627	5,524	183,059	829,210	19.57	21.27	29.27	21.06
Texas	....	....	....	....	....	....	....	....
Vermont	291,218	730	....	291,948	4.09	17.13*l*	....	4.02
Virginia	740,858	49,852	449,087	1,239,797	6.07	5.28	4.04*l*	2.34
Wisconsin	30,749 ‡6,100	185	11	30,945 ‡6,100	....	....	....	....
	14,165,038	377,942	2,482,761	17,025,741	34.78	20 57	23.96	32.74
TERRITORIES.								
Colorado	....	....	....	....	....	....	....	....
Dakota	....	....	....	....	....	....	....	....
Nebraska	....	....	....	....	....	....	....	....
Nevada	....	....	....	....	....	....	....	....
New Mexico	....	....	....	....	....	....	....	....
Utah	....	....	....	....	....	....	....	....
Washington	....	....	....	....	....	....	....	....
District of Columbia	30,657	8,361	4,694	43,712	11.22	35.09	23.28*l*	9.74
	14,195,695	386,303	2,487,455	17,069,453	34.72	20.87	23.81	32.67

TABLE No. 1.—*Population of the States and Territories, &c.*—1850.

STATES.	CENSUS OF 1850.				RATIO OF INCREASE FROM 1840 TO 1850.			
	White.	Free colored.	Slave.	Total.	White.	Free colored.	Slave.	Total.
Alabama	426,514	2,265	342,844	771,623	27.24	11.08	35.22	30.62
Arkansas	162,189	608	47,100	209,897	110.16	30.75	136.26	115.12
California	91,635	962	....	92,597	....	....	....	....
Connecticut	363,099	7,693	....	370,792	0.28	5.08 *l*	....	19.62
Delaware	71,169	18,073	2,290	91,532	21.52	6.82	12.09 *l*	17.22
Florida	47,203	932	39,310	87,445	68.92	14.07	52.85	60.52
Georgia	521,572	2,931	381,682	906,185	27.93	6.46	35.85	31.07
Illinois	846,034	5,436	....	851,470	79.14	51.08	....	78.81
Indiana	977,154	11,262	....	988,416	43.97	57.55	....	44.11
Iowa	191,881	333	....	192,214	347.02	93.60	....	345.85
Kansas	....	....	....	....	....	....	....	....
Kentucky	761,413	10,011	210,981	982,405	28.99	36.81	15.75	25.98
Louisiana	255,491	17,462	244,809	517,762	61.23	31.52 *l*	45.32	46.92
Maine	581,813	1,356	....	583,169	16.26	0.07	....	16.22
Maryland	417,943	74,723	90,368	583,034	31.34	20.36	0.70	24.04
Massachusetts	985,450	9,064	....	994,514	35.17	4 55	....	34.81
Michigan	395,071	2,583	....	397,654	86.74	265.34	....	87.34
Minnesota	6,038	39	....	6,077	....	....	....	....
Mississippi	295,718	930	309,878	606,526	65.13	31.91 *l*	58.74	61.46
Missouri	592,004	2,618	87,422	682,044	82.78	66.32	50.10	77.75
New Hampshire	317,456	520	....	317,976	11.76	3.16 *l*	....	11.74
New Jersey	465,509	23,810	236	489,555	32.04	13.14	64.98 *l*	31.14
New York	3,048,325	49,069	....	3,097,394	28.14	1.91 *l*	....	27.52
North Carolina	553,028	27,463	288,548	869,039	14.05	20.81	17.38	15.35
Ohio	1,955,050	25,279	....	1,980,329	30.15	45.76	....	30.33
Oregon	13,087	207	....	13,294	....	....	....	....
Pennsylvania	2,258,160	53,626	....	2,311,786	34.72	12.06	....	34.09
Rhode Island	143,875	3,670	....	147,545	36.26	13.34	....	35.57
South Carolina	274,563	8,960	384,984	668,507	5.97	8.26	17.71	12.47
Tennessee	756,836	6,422	239,459	1,002,717	18.13	16.25	30.80	20.92
Texas	154,034	397	58,161	212,592	....	....	....	....
Vermont	313,402	718	....	314,120	7.61	1.64 *l*	....	7.59
Virginia	894,800	54,333	472,528	1,421,661	20.77	8.98	5.21	14.60
Wisconsin	304,756	635	....	305,391	891.01	243.24	....	886.88
	19,442,272	424,390	3,200,600	23,067,262	37.25	12.28	28.91	35.48
TERRITORIES.								
Colorado	....	....	....	....	....	....	....	....
Dakota	....	....	....	....	....	....	....	....
Nebraska	....	....	....	....	....	....	....	....
Nevada	....	....	....	....	....	....	....	....
New Mexico	61,547	....	....	61,547	....	....	....	....
Utah	11,354	....	26	11,380	....	....	....	....
Washington	....	....	....	....	....	....	....	....
District of Columbia	37,941	10,059	3,687	51,687	23.75	20.30	21.45 *l*	18.24
	19,553,114	434,449	3,204,313	23,191,876	37.74	12.46	28.82	35.87

TABLE No. 1.—*Population of the States and Territories, &c.*—1860.

STATES.	CENSUS OF 1860.				RATIO OF INCREASE FROM 1850 TO 1860.			
	White.	Free colored.	Slave.	Total.	White.	Free colored	Slave.	Total.
Alabama	526,431	2,690	435,080	964,201	23.43	18.76	27.18	24.96
Arkansas	324,191	144	111,115	435,450	99.88	81.25 *l*	135.91	107.46
California	361,353	4,086	....	[*14,555] 365,439	294.34	324.74	....	310.37
Connecticut	451,520	8,627	....	460,147	24.35	12.14	....	42.10
Delaware	90,589	19,829	1,798	112,216	27.28	9.72	21.48 *l*	22.60
Florida	77,748	932	61,745	140,425	64.70	....	57.07	60.59
Georgia	591,588	3,500	462,198	1,057,286	13.42	19.41	21.10	16.67
Illinois	1,704,323	7,628	....	1,711,951	101.45	40.32	....	101.06
Indiana	1,339,000	11,428	....	1,350,428	37.03	1.47	....	36.63
Iowa	673,844	1,069	....	674,913	251.18	231.53	....	251.14
Kansas	106,579	625	2	107,206	....	....	....	....
Kentucky	919,517	10,684	225,483	1,155,684	20.76	6.72	6.87	17.64
Louisiana	357,629	18,647	331,726	708,002	39.98	6.78	35.50	36.74
Maine	626,952	1,327	....	628,279	7.76	2.14 *l*	....	7.74
Maryland	515,918	83,942	87,189	687,049	23.14	12.35	3.52 *l*	17.84
Massachusetts	1,221,464	9,602	....	1,231,066	23.95	5.93	....	23.79
Michigan	742,314	6,799	....	749,113	87.89	163.22	....	88.38
Minnesota	171,864	259	....	172,123	2,775.06	709.38	....	2,760.87
Mississippi	353,901	773	436,631	791,305	19.68	16.88 *l*	40.90	30.47
Missouri	1,063,509	3,572	114,931	1,182,012	79.64	36.44	31.47	73.30
New Hampshire	325,579	494	....	326,073	2.56	5.00 *l*	....	2.55
New Jersey	646,699	25,318	18	672,035	38.92	6.33	92.37 *l*	37.27
New York	3,831,730	49,005	....	3,880,735	25.70	0.13 *l*	....	25.29
North Carolina	631,100	30,463	331,059	992,622	14.12	10.92	14.73	14.20
Ohio	2,302,838	36,673	....	2,339,511	17.79	41.12	....	18.14
Oregon	52,337	128	....	52,465	299.92	38.16 *l*	....	294.65
Pennsylvania	2,849,266	56,849	....	2,906,115	26.18	6.01	....	25.71
Rhode Island	170,668	3,952	....	174,620	18.62	7.68	....	18.35
South Carolina	291,388	9,914	402,406	703,708	6.13	10.65	4.53	5.27
Tennessee	826,782	7,300	275,719	1,109,801	9.24	13.67	15.14	10.68
Texas	421,294	355	182,566	604,215	173.51	10.58 *l*	213.89	184.22
Vermont	314,389	709	....	315,098	0.31	1.25 *l*	....	0.31
Virginia	1,047,411	58,042	490,865	1,596,318	17.06	6.83	3.88	12.29
Wisconsin	774,710	1,171	....	775,881	154.20	8.44	....	154.06
	26,706,425	476,536	3,950,531	31,148,047	37.37	12.30	23.44	35.04
TERRITORIES.								
Colorado	34,231	46	....	34,277	....	....	....	....
Dakota	2,576	....	....	*a*2,261 2,576	....	....	....	....
Nebraska	28,759	67	15	28,841	....	....	....	....
Nevada	6,812	45	....	6,857	....	....	....	....
New Mexico	82,924	85	....	*a*10,507 83,009	34.73	....	....	51.94
Utah	40,214	30	29	40,273	254.18	....	11.53	253.89
Washington	11,138	30	....	*a*426 11,168	....	....	....	....
District of Columbia	60,764	11,131	3,185	75,080	60.15	10.66	13.62 *l*	45.26
	26,973,843	487,970	3,953,760	31,443,322	37.97	12.33	23.39	35.59

a Indians.

TABLE No. 1—Continued.

Ratio of increase of population of the States and Territories, &c.

STATES.	RATIO OF INCREASE FROM 1790 TO 1860.				Representative population.	Representation under the apportionment.			Representation as increased by the law of Mar. 4, 1862, in the 38th Congress.
	White.	Free colored.	Slave.	Total.		In the 38th Congress.	Loss.	Gain.	
Alabama	*a*516.06	371.10	938.90	653.87	790,169	6	1	....	6
Arkansas	*a*2,477.24	144.07	6,771.68	2,950.87	391,004	3	....	1	3
California	*b*294.34	324.74	....	310.37	365,439	3	....	1	3
Connecticut	94.13	208.00	....	93.22	460,147	4	....	....	4
Delaware	95.61	408.57	*l*79.76	89.88	111,496	1	....	....	1
Florida	*c*322.89	10.43	298.33	304.33	115,727	1	....	....	1
Georgia	1,018.60	779.40	1,479 41	1,180.81	872,406	7	1	....	7
Illinois	*d*14,718.92	1,144.37	....	13,838.70	1,711,951	13	....	4	14
Indiana	*e*29,154.97	6,911.04	....	27,601.09	1,350,428	11	...	....	11
Iowa	*f*1,469.85	541.86	....	1,465.57	674,913	5	....	3	6
Kansas	....	....	....	....	107,206	1	....	....	1
Kentucky	1,404.13	9,271.92	1,806.03	1,481.46	1,065,490	8	2	....	9
Louisiana	*d*942.32	145.84	857.09	824.82	575,311	5	....	1	5
Maine	553.06	146.65	....	550.80	628,279	5	1	....	5
Maryland	147.27	943.67	*l*15.38	114.88	652,173	5	1	....	5
Massachusetts	227.25	75.76	....	225.06	1,231,066	10	1	....	10
Michigan	*d*15,974.36	5,565.83	....	15,631.06	749,113	6	....	2	6
Minnesota	*b*2,775.06	564.10	....	2,760.87	172,123	1	1	....	2
Mississippi	*e*6,733.38	324.73	12,414.50	8,841.30	616,652	5	....	....	5
Missouri	*d*6,073.50	488.47	3,717.03	5,570.48	1,136,039	9	....	2	9
New Hampshire	130.73	*l*21.59	....	129 79	326,073	3	....	....	3
New Jersey	280.51	816.65	*l*63,361.11	264.96	672,027	5	....	....	5
New York	1,119.74	952.96	....	1,040.99	3,880,735	31	2	....	31
North Carolina	118.98	512.32	229 18	152.09	860,198	7	1	....	7
Ohio	*e*5,014.24	10,782.19	....	5,057.08	2,339,511	18	3	....	19
Oregon	*b*299.92	*l*38.16	....	294.65	52,465	1	...	....	1
Pennsylvania	571.80	769.65	....	569.03	2,906,115	23	2	....	24
Rhode Island	163.82	13.92	....	152.67	174,620	1	1	....	2
South Carolina	107.87	450.47	275.75	182.53	542,745	4	2	....	4
Tennessee	2,482.65	1,922.16	7,969.04	3,000.78	999,513	8	2	....	8
Texas	*b*173.51	*l*10.58	213.89	184.22	531,188	4	....	2	4
Vermont	269.24	178.04	....	268.90	315,098	2	1	....	3
Virginia	136.90	354.66	67.29	113.32	1,399,972	11	2	....	11
Wisconsin	*f*2,219.46	532.97	....	2,407.29	775,881	6	....	3	6
	741.87	701.41	466.06	692.65	29,553,273	233	....	....	241
TERRITORIES.									
Colorado	....	....	....	....	....	......	...	....	......
Dakota	....	....	....	....	....	......	...	....	......
Nebraska	....	....	....	....	....	......	...	....	......
Nevada	....	....	....	....	....	......	...	....	......
New Mexico	*b*34.73	....	....	51.94	....	......	...	....	......
Utah	*b*254.18	....	11.53	253.89	....	......	...	....	......
Washington	....	....	....	....	....	......	...	....	......
District of Columbia	*e*503.66	1,321.58	*l*1.82	432 75	....	......	...	....	......
	750.30	720.65	466.53	700.16	....	......	...	....	......

a From 1820. *b* From 1850. *c* From 1830. *d* From 1810. *e* From 1800. *f* From 1840.

Table No. 1—Continued.

Table showing the number of the Inhabitants of the States and Territories at each Census from 1790 *to* 1860, *inclusive, and the number of Whites, Free Colored, and Slaves, respectively, together with the rate of increase of each class during the several decennial terms and for the whole period.*

Aggregate population.	1790.	1800.	Rate per cent. of increase.	1810.	Rate per cent. of increase.	1820.	Rate per cent. of increase.	1830.	Rate per cent. of increase.	1840.	Rate per cent. of increase.	1850.	Rate per cent. of increase.	1860.	Rate per cent. of increase.	Rate per cent. of increase from 1790 to 1860.
Total population............	3,929,827	5,305,925	35.02	7,239,814	36.45	9,638,131	33.13	12,866,020	33.49	17,069,453	32.67	23,191,876	35.87	31,443,322	35.59	700.16
Total white population.......	3,172,464	4,304,489	35.68	5,862,004	36.18	7,861,937	34.11	10,537,378	34.03	14,195,695	34.72	19,553,114	37.74	26,973,843	37.97	750.30
Total free colored population.	59,466	108,395	82 28	186,446	72.00	233,524	25.23	319,599	36.87	386,303	20.87	434,449	12.46	487,970	12.33	720.65
Total free population	3,231,930	4,412,884	36.54	6,048,450	37.06	8,095,461	33.84	10,856,977	34.11	14,581,998	34.31	19,987,563	37.07	27,461,813	37.40	747.66
Total slave population	697,897	893,041	27.97	1,191,364	33.40	1,538,038	28.79	2,009,043	30.61	2,487,455	23.81	3,204,313	28.82	3,953,760	23.39	466.53
Total colored population	757,363	1,001,436	32.23	1,377,810	37.58	1,771,562	28.58	2,328,642	31.45	2,873,758	23.41	3,638,762	26.62	4,441,730	22.07	486.48

Total population in 1860, *including Indian tribes.*

Total population of the States and Territories	31,443,322
White population of Indian Territory west of Arkansas....................................	1,988
Free colored population of Indian Territory west of Arkansas	404
Slave population of Indian Territory west of Arkansas....................................	7,369
Population of Indian tribes, (according to table on page 136)	294,431
	31,747,514

TABLE No. 2.

Table showing the population of the States and Territories by Sexes, according to the Eighth Census, 1860.

STATES.	WHITE.			FREE COLORED.			INDIANS.			Total free.	SLAVES.			Aggregate population.
	Male.	Female.	Total.	Male.	Female.	Total.	Male.	Female.	Total.		Male.	Female.	Total.	
Alabama	270,190	256,081	526,271	1,254	1,436	2,690	81	79	160	529,121	217,766	217,314	435,080	964,201
Arkansas	171,477	152,666	324,143	72	72	144	24	24	48	324,335	56,174	54,941	111,115	435,450
California	239,856 *22,385	98,149 *963	338,005 *23,348	2,827	1,259	4,086	8,269	6,286	14,555	379,994	....	....	....	379,994
Connecticut	221,851	229,653	451,504	4,136	4,491	8,627	7	9	16	460,147	....	....	....	460,147
Delaware	45,940	44,649	90,589	9,889	9,940	19,829	....	....	....	110,418	860	938	1,798	112,216
Florida	41,128	36,619	77,747	454	478	932	1	....	1	78,680	31,348	30,397	61,745	140,425
Georgia	301,066	290,484	591,550	1,669	1,831	3,500	17	21	38	595,088	229,193	233,005	462,198	1,057,286
Illinois	898,941	805,350	1,704,291	3,809	3,819	7,628	11	21	32	1,711,951	....	....	....	1,711,951
Indiana	693,348	645,362	1,338,710	5,791	5,637	11,428	121	169	290	1,350,428	....	....	....	1,350,428
Iowa	353,900	319,879	673,779	566	503	1,069	27	38	65	674,913	....	....	....	674,913
Kansas	58,806	47,584	106,390	286	339	625	86	103	189	107,204	....	2	2	107,206
Kentucky	474,193	445,291	919,484	5,101	5,583	10,684	18	15	33	930,201	113,009	112,474	225,483	1,155,684
Louisiana	189,648	167,808	357,456	8,279	10,368	18,647	90	83	173	376,276	171,977	159,749	331,726	708,002
Maine	316,527	310,420	626,947	659	668	1,327	3	2	5	628,279	....	....	....	628,279
Maryland	256,839	259,079	515,918	39,746	44,196	83,942	....	....	....	599,860	44,313	42,876	87,189	687,049
Massachusetts	592,231	629,201	1,221,432	4,469	5,133	9,602	13	19	32	1,231,066	....	....	....	1,231,066
Michigan	389,919	349,880	739,799	3,567	3,232	6,799	1,208	1,307	2,515	749,113	....	....	....	749,113
Minnesota	91,804	77,691	169,495	126	133	259	1,254	1,115	2,369	172,123	....	....	....	172,123
Mississippi	186,273	167,626	353,899	372	401	773	2	....	2	354,674	219,301	217,330	436,631	791,305
Missouri	563,131	500,358	1,063,489	1,697	1,875	3,572	13	7	20	1,067,081	57,360	57,571	114,931	1,182,012
New Hampshire	159,563	166,016	325,579	253	241	494	....	....	....	326,073	....	....	....	326,073
New Jersey	322,733	323,966	646,699	12,312	13,006	25,318	....	....	....	672,017	6	12	18	672,035
New York	1,910,279	1,921,311	3,831,590	23,178	25,827	49,005	75	65	140	3,880,735	....	....	....	3,880,735
North Carolina	313,670	316,272	629,942	14,880	15,583	30,463	597	561	1,158	661,563	166,469	164,590	331,059	992,622

Ohio	1,171,698	1,131,110	2,302,808	18,442	18,231	36,673	22	8	30	2,339,511	....	....	....	2,339,511
Oregon	31,451	20,709	52,160	76	52	128	64	113	177	52,465	....	....	....	52,465
Pennsylvania	1,427,943	1,421,316	2,849,259	26,373	30,476	56,849	3	4	7	2,906,115	....	....	....	2,906,115
Rhode Island	82,294	88,355	170,649	1,831	2,121	3,952	8	11	19	174,620	....	....	....	174,620
South Carolina	146,160	145,140	291,300	4,548	5,366	9,914	41	47	88	301,302	196,571	205,835	402,406	703,708
Tennessee	422,779	403,943	826,722	3,538	3,762	7,300	31	29	60	834,082	136,370	139,349	275,719	1,109,801
Texas	228,585	192,306	420,891	181	174	355	212	191	403	421,649	91,189	91,377	182,566	604,215
Vermont	158,406	155,963	314,369	371	338	709	9	11	20	315,098	....	....	....	315,098
Virginia	528,842	518,457	1,047,299	27,721	30,321	58,042	55	57	112	1,105,453	249,483	241,382	490,865	1,596,318
Wisconsin	406,309 †199	367,384 †205	773,693 †404	653	518	1,171	288	325	613	775,881	....	....	....	775,881 ....
Total	13,690,364	13,007,246	26,697,610	229,126	247,410	476,536	12,650	10,720	23,370	27,197,516	1,981,389	1,969,142	3,950,531	31,148,047
TERRITORIES.														
Colorado	32,654	1,577	34,231	37	9	46	....	....	....	34,277	....	....	....	34,277
Dakota	1,592	984	2,576	....	....	....	1,205	1,056	2,261	4,837	....	....	....	4,837
District of Columbia	29,584	31,179	60,763	4,702	6,429	11,131	1	....	1	71,895	1,212	1,973	3,185	75,080
Nebraska	16,689	12,007	28,696	35	32	67	30	33	63	28,826	6	9	15	28,841
Nevada	6,102	710	6,812	35	10	45	....	....	....	6,857	....	....	....	6,857
New Mexico	43,679 †20	39,245 †35	82,924 †55	45	40	85	5,347	5,105	10,452	93,516	....	....	....	93,516
Utah	20,178	19,947	40,125	13	17	30	46	43	89	40,244	18	11	29	40,273
Washington	8,225	2,913	11,138	26	4	30	195	231	426	11,594	....	....	....	11,594
Total	158,723	108,597	267,320	4,893	6,541	11,434	6,824	6,468	13,292	292,046	1,236	1,903	3,229	295,275
Total in States and Territories	13,849,087	13,115,843	26,964,930	234,019	253,951	487,970	19,474	17,188	36,662	27,489,562	1,982,625	1,971,135	3,953,760	31,443,322

* Chinese and half-breeds.

† Half-breeds.

TABLE No. 3.—*Indian Territory west of Arkansas, Whites, Free Colored, and Slaves.*

Subdivision.	White.		Total.	Free colored.		Total.	Total free.	Slave.		Total.	Aggregate.
	Males.	Fems.		Males.	Fems.			Males.	Fems.		
CHOCTAW NATION.											
Counties.											
Boklookloo	6	4	10	......	......	......	10	5	8	13	23
Eagle	16	10	26	......	......	......	26	90	92	182	208
Red River	9	4	13	......	......	......	13	177	167	344	357
Towson	86	63	149	2	3	5	154	135	144	279	433
Nashoba	10	5	15	24	23	47	62	5	5	10	72
Kiamitia	39	20	59	......	......	......	59	179	201	380	439
Cedar	7	10	17	......	......	......	17	31	49	80	97
Blue	183	90	273	4	3	7	280	144	115	259	539
Gaines	30	2	32	5	3	8	40	45	51	96	136
Sugar Loaf and Skallyville	24	16	40	......	......	......	40	27	24	51	91
Skallyville	70	58	128	......	......	......	128	93	108	201	329
Samboy and Skallyville	27	13	40	......	......	......	40	14	17	31	71
Wade	......	......	......	......	......	......	......	17	25	42	42
Jacksfork	......	......	......	......	......	......	......	27	21	48	48
Atoka	......	......	......	......	......	......	......	7	5	12	12
Cole	......	......	......	......	......	......	......	129	140	269	269
	507	295	802	35	32	67	869	1,125	1,172	2,297	3,166
CHEROKEE NATION.											
Cherokee Nation	502	211	713	8	9	17	730	1,222	1,282	2,504	3,234
CREEK NATION.											
Creek Nation	204	115	319	151	126	277	596	811	840	1,651	2,247
CHICKASAW NATION.											
Counties.											
Tishomingo	53	26	79	1	......	1	80	119	121	240	320
Panola	26	14	40	......	......	......	40	150	170	320	360
Pickens	18	9	27	5	7	12	39	121	119	240	279
Pontotoc	......	......	......	......	......	......	......	58	59	117	117
	97	49	146	6	7	13	159	448	469	917	1,076
SEMINOLE COUNTY.											
Seminole County	6	2	8	18	12	30	38	......	......	......	38
Total	1,316	672	1,988	218	186	404	2,392	3,606	3,763	7,369	9,761

Indian population in the States and Territories not enumerated in the Census and retaining their tribal character.

West of Arkansas	65,680	Oregon	7,000
California	13,540	Tennessee	181
Georgia	377	Wisconsin	2,833
Indiana	384	Colorado Territory	6,000
Kansas	8,189	Dakota Territory	39,664
Michigan	7,777	Nebraska Territory	5,072
Minnesota	17,900	Nevada Territory	7,550
Mississippi	900	New Mexico	55,100
New York	3,785	Utah Territory	20,000
North Carolina	1,499	Washington Territory	31,000
			294,431

TABLE No. 4.

Manumitted slaves, according to the Seventh Census (1850) *and the Eighth Census,* (1860,) *respectively.*

STATES.	SEVENTH CENSUS.				EIGHTH CENSUS.			
	Slaves.	Manumitted.	One out of—	Per cent.	Slaves.	Manumitted.	One out of—	Per cent.
Alabama	342,844	16	21,427	.0046	435,080	101	4,310	.0231
Arkansas	47,100	1	47,100	.0021	111,115	41	2,711	.0369
Delaware	2,290	277	8	12.0960	1,798	12	149	.6674
Florida	39,310	22	1,786	.0559	61,745	17	3,632	.0275
Georgia	381,682	19	20,088	.0049	462,198	160	4,360	.0229
Kentucky	210,981	152	1,388	.0720	225,483	176	1,281	.0780
Louisiana	244,809	159	1,539	.0649	331,726	517	641	.1558
Maryland	90,368	493	183	.5455	87,189	1,017	85	1.1664
Mississippi	309,878	6	51,646	.0019	436,631	182	2,399	.0416
Missouri	87,422	50	1,748	.0571	114,931	89	1,291	.0774
North Carolina	288,548	2	144,274	.0006	331,059	258	1,283	.0779
South Carolina	384,984	2	192,492	.0005	402,406	12	33,533	.0029
Tennessee	239,459	45	5,321	.0187	275,719	174	1,584	.0630
Texas	58,161	5	11,632	.0085	182,566	31	5,889	.0169
Virginia	472,528	218	2,167	.0461	490,865	277	1,771	.0564
District of Columbia	....	....	....	....	3,185	8	398	.2514
	3,200,364	1,467	2,181	.0458	3,953,696	3,018	1,309	.0763

TABLE No. 5.

Fugitive slaves, according to the Seventh Census (1850) *and the Eighth Census,* (1860,) *respectively.*

STATES.	SEVENTH CENSUS.				EIGHTH CENSUS.			
	Slaves.	Fugitives.	One out of—	Per cent.	Slaves.	Fugitives.	One out of—	Per cent.
Alabama	342,844	29	11,822	.0084	435,080	36	12,086	.0082
Arkansas	47,100	21	2,242	.0445	111,115	28	3,968	.0252
Delaware	2,290	26	88	1.1353	1,798	12	150	.6674
Florida	39,310	18	2,184	.0457	61,745	11	5,613	.0177
Georgia	381,682	89	4,288	.0233	462,198	23	20,096	.0049
Kentucky	210,981	96	2,198	.0455	225,483	119	1,895	.0527
Louisiana	244,809	90	2,720	.0366	331,726	46	7,211	.0138
Maryland	90,368	279	324	.3088	87,189	115	758	.1318
Mississippi	309,878	41	7,558	.0132	436,631	68	6,422	.0155
Missouri	87,422	60	1,457	.0686	114,931	99	1,161	.0860
North Carolina	288,548	64	4,508	.0222	331,059	61	5,262	.0184
South Carolina	384,984	16	24,061	.0041	402,406	23	17,501	.0057
Tennessee	239,459	70	3,421	.0292	275,719	29	9,509	.0105
Texas	58,161	29	2,005	.0498	182,566	16	11,410	.0087
Virginia	472,528	83	5,693	.0175	490,865	117	4,194	.0238
	3,200,364	1,011	3,165	.0315	3,950,511	803	4,919	.0203

TABLE

Table of Mortality in the United States from June 1, 1859,

STATES AND TERRITORIES.	JANUARY.		FEBRUARY.		MARCH.		APRIL.		MAY.		JUNE.	
	Male.	Female.	Male.	Female.	Male.	Female.	Male.	Female.	Male.	Female.	Male.	Female.
Alabama	638	482	554	526	628	530	634	521	781	667	477	475
Arkansas	496	376	505	367	545	453	478	386	414	353	288	295
California	231	124	182	105	210	106	247	103	268	148	196	75
Connecticut	274	241	265	248	306	273	309	297	289	308	207	189
Delaware	52	54	51	54	54	54	48	60	42	74	43	40
District of Columbia	63	63	49	42	70	75	58	45	60	50	54	30
Florida	93	62	102	70	85	64	77	73	98	91	47	50
Georgia	576	507	610	593	588	554	557	555	733	699	515	511
Illinois	779	690	843	741	1,078	885	866	767	834	728	588	572
Indiana	622	549	649	708	813	784	715	678	731	679	481	444
Iowa	290	241	315	309	394	348	355	283	319	303	170	157
Kansas	66	48	53	30	67	43	74	58	51	58	37	37
Kentucky	749	646	775	701	752	750	832	735	845	820	652	566
Louisiana	691	420	560	369	592	413	619	550	809	615	633	524
Maine	305	295	313	322	384	409	379	345	402	443	226	245
Maryland	319	284	319	294	358	336	379	340	378	368	299	285
Massachusetts	825	884	804	763	946	938	863	895	940	937	750	677
Michigan	338	279	347	322	406	355	359	358	399	325	206	207
Minnesota	34	43	56	44	57	55	50	50	73	60	34	28
Mississippi	558	456	501	490	542	515	576	564	783	689	486	482
Missouri	769	596	758	683	911	728	831	759	849	671	620	472
New Hampshire	157	165	197	212	250	218	220	268	216	211	125	129
New Jersey	357	286	353	326	429	410	411	351	464	409	285	224
New York	2,232	1,975	2,303	1,987	2,689	2,300	2,442	2,182	2,649	2,447	1,629	1,465
North Carolina	544	483	505	526	563	566	586	579	808	791	555	605
Ohio	1,058	981	1,172	1,117	1,340	1,301	1,253	1,123	1,382	1,210	860	794
Oregon	17	9	14	15	10	15	14	10	13	17	3	9
Pennsylvania	1,418	1,250	1,547	1,343	1,841	1,644	1,687	1,443	1,785	1,495	1,108	902
Rhode Island	104	103	74	95	126	100	112	103	116	121	78	76
South Carolina	422	362	378	397	483	425	433	389	538	594	403	452
Tennessee	678	579	671	596	789	680	693	660	757	707	552	594
Texas	439	375	452	395	435	404	490	414	547	447	327	316
Vermont	118	125	155	146	182	196	147	184	170	173	109	107
Virginia	861	804	924	885	1,112	1,120	1,067	1,035	1,360	1,269	1,011	1,004
Wisconsin	296	284	394	319	472	380	420	382	399	352	216	157
Dakota	1	......	......	....	1	......	......	......	......	......	......	......
Nebraska	16	13	16	20	17	12	17	12	17	19	16	11
New Mexico	71	38	69	72	77	55	55	59	81	81	64	46
Utah	16	17	10	5	12	11	16	15	35	10	8	13
Washington	3	1	2	2	3	7	5	1	3	2	2	1
Total	17,576	15,190	17,847	16,239	20,617	18,512	19,376	17,632	21,438	19,441	14,360	13,266
Grand total	32,766		34,086		39,129		37,008		40,879		27,626	

No. 6.

to May 31, 1860, *inclusive, by months, ages, and sexes.*

JULY.		AUGUST.		SEPTEMBER.		OCTOBER.		NOVEMBER.		DECEMBER.		Unknown male.	Unknown female.	Total male.	Total female.	Total.
Male.	Female.	Male.	Female.	Male.	Female.	Male.	Female.	Male.	Female.	Male.	Female.					
536	526	554	486	560	509	499	461	400	374	464	415	28	35	6,753	6,007	12,760
367	350	351	377	375	367	304	283	281	229	301	264	35	22	4,738	4,122	8,860
179	81	158	74	182	79	189	111	195	106	225	112	11	8	2,473	1,232	3,705
247	187	289	279	244	250	262	254	219	208	252	234	5	2	3,168	2,970	6,138
76	55	79	84	44	45	50	36	38	30	40	42	1	...	618	628	1,246
79	72	68	56	47	33	31	35	48	32	48	37	10	20	685	590	1,275
63	60	76	60	78	64	88	72	67	51	83	62	22	11	979	790	1,769
535	509	527	476	523	498	491	429	433	355	480	419	83	51	6,651	6,156	12,807
764	643	1,050	924	1,149	977	957	794	686	528	680	624	66	50	10,340	8,923	19,263
534	489	769	731	843	790	684	680	481	438	507	394	12	..	7,841	7,364	15,205
217	186	391	309	478	433	409	370	271	227	259	213	8	5	3,876	3,384	7,260
78	46	89	71	101	84	80	62	59	49	52	50	....	...	807	636	1,443
737	640	736	646	688	645	618	620	592	490	594	565	39	32	8,611	7,856	16,467
597	394	564	386	530	367	496	335	508	271	575	370	80	61	7,254	5,075	12,329
265	228	312	315	343	340	294	310	260	306	294	265	8	6	3,785	3,829	7,614
359	311	359	353	276	268	208	211	241	207	269	234	67	48	3,831	3,539	7,370
843	851	1,232	1,212	1,082	1,044	877	873	706	741	790	794	25	12	10,683	10,621	21,304
278	269	428	342	351	344	261	217	265	218	269	229	14	13	3,921	3,478	7,399
47	23	42	46	47	60	62	48	44	30	44	28	4	..	594	515	1,109
569	546	554	534	454	427	427	342	347	241	451	365	177	138	6,425	5,789	12,214
783	645	976	863	994	922	820	678	623	497	624	456	29	...	9,587	7,970	17,557
145	145	199	217	177	216	167	161	166	167	163	168	4	6	2,186	2,283	4,469
311	276	361	307	282	284	241	204	227	183	278	229	25	12	4,024	3,501	7,525
1,860	1,511	2,172	1,942	1,914	1,677	1,633	1,405	1,607	1,340	1,803	1,464	147	106	25,080	21,801	46,881
451	523	499	517	458	470	447	475	389	399	427	367	33	41	6,265	6,342	12,607
1,068	943	1,100	992	1,019	984	943	823	788	716	857	808	46	46	12,886	11,838	24,724
6	7	7	4	4	9	12	10	13	9	17	7	....	...	130	121	251
1,222	1,067	1,274	1,122	1,123	910	1,108	915	905	837	1,165	1,014	49	40	16,232	13,982	30,214
106	92	153	124	129	130	89	82	78	97	106	83	1	1	1,272	1,207	2,479
451	434	417	367	372	420	379	354	293	282	352	289	38	21	4,959	4,786	9,745
665	696	637	665	678	679	616	565	466	411	528	528	39	47	7,769	7,407	15,176
328	303	377	305	347	246	487	330	430	313	391	354	71	46	5,121	4,248	9,369
120	102	109	145	148	132	119	127	127	132	141	138	2	1	1,647	1,708	3,355
994	953	1,011	925	834	824	752	771	663	629	767	715	115	68	11,472	11,002	22,474
244	193	336	269	319	278	301	215	219	194	265	218	1	6	3,882	3,247	7,129
......	......	1	......	......	......	.....	1	......	......	.....	......	....	...	3	1	4
12	3	25	26	26	26	20	17	12	6	7	15	....	...	201	180	381
63	37	43	45	53	33	53	33	49	26	56	41	2	3	736	569	1,305
18	6	21	10	17	23	25	23	22	12	15	14	....	...	215	159	374
2	......	1	2	......	......	1	.....	2	2	3	5	....	...	27	23	50
16,220	14,402	18,347	16,608	17,289	15,887	15500	13732	13,220	11,383	14,642	12,629	1295	958	207,727	185,879	393,606
30,622		34,955		33,176		29,232		24,603		27,271		2,253		393,606		393,606

TABLE No. 6.—*Table of Mortality*

STATES AND TERRITORIES.	Under 1.		Under 2.		Under 3.		Under 4.		Under 5.		Under 10.		Under 15.		Under 20.	
	Male.	Female.	Male.	Female.	Male.	Female.	Male.	Female.	Male.	Female.	Male.	Female.	Male.	Female.	Male.	Female.
Alabama	1,787	1,506	825	614	388	331	194	181	141	147	379	371	233	246	322	300
Arkansas	914	772	402	336	272	244	163	175	138	156	410	383	274	246	308	309
California	340	252	146	156	127	99	94	75	71	57	127	121	30	30	47	40
Connecticut	492	399	208	168	134	130	100	80	77	74	183	165	55	84	116	118
Delaware	120	112	55	59	38	40	18	19	17	9	41	48	27	24	27	39
Dist. of Columbia	166	150	75	45	19	32	22	18	13	15	37	35	12	22	30	33
Florida	164	155	84	77	57	40	36	31	29	37	82	59	48	35	32	37
Georgia	1,889	1,585	800	659	382	322	184	202	144	129	299	359	230	241	282	305
Illinois	2,412	1,970	1,384	1,177	825	672	459	431	297	274	733	773	309	305	381	388
Indiana	1,696	1,438	880	839	566	533	341	350	247	230	640	711	241	302	342	384
Iowa	971	805	546	412	277	274	154	155	106	100	260	260	117	105	139	149
Kansas	164	185	75	71	55	37	30	29	18	20	52	52	35	22	33	20
Kentucky	2,123	1,677	898	735	501	456	334	265	218	228	684	635	326	367	349	493
Louisiana	1,126	1,001	592	529	407	370	220	197	158	141	438	432	213	214	288	292
Maine	496	427	222	196	156	142	81	80	72	63	180	172	89	147	211	304
Maryland	805	716	367	320	236	242	127	121	96	75	229	194	109	98	138	170
Massachusetts	2,250	1,920	910	744	464	440	247	300	224	211	508	492	216	235	348	492
Michigan	753	672	353	300	231	229	148	151	117	94	262	274	126	95	151	177
Minnesota	154	129	65	44	35	38	17	17	19	10	30	32	14	14	13	22
Mississippi	1,581	1,411	745	613	382	334	237	200	154	162	443	441	264	276	295	325
Missouri	2,239	1,765	1,187	1,055	690	584	370	315	235	260	665	682	281	313	396	393
New Hampshire	343	275	108	100	71	68	33	37	31	31	91	80	53	67	94	119
New Jersey	809	689	366	318	243	192	168	176	119	113	296	264	107	105	125	119
New York	4,458	3,545	2,313	2,046	1,580	1,430	1103	1022	717	685	1,784	1,702	639	636	816	876
North Carolina	1,629	1,391	715	611	399	333	171	204	142	140	354	376	216	253	253	306
Ohio	2,594	2,054	1,221	1,149	896	873	608	563	462	458	1,078	1,126	377	444	459	585
Oregon	32	30	12	8	9	11	9	4	8	3	13	15	3	8	3	8
Pennsylvania	3,185	2,475	1,432	1,200	982	889	668	606	438	442	1,162	1,110	482	485	556	636
Rhode Island	237	183	121	101	57	51	33	35	29	15	77	53	25	33	38	51
South Carolina	1,281	1,191	520	467	285	272	155	134	105	104	347	305	173	218	219	251
Tennessee	1,988	1,675	790	709	431	377	277	210	193	163	508	476	296	304	370	445
Texas	1,115	932	508	432	284	261	165	146	117	107	316	328	187	186	266	281
Vermont	190	157	81	73	62	51	47	45	38	21	87	67	55	60	64	109
Virginia	2,864	2,376	1,094	976	627	503	370	330	228	256	696	730	374	429	462	548
Wisconsin	981	675	433	347	300	229	169	153	108	95	284	285	121	107	133	115
Dakota	......	......	1	......	......	......	....	....	....	....	......	......	....	....	....	....
Nebraska	64	60	15	17	9	11	4	9	3	9	14	12	7	7	7	6
New Mexico	140	112	44	63	44	28	13	11	12	16	32	29	24	20	25	38
Utah	82	45	39	31	14	9	4	4	1	6	7	10	5	....	4	6
Washington	2	3	1	1	2	1	....	3	....	....	2	3	....	1	....	3
Total	44,636	36,915	20,633	17,798	12,537	11,178	7573	7084	5342	5156	13,830	13,662	6393	6784	8142	9292
Grand total	81,551		38,431		23,715		14,657		10,498		27,492		13,177		17,434	

in the United States, &c.—Continued.

Under 25.		Under 30.		Under 40.		Under 50.		Under 60.		Under 70.		Under 80.		Under 90.		Over 90.		Unk'wn ages.	
Male.	Female.	Male.	Female.	Male.	Female.	Male.	Female.	Male.	Female.	Male.	Female.	Male.	Female.	Male.	Female.	Male.	Female.	Male.	Female.
426	376	267	267	436	477	386	351	319	240	328	252	190	198	74	83	50	56	8	11
370	317	239	231	418	422	318	213	217	140	163	97	87	49	29	20	8	10	8	2
139	70	289	82	565	130	259	48	148	31	48	21	19	5	5	3	....	4	19	8
112	154	149	162	269	280	252	182	233	183	286	245	276	269	177	209	40	62	9	6
35	40	25	37	54	43	42	40	37	27	32	37	36	32	10	17	2	5	2	....
21	35	36	42	72	45	53	30	48	27	39	25	28	21	12	10	2	5	....	....
65	53	43	52	80	64	56	50	73	31	49	28	29	19	13	10	11	9	28	3
338	361	235	292	433	451	343	334	287	257	363	279	221	193	122	119	65	61	34	7
487	472	412	408	691	660	579	399	525	338	425	296	244	204	100	86	18	14	59	56
384	412	307	333	551	608	455	375	423	315	391	282	244	219	108	9	19	24	6	....
144	156	163	138	230	299	216	148	211	140	180	124	97	87	49	23	10	8	6	1
47	33	55	37	89	54	52	37	54	19	28	12	15	7	4	1	....	....	1	....
433	533	346	358	550	592	450	406	434	345	398	271	310	250	184	166	50	69	23	10
516	288	558	305	981	480	750	316	483	183	260	159	135	75	55	49	40	33	34	11
261	283	224	260	278	350	242	244	264	222	337	306	368	335	258	230	46	67	....	1
195	204	146	183	288	282	287	233	249	193	240	209	201	161	97	96	21	41	....	1
425	564	669	767	965	1,039	834	763	764	627	738	682	686	732	363	477	69	132	3	4
209	221	170	187	283	298	262	226	312	169	258	169	192	134	70	56	19	23	5	3
24	30	37	35	63	47	47	44	36	26	19	13	13	9	7	5	1	....	....	....
371	372	286	283	472	449	391	306	285	208	271	199	128	106	60	57	55	43	5	4
542	467	452	388	772	623	606	380	487	309	345	250	186	90	72	78	20	18	42	....
110	144	103	174	159	190	149	140	183	156	191	180	252	250	169	231	43	39	3	2
160	182	157	167	287	298	294	172	232	172	260	160	233	210	121	129	23	28	24	7
1,034	1,039	1163	1135	2,174	1,871	1,801	1,337	1,597	1084	1,575	1215	1357	1202	752	741	161	194	56	41
308	346	231	328	380	479	331	347	325	312	296	357	297	272	162	187	56	88	....	12
586	612	474	555	861	895	777	605	675	488	703	541	630	504	371	275	61	68	53	43
3	7	8	12	11	11	6	2	6	2	2	2	1	1	....	1	....	....	....	....
760	771	659	685	1,262	1,066	1,075	784	1,010	646	1,044	776	929	820	465	470	80	93	43	28
61	64	52	65	109	119	85	82	84	75	102	84	76	98	47	50	13	27	26	21
236	242	185	157	305	367	257	264	239	223	272	246	215	166	98	111	60	65	7	3
428	517	316	430	525	598	419	417	373	299	364	289	256	271	164	144	60	67	11	16
358	295	342	231	488	393	352	257	267	152	170	115	83	64	32	29	16	11	55	28
87	104	62	88	104	146	101	138	118	138	152	146	215	180	148	143	34	41	2	1
543	609	385	496	672	898	657	634	645	555	741	626	612	508	326	354	116	164	60	10
124	163	142	166	258	285	229	191	208	164	193	125	140	93	57	46	2	8	....	....
......	......	....	....	......	1	......	......	2	....	......	...	....	....	....	....	....	....	....	....
12	6	11	8	17	13	19	8	10	10	6	2	1	....	1	1	....	....	1	1
55	38	56	39	99	65	69	35	49	28	33	21	11	9	7	11	11	5	12	1
14	7	14	5	12	13	2	8	10	9	4	3	1	1	2	2	....	....	....	....
2	2	5	1	7	4	3	......	3	....	......	1	....	....	....	...	....	....	....	....
10,425	10,589	9477	9585	16,270	15,405	13,508	10,546	11,925	8543	11,306	8845	9014	7844	4791	4729	1282	1582	645	342
21,014		19,062		31,675		24,052		20,468		20,151		16,858		9,520		2,864		987	

TABLE No. 6—Continued.

Table of Mortality, distinguishing by Sex the number of Deaths in the United States and Territories from divers specific causes, (alphabetically arranged,) during the year from the 1st day of June, 1859, to the 31st day of May, 1860, inclusive.

Causes of death.	ALABAMA.		ARKANSAS.		CALIFORNIA.		CONNECTICUT.		DELAWARE.		DIST. COLUMBIA.		FLORIDA.		GEORGIA.		ILLINOIS.	
	Male.	Female.	Male.	Female.	Male.	Female.	Male.	Female.	Male.	Female.	Male.	Female.	Male.	Female.	Male.	Female.	Male.	Female.
Abscess	7	3	4	5	15	4	9	6	1	1	1	2	5	......	9	6	11	5
Abscess, lumbar	......	......	......	......	4	......	......	......	......	......	......	......	......	......	......	......	2	......
Anæmia	......	......	......	......	......	......	......	1	......	......	......	......	......	......	......	......	......	1
Angina pectoris	......	......	......	......	......	......	......	......	......	......	......	......	......	......	......	......	1	......
Aneurism	......	......	1	......	5	1	......	......	......	......	......	......	......	......	......	......	2	......
Apoplexy	57	50	13	16	30	11	57	39	2	1	6	1	2	5	35	27	54	35
Ascites	1	......	......	......	3	......	......	......	......	1	1	......	......	......	......	......	......	......
Asthma	15	21	3	1	6	1	1	......	2	1	2	1	3	4	17	12	9	10
Bowels, disease of	67	63	9	13	13	6	15	10	2	......	1	......	6	......	69	51	15	11
Brain, disease of	89	58	111	85	40	27	42	26	4	1	12	7	16	17	51	36	160	125
Brain, softening of	......	......	......	1	3	......	......	4	......	......	......	......	......	......	......	......	2	1
Bronchitis	36	28	20	12	11	9	11	3	5	7	2	4	......	......	41	26	41	33
Cancer	24	49	14	18	11	7	26	48	2	9	6	5	5	6	35	46	50	69
Canker	......	......	......	1	......	......	2	5	......	......	......	......	......	......	......	......	19	16
Carbuncle	1	1	3	......	......	1	1	......	......	1	1	......	......	......	1	4	......	......
Cephalitis	221	144	197	181	63	58	79	51	17	18	17	8	25	28	158	112	380	321
Child-birth	......	124	......	86	......	49	......	53	......	17	......	6	......	30	......	135	......	223
Cholera	18	7	5	4	1	1	14	5	4	1	1	1	3	......	6	5	52	18
Cholera infantum	67	33	25	17	16	10	71	52	13	20	15	15	3	3	65	63	167	148
Chorea	......	1	......	......	......	......	1	1	......	......	......	......	......	1	2	1	2	4
Cold water	......	......	......	......	......	......	......	......	1	......	......	......	......	......	......	......	......	......
Colitis	44	20	11	15	4	......	9	......	5	2	1	1	9	2	29	20	23	23
Consumption	252	344	160	169	367	157	596	673	94	107	132	123	53	44	196	295	986	962
Convulsions	48	56	42	22	12	12	33	37	5	2	23	13	3	5	64	49	143	85
Croup	222	203	218	159	43	30	83	81	36	23	17	14	12	11	239	184	622	536
Cyanosis	......	......	......	......	......	......	......	1	......	......	......	1	......	......	1	......	......	1
Cystitis	4	1	......	1	3	......	2	1	1	......	1	......	......	......	8	......	6	......

Debility	28	29	4	2	18	12	13	28	6	8	3	3	1	1	27	31	32	39
Delirium tremens	5	...	3	...	13	1	18	2	2	...	2	...	1	...	10	2	27	3
Diarrhœa	202	126	40	50	24	15	13	7	8	20	26	19	40	31	209	158	313	294
Diabetes	7	1	...	1	3	...	5	1	...	...	...	...	1	...	9	5	12	5
Diptheria	16	31	4	6	34	24	13	12	...	1	2	...	...	...	8	9	22	19
Dropsy	277	265	111	120	56	10	80	122	16	19	9	10	64	47	283	293	205	203
Dysentery	167	146	101	77	48	22	65	58	23	24	14	6	26	21	223	171	457	388
Dyspepsia	22	11	8	2	2	2	...	2	2	3	...	...	4	3	28	15	24	7
Enteritis	58	55	67	39	41	36	47	34	18	8	10	9	8	11	63	52	155	123
Epilepsy	9	3	...	4	4	1	5	3	...	...	1	...	...	...	14	8	14	7
Erysipelas	23	34	50	26	7	5	34	35	5	1	4	2	4	5	35	40	85	96
Fever, intermittent	106	83	207	187	41	22	1	1	1	3	6	5	26	16	82	81	259	205
Fever, remittent	233	208	303	299	85	39	65	58	10	7	2	4	56	49	199	206	361	321
Fever, typhoid	450	386	287	227	84	30	125	91	22	34	16	27	50	38	472	415	654	529
Fistula	...	1	...	...	3	...	1	...	...	...	...	...	...	...	...	...	1	...
Fits	35	34	34	36	9	13	66	51	5	10	7	3	7	8	31	42	78	69
Gastritis	15	28	16	29	2	7	4	7	1	3	...	3	...	2	12	10	15	15
Gout	1	1	...	...	1	...	1	...	...	...	1	...	...	...	...	1	...	...
Heart, disease of	33	51	19	13	67	23	103	72	8	15	17	15	11	4	59	53	106	86
Heat	8	3	7	3	4	...	2	...	...	...	2	...	...	1	5	4	20	1
Hemorrhage	23	20	10	10	17	7	20	22	2	2	10	3	9	3	21	17	23	16
Hepatitis	1	3	3	2	3	...	3	3	...	1	...	...	...	...	1	1	3	7
Hernia	5	...	2	...	9	1	3	4	2	...	1	1	2	...	5	2	9	7
Hip disease	2	1	...	...	3	...	3	...	...	1	...	2	...	...	1	...	3	1
Hydrocephalus	15	12	3	3	18	16	42	45	2	2	13	20	1	2	13	14	104	52
Hydrophobia	1	...	...	...	...	...	...	...	1	...	...	...	...	...	2	1	1	3
Hydrothorax	20	34	5	9	4	1	2	5	...	...	3	...	2	2	15	19	4	...
Ileus	...	...	...	1	...	...	...	...	...	...	...	...	...	...	...	...	...	...
Infantile	144	120	27	13	17	14	15	16	10	7	28	29	23	22	104	86	189	184
Inflammation	14	10	11	13	10	1	11	8	1	2	1	1	2	4	37	35	37	25
Influenza	9	9	3	6	...	2	3	4	1	...	1	...	1	...	11	6	9	5
Insanity	2	7	4	...	5	1	6	7	4	6	9	6	...	...	4	5	11	6
Intemperance	32	2	11	...	25	4	16	1	10	2	4	...	5	1	35	...	22	2
Intussusception	1	1	1	1	2	...	...	...	...	...	...	...	...	...	1	1	3	...
Ischuria	...	...	...	...	...	...	...	...	...	...	...	...	...	...	...	...	...	...
Jaundice	13	6	7	11	2	...	5	6	3	...	4	3	...	1	11	15	18	15

Table of Mortality, distinguishing by Sex the number of Deaths in the United States, &c.—Continued.

Causes of death.	ALABAMA.		ARKANSAS.		CALIFORNIA.		CONNECTICUT.		DELAWARE.		DIST. COLUMBIA.		FLORIDA.		GEORGIA.		ILLINOIS.	
	Male.	Female.	Male.	Female.	Male.	Female.	Male.	Female.	Male.	Female.	Male.	Female.	Male.	Female.	Male.	Female.	Male.	Female.
Joints, disease of	......	......	......	......	......	......	2	2	......	......	......	......	......	......	......	......	......	......
Kidney, disease of	13	2	2	1	4	1	13	3	1	......	2	......	3	1	11	1	13	5
Laryngitis	3	1	......	......	2	......	......	1	......	......	......	......	......	......	......	2	4	3
Liver, disease of	40	31	24	17	17	10	32	31	10	3	1	3	12	4	44	34	81	62
Lungs, disease of	40	34	32	15	28	12	33	31	2	5	8	2	1	5	33	38	79	63
Malformation	5	2	3	......	......	......	3	......	1	......	......	......	1	1	1	4	2	1
Marasmus	7	8	5	5	3	2	15	9	3	2	2	1	3	1	6	5	4	3
Measles	31	31	20	31	9	7	48	37	2	2	2	......	......	1	21	26	56	53
Metritis	......	4	......	5	......	......	......	......	......	1	......	......	......	......	......	9	......	......
Mortification	2	3	1	1	5	......	6	2	2	......	......	1	......	1	3	2	2	3
Necrosis	6	3	2	......	1	......	......	......	......	......	......	1	2	......	11	6	2	2
Nephria	......	......	1	......	1	......	......	......	......	......	......	......	......	......	......	......	1	......
Nephritis	1	......	......	1	......	......	1	......	......	......	......	......	......	1	1	1	5	1
Neuralgia	18	18	9	12	2	2	6	7	......	......	......	......	1	......	17	14	30	25
Old age	122	141	34	35	7	6	183	211	6	23	7	17	17	11	126	175	124	138
Ovarian dropsy	......	......	......	......	......	1	......	......	......	......	......	......	......	......	......	......	......	......
Paralysis	45	38	21	15	32	8	57	55	18	10	13	6	8	6	56	65	62	65
Paramenia	......	24	......	11	......	......	......	1	......	1	......	......	......	1	......	7	......	7
Parotitis	2	2	1	......	......	......	......	......	2	......	......	1	......	......	1	......	7	5
Pericarditis	......	......	......	......	1	......	......	......	1	2	......	......	......	......	......	......	4	3
Peritonitis	......	......	......	......	1	......	......	2	......	2	......	......	......	......	1	......	4	5
Phlebitis	2	......	......	......	2	3	......	......	......	......	......	......	......	......	1	......	......	1
Pleurisy	11	10	18	11	5	......	13	8	3	1	3	2	3	3	11	13	23	23
Pneumonia	837	540	932	593	88	29	155	147	21	19	23	45	117	73	737	530	772	585
Prostate, disease of	......	......	......	......	......	......	......	......	......	......	......	......	......	......	......	......	......	......
Puerperal fever	......	50	......	63	......	3	......	12	......	1	......	2	......	5	......	59	......	53
Purpura and scurvy	1	3	......	......	1	1	......	......	1	......	......	......	......	1	4	......	1	......
Quinsy	28	28	29	30	......	2	1	2	1	3	......	......	3	1	24	38	19	16

Rheumatism	53	33	13	8	8	3	18	17	6	6	8	2	5	2	35	29	56	22
Scarlatina	118	133	222	215	239	202	188	201	36	38	34	27	3	......	111	106	855	843
Scrofula	39	41	14	25	6	7	19	19	2	1	1	1	1	2	35	24	68	60
Skin, disease of	88	82	102	55	1	......	1	2	1	3	......	......	6	7	115	78	43	40
Smallpox	......	2	4	......	4	......	5	8	2	......	......	......	......	......	7	1	4	4
Spina bifida	......	......	......	......	......	......	1	1	......	......	......	......	......	......	......	......	......	......
Spine, disease of	26	14	8	4	6	......	7	4	5	1	1	3	4	......	15	13	28	25
Splenitis	2	1	4	3	1	......	......	1	......	......	......	......	......	......	1	......	6	1
Still-born	33	27	6	8	20	22	17	9	......	......	......	......	3	4	35	22	59	36
Stomach, disease of	3	5	3	1	1	1	1	2	......	......	1	2	1	......	4	4	3	8
Stone	16	5	5	2	1	......	13	1	4	1	1	......	3	1	26	3	23	2
Stricture of urethra	2	1	1	......	2	......	......	......	......	......	......	......	......	......	3	......	1	......
Sudden death	28	10	6	10	4	6	13	7	1	......	3	3	3	1	18	20	9	10
Syphilis	9	5	......	1	23	1	1	1	......	......	......	1	......	......	4	6	4	1
Tabes mesenteria	......	......	......	......	2	......	......	......	......	......	......	......	......	......	......	......	......	1
Teething	230	177	33	33	26	28	31	21	2	4	16	10	27	22	168	151	96	102
Tetanus	91	60	12	3	9	1	13	3	2	......	2	2	11	11	40	38	29	28
Throat, disease of	33	33	23	25	16	9	22	25	3	7	1	......	3	......	26	20	81	86
Thrush	15	17	7	8	2	1	2	3	1	4	3	2	1	2	19	10	16	23
Tumor	3	4	1	1	4	2	1	18	1	2	1	1	2	......	7	12	11	14
Ulcers	12	12	7	12	6	2	3	1	......	......	......	1	2	2	12	11	14	9
Ulcer of intestines	1	3	......	......	......	3	......	......	......	......	......	......	......	......	......	2	2	3
Unknown	808	800	532	575	145	103	168	127	69	64	68	61	118	108	984	982	819	706
Uterus, disease of	......	17	......	9	......	1	......	2	......	......	......	......	......	5	......	24	......	3
Whooping cough	153	181	87	100	7	16	40	57	6	11	18	15	4	10	159	174	183	199
Worms	75	88	64	69	1	1	2	3	3	6	1	......	22	17	112	84	18	26
Yellow fever	2	......	2	......	......	......	......	......	......	......	......	......	11	2	3	1	1	......
Totals	6,204	5,651	4,474	4,009	2,054	1,189	2,976	2,896	575	614	655	585	890	740	6,104	5,714	9,747	8,734
Aggregates	11,855		8,483		3,243		5,872		1,189		1,240		1,630		11,818		18,481	
Total of violent deaths	905		377		462		266		57		35		139		989		782	
Grand totals	12,760		8,860		3,705		6,138		1,246		1,275		1,769		12,807		19,263	

Table of Mortality, distinguishing by Sex the number of Deaths in the United States, &c.—Continued.

Causes of death.	INDIANA.		IOWA.		KANSAS.		KENTUCKY.		LOUISIANA.		MAINE.		MARYLAND.		MASSACHUSETTS.		MICHIGAN.	
	Male.	Female.	Male.	Female.	Male.	Female.	Male.	Female.	Male.	Female.	Male.	Female.	Male.	Female.	Male.	Female.	Male.	Female.
Abscess	5	2	3	2			12	4	9	10	8	6	2	7	21	12	5	6
Abscess, lumbar	1											2					1	
Anæmia	1	1					1		4	2			1		1	6		
Angina pectoris									1	1					2			
Aneurism	1								6	2					6	1		
Apoplexy	42	30	22	20	1	1	47	34	79	25	33	13	34	20	110	84	24	21
Ascites									20	7					2	1	1	
Asthma	10	7	3	7			5	9	17	5	5	4	8	8	26	19	6	4
Bowels, disease of	24	12	6	5	3	2	19	14	20	13	31	28	12	10	150	121	12	12
Brain, disease of	116	111	57	58	12	16	91	57	131	77	84	72	52	42	247	182	104	81
Brain, softening of			1	1	1		5		3		3		2		21	12	1	
Bronchitis	39	31	17	28	3	1	46	38	38	25	6	7	21	7	32	21	8	6
Cancer	30	56	18	38	4	5	26	66	18	36	50	62	21	41	95	199	29	30
Canker	6	10	7	3		1			1	1	35	33			80	80	6	12
Carbuncle	6	2		1			5	1	2		3			1	2	1		
Cephalitis	345	297	173	141	31	21	284	214	157	131	69	44	99	89	92	84	116	77
Child-birth		150		61		11		135		148		58		84		251		97
Cholera	24	11	10	3	6		21	15	29	20	20	16	13	7	43	33	15	5
Cholera infantum	81	75	51	50	10	8	81	68	53	40	20	16	39	43	436	367	17	15
Chorea	2	2		1			1					1	1		1			1
Cold water																		
Colitis	31	23	14	5	3	2	25	20	26	10	15	8	10	10	7	8	14	3
Consumption	848	856	317	431	53	54	722	1,020	547	296	871	1,298	541	656	2,168	2,677	553	634
Convulsions	99	77	65	48	8	7	85	63	60	61	8	9	42	46	133	76	71	64
Croup	400	378	235	225	39	31	441	346	91	80	68	51	150	149	307	294	140	111
Cyanosis	1	1				1							2		2	3		
Cystitis	3	1	3	2			9	1	7	2	3				1		8	1
Debility	20	22	11	6	3	4	26	23	66	62	14	19	14	19	70	80	11	15

Delirium tremens	17	...	6	...		...	22	1	70	15	3	...	4	...	27	3	5	...
Diarrhœa	151	127	125	99	25	15	106	84	326	143	52	49	106	75	86	60	61	47
Diabetes	12	2	5	1	...	1	14	...	1	1	13	7	2	...	21	8	5	1
Diptheria	21	30	26	17	...	1	45	36	43	45	...	1	4	10	13	14	2	...
Dropsy	171	165	71	84	16	13	246	227	175	144	108	138	124	122	240	302	94	128
Dysentery	293	291	152	112	17	24	126	103	265	165	66	71	132	109	278	290	114	117
Dyspepsia	27	13	10	1	2	1	21	15	12	4	8	6	10	15	14	2	10	4
Enteritis	125	73	60	58	14	7	113	79	83	66	35	31	38	39	92	118	60	61
Epilepsy	12	8	6	8	1	1	9	13	5	6	6	1	5	3	27	12	8	4
Erysipelas	87	74	41	24	9	7	60	62	24	24	33	20	17	9	83	70	37	35
Fever, intermittent	185	180	122	108	69	76	116	123	116	72	1	1	3	5	2	3	50	43
Fever, remittent	221	215	124	111	58	32	260	274	384	254	85	95	64	65	136	124	112	104
Fever, typhoid	490	472	225	188	59	40	473	423	317	241	212	222	132	123	363	337	164	163
Fistula	1	...	...	...	...	...	5	1	3	...	1	...	1	...	2	3	...	...
Fits	68	62	27	22	3	2	54	47	49	48	44	44	37	39	120	116	62	47
Gastritis	17	33	8	8	3	1	33	44	17	18	2	1	13	18	26	22	8	5
Gout	1	...	...	...	...	...	1	...	2	1	1	...	4	...	2	...	...	...
Heart, disease of	62	76	34	37	2	4	85	77	79	56	139	107	99	82	389	316	59	58
Heat	10	1	12	...	...	...	13	1	35	9	1	...	5	...	7	1	4	...
Hemorrhage	15	24	9	4	...	1	26	22	12	18	17	7	15	11	44	40	12	10
Hepatitis	4	6	3	...	...	...	6	2	13	7	...	2	4	...	2	...	1	1
Hernia	9	4	5	5	1	...	9	5	9	4	11	5	2	2	6	4	8	1
Hip disease	2	1	...	...	...	...	2	2	2	...	2	3	...	...	11	8	1	1
Hydrocephalus	32	28	29	20	1	1	30	23	12	8	63	73	34	25	241	237	55	39
Hydrophobia	...	...	1	1	...	...	1	1	...	...	...	...	...	...	2	...	...	...
Hydrothorax	3	7	3	6	...	...	2	4	8	7	3	3	5	2	19	9	3	2
Ileus	...	...	...	...	...	...	...	...	1	...	...	...	...	...	...	...	...	...
Infantile	102	92	91	56	12	23	215	172	91	62	26	18	37	64	337	283	34	24
Inflammation	14	13	9	9	2	...	11	12	25	14	12	10	1	7	28	26	35	23
Influenza	4	4	2	3	...	1	7	8	14	5	10	13	...	1	19	26	1	1
Insanity	4	2	3	1	...	...	3	9	11	5	6	5	6	1	34	28	4	...
Intemperance	26	...	6	...	5	...	48	4	47	9	5	...	22	1	38	20	19	1
Intussusception	2	...	...	...	...	...	1	...	2	...	...	1	...	...	3	1	1	1
Ischuria	...	...	...	...	...	...	...	...	1	...	...	...	...	...	1	...	...	...
Jaundice	17	13	8	8	2	1	14	9	8	8	4	4	4	9	11	13	13	5
Joints, disease of	...	...	...	...	...	...	...	...	...	...	...	...	...	...	8	1	...	...

Table of Mortality, distinguishing by Sex the number of Deaths in the United States, &c.—Continued.

Causes of death.	INDIANA.		IOWA.		KANSAS.		KENTUCKY.		LOUISIANA.		MAINE.		MARYLAND.		MASSACHUSETTS.		MICHIGAN.	
	Male.	Female.	Male.	Female.	Male.	Female.	Male.	Female.	Male.	Female.	Male.	Female.	Male.	Female.	Male.	Female.	Male.	Female.
Kidney, disease of	19	2	8	2	1	......	22	4	19	3	29	3	9	2	46	13	9	2
Laryngitis	3	......	......	1	......	......	2	1	1	......	......	......	......	......	3	2	1	1
Liver, disease of	59	44	32	18	7	3	44	38	29	16	41	21	27	23	72	83	36	30
Lungs, disease of	42	33	56	30	9	8	64	64	36	23	65	55	25	15	171	143	68	22
Malformation	2	2	1	......	......	......	3	2	3	2	1	......	......	......	1	......	2	1
Marasmus	2	3	......	3	2	......	10	10	21	20	......	......	5	4	20	22	......	3
Measles	92	104	20	24	......	2	73	80	121	95	15	16	61	59	81	60	20	33
Metritis	......	4	......	2	......	......	......	2	......	5	......	......	......	7	......	......	......	1
Mortification	4	2	1	1	1	1	8	2	14	1	6	1	1	......	9	14	7	2
Necrosis	7	4	20	12	......	......	8	3	2	6	......	......	3	......	......	......	3	......
Nephria	......	......	......	......	......	......	......	......	......	......	......	......	......	......	......	......	......	1
Nephritis	1	1	2	......	......	......	1	1	3	......	......	......	1	......	5	1	2	3
Neuralgia	21	31	12	12	2	......	19	25	2	5	3	7	3	7	7	20	10	3
Old age	114	128	65	46	8	3	185	217	128	94	196	235	104	159	361	535	87	104
Ovarian dropsy	......	......	......	......	......	......	......	......	......	......	......	1	......	1	......	2	......	......
Paralysis	58	72	26	22	3	6	88	80	33	17	88	82	66	68	170	206	34	24
Paramenia	......	2	......	3	......	......	......	9	......	5	......	......	......	......	......	1	......	3
Parotitis	2	3	4	......	1	......	......	1	1	2	1	1	......	1	4	......	2	......
Pericarditis	......	1	......	......	......	......	1	......	1	......	1	......	......	......	1	2	1	......
Peritonitis	2	1	......	......	......	......	2	1	6	3	......	1	......	......	7	8	......	2
Phlebitis	1	1	......	1	......	......	......	......	1	......	1	......	2	......	1	2	......	......
Pleurisy	10	16	7	8	3	2	17	15	75	35	10	7	38	16	51	50	15	6
Pneumonia	688	461	343	238	91	50	589	430	774	449	160	133	200	117	534	467	320	246
Prostate, disease of	1	......	......	......	......	......	......	......	3	......	1	......	......	......	......	......	......	......
Puerperal fever	......	47	......	15	......	3	......	58	......	34	......	4	......	9	......	26	......	16
Purpura and scurvy	......	1	1	......	......	1	1	3	1	......	......	......	1	1	1	2	......	......
Quinsy	18	23	4	3	1	......	19	19	7	5	2	1	4	2	1	......	6	3
Rheumatism	40	30	9	8	7	1	41	35	39	17	18	12	34	15	37	36	11	12

Scarlatina	677	755	177	160	31	27	772	733	211	196	182	165	182	159	382	427	336	321
Scrofula	90	62	30	27	7	2	102	99	20	15	29	10	27	21	55	55	28	12
Skin, disease of	28	18	6	6		2	79	70	22	16	5	5	2	1	10	5	2	2
Smallpox	7	2		5		1	8	7	7	9	35	21	5	2	297	174	6	2
Spina bifida															2	4		
Spine, disease of	20	29	7	7		4	18	23	15	4	11	14	15	13	33	29	12	12
Splenitis	3	2				1	4	1	1	1					1		1	3
Still-born	19	21	69	58	2	8	71	49	13	7	1		10	5	70	28	5	5
Stomach, disease of	4	5	2				1	3	4	7	6	3	7	3	2	2	2	4
Stone	23	2	8		1	1	29	2	2	1	19	4	8	2	30	7	13	
Stricture of urethra			4	2			2	1	4				1					
Sudden death	13	6	5	2	2	1	15	12	12	5	6	8	22	15	23	9	4	8
Syphilis	2		1	1			9	4	12	6	1	3		1	15	11	3	
Tabes mesenteria	1	1			1		1		1						2	4		
Teething	30	27	29	18	3	3	37	27	238	251	23	13	61	54	167	126	22	29
Tetanus	10	8	4	2			41	20	148	96	2	1	14	1	16	4	5	5
Throat, disease of	119	169			2	2	65	61	79	99	25	39	23	18	57	71	16	19
Thrush	17	14	10	3		2	8	13	8	8			12	10	5	7	3	6
Tumor	8	10	3	2	1		6	9	3	7	9	23	7	6	26	50	5	7
Ulcers	7	4	3	5	1	2	10	11	9	2	1	2		2	9	3	2	2
Ulcer of intestines	3	1	1	1			2	2	1	1	1	1	1		1	2	1	2
Unknown	650	649	349	291	61	46	1,178	1,071	598	493	139	137	512	444	303	320	237	218
Uterus, disease of		3		1				21		17		1		1		8		1
Whooping cough	138	184	84	128	21	17	197	239	143	177	33	39	104	102	139	213	52	66
Worms	25	22	6	3			40	29	115	82	7	5	12	12	10	5	12	10
Yellow fever	1						6	1	118	36			14	6				
Totals	7,421	7,181	3,645	3,298	749	616	8,027	7,622	6,751	4,886	3,488	3,759	3,617	3,460	10,025	10,368	3,585	3,373
Aggregates	14,602		6,943		1,365		15,649		11,637		7,247		7,077		20,393		6,958	
Total of violent deaths	603		317		78		818		692		367		293		911		441	
Grand totals	15,205		7,260		1,443		16,467		12,329		7,614		7,370		21,304		7,399	

Table of Mortality, distinguishing by Sex the number of Deaths in the United States, &c.—Continued.

Causes of death.	MINNESOTA.		MISSISSIPPI.		MISSOURI.		NEW HAMPSHIRE.		NEW JERSEY.		NEW YORK.		NOR'H CAROLINA.		OHIO.		OREGON.	
	Male.	Female.	Male.	Female.	Male.	Female.	Male.	Female.	Male.	Female.	Male.	Female.	Male.	Female.	Male.	Female.	Male.	Female.
Abscess		1	2	1	14	8	6	5	10	9	61	51	1	2	20	11		1
Abscess, lumbar								1	1		6				4	1		
Anæmia					1	1			1	1	8	2		1		1		
Angina pectoris												1						
Aneurism			1							1	7	4			2			
Apoplexy	3	4	36	21	50	27	22	17	57	35	307	197	42	45	99	77	1	1
Ascites					8						6		1	1				
Asthma			3	12	4	3	2	1	8	7	49	36	16	13	22	27		
Bowels, disease of	2	5	38	26	27	22	15	11	7	5	55	62	28	28	31	13		1
Brain, disease of	15	8	109	64	119	92	36	25	91	38	526	379	36	43	194	136	2	2
Brain, softening of			2		2		5	3		1	28	10	1		1	1		
Bronchitis	1		26	14	62	51	3	5	60	39	99	74	26	23	48	48		1
Cancer	1	6	17	44	32	47	36	66	36	39	216	306	28	80	98	131	2	
Canker	3				5	2	12	17	1		10	17	1		5	5		
Carbuncle		1	1	1	4	1		1	2		8	2	1		3	1		
Cephalitis	17	24	206	169	377	297	23	23	100	100	525	429	127	98	434	341	4	2
Child-birth		33		112		161		20		87		426		156		228		1
Cholera	3	1	14	10	40	21	5	4	16	8	87	72	6	8	34	32	1	
Cholera infantum	22	24	69	54	97	79	39	40	77	56	367	323	47	39	143	117		
Chorea			1							1	3	6		3	3	2		
Cold water					1										1			
Colitis	1		20	10	27	20	5		16	7	56	43	39	33	54	31		
Consumption	67	84	239	315	650	652	508	655	667	683	4,021	4,186	308	453	1,669	1,826	9	12
Convulsions	22	11	57	52	243	161	7	3	82	60	435	398	32	20	271	183	1	3
Croup	27	18	224	204	621	480	39	33	158	160	972	825	235	192	476	401	9	6
Cyanosis											1	4	1	1	1	1		
Cystitis		1	3		6	3	2		1		18	5	6	3	14			
Debility	3	5	26	25	44	51	15	10	37	30	179	179	24	25	35	47		

Delirium tremens	1		7		29	2	8		9		91	13	5		26	2		
Diarrhœa	6	5	167	96	398	309	13	14	67	57	411	375	229	235	237	241	1	
Diabetes			4		7		9	5	6	2	64	19	4	4	24	10	1	
Diptheria			48	51	36	32			8	8	150	187	11	11	27	27		
Dropsy	11	13	198	180	202	188	77	73	121	127	599	712	249	339	293	343		2
Dysentery	9	8	139	132	257	186	46	39	64	75	554	477	239	192	303	227	1	
Dyspepsia	1		18	15	16	4	3	2	7	8	50	26	21	14	43	29		
Enteritis	5	6	61	65	139	119	20	24	78	62	418	372	35	49	210	156	3	3
Epilepsy			2	6	11	5	3		10	4	49	36	2	7	17	19		
Erysipelas	4	3	29	30	71	61	23	21	31	25	198	165	24	36	109	89	3	4
Fever, intermittent	5	3	142	116	300	209	1		18	10	48	39	46	70	110	89	1	1
Fever, remittent	19	19	335	309	399	399	39	61	75	52	329	226	162	216	219	194	3	4
Fever, typhoid	24	13	414	394	603	453	121	118	90	69	592	429	517	492	553	485	4	4
Fistula				1	4						1				1			
Fits	2	3	40	56	84	62	38	18	66	48	400	332	43	34	118	96	2	4
Gastritis	2		28	22	30	26	5	8	1	2	45	46	20	9	20	38		1
Gout		1			1				2		3	1	1	1	1			
Heart, disease of	4	7	50	45	80	57	85	73	106	84	732	575	68	47	202	185		
Heat	2		11	6	20	4		1	2		30	7	3	1	36	4	1	
Hemorrhage	2	4	19	15	24	16	9	5	17	12	111	59	26	16	46	37	1	
Hepatitis	1		6	1	7	4			4	3	15	11	3	1	9	4		
Hernia	1	1	9	3	8	3	3		9	4	22	13	14	1	15	6		
Hip disease			1	2	2			2	3	4	17	13	1		3	2		
Hydrocephalus	5	3	17	10	27	27	22	15	53	49	591	479	12	6	103	72	2	
Hydrophobia					4				3	1	4			1	1			
Hydrothorax	1	2	18	16	4	4	2	2	10	2	25	29	27	18	15	5		
Ileus													1					
Infantile	5	2	100	106	129	95	56	30	49	39	303	219	166	134	159	143	1	
Inflammation	2	3	19	14	21	17	13	9	18	17	148	141	14	13	33	29	2	2
Influenza			5	10	2	3	6	8		1	25	21	8	6	10	5		
Insanity		1	3	1	17	11	4	3	3	3	37	25	2	6	10	9		
Intemperance	3		19		27	3	8		20	2	88	13	31		31	5	1	
Intussusception			2		1						1	1		1	1	1		
Ischuria											2							
Jaundice		1	6	4	28	12	1	1	6	9	42	42	20	12	36	25		1
Joints, disease of												1						

Table of Mortality, distinguishing by Sex the number of Deaths in the United States, &c.—Continued.

Causes of death.	MINNESOTA.		MISSISSIPPI.		MISSOURI.		NEW HAMPSHIRE.		NEW JERSEY.		NEW YORK.		NOR'H CAROLINA.		OHIO.		OREGON.	
	Male.	Female.	Male.	Female.	Male.	Female.	Male.	Female.	Male.	Female.	Male.	Female.	Male.	Female.	Male.	Female.	Male.	Female.
Kidney, disease of			13	2	25	3	12	3	10	5	93	26	14	2	30	6		
Laryngitis					5	1					3	1	8	4	3	2		
Liver, disease of	6	9	33	24	64	35	21	28	21	25	194	144	48	42	88	68	1	5
Lungs, disease of	11	2	39	35	65	75	35	24	39	26	431	324	15	18	143	113	3	1
Malformation		1	4	1	4	3	1				4	5	2	3	3	3		
Marasmus		2	7	3	12	4			24	14	165	177	14	9	12	6		
Measles		3	98	82	131	116	3	2	30	46	379	367	58	68	216	233	1	
Metritis				3		2				3		8		6		7		
Mortification			3	1	4	2	9	6	4	2	32	14	5	1	7	3		
Necrosis			5	4	9	1	1		1	2	7		5	4	14	6		
Nephria				1					1		8	8	1		2			
Nephritis	1					1	3		2		29	6	1		8	2		
Neuralgia	2	1	10	8	29	28		5	4	5	43	66	19	13	26	37		
Old age	6	12	98	108	90	123	122	168	114	160	687	858	137	228	374	356		
Ovarian dropsy												2				1		
Paralysis	2	5	19	29	44	36	48	88	75	65	379	310	90	76	153	178		1
Paramenia				10		11						4		5		13		
Parotitis	1		6	5	11	10					15	6	1		1	2		
Pericarditis					1						5	3		1	7	5		
Peritonitis				1		2		1			10	9	1	6	7	5		
Phlebitis						1										1		
Pleurisy			12	9	30	22	5	10	18	15	76	51	31	11	28	16		
Pneumonia	42	25	940	600	831	575	107	117	159	120	1,251	850	499	418	717	594	5	7
Prostate, disease of																		
Puerperal fever		3		57		74		7		14		42		38		63		1
Purpura and scurvy			1	1	4	2	1	1	1		4		2		7	1		
Quinsy		1	22	23	32	32			3	3	8	13	17	19	14	15		
Rheumatism	2	2	23	19	41	28	11	7	20	15	139	83	43	31	55	59		1

Scarlatina	38	18	149	119	440	456	82	87	365	329	2,350	2,332	179	184	1,636	1,781	19	18
Scrofula	4	7	42	40	62	65	18	22	19	21	105	94	52	49	84	94	2	
Skin, disease of			52	49	72	62	4		2	1	8	6	55	41	24	10		
Smallpox					12	6	16	6	7	1	163	129	1		59	76		
Spina bifida								1										
Spine, disease of	2		17	17	21	23	5	9	16	7	81	44	14	8	47	30		1
Splenitis	1		1	2	6	1					4	2	2	2	3	2		
Still-born			33	30	28	19	2		7	2	86	70	30	25	58	55		
Stomach, disease of		1	3	6	10	6		3		1	21	10	3	1	14	14		
Stone		1	13		12		13	1	9	1	82	4	33	1	51	3	1	
Stricture of urethra			3	1	1	1			2		4		3	2		1		
Sudden death			5	3	12	5	6	4	11	12	38	33	22	23	32	21	2	1
Syphilis			6	3	1			1	1		16	12	3	4	5	3		
Tabes mesenteria			1		2						15	14	1	1				
Teething	7	1	150	142	111	125	6	14	42	41	263	230	52	45	69	67	2	
Tetanus	7	1	57	32	53	25	1	1	14	3	51	39	18	9	32	17		
Throat, disease of			37	39	74	78	11	16	49	51	215	217	29	30	236	246	7	10
Thrush		1	10	8	19	21		1	3	4	10	11	18	20	10	6		
Tumor	1		3	3	6	3	4	11	12	12	50	62	5	12	19	15		
Ulcers	3		9	4	6	15	2		5	3	12	10	8	4	8	5	1	
Ulcer of intestines				1	1			1	1		8	4			4	3		
Unknown	66	53	754	726	1,054	932	96	101	205	168	1,464	1,068	1,033	1,056	959	824	9	13
Uterus, disease of				35		8		1		1		8		15		6		
Whooping cough	13	15	172	196	158	193	20	28	84	88	307	397	199	201	169	239	2	2
Worms	3	1	73	56	41	34	1	4	4	3	41	47	78	66	13	26	1	
Yellow fever			3	3	5	2							2		2	1		
Totals	520	489	5,937	5,461	9,061	7,757	2,061	2,251	3,768	3,415	23,571	21,361	5,861	6,041	12,132	11,578	112	117
Aggregates	1,009		11,398		16,818		4,312		7,183		44,932		11,902		23,710		229	
Total of violent deaths	100		816		739		157		342		1,949		705		1,014		22	
Grand totals	1,109		12,214		17,557		4,469		7,525		46,881		12,607		24,724		251	

Table of Mortality, distinguishing by Sex the number of Deaths in the United States, &c.—Continued.

Cause of death.	PENNSYLVANIA.		RHODE ISLAND.		SOUTH CAROLINA.		TENNESSEE.		TEXAS.		VERMONT.		VIRGINIA.		WISCONSIN.	
	Male.	Female.	Male.	Female.	Male.	Female.	Male.	Female.	Male.	Female.	Male.	Female.	Male.	Female.	Male.	Female.
Abscess	27	15	3	2	9	9	11	3	9	2	7	2	18	7	3	3
Abscess, lumbar																
Anæmia	1	1											2			
Angina pectoris																
Aneurism	2			1										1		
Apoplexy	235	176	15	24	50	50	40	35	22	28	21	25	80	66	41	29
Ascites																
Asthma	44	32	1	3	14	9	8	11	7	5	3	1	22	28	9	5
Bowels, disease of	38	25	9	3	53	37	32	19	19	16	2	6	62	49	10	4
Brain, disease of	232	156	19	12	60	49	70	60	84	56	27	24	142	72	29	25
Brain, softening of	10	8	3	1	3	2	1	2		1	5	2	6	2	1	2
Bronchitis	169	140	4	6	35	35	37	45	25	24	3	1	65	68	8	6
Cancer	99	208	14	31	16	48	25	62	19	25	30	52	66	102	26	23
Canker	6	4	7	2						1	4	1	1		8	13
Carbuncle	9	6			2	2	3	4	2	2			2	1	1	
Cephalitis	439	334	27	17	93	66	330	250	176	112	23	20	231	183	89	71
Child-birth		323		16		113		122		100		27		238		131
Cholera	30	34	3	2	11	6	16	7	6	5	5	3	24	18	4	5
Cholera infantum	191	182	39	30	42	58	64	60	18	25	10	7	99	70	19	16
Chorea		4				1	2	2		1	1	1	1	1		
Cold water									1						1	
Colitis	54	21	3		25	19	29	14	19	14	1	2	62	50	20	11
Consumption	2,567	2,445	254	313	173	217	593	847	221	199	314	465	855	1,254	417	493
Convulsions	345	287	34	18	48	40	77	55	50	41	2	3	191	121	111	87
Croup	736	583	43	25	128	126	489	415	172	126	40	38	339	279	136	123
Cyanosis	1	4		1										1	1	
Cystitis	11	2			1	1	3			1	1		16	4	2	
Debility	172	152	16	12	29	29	30	17	21	14	8	10	36	33	30	21

Delirium tremens	56	9	5	1	8	....	4	1	10-	....	1	....	15	1	7	....
Diarrhœa	218	178	25	16	119	142	118	96	125	79	7	9	191	177	78	53
Diabetes	17	3	3	2	3	2	6	1	7	1	14	3	3	5	6	4
Diptheria	118	128	12	11	....	....	2	2	2	2	4	2	115	155	1	1
Dropsy	497	510	27	33	257	308	209	230	100	122	49	75	469	452	77	82
Dysentery	390	332	32	28	139	138	137	158	169	164	25	23	388	340	139	103
Dyspepsia	52	36	1	1	16	19	20	18	8	1	1	3	40	33	11	1
Enteritis	262	175	18	7	40	24	97	86	73	61	43	28	104	72	71	43
Epilepsy	28	24	6	....	3	3	9	5	2	2	1	1	5	9	9	13
Erysipelas	134	116	5	17	13	4	48	40	23	32	20	10	48	43	33	26
Fever, intermittent	40	33	....	....	28	27	107	116	61	72	1	3	44	24	27	13
Fever, remittent	280	235	9	6	201	199	284	320	254	258	20	19	174	155	85	99
Fever, typhoid	763	579	37	29	333	332	482	436	351	350	111	99	565	491	151	110
Fistula	3	....	1	....	....	....	....	....	....	....	....	....	1	1	1	....
Fits	186	166	14	12	53	42	56	40	32	15	20	22	101	70	60	59
Gastritis	37	24	2	2	11	9	24	33	22	23	6	6	16	24	10	8
Gout	5	....	....	....	....	....	....	....	....	....	....	....	4	1	1	1
Heart, disease of	322	327	36	32	43	53	66	45	30	25	79	71	129	142	38	31
Heat	19	....	....	....	7	2	8	5	5	3	....	....	9	4	8	....
Hemorrhage	67	58	9	7	15	10	30	22	12	14	7	3	46	51	12	8
Hepatitis	14	11	2	1	1	1	4	4	1	1	....	1	....	1	4	3
Hernia	22	6	....	1	10	2	12	2	6	1	....	2	25	7	6	3
Hip disease	8	3	....	....	1	....	....	....	....	....	2	1	5	1	....	....
Hydrocephalus	172	129	34	17	11	13	20	11	9	7	13	15	39	32	38	29
Hydrophobia	3	....	....	....	....	....	....	1	2	1	....	....	....	....	1	1
Hydrothorax	20	23	3	4	20	14	15	5	2	3	6	3	35	17	3	....
Ileus	....	....	....	....	1	....	....	....	....	....	....	....	....	....	....	....
Infantile	256	184	6	14	79	95	103	103	65	50	6	5	252	257	73	56
Inflammation	68	57	5	1	18	10	18	16	24	19	2	3	21	12	22	12
Influenza	3	11	....	....	15	6	6	5	5	6	1	2	9	8	3	5
Insanity	32	21	3	2	3	5	8	3	3	7	1	2	4	8	5	4
Intemperance	54	3	10	4	16	4	45	1	17	....	3	....	73	6	10	....
Intussusception	....	....	1	....	1	....	2	....	....	1	....	....	3	2	....	....
Ischuria	....	....	....	....	....	....	....	....	....	....	....	....	....	....	....	....
Jaundice	32	28	1	2	9	2	9	12	4	4	2	2	24	21	3	7

Table of Mortality, distinguishing by Sex the number of Deaths in the United States, &c.—Continued.

Cause of death.	PENNSYLVANIA.		RHODE ISLAND.		SOUTH CAROLINA.		TENNESSEE.		TEXAS.		VERMONT.		VIRGINIA.		WISCONSIN.	
	Male.	Female.	Male.	Female.	Male.	Female.	Male.	Female.	Male.	Female.	Male.	Female.	Male.	Female.	Male.	Female.
Joints, disease of	......	......	......	......	......	......	......	......	......	......	......	......	......	......	......	......
Kidney, disease of	43	9	2	2	9	2	16	7	13	4	8	......	24	5	3	2
Laryngitis	5	1	1	......	......	......	1	1	1	3	......	1	2	......	......	......
Liver, disease of	120	99	12	9	42	30	46	39	29	24	12	14	65	58	39	36
Lungs, disease of	151	115	8	7	23	30	45	47	42	25	31	39	61	58	54	37
Malformation	6	4	7	5	5	3	6	4	1	1	......	1	3	4	1	2
Marasmus	64	63	8	13	13	13	3	2	1	1	......	......	11	5	2	2
Measles	96	121	......	3	15	34	63	58	59	76	5	5	80	60	29	26
Metritis	......	9	......	......	......	3	......	5	......	3	......	......	......	9	......	......
Mortification	21	12	1	4	2	1	3	1	1	......	5	......	7	7	7	3
Necrosis	11	4	......	......	7	2	8	4	......	1	......	......	7	4	......	1
Nephria	2	......	......	......	......	......	......	......	......	......	......	1	......	......	......	......
Nephritis	8	2	2	2	1	2	3	......	1	......	......	1	5	8	2	......
Neuralgia	50	34	1	1	2	5	19	35	17	11	4	5	14	28	14	17
Old age	398	500	42	64	152	153	154	199	47	61	122	133	379	495	83	80
Ovarian dropsy	......	1	......	......	......	......	......	......	......	......	......	......	......	......	......	......
Paralysis	279	268	21	11	46	52	64	65	16	18	33	39	163	208	22	23
Paramenia	......	3	......	1	......	4	......	11	......	7	......	......	......	6	......	2
Parotitis	2	1	......	......	......	......	......	1	......	3	......	......	8	3	2	......
Pericarditis	3	3	......	......	......	1	......	......	......	......	......	......	......	......	......	1
Peritonitis	1	5	3	5	......	1	......	......	......	1	1	1	2	2	1	......
Phlebitis	1	1	......	1	......	1	......	......	......	......	......	......	......	1	......	......
Pleurisy	72	49	1	5	11	14	12	6	6	8	2	6	60	34	10	5
Pneumonia	626	494	64	72	621	443	690	475	552	412	94	66	956	649	244	186
Prostate, disease of	......	......	......	......	......	......	2	......	......	......	......	......	......	......	......	......
Puerperal fever	......	44	......	3	......	40	......	94	......	39	......	3	......	100	......	14
Purpura and scurvy	4	3	1	1	2	......	3	......	2	1	......	1	5	3	......	......
Quinsy	15	10	......	1	9	6	23	11	35	34	......	......	13	14	5	3

Rheumatism	85	66	6	5	28	15	62	46	28	16	5	5	78	64	27	14
Scarlatina	1,595	1,561	48	42	84	78	452	427	109	112	134	110	294	307	480	417
Scrofula	84	74	5	6	28	29	88	99	24	22	6	9	172	163	20	15
Skin, disease of	19	17	1	....	20	17	92	99	66	48	1	3	44	22	6	1
Smallpox	41	46	7	1	....	....	5	5	....	1	4	7	15	9	8	7
Spina bifida	....	....	....	....	1	....	4	1	....	....	....	....	....	....	....	....
Spine, disease of	56	48	6	4	12	5	24	17	13	7	5	6	45	26	13	3
Splenitis	....	....	....	....	....	1	2	1	2	1	2	....	....	3	....	....
Still-born	59	44	3	1	20	29	54	37	15	20	2	2	79	40	15	6
Stomach, disease of	18	11	....	1	1	....	6	10	2	....	....	....	4	11	3	2
Stone	60	3	....	....	16	3	24	6	7	1	14	....	34	6	11	2
Stricture of urethra	3	....	....	....	3	....	1	....	....	1	....	....	7	1	....	....
Sudden death	44	21	5	1	20	18	27	24	8	4	1	....	43	38	5	6
Syphilis	8	3	2	2	6	7	4	5	1	1	....	....	1	8	....	....
Tabes mesenteria	....	1	....	....	....	....	....	....	....	....	....	....	2	....	....	....
Teething	74	70	21	16	187	173	83	72	105	95	3	1	92	112	50	39
Tetanus	40	23	2	1	49	57	77	34	56	31	....	3	62	32	25	32
Throat, disease of	107	150	2	5	29	33	37	46	17	19	4	3	166	196	20	26
Thrush	8	9	....	2	11	7	17	14	5	5	1	....	37	30	3	....
Tumor	26	31	1	3	4	1	7	8	1	2	6	9	6	10	2	3
Ulcers	11	13	....	....	6	4	13	12	1	1	2	1	10	7	3	6
Ulcer of intestines	1	4	....	....	2	....	1	1	1	....	2	....	....	1	2	....
Unknown	982	833	56	66	608	568	1,018	995	619	593	88	75	1,881	1,786	328	237
Uterus, disease of	....	3	....	1	....	5	....	20	....	16	....	2	....	7	....	3
Whooping cough	224	253	33	27	173	165	122	169	77	77	15	17	412	509	63	49
Worms	19	19	1	4	76	62	49	48	31	24	3	1	71	93	13	6
Yellow fever	....	....	....	....	2	....	1	....	327	103	....	....	2	....	....	....
Totals	15,138	13,708	1,174	1,167	4,612	4,501	7,240	7,108	4,633	4,056	1,567	1,673	10,699	10,512	3,574	3,157
Aggregates	28,846		2,341		9,113		14,348		8,689		3,240		21,211		6,731	
Total of violent deaths	1,368		138		632		828		680		115		1,263		398	
Grand totals	30,214		2,479		9,745		15,176		9,369		3,355		22,474		7,129	

Table of Mortality, distinguishing by Sex the number of Deaths in the United States, &c.—Continued.

Causes of death.	DAKOTA.		NEBRASKA.		NEW MEXICO.		UTAH.		WASHINGTON.		TOTALS.		Grand totals.
	Male.	Female.	Male.	Female.	Male.	Female.	Male.	Female.	Male.	Female.	Male.	Female.	
Abscess	....	....	1	....	....	2	....	....	....	....	329	215	544
Abscess, lumbar	....	....	....	....	....	....	....	....	....	....	19	4	23
Anæmia	....	....	....	....	....	....	....	....	....	....	21	18	39
Angina pectoris	....	....	....	....	....	....	....	....	....	....	4	2	6
Aneurism	....	....	....	....	....	....	....	....	....	....	33	11	44
Apoplexy	....	....	....	3	7	4	....	1	....	....	1,776	1,302	3,078
Ascites	....	....	....	....	....	....	....	....	....	....	43	10	53
Asthma	....	....	1	....	7	5	....	....	....	....	358	312	670
Bowels, disease of	....	....	....	....	2	3	....	2	....	....	904	708	1,612
Brain, disease of	....	....	2	2	6	3	1	1	....	1	3,219	2,326	5,545
Brain, softening of	....	....	....	....	....	....	....	....	....	....	110	54	164
Bronchitis	....	....	1	....	4	1	....	....	....	....	1,053	867	1,920
Cancer	....	....	1	2	2	2	....	....	....	....	1,228	2,064	3,292
Canker	....	....	2	1	....	....	10	5	....	....	231	230	461
Carbuncle	....	....	....	....	....	....	....	....	....	....	63	35	98
Cephalitis	....	....	8	13	3	2	6	2	1	1	5,762	4,573	10,335
Child-birth	....	....	....	3	....	40	....	7	....	3	....	4,065	4,065
Cholera	1	....	....	....	4	2	....	....	....	....	595	390	985
Cholera infantum	1	....	....	2	1	....	4	....	....	....	2,579	2,225	4,804
Chorea	....	....	....	....	....	....	....	....	....	....	21	35	56
Cold water	....	....	....	....	....	....	....	....	....	....	5	....	5
Colitis	....	....	....	....	2	....	....	....	....	....	713	447	1,160
Consumption	....	....	13	15	18	16	8	10	2	6	23,029	25,942	48,971
Convulsions	....	....	5	2	....	....	4	1	....	2	2,961	2,280	5,241
Croup	....	....	2	1	7	2	13	10	3	3	8,232	6,956	15,188
Cyanosis	....	....	....	....	....	....	....	....	....	....	11	20	31
Cystitis	....	....	....	....	6	1	....	....	....	....	149	31	180
Debility	....	....	....	1	2	1	1	1	....	1	1,075	1,067	2,142

Delirium tremens			1								520	56	576
Diarrhœa			3	2	6	2	5	5			4,337	3,510	7,847
Diabetes							1				289	95	384
Diptheria			1	2							788	875	1,663
Dropsy			2	3	21	20		3		2	5,804	6,230	12,034
Dysentery			6	6	12	13	3	5	1		5,620	4,841	10,461
Dyspepsia			1		4	2		1			517	319	836
Enteritis			5	3	4	7	17	7	1		2,791	2,268	5,059
Epilepsy					1	1			1		285	217	502
Erysipelas			1	2	3	2	2	1			1,460	1,296	2,756
Fever, intermittent			12	15	8	1					2,392	2,055	4,447
Fever, remittent			13	8	98	94	4	4			5,760	5,342	11,102
Fever, typhoid			10	8	3	3	2	6			10,321	8,886	19,207
Fistula											30	7	37
Fits			4	3	1	1	1	2			2,057	1,778	3,835
Gastritis				1	7	4					478	540	1,018
Gout											33	8	41
Heart, disease of			1	1	9	6	1	1	1		3,453	2,952	6,405
Heat			1		2						299	61	360
Hemorrhage			1	1	2	2					741	577	1,318
Hepatitis											118	82	200
Hernia											260	100	360
Hip disease											75	47	122
Hydrocephalus			1	1			3				1,880	1,535	3,415
Hydrophobia						1					27	12	39
Hydrothorax			2								309	257	566
Ileus											3	1	4
Infantile			9	6	8	5	37	20			3,364	2,848	6,212
Inflammation				1	14		3	7			726	596	1,322
Influenza				1		1	1				194	193	387
Insanity											251	200	451
Intemperance			1		7						840	88	928
Intussusception											29	12	41
Ischuria											4		4
Jaundice				1		1					367	314	681
Joints, disease of											10	4	14

Table of Mortality, distinguishing by Sex the number of Deaths in the United States, &c.—Continued.

Causes of death.	DAKOTA.		NEBRASKA.		NEW MEXICO.		UTAH.		WASHINGTON.		TOTALS.		Grand totals.
	Male.	Female.	Male.	Female.	Male.	Female.	Male.	Female.	Male.	Female.	Male.	Female.	
Kidney, disease of					1	1					540	124	664
Laryngitis											48	26	74
Liver, disease of				1	11	3	3	1	1		1,464	1,165	2,629
Lungs, disease of			2		7	2	2				1,999	1,576	3,575
Malformation											76	55	131
Marasmus						1					444	416	860
Measles			1	2			1				1,937	1,963	3,900
Metritis				1		1						100	100
Mortification			1			1			1		185	95	280
Necrosis						1					142	71	213
Nephria											17	11	28
Nephritis											89	34	123
Neuralgia			1		1	4					418	491	909
Old age			2	1	11	14	2	1	1		4,895	5,992	10,887
Ovarian dropsy												9	9
Paralysis			2		1	2	2		1		2,308	2,319	4,627
Paramenia						5						157	157
Parotitis											75	47	122
Pericarditis											27	22	49
Peritonitis											49	64	113
Phlebitis											12	14	26
Pleurisy					38	46		1			728	534	1,262
Pneumonia			20	13		2	4	2	1		15,804	11,272	27,076
Prostate, disease of											7		7
Puerperal fever				1								1,097	1,097
Purpura and scurvy					2						52	27	79
Quinsy					1		3				367	361	728
Rheumatism					10	7		1			1,101	772	1,873

Scarlatina			3	7	1	1	2		1	2	13,217	13,176	26,393
Scrofula			1	1		1					1,389	1,294	2,683
Skin, disease of			1	1	2	1	1	1			981	771	1,752
Smallpox				1		1					729	534	1,263
Spina bifida											8	7	15
Spine, disease of					1						609	454	1,063
Splenitis											47	29	76
Still-born					2	2					926	691	1,617
Stomach, disease of					4	6					134	133	267
Stone					1	1					606	67	673
Stricture of urethra					1						48	11	59
Sudden death					1						469	347	816
Syphilis						2					138	93	231
Tabes mesenteria											29	22	51
Teething			2				6	5		1	2,564	2,345	4,909
Tetanus					1	1					994	624	1,618
Throat, disease of			1		11	2		1			1,646	1,851	3,497
Thrush							1				282	272	554
Tumor					4	2					256	355	611
Ulcers					1	3	1				200	171	371
Ulcer of intestines									1		38	36	74
Unknown	1	1	23	18	151	157	18	31		1	19,151	17,497	36,648
Uterus, disease of						1						246	246
Whooping cough			9	12	5	10					3,825	4,575	8,400
Worms				1	1			1	1		1,045	958	2,003
Yellow fever											502	155	657
Totals	3	1	180	170	551	531	173	147	18	23	193,572	179,919	373,491
Aggregates	4		350		1,082		320		41		373,491		
Total of violent deaths			31		223		54		9		20,115		
Grand totals	4		381		1,305		374		50		393,606		

TABLE NO. 6.—

DEATHS.	Alabama.		Arkansas.		California.		Connecticut.		Delaware.		District of Columbia.	
	M.	F.	M.	F.	M.	F.	M.	F.	M.	F.	M.	F.
I. ACCIDENTAL:												
Accidents not specified..	103	35	79	9	126	2	61	9	10	2	6	.....
Burns and scalds........	90	152	26	35	16	17	13	34	3	5	2	3
Drowning	61	12	38	9	87	8	47	6	15	1	7	......
Fall	27	7	13	4	15	4	10	5	5	2	3	1
Fire-arms	36	2	22	1	43	.....	7	1	1	......	6	.....
Freezing	2	......	4	......	2	.....	.....	....	......	1	.....	......
Lightning	3	6	1	2	......	.....	2	......	......	......	......	......
Neglect and exposure....	1	......	2	2	2	......	2	......	......	......	......	......
Poison	20	14	14	9	12	3	6	2	1	2	3	1
Railroad..............	7	......	......	......	1	.....	9	3	1	......	.....	....
Strangulation	10	4	1	2	1	.....	1	3	.....	......	...	......
Suffocation	135	121	35	36	5	1	5	3	1	.....	1	......
Total accidents	495	353	235	109	310	35	163	66	37	13	28	5
II. SUICIDE:												
Cutting throat	......	......	......	......	5	.....	2	......	.....	.....	......	.....
Drowning	......	1	1	......	.....	.....	2	3	......	......	......	......
Fire-arms..............	3	.....	......	......	12	.....	2	.....	......	......	1	......
Hanging...............	10	1	......	......	5	1	5	......	1	......	.....	......
Poison	2	.....	1	1	6	3	5	3	.....	......	......	......
Strangulation..........	......	......	......	......	.....	......	......	......	.....	......	......	......
Suicides not specified ...	3	1	.....	......	6	......	9	......	1	......	1	.....
Total suicides.......	18	3	2	1	34	4	25	6	2	......	2	......
III. HOMICIDE	17	......	8	......	40	1	1	.....	2	......	......	......
IV. MURDER	18	......	17	3	31	3	3	2	1	1	......	......
V. EXECUTED	1	......	2	......	4	......	......	......	1	......	......	......
Total violent deaths..	549	356	264	113	419	43	192	74	43	14	30	5

Violent Deaths.

Florida.		Georgia.		Illinois.		Indiana.		Iowa.		Kansas.		Kentucky.		Louisiana.	
M.	F.	M.	F.	M.	F.	M.	F.	M.	F.	M.	F.	M.	F.	M.	F.
10	5	102	30	168	23	130	24	70	9	13	2	130	23	134	23
18	28	121	195	79	69	63	86	25	41	6	11	72	84	52	82
14	2	40	15	102	19	75	10	47	8	6	1	82	15	103	12
3	1	32	14	42	13	22	14	15	6	1	......	42	18	31	5
8	......	23	......	30	3	11	3	11	2	9	......	35	1	46	1
......	1	6	1	3	......	2	......	6	......	......	......	4	......	2	1
......	2	4	1	16	2	1	3	7	1	2	......	4	1	2	2
......	......	8	5	2	2	1	......	......	......	......	......	1	2	3	......
3	4	18	16	34	33	37	26	15	9	3	2	37	28	29	13
5	......	11	......	33	7	27	2	2	......	......	......	9	2	1	......
1	2	10	5	11	3	10	4	7	4	......	......	7	3	1	3
7	5	125	146	5	3	4	6	2	2	......	......	79	51	34	39
69	50	500	428	525	177	383	178	207	82	40	16	502	228	438	181
1	......	1	......	2	......	1	......	......	......	......	......	......	......	2	......
......	......	......	......	......	2	......	......	1	......	......	......	1	2	3	1
......	......	3	......	8	......	4	......	3	......	......	1	5	......	5	......
1	......	2	3	11	3	6	1	5	1	1	......	14	2	3	......
2	......	1	1	4	......	3	......	5	1	1	2	1	......	1	1
......	......	......	......	......	......	......	......	......	......	......	......	......	......	......	......
......	......	7	3	9	5	7	3	......	2	1	......	6	1	4	1
4	......	14	7	34	10	21	4	14	4	3	3	27	5	18	3
4	......	15	5	12	1	8	......	5	......	8	1	30	......	15	2
5	......	17	2	22	1	8	1	4	......	7	......	23	1	29	3
7	......	1	......	......	......	......	......	1	......	......	......	2	......	3	......
89	50	547	442	593	189	420	183	231	86	58	20	584	234	503	189

TABLE No. 6—*Violent*

DEATHS.	Maine.		Maryland.		Massachusetts.		Michigan.		Minnesota.		Mississippi.	
	M.	F.	M.	F.	M.	F.	M.	F.	M.	F.	M.	F.
I. ACCIDENTAL:												
Accidents not specified..	45	4	51	10	140	88	96	12	16	1	113	36
Burns and scalds........	26	25	29	43	48	62	32	46	8	10	65	108
Drowning..............	139	13	48	8	218	27	84	18	32	9	45	12
Fall..................	33	10	14	3	69	15	26	11	1	......	15	6
Fire-arms..............	5	1	10	1	8	......	20	2	2	1	28	6
Freezing...............	2	1	2	......	1	......	12	......	2	......	9	1
Lightning..............	......	2	5	......	1	......	2	2	1	1	8	4
Neglect and exposure...	2	2	2	......	6	11	2	......	......	......	8	6
Poison.................	5	2	7	2	6	7	9	3	2	1	22	15
Railroad...............	8	1	13	......	44	8	11	......	......	......	7	1
Strangulation..........	3	......	5	1	4	2	4	2	......	1	9	3
Suffocation............	......	......	9	6	12	5	2	......	1	......	116	123
Total accidents.......	268	61	195	74	557	225	300	96	65	24	445	321
II. SUICIDE:												
Cutting throat.........	3	......	1	......	7	1	......	2	......	......	......	......
Drowning...............	4	3	1	......	4	4	......	......	......	......	2	1
Fire-arms..............	......	......	1	......	7	......	2	......	......	......	3	......
Hanging................	12	4	2	2	19	2	14	2	3	......	2	1
Poison.................	3	1	......	......	8	5	5	1	......	......	......	1
Strangulation..........	......	......	......	......	2	......	......	......	......	......	......	......
Suicides not specified...	2	1	6	2	43	8	8	2	1	......	8	3
Total suicides........	24	9	11	4	90	20	29	7	4	......	15	6
III. HOMICIDE..........	4	......	4	......	6	8	5	......	3	1	21	1
IV. MURDER.............	1	......	4	1	5	......	2	2	2	......	5	......
V. EXECUTED............	......	......	......	......	......	......	......	......	......	1	2	......
Total violent deaths...	297	70	214	79	658	253	336	105	74	26	488	328

Deaths—Continued.

Missouri.		New Hampshire.		New Jersey.		New York.		North Carolina.		Ohio.		Oregon.		Pennsylvania.	
M.	F.	M.	F.	M.	F.	M.	F.	M.	F.	M.	F.	M.	F.	M.	F.
125	23	30	7	63	7	467	72	74	15	216	39	1	......	342	34
75	77	6	10	34	40	155	186	80	149	105	121	3	1	149	125
79	15	34	2	71	8	353	41	51	8	140	28	3	2	225	45
30	18	10	4	22	5	166	37	20	7	81	23	......	......	101	14
33	5	4	1	4	1	39	2	14	2	38	1	......	......	33	......
3	......	1	......	3	......	10	1	5	.....	4	......	......	......	7	......
10	2	1	1	1	......	7	1	6	2	7	1	......	......	5	3
5	......	3	......	1	......	15	7	5	......	6	3	......	......	6	5
36	21	3	.....	5	3	34	30	14	9	23	22	......	1	22	8
11	1	4	......	24	6	96	10	2	2	53	1	......	......	96	8
10	7	1	1	1	3	15	5	10	7	9	6	......	......	9	10
37	38	1	......	3	6	21	12	88	95	6	2	......	......	7	5
454	207	98	26	232	79	1,378	404	369	296	688	247	7	4	1,002	257
1	......	5	......	......	2	9	1	2	1	3	......	......	......	7	3
1	1	3	1	1	......	2	5	......	......	4	.....	......	......	4	1
4	....	2	.....	2	......	8	1	2	......	3	1	......	......	5	......
10	2	12	1	8	1	36	6	2	1	9	3	......	......	26	7
4	......	2	1	1	2	10	10	3	......	4	1	......	......	10	4
......	......	......	......	......	......	......	......	......	......	......	1	......	......	......	......
5	2	3	1	5	2	31	11	3	1	14	4	1	......	15	1
25	5	27	4	17	7	96	34	12	3	37	10	1	......	67	16
26	......	......	......	2	......	19	2	6	1	18	3	5	......	17	......
21	1	......	2	3	......	13	......	15	1	11	......	2	......	8	1
......	......	......	.....	2	......	3	......	2	......	......	......	3	......	......	.....
526	213	125	32	256	86	1,509	440	404	301	754	260	18	4	1,094	274

TABLE No. 6.—*Violent*

DEATHS.	Rhode Island.		South Carolina.		Tennessee.		Texas.		Vermont.		Virginia.	
	M.	F.	M.	F.	M.	F.	M.	F.	M.	F.	M.	F.
I. ACCIDENTAL:												
Accidents not specified..	26	1	80	24	112	20	79	91	21	2	164	42
Burns and scalds........	8	16	82	124	64	108	37	74	11	14	142	231
Drowning	28	7	47	24	42	14	60	12	18	5	108	20
Fall	10	2	26	13	27	7	30	6	6	3	41	22
Fire-arms	1	......	11	......	35	3	49	2	1	......	33	1
Freezing	2	......	1	1	4	2	9	1	......	1	7	......
Lightning	......	......	6	6	2	1	7	1	1	......	11	6
Neglect and exposure ...	2	2	......	6	7	......	4	6	......	......	2	1
Poison	4	5	8	7	33	33	25	19	1	4	34	22
Railroad	4	1	7	1	12	......	1	1	2	......	15	......
Strangulation	1	1	7	2	9	3	5	4	1	......	21	5
Suffocation	......	......	56	74	111	101	39	38	1	2	139	122
Total accidents.....	86	35	331	282	458	292	345	183	63	31	717	427
II. SUICIDE:												
Cutting throat	......	......	......	......	1	......	......	......	1	......	2	......
Drowning	2	1	1	......	3	......	......	......	......	1	......	2
Fire-arms	2	......	......	......	8	1	6	......	......	......	6	......
Hanging	1	......	2	......	5	......	4	1	7	3	5	6
Poison	2	3	......	......	2	2	3	2	6	......	3	......
Strangulation	......	......	......	......	......	......	......	......	......	......	......	......
Suicides not specified ...	2	1	4	1	6	2	14	......	3	......	5	2
Total suicides	9	5	7	1	25	5	27	3	17	4	21	10
III. HOMICIDE	......	......	3	......	19	......	53	3	......	......	9	3
IV. MURDER	3	......	3	2	20	1	62	3	......	......	19	3
V. EXECUTED	......	......	3	......	7	1	1	......	......	......	7	2
Total violent deaths.	98	40	347	285	529	299	488	192	80	35	773	490

NOTES.

Under "accidents not specified," are included deaths of 20 males and 57 females by the fall of Pemberton Mills, at Lawrence, Massachusetts.

Under accidental deaths by "poison," are counted deaths of 3 males and 2 females by arsenic, 3 males by corrosive sublimate, and 9 males and 3 females by strychnine.

Deaths—Continued.

Wisconsin.		Dakota.		Nebraska.		New Mexico.		Utah.		Washington.		Total.		Aggregate.
M.	F.	M.	F.	M.	F.	M.	F.	M.	F.	M.	F.	M.	F.	M. & F.
75	10	......	......	5	......	12	2	7	......	......	......	3,502	664	4,166
41	41	......	......	1	3	7	16	4	5	......	......	1,798	2,477	4,275
88	11	......	......	2	3	7	4	9	5	5	......	2,660	459	3,119
25	1	......	......	......	1	2	1	1	......	1	......	1,018	303	1,321
......	1	......	......	6	1	15	......	6	1	1	......	684	46	730
6	1	......	......	......	1	4	......	......	......	......	......	125	14	139
3	2	......	......	1	......	5	3	2	......	......	......	134	58	192
......	......	......	......	1	......	3	......	......	......	1	......	103	60	163
20	14	......	......	3	1	4	......	......	......	......	......	552	391	943
28	......	......	......	......	......	......	......	......	......	......	......	544	55	599
3	1	......	......	......	......	1	......	......	......	......	......	188	97	285
2	3	......	......	......	......	2	......	......	......	......	......	1,091	1,045	2,136
291	85	......	......	19	10	62	26	29	11	8	......	12,399	5,669	18,068
1	......	......	......	......	......	......	......	......	......	......	......	57	10	67
......	2	......	......	......	......	......	......	......	......	......	......	40	31	71
1	......	......	......	......	......	1	......	......	......	......	......	109	4	113
6	1	......	......	......	......	......	......	......	......	......	......	249	55	304
1	......	......	......	......	......	......	......	......	1	......	......	99	46	145
......	......	......	......	......	......	......	......	......	......	......	......	2	1	3
5	1	......	......	......	......	......	......	......	......	......	......	238	61	299
14	4	......	......	......	......	1	......	......	1	......	......	794	208	1,002
2	......	......	......	2	......	23	......	13	......	1	......	426	32	458
1	1	......	......	......	......	94	12	......	......	......	......	479	47	526
......	......	......	......	......	......	5	......	......	......	......	......	57	4	61
308	90	......	......	21	10	185	38	42	12	9	......	14,155	5,960	20,115

NOTE.

Among the suicides by "poison," are included 3 males and 3 females by arsenic, 1 male by corrosive sublimate, and 12 males and 3 females by strychnine.

Table No. 7.

Table showing the number of Deaf and Dumb in the United States and Territories, according to the Eighth Census, 1860.

STATES.	DEAF AND DUMB.	
	Free.	Slave.
Alabama	235	67
Arkansas	127	15
California	68	....
Connecticut	473	....
Delaware	57	1
Florida	18	9
Georgia	345	83
Illinois	801	....
Indiana	691	....
Iowa	282	....
Kansas	30	....
Kentucky	641	75
Louisiana	215	38
Maine	354	....
Maryland	246	35
Massachusetts	512	....
Michigan	335	....
Minnesota	33	....
Mississippi	164	55
Missouri	520	46
New Hamphsire	212	....
New Jersey	282	....
New York	2,077	....
North Carolina	440	106
Ohio	1,171	....
Oregon	16	....
Pennsylvania	1,587	....
Rhode Island	62	....
South Carolina	170	59
Tennessee	422	73
Texas	180	24
Vermont	180	....
Virginia	768	121
Wisconsin	378	....
TERRITORIES.		
District of Columbia	54	1
Dakota	....	....
Nebraska	15	....
New Mexico	85	....
Utah	14	....
Washington	9	....
	14,269	808 14,269
Total	....	15,077

TABLE No. 8.

Value of Agricultural Implements produced in the United States during the year ending June 1, 1860.

States and Territories.	Value of products in 1850.	Value of products in 1860.	Per cent. increase.
Maine	$259,787	*$339,180	30.5
New Hampshire	119,096	*134,935	12.4
Vermont	133,355	157,647	10.7
Massachusetts	820,141	*1,740,943	112.2
Rhode Island	72,000	*117,845	63.6
Connecticut	258,047	266,162	3.1
Total in New England States	1,662,426	2,756,712	65.8
New York	1,266,276	3,429,037	170.8
Pennsylvania	853,513	1,455,760	70.5
New Jersey	72,636	198,211	172.9
Delaware	15,175	90,581	49.7
Maryland	257,656	318,980	23.8
District of Columbia	6,550	....	....
Total in Middle States	2,471,806	5,492,569	122.2
Ohio	557,932	2,690,943	382.3
Indiana	146,025	709,645	386.1
Michigan	30,600	412,192	1250.3
Illinois	761,970	2,552,165	235.0
Wisconsin	187,335	563,855	201.0
Minnesota	....	17,000	....
Iowa	17,900	112,590	529.0
Missouri	37,550	280,037	645.7
Kentucky	184,615	597,118	245.1
Kansas	....	20,000	....
Total in Western States	1,923,927	7,955,545	313.7
Virginia	213,906	339,959	58.9
North Carolina	32,930	40,000	21.4
South Carolina	29,939	4,800	Decrease.
Georgia	228,837	252,075	10.1
Florida	....	17,600	....
Alabama	34,500	†583,678	16.9
Louisiana	25,610	86,408	237.5
Texas	....	140,000	Decrease.
Mississippi	109,260	94,283	Decrease.
Arkansas	11,900	5,700	Decrease.
Tennessee	97,570	17,980	Decrease.
Total in Southern States	784,452	1,582,483	101.7
California	....	9,375	....
Oregon	....	5,830	....
Total in Pacific States	....	15,205	....
Aggregate in United States	6,842,611	17,802,514	160.1

* Including forks, shovels, and scythes. † This amount includes $418,925 worth of cotton gins.

TABLE No. 9.—*Statistics of Pig Iron produced in the United States during the year ending June* 1, 1860.

States.	Tons of ore mined.	Tons of pig iron.	Value.
New Hampshire	1,000	3,224	$92,910
Vermont	4,500		
Massachusetts	25,000	13,700	403,000
Connecticut	20,700	11,000	379,500
New York	176,375	63,145	1,385,208
Pennsylvania	1,706,476	553,560	*11,427,379
New Jersey	57,800	29,048	574,820
Maryland	79,200	30,500	739,600
Ohio	228,794	94,647	2,327,261
Indiana	....	375	9,375
Michigan	17,900	10,400	291,400
Wisconsin	4,500	2,000	40,000
Missouri	42,000	22,000	575,000
Kentucky	73,600	23,362	534,164
Virginia	23,217	9,096	251,173
Tennessee	53,220	18,417	457,000
Total	2,514,282	884,474	19,487,790
Product in 1850	....	....	13,491,898
Increase, (44.4 per cent.)	....	....	5,995,892

* Pennsylvania makes 62.5 per cent. of the quantity, and 58.6 per cent. of the value of the whole production.

TABLE No. 10.—*Statement of quantity and value of Bar and other Rolled Iron made in the United States during the year ending June* 1, 1860.

States.	Tons.	Value.
Maine	5,300	$332,000
New Hampshire	70	7,000
Massachusetts	20,285	1,291,200
Vermont	1,100	63,250
Connecticut	2,060	175,500
New York	38,275	2,215,250
New Jersey	25,006	1,370,725
Pennsylvania	259,709	12,643,500
Maryland	7,000	556,000
Ohio	10,439	692,000
Indiana	2,000	105,000
Missouri	4,678	535,000
Kentucky	6,200	514,000
Tennessee	5,024	483,248
North Carolina	1,007	92,948
Virginia	17,870	1,147,425
South Carolina	275	24,750
Total	406,298	22,248,796
Product in 1850	....	15,938,786
Increase, (39.5 per cent.)	....	6,310,010

TABLE No. 11.

Value of Steam Engines and Machinery produced in the United States during the year ending June 1, 1860.

States and Territories.	Value of product in 1850.	Value of product in 1860.	Per cent. increase.
Maine	$648,180	$681,295	5.1
New Hampshire	606,170	898,560	48.0
Vermont	363,494	493,836	36.0
Massachusetts	5,220,482	5,131,238	Decrease.
Rhode Island	1,210,728	1,068,825	Decrease.
Connecticut	735,455	1,953,535	165.0
Total in New England States	8,784,509	10,227,289	16.4
New York	8,422,744	10,484,863	24.0
Pennsylvania	4,214,213	7,243,453	71.1
New Jersey	890,123	3,215,673	260.0
Delaware	301,044	550,500	82.0
Maryland	910,100	1,285,000	41.0
District of Columbia	17,000	130,583	668.0
Total in Middle States	14,755,224	22,910,072	55.2
Ohio	2,153,297	4,855,005	120.0
Indiana	215,970	426,805	97.0
Michigan	329,050	309,082	Decrease.
Illinois	247,595	307,500	24.0
Wisconsin	124,790	384,600	208.0
Iowa	6,200	186,720	2911.0
Missouri	228,675	719,500	210.0
Kentucky	319,740	1,004,664	214.0
Kansas	....	40,000	....
Total in Western States	3,625,317	8,233,876	127.1
Virginia	439,455	1,478,036	236.0
North Carolina	34,300	92,750	170.0
South Carolina	73,400	462,192	529.0
Georgia	69,000	375,325	443.9
Florida	....	31,000	....
Alabama	140,075	524,350	274.0
Louisiana	....	318,400	....
Texas	5,850	55,000	840.0
Mississippi	30,000	528,000	1660.0
Arkansas	9,600	21,750	126.0
Tennessee	31,604	174,000	450.0
Total in Southern States	833,284	4,060,803	387.3
Utah	....	15,000	....
California	....	1,600,510	....
Oregon	....	71,000	....
Total in Pacific States	....	1,686,510	....
Aggregate	27,998,334	47,118,550	68.2

TABLE No. 12.

Statistics of Iron Founding in the United States during the year ending June 1, 1860.

States	Value in 1850.	Value in 1860.
Maine	$309,671	$429,896
New Hampshire	256,129	379,923
Vermont	413,501	296,430
Massachusetts	1,921,895	1,801,035
Rhode Island	195,700	336,600
Connecticut	851,888	752,895
Total in New England States	3,948,784	3,996,779
New York	5,912,698	8,216,124
Pennsylvania	3,092,347	4,977,793
New Jersey	1,016,151	2,203,338
Delaware	156,462	640,000
Maryland	515,862	742,876
District of Columbia	41,296	94,400
Total in Middle States	10,734,816	16,874,531
Ohio	2,484,878	1,650,323
Indiana	296,080	168,575
Michigan	61,000	383,002
Illinois	347,180	605,428
Wisconsin	114,214	377,301
Iowa	8,800	187,435
Missouri	341,495	1,041,520
Kentucky	186,340	757,400
Total in Western States	3,839,987	5,170,984
Virginia	409,836	809,955
North Carolina	48,577	56,650
South Carolina	96,959	5,000
Georgia	99,040	79,000
Florida	....	63,000
Alabama	238,500	142,480
Louisiana	312,500	525,800
Texas	60,500	70,877
Mississippi	84,400	147,550
Arkansas	....	52,000
Tennessee	235,618	552,050
Total in Southern States	6,587,930	2,504,362
Aggregate in United States	20,111,517	28,546,656
Increase, (42 per cent.)	....	8,435,139

TABLE No. 13.—*Statistics of Coal produced in the United States during the year ending June 1, 1860.*

STATES.	BITUMINOUS.		ANTHRACITE.	
	Bushels.	Value.	Tons.	Value.
Rhode Island	95,000	$28,500	1,000	$5,000
Pennsylvania	66,994,295	2,833,859	*9,397,332	11,869,574
Maryland	14,200,000	464,338	....	....
Ohio	28,339,900	1,539,713	....	....
Indiana	379,035	27,000	....	....
Illinois	14,258,120	964,187	....	....
Iowa	72,500	6,500	....	....
Missouri	97,000	8,200	....	....
Kentucky	6,732,000	476,800	....	....
Virginia	9,542,627	690,188	....	....
Georgia	48,000	4,800	....	....
Alabama	10,000	1,200	....	....
Tennessee	3,474,100	413,662	....	....
Washington Territory	134,350	32,244	....	....
	144,376,927	7,491,191	9,398,332	11,874,574

Anthracite—tons	9,398,332	$11,874,574
Bituminous—tons	5,775,077	7,491,191
Aggregate tons	15,173,409	19,365,765
Value of coal mined in 1850		7,173,750
Increase, (169.9 per cent.)		12,192,015

* Of bituminous coal, Pennsylvania produced 46.4 per cent. of the quantity, and 37.8 per cent. of the value of the whole; of all kinds of coal, 75.9 per cent. of the whole value.

TABLE No. 14.—*Statistics of Copper and other metals mined in the United States during the year ending June 1, 1860.*

STATES.	NICKEL.		ZINC.		LEAD.		COPPER.	
	Tons of ore.	Value.	Tons of ore.	Value.	Tons of ore.	Value.	Tons of ore.	Value.
New York	....	....	....	....	....	$800	....	....
Pennsylvania	2,348	$28,176	11,800	$72,600	....	....	70	$2,450
Maryland	....	....	....	....	....	....	1,500	60,000
Michigan	....	....	....	....	....	....	6,283	2,292,186
Illinois	....	....	....	....	....	72,953	....	....
Wisconsin	....	....	....	....	....	325,368	....	....
Iowa	....	....	....	....	....	160,500	....	....
Missouri	....	....	....	....	4,164	356,660	50	6,000
Virginia	....	....	....	....	....	61,000	1,500	31,880
North Carolina	....	....	....	....	....	....	2,000	105,000
Tennessee	....	....	....	....	....	....	2,379	404,000
New Mexico	....	....	....	....	....	....	650	415,000
Total.	2,348	28,176	11,800	72,600	....	977,281	14,432	3,316,516

TABLE No. 15.

Statistics of Printing in the following States during the year ending June 1, 1860

States.	Books.	Jobs.	Newspapers.	Value in 1860.	Value in 1850.
Maine	$54,000	$63,836	$177,103	$294,939	$119,988
New Hampshire	....	120,080	124,790	244,879	44,706
Vermont	9,975	36,450	53,276	99,701	19,980
Massachusetts	397,500	529,347	1,979,069	2,905,916	1,493,232
Connecticut	487,900	36,000	117,600	641,500	577,850
Rhode Island	20,500	70,062	114,700	205,262	....
New York	6,920,102	2,574,529	13,422,254	22,916,385	6,163,809
New Jersey	24,163	43,469	149,638	217,270	36,142
Pennsylvania	2,264,250	1,905,205	2,112,132	6,281,587	1,717,612
Delaware	....	81,400	23,932	105,332	....
Maryland	58,000	122,800	169,355	350,155	379,569
District of Columbia	635,000	39,500	104,000	778,500	77,736
Michigan	4,200	83,281	122,248	209,729	20,000
Illinois	13,900	327,925	412,148	753,973	18,475
Wisconsin	15,419	74,070	90,955	180,444	28,698
Iowa	15,000	76,077	49,136	140,213	5,450
Missouri	10,000	119,753	139,996	269,749	22,150
Kentucky	64,000	49,500	191,100	304,600	131,200
Ohio	673,800	632,606	844,377	2,150,783	357,565
Indiana	....	62,123	73,292	135,415	92,648
Tennessee	175,750	133,200	182,270	491,220	45,895
Aggregate	11,843,459	7,181,213	20,653,371	39,678,043	11,352,705

TABLE No. 16.

Statistics of Sewing Machines produced in the United States during the year ending June 1, 1860.

STATES	No. of establishments.	Capital invested in real and personal estate in the business.	Value of raw material, including fuel.	AVERAGE NUMBER OF HANDS EMPLOYED.		Cost of labor.	Number of machines.	Value.
				Male.	Fem.			
New Hampshire	5	$20,350	$25,160	97	.....	$39,540	6,000	$134,500
Vermont	......	25,000	8,320	40	......	19,200	3,500	42,000
Massachusetts	......	253,000	61,171	509	8	244,560	21,400	1,067,300
Rhode Island	1	35,000	6,745	60	......	21,600	6,000	90,000
Connecticut	......	420,000	162,450	679	......	443,400	39,268	2,784,600
New York	19	368,200	212,440	412	......	132,720	27,230	1,043,805
Pennsylvania	12	212,500	52,598	240	20	115,440	5,149	249,355
Ohio	8	46,200	36,072	114	......	40,776	7,283	178,785
Delaware	1	10,000	2,875	15	......	6,000	500	15,000
Aggregate	46	1,390,250	567,831	2,166	28	1,063,236	116,330	5,605,345

TABLE No. 17.

Clothing made in the following States during the year ending June 1, 1860.

STATES.	Number of establishments.	Capital invested, in real and personal estate, in the business.	Raw material used, including fuel.	AVERAGE NUMBER OF HANDS EMPLOYED.		Annual cost of labor.	ANNUAL PRODUCTS.	
				Male.	Female.		Value in 1850.	Value in 1860.
Maine	93	$352,750	$940,709	258	2,218	$359,324	$917,311	$1,632,946
New Hampshire	67	144,180	334,589	136	1,046	212,664	616,233	669,044
Vermont	39	72,100	131,899	83	239	68,832	124,560	250,669
Massachusetts	194	1,303,100	4,084,771	1,503	3,180	1,134,400	8,757,156	6,440,671
Rhode Island	65	316,700	604,831	398	970	268,260	422,372	1,138,086
Connecticut	57	337,000	782,105	406	1,085	275,604	1,519,433	1,338,985
New York	842	8,028,811	14,341,094	14,576	17,732	6,265,015	16,007,534	24,969,852
Pennsylvania	667	5,325,088	6,244,185	7,776	10,152	2,911,612	6,988,498	12,192,603
New Jersey	137	1,592,775	2,232,145	2,224	4,922	1,164,854	2,484,594	3,975,436
Delaware	20	69,675	102,208	64	167	46,176	83,602	179,840
Maryland	148	1,266,150	1,909,676	2,233	3,779	931,056	2,694,377	3,256,716
District of Columbia	34	125,150	191,668	150	177	91,860	297,900	342,798
Ohio	436	3,021,221	4,339,684	6,348	6,848	2,264,352	2,765,232	8,615,329
Aggregate in 12 States and D. C.	2,799	21,954,700	36,239,564	36,155	52,515	15,994,009	43,678,802	64,002,975
Increase, (47. per cent.)	....	....	....	....	....	....	....	20,324,173

TABLE No. 18.—*Value of Sawed and Planed Lumber produced during the year ending June 1, 1860.*

States and Territories.	Value of product in 1850.	Value of product in 1860.	Per cent. increase.
Maine	$5,872,573	$6,784,981	15.5
New Hampshire	1,099,492	1,226,784	11.6
Vermont	618,065	1,065,886	72.4
Massachusetts	1,552,265	2,288,419	47.4
Rhode Island	241,556	172,174	Decrease.
Connecticut	534,794	531,651	Decrease.
Total in New England States	9,918,745	12,069,895	21.5
New York	13,126,759	12,485,418	Decrease.
Pennsylvania	7,729,058	11,311,149	46.3
New Jersey	1,123,052	1,602,319	42.6
Delaware	236,863	261,172	10.0
Maryland	585,168	724,122	23.7
District of Columbia	29,000	70,825	144.2
Total in Middle States	22,829,900	26,455,005	15.8
Ohio	3,864,452	5,600,045	47.5
Indiana	2,195,351	3,169,843	44.3
Michigan	2,464,329	7,033,427	185.4
Illinois	1,324,484	2,275,124	71.8
Wisconsin	1,218,516	4,836,159	297.0
Minnesota	57,800	816,808	131.3
Iowa	470,760	2,378,529	405.9
Missouri	1,479,124	3,702,992	150.3
Kentucky	1,502,434	2,200,674	46.4
Kansas	....	945,088	....
Nebraska	....	316,104	....
Total in Western States	14,577,250	33,274,793	128.2
Virginia	977,412	2,537,130	159.5
North Carolina	985,075	1,073,968	9.0
South Carolina	1,108,880	1,077,712	Decrease.
Georgia	923,403	2,064,026	123.5
Florida	391,034	1,475,240	277.3
Alabama	1,103,481	2,017,641	82.8
Louisiana	1,129,677	1,018,554	Decrease.
Texas	466,012	1,612,829	246.1
Mississippi	913,197	2,055,396	125.1
Arkansas	122,918	1,033,185	746.0
Tennessee	725,387	1,975,481	172.4
Total in Southern States	8,846,476	17,941,162	102.3
New Mexico	20,000	65,150	....
Utah	14,620	132,565	807.8
California	959,485	4,214,596	339.4
Oregon	1,355,500	586,600	29.7
Washington	....	1,172,520	
Total in Pacific States	2,349,605	6,171,431	162.7
Aggregate in United States	58,521,976	95,912,286	63.9

TABLE No. 19.—*Value of Flour and Meal produced during the year ending June* 1, 1860.

States and Territories.	Value of product in 1850.	Value of product in 1860.	Per cent. increase.
Maine	$946,358	$1,576,863	64.8
New Hampshire	1,127,016	1,486,981	31.9
Vermont	719,231	1,659,898	130.7
Massachusetts	2,475,553	4,196,710	69.5
Rhode Island	90,651	515,699	469.9
Connecticut	961,677	1,719,294	78.7
Total in New England States	6,320,486	11,155,445	76.5
New York	33,037,121	35,064,906	6.1
Pennsylvania	24,115,575	26,572,261	10.1
New Jersey	4,056,761	6,399,610	57.7
Delaware	1,214,017	1,844,919	52.0
Maryland	5,499,265	8,020,122	45.6
District of Columbia	510,440	1,184,593	132.1
Total in Middle States	68,433,179	79,086,411	15.5
Ohio	14,372,270	27,129,405	88.7
Indiana	5,564,091	11,292,665	104.9
Michigan	4,093,681	8,663,288	111.1
Illinois	5,781,483	18,104,804	213.0
Wisconsin	3,536,293	8,161,183	130.7
Minnesota	500	1,310,000	2619.0
Iowa	2,019,448	6,950,949	239.0
Missouri	5,124,003	8,997,083	75.5
Kentucky	2,182,223	5,034,745	130.7
Kansas	....	284,281	....
Nebraska	....	110,391	....
Total in Western States	42,673,992	96,038,794	125.0
Virginia	9,408,892	15,212,060	61.6
North Carolina	1,447,211	3,185,251	120.1
South Carolina	1,151,128	876,250	Decrease.
Georgia	1,362,437	3,323,730	143.9
Florida	28,575	355,066	1145.5
Alabama	860,241	807,502	Decrease.
Louisiana	93,939	11,694	Decrease.
Texas	50,540	2,179,610	4324.6
Mississippi	461,838	541,994	17.3
Arkansas	115,875	453,999	294.0
Tennessee	1,601,141	3,820,301	138.6
Total in Southern States	16,581,817	30,767,457	85.5
New Mexico	....	374,190	....
Utah	253,000	237,635	Decrease.
California	754,192	4,335,809	475.0
Oregon	881,140	1,074,828	219.8
Washington	....	73,800	....
Total in Pacific States	1,888,332	6,096,262	222.8
Aggregate in United States	135,897,806	223,144,369	64.2

TABLE No. 20.

Spirituous Liquors distilled during the year ending June 1, 1860.

States and Territories.	No. of establishments.	Gallons of whiskey, high wines, and alcohol.	Gallons of brandy, gin, &c.	Gallons of New England rum.	Total gallons.	Value.
Maine	1	....	....	452,000	452,000	$142,500
Massachusetts	11	972,000	....	2,396,800	3,368,800	1,266,570
Connecticut	7	....	203,100	....	203,100	109,250
Total in N. England States	19	972,000	203,100	2,848,800	4,023,900	1,518,320
New York	77	21,923,732	2,924,800	1,303,680	26,152,212	7,698,464
New Jersey	52	1,517,985	....	....	1,517,985	490,842
Pennsylvania	191	8,335,302	....	....	8,335,302	2,183,421
Maryland	20	1,182,700	....	....	1,182,700	329,641
Total in Middle States	340	32,959,719	2,924,800	1,303,680	37,188,199	10,702,368
Ohio	137	15,140,475	20,500	....	15,160,975	4,197,429
Indiana	32	8,358,560	....	....	8,358,560	1,951,530
Kentucky	166	3,247,203	880	....	3,248,083	959,651
Illinois	42	15,165,760	....	....	15,165,760	3,204,176
Michigan	7	251,320	....	....	251,320	73,704
Wisconsin	15	531,250	....	....	531,250	101,346
Minnesota	8	58,000	....	....	58,000	15,950
Iowa	13	383,320	....	....	383,320	81,830
Missouri	19	1,572,200	....	....	1,572,200	309,000
Kansas	1	1,800	....	....	1,800	3,750
New Mexico	12	10,750	1,575	....	12,325	22,425
Utah	3	2,600	....	....	2,600	6,800
Total in Western States	455	44,723,238	22,955	....	44,746,193	10,927,591
California	24	526,965	236,300	....	763,265	349,410
Oregon	1	40,000	....	....	40,000	40,000
Total in Pacific States	25	566,965	236,300	....	803,265	389,410
Tennessee	85	272,930	10,264	....	283,194	176,648
Virginia	62	757,980	....	....	757,980	391,143
North Carolina	100	100,155	....	....	100,155	72,341
South Carolina	29	33,532	....	....	33,532	31,982
Georgia	8	16,620	....	....	16,620	11,804
Alabama	5	28,800	....	....	28,800	13,044
Texas	8	12,650	....	....	12,650	12,400
Arkansas	2	8,500	....	....	8,500	6,125
Total in Southern States	299	1,231,167	10,264	....	1,241,431	715,487
Aggregate in United States	1,138	80,453,089	3,397,419	4,152,480	88,002,988	24,253,176

Table No. 21.

Malt Liquors brewed in the following States and Territories during the year ending June 1, 1860.

States and Territories.	No. of establishments.	Barrels.	Value.
Maine	5	7,230	$36,169
New Hampshire	3	17,200	86,000
Massachusetts	13	133,600	658,700
Rhode Island	4	6,400	31,267
Connecticut	6	16,030	91,210
Total in New England States	31	180,460	903,346
New York	175	990,767	4,996,151
New Jersey	22	155,430	865,910
Pennsylvania	172	585,206	3,246,681
Maryland	26	44,664	242,286
District of Columbia	4	13,484	84,300
Total in Middle States	399	1,789,551	9,435,328
Ohio	29	402,035	1,912,419
Indiana	50	66,338	328,116
Kentucky	17	74,850	219,700
Illinois	75	218,043	1,309,180
Michigan	42	57,671	354,758
Wisconsin	121	124,956	702,812
Minnesota	24	14,080	77,740
Iowa	39	35,588	221,495
Missouri	55	172,570	1,143,450
Kansas	4	5,100	52,800
Nebraska	2	2,200	16,400
Utah	2	145	4,200
Total in Western States	460	1,173,576	6,343,070
California	71	87,806	1,211,641
Oregon	8	4,152	83,750
Total in Pacific States	89	91,958	1,295,391
Tennessee	1	4,000	24,000
Aggregate	970	3,239,545	18,001,135

TABLE No. 22.

Cotton Goods produced during the year ending June 1, 1860.

STATES.	No. of establishments.	Capital invested.	Pounds of cotton.	Value of raw material.	NUMBER OF—		AVERAGE NUMBER OF HANDS EMPLOYED.		Annual cost of labor.	ANNUAL PRODUCT.		Per cent. increase.
					Spindles.	Looms.	Male.	Female.		In 1850.	In 1860.	
Maine	19	$6,108,325	23,438,723	$3,000,000	300,000	6,000	1,908	4,342	$1,244,928	$2,630,616	$6,636,623	152.3
New Hampshire	44	13,878,000	39,212,644	9,758,921	669,885	17,015	6,300	13,859	4,574,520	8,861,749	16,661,531	87.0
Vermont	10	321,000	1,057,250	133,000	19,712	424	142	225	78,468	280,300	357,400	27.5
Massachusetts	200	33,300,000	126,666,089	14,778,344	1,739,700	44,978	12,635	22,353	7,221,156	21,394,401	36,745,864	68.9
Rhode Island	135	11,500,000	38,521,608	5,281,000	766,000	26,000	5,474	6,615	2,417,640	6,495,972	12,258,657	88.7
Connecticut	64	6,000,000	15,799,140	4,000,000	464,000	8,787	3,314	4,275	1,453,128	4,122,952	7,641,460	87.0
Total in N. E. States	472	71,107,325	244,695,454	36,951,265	3,959,297	103,204	29,773	51,669	16,989,840	43,785,990	80,301,535	83.4
New York	70	5,427,079	25,910,876	2,988,270	328,816	7,511	3,043	4,288	1,271,592	5,019,323	7,471,961	48.8
Pennsylvania	151	8,253,640	32,855,669	6,732,275	358,578	10,678	5,350	7,370	2,265,912	5,812,126	11,759,000	102.0
New Jersey	29	1,845,000	2,257,885	1,693,663	96,112	1,181	853	1,371	435,684	1,289,648	3,250,770	152.1
Delaware	11	572,000	2,717,000	521,492	25,704	494	486	521	202,884	538,439	919,103	70.7
Maryland	19	2,214,500	12,020,119	1,641,913	49,891	1,520	947	1,568	464,112	2,021,396	2,796,877	38.3
District of Columbia	1	45,000	294,117	47,403	2,560	82	70	25	19,800	100,000	74,400	Dec.
Total in Middle States	281	18,357,219	76,055,666	13,625,016	861,661	21,466	10,749	15,143	4,659,984	14,780,932	26,272,111	77.7
Virginia	13	1,325,243	7,302,797	770,977	28,700	524	741	952	262,440	1,446,109	1,063,611	Dec.
North Carolina	36	1,049,750	5,152,750	564,612	30,144	479	416	1,210	168,840	985,411	930,567	Dec.

South Carolina	17	827,825	3,845,811	419,500	16,461	931	372	584	133,180	842,440	588,950	Dec.
Georgia	32	1,854,603	12,977,904	1,689,075	44,312	1,058	1,376	1,909	483,520	1,395,056	2,215,636	58.8
Florida	1	30,000	200,000	22,000	....	....	40	25	7,872	49,920	40,000	Dec.
Alabama	11	1,306,500	4,389,641	623,963	26,540	663	567	765	206,124	398,585	917,105	130.0
Louisiana	2	1,075,000	1,995,700	283,900	4,225	150	70	70	24,000	....	509,700	....
Texas	1	500,000	588,000	78,920	2,700	100	160	....	36,480	....	99,241	....
Mississippi	4	350,000	534,400	163,419	1,844	28	155	155	33,996	22,000	261,135	108.7
Arkansas	1	55,000	60,000	6,750	....	....	20	10	7,200	17,360	13,000	Dec.
Tennessee	25	930,000	3,172,000	283,838	7,914	80	214	437	109,764	508,481	533,348	4.8
Total in Southern States	143	9,303,921	40,219,003	4,906,954	164,840	4,013	4,161	6,117	1,471,416	5,665,362	7,172,293	26.6
Ohio	7	250,000	1,815,000	250,000	15,000	400	270	340	112,400	594,204	629,500	5.9
Indiana	2	250,000	800,000	100,000	11,000	375	176	190	72,468	86,660	349,000	32.0
Illinois	3	10,000	40,000	8,000	....	....	8	8	1,980	....	15,987	....
Missouri	3	169,000	100,000	14,500	14,500	....	85	85	31,080	142,900	230,000	60.8
Kentucky	4	104,000	311,000	139,000	9,500	....	93	53	21,000	445,639	167,500	Dec.
Total in Western States	19	783,000	3,066,000	511,500	50,000	775	632	676	238,928	1,269,403	1,391,987	9.6
Aggregate	915	99,551,465	364,036,123	55,994,735	5,035,798	129,458	45,315	73,605	23,360,168	65,501,687	115,137,926	75.78

TABLE No. 23.

Woollen Goods, (including Carding and Fulling and Mixed Goods,) produced during the year ending June 1, 1860.

STATES AND TERRITORIES.	Number of establishments.	Capital invested.	Pounds of wool.	Pounds of cotton used in mixed goods.	Value of raw material.	NUMBER OF—		AVERAGE NUMBER OF HANDS EMPLOYED.		Annual cost of labor.	ANNUAL PRODUCT.	
						Spindles.	Looms.	Male.	Female.		In 1850.	In 1860.
Maine	61	$989,400	2,646,200	100,000	$1,047,496	11,765	185	604	499	$277,440	$1,022,929	$1,674,800
New Hampshire	71	1,519,550	3,596,730	321,280	1,732,074	36,320	696	1,003	1,003	499,764	2,139,967	2,876,000
Vermont	50	1,781,550	3,303,500	59,300	1,679,594	23,371	463	830	1,065	388,956	1,820,769	2,550,000
Massachusetts	131	10,179,500	26,271,200	3,589,500	11,613,174	159,651	4,237	6,645	4,608	2,645,868	12,781,514	18,930,000
Rhode Island	50	2,986,000	5,000,000	1,881,200	3,920,155	86,048	1,586	2,483	1,568	1,012,836	2,504,700	6,599,280
Connecticut	90	2,494,000	8,000,000	995,932	4,206,000	76,178	1,753	2,291	1,460	917,437	4,974,959	5,879,000
Total in N. E. States	453	19,950,000	48,817,630	6,947,212	24,198,493	393,333	8,920	13,856	10,203	5,742,301	25,244,838	38,509,080
New York	235	4,598,233	11,708,230	2,685,000	4,979,631	87,887	1,686	3,786	4,255	1,591,248	7,605,774	9,090,316
Pennsylvania	447	5,642,425	6,223,850	4,753,413	6,770,347	108,326	4,334	6,682	4,022	2,229,936	5,792,566	12,744,373
New Jersey	35	937,400	1,712,000	656,000	682,743	10,361	270	812	587	320,304	1,020,941	1,527,209
Delaware	6	98,000	147,500	120,000	78,807	1,000	76	79	38	27,888	249,510	156,635
Maryland	25	287,200	955,800	77,000	254,874	2,480	66	228	127	77,868	319,240	581,955
Total in Middle States	748	11,563,258	20,747,380	8,291,413	12,766,402	210,054	6,432	11,587	8,969	4,247,244	14,988,031	24,100,488
Virginia	69	476,380	1,329,738	70,000	466,020	7,574	121	517	108	114,636	826,746	809,760
North Carolina	22	286,700	441,290	125,000	170,111	1,000	20	145	149	46,092	71,470	260,279
South Carolina	8	9,500	37,800	....	13,420	....	....	10	....	1,964	15,100	17,177
Georgia	28	174,600	1,500,000	150,000	243,700	1,480	20	62	45	17,480	....	465,000
Alabama	15	100,000	342,235	20,000	90,000	1,000	20	46	28	18,000	21,800	218,000

Texas	9	24,100	106,250	18,000	30,950	....	....	17	7	6,780	22,000	49,125
Mississippi	9	109,500	376,400	107,000	133,290	1,000	21	204	20	12,408	31,670	184,500
Arkansas	8	8,550	90,800	20,000	26,960	....	....	9	....	1,680	8,800	31,840
Tennessee........	59	128,650	570,865	260,000	143,151	500	....	145	58	36,636	111,225	267,622
Total in Southern States	227	1,317,980	4,795,378	770,000	1,317,602	12,554	202	1,155	415	255,676	1,108,811	2,303,303
Ohio	113	623,650	1,054,540	....	393,344	5,827	96	356	153	137,064	1,513,978	692,333
Indiana	84	458,144	1,009,000	....	344,500	8,266	177	561	93	165,108	528,700	695,3[illegible]0
Illinois..................	33	233,450	545,000	....	182,320	1,000	20	173	33	51,072	370,870	266,230
Michigan	20	139,500	223,100	....	91,090	1,000	20	98	50	38,316	192,043	174,398
Wisconsin	15	96,800	212,400	....	56,820	1,000	20	78	24	26,868	60,105	167,600
Iowa......................	23	109,100	265,200	....	103,373	1,000	20	120	21	35,916	112,454	167,960
Missouri..................	99	212,845	856,244	....	230,911	896	29	190	14	47,172	358,427	425,319
Kentucky	92	645,800	1,310,700	....	598,445	3,990	94	539	112	131,340	803,507	1,128,882
Total in Western States.	479	2,519,289	5,476,184	....	2,000,803	22,979	476	2,115	500	632,856	3,940,084	3,718,092
California	1	100,000	400,000	....	50,000	500	30	40	20	33,600	....	150,000
Oregon	1	70,000	150,000	....	27,000	280	15	27	13	16,200	....	85,000
Total in Pacific States...	2	170,000	550,000	....	77,000	780	45	67	33	49,800	....	2[illegible]5,000
Aggregate..........	1,909	35,520,527	80,386,572	16,008,625	40,360,300	639,700	16,075	28,780	20,120	10,927,877	45,281,764	68,865,963

TABLE No. 24.

Leather produced during the year ending June 1, 1860.

States and Territories.	Value of product in 1850.	Value of product in 1860.	Per cent. increase.
Maine	$1,701,299	$2,011,034	18.2
New Hampshire	944,554	1,933,949	104.7
Vermont	640,665	1,000,153	56.1
Massachusetts	5,672,559	10,354,056	82.3
Rhode Island	133,050	80,897	Decrease.
Connecticut	775,325	953,782	23.0
Total in New England States	9,867,452	16,333,871	66.6
New York	9,802,670	20,753,017	111.7
Pennsylvania	6,296,363	12,491,631	98.4
New Jersey	1,269,982	1,297,627	2.1
Delaware	213,742	37,240	Decrease.
Maryland	1,426,734	1,723,033	17.2
District of Columbia	56,000	37,000	Decrease.
Total in Middle States	19,065,491	36,344,548	90.7
Ohio	2,110,982	2,799,239	32.6
Indiana	750,801	800,387	6.6
Michigan	401,730	574,172	42.4
Illinois	337,384	150,000	Decrease.
Wisconsin	181,010	498,268	175.2
Minnesota	....	11,400	....
Iowa	24,550	81,760	23.3
Missouri	366,361	368,826	.6
Kentucky	1,108,533	701,555	Decrease.
Kansas	....	850	....
Total in Western States	5,281,351	5,986,457	13.3
Utah	....	93,255	....
California	....	226,214	....
Oregon	....	14,500	....
Washington	....	17,500	....
Total in Pacific States	....	351,469	....
Virginia	927,877	1,218,700	31.3
North Carolina	363,647	343,020	Decrease.
South Carolina	282,399	150,985	Decrease.
Georgia	403,439	393,164	Decrease.
Alabama	344,445	340,400	Decrease.
Louisiana	78,085	47,000	Decrease.
Texas	52,600	123,050	132.0
Mississippi	241,632	223,862	Decrease.
Arkansas	78,824	115,375	46.3
Tennessee	804,631	1,118,850	38.9
Total in Southern States	3,577,579	4,074,406	13.8
Aggregate in United States	37,791,873	63,090,751	66.9

TABLE No. 25.—*Boots and Shoes manufactured in the following States during the year ending June* 1, 1860.

STATES AND TERRITORIES.	Number of establishments.	Capital invested in real and personal estate in the business.	Value of raw material, including fuel.	AVERAGE NUMBER OF HANDS EMPLOYED.		Cost of labor.	ANNUAL PRODUCTS.		Per cent. increase.
				Male.	Female.		Value in 1850.	Value in 1860.	
Maine	295	$420,984	$879,031	1,820	702	$592,032	$961,556	$1,661,915	72.8
New Hampshire	337	583,285	2,497,471	3,479	1,365	1,077,048	2,610,169	3,863,866	48.0
Vermont	148	133,962	210,595	484	58	169,224	342,353	440,366	25 6
Massachusetts	1,497	11,169,277	24,497,344	47,353	22,045	17,226,408	24,102,366	46,440,209	92.6
Rhode Island	66	104,495	155,937	382	31	86,028	69,098	315,959	357.2
Connecticut	211	510,400	839,435	2,521	777	831,168	1,861,783	2,044,762	9.8
Total in N. E. States	2,554	12,922,403	29,079,813	56,039	24,978	19,981,848	29,947,325	54,767,077	82.8
New York	2,276	3,212,423	4,848,877	11,838	2,028	3,567,636	7,766,428	10,878,797	39.8
Pennsylvania	2,178	2,823,672	3,127,628	10,826	2,344	3,102,128	5,636,733	8,178,935	36 0
New Jersey	373	574,055	814,926	2,357	482	761,976	1,698,877	1,850,137	8.9
Maryland	453	333,955	515,254	1,577	292	....	1,372,358	1,244,167	Dec.
Delaware	53	85,026	98,107	263	58	80,664	157,254	226,470	37.7
District of Columbia	56	67,505	96,549	273	20	....	144,597	209,785	45.2
Total in Middle States	5,389	7,096,636	9,501,341	27,134	5,224	7,512,404	16,776,247	22,588,291	34 6
Ohio	950	1,115,476	1,455,686	4,259	342	1,340,712	2,320,096	3,623,827	56.1
Michigan	273	339,167	380,676	976	58	295,392	527,479	863,315	63.7
Indiana	461	347,370	428,614	1,148	51	381,516	506,039	1,034,341	104.4
Illinois	321	378,110	400,348	1,047	27	292,292	478,925	963,052	101.2
Wisconsin	217	266,065	431,175	917	50	204,964	289,998	901,944	211.7
Minnesota	60	45,980	59,578	120	20	....	....	133,395	.....
Iowa	118	125,377	141,922	336	10	109,404	56,533	325,296	475.6
Missouri	277	291,680	326,699	904	43	331,704	559,238	868,768	55.5
Kentucky	264	218,215	290,766	828	29	255,840	403,212	685,783	70.1
Utah	13	4,520	17,535	28	....	15,480	....	36,833	.....
Nebraska	9	9,950	9,824	33	1	12,072	....	28,651	.....
Total in Western States	2,963	3,141,910	3,942,823	10,596	631	3,239,376	5,141,520	9,465,205	84.1
Virginia	250	263,547	265,113	879	116	258,768	596,883	718,591	20.4
Louisiana	497	388,440	547,001	1,137	170	382,572	406,825	1,391,121	242.4
Tennessee	94	84,617	111,681	153	11	72,684	243,976	262,348	7.5
Georgia	117	153,430	173,666	349	10	92,904	244,260	357,267	46.3
Tot. in 4 South'n States	958	890,034	1,097,461	2,518	307	806,928	1,491,944	2,729,327	80.3
Aggregate	11,864	24,050,983	43,621,438	96,287	31,140	31,540,556	53,357,036	89,549,900	67.8

India-rubber Goods produced in the following States during the year ending June 1, 1860.

Massachusetts	5	638,000	532,900	324	74	107,832	276,080	803,000	190.9
Rhode Island	2	156,000	105,011	60	44	29,434	215,000	246,700	14.7
Connecticut	13	1,415,000	1,245,800	662	347	320,436	1,218,500	2,676,000	119.6
New York	6	625,000	369,000	458	207	153,924	548,500	977,700	78.3
Pennsylvania	2	7,500	5,300	6	4	3,106	19,400	13,500	Dec.
New Jersey	3	720,000	502,900	315	382	186,768	723,605	1,013,000	40.0
Aggregate	31	3,561,500	2,760,911	1,825	1,058	801,500	3,001,085	5,729,900	90.9

TABLE No. 26.—*Furniture produced during the year ending June 1, 1860.*

STATES.	No. of establishments.	Capital invested in real and personal estate in the business.	Raw materials used, including fuel.	AVERAGE NUMBER OF HANDS EMPLOYED.		Value of product in 1850.	Value of product in 1860.
				Male.	Female		
Maine	55	103,717	73,329	263	10	$164,112	$236,534
New Hampshire	59	179,000	119,397	348	7	191,048	357,195
Vermont	64	149,200	82,248	340	2	123,960	268,735
Massachusetts	190	1,521,858	1,114,483	3,216	1,269	2,635,216	3,365,415
Rhode Island	23	140,500	97,843	166	12	59,036	217,472
Connecticut	44	277,900	207,025	400	6	358,310	514,425
Total in New England States	435	2,372,175	1,694,325	4,733	1,306	3,531,682	4,959,776
New York	625	3,723,931	2,325,015	6,295	380	4,966,092	7,175,060
Pennsylvania	494	1,725,436	948,969	3,109	17	2,553,790	2,938,503
New Jersey	60	170,250	100,106	252	17	384,807	232,500
Delaware	15	55,700	20,007	36	4	42,905	50,052
Maryland	63	301,700	210,869	507	....	705,165	626,154
District of Columbia	12	22,950	15,630	28	2	85,975	44,420
Total in Middle States	1,269	5,999,987	3,620,596	10,227	420	8,738,734	11,066,689
Ohio	355	2,273,743	844,797	3,993	97	1,809,390	3,703,605
Indiana	153	291,692	160,767	675	....	430,393	601,124
Michigan	105	269,955	107,949	604	12	196,255	450,028
Illinois	130	442,060	166,889	634	6	357,203	873,609
Wisconsin	85	228,500	97,598	351	39	177,377	366,525
Minnesota	29	47,000	17,705	93	....	....	63,269
Iowa	60	134,950	35,282	224	....	51,805	157,491
Missouri	47	128,095	66,052	157	....	258,391	203,142
Kentucky	68	155,915	66,688	262	....	680,179	256,046
Total in Western States	1,032	3,971,910	1,563,727	6,993	154	3,960,993	6,674,839
Agg'te of 20 States and Dis. Col.	2,736	12,344,072	6,878,648	21,953	1,880	16,231,409	22,701,304
Increase, (39.8 per cent.)	....	....	....	....	....	....	6,469,895

TABLE No. 27.—*Musical Instruments produced in the following States during the year ending June 1, 1860.*

STATES.	No. of establishments.	Capital invested in real and personal estate in the business.	Raw materials used, including fuel.	MONTHLY AVERAGE NUMBER OF HANDS EMPLOYED.		Monthly cost of labor.	Value of annual product.
				Male.	Female.		
Maine	5	37,000	9,075	23	....	$965	$32,850
New Hampshire	6	34,200	16,375	76	....	2,564	64,800
Vermont	4	25,500	17,840	42	....	1,560	57,960
Massachusetts	36	980,500	608,927	945	....	53,424	1,762,470
Rhode Island	1	500	50	3	....	100	1,200
Connecticut	1	4,000	1,495	4	....	140	4,000
New York	77	2,654,700	1,083,419	2,449	4	....	3,392,577
Pennsylvania	27	265,000	108,050	323	....	....	475,950
Total in 8 States	157	4,001,400	1,840,231	3,865	4	58,753	5,791,807

TABLE No. 28.—*Jewelry, Silverware, &c., produced during the year ending June 1, 1860.*

States.	Value of gold assayed and refined.	Value of watches.	Value of gold-leaf and foil.	Value of silverware.	Val. of silver plated & Britannia ware.	Val. of jewelry, watch-cases, &c.	Total value.
Maine	....	....	....	....	$23,000	$11,240	$34,240
New Hampshire	....	....	....	....	....	11,300	11,300
Vermont	....	....	....	$24,700	7,500	5,750	37,950
Massachusetts	....	$348,900	$17,700	196,360	341,375	1,744,306	2,648,641
Rhode Island	$269,500	....	9,000	490,000	....	2,238,178	3,006,678
Connecticut	....	....	80,000	32,600	1,579,760	195,124	1,887,484
New York	420,570	....	108,372	1,593,795	563,745	2,779,981	5,466,463
Pennsylvania	430,000	....	264,600	519,650	561,650	2,356,230	4,132,130
New Jersey	....	4,500	....	7,000	665,500	1,604,344	2,281,344
Delaware	....	....	....	....	....	1,800	1,800
Maryland	....	....	....	30,000	....	600	30,600
District of Columbia	....	....	....	....	....	15,950	15,950
	1,120,070	353,400	479,672	2,894,105	3,742,530	10,964,803	19,554,580

TABLE No. 29.—*Illuminating Gas produced during the year ending June 1, 1860.*

STATES AND TERRITORIES.	No. of establishments.	Capital invested in real and personal estate in the business.	RAW MATERIAL USED, INCLUDING FUEL.		No. of men employed.	Cost of labor.	ANNUAL PRODUCTS.	
			Tons of coal.	Val. of raw material.			Quantities, in 1,000 ft.	Value, includ'g coke.
Maine	10	$840,000	5,482	$41,865	59	$21,732	44,087	$143,852
New Hampshire	5	248,000	3,436	36,226	31	5,760	25,980	86,843
Vermont	2	106,000	570	4,600	7	2,640	2,824	15,215
Massachusetts	10	2,686,500	59,200	362,565	225	109,404	366,553	967,058
Rhode Island	4	792,600	8,383	62,213	64	22,320	68,450	197,735
Connecticut	8	566,000	14,664	56,473	53	20,196	70,338	232,054
Total in New England	39	5,239,100	91,735	563,942	439	182,052	578,232	1,642,757
New York	43	7,558,150	215,516	1,564,884	2,691	979,464	1,809,921	4,881,805
Pennsylvania	30	5,248,554	120,131	651,919	1,006	472,452	828,553	2,147,802
New Jersey	15	986,130	7,660	64,004	86	45,156	70,599	239,474
Delaware	2	177,300	1,520	10,500	12	5,220	12,800	33,175
Maryland	2	87,000	550	5,200	9	3,600	2,800	13,500
District of Columbia	2	612,000	10,500	52,625	108	4,800	77,764	242,388
Total in Middle States	94	14,669,134	355,877	2,349,132	3,912	1,510,692	2,802,437	7,558,144
Ohio	22	1,668,650	30,173	92,470	356	135,936	195,701	491,748
Indiana	7	388,850	6,470	24,426	49	23,772	36,628	96,012
Illinois	8	1,335,000	5,083	81,096	182	65,700	105,029	342,142
Wisconsin	4	100,000	....	....	......	....	30,000	94,176
Iowa	4	....	....	....	......	....	12,900	55,900
Missouri	2	605,000	15,317	48,750	61	30,480	101,817	419,306
Kentucky	2	117,966	5,625	25,220	88	38,040	60,857	96,449
California	4	270,000	1,815	62,975	20	26,880	16,950	146,200
Total in Western States	53	4,485,466	64,483	334,937	756	320,808	559,882	1,741,933
Virginia	15	264,000	1,840	12,955	31	6,396	22,580	59,700
North Carolina	1	27,000	....	788	3	900	674	4,046
Georgia	2	273,000	2,500	31,100	35	17,520	21,058	96,000
Alabama	1	125,000	3,000	22,000	20	21,600	13,218	58,000
Tennessee	1	200,000	....	....	25	13,200	16,000	63,800
Total in Southern States	20	889,000	7,340	66,843	114	59,616	73,530	281,546
Aggregate United States	206	25,282,700	519,435	3,314,854	5,221	2,073,168	4,014,081	11,224,380

TABLE NO. 30.

Quantity and value of Salt made in the following States during the year ending June 1, 1860.

States.	Bushels.	Value.
Massachusetts	30,900	$7,874
New York	7,521,335	1,289,511
Pennsylvania	604,300	154,264
Ohio	1,744,240	276,879
Virginia	2,056,513	478,684
Kentucky	69,665	21,190
Texas	120,000	29,800
California	44,000	7,100
Total	12,190,953	2,265,302

TABLE NO. 31.

Product of the Fisheries during the year ending June 1, 1860.

States and Territories.	Value of the product of whale fisheries.	Value of codfish, mackerel, &c.	Value of shad, &c.	Value of white fish.	Value of salmon.	Value of oysters.	Total.
Maine		$1,050,755					$1,050,755
New Hampshire			$64,500				64,500
Massachusetts	$6,526,238	2,774,204					9,300,442
Rhode Island	246,350	62,400					308,750
Connecticut	731,000	281,189					1,012,189
New York		14,955	6,815	$36,000		$93,270	151,040
New Jersey			41,617			167,660	209,277
Maryland			5,800			15,305	21,105
Indiana				17,500			17,500
Michigan				250,467			250,467
Wisconsin				83,512			83,512
Virginia			33,600			53,145	86,745
North Carolina			99,768			2,100	101,868
Florida			68,952				68,952
Texas						6,093	6,093
California	18,000			77,000	$18,950		113,950
Oregon					13,450		13,450
Washington					18,900	44,597	63,497
Aggregate	7,521,588	4,183,503	321,052	464,479	51,300	382,170	12,924,092

TABLE No. 32.

Soap and Candles produced during the year ending June 1, 1860.

STATES.	Number of establishments.	Capital invested in real and personal estate in the business.	Raw material used, including fuel.	AVERAGE NUMBER OF HANDS EMPLOYED.		ANNUAL PRODUCTS.		Per cent. increase.
				Male.	Female.	Value in 1850.	Value in 1860.	
Maine	13	$25,100	$37,954	35	......	$52,180	$53,637	......
New Hampshire	11	31,800	34,756	31	......	30,165	64,514	114.4
Massachusetts	76	632,650	1,348,481	389	18	1,263,678	1,910,206	51.1
Rhode Island	6	47,000	81,698	22	......	525,370	107,332	Dec.
Connecticut	31	140,650	259,836	84	2	124,285	396,045	219.0
Total in New England	137	877,200	1,762,725	561	20	1,995,678	2,531,734	26.8
New York	130	1,378,600	2,692,836	410	......	3,363,207	3,836,503	14.0
Pennsylvania	92	1,302,458	2,011,665	507	......	1,496,209	2,937,798	96.0
New Jersey	10	73,000	224,825	42	4	444,885	595,075	33.0
Delaware	2	32,000	30,730	12	......	43,000	61,500	41.8
Maryland	10	143,700	346,703	4	......	579,553	433,345	Dec.
District of Columbia	3	10,000	42,930	15	......	18,100	62,587	247.6
Total in Middle States	247	2,939,758	5,349,689	990	4	5,944,954	7,926,808	33.3
Ohio	25	621,927	1,778,642	212	32	611,193	2,418,972	294.0
Indiana	16	89,100	198,900	58	......	52,262	256,535	388.0
Michigan	9	46,200	83,200	42	2	86,032	108,478	25.0
Illinois	22	113,500	258,939	73	......	184,739	386,442	109.0
Wisconsin	12	67,100	113,760	37	......	149,374	187,010	25.2
Iowa	7	35,000	69,805	20	......	......	113,470	......
Missouri	12	620,800	1,313,328	246	55	513,593	1,649,380	207.0
Kentucky	10	189,500	166,162	105	25	239,609	486,900	103.0
Total in Western States	113	1,783,127	3,982,736	793	114	1,836,802	5,607,187	205.0
Virginia	18	146,800	187,496	83	4	179,073	279,903	56.0
Louisiana	16	27,700	76,261	50	......	175,000	156,310	Dec.
Texas	1	10,000	995	4	......	......	9,700	......
Tennessee	2	20,000	27,800	9	......	40,705	44,000	......
Total in Southern States	37	204,500	292,552	146	4	394,778	489,913	24.0
California	11	57,300	124,551	23	......	......	204,900	......
Other States, (estimated)	......	......	......	......	......	27,518	200,000	......
Aggregate in U. States	545	5,861,885	11,512,253	2,513	142	10,199,730	16,960,542	66.0

TABLE No. 33.—*Approximate statistics of the Products of Industry for the year ending June* 1, 1860.

STATES AND TERRITORIES.	Number of establishments.	Capital invested, in real and personal estate, in the business.	Value of raw material used, including fuel.	AVERAGE NUMBER OF HANDS EMPLOYED.		Value of annual product.
				Male.	Female.	
Maine	3,582	$22,000,000	$20,861,452	25,000	14,710	$36,075,498
New Hampshire	2,582	25,900,000	21,400,000	19,200	16,900	45,500,000
Vermont	1,501	9,500,000	8,110,000	8,940	1,860	16,000,000
Massachusetts	7,766	133,000,000	141,000,000	148,800	68,300	266,000,000
Rhode Island	1,160	23,300,000	23,400,000	21,200	12,000	47,500,000
Connecticut	2,923	45,720,000	40,140,000	44,160	21,620	83,000,000
Total in New England States.	19,514	259,420,000	257,911,452	267,300	135,390	494,075,498
New York	23,236	175,449,206	209,899,890	174,059	47,422	379,623,560
Pennsylvania	21,100	189,000,000	145,300,000	185,141	38,000	285,500,000
New Jersey	4,060	40,000,000	42,600,000	114,660	13,060	81,000,000
Delaware	564	5,360,000	5,375,000	5,332	860	9,920,000
Maryland	2,980	51,800,000	21,900,000	20,800	20,100	42,576,000
District of Columbia	424	2,650,000	2,801,000	2,556	387	5,512,000
Total in Middle States	52,364	464,259,206	427,875,890	502,548	119,829	804,131,560
Ohio	10,710	58,000,000	70,000,000	69,800	11,400	125,000,000
Indiana	5,120	18,875,000	27,360,000	20,600	710	43,250,000
Michigan	2,530	24,000,000	19,000,000	22,860	1,260	35,200,000
Illinois	4,100	27,700,000	33,800,000	23,500	870	56,750,000
Wisconsin	3,120	16,580,000	17,250,000	16,320	770	28,500,000
Minnesota	565	2,400,000	2,060,000	2,215	15	3,600,000
Iowa	1,790	7,500,000	8,500,000	6,475	102	14,900,000
Missouri	2,800	20,500,000	24,000,000	20,130	1,200	43,500,000
Kentucky	3,160	20,000,000	21,380,000	20,580	1,460	36,330,000
Kansas	299	1,063,000	669,269	1,719	....	2,800,000
Nebraska	107	271,475	238,225	331	8	581,942
Total in Western States	34,301	196,889,475	224,257,494	204,530	17,795	390,411,942
Virginia	4,890	26,640,000	30,880,000	33,050	3,540	51,300,000
North Carolina	2,790	9,310,000	9,860,000	11,760	2,130	14,450,000
South Carolina	1,050	5,610,000	3,620,000	6,000	800	6,800,000
Georgia	1,724	11,160,000	10,000,000	9,910	2,180	13,700,000
Florida	180	6,675,000	965,000	2,310	170	2,700,000
Alabama	1,117	8,260,000	4,400,000	6,620	1,140	9,400,000
Louisiana	1,710	7,110,000	7,380,000	7,610	80	15,500,000
Texas	910	3,850,000	2,770,000	3,360	110	6,250,000
Mississippi	860	3,740,000	2,460,000	4,540	150	6,000,000
Arkansas	375	1,040,000	909,000	1,520	35	2,150,000
Tennessee	2,420	17,270,000	9,365,000	11,960	1,135	17,100,000
Total in Southern States	18,026	100,665,000	82,609,000	98,640	11,470	145,350,000
Utah	152	412,126	398,528	348	9	823,000
California	3,505	23,682,593	16,558,636	23,803	463	59,500,000
Oregon	300	1,293,000	1,452,000	996	10	3,138,000
Washington	52	1,296,700	505,000	886	4	1,405,000
New Mexico	86	2,081,900	432,000	949	30	1,165,000
Total in Pacific States	4,095	28,765,319	19,346,164	26,982	516	65,031,000
Aggregate in United States	128,300	1,050,000,000	1,012,000,000	1,100,000	285,000	1,900,000,000

TABLE No. 33 *a*.

Statement of the Leading Manufactures, and the value of product of each for the year ending June 1, 1860.

No.	Leading manufactures.	Value of product in round numbers.
1	Flour and meal	$224,000,000
2	Cotton goods	115,000,000
3	Lumber	95,000,000
4	Boots and shoes	90,000,000
5	Leather, including morocco and patent leather	72,000,000
6	Clothing	70,000,000
7	Woollen goods	69,000,000
8	Machinery, steam engines, &c	47,000,000
9	Printing: Book, job, and newspaper	42,000,000
10	Sugar refining	38,500,000
11	Iron founding	28,500,000
12	Spirituous liquors	25,000,000
13	Cabinet furniture	24,000,000
14	Bar and other rolled iron	22,000,000
15	Pig iron	19,500,000
16	Malt liquors	18,000,000
17	Agricultural implements	17,800,000
18	Paper	17,500,000
19	Soap and candles	17,000,000

TABLE No. 34.

A comparative statement showing by States the number of Banks, the capital, loans, specie, circulation, and deposits.

STATES.	SEVENTH CENSUS, 1850.					
	No. of banks and branches.	Capital.	Loans.	Specie.	Circulation.	Deposits.
Alabama	2	$1,800,580	$4,670,458	$1,998,820	$3,568,285	$1,474,963
Connecticut	43	9,907,503	15,607,315	640,622	5,253,884	2,395,311
Delaware	9	1,293,185	2,264,313	159,773	833,960	502,765
Florida	......	......	......	......	......	......
Georgia	21	13,482,198	11,421,626	2,112,446	9,898,827	2,580,826
Illinois	......	......	......	......	......	......
Indiana	14	2,082,950	4,395,099	1,197,880	3,422,445	630,325
Iowa	......	......	......	......	......	......
Kansas	......	......	......	......	......	......
Kentucky	26	7,536,927	12,506,305	2,794,351	7,643,075	2,323,657
Louisiana	25	12,370,390	19,309,108	5,716,001	5,059,229	8,464,389
Maine	32	3,248,000	5,830,230	475,589	2,654,208	1,233,671
Maryland	25	8,128,881	14,900,816	2,709,699	3,532,869	5,838,766
Massachusetts	126	36,925,050	63,330,024	2,993,178	17,005,826	11,176,827
Michigan	6	764,022	1,319,305	125,722	897,364	416,147
Missouri	6	1,209,131	3,533,463	1,198,268	2,522,500	1,098,981
New Hampshire	22	2,375,900	3,821,120	129,399	1,897,111	566,634
New Jersey	26	3,754,900	7,158,977	622,885	3,046,658	2,411,861
New York	198	48,618,762	107,132,389	10,045,330	26,415,526	50,774,193
North Carolina	18	3,789,250	6,056,726	1,645,028	4,249,883	942,098
Ohio	57	8,718,366	17,059,593	2,750,587	11,059,700	5,310,555
Pennsylvania	52	17,701,206	38,423,274	4,327,394	11,798,996	17,689,212
Rhode Island	63	11,645,492	15,492,547	297,661	2,553,865	1,488,596
South Carolina	14	13,213,031	23,312,330	2,218,228	11,771,270	3,065,686
Tennessee	23	6,881,568	10,992,139	1,456,778	6,814,376	1,917,757
Vermont	27	2,197,240	4,423,719	127,325	2,856,027	546,703
Virginia	37	9,824,545	19,646,777	2,928,174	10,256,997	4,717,732
Wisconsin	......	......	......	......	......	......
Total	872	227,469,077	412,607,653	48,671,138	155,012,881	127,567,655

TABLE No. 34.—*Statement of the number of Banks, &c.*—Continued.

STATES.	EIGHTH CENSUS, 1860.					
	No. of banks and branches.	Capital.	Loans.	Specie.	Circulation.	Deposits.
Alabama	8	$4,901,000	$13,570,027	$2,747,174	$7,477,976	$4,851,153
Connecticut	74	21,512,176	27,856,785	989,920	7,561,519	5,574,900
Delaware	12	1,640,775	3,150,215	208,924	1,135,772	976,226
Florida	2	300,000	464,630	32,876	183,640	129,518
Georgia	29	16,689,560	16,776,282	3,211,974	8,798,100	4,738,289
Illinois	74	5,251,225	387,229	223,812	8,981,723	697,037
Indiana	97	4,343,210	7,675,861	1,583,140	5,390,245	1,700,479
Iowa	12	460,450	724,228	225,545	563,806	527,378
Kansas	1	52,000	48,256	8,268	8,895	2,695
Kentucky	45	12,835,670	25,284,869	4,502,250	13,520,207	5,662,892
Louisiana	13	24,496,866	35,401,609	12,115,431	11,579,313	19,777,812
Maine	68	7,506,890	12,654,794	670,979	4,149,718	2,411,022
Maryland	31	12,568,962	20,898,762	2,779,418	4,106,869	8,874,180
Massachusetts	174	64,519,200	107,417,323	7,532,647	22,086,920	27,804,699
Michigan	4	755,465	892,949	24,175	222,197	375,397
Missouri	38	9,082,951	15,461,192	4,160,912	7,884,885	3,357,176
New Hampshire	52	5,016,000	8,591,688	255,278	3,271,183	1,187,991
New Jersey	49	7,884,412	14,909,174	940,700	4,811,832	5,741,465
New York	303	111,441,320	200,351,332	20,921,545	29,959,506	104,070,273
North Carolina	50	6,626,478	12,213,272	1,617,687	5,594,047	1,487,273
Ohio	52	6,890,839	11,100,462	1,828,640	7,983,889	4,039,614
Pennsylvania	90	25,565,582	50,327,157	8,378,474	13,132,892	26,167,843
Rhode Island	91	20,865,569	26,719,877	450,920	3,558,295	3,553,104
South Carolina	20	14,962,062	27,801,912	2,324,121	11,475,634	4,165,615
Tennessee	34	8,067,037	11,751,019	2,267,710	5,538,378	4,324,799
Vermont	46	4,029,240	6,496,523	198,409	3,882,983	787,834
Virginia	65	16,005,156	24,975,792	2,943,652	9,812,197	7,729,652
Wisconsin	108	7,620,000	7,592,361	419,947	4,429,855	3,085,813
Total	1,642	421,890,095	691,495,580	83,564,528	207,102,477	253,802,129
Total Seventh Census.	872	227,469,077	412,607,653	48,671,138	155,012,881	127,567,655
Increase	770	194,421,018	278,887,927	34,893,390	52,089,596	126,234,474

Table No. 35.

The assessed value of Real Estate and Personal Property, according to the Eighth Census, 1860.

States and Territories.	Real estate.	Personal property.
Alabama	$155,034,089	$277,164,673
Arkansas	63,254,740	116,956,590
California	66,906,631	72,748,036
Connecticut	191,478,842	149,778,134
Delaware	26,273,803	13,493,430
Florida	21,722,810	47,206,875
Georgia	179,801,441	438,430,946
Illinois	287,219,940	101,987,432
Indiana	291,829,992	119,212,432
Iowa	149,433,423	55,733,560
Kansas	16,088,602	6,429,630
Kentucky	277,925,054	250,287,639
Louisiana	280,704,988	155,082,277
Maine	86,717,716	67,662,672
Maryland	65,341,438	231,793,800
Massachusetts	475,413,165	301,744,651
Michigan	123,605,084	39,927,921
Minnesota	25,391,771	6,727,002
Mississippi	157,836,737	351,636,175
Missouri	153,450,577	113,485,274
New Hampshire	59,638,346	64,171,743
New Jersey	151,161,942	145,520,550
New York	1,069,658,080	320,806,558
North Carolina	116,366,573	175,931,029
Ohio	687,518,121	272,348,980
Oregon	6,279,602	12,745,313
Pennsylvania	561,192,980	158,060,355
Rhode Island	83,778,204	41,326,101
South Carolina	129,772,684	359,546,444
Tennessee	219,991,180	162,504,020
Texas	112,476,013	155,316,322
Vermont	65,639,973	19,118,646
Virginia	417,952,228	239,069,108
Wisconsin	148,238,766	37,706,723
District of Columbia	33,097,542	7,987,403
Nebraska Territory	5,732,145	1,694,804
New Mexico Territory	7,018,260	13,820,520
Utah Territory	286,504	3,871,516
Washington Territory	1,876,063	2,518,672
	6,973,106,049	5,111,553,956

TABLE No. 35—Continued.

The true value of Real Estate and Personal Property according to the Seventh Census (1850) and the Eighth Census, (1860,) respectively; also the increase, and increase per cent.

STATES AND TERRITORIES.	REAL ESTATE AND PERSONAL PROPERTY.		Increase.	Increase per cent.
	1850.	1860.		
Alabama	$228,204,332	$495,237,078	$267,032,746	117.01
Arkansas	39,841,025	219,256,473	179,415,448	450 32
California	22,161,872	207,874,613	185,712,741	837.98
Connecticut	155,707,980	444,274,114	288,566,134	185.32
Delaware	21,062,556	46,242,181	25,179,625	119.54
Florida	22,862,270	73,101,500	50,239,230	219.74
Georgia	335,425,714	645,895,237	310,469,523	92.56
Illinois	156,265,006	871,860,282	715,595,276	457.93
Indiana	202,650,264	528,835,371	326,185,107	160.95
Iowa	23,714,638	247,338,265	223,623,627	942.97
Kansas	....	31,327,895	....	....
Kentucky	301,628,456	666,043,112	364,414,656	120.81
Louisiana	233,998,764	602,118,568	368,119,804	157.31
Maine	122,777,571	190,211,600	67,434,029	54.92
Maryland	219,217,364	376,919,944	157,702,580	71.93
Massachusetts	573,342,286	815,237,433	241,895,147	42.19
Michigan	59,787,255	257,163,983	197,376,728	330.13
Minnesota	Not returned.	52,294,413	....	....
Mississippi	228,951,130	607,324,911	378,373,781	165.26
Missouri	137,247,707	501,214,398	363,966,691	265.18
New Hampshire	103,652,835	156,310,860	52,658,025	50.80
New Jersey*	200,000,000	467,918,324	267,918,324	133.95
New York	1,080,309,216	1,843,338,517	763,029,301	70.63
North Carolina	226,800,472	358,739,399	131,938,927	58.17
Ohio	504,726,120	1,193,898,422	689,172,302	136.54
Oregon	5,063,474	28,930,637	23,867,163	471.35
Pennsylvania	722,486,120	1,416,501,818	694,015,698	96.05
Rhode Island	80,508,794	135,337,588	54,828,794	68.10
South Carolina	288,257,694	548,138,754	259,881,060	90.15
Tennessee	201,246,686	493,903,892	292,657,206	145.42
Texas	52,740,473	365,200,614	312,460,141	592.44
Vermont	92,205,049	122,477,170	30,272,121	32.83
Virginia	430,701,082	793,249,681	362,548,599	84.17
Wisconsin	42,056,595	273,671,668	231,615,073	550.72
District of Columbia	14,018,874	41,084,945	27,066,071	193.06
Nebraska Territory	....	9,131,056	....	....
New Mexico Territory	5,174,471	20,813,768	15,639,298	302.24
Utah Territory	986,083	5,596,118	4,610,035	467.50
Washington Territory	....	5,601,466	....	....
	7,135,780,228	16,159,616,068	8,925,481,011	126.45

* Partly estimated.

TABLE No. 36.—*Productions of Agriculture for* 1850 *and* 1860.

STATES.	LANDS IMPROVED.		LANDS UNIMPROVED.	
	1850.	1860.	1850.	1860.
	Acres.	*Acres.*	*Acres.*	*Acres.*
Alabama	4,435,614	6,462,987	7,702,067	12,687,913
Arkansas	781,530	1,933,036	1,816,684	7,609,938
California	32,454	2,430,882	3,861,531	6,533,858
Connecticut	1,768,178	1,830,808	615,701	673,457
Delaware	580,862	637,065	375,282	367,230
Florida	349,049	676,464	1,246,240	2,273,008
Georgia	6,378,479	8,062,758	16,442,900	18,587,732
Illinois	5,039,545	13,251,473	6,997,867	7,993,557
Indiana	5,046,543	8,161,717	7,746,879	8,154,059
Iowa	824,682	3,780,253	1,911,382	5,649,136
Kansas	....	372,835	....	1,284,626
Kentucky	5,968,270	7,644,217	10,981,478	11,519,059
Louisiana	1,590,025	2,734,901	3,399,018	6,765,879
Maine	2,039,596	2,677,216	2,515,797	3,023,539
Maryland	2,797,905	3,002,269	1,836,445	1,833,306
Massachusetts	2,133,436	2,155,512	1,222,576	1,183,212
Michigan	1,929,110	3,419,861	2,454,780	3,511,581
Minnesota	5,035	554,397	23,846	2,222,734
Mississippi	3,444,358	5,150,008	7,046,061	11,703,556
Missouri	2,938,425	6,246,871	6,794,245	13,737,938
New Hampshire	2,251,488	2,367,039	1,140,926	1,377,591
New Jersey	1,767,991	1,944,445	984,955	1,039,086
New York	12,408,964	14,376,397	6,710,120	6,616,553
North Carolina	5,453,975	6,517,284	15,543,008	17,245,685
Ohio	9,851,493	12,665,587	8,146,000	8,075,551
Oregon	132,857	895,375	299,951	5,316,817
Pennsylvania	8,623,619	10,463,306	6,294,728	6,548,847
Rhode Island	356,487	329,884	197,451	189,814
South Carolina	4,072,551	4,572,060	12,145,049	11,623,860
Tennessee	5,175,173	6,897,974	13,808,849	13,457,960
Texas	643,976	2,649,207	10,852,363	20,486,990
Vermont	2,601,409	2,758,443	1,524,413	1,402,396
Virginia	10,360,135	11,435,954	15,792,176	19,578,946
Wisconsin	1,045,499	3,746,036	1,931,159	4,153,134
Total States	112,833,813	162,804,521	180,361,927	244,428,549
TERRITORIES.				
Columbia, District of	16,267	17,474	11,187	16,789
Dakota	....	2,115	....	24,333
Nebraska	....	122,582	....	501,723
New Mexico	166,201	149,415	124,370	1,177,055
Utah	16,333	82,260	30,516	58,898
Washington	....	83,022	....	300,897
Total Territories	198,801	456,868	166,073	2,079,695
Aggregate	113,032,614	163,261,389	180,528,000	246,508,244

TABLE No. 36.—*Productions of Agriculture for* 1850 *and* 1860—Continued.

STATES.	CASH VALUE OF FARMS.		VALUE OF FARMING IMPLEMENTS AND MACHINERY.	
	1850.	1860.	1850.	1860.
	Dollars.	*Dollars.*	*Dollars.*	*Dollars.*
Alabama	64,323,224	172,176,168	5,125,663	7,287,599
Arkansas	15,265,245	91,673,403	1,601,296	4,024,114
California	3,874,041	46,571,994	103,483	2,443,297
Connecticut	72,726,422	90,830,005	1,892,541	2,339,481
Delaware	18,880,031	31,426,357	510,279	817,883
Florida	6,323,109	16,371,684	658,795	888,930
Georgia	95,753,445	157,072,803	5,894,150	6,844,387
Illinois	96,133,290	432,531,072	6,405,561	18,276,160
Indiana	136,385,173	344,902,776	6,704,444	10,420,826
Iowa	16,657,567	118,741,405	1,172,869	5,190,042
Kansas	....	11,394,184	....	675,336
Kentucky	155,021,262	291,496,955	5,169,037	7,474,573
Louisiana	75,814,398	215,565,421	11,576,938	20,391,883
Maine	54,861,748	78,690,725	2,284,557	3,298,327
Maryland	87,178,545	145,973,677	2,463,443	4,010,529
Massachusetts	109,076,347	123,255,948	3,209,584	3,894,998
Michigan	51,872,446	163,279,087	2,891,371	5,855,642
Minnesota	161,948	19,070,737	15,981	1,044,009
Mississippi	54,738,634	186,866,914	5,762,927	8,664,816
Missouri	63,225,543	230,632,126	3,981,525	8,711,508
New Hampshire	55,245,997	69,689,761	2,314,125	2,682,412
New Jersey	120,237,511	180,250,338	4,425,503	5,746,567
New York	554,546,642	803,343,593	22,084,926	29,166,565
North Carolina	67,891,766	143,301,065	3,931,532	5,873,942
Ohio	358,758,603	666,564,171	12,750,585	16,790,226
Oregon	2,849,170	14,765,355	183,423	949,103
Pennsylvania	407,876,099	662,050,707	14,722,541	22,442,842
Rhode Island	17,070,802	19,385,573	497,201	587,241
South Carolina	82,431,684	139,652,508	4,136,354	6,151,657
Tennessee	97,851,212	272,555,054	5,360,210	8,371,095
Texas	16,550,008	104,007,689	2,151,704	6,114,362
Vermont	63,367,227	91,511,673	2,739,282	3,554,728
Virginia	216,401,543	371,696,211	7,021,772	9,381,008
Wisconsin	28,528,563	131,117,082	1,641,568	5,758,847
Total States	3,267,879,245	6,638,414,221	151,385,170	246,125,065
TERRITORIES.				
Columbia, District of	1,730,460	2,989,267	40,220	54,410
Dakota	....	97,335	....	15,574
Nebraska	....	3,916,002	....	180,082
New Mexico	1,653,922	2,701,626	77,960	194,005
Utah	311,799	1,637,854	84,288	255,854
Washington	....	1,116,202	....	202,506
Total Territories	3,696,181	12,458,286	202,468	902,431
Aggregate	3,271,575,426	6,650,872,507	151,587,638	247,027,496

TABLE No. 36.—*Productions of*

STATES.	LIVE STOCK.							
	Horses.		Asses and mules.		Milch cows.		Working oxen.	
	1850.	1860.	1850.	1860.	1850.	1860.	1850.	1860.
	Number.	*Number.*	*Number.*	*Number.*	*Number.*	*Number.*	*Number.*	*Number.*
Alabama	128,001	127,205	59,895	108,701	227,791	234,045	66,961	92,495
Arkansas	60,197	101,249	11,559	44,158	93,151	158,873	34,239	70,944
California	21,719	160,395	1,666	13,744	4,280	198,859	4,780	31,527
Connecticut	26,879	33,276	49	82	85,461	98,877	46,988	47,939
Delaware	13,852	16,562	791	2,294	19,248	22,595	9,797	9,530
Florida	10,848	13,424	5,002	10,909	72,876	92,704	5,794	7,787
Georgia	151,331	130,771	57,379	101,069	334,223	299,688	73,286	74,487
Illinois	267,653	575,161	10,573	38,881	294,671	532,731	76,156	90,973
Indiana	314,299	409,504	6,599	18,627	284,554	491,033	40,221	95,982
Iowa	38,536	174,957	754	5,713	45,704	188,546	21,892	56,563
Kansas	....	18,882	....	1,430	....	26,726	....	20,133
Kentucky	315,682	355,704	65,609	117,635	247,475	269,215	62,274	108,999
Louisiana	89,514	79,068	44,849	92,259	105,576	130,672	54,968	61,008
Maine	41,721	60,638	55	104	133,556	147,315	83,893	79,792
Maryland	75,684	93,406	5,644	9,829	86,856	99,463	34,135	34,524
Massachusetts	42,216	47,786	34	108	130,099	144,492	46,611	38,221
Michigan	58,506	154,168	70	359	99,676	200,635	55,350	65,949
Minnesota	860	17,122	14	395	607	40,386	655	27,574
Mississippi	115,460	117,134	54,547	112,488	214,231	207,134	83,485	104,184
Missouri	225,319	361,874	41,667	80,941	230,169	345,243	112,168	166,588
New Hampshire	34,233	41,101	19	10	94,277	94,880	59,027	51,512
New Jersey	63,955	79,707	4,089	6,362	118,736	138,818	12,070	10,067
New York	447,014	503,725	963	1,553	931,324	1,123,634	178,909	121,702
North Carolina	148,693	150,661	25,259	51,388	221,799	228,623	37,309	48,511
Ohio	463,397	622,829	3,423	6,917	544,499	696,309	65,381	61,760
Oregon	8,046	36,600	420	990	9,427	53,072	8,114	7,426
Pennsylvania	350,398	437,654	2,259	8,832	530,224	673,547	61,527	60,371
Rhode Island	6,168	7,121	1	10	18,698	19,700	8,139	7,857
South Carolina	97,171	81,125	37,483	56,456	193,244	163,938	20,507	22,629
Tennessee	270,636	289,548	75,303	119,221	250,456	247,105	86,255	104,495
Texas	76,760	320,621	12,463	63,000	217,811	598,086	51,285	172,243
Vermont	61,057	67,250	218	35	146,218	171,698	48,577	42,860
Virginia	272,403	287,522	21,483	41,014	317,619	330,627	89,513	97,862
Wisconsin	30,179	116,192	156	1,019	64,339	193,996	42,801	93,660
Total States	4,328,387	6,089,942	550,295	1,116,533	6,368,785	8,663,265	1,683,067	2,188,154
TERRITORIES.								
Columbia, District of	824	641	57	122	813	639	104	69
Dakota	....	84	....	19	....	286	....	348
Nebraska	....	4,522	....	473	....	7,125	....	12,720
New Mexico	5,079	10,119	8,654	11,255	10,635	34,461	12,557	26,104
Utah	2,429	5,145	325	973	4,861	13,052	5,266	9,903
Washington	....	5,005	....	178	....	10,034	....	2,777
Total Territories	8,332	25,516	9,036	13,020	16,309	65,597	17,627	51,921
Aggregate	4,336,71[illegible]	6,115,458	559,331	1,129,553	6,385,094	8,728,862	1,700,694	2,240,075

Agriculture for 1850 *and* 1860—Continued.

LIVE STOCK.

Other cattle.		Sheep.		Swine.		Value of live stock.	
1850.	1860.	1850.	1860.	1850.	1860.	1850.	1860.
Number.	*Number.*	*Number.*	*Number.*	*Number.*	*Number.*	*Dollars.*	*Dollars.*
433,263	452,643	371,880	369,061	1,904,540	1,736,959	21,690,112	43,061,805
165,320	318,355	91,256	202,674	836,727	1,155,379	6,647,969	22,040,211
253,599	952,048	17,574	1,075,718	2,776	453,523	3,351,058	36,601,154
80,226	95,091	174,181	117,107	76,472	75,120	7,467,490	11,311,079
24,166	25,596	27,503	18,857	56,261	47,848	1,849,281	3,144,706
182,415	284,736	23,311	29,958	209,453	274,314	2,880,058	5,480,789
690,019	631,707	560,435	512,618	2,168,617	2,036,116	25,728,416	38,372,734
541,209	881,877	894,043	775,230	1,915,907	2,279,722	24,209,258	73,434,621
389,891	582,990	1,122,493	2,157,375	2,263,776	2,498,528	22,478,555	50,116,964
69,025	291,145	149,960	258,228	323,247	921,161	3,689,275	21,776,786
....	41,000	....	15,702	....	128,309	....	3,205,522
442,763	457,845	1,102,091	938,990	2,891,163	2,330,595	29,661,436	61,868,237
414,798	329,855	110,333	180,855	597,301	642,855	11,152,275	24,751,822
125,890	149,827	451,577	452,472	54,598	54,783	9,705,726	15,437,533
98,595	119,254	177,902	155,765	352,911	387,756	7,997,634	14,667,853
83,284	97,201	188,651	114,829	81,119	73,948	9,647,710	12,737,744
119,471	267,683	746,435	1,465,477	205,847	374,664	8,008,734	23,220,026
740	51,043	80	13,123	734	101,252	92,859	3,655,366
436,254	415,559	304,929	337,754	1,582,734	1,534,097	19,403,662	40,245,079
449,173	657,153	762,511	937,445	1,702,625	2,354,425	19,887,580	53,693,673
114,606	118,075	384,756	310,534	63,487	51,935	8,871,901	10,924,627
80,455	89,909	160,488	135,228	250,370	236,089	10,679,291	16,134,693
767,406	727,837	3,453,241	2,617,855	1,018,252	910,178	73,570,499	103,856,296
434,402	416,676	595,249	546,749	1,812,813	1,883,214	17,717,647	31,130,805
749,067	901,781	3,942,929	3,063,887	1,964,770	2,175,623	44,121,741	80,433,780
24,188	93,001	15,382	75,936	30,235	79,660	1,876,189	6,272,892
562,195	685,575	1,822,357	1,631,540	1,040,366	1,031,266	41,500,053	69,672,726
9,375	11,548	44,296	32,624	19,509	17,478	1,532,637	2,042,044
563,935	320,209	285,551	233,509	1,065,503	965,779	15,060,015	23,934,465
414,051	408,574	811,591	773,317	3,104,800	2,343,948	29,978,016	61,257,374
661,018	2,733,267	100,530	783,618	692,022	1,368,378	10,412,927	52,892,934
154,143	149,359	1,014,122	721,993	66,296	49,433	12,643,228	15,884,393
669,137	615,696	1,310,004	1,042,946	1,829,843	1,589,519	33,656,659	47,794,256
76,293	225,210	124,896	332,454	159,276	333,957	4,897,385	17,807,366
10,280,372	14,599,325	21,342,537	22,431,428	30,344,350	32,497,811	542,067,276	1,098,862,355
123	198	150	40	1,635	1,099	71,643	109,640
....	338	....	22	....	287	....	39,116
....	8,870	....	1,757	....	25,965	....	1,216,328
10,085	29,228	377,271	836,459	7,314	9,489	1,494,629	4,386,084
2,489	17,369	3,262	37,888	914	10,780	546,968	1,729,012
....	16,072	....	10,162	....	9,836	....	1,147,681
12,697	72,075	380,683	886,328	9,863	57,456	2,113,240	8,627,861
10,293,069	14,671,400	21,723,220	23,317,756	30,354,213	32,555,267	544,180,516	1,107,490,216

TABLE NO. 36.—*Productions of Agriculture*

STATES.	WHEAT.		RYE.		INDIAN CORN.	
	1850.	1860.	1850.	1860.	1850.	1860.
	Bushels.	*Bushels.*	*Bushels.*	*Bushels.*	*Bushels.*	*Bushels.*
Alabama	294,044	1,222,487	17,261	73,942	28,754,048	32,761,194
Arkansas	199,639	955,298	8,047	77,869	8,893,939	17,758,665
California	17,228	5,946,619	....	51,244	12,236	524,857
Connecticut	41,762	52,401	600,893	618,702	1,935,043	2,059,835
Delaware	482,511	912,941	8,066	27,209	3,145,542	3,892,337
Florida	1,027	2,808	1,152	21,314	1,996,809	2,824,538
Georgia	1,088,534	2,544,913	53,750	115,532	30,080,099	30,776,293
Illinois	9,414,575	24,159,500	83,364	981,322	57,646,984	115,296,779
Indiana	6,214,458	15,219,120	78,792	400,226	52,964,363	69,641,591
Iowa	1,530,581	8,433,205	19,916	176,055	8,656,799	41,116,994
Kansas	....	168,527	....	3,928	....	5,678,834
Kentucky	2,142,822	7,394,811	415,073	1,055,262	58,672,591	64,043,633
Louisiana	417	29,283	475	12,789	10,266,373	16,205,856
Maine	296,259	233,877	102,916	123,290	1,750,056	1,546,071
Maryland	4,494,680	6,103,480	226,014	518,901	10,749,858	13,444,922
Massachusetts	31,211	119,783	481,021	388,085	2,345,490	2,157,063
Michigan	4,925,889	8,313,185	105,871	494,197	5,641,420	12,152,110
Minnesota	1,401	2,195,812	125	124,259	16,725	2,987,570
Mississippi	137,990	579,452	9,606	41,260	22,446,552	29,563,735
Missouri	2,981,652	4,227,586	44,268	293,262	36,214,537	72,892,157
New Hampshire	185,658	238,966	183,117	128,248	1,573,670	1,414,628
New Jersey	1,601,190	1,763,128	1,255,578	1,439,497	8,759,704	9,723,336
New York	13,121,498	8,681,100	4,148,182	4,786,905	17,858,400	20,061,048
North Carolina	2,130,102	4,743,706	229,563	436,856	27,941,051	30,078,564
Ohio	14,487,351	14,532,570	425,918	656,146	59,078,695	70,637,140
Oregon	211,943	822,408	106	2,714	2,918	74,566
Pennsylvania	15,367,691	13,045,231	4,805,160	5,474,792	19,835,214	28,196,821
Rhode Island	49	1,131	26,409	28,259	539,201	458,912
South Carolina	1,066,277	1,285,631	43,790	89,091	16,271,454	15,065,606
Tennessee	1,619,386	5,409,863	89,137	265,344	52,276,223	50,748,266
Texas	41,729	1,464,273	3,108	95,012	6,028,876	16,521,593
Vermont	535,955	431,127	176,233	130,676	2,032,396	1,463,020
Virginia	11,212,616	13,129,180	458,930	944,024	35,254,319	38,360,704
Wisconsin	4,286,131	15,812,625	81,253	888,534	1,988,979	7,565,290
Total States	100,164,356	170,176,027	14,183,094	20,965,046	591,630,564	827,694,528
TERRITORIES.						
Columbia, District of	17,370	12,760	5,509	6,939	65,230	80,840
Dakota	....	945	....	700	....	20,296
Nebraska	....	72,268	....	1,185	....	1,846,785
New Mexico	196,516	446,075	....	1,300	365,411	710,605
Utah	107,702	382,697	210	872	9,899	93,861
Washington	....	92,609	....	244	....	4,792
Total Territories	321,588	1,007,354	5,719	11,240	440,540	2,757,179
Aggregate	100,485,944	171,183,381	14,188,813	20,976,286	592,071,104	830,451,707

for 1850 *and* 1860—Continued.

OATS.		RICE.		TOBACCO.		GINNED COTTON.	
1850.	1860.	1850.	1860.	1850.	1860.	1850.	1860.
Bushels.	*Bushels.*	*Pounds.*	*Pounds.*	*Pounds.*	*Pounds*	*Bales.**	*Bales.**
2,965,696	716,435	2,312,252	499,559	164,990	221,284	564,429	997,978
656,183	502,866	63,179	215	218,936	999,757	65,344	367,485
....	957,684	....	1,800	1,000	3,150	....	....
1,258,738	1,522,218	....	....	1,267,624	6,000,133	....	....
604,518	1,046,910	....	....	....	9,699	....	....
66,586	46,779	1,075,090	223,209	998,614	758,015	45,131	63,322
3,820,044	1,231,817	38,950,691	52,507,652	423,924	919,316	499,091	701,840
10,087,241	15,336,072	....	....	841,394	7,014,230	....	6
5,655,014	5,028,755	....	1,219	1,044,620	7,246,132	14	....
1,524,345	5,879,653	....	....	6,041	312,919	....	....
....	80,744	....	....	....	16,978	....	....
8,201,311	4,617,0[illegible]9	5,688	24,407	55,501,196	108,102,433	758	4,092
89,637	65,845	4,425,349	6,455,017	26,878	40,610	178,737	722,218
2,181,037	2,988,939	....	....	....	1,583	....	....
2,242,151	3,959,298	....	....	21,407,497	38,410,965	....	....
1,165,146	1,180,075	....	....	138,246	3,233,198	....	....
2,866,056	4,073,098	....	....	1,245	120,621	....	....
30,582	2,202,050	....	....	....	38,510	....	....
1,503,288	121,033	2,719,856	657,293	49,960	127,736	484,292	1,195,699
5,278,079	3,680,870	700	9,767	17,113,784	25,086,196	....	100
973,381	1,329,213	....	....	50	21,281	....	....
3,378,063	4,539,132	....	....	310	149,485	....	....
26,552,814	35,175,133	....	1,120	83,189	5,764,582	....	....
4,052,078	*2,781,860*	*5,465,868*	*7,593,976*	11,984,786	32,853,250	50,545	145,514
13,472,742	15,479,133	....	....	10,454,449	25,528,972	....	....
61,214	900,204	....	....	325	215	....	....
21,538,156	27,387,149	....	....	912,651	3,181,586	....	....
215,232	234,453	....	....	....	705	....	....
2,322,155	936,974	159,930,613	119,100,528	74,285	104,412	300,901	353,413
7,703,086	2,343,122	258,854	30,516	20,148,932	38,931,277	194,532	227,450
199,017	988,812	88,203	25,670	66,897	98,016	58,072	405,100
2,307,734	3,511,605	....	....	....	12,153	....	....
10,179,144	10,184,865	17,154	8,225	56,803,227	123,967,757	3,947	12,727
3,414,672	11,059,270	....	....	1,268	87,595	....	....
146,565,140	172,089,095	215,313,497	187,140,173	199,736,318	429,364,751	2,445,793	5,196,9[illegible]4
8,134	29,548	....	....	7,800	15,200	....	....
....	2,540	....	....	....	....	....	....
....	79,977	....	....	....	3,801	....	....
5	7,491	....	....	8,467	6,999	....	....
10,900	188,036	....	....	70	10	....	1,133
....	158,001	....	....	....	10	....	....
19,039	465,593	....	....	16,337	26,020	....	1,133
146,584,179	172,554,688	215,313,497	187,140,173	199,752,655	429,390,771	2,445,793	5,198,077

* Of 400 pounds each.

TABLE No. 36.—*Productions of Agriculture*

STATES.	WOOL.		PEAS AND BEANS.		IRISH POTATOES.	
	1850.	1860.	1850.	1860.	1850.	1860.
	Pounds.	*Pounds.*	*Bushels.*	*Bushels.*	*Bushels.*	*Bushels.*
Alabama	657,118	681,404	892,701	1,483,609	246,001	397,566
Arkansas	182,595	410,285	285,738	439,412	193,832	418,000
California	5,520	2,681,922	2,292	184,962	9,292	1,647,293
Connecticut	497,454	335,986	19,090	25,864	2,689,725	1,833,148
Delaware	57,768	50,201	4,120	7,438	240,542	377,931
Florida	23,247	58,594	135,359	364,738	7,828	18,549
Georgia	990,019	946,229	1,142,011	1,765,214	227,379	316,552
Illinois	2,150,113	2,477,563	82,814	112,624	2,514,861	5,799,964
Indiana	2,610,287	2,466,264	35,773	77,701	2,083,337	3,873,130
Iowa	373,898	653,036	4,775	45,570	276,120	2,700,515
Kansas	....	22,593	....	10,167	....	283,968
Kentucky	2,297,433	2,325,124	202,574	288,349	1,492,487	1,756,532
Louisiana	109,897	296,187	161,732	430,410	95,632	332,725
Maine	1,364,034	1,495,063	205,541	246,918	3,436,040	6,374,617
Maryland	477,438	491,511	12,816	34,407	764,939	1,264,429
Massachusetts	585,136	377,267	43,709	45,346	3,585,384	3,201,901
Michigan	2,043,283	4,062,858	74,254	182,195	2,359,897	5,264,733
Minnesota	85	22,740	10,002	18,802	21,145	2,027,945
Mississippi	559,619	637,729	1,072,757	1,986,558	261,482	401,804
Missouri	1,627,164	2,069,778	46,017	107,999	939,006	1,990,850
New Hampshire	1,108,476	1,160,212	70,856	79,455	4,304,919	4,137,543
New Jersey	375,396	349,250	14,174	27,675	3,207,236	4,171,690
New York	10,071,301	9,454,473	741,546	1,609,334	15,398,368	26,447,389
North Carolina	970,738	883,473	1,584,252	1,932,204	620,318	830,565
Ohio	10,196,371	10,648,161	60,168	105,219	5,057,769	8,752,873
Oregon	29,686	208,943	6,566	34,616	91,326	311,700
Pennsylvania	4,481,570	4,752,523	55,231	123,094	5,980,732	11,687,468
Rhode Island	129,692	90,699	6,846	7,699	651,029	542,909
South Carolina	487,233	427,102	1,026,900	1,728,074	136,494	226,735
Tennessee	1,364,378	1,400,508	369,321	550,913	1,067,844	1,174,647
Texas	131,917	1,497,748	179,350	359,560	94,645	168,937
Vermont	3,400,717	2,975,544	104,649	68,912	4,951,014	5,147,908
Virginia	2,860,765	2,509,443	521,579	515,004	1,316,933	2,292,118
Wisconsin	253,963	1,011,915	20,657	99,804	1,402,077	3,848,505
Total States	52,474,311	59,932,328	9,196,170	15,099,746	65,725,633	110,023,139
TERRITORIES.						
Columbia, District of	525	100	7,754	3,749	28,292	31,733
Dakota	....	....	....	286	....	9,489
Nebraska	....	3,312	....	4,508	....	169,762
New Mexico	32,901	479,245	15,688	38,584	3	5,354
Utah	9,222	75,638	289	3,135	43,968	140,370
Washington	....	20,720	....	38,005	....	191,354
Total Territories	42,648	579,015	23,731	88,267	72,263	548,062
Aggregate	52,516,959	60,511,343	9,219,901	15,188,013	65,797,896	110,571,201

for 1850 *and* 1860—Continued.

SWEET POTATOES.		BARLEY.		BUCKWHEAT.		VALUE OF ORCHARD PRODUCTS.	
1850.	1860.	1850.	1860.	1850.	1860.	1850.	1860.
Bushels.	*Bushels.*	*Bushels.*	*Bushels.*	*Bushels.*	*Bushels.*	*Dollars.*	*Dollars.*
5,475,204	5,420,987	3,958	14,703	348	1,334	15,408	213,323
788,149	1,462,714	177	3,079	175	488	40,141	56,230
1,000	158,001	9,712	4,307,775	....	36,486	17,700	607,459
80	2,710	19,099	20,813	229,297	309,107	175,118	508,848
65,443	142,213	56	3,646	8,615	16,355	46,574	114,225
757,226	1,213,493	....	15	55	....	1,280	21,716
6,986,428	6,508,541	11,501	14,682	250	2,023	92,776	176,048
157,433	341,443	110,795	1,175,651	184,504	345,069	446,049	1,145,936
201,711	284,304	45,483	296,374	149,740	367,797	324,940	1,212,142
6,243	50,938	25,093	454,116	52,516	216,524	8,434	131,234
....	9,221	....	4,128	....	36,799	....	724
998,179	1,057,558	95,343	270,685	16,097	18,929	106,230	604,851
1,428,453	2,070,901	....	144	3	160	22,359	110,923
....	1,435	151,731	802,109	104,523	339,520	342,865	501,767
208,993	23,744	745	17,350	103,671	212,338	164,051	252,196
....	616	112,385	134,891	105,895	123,202	463,995	925,519
1,177	36,285	75,249	305,914	472,917	600,435	132,650	1,137,678
200	781	1,216	125,130	515	27,677	....	298
4,741,795	4,348,491	228	1,596	1,121	1,740	50,405	259,380
335,505	335,102	9,631	228,502	23,641	182,292	514,711	810,975
....	161	70,256	121,103	65,265	89,996	248,563	557,934
508,015	1,034,832	6,492	24,915	878,934	877,386	607,268	429,402
5,629	7,523	3,585,059	4,186,667	3,183,955	5,126,305	1,761,950	3,726,380
5,095,709	6,140,039	2,735	3,445	16,704	35,924	34,348	643,688
187,991	297,908	354,358	1,601,082	638,060	2,327,005	695,921	1,858,673
....	335	....	26,463	....	2,685	1,271	474,934
52,172	103,190	165,584	530,716	2,193,692	5,572,026	723,389	1,479,938
....	946	18,875	40,993	1,245	3,573	63,994	83,691
4,337,469	4,115,698	4,583	11,490	283	602	35,108	213,989
2,777,716	2,614,558	2,737	23,489	19,427	14,421	52,894	314,269
1,332,158	1,853,306	4,776	38,905	59	1,612	12,505	46,802
....	623	42,150	75,282	209,819	215,821	315,255	198,427
1,813,634	1,960,808	25,437	68,759	214,898	477,808	177,137	800,650
879	2,345	209,692	678,992	79,878	67,622	4,823	76,096
38,264,591	41,601,750	5,165,136	15,613,604	8,956,102	17,651,061	7,700,112	19,696,345
3,497	4,191	75	175	378	445	14,843	9,980
....	....	....	....	....	....	....	115
....	163	....	1,243	....	12,329	....	161
....	180	5	6,099	100	6	8,231	19,701
60	....	1,799	12,283	332	96	....	9,280
....	18	....	1,715	....	977	....	23,779
3,557	4,552	1,879	21,515	810	13,853	23,074	63,016
38,268,148	41,606,302	5,167,015	15,635,119	8,956,912	17,664,914	7,723,186	19,759,361

TABLE No. 36.—*Productions of Agriculture*

STATES.	WINE.		VALUE OF PRODUCTIONS OF MARKET GARDENS.		BUTTER.	
	1850.	1860.	1850.	1860.	1850.	1860.
	Gallons.	*Gallons.*	*Dollars.*	*Dollars.*	*Pounds.*	*Pounds.*
Alabama	220	19,130	84,821	135,181	4,008,811	6,125,708
Arkansas	35	1,005	17,150	38,094	1,854,239	4,062,481
California	58,055	494,516	75,275	1,074,143	705	3,338,590
Connecticut	4,269	46,783	196,874	337,025	6,498,119	7,620,912
Delaware	145	683	12,714	37,797	1,055,308	1,430,502
Florida	10	1,661	8,721	18,213	371,498	404,470
Georgia	796	27,646	76,500	201,916	4,640,559	5,439,765
Illinois	2,997	47,093	127,494	418,195	12,526,543	28,337,516
Indiana	14,055	88,275	72,864	288,070	12,881,535	17,934,767
Iowa	420	3,706	8,848	141,549	2,171,188	11,526,002
Kansas	....	241	....	36,353	....	1,012,975
Kentucky	8,093	179,949	303,120	458,246	9,947,523	11,716,609
Louisiana	15	5,030	148,329	390,742	683,069	1,440,943
Maine	724	3,165	122,387	194,006	9,243,811	11,687,781
Maryland	1,431	3,222	200,869	530,221	3,806,160	5,265,295
Massachusetts	4,688	20,915	600,020	1,397,623	8,071,370	8,297,936
Michigan	1,654	13,733	14,738	145,058	7,065,878	14,650,384
Minnesota	....	394	150	94,681	1,100	2,961,591
Mississippi	407	10,106	46,250	124,608	4,346,234	5,111,185
Missouri	10,563	27,827	99,454	346,405	7,834,359	12,704,837
New Hampshire	344	9,401	56,810	76,256	6,977,056	6,956,764
New Jersey	1,811	21,083	475,242	1,542,155	9,487,210	10,714,447
New York	9,172	61,404	912,047	3,381,596	79,766,094	103,097,279
North Carolina	11,058	54,064	39,462	75,663	4,146,290	4,735,495
Ohio	48,207	562,640	214,004	860,313	34,449,379	50,495,745
Oregon	....	2,603	90,241	86,335	211,464	1,012,339
Pennsylvania	25,590	38,623	688,714	1,384,970	39,878,418	58,653,511
Rhode Island	1,013	507	98,298	146,661	995,670	1,014,856
South Carolina	5,880	24,964	47,286	187,348	2,981,850	3,177,934
Tennessee	92	13,562	97,183	274,163	8,139,585	10,000,823
Texas	99	13,946	12,354	55,943	2,344,900	5,948,611
Vermont	659	2,923	18,853	24,792	12,137,980	15,681,834
Virginia	5,408	40,508	183,047	589,411	11,089,359	13,461,712
Wisconsin	113	9,511	32,142	207,153	3,633,750	13,651,053
Total States	218,023	1,850,819	5,182,261	15,300,885	313,247,014	459,672,652
TERRITORIES.						
Columbia, District of	863	118	67,222	139,108	14,872	18,835
Dakota	....	....	....	500	....	1,670
Nebraska	....	631	....	9,680	....	352,697
New Mexico	2,363	8,201	6,679	17,640	111	13,133
Utah	....	60	23,868	45,465	83,309	293,065
Washington	....	179	....	27,749	....	157,802
Total Territories	3,226	9,189	97,769	240,142	98,292	837,202
Aggregate	221,249	1,860,008	5,280,030	15,541,027	313,345,306	460,509,854

for 1850 *and* 1860—Continued.

CHEESE.		HAY.		CLOVER SEED.		GRASS SEED.	
1850.	1860.	1850.	1860.	1850.	1860.	1850.	1860.
Pounds.	*Pounds.*	*Tons.*	*Tons.*	*Bushels.*	*Bushels.*	*Bushels.*	*Bushels.*
31,412	9,607	32,685	55,219	138	187	547	653
30,088	16,952	3,976	8,276	90	60	436	3,110
150	1,564,857	2,038	306,741	....	4	....	162
5,363,277	3,898,411	516,131	562,425	13,841	13,671	16,628	13,024
3,187	6,579	30,159	36,973	2,525	3,595	1,403	1,165
18,015	3,784	2,510	7,594	....	....	2	....
46,976	15,587	23,449	46,448	132	635	428	1,914
1,278,225	1,595,358	601,952	1,834,265	3,427	16,687	14,380	202,808
624,564	569,574	403,230	635,322	18,320	45,321	11,951	31,866
209,840	901,220	89,055	707,260	342	1,564	2,096	69,432
....	28,053	....	50,812	....	98	....	2,633
213,954	190,400	113,747	158,484	3,230	2,308	21,481	62,563
1,957	5,494	25,752	46,999	2	....	97	701
2,434,454	1,799,862	755,889	975,716	9,097	48,851	9,214	6,307
3,975	8,342	157,956	191,744	15,217	39,811	2,561	3,195
7,088,142	5,294,090	651,807	665,331	1,002	1,295	5,085	4,852
1,011,492	2,009,064	404,934	756,908	16,989	49,480	9,285	6,555
....	198,904	2,019	274,952	....	156	....	2,314
21,191	3,419	12,504	32,885	84	217	533	1,175
203,572	259,633	116,925	401,070	619	2,216	4,346	55,713
3,196,563	2,232,092	598,854	642,741	829	11,992	8,071	5,573
365,756	182,172	435,950	508,729	28,280	39,208	63,051	85,410
49,741,413	48,548,288	3,728,797	3,564,786	88,222	106,933	96,493	81,622
95,921	51,119	145,653	181,365	576	332	1,275	3,008
20,819,542	23,758,738	1,443,142	1,602,513	103,197	216,545	37,310	53,475
36,980	82,456	373	26,441	4	307	22	3,793
2,505,034	2,508,556	1,842,970	2,245,420	125,030	274,363	53,913	57,204
316,508	177,252	74,418	82,725	1,328	1,221	3,708	4,229
4,970	1,543	20,925	87,592	376	28	30	38
177,681	126,794	74,091	146,027	5,096	8,062	9,118	41,532
95,299	277,512	8,354	11,349	10	449	....	2,976
8,720,834	8,077,689	866,153	919,066	760	2,444	14,936	11,420
436,292	280,792	369,098	445,529	29,727	36,961	23,428	53,063
400,283	1,104,459	275,662	853,799	483	3,848	5,003	26,383
105,497,547	105,788,652	13,831,558	19,073,506	468,973	928,849	416,831	899,868
1,500	....	2,279	3,180	3	....	....	....
....	....	....	1,122	....	35	....	....
....	15,762	....	25,320	....	5	....	206
5,848	37,250	....	1,103	....	2	....	....
30,998	21,325	4,805	20,026	2	3	....	101
....	12,146	....	4,871	....	116	....	211
38,346	86,483	7,084	55,622	5	161	....	518
105,535,893	105,875,135	13,838,642	19,129,128	468,978	929,010	416,831	900,386

TABLE No. 36.—*Productions of Agriculture*

STATES.	HEMP.						HOPS.	
	Dew-rotted.		Water-rotted.		Other prepared.			
	1850.	1860.	1850.	1860.	1850.	1860.	1850.	1860.
	Tons.	*Tons.*	*Tons.*	*Tons.*	*Tons.*	*Tons.*	*Pounds.*	*Pounds.*
Alabama	....	....	....	....	....	....	276	1,069
Arkansas	....	140	15	30	....	676	157	164
California	....	....	....	....	....	....	....	10
Connecticut	....	3	....	....	....	....	554	959
Delaware	....	....	....	....	....	....	348	414
Florida	....	....	....	....	....	1	14	....
Georgia	....	1	....	....	....	30	261	199
Illinois	....	....	....	....	....	....	3,551	7,129
Indiana	....	....	....	....	....	1	92,796	75,053
Iowa	....	....	....	....	....	....	8,242	1,797
Kansas	....	44	....	....	....	....	....	130
Kentucky	16,432	33,044	1,355	2,026	....	4,344	4,309	5,899
Louisiana	....	....	....	....	....	....	125	8
Maine	....	....	....	....	....	50	40,120	102,987
Maryland	63	18	....	....	....	254	1,870	2,943
Massachusetts	....	....	....	....	....	....	121,595	111,301
Michigan	....	....	....	....	....	....	10,663	61,704
Minnesota	....	....	....	....	....	....	....	149
Mississippi	7	6	....	....	....	....	473	221
Missouri	15,968	15,789	60	1,507	....	1,972	4,130	2,265
New Hampshire	....	18	....	50	....	13	257,174	130,428
New Jersey	....	230	....	....	....	200	2,133	3,722
New York	1	32,191	3	99	....	3,531	2,536,299	9,655,542
North Carolina	36	....	3	....	....	3,016	9,246	1,767
Ohio	100	....	50	....	....	3	63,731	22,344
Oregon	....	5	....	....	....	....	8	187
Pennsylvania	44	1,640	....	189	....	2,174	22,088	41,576
Rhode Island	....	....	....	....	....	....	277	50
South Carolina	....	1	....	....	....	....	26	122
Tennessee	454	6	141	10	....	787	1,032	2,329
Texas	....	....	....	10	....	....	7	122
Vermont	....	2	....	1	....	....	288,023	631,641
Virginia	88	5	51	3	....	4	11,506	10,015
Wisconsin	....	97	....	15	....	244	15,930	135,587
Total States	33,193	83,240	1,678	3,940	....	17,300	3,496,964	11,009,833
TERRITORIES.								
Columbia, District of	....	....	....	....	....	....	15	15
Dakota	....	....	....	....	....	....	....	....
Nebraska	....	7	....	2	....	....	....	41
New Mexico	....	....	....	....	....	....	....	....
Utah	....	....	....	1	....	....	50	95
Washington	....	....	....	....	....	....	....	28
Total Territories	....	7	....	3	....	....	65	179
Aggregate	33,193	83,247	1,678	3,943	....	17,300	3,497,029	11,010,012

for 1850 *and* 1860—Continued.

FLAX.		FLAXSEED.		SILK COCOONS.		MAPLE SUGAR.	
1850.	1860.	1850.	1860.	1850.	1860.	1850.	1860.
Pounds.	*Pounds.*	*Bushels.*	*Bushels.*	*Pounds.*	*Pounds.*	*Pounds.*	*Pounds.*
3,921	109	69	68	167	......	643	543
12,291	3,233	321	541	38	1	9,330	3,097
......	......	......	......	......	......	......	......
17,928	1,187	703	109	328	18	50,796	44,259
11,174	8,112	904	2,126	......	9	......	......
50	......	......	......	6	......	......	......
5,387	3,303	622	96	813	72	50	991
160,063	32,636	10,787	11,202	47	436	248,904	131,751
584,469	73,112	36,888	155,159	387	959	2,921,192	1,515,594
62,660	28,888	1,959	6,130	246	217	78,407	248,951
......	13	......	9	......	......	......	1,548
2,100,116	728,234	75,801	28,881	1,281	340	437,405	380,941
......	......	......	......	29	......	255	......
17,081	2,997	580	489	252	73	93,542	306,742
35,686	14,481	2,446	1,570	39	3	47,740	63,281
1,162	165	72	7	7	......	795,525	1,006,078
7,152	3,359	519	223	108	1,043	2,439,794	2,988,018
......	1,968	......	73	......	......	2,950	370,947
665	......	26	10	2	......	......	99
627,160	109,837	13,696	4,656	186	127	178,910	142,430
7,652	1,347	189	31	191	1	1,298,863	2,255,012
182,965	48,651	16,525	3,241	23	......	2,197	3,455
940,577	1,514,476	57,963	56,986	1,774	259	10,357,487	10,816,458
593,796	216,490	38,196	20,008	229	338	27,932	30,845
446,932	......	188,880	250,768	1,552	2,166	4,588,209	3,323,942
640	50	......	4	......	......	......	......
530,307	310,030	41,728	24,209	285	163	2,326,525	2,768,965
85	......	......	......	......	......	28	......
333	344	55	313	123	20	200	205
368,131	161,740	18,904	9,611	1,923	50	158,557	117,359
1,048	......	26	......	22	26	......	69
20,852	5,107	939	331	268	......	6,349,357	9,819,939
1,000,450	487,330	52,318	30,673	517	225	1,227,665	937,643
68,393	21,644	1,191	4,256	......	15	610,976	1,584,406
7,709,126	3,778,843	562,307	611,780	10,843	6,561	34,253,436	38,863,568
......	......	......	......	......	......	......	......
......	......	......	......	......	......	......	......
......	......	......	2	......	......	......	316
......	......	......	......	......	......	......	......
550	4,197	5	145	......	1	......	......
......	39	......	......	......	......	......	......
550	4,236	5	147	......	1	......	316
7,709,676	3,783,079	562,312	611,927	10,843	6,562	34,253,436	38,863,884

TABLE No. 36.—*Productions of Agriculture*

STATES.	CANE SUGAR.		CANE MOLASSES.		SORGHUM MOLASSES.	MAPLE MOLASSES.
	1850.	1860.	1850.	1860.	1860.	1860.
	*Hhds.**	*Hhds.**	*Gallons.*	*Gallons.*	*Gallons.*	*Gallons.*
Alabama	87	108	83,428	81,694	67,172	...
Arkansas	...	...	18	...	...	115,673
California	...	...	...	...	100	...
Connecticut	...	...	665	...	395	2,277
Delaware	...	...	50	761	852	...
Florida	2,750	1,761	352,893	435,890	...	...
Georgia	846	1,167	216,245	546,770	103,450	20
Illinois	...	...	8,354	...	797,096	21,423
Indiana	...	...	180,325	...	827,777	203,028
Iowa	...	...	3,162	...	1,993,474	97,751
Kansas	...	...	...	...	79,482	2
Kentucky	10	...	30,079	...	365,861	139,036
Louisiana	226,001	297,816	10,931,177	14,535,157	...	66,470
Maine	...	...	3,167	...	...	...
Maryland	...	...	1,430	45	862	2,404
Massachusetts	...	...	4,693	...	...	...
Michigan	...	...	19,823	...	266,509	384,521
Minnesota	...	...	...	...	14,974	21,829
Mississippi	8	244	18,318	3,445	8,207	...
Missouri	...	...	5,636	22,305	776,101	18,289
New Hampshire	...	...	9,811	...	...	...
New Jersey	...	...	954	36	360	8,088
New York	...	...	56,539	15	265	131,841
North Carolina	...	38	704	12,494	263,475	17,759
Ohio	...	...	197,308	...	707,416	392,932
Oregon	...	...	24	...	419	...
Pennsylvania	...	...	50,652	...	9,605	127,455
Rhode Island	...	...	4	15	...	5
South Carolina	77	198	15,904	15,144	51,041	...
Tennessee	3	...	7,223	294,322	485,828	6,754
Texas	7,351	590	441,918	388,937	115,051	3,600
Vermont	...	...	5,997	...	...	...
Virginia	...	...	40,322	50	221,017	100,139
Wisconsin	...	283	9,874	...	19,253	83,003
Total States	237,133	302,205	12,696,697	16,337,080	7,176,042	1,944,299
TERRITORIES.						
Columbia, District of	...	...	...	...	...	...
Dakota	...	...	...	...	...	20
Nebraska	...	...	...	...	23,105	275
New Mexico	...	...	4,236	...	3,369	...
Utah	...	...	58	...	32,509	...
Washington	...	...	...	...	...	...
Total Territories	...	...	4,294	...	58,983	295
Aggregate	237,133	302,205	12,700,991	16,337,080	7,235,025	1,944,594

* Of 1,000 pounds each.

for 1850 *and* 1860—Continued.

BEESWAX AND HONEY.	BEESWAX.	HONEY.	TOTAL BEESWAX & HONEY.	VALUE OF HOME-MADE MANUFACTURES.		VALUE OF ANIMALS SLAUGHTERED.	
1850.	1860.	1860.	1860.	1850.	1860.	1850.	1860.
Pounds.	*Pounds.*	*Pounds.*	*Pounds.*	*Dollars.*	*Dollars.*	*Dollars.*	*Dollars.*
897,021	153,018	1,189,073	1,342,091	1,934,120	1,920,175	4,823,485	10,325,022
192,338	50,797	802,748	853,545	638,217	928,481	1,163,313	3,895,399
....	570	2,370	2,940	7,000	265,674	107,173	3,562,887
93,304	4,371	62,730	67,101	192,252	48,954	2,202,266	3,181,992
41,248	1,993	66,137	68,130	38,121	17,591	373,665	573,075
18,971	10,883	1,163,540	1,174,423	75,582	62,243	514,685	1,201,441
732,514	61,505	953,915	1,015,420	1,838,968	1,431,413	6,339,762	10,908,204
869,444	56,874	1,333,280	1,390,154	1,155,902	933,815	4,972,286	15,159,343
935,329	35,074	1,186,865	1,221,939	1,631,039	847,251	6,567,935	9,592,322
321,711	32,802	919,750	952,552	221,292	314,016	821,164	4,403,463
....	467	14,942	15,409	....	15,371	....	547,450
1,158,019	68,340	1,768,692	1,837,032	2,459,128	2,095,578	6,462,598	11,640,740
96,701	4,748	90,770	95,518	139,232	503,124	1,458,990	2,083,736
189,618	8,769	314,685	323,454	513,599	490,787	1,646,773	2,780,179
74,802	6,960	193,354	200,314	111,828	67,003	1,954,800	2,821,510
59,508	3,289	59,125	62,414	205,333	245,886	2,500,924	2,915,045
359,232	41,972	728,900	770,872	340,947	143,181	1,328,327	4,080,720
80	2,083	32,840	34,923	....	8,057	2,840	732,418
397,460	40,449	595,859	636,308	1,164,020	1,318,426	3,636,582	7,528,007
1,328,972	79,190	1,585,983	1,665,173	1,674,705	1,984,262	3,367,106	9,844,449
117,140	4,936	125,142	130,078	393,455	251,013	1,522,873	3,787,500
156,694	8,130	185,925	194,055	112,781	27,588	2,638,552	4,120,276
1,755,830	121,019	2,369,751	2,490,770	1,280,333	717,865	13,573,883	15,841,403
512,289	170,495	2,055,969	2,226,464	2,086,522	2,045,372	5,767,866	10,414,546
804,275	52,415	1,389,292	1,441,707	1,712,196	600,081	7,439,243	14,293,972
....	334	627	961	....	45,914	164,530	640,196
839,509	52,570	1,402,128	1,454,698	749,132	544,732	8,219,848	13,399,378
6,347	540	5,261	5,801	26,495	7,824	667,486	713,725
216,281	40,479	526,077	566,556	909,525	815,117	3,502,637	6,072,822
1,036,572	104,286	1,494,680	1,598,966	3,137,790	3,166,195	6,401,765	12,345,696
380,825	26,585	550,708	577,293	266,984	596,169	1,116,137	5,218,987
249,422	8,258	204,647	212,905	267,710	63,295	1,861,336	2,549,001
880,767	94,861	1,430,811	1,525,672	2,156,312	1,575,585	7,502,986	11,488,441
131,005	8,009	207,184	215,193	43,624	128,423	920,178	3,368,710
14,853,128	1,357,071	25,013,760	26,370,831	27,484,144	24,226,461	111,543,994	212,032,055
550	24	510	534	2,075	440	9,038	55,440
....	....	....	....	....	....	....	375
....	202	9,465	9,667	....	1,776	....	100,755
2	....	....	....	6,033	26,396	82,125	309,168
10	3	....	3	1,392	69,643	67,985	268,752
....	564	5,256	5,820	....	33,506	....	105,108
562	793	15,231	16,024	9,500	131,761	159,148	839,598
1,453,790	1,357,864	25,028,991	26,386,855	27,493,644	24,358,222	111,703,142	212,871,653

TABLE No. 36—Continued.

The number of Horses, Asses and Mules, Neat Cattle, Sheep, and Swine, as returned by circular of assistant marshals of Census, 1860.

STATES.	Horses.	Asses and mules.	Neat cattle.	Sheep.	Swine.
Alabama	11,692	3,975	40,208	12,404	63,528
Arkansas	5,329	4,035	22,731	6,481	18,919
California	12,769	3,452	53,795	23,414	3,762
Connecticut	16,239	135	22,104	2,700	26,034
Delaware	3,791	440	6,779	559	7,969
Florida	4,562	2,145	78,836	1,675	26,092
Georgia	43,641	19,000	203,070	120,596	375,350
Illinois	114,163	7,700	218,459	33,822	254,380
Indiana	39,425	3,074	79,340	32,012	146,034
Iowa	36,018	2,054	94,184	22,267	130,891
Kansas	8,124	1,234	34,938	1,145	16,500
Kentucky	61,209	18,427	128,045	67,161	234,255
Louisiana	24,197	14,916	76,331	21,643	50,755
Maine	28,296	98	77,240	61,926	21,196
Maryland	9,224	880	9,555	1,135	15,113
Massachusetts	56,745	2	48,329	8,616	43,146
Michigan	30,601	151	80,760	47,916	57,316
Minnesota	8,063	479	29,823	2,473	19,718
Mississippi	2,445	596	6,881	1,062	3,175
Missouri	80,569	10,625	118,181	96,005	412,368
New Hampshire	12,881	6	21,254	6,191	17,423
New Jersey	28,519	6,022	41,664	12,093	71,516
New York	92,458	2,293	31,801	3,065	100,791
North Carolina	29,955	8,494	113,241	77,296	206,976
Ohio	117,101	3,240	222,956	132,653	317,116
Oregon	16,690	7,302	59,199	10,788	10,728
Pennsylvania	66,180	6,407	168,104	53,225	200,236
Rhode Island	7,191	49	6,144	5,455	7,242
South Carolina	....	....	....	....	....
Tennessee	21,925	8,871	58,512	29,854	108,577
Texas	95,497	13,082	861,646	320,926	198,261
Vermont	17,201	12	26,686	18,015	18,526
Virginia	42,786	6,608	143,535	112,591	198,121
Wisconsin	27,869	505	120,450	11,885	70,866
TERRITORIES.					
Columbia, District of	1,233	159	1,092	62	1,744
Nebraska	1,779	951	2,484	52	1,376
New Mexico	6,541	8,536	27,116	142,110	7,624
Utah	1,400	375	9,875	4,325	3,625
Washington	1,206	457	1,661	212	656
Total	1,185,514	166,786	3,347,009	1,505,810	3,467,905

Table No. 37.

Newspapers and Periodicals in the United States in 1860.

States and Territories.	Political.								Religious.				
	Daily.	Bi-weekly.	Tri-weekly.	Weekly.	Monthly.	Quarterly.	Annual.	Total.	Weekly.	Monthly.	Quarterly.	Annual.	Total.
Alabama	9	1	6	73	....	....	....	89	2	....	....	....	2
Arkansas	....	....	....	34	....	....	....	34	2	....	....	....	2
California	22	3	2	68	1	....	....	96	4	2	....	....	6
Connecticut	14	1	....	30	....	....	....	45	3	....	....	....	3
Delaware	....	4	....	9	....	....	....	13	....	....	....	....	....
Florida	....	1	2	17	....	....	....	20	....	....	....	....	....
Georgia	12	1	5	56	1	....	....	75	2	2	....	....	4
Illinois	23	1	6	228	1	....	....	259	5	6	....	....	11
Indiana	13	5	....	154	....	....	....	172	3	3	....	....	6
Iowa	9	2	2	106	....	....	....	119	....	1	....	....	1
Kansas	3	....	....	21	....	....	....	24	....	....	....	....	....
Kentucky	4	1	3	57	....	....	....	65	4	1	....	....	5
Louisiana	4	2	....	62	....	....	....	68	2	....	....	....	2
Maine	7	....	4	37	....	....	....	48	6	....	....	....	6
Maryland	6	....	2	49	....	....	....	57	....	....	....	....	....
Massachusetts	17	13	3	78	1	....	....	112	18	10	3	....	31
Michigan	8	3	1	96	1	....	....	109	3	1	....	....	4
Minnesota	4	....	....	43	....	....	....	47	1	....	....	....	1
Mississippi	5	1	2	62	....	....	....	70	1	....	....	....	1
Missouri	15	....	3	122	1	....	....	141	9	2	....	....	11
New Hampshire	....	....	....	17	....	....	....	17	1	....	....	....	1
New Jersey	15	1	....	63	....	....	....	79	1	1	....	....	2
New York	68	8	5	280	2	....	2	365	24	25	5	2	56
North Carolina	8	4	1	47	....	....	....	60	5	1	....	....	6
Ohio	22	4	8	219	3	....	....	256	27	8	....	2	37
Oregon	2	....	....	11	....	....	....	13	1	....	....	....	1
Pennsylvania	28	3	1	242	3	....	....	277	20	17	4	2	43
Rhode Island	5	1	....	12	....	....	....	18	....	....	....	....	....
South Carolina	2	....	4	27	....	....	....	33	1	1	1	....	3
Tennessee	8	....	7	51	....	....	....	66	7	2	1	....	10
Texas	3	....	3	65	....	....	....	71	4	....	....	....	4
Vermont	2	....	....	24	....	....	....	26	4	....	....	....	4
Virginia	15	11	5	85	1	....	....	117	11	2	....	....	13
Wisconsin	14	....	8	127	....	....	....	149	....	1	....	....	1
District of Columbia	5	2	1	4	....	1	....	13	....	....	....	....	....
Nebraska Territory	....	1	....	12	....	....	....	13	....	....	....	....	....
New Mexico Ter.	....	....	....	2	....	....	....	2	....	....	....	....	....
Utah Territory	....	....	....	....	....	....	....	....	....	....	....	....	....
Washington Territory	....	....	....	4	....	....	....	4	....	....	....	....	....
Total	372	74	84	2,694	15	1	2	3,242	171	86	14	6	277

TABLE No. 37.—*Newspapers and Periodicals*

STATES AND TERRITORIES.	LITERARY.						MISCELLANEOUS.							
	Daily.	Weekly.	Monthly.	Quarterly.	Annual.	Total.	Daily.	Bi-weekly.	Tri-weekly.	Weekly.	Monthly.	Quarterly.	Annual.	Total.
Alabama		2	2			4					1			1
Arkansas		1				1								
California		9	1			10				8	1			9
Connecticut		2	1	2		5				2				2
Delaware		1				1								
Florida		2				2								
Georgia		13	8	1		22				2	2			4
Illinois		3	5			8		1		2	5			8
Indiana		3	2			5					3			3
Iowa			1			1				6	3			9
Kansas										3				3
Kentucky		3	1			4					3			3
Louisiana		2				2	4	1		4				9
Maine		4	3			7	1			5	3			9
Maryland														
Massachusetts		31	18	2		51		1		18	7	1	1	28
Michigan		3				3				1	1			2
Minnesota										1				1
Mississippi		1				1				1				1
Missouri		5	4			9	1			7	4			12
New Hampshire		2				2								
New Jersey		6			1	7					2			2
New York	1	33	24	5		63	5	2	2	29	18		2	58
North Carolina		5	2			7					1			1
Ohio	1	6	17			24	1			8	13		1	23
Oregon												1	1	2
Pennsylvania		17	6	1	1	25	1			18	2	1		22
Rhode Island		5	1			6				2				2
South Carolina		4	1			5				3	1			4
Tennessee		2	1	1	1	5				1	1			2
Texas		9	3			12				1	1			2
Vermont			1			1								
Virginia		2	1			3				5	1			6
Wisconsin		1	1			2				2	1			3
District of Columbia														
Nebraska Territory											1			1
New Mexico Ter														
Utah Territory										2				2
Washington Territory														
Total	2	177	104	12	3	298	13	5	2	131	75	3	5	234

in the United States in 1860—Continued.

NUMBER OF COPIES.							
Daily.	Tri-weekly.	Bi-weekly.	Weekly.	Monthly.	Quarterly.	Annually.	Whole number annually.
8,820	2,886	400	74,289	7,200	....	....	7,175,444
....	....	1,000	38,812	....	....	....	2,122,224
58,444	3,300	2,300	131,249	34,600	....	....	26,111,788
19,100	....	400	68,436	500	7,100	....	9,555,672
....	....	3,294	12,850	....	....	....	1,010,776
....	1,400	2,500	11,600	....	....	....	1,081,600
18,650	3,600	900	127,322	29,500	1,000	....	13,415,444
38,100	2,936	1,026	282,997	31,100	....	....	27,464,764
8,881	....	1,600	134,600	14,300	....	....	10,090,310
7,700	695	500	76,945	3,400	....	....	6,589,360
1,650	....	....	20,270	....	....	....	1,565,540
19,500	2,750	2,000	123,947	31,400	....	....	13,504,044
41,000	....	1,850	77,800	....	....	....	16,948,000
8,141	3,978	....	95,510	18,540	....	....	8,333,278
53,200	6,146	....	62,898	....	....	....	20,721,472
169,600	2,400	40,700	778,680	353,100	21,500	3,000	102,000,760
14,150	9,000	9,150	92,648	3,900	....	....	11,606,596
2,524	....	....	30,030	....	....	....	2,344,000
15,370	2,500	5,000	65,867	....	....	....	9,099,784
44,550	7,800	....	277,357	24,300	....	....	29,741,464
....	....	....	19,700	....	....	....	1,024,400
18,510	....	1,000	131,506	10,000	....	1,000	12,801,412
487,340	18,900	58,871	2,600,925	2,045,000	57,600	766,000	320,930,884
3,550	200	2,162	65,612	7,850	....	....	4,862,572
84,560	4,212	3,500	805,810	218,850	....	4,750	71,767,742
800	....	....	14,820	4,000	....	8,000	1,074,640
233,550	3,900	9,800	700,961	464,684	6,800	13,000	116,094,480
10,300	....	2,000	35,990	1,400	....	....	5,289,280
1,600	6,200	....	41,070	4,500	500	....	3,654,840
11,300	4,509	....	101,839	43,760	3,500	12,000	10,053,152
5,360	9,288	....	90,615	2,775	....	....	7,855,808
750	....	....	44,665	2,000	....	....	2,579,080
44,400	2,750	21,212	189,360	43,900	....	....	26,772,568
14,125	3,220	....	111,400	10,400	....	....	10,798,670
32,910	4,600	3,000	26,000	....	3,000	....	10,881,100
....	....	1,000	7,750	1,000	....	....	519,000
....	....	....	1,150	....	....	....	59,800
....	....	....	6,300	....	....	....	327,600
....	....	....	2,350	....	....	....	122,200
1,478,435	107,170	175,165	7,581,930	3,411,959	101,000	807,750	927,951,548

TABLE No. 38.

RAILROADS OF THE UNITED STATES.

A comparative statement of the extent of line completed, and the cost of construction and equipment thereof, in the years 1850 *and* 1860, *respectively.*

[In these tables, when a road is found to extend over two or more States, the length and cost are adjusted to the States accordingly. When, however, the length so overlapping does not exceed a few miles, the whole is given to the State in which the owners are domiciled.]

STATE OF MAINE.

RAILROADS.	MILEAGE.		COST OF CONSTRUCTION, ETC.	
	1850.	1860.	1850.	1860.
Androscoggin	....	37.00	....	$757,381
Androscoggin and Kennebec	55.00	55.00	$1,816,670	2,218,318
Atlantic and St. Lawrence	48.00	149.00	1,642,214	7,559,066
Bangor, Oldtown, and Milford	11.00	12.50	135,000	244,726
Calais and Baring	....	6.00	....	226,160
Great Falls and South Berwick	....	6.00	....	169,210
Kennebec and Portland (with branch)	59.50	72.50	1,742,370	2,871,264
Lewy's Island	....	16.50	....	315,397
Machiasport	7.75	7.75	110,000	100,000
Penobscot and Kennebec	....	54.78	....	1,879,986
Portland and Oxford Central	13.00	18.50	260,000	370,000
Portland, Saco, and Portsmouth	51.34	51.34	1,293,640	1,500,000
Somerset and Kennebec	....	37.00	....	835,946
York and Cumberland	....	18.50	....	1,090,317
	245.59	542.37	6,999,894	20,137,771
Deduct—				
Atlantic and St. Lawrence, in N. H. and Vt	....	70.20	....	3,561,386
Total in Maine	245.59	472.17	6,999,894	16,576,385

STATE OF NEW HAMPSHIRE.

RAILROADS.	Mileage 1850.	Mileage 1860.	Cost 1850.	Cost 1860.
Ashuelot	23.76	23.76	506,018	506,018
Boston, Concord, and Montreal	51.34	93.54	1,282,945	2,863,584
Cheshire	53.64	53.64	2,739,318	3,075,964
Cochecho	17.53	28.12	421,715	847,007
Concord	34.53	34.53	1,386,788	1,500,000
Concord and Portsmouth	18.23	47.00	478,464	1,108,859
Contoocook River	14.16	14.64	209,063	257,069
Eastern	16.55	16.55	525,205	525,205
Great Falls and Conway	6.59	20.09	133,520	433,565
Manchester and Lawrence	26.47	26.47	732,796	1,000,000
Merrimack and Connecticut Rivers	43.30	52.68	821,986	1,282,504
Northern (with branch)	82.57	82.57	2,795,603	3,343,167
Peterboro' and Shirley	....	9.36	....	245,643

TABLE No. 38.—*Railroads of the United States*—Continued.

STATE OF NEW HAMPSHIRE.

RAILROADS.	MILEAGE.		COST OF CONSTRUCTION, ETC.	
	1850.	1860.	1850.	1860.
Sullivan	24.68	25.26	$930,063	$1,250,000
White Mountains	....	20.78	....	371,037
Wilton	11.80	15.43	159,257	226,979
	425.15	564.42	13,122,741	18,836,601
Add—				
Atlantic and St. Lawrence, from Maine	....	52.00	....	2,638,064
Boston and Maine, from Massachusetts	40.17	40.17	1,651,392	1,793,994
Total in New Hampshire	465.32	656.59	14,774,133	23,268,659

STATE OF VERMONT.

RAILROADS.	MILEAGE 1850.	MILEAGE 1860.	COST 1850.	COST 1860.
Connecticut and Passumpsic Rivers	40.03	90.70	1,323,039	2,531,146
Rutland and Burlington	119.54	119.54	4,343,441	4,607,451
Rutland and Washington	....	44.73	....	1,771,683
Rutland and Whitehall (with branch)	....	8.39	....	255,700
Southern Vermont	....	8.00	....	200,000
Vermont and Canada	....	47.00	....	1,350,695
Vermont Central (with branch)	120.00	120.00	5,134,421	8,402,055
Vermont Valley	....	23.69	....	1,301,886
Western Vermont (with branch)	....	59.50	....	1,083,500
	279.57	521.55	10,800,901	21,504,116
Add—				
Atlantic and St. Lawrence, from Maine	....	18.20	....	923,322
St. Lawrence and Atlantic, from Canada	....	17.00	....	908,777
Total in Vermont	279.57	556.75	10,800,901	23,336,215

STATE OF MASSACHUSETTS.

RAILROADS.	MILEAGE 1850.	MILEAGE 1860.	COST 1850.	COST 1860.
Agricultural Branch	....	15.03	....	360,017
Amherst, Belchertown and Palmer	....	19.50	....	295,337
Berkshire	21.14	21.14	600,000	600,000
Boston and Lowell (with branch)	27.62	28.62	1,945,646	2,428,593
Boston and Maine (with branches)	83.05	83.05	4,021,606	4,303,499
Boston and Providence (with branches)	47.47	47.47	3,416,323	3,161,000
Boston and Worcester (with branches)	68.40	68.40	4,882,648	4,738,442
Cape Cod Branch (with branch)	28.84	47.14	626,543	1,031,625
Connecticut River (with branch)	52.35	52.35	1,798,825	1,802,043
Danvers Branch	....	9.20	....	233,124
Dorchester and Milton Branch	3.26	3.26	132,171	136,789
Eastern (with branches)	58.51	72.50	3,095,186	4,168,949
Easton Branch	....	3.78	....	55,894

TABLE No. 38.—*Railroads of the United States*—Continued.

STATE OF MASSACHUSETTS.

RAILROADS.	MILEAGE.		COST OF CONSTRUCTION, ETC.	
	1850.	1860.	1850.	1860.
Essex (with branch)	21.18	21.18	$537,869	$747,008
Fairhaven Branch	....	15.11	....	400,055
Fitchburg (with branches)	65.78	67.78	3,552,282	3,540,000
Fitchburg and Worcester	13.99	13.99	259,073	333,884
Grand Junction, (Boston)	6.18	9.00	763,844	1,946,942
Hampshire and Hampden	....	24.96	....	596,651
Horn Pond Branch	....	0.66	....	13,075
Lexington and West Cambridge	6.63	6.63	242,160	251,258
Lowell and Lawrence	12.35	12.35	333,254	363,158
Marlboro' Branch	....	3.90	....	157,500
Medway Branch	....	3.60	....	37,909
Middleboro' and Taunton	....	8.55	....	156,257
Midland (Norfolk county, &c.)	25.96	61.34	1,060,990	3,692,144
Nashua and Lowell	14.58	14 58	651,214	654,663
New Bedford and Taunton (with branches)	21.08	21.59	498,751	553,014
Newburyport	8.55	26 97	106,825	597,386
New York and Boston	....	21.50	....	744,130
Old Colony and Fall River	87.26	87.26	3,361,701	3,434,164
Peterboro' and Shirley	14.10	14.10	272,647	265,327
Pittsfield and North Adams	18.65	18.65	443,678	443,678
Providence and Worcester	43.41	43.41	1,824,796	1,761,543
Rockport	....	4.01	....	83,718
Salem and Lowell	16.88	16.88	316,943	464,013
South Reading Branch	8.15	8.15	293,759	299,628
South Shore	11.50	11.50	420,434	501,593
Stockbridge and Pittsfield	21.93	21.93	448,700	448,700
Stony Brook	13.16	13.16	265,526	267,383
Stoughton Branch	4.04	4.04	93,433	99,478
Taunton Branch (with branch)	11.68	11.68	307,136	313,156
Troy and Greenfield (tunnel)	....	7.00	....	1,040,238
Vermont and Massachusetts (with branch)	69.00	77.00	3,406,244	3,268,415
Western	117.81	117.81	8,033,708	8,443,881
West Stockbridge	2.75	2.75	41,516	39,600
Worcester and Nashua	45.67	45.67	1,410,197	1,378,898
	1,072.91	1,310.13	49,465,628	60,653,699
Deduct—				
Boston and Maine, in New Hampshire	40.17	40.17	1,651,392	1,793,994
Providence and Worcester, in Rhode Island	18.00	18.00	756,648	808,398
	58.17	58.17	2,408,040	2,602,392
	1,014.74	1,251.96	47,057,588	58,051,307
Add—				
Norwich and Worcester, from Connecticut	21.00	21.00	829,317	831,021
Total in Massachusetts	1,035.74	1,272.96	47,886,905	58,882,328

TABLE No. 38.—*Railroads of the United States*—Continued.

STATE OF RHODE ISLAND.

RAILROADS.	MILEAGE.		COST OF CONSTRUCTION, ETC.	
	1850.	1860.	1850.	1860.
New York, Providence, and Boston	50.00	50.00	$2,045,946	$2,158,000
Providence, Warren, and Bristol	....	13.60	....	448,667
	50.00	63.60	2,045,946	2,606,667
Add—				
Hartford, Providence, and Fishkill, from Connecticut	....	26.32	....	903,762
Providence and Worcester, from Massachusetts	18.00	18.00	756,648	808,398
Total in Rhode Island	68.00	107.92	2,802,594	4,318,827

STATE OF CONNECTICUT.

RAILROADS.	Mileage 1850.	Mileage 1860.	Cost 1850.	Cost 1860.
Danbury and Norwalk	....	23.81	....	$402,476
Hartford and New Haven (with branches)	72.38	72.38	$2,631,541	3,461,396
Hartford, Providence, and Fishkill	50.77	122.36	2,076,854	4,205,966
Housatonic	74.00	74.00	2,400,000	2,439,775
Naugatuck	57.00	57.00	1,335,001	1,578,301
New Haven, New London, and Stonington	....	61.00	....	1,851,877
New Haven and Northampton (with branches)	....	59.66	....	1,400,000
New London, Northern	66.00	66.00	1,450,410	1,578,568
New York and New Haven	62.25	62.25	3,005,395	5,315,871
Norwich and Worcester	66.00	66.00	2,598,514	2,613,694
	448.40	664.46	15,497,715	24,847,924
Deduct—				
Hartford, Providence, and Fishkill, in Rhode Island	....	26.32	....	903,762
New York and New Haven, in New York	14.14	14.14	678,624	1,129,041
Norwich and Worcester, in Massachusetts	21.00	21.00	829,317	831,021
	35.14	61.46	1,507,941	2,863,824
Total in Connecticut	413.26	603.00	13,989,774	21,984,100

STATE OF NEW YORK.

RAILROADS.	Mileage 1850.	Mileage 1860.	Cost 1850.	Cost 1860.
Albany and Vermont	....	32.95	....	2,020,667
Albany and West Stockbridge	38.25	38.25	1,930,317	2,392,984
Avon, Genesee, and Mount Morris	....	15.53	....	329,225
Black River and Utica (with branch)	....	37.53	....	1,237,553
Blossburg and Corning	14.81	14.81	250,000	496,661
Brooklyn and Jamaica	11.00	11.00	369,856	369,856
Buffalo, New York, and Erie	....	142.00	....	3,150,762
Buffalo and New York City	....	60.00	....	2,901,868
Buffalo and State Line	....	68.34	....	2,788,284
Cayuga and Susquehanna	34.61	34.61	580,310	1,095,600
Chemung	17.36	17.36	400,000	400,000

TABLE No. 38.—*Railroads of the United States*—Continued.

STATE OF NEW YORK.

RAILROADS.	MILEAGE.		COST OF CONSTRUCTION, ETC.	
	1850.	1860.	1850.	1860.
Elmira, Jefferson, and Canandaigua	....	46.84	....	$1,274,779
Hicksville and Cold Spring	....	4.00	....	45,263
Hudson and Boston	31.50	17.33	$821,331	175,000
Hudson River	74.71	143.72	6,666,681	11,388,279
Long Island (with branch)	86.50	86.50	2,191,812	2,566,270
New York Central (with branches)	447.00	555.88	20,023,863	30,840,713
New York and Flushing	....	7.80	....	245,000
New York and Erie (with branch)	337.00	465.00	20,066,208	35,320,907
New York and Harlem (with branch)	80.17	132.87	4,666,372	8,022,788
Niagara Bridge and Canandaigua	....	100.21	....	3,210,616
Niagara Falls and Lake Ontario	....	13.15	....	393,775
Ogdensburg, Northern (with branch)	58.00	119.50	2,979,937	4,809,856
Oswego and Syracuse	35.91	35.91	548,353	791,002
Plattsburg and Montreal	....	23.17	....	349,775
Potsdam and Watertown	....	75.36	....	1,600,026
Rensselaer and Saratoga	25.26	25.26	687,324	912,172
Rochester and Genesee Valley	....	18.45	....	654,021
Sackett's Harbor, Rome, and New York	....	18.50	....	389,310
Saratoga and Schenectady	21.50	21.50	396,379	480,684
Saratoga and White Hall (with branch)	45.38	47.52	1,312,772	901,684
Staten Island	....	13.20	....	287,832
Syracuse, Binghampton, and New York	....	80.94	....	2,854,212
Troy and Bennington	....	5.38	....	235,924
Troy and Boston	....	34.91	....	1,534,763
Troy and Greenbush	6.00	6.00	282,527	294,908
Troy and Rutland	....	17.27	....	349,939
Troy, Union, and Depot	....	2.14	....	752,601
Union Ramapo	....	0.25	....	50,000
Watertown and Rome	24.00	96.76	603,457	2,275,944
	1,388.96	2,687.70	64,777,499	130,191,501
Add—				
New York and New Haven, from Connecticut	14.14	14.14	678,624	1,129,041
Total in New York	1,403.10	2,701.84	65,456,123	131,320,542

STATE OF NEW JERSEY.

RAILROADS.	1850.	1860.	1850.	1860.
Belvidere Delaware	....	64.21	....	3,134,656
Burlington and Mount Holly	7.12	7.12	99,551	120,000
Camden and Amboy (with branches)	92.37	92.37	4,000,000	5,918,658
Camden and Atlantic	....	60.23	....	1,833,935
Central, of New Jersey	9.50	63.80	236,461	5,835,576
Flemington	....	12.00	....	287,087
Freehold and Jamesburg	....	11.50	....	231,174
Millstone and New Brunswick	....	6.62	....	111,114
Millville and Glassboro'	....	22.30	....	190,422
Morris and Essex	34.02	52.52	1,231,792	1,757,991
Newark and Bloomfield	....	6.00	....	110,098

TABLE No. 38.—*Railroads of the United States*—Continued.

STATE OF NEW JERSEY.

RAILROADS.	MILEAGE.		COST OF CONSTRUCTION, ETC.	
	1850.	1860.	1850.	1860.
New Jersey	33.80	33.80	$2,800,691	$4,933,259
Northern New Jersey	....	21.27	....	411,929
Paterson and Hudson	14.00	14.00	630,000	630,000
Paterson and Ramapo	15.12	15.12	350,000	350,000
Raritan and Delaware Bays (with branch)	....	22.00	....	330,000
Sussex	....	12.00	....	417,143
Warren	....	21.04	....	1,876,712
West Jersey	....	22.00	....	517,279
Total in New Jersey	205.93	559.90	9,348,495	28,997,033

STATE OF PENNSYLVANIA.

RAILROADS.	MILEAGE. 1850.	MILEAGE. 1860.	COST 1850.	COST 1860.
Alleghany Valley	....	45.00	....	1,765,300
Bald Eagle Valley	....	7.00	....	411,000
Barclay Coal	....	16.50	....	261,906
Beaver Meadow (with branches)	20.47	52.23	417,819	1,226,762
Bellefonte and Snowshoe	....	18.33	....	366,600
Catasauqua	....	13.00	....	150,000
Catawissa	....	64.00	....	4,059,707
Chester Valley	....	21.50	....	1,371,900
Chestnut Hill	....	4.16	....	121,400
Cumberland Valley	52.00	52.00	1,187,750	1,192,111
Delaware, Lackawanna, and Western	....	113.50	....	9,145,950
Delaware and Hudson Canal Companies	26.50	27.50	741,576	1,792,829
East Brandywine	....	17.50	....	350,000
East Pennsylvania (with branch)	....	36.52	....	1,098,602
Erie and Northeast	....	18.50	....	700,000
Erie and Pittsburg	....	40.25	....	800,000
Fayette County	....	12.69	....	153,800
Franklin	22.50	22.50	225,000	525,000
Gettysburg	....	17.12	....	274,481
Hanover Branch	....	12.20	....	202,095
Harrisburg and Lancaster (with branch)	36.00	54.00	1,250,057	1,882,550
Hazleton and Lehigh	....	14.50	....	290,000
Hempfield	....	32.00	....	1,809,563
Huntingdon and Broad Top (with branches)	....	42.50	....	1,354,930
Lackawanna	....	9.00	....	180,000
Lackawanna and Bloomsburg	....	80.00	....	2,400,000
Lehigh and Luzerne (with branches)	....	10.50	....	253,466
Lehigh and Susquehanna	19.71	19.71	1,000,000	1,380,000
Lehigh Valley	....	45.50	....	3,787,533
Little Schuylkill (and branches)	....	33.50	....	3,299,605
Littlestown	....	7.25	....	76,000
Lorberry Creek	5.13	5.13	10,000	10,000
Lyken's Valley (with branches)	15,50	19.70	300,000	429,000
McCauley's Mountain	....	6.00	....	200,000
Mauch Chunk and Summit Hill	13.00	26.25	200,000	400,000
Mill Creek and Mine Hill (with branches)	8.29	12.52	233,715	310,850

TABLE No. 38.—*Railroads of the United States*—Continued.

STATE OF PENNSYLVANIA.

RAILROADS.	MILEAGE.		COST OF CONSTRUCTION, ETC.	
	1850.	1860.	1850.	1860.
Mine Hill and Schuylkill Haven (with branches)	39.08	72.28	$800,000	$2,861,066
Mount Carbon (with branches)	6.26	6.26	178,735	204,501
Mount Carbon and Port Carbon	2.50	2.50	230,700	282,350
North Lebanon (with branches)	....	8.20	....	309,195
North Pennsylvania (with branches)	....	67.15	....	5,868,586
Pennsylvania (with branches)	218.14	359.21	10,112,452	26,646,447
Pennsylvania (coal company's)	47.00	47.00	1,604,837	1,998,819
Philadelphia and Baltimore Central	....	36.50	....	874,690
Philadelphia (Sunbury) and Erie	....	148.00	....	9,575,699
Philadelphia, Norristown, and Germantown	20.20	20.20	954,635	1,674,378
Philadelphia and Reading (with branches)	95.00	154.00	16,325,332	24,125,701
Philadelphia and Trenton	28.20	28.20	564,000	607,666
Philadelphia, Wilmington, and Baltimore	98.00	98.00	6,052,037	7,788,786
Pittsburg and Connellsville	....	59.00	....	2,919,698
Pittsburg, Fort Wayne, and Chicago	....	467.50	....	17,479,905
Quakake Valley	....	14.09	....	668,933
Schuylkill and Susquehanna	....	54.00	....	1,258,700
Schuylkill Valley (with branches)	18.46	24.45	437,600	573,616
Strasburg	4.25	4.25	42,500	42,500
Shamokin Valley and Pottsville	28.05	29.15	560,000	1,696,406
Swatara	6.00	6.00	100,000	100,000
Tioga (with branch)	25.85	29.61	427,316	789,281
Trevorton	....	14.50	....	762,000
Tyrone and Clearfield	....	22.00	....	440,000
Union Canal Company's	....	5.75	....	57,500
Westchester (with branch)	10.25	10.25	100,000	106,888
Westchester and Philadelphia	....	26.38	....	1,485,315
Williamsport and Elmira	....	78.00	....	4,050,314
Wrightsville, York, and Gettysburg	13.00	13.00	425,708	400,046
	879.34	2,935.49	44,481,769	159,681,986
Deduct—				
Philadelphia, Wilmington, and Baltimore, in Del. & Md.	79.00	79.00	4,878,636	6,278,684
Pittsburg, Fort Wayne, and Chicago, in Ohio, Ind. & Ill.	....	416.00	....	15,554,240
	79.00	495.00	4,878,636	21,832,924
Add—	800.34	2,440.49	39,603,133	137,849,062
Northern Central, from Maryland	22.00	102.00	2,079,921	5,622,648
Total in Pennsylvania	822.34	2,542.49	41,683,054	143,471,710

STATE OF DELAWARE.

RAILROADS.	Mileage 1850.	Mileage 1860.	Cost 1850.	Cost 1860.
Delaware	....	84.00	....	1,552,257
Junction and Breakwater	....	8.50	....	77,040
Newcastle and Frenchtown	16.19	16.19	861,325	744,520
Newcastle and Wilmington	....	5.00	....	150,000
Add—	16.19	113.69	861,325	2,523,817
Philadelphia, Wilmington, and Baltimore, from Penn.	23.00	23.00	1,420,365	1,827,972
Total in Delaware	39.19	136.69	2,281,690	4,351,789

TABLE No. 38.—*Railroads of the United States, &c.*—Continued.

STATE OF MARYLAND.

RAILROADS.	MILEAGE.		COST OF CONSTRUCTION, ETC.	
	1850.	1860.	1850.	1860.
Annapolis and Elkridge	21.50	21.50	$442,000	$442,000
Baltimore and Ohio (with branches)	178.00	386.80	8,798,619	24,918,773
Washington branch (of B. & O. R.)	30.00	30.00	1,650,000	1,650,000
Cumberland Coal and Iron (with branches)	10.40	14.00	300,000	560,000
Cumberland and Pennsylvania (with branches)	9.00	27.50	300,000	1,254,992
Eastern Shore	....	6.50	....	125,000
George's Creek	....	21.00	....	600,000
Northern Central (with branch)	67.50	142.00	3,506,637	8,228,731
Western Maryland	....	18.00	....	300,000
	316.40	667.30	14,997,256	38,079,496
Deduct—				
Baltimore and Ohio, in Virginia	97.00	241.00	4,794,807	15,520,403
Northern Central, in Pennsylvania	22.00	102.00	2,079,921	5,622,648
	119.00	343.00	6,874,728	21,143,051
Add—	197.40	324.30	8,122,528	16,936,445
Philadelphia, Wilmington, and Baltimore, from Penn.	56.00	56.00	3,458,280	4,450,712
Total in Maryland	253.40	380.30	11,580,808	21,387,157

STATE OF VIRGINIA.

RAILROADS.	MILEAGE 1850.	MILEAGE 1860.	COST 1850.	COST 1860.
Alexandria, Loudoun, and Hampshire	....	41.51	....	1,533,038
Alexandria and Washington	....	6.12	....	122,400
Blue Ridge (State road)	....	16.81	....	1,604,761
Clover Hill	18.50	18.50	185,000	185,000
Manassas Gap (with branches)	....	86.73	....	3,153,228
Norfolk and Petersburg	....	80.00	....	2,129,029
Northwestern Virginia (by B. & O. R. Co.)	....	103.50	....	5,683,753
Orange and Alexandria (with branches)	....	156.70	....	6,421,798
Petersburg (with branches)	80.00	80.00	1,123,821	1,259,854
Richmond and Danville (with branches)	27.69	143.19	1,405,538	3,726,037
Richmond, Fredericksburg, and Potomac (with branch)	75.00	78.50	1,509,959	1,985,579
Richmond and Petersburg (with branch)	24.89	24.89	943,291	1,222,523
Richmond and York River	....	23.66	....	725,394
Roanoke Valley	....	22.00	....	476,612
Seaboard and Roanoke	80.00	80.00	1,000,000	1,469,246
South Side (with branch)	10.00	132.00	120,000	4,239,537
Virginia Central	70.07	189.19	943,984	5,493,950
Virginia and Tennessee (with branches)	....	214.86	....	7,430,835
Winchester and Potomac	32.00	32.00	558,912	575,830
Add—	418.15	1,530.16	7,790,505	49,438,404
Baltimore and Ohio, from Maryland	97.00	241.00	4,794,807	15,520,403
Total in Virginia	515.15	1,771.16	12,585,312	64,958,807

TABLE No. 38.—*Railroads of the United States*—Continued.

STATE OF NORTH CAROLINA.

RAILROADS.	MILEAGE.		COST OF CONSTRUCTION, ETC.	
	1850.	1860.	1850.	1860.
Atlantic and North Carolina	....	94.92	....	$2,157,503
North Carolina	....	223.00	....	4,235,072
Raleigh and Gaston	87.00	97.00	$870,000	1,240,241
Western	....	41.50	....	830,000
Western North Carolina	....	84.00	....	1,740,000
Wilmington, Charlotte, and Rutherfordton	....	110.00	....	2,200,000
Wilmington and Manchester	....	161.50	....	2,869,223
Wilmington and Weldon (with branch)	161.50	176.50	2,411,623	3,196,588
Deduct—	248.50	988.42	3,281,623	18,468,627
Wilmington and Manchester, in South Carolina	....	99.00	....	1,758,834
Total in North Carolina	248.50	889.42	3,281,623	16,709,793

STATE OF SOUTH CAROLINA.

RAILROADS.	1850.	1860.	1850.	1860.
Blue Ridge (with branch)	....	33.00	....	2,989,165
Charleston and Savannah	....	103.32	....	2,319,784
Charlotte and South Carolina	....	109.60	....	1,719,043
Cheraw and Darlington	....	40.30	....	612,316
Greenville and Columbia (with branches)	47.00	164.25	876.776	2,762,930
King's Mountain	....	22.50	....	225,000
Laurens	....	32.00	....	543,403
Northeastern	....	102.00	....	2,054,315
South Carolina (with branches)	242.00	242.00	6,649,205	6,503,106
Spartanburg and Union	....	40.00	....	897,391
Add—	289.00	888.97	7,525,981	20,626,453
Wilmington and Manchester, from North Carolina	....	99.00	....	1,758,834
Total in South Carolina	289.00	987.97	7,525,981	22,385,287

STATE OF GEORGIA.

RAILROADS.	1850.	1860.	1850.	1860.
Atlanta and West Point	....	86.74	....	1,192,389
Augusta and Savannah	....	53.00	....	1,032,298
Barnesville and Thomaston	....	16.00	....	240,000
Brunswick and Florida	....	43.50	....	755,919
Central, of Georgia	190.72	190.72	2,996,118	3,700,000
Etowah	....	8 87	....	112,526
Georgia (with branches)	213.00	232.00	4,000,000	4,156,000
Macon and Brunswick	....	37.50	....	927,349
Macon and Western	102.00	102.00	1,276,422	1,501,964
Main Trunk (Atlantic and Gulf)	....	109.69	....	2,193,817
Milledgeville and Eatonton	....	22.00	....	275,901
Milledgeville and Gordon	....	17.00	....	213,500
Muscogee	....	50.00	....	1,000,000
Rome and Kingston	....	20.00	....	250,000
Savannah, Albany, and Gulf	....	68.13	....	1,386,634
Southwestern (with branches)	....	209.07	....	4,217,948
Western and Atlantic	138.00	138.00	5,000,000	5,901,497
Total in Georgia	643.72	1,404.22	13,272,540	29,057,742

TABLE NO. 38.—*Railroads of the United States*—Continued.

STATE OF FLORIDA.

RAILROADS.	MILEAGE.		COST OF CONSTRUCTION, ETC.	
	1850.	1860.	1850.	1860.
Florida	....	154.20	....	$3,084,000
Florida and Alabama	....	45.10	....	1,133,000
Florida, Atlantic, and Gulf Central	....	59.30	....	1,212,000
Pensacola and Georgia	....	115.90	....	2,719,000
Perdido and Junction	....	6.00	....	60,000
Tallahassee	21.00	21.00	$210,000	420,000
Total in Florida	21.00	401.50	210,000	8,628,000

STATE OF ALABAMA.

RAILROADS.	MILEAGE 1850.	MILEAGE 1860.	COST 1850.	COST 1860.
Alabama and Florida	....	115 60	....	2,981,716
Alabama and Mississippi River	....	30.30	....	618,965
Alabama and Tennessee River	....	109.80	....	2,446,833
Marion and Cahawba	....	14 00	....	280,000
Mobile and Girard	....	57.30	....	1,500,000
Mobile and Great Northern	....	49.16	....	1,094,603
Mobile and Ohio	....	482.80	....	14,484,000
Montgomery and West Point (with branch)	88.50	116.90	1,286,209	2,265,983
Tennessee and Alabama Central	....	26.10	....	781,591
Tuscumbia and Decatur	44.00	....	660,000	....
	132.50	1,001.96	1,946,209	26,453,691
Deduct—				
Mobile and Ohio, in Mississippi, Tenn., and Kentucky	....	419.80	....	12,594,000
	132.50	582.16	1,946,209	13,859,69
Add—				
Memphis and Charleston, from Tennessee	....	161.00	....	3,731,497
Total in Alabama	132.50	743.16	1,946,209	17,591,188

STATE OF MISSISSIPPI.

RAILROADS.	MILEAGE 1850.	MILEAGE 1860.	COST 1850.	COST 1860.
Grand Gulf and Port Gibson	8.00	8.00	120,000	120,000
Mississippi Central	....	187.00	....	4,534,937
Mississippi and Tennessee	....	99.20	....	2,149,319
Raymond	7.00	7.00	100,000	100,000
Western Mississippi	60.00	143.60	1,800,000	4,308,000
	75.00	444.80	2,020,000	11,212,256
Add—				
Mobile and Ohio, from Alabama	....	282.50	....	8,475,000
N. Orleans, Jackson, and Gt. Northern, from Louisiana	....	118.00	....	3,786,974
Memphis and Charleston, from Tennessee	....	27.00	....	625,779
Total in Mississippi	75.00	872.30	2,020,000	24,100,009

TABLE No. 38.—*Railroads of the United States*—Continued.

STATE OF LOUISIANA.

RAILROADS.	MILEAGE.		COST OF CONSTRUCTION, ETC.	
	1850.	1860.	1850.	1860.
Baton Rouge, Grosse-Tete, and Opelousas	....	17.00	....	$327,112
Clinton and Port Hudson	14.00	22.00	$400,000	750,666
Mexican Gulf	27.00	27.00	500,000	662,910
Milnburg and Lake Pontchartrain	4.50	6.00	120,000	212,938
New Orleans and Carrollton (with branches)	8.00	15.00	300,000	500,000
New Orleans, Jackson, and Great Northern	....	80.00	....	4,459,680
New Orleans, Opelousas, and Great Western	....	206.00	....	6,611,181
Vicksburg, Shreveport, and Texas	....	53.75	....	1,662,691
West Feliciana	26.00	26.00	....	620,000
	79.50	452.75	1,320,000	15,807,178
Deduct—				
N. Orleans, Jackson, and Gt. Northern, in Mississippi	....	118.00	....	3,786,974
Total in Louisiana	79.50	334.75	1,320,000	12,020,204

STATE OF TEXAS.

RAILROADS.	1850.	1860.	1850.	1860.
Buffalo Bayou, Brazos, and Colorado	....	32.00	....	1,000,000
Galveston, Houston, and Henderson	....	72.00	....	2,500,000
Houston, Tap, and Brazoria	....	60.00	....	2,000,000
Houston and Texas Central	....	90.00	....	4,232,345
San Antonio and Mexican Gulf	....	25.00	....	500,000
Southern Pacific	....	27.00	....	1,000,000
Total in Texas	....	306.00	....	11,232,345

STATE OF ARKANSAS.

RAILROADS.	1850.	1860.	1850.	1860.
Memphis and Little Rock	....	38.50	....	1,155,000

STATE OF TENNESSEE.

RAILROADS.	1850.	1860.	1850.	1860.
Central Southern	....	47.58	....	1,079,572
Cleveland and Chattanooga	....	30.62	....	867,210
East Tennessee and Georgia	....	110.80	....	3,637,367
East Tennessee and Virginia	....	130.28	....	2,866,297
Edgefield and Kentucky	....	46.70	....	1,289,771
Memphis and Charleston (with branch)	....	290.96	....	6,744,647
Memphis and Ohio	....	130.60	....	2,612,019
Memphis, Clarksville, and Louisville	....	56.80	....	1,592,518
McMinnville and Manchester	....	34.20	....	590,623
Mississippi Central and Tennessee	....	49.00	....	1,188,377
Nashville and Chattanooga (with branch)	....	158.75	....	3,632,882

TABLE No. 38.—*Railroads of the United States*—Continued.

STATE OF TENNESSEE.

RAILROADS.	MILEAGE.		COST OF CONSTRUCTION, ETC.	
	1850.	1860.	1850.	1860.
Nashville and Northwestern	....	98.40	....	$2,460,000
Tennessee and Alabama	....	45.81	....	1,185,053
Winchester and Alabama	....	38.12	....	629,662
		1,268.62	....	30,375,998
Deduct—				
Memphis and Charleston, in Mississippi and Alabama	....	188.00	....	4,357,276
		1,080.62	....	26,018,722
Add—				
Mobile and Ohio, from Alabama	....	117.30	....	3,519,000
Total in Tennessee	....	1,197.92	....	29,537,722

STATE OF KENTUCKY.

RAILROADS.	MILEAGE 1850.	MILEAGE 1860.	COST 1850.	COST 1860.
Breckenridge	....	8.53	....	312,000
Covington and Lexington	....	80.22	....	4,019,995
Lexington and Big Sandy	....	17.09	....	694,024
Lexington and Danville	....	13.16	....	824,448
Lexington and Frankford	29.18	29.18	$551,226	645,702
Louisville and Frankford	49.03	65.10	1,279,315	1,567,894
Louisville and Nashville (with branches)	....	253.20	....	8,530,718
Maysville and Lexington	....	18.80	....	601,298
New Orleans and Ohio (Paducah branch)	....	59.65	....	1,172,398
Portland and Louisville	....	5.00	....	100,000
	78.21	549.93	1,830,541	18,468,477
Add—				
Mobile and Ohio, from Alabama	....	20.00	....	600,000
Total in Kentucky	78.21	569.93	1,830,541	19,068,477

STATE OF OHIO.

RAILROADS.	MILEAGE 1850.	MILEAGE 1860.	COST 1850.	COST 1860.
Bellefontaine and Indiana	....	118.23	....	3,088,218
Carrolton	....	11.50	....	225,000
Central Ohio	....	137.06	....	6,502,178
Cincinnati, Hamilton, and Dayton	....	60.30	....	3,153,188
Cincinnati and Indianapolis Junction	....	42.00	....	1,050,387
Cincinnati, Wilmington, and Zanesville	....	132.80	....	6,250,841
Cleveland, Columbus, and Cincinnati	135.41	141.20	3,008,616	4,772,526
Cleveland and Mahoning	....	67.00	....	2,768,320
Cleveland, Painesville, and Ashtabula	....	96.60	....	3,987,076
Cleveland and Pittsburg (with branches)	....	203.50	....	9,320,288
Cleveland and Toledo	....	188.60	....	7,187,250
Cleveland, Zanesville, and Cincinnati	....	61.39	....	1,574,693

TABLE No. 38.—*Railroads of the United States*—Continued.

STATE OF OHIO.

RAILROADS.	MILEAGE.		COST OF CONSTRUCTION, ETC.	
	1850.	1860.	1850.	1860.
Columbus and Indianapolis	....	103.00	....	$3,090,618
Columbus and Xenia	54.56	54.56	$721,720	1,781,938
Dayton and Michigan	....	144.00	....	5,200,215
Dayton and Western	....	36.30	....	1,104,085
Dayton, Xenia, and Belpre	....	16.13	....	860,496
Eaton and Hamilton	....	45.08	....	1,101,744
Fremont and Indiana	....	36.00	....	1,310,922
Greenville and Miami	....	32.00	....	888,000
Iron	....	13.00	....	219,121
Little Miami	83.40	83.40	1,418,875	4,290,423
Marietta and Cincinnati (with branch)	....	204.40	....	10,683,687
Ohio and Mississippi	....	192.30	....	18,635,688
Pittsburg, Columbus, and Cincinnati (with branch)	....	125.00	....	4,772,951
Sandusky, Dayton, and Cincinnati (with branch)	173.90	173.90	3,662,349	4,594,178
Sandusky, Mansfield, and Newark (with branch)	116.00	126.00	1,692,840	2,309,126
Scioto and Hocking Valley	....	55.60	....	1,103,975
Springfield and Columbus	....	29.50	....	346,589
Springfield, Mount Vernon, and Pittsburg	....	49.80	....	2,205,039
Toledo, Wabash, and Western	....	243.00	....	8,019,539
	563.27	3,013.15	10,504,400	122,398,299
Deduct—				
Ohio and Mississippi, in Indiana	....	173.30	....	16,794,417
Toledo, Wabash, and Western, in Indiana	....	172.00	....	5,676,344
	....	345.30	....	22,470,761
	563.27	2,667.85	10,504,400	99,927,538
Add—				
Michigan Southern, from Michigan	12.00	82.60	180,000	2,657,407
Pittsburg, Fort Wayne, and Chicago, from Penn	....	249.00	....	9,311,406
Total in Ohio	575.27	2,999.45	10,684,400	111,896,351

STATE OF INDIANA.

RAILROADS.	MILEAGE 1850.	MILEAGE 1860.	COST 1850.	COST 1860.
Chicago and Cincinnati	....	61.00	....	1,250,000
Cincinnati and Chicago	....	108.00	....	2,080,433
Cincinnati, Peru, and Chicago	....	29.13	....	1,161,209
Evansville and Crawfordsville	....	132.00	....	2,465,792
Indiana Central	....	72.40	....	2,233,361
Indianapolis and Cincinnati (with extension)	....	109.80	....	3,457,108
Indianapolis, Pittsburg, and Cleveland	28.00	82.77	312,579	1,902,693
Jeffersonville	16.00	78.00	170,000	2,182,004
Joliet and Northern Indiana	....	45.00	....	1,172,908
Knightstown and Shelbyville	27.00	27.00	270,000	270,000
Lafayette and Indianapolis	....	64.00	....	1,856,287

TABLE No. 38.—*Railroads of the United States*—Continued.

STATE OF INDIANA.

RAILROADS.	MILEAGE.		COST OF CONSTRUCTION, ETC.	
	1850.	1860.	1850.	1860.
Louisville, New Albany, and Chicago	35.00	288.00	$417,954	$7,029,494
Madison and Indianapolis (with branches)	86.00	135.00	1,800,000	2,667,704
Peru and Indianapolis		74.00		2,371,554
Rushville and Shelbyville	20.00	20.00	250,000	320,000
Shelbyville Lateral	16.00	16.00	160,000	160,000
Terre Haute and Richmond		73.00		1,611,450
Union Track and Depot		3.54		265,033
	228.00	1,418.60	3,380,533	34,457,030
Deduct—				
Joliet and Northern Indiana, in Illinois		30.00		781,950
	228.00	1,388.60	3,380,533	33,675,080
Add—				
Michigan Central, from Michigan		52.00		2,402,608
Michigan Southern, from Michigan		185.00		5,951,820
Ohio and Mississippi, from Ohio		173.30		16,794,417
Pittsburg, Fort Wayne, and Chicago, from Penn		155.00		5,794,879
Toledo, Wabash, and Western, from Ohio		172.00		5,676,344
Total in Indiana	228.00	2,125.90	3,380,533	70,295,148

STATE OF MICHIGAN.

RAILROADS.	MILEAGE 1850.	MILEAGE 1860.	COST 1850.	COST 1860.
Bay de Noquet and Marquette		20.50		410,000
Chicago, Detroit, and Canada Grand Junction		57.00		1,710,000
Detroit and Milwaukie	25.00	188.00	408,000	9,118,219
Detroit, Monroe, and Toledo		51.00		1,522,821
Flint and Pere Marquette		33.00		1,000,000
Iron Mountain (Northern Michigan)		25.00		500,000
Michigan Central	226.00	284.80	6,339,667	13,158,958
Michigan Southern & Northern Indiana (with branches)	103.00	484.60	2,378,082	15,590,952
	354.00	1,143.90	9,125,749	43,010,950
Deduct—				
Michigan Southern, in Ohio, Indiana, and Illinois	12.00	279.60	180,000	8,995,291
Michigan Central, in Indiana and Illinois		65.00		3,003,260
	12.00	344.60	180,000	11,998,551
Total in Michigan	342.00	799.30	8,945,749	31,012,399

STATE OF ILLINOIS.

RAILROADS.	MILEAGE 1850.	MILEAGE 1860.	COST 1850.	COST 1860.
Chicago, Alton, and St. Louis		220.00		10,000,000
Chicago, Burlington, and Quincy	13.00	138.00	195,000	7,468,926
Chicago and Milwaukie		45.00		1,884,344
Chicago and Northwestern		213.00		10,684,922

TABLE No. 38.—*Railroads of the United States*—Continued.

STATE OF ILLINOIS.

RAILROADS.	MILEAGE.		COST OF CONSTRUCTION, ETC.	
	1850.	1860.	1850.	1860.
Chicago and Rock Island	....	181.50	....	$6,913,554
Elgin and State Line	....	32.20	....	581,317
Galena and Chicago Union (with branches)	42.50	261.25	$695,507	9,352,481
Great Western (with branch)	55.00	182.00	550,000	5,086,206
Illinois Central	....	738.25	....	27,195,391
Illinois Coal	....	4.00	....	100,000
Joliet and Chicago	....	35.80	....	1,000,000
Logansport, Peoria, and Burlington	....	171.00	....	5,000,000
Mound City	....	3.00	....	60,000
Ohio and Mississippi	....	148.00	....	4,870,686
Peoria and Bureau Valley	....	46.60	....	2,106,000
Peoria and Oquawka	....	94.00	....	3,769,889
Quincy and Chicago	....	100.00	....	1,978,550
Quincy and Toledo	....	34.00	....	750,000
Rockford	....	28.00	....	560,000
Rock Island and Peoria	....	11.00	....	220,000
Sycamore and Cortlandt	....	5.00	....	75,000
Terre Haute, Alton, and St. Louis (with branches)	....	208.30	....	8,865,252
Warsaw and Peoria	....	13.00	....	300,000
	110.50	2,912.90	1,440,507	108,822,518
Add—				
Joliet and Northern Indiana, from Indiana	....	30.00	....	781,950
Michigan Southern, from Michigan	....	12.00	....	386,064
Michigan Central, from Michigan	....	13.00	....	600,652
Pittsburg, Fort Wayne, and Chicago, from Penn	....	12.00	....	447,955
Racine and Mississippi, from Wisconsin	....	35.00	....	1,279,530
	110.50	3,014.90	1,440,507	112,318,669
Deduct—				
Chicago and Northwestern, in Wisconsin	....	147.00	....	7,374,108
Total in Illinois	110.50	2,867.90	1,440,507	104,944,561

STATE OF WISCONSIN.

RAILROADS.	MILEAGE 1850.	MILEAGE 1860.	COST 1850.	COST 1860.
Beloit and Madison	....	17.30	....	350,000
Kenosha, Rockford, and Rock Island	....	28.30	....	1,069,069
Manitowoc and Mississippi	....	7.50	....	200,000
Milwaukie and Chicago	....	40.00	....	1,830,073
Milwaukie and Horicon	....	42.00	....	1,137,912
Milwaukie and Minnesota	....	199.89	....	7,400,000
Milwaukie and Prairie du Chien (with branches)	20.00	234.40	612,382	7,500,000
Milwaukie and Superior	....	18.00	....	360,000
Milwaukie and Western	....	57.22	....	1,498,762
Mineral Point	....	32.00	....	1,813,927
Racine and Mississippi	....	104.00	....	3,802,016
Sheboygan and Fond du Lac	....	20.00	....	500,000

TABLE No. 38.—*Railroads of the United States*—Continued.

STATE OF WISCONSIN.

RAILROADS.	MILEAGE.		COST OF CONSTRUCTION, ETC.	
	1850.	1860.	1850.	1860.
Wisconsin Central	....	10.00	....	$250,000
	20.00	810.61	$612,382	27,711,759
Add— Chicago and Northwestern, from Illinois	....	147.00	....	7,123,282
	20.00	957.61	612,382	34,835,041
Deduct— Racine and Mississippi, in Illinois	....	35.00	....	1,279,435
Total in Wisconsin	20.00	922.61	612,382	33,555,606

STATE OF IOWA.

RAILROADS.	MILEAGE 1850.	MILEAGE 1860.	COST 1850.	COST 1860.
Burlington and Missouri	....	93.30	....	2,492,758
Cedar Rapids and Missouri	....	25.35	....	612,359
Chicago, Iowa, and Nebraska	....	82.11	....	1,860,251
Dubuque and Pacific	....	111.18	....	2,836,833
Dubuque, Marion, and Western	....	51.00	....	1,351,790
Keokuk, Fort Des Moines, and Minnesota	....	92.00	....	2,879,615
Keokuk, Mt. Pleasant, and Muscatine	....	25.20	....	1,022,306
Mahaska County	....	12.00	....	120,000
Mississippi and Missouri (with branches)	....	187.63	....	6,318,721
Total in Iowa	....	679.77	....	19,494,633

STATE OF MISSOURI.

RAILROADS.	MILEAGE 1850.	MILEAGE 1860.	COST 1850.	COST 1860.
Cairo and Fulton	....	37.00	....	1.213,497
Hannibal and St. Joseph	....	206.80	....	12,364,139
North Missouri	....	168.80	....	6,966,144
Pacific (main line)	....	189.70	....	11,219,541
Southwestern Branch	....	77.50	....	3,872,510
Platte County	....	37.00	....	925,000
Quincy and Palmyra	....	10.50	....	250,000
St. Louis and Iron Mountain, (with branch)	....	90.15	....	5,531,981
Total in Missouri	....	817.45	....	42,342,812

STATE OF CALIFORNIA.

RAILROADS.	MILEAGE 1850.	MILEAGE 1860.	COST 1850.	COST 1860.
California Central	....	43.80	....	1,900,000
Sacramento Valley	....	22.50	....	1,600,000
Las Mariposas	....	3.75	....	100,000
Total in California	....	70.05	....	3,600,000

STATE OF OREGON.

RAILROADS.	MILEAGE 1850.	MILEAGE 1860.	COST 1850.	COST 1860.
Cascade Transit	....	3.80	....	80,000

TABLE No. 38.—*Railroads of the United States*—Continued.

RECAPITULATION.

STATES.	MILEAGE.		COST OF CONSTRUCTION, ETC.	
	1850.	1860.	1850.	1860.
Maine	245.59	472.17	$6,999,894	$16,576,385
New Hampshire	465.32	656.59	14,774,133	23,268,659
Vermont	279.57	556.75	10,800,901	23,336,215
Massachusetts	1,035.74	1,272.96	47,886,905	58,882,328
Rhode Island	68.00	107.92	2,802,594	4,318,827
Connecticut	413.26	603.00	13,989,774	21,984,100
New England States	2,507.48	3,669.39	97,254,201	148,366,514
New York	1,403.10	2,701.84	65,456,123	131,320,542
New Jersey	205.93	559.90	9,348,495	28,997,033
Pennsylvania	822.34	2,542.49	41,683,054	143,471,710
Delaware	39.19	136.69	2,281,690	4,351,789
Maryland	253.40	380.30	11,580,808	21,387,157
Middle Atlantic States	2,723.96	6,321.22	130,350,170	329,528,231
Virginia	515.15	1,771.16	12,585,312	64,958,807
North Carolina	248.50	889.42	3,281,623	16,709,793
South Carolina	289.00	987.97	7,525,981	22,385,287
Georgia	643.72	1,404.22	13,272,540	29,057,742
Florida	21.00	401.50	210,000	8,628,000
Southern Atlantic States	1,717.37	5,454.27	36,875,456	141,739,629
Alabama	132.50	743.16	1,946,209	17,591,188
Mississippi	75.00	872.30	2,020,000	24,100,009
Louisiana	79.50	334.75	1,320,000	12,020,204
Texas	....	306.00	....	11,232,345
Gulf States	287.00	2,256.21	5,286,209	64,943,746
Arkansas	....	38.50	....	1,155,000
Tennessee	....	1,197.92	....	29,537,722
Kentucky	78.21	569.93	1,830,541	19,068,477
Interior States, South	78.21	1,806.35	1,830,541	49,761,199
Ohio	575.27	2,999.45	10,684,400	111,896,351
Indiana	228.00	2,125.90	3,380,533	70,295,148
Michigan	342.00	799.30	8,945,749	31,012,399
Illinois	110.50	2,867.90	1,440,507	104,944,561
Wisconsin	20.00	922.61	612,382	33,555,606
Minnesota	....	....	....	....
Iowa	....	679.77	....	19,494,633
Missouri	....	817.45	....	42,342,812
Kansas	....	....	....	....
Interior States, North	1,275.77	11,212.38	25,063,571	413,541,510

TABLE No. 38.—*Railroads of the United States*—Continued.

RECAPITULATION.

STATES.	MILEAGE.		COST OF CONSTRUCTION, ETC.	
	1850.	1860.	1850.	1860.
California	....	70.05	....	$3,600,000
Oregon	....	3.80	....	80,000
Pacific States	....	73.85	....	3,680,000
New England States	2,507.48	3,669.39	$97,254,201	148,366,514
Middle Atlantic States	2,723.96	6,321.22	130,350,170	329,528,231
Southern Atlantic States	1,717.37	5,454.27	36,875,456	141,739,629
Gulf States	287.00	2,256.21	5,286,209	64,943,746
Interior States, South	78.21	1,806.35	1,830,541	49,761,199
Interior States, North	1,275.77	11,212.38	25,063,571	413,541,510
Pacific States	....	73.85	....	3,680,000
Total United States	8,539.79	30,793.67	296,660,148	1,151,560,829
City railroads in 1860	....	402.57	....	14,862,840
Total	....	31,196¼	....	1,166,422,729

City Passenger Railroads, 1860, *not included in Tables of Commercial Railroads.*

CITY OF BOSTON.

RAILROADS.	Length of track.	Cost of roads, equipment, &c.
	Miles.	
Boston and Chelsea	2.18	$140,000
Broadway	2.93	63,496
Cambridge	4.80	481,377
Charleston and Medford	2.96	34,000
Chelsea Beach*	....	....
Cliftondale	6.74	110,200
Dorchester	4.77	155,623
Dorchester Extension	1.48	12,800
Lynn and Boston*	....	27,800
Malden and Melrose	3.41	420,183
Metropolitan	13.27	684,325
Middlesex	5.77	348,000
Newton	2.87	26,845
Somerville	2.68	43,345
Stoneham street	2.42	11,750
Suffolk	3.31	138,673
Union, (equipment only)	....	157,971
Waltham and Watertown	2.13	19,700
West Cambridge	1.57	12,850
West Roxbury	1.85	53,737
Winnisimmet	2.25	50,000
Total	67.39	2,964,875

*Not completed.

TABLE No. 38—*City Passenger Railroads*, 1860—Continued.

CITY OF NEW YORK.

RAILROADS.	Length of track.	Cost of roads, equipment, &c.
	Miles.	
Eighth Avenue	11.13	$859,834
Ninth Avenue	9.22	397,832
Second Avenue	16.57	1,181,537
Sixth Avenue	8.37	946,961
Third Avenue	16.50	1,616,671
Total	61.79	5,002,835

CITY OF BROOKLYN.

RAILROADS.	Length of track.	Cost of roads, equipment, &c.
Broadway	9.26	222,834
Brooklyn Central	21.53	586,619
Brooklyn City	49.13	1,262,225
Total	79.92	2,071,678

HOBOKEN CITY.

RAILROADS.	Length of track.	Cost of roads, equipment, &c.
Hoboken and Hudson City	1.79	32,000

CITY OF PHILADELPHIA.

RAILROADS.	Length of track.	Cost of roads, equipment, &c.
Citizens	8.50	200,000
Delaware County	3.00	27,500
Frankford and Southwark	16.50	551,000
Fairmount	5.00	140,000
Fairmount and Arch Street	5.00	180,000
Germantown, 4th and 8th streets	17.25	300,000
Girard College	5.50	160,000
Green and Coates Streets	5.25	220,000
Heston, Mantua and Fairmount	7.00	100,000
North Philadelphia	5.50	300,000
Philadelphia and Gray's Ferry	7.00	176,000
Philadelphia City	4.00	100,000
Philadelphia and Darby	4.25	117,200
Richmond and Schuylkill	5.25	130,000
Ridge Avenue and Manayunk	9.00	185,000
Second and Third Streets	18.75	450,000
Seventeenth and Nineteenth Streets	6.00	120,000
Thirteenth and Fifteenth Streets	6.00	100,000
West Philadelphia	9.25	255,000
Total	148.00	3,811,700

TABLE No. 38—*City Passenger Railroads*, 1860—Continued.

CITY OF CINCINNATI.

RAILROADS.	Length of track.	Cost of roads, equipment, &c.
	Miles.	
Cincinnati Street	5	$151,913
City Passenger	5	111,412
Passenger	3¾	69,837
Pendleton and Fifth Street Market Company	3⅝	70,000
Total	17⅜	403,162

CITY OF ST. LOUIS.

St. Louis	10.20	298,604
Citizens'	8.29	117,437
People's	4.48	83,875
Missouri	3.33	76,674
Total	26.30	576,590

RECAPITULATION.

CITIES.	Length.	Cost of roads, &c.
	Miles.	
Boston, Mass	67.39	2,964,875
New York, N. Y.	61.79	5,002,835
Brooklyn, N. Y	79.92	2,071,678
Hoboken, N. J	1.79	32,000
Cincinnati, Ohio	17.38	403,163
St. Louis, Mo	26.30	576,590
Philadelphia, Pa	148.00	3,811,700
Total	402.57	14,862,840

NOTE.

We doubt not that the sum stated (page 231) as the aggregate cost of our roads is considerably too small, and for the reason that the leading roads in furnishing and perfecting their works have expended large sums out of their earnings which have not gone to capital stock or bonded debt. We know of one road which has thus expended near $2,000,000.

TABLE No. 38.—Continued.

Number of miles of Railroads in operation at the end of each year, from 1850 to 1860, inclusive.

STATES.	1850.	1851.	1852.	1853.	1854.	1855.	1856.	1857.	1858.	1859.	1860.
Maine	245.59	292.47	322.47	333.47	359.97	414.67	429.17	451.17	467.67	472.17	472.17
New Hampshire	465.32	536.78	567.78	643.86	643.86	656.59	656.59	656.59	656.59	656.59	656.59
Vermont	279.57	413.29	471.32	506.22	511.72	529.42	529.42	529.42	529.42	548.75	556.75
Massachusetts	1,035.74	1,037.74	1,047.44	1,105.34	1,144.27	1,272.96	1,272.96	1,272.96	1,272.96	1,272.96	1,272.96
Rhode Island	68.00	68.00	68.00	68.00	94.32	107.92	107.92	107 92	107.92	107.92	107.92
Connecticut	412.26	463.26	506.96	506.96	506.96	506.96	589.34	589.34	589.34	603.00	603.00
New England States	2,506.48	2,811 54	2,983 97	3,163.85	3,261.10	3,468.52	3,585.40	3,607.40	3,623.90	3,661.39	3,669.39
New York	1,403.10	1,845.55	2,249.77	2,406.10	2,567.40	2,595.35	2,641.70	2,674.06	2,675.31	2,690.84	2,701.84
New Jersey	205.93	303.37	317.87	347.17	375.17	466.02	485.29	507.33	516.33	535 60	559.90
Pennsylvania	822.34	1,030.15	1,113.05	1,144.55	1,404.22	1,537.22	1,799.17	1,925.42	2,081.07	2,339.99	2,442.49
Delaware	39.19	39.19	39.19	39.19	44.19	56.19	79.19	115.19	123.69	136.69	136.69
Maryland	253.40	274.26	326.80	326.80	326.80	326.80	326 80	351.80	361.80	370.80	380.30
Middle Atlantic States	2,723.96	3,492.52	4,046.68	4,263.81	4,717.78	4,981 58	5,332.15	5,573.80	5,758.20	6,073.92	6,221.22
Virginia	515.15	652.44	954.33	1,099.96	1,218 82	1,269.41	1,341.21	1,531.17	1,594.19	1,658.25	1,771.16
North Carolina	248.50	248.50	311.00	386.00	534.00	544.00	638.92	689 92	789.92	889.42	889.42
South Carolina	289.00	378.50	598.35	652.35	669.35	759.65	847.65	878.65	906.35	987.97	987.97
Georgia	643.72	794.72	909.72	962.46	983.46	1,020.46	1,165.43	1,241.70	1,297.32	1,355.90	1,404.22
Florida	21.00	21.00	21.00	....	....	....	56.00	128.00	198.30	289.80	401.50
Southern Atlantic States	1,717.37	2,095.16	2,794.40	3,100.77	3,405.63	3,593.52	4,049.21	4,469.44	4,786.08	5,181.34	5,454.27
Alabama	132.50	132.50	161.00	214.72	304.00	334.54	454.00	531.80	531.80	628.40	743.16
Mississippi	75.00	75.00	96.20	96.20	222.30	278.00	413.00	483.50	604.13	697.80	872.30
Louisiana	79.50	79.50	79.50	89.00	198.00	203.00	249.50	261.00	281.00	294.75	334.75

Texas	......	......	......	......	32.00	40.00	71.00	157.00	205.50	284.50	306.00
Gulf States	287.00	287.00	336.70	399.92	756.30	855.54	1,187.50	1,433.30	1,622.43	1,905.45	2,256.21
Arkansas	......	......	......	......	......	......	......	......	......	......	38.50
Tennessee	......	112.33	185.44	291.25	329.25	466.05	541.21	769.69	887.60	963.10	1,197.92
Kentucky	78.21	94.10	94.10	167.10	241.90	241.90	267.90	304.90	458.50	537.00	567.93
Interior States, South	78.21	206.43	279.54	458.35	571.15	707.95	809.11	1,074.59	1,346.10	1,500.10	1,804.35
Ohio	575.27	895.42	1,385.94	1,777.37	2,001.28	2,453.16	2,522.73	2,619.57	2,651.23	2,811.61	2,900.75
Indiana	228.00	538.50	755.92	1,208.61	1,317.29	1,406.52	1,806.84	1,894.79	1,994.70	2,013.62	2,125.90
Michigan	342.00	379.27	431.27	431.27	444.17	474.23	500.49	602.50	642.37	737.40	799.30
Illinois	110.50	271.39	412.19	759.62	788.40	886.79	2,135.33	2,501.65	2,733.92	2,781.20	2,867.90
Wisconsin	20.00	50.00	70.60	70.60	97.25	187.50	276.40	629.92	647.35	826.00	922.61
Minnesota	......	......	......	......	......	......	......	......	......	......	......
Iowa	......	......	......	......	......	68.50	253.86	343.71	379.36	532.80	679.67
Missouri	......	......	......	37.50	37.50	138.70	144.22	317.63	547.20	724.25	817.45
Kansas	......	......	......	......	......	......	......	......	......	......	......
Interior States, North	1,275.77	2,134.58	3,055.92	4,284.97	4,685.89	5,615.40	7,639.87	8,909.77	9,596.13	10,426.88	11,113.58
California	......	......	......	......	......	8.00	22.00	22.00	22.00	22.00	70.05
Oregon	......	......	......	......	......	......	......	......	......	......	3.80
Pacific States	......	......	......	......	......	8.00	22.00	22.00	22.00	22.00	73.85
New England States	2,506.48	2,811.54	2,983.97	3,163.85	3,261.10	3,488.52	3,585.40	3,607.40	3,623.90	3,661.39	3,669.39
Middle Atlantic States	2,723 96	3,492.52	4,646.68	4,263.81	4,717.78	4,981.58	5,332.15	5,573.80	5,758.20	6,073.92	6,221.22
Southern Atlantic States	1,717.37	2,095.16	2,794.40	3,100.77	3,405.63	3,593.52	4,049.21	4,469.44	4,786.08	5,181.34	5,454.27
Gulf States	287.00	287.00	336.70	399.92	756.30	855.54	1,187.50	1,433.30	1,622.43	1,905.45	2,256.21
Interior States, South	78.21	206.43	279.54	458.35	571.15	707.95	809.11	1,074.59	1,346.10	1,500.10	1,804.35
Interior States, North	1,275.77	2,134.58	3,055.92	4,284.97	4,685.89	5,615.40	7,639.87	8,909.77	9,596.13	10,426.88	11,113.58
Pacific States	......	......	......	......	......	8.00	22.00	22.00	22.00	22.00	73.85
Total United States	8,588.79	11,027.23	13,497.21	15,671.67	17,397.85	19,250.51	22,625.24	25,090.30	26,754.84	28,771.08	30,592.87

TABLE No. 38—Continued.

Number of miles of Railroads brought into use during each year from 1851 *to* 1860, *inclusive.*

STATES.	1851.	1852.	1853.	1854.	1855.	1856.	1857.	1858.	1859.	1860.	Miles of rail-road built in ten years.
Maine	46.88	30.00	11.00	26.50	54.70	14.50	22.00	16.50	4.50	....	226.58
New Hampshire	71.46	31.00	76.08	....	12.73	....	....	....	....	....	191.27
Vermont	133.72	58.03	34.90	5.50	17.70	....	....	....	19.33	8.00	277.18
Massachusetts	2.00	9.70	57.90	38.93	128.69	....	....	....	....	....	237.22
Rhode Island	....	....	....	26.32	13.60	....	....	....	....	....	39.92
Connecticut	51.00	43.70	....	....	....	82.38	....	....	13.66	....	190.74
New England States	305.06	172.43	179.88	97.25	227.42	96.88	22.00	16.50	37.49	8.00	1,162.91
New York	442.45	404.22	156.33	161.30	27.95	46.35	32.36	1.25	15.53	11.00	1,298.74
New Jersey	97.44	14.50	29.30	28.00	90.85	19.27	22.04	9.00	19.27	24.30	353.97
Pennsylvania	207.81	82.90	31.50	259.67	133.00	261.95	126.25	155.65	258.92	102.50	1,620.15
Delaware	....	....	....	5.00	12.00	23.00	36.00	8.50	13.00	....	97.50
Maryland	20.86	52.24	....	....	....	....	25.00	10.00	9 00	9.50	126.90
Middle Atlantic States	768.56	554.16	217.13	453.97	263.80	350.57	241.65	184.40	315.72	147.30	3,497.26
Virginia	137.29	301.89	145.63	118.86	50.59	71.80	189.96	63.02	64.06	112.91	1,256.01
North Carolina	....	62.50	75.00	148.00	10.00	94.92	51.00	100.00	99.50	....	640.92
South Carolina	89.50	219.85	54.00	17.00	90.30	88.00	31.00	27.70	81.62	....	698.97
Georgia	151.00	115.00	52.74	21.00	37.00	144.97	76.27	55.62	58.58	48.32	760.50
Florida	....	....	....	....	....	35.00	72.00	70.30	91.50	111.70	380.50
Southern Atlantic States	377.79	699.24	327.37	304.86	187.89	434.69	420.23	316.64	395.26	272.93	3,736.90
Alabama	....	28.50	53.72	89.28	30.54	119.46	77.80	....	96.60	114.76	610.66
Mississippi	....	21.20	....	126.10	55.70	135.00	70.50	120.63	93.67	174.50	797.30
Louisiana	....	....	9.50	109.00	5.00	46.50	11.50	20.00	13.75	40.00	255.25

Texas				32.00	8.00	31.00	86.00	48.50	79.00	21.50	306.00
Gulf States		49.70	63.22	356.38	99.24	331.96	245.80	189.13	283.02	350.76	1,969.21
Arkansas										38.50	38.50
Tennessee	112.33	73.11	105.81	38.00	136.80	75.16	228.48	117.91	75.50	234.82	1,197.92
Kentucky	15.89		73.00	74.80		26.00	37.00	153.60	78.50	30.93	489.72
Interior States, South	128.22	73.11	178.81	112.80	136.80	101.16	265.48	271.51	154.00	304.25	1,726.14
Ohio	320.15	490.52	391.43	223.91	451.88	69.57	96.84	31.66	160.38	89.14	2,325.48
Indiana	310.50	217.42	452.69	108.68	89.23	400.32	87.95	99.91	18.92	112.28	1,897.90
Michigan	37.27	52.00		12.90	30.06	26.26	102.01	39.87	95.03	61.90	457.30
Illinois	160.89	140.80	347.43	28.78	98.39	1,248.54	366.32	232.27	47.28	86.70	2,757.40
Wisconsin	30.00	20.60		26.65	90.25	88.90	353.52	17.43	178.65	96.61	902.61
Minnesota											
Iowa					68.50	185.36	89.85	35.65	153.44	146.87	679.67
Missouri			37.50		101.20	5.52	173.41	229.57	177.05	93.20	817.45
Kansas											
Interior States, North	858.81	921.34	1,229.05	400.92	929.51	2,024.47	1,269.90	686.36	830.75	686.70	9,837.81
California					8.00	14.00				48.05	70.05
Oregon										3.80	3.80
Pacific States					8.00	14.00				51.85	73.85
New England States	305.06	172.43	179.88	97.25	227.42	96.88	22.00	16.50	37.49	8.00	1,162.91
Middle Atlantic States	768.56	554.16	217.13	453.97	263.80	350.57	241.65	184.40	315.72	147.30	3,497.26
Southern Atlantic States	377.79	699.24	327.37	304.86	187.89	434.69	420.23	316.64	395.26	272.93	3,736.90
Gulf States		49.70	63.22	356.38	99.24	331.96	245.80	189.13	283.02	350.76	1,969.21
Interior States, South	128.22	73.11	178.81	112.80	136.80	101.16	265.48	271.51	154.00	304.25	1,726.14
Interior States, North	858.81	921.34	1,229.05	400.92	929.51	2,024.47	1,269.90	686.36	830.75	686.70	9,837.81
Pacific States					8.00	14.00				51.85	73.85
Total United States	2,438.44	2,469.98	2,195.46	1,726.18	1,852.66	3,353.73	2,465.06	1,664.54	2,016.24	1,821.79	22,004.08

TABLE No. 39.—*Canals and River Improvements.*

Canals and river improvements.	States.	Points connected.	Miles of navigat'n. Canal.	Miles of navigat'n. Slack water.	Dimensions. Width in feet.	Dimensions. Depth in feet.	Locks. No. of structures.	Locks. Chambers. Length in feet.	Locks. Chambers. Width in feet.	Total rise and fall in feet.	Cost of construction in dollars.
Cumberland and Oxford	Maine	Portland—Sebago Pond	20.50	....	34	4	25	......	......	168	50,000 (Cumberland and Oxford and Songo River Improvement together)
Songo River Improvement	do	Sebago Pond—Brandy and Long Ponds	....	30.00	......	4	1	......	......	8	
Bon Falls	N. Hampshire	Around the Falls so called in the Merrimac river (Bon Falls to Pawtucket)	0.75	....	......	......	4	......	......	25	25,000
Hooksett Falls	do		0.13	....	......	......	3	......	......	16	17,000
Amoskeag Falls	do		1.00	....	......	......	9	......	......	45	50,000
Union	do		3.00	6.00	......	......	7	......	......	....	....
Sewall's Falls	do		0.25	....	......	......	2	......	......	....	....
Pawtucket	Massachusetts		1.65	....	60	4	5	......	......	32	....
White River	Vermont	Around the Falls so called in the Connecticut river (White River to Enfield Falls)	0 50	....	......	......	......	......	......	....	....
Watuguuchy	do		0.40	....	......	......	......	......	......	....	....
Bellows' Falls	do		0.16	....	......	......	9	......	......	50	....
Montague	Massachusetts		3.00	....	25	3	8	......	......	75	....
South Hadley	do		2.00	....	......	......	5	......	......	50	....
Enfield Falls	Connecticut		5.50	....	......	......	3	90	20	30	....
Erie	New York	Albany (Hudson river) and Buffalo (Lake Erie)	350.58	....	70	7	71	110	18	582	41,873,738 (Erie to Glenn's Falls Feeder together)
Champlain	do	Grand Junction (Erie canal) and Whitehall (Lake Champlain)	64.00	....	70	7	20	110	18	180	
Waterford Side-cut	do	Waterford—Hudson River	2.75	....	70	7	3	110	18	133	
Glenn's Falls Feeder	do	Upper Hudson—Summit Level	7.00	....	40	4	13	90	15	132	
Black River	do	Rome (Erie canal)—High Falls of Black river	35.62	....	70	7	109	110	18	1,079	*3,019,832 (Black River and Summit Feeder together)
Summit Feeder	do	Black River and Elder Creek—Summit, 23 miles from Rome	12.48	....	......	......	......	......	......	....	
Black River Improvement	do	High Falls—Carthage	....	42.50	60	5	1	110	18	....	†3,019,832 (Black River Improvement and Feeders, etc. together)
Feeders, etc	do	....	....	12.95	......	......	......	......	......	....	
Chenango	do	Utica (Erie canal) and Binghamton (Susquehanna river)	97.17	....	70	7	114	110	18	1,016	2,439,676 (Chenango and Feeders together)
Feeders	do	....	17.50	....	......	......	......	......	......	....	

Oneida Lake	....do	Higginsville (Erie canal)—Oneida Lake	6.00	......	......	......	7	......	......	58	50,000
Oneida River Improvement	....do	Oneida Lake—Oswego River and Canal	......	20.00	......	......	2	......	......	......	91,977
Oswego	....do	Syracuse (Erie canal)—Oswego (Lake Ontario)	18.25	20.00	70	7	18	110	18	157	2,806,187
Baldwinsville Side-cut	....do	Baldwinsville—Seneca River	1.00	......	......	......	......	......	......	......	......
Cayuga and Seneca	....do	Montezuma (Erie canal)—Geneva (Seneca lake)	20.71	......	......	......	10	110	18	76	} 1,169,276
Cayuga Lake Branch	....do	Foot of Cayuga Lake—East Cayuga	2.06	......	......	......	1	110	18	10	
Seneca River Towing Path	....do	(Along the Seneca river)	......	5.00	......	......	......	......	......	......	......
Crooked Lake	....do	Dresden (Seneca lake)—Penn Yan (Crooked lake)	7.69	......	......	......	38	......	......	273	305,245
Chemung	....do	Head of Seneca lake—Elmira (Chemung river)	23.00	......	......	......	49	......	......	491	} 949,603
Feeder	....do	Horsehead's (Chemung canal)—Knoxville	16.75	......	......	......	3	......	......	27	
Genesee Valley	....do	Rochester (Erie canal)—Olean (Alleghany river)	107.00	......	......	......	106	......	......	1,064	
Dansville Branch	....do	Shakers (Genesee Valley canal)—Dansville	6.75	......	......	......	8	......	......	82	} 5,601,606
Millgrove Extension	....do	Olean—Millgrove (Alleghany river)	11.20	......	......	......	......	......	......	......	‡240,000
Junction	....do	Elmira (Chemung canal)—Pennsylvania State Line	§11.00	......	......	......	......	......	......	......	......
Delaware and Hudson	N. Y. and Pa.	Eddyville (Hudson river)—Honesdale, Pa.	108.00	......	50	6	105	100	19	950	6,185,616
Delaware and Raritan	New Jersey	Bordentown (Del. river)—New Brunswick (Raritan river)	43.00	......	75	8	15	220	24	150	} 3,935,287
Delaware Feeder	....do	Bull's Island (Delaware river)—Trenton	22.50	......	60	6	1	100	24	4	
Morris	....do	Jersey City (Hudson river)—Philipsburg (Delaware river)	101.00	......	40	5	23	98	22	1,674	2,825,997
Lehigh Navigation	Pennsylvania	Stoddardsville (Lehigh river)—Easton (Delaware river)	39.25	45.32	60	5	78	100	12	1,297	4,455,000
Schuylkill Navigation	....do	Philadelphia (Delaware river)—Port Carbon	108.50	......	70	6	70	110	18	616	10,285,000
Delaware Division	....do	Easton (Lehigh river)—Bristol (Delaware river)	59.80	......	40	6	24	100	12	167	2,433,350
North Branch	....do	Wilkesbarre—State Line of New York	105.00	......	40	5	27	90	15	258	1,000,000
Wyoming	....do	Wilkesbarre—Northumberland	64.00	......	40	5	8	90	15	69	1,889,000
West Branch & Susquehanna	....do	Farrandsville—Duncan Island	117.00	......	40	5	31	90	15	225	} 2,729,743
Bald Eagle Branch	....do	Lock Haven, W. B. and S. canal—Bald Eagle	3.00	......	40	5	......	......	......	......	
Lewisburg Cross-cut	....do	......	1.00	......	40	5	......	......	......	......	
Union	....do	Reading (Schuylkill river)—Middletown (Susquehanna river)	77.00	......	36	4	84	90	17	503	} 6,125,000
Pine Grove Branch	....do	Union Canal—Pine Grove	22.00	......	36	4	......	......	......	......	
Susquehanna and Tide-water	Pa. and Md.	Wrightsville—Havre de Grace, Md	45.00	......	50	5	29	110	17	233	4,668,486
Pennsylvania	Pennsylvania	Columbia (Susquehanna river)—Hollidaysburg	156.00	17.00	40	4	76	90	15	671	} 1,000,000
Western Division	....do	Johnstown—Pittsburg	76.00	27.00	40	4	45	90	15	469	
Monongahela Navigation	....do	Pittsburg (Ohio river)—Geneva	......	83.00	......	5	......	......	......	......	905,837
Youghiogeny	....do	McKeesport—West Newton	......	18.00	......	5	2	......	......	27	200,000

* Completed in 1860. † Probably in use in 1861. ‡ Completed in 1861. § Completed in 1859.

TABLE No. 39.—*Canals and River Improvements*—Continued.

Canals and river improvements.	States.	Points connected.	MILES OF NAVIGAT'N.		DIMENSIONS.		LOCKS.			Total rise and fall in feet.	Cost of construction in dollars.
			Canal.	Slack water.	Width in feet	Depth in feet.	No. of structures.	Chambers. Length in feet.	Chambers. Width in feet.		
Erie	Pennsylvania	Bridgewater (Ohio river)—Erie City (Lake Erie)	136.00		40	4	133	90	15	930	$5,285,291
French Creek Feeder	do	Bemus Dam—Main Canal	27.00		40	4	16	90	15	128	
Wiconisco	do	Wiconisco Creek—Duncan's Island	12.25		40	4	6	90	15	35	393,440
Chesapeake and Delaware	Delaware	Delaware City—Back Creek (Elk river)	12.63		66	10	3	220	24	32	3,547,561
Chesapeake and Ohio	Maryland	Georgetown, D. C.—Cumberland, Md.	184.50		50	6	74	100	15	606	10,506,309
Alexandria	Virginia	Alexandria—Washington Aqueduct	7.20		50	6					1,068,762
James River and Kanawha	do	Richmond—Buchanan	147.78								6,139,280
Dismal Swamp	Va. and N. C.	Deep Creek, of Elizabeth river—Joyce's Creek, Pasquotank river.	22.50		40	$6\frac{1}{2}$	4	100	22	33	
Northwest Branch	do	Northwest River—Main Canal	6.00		24	4	1	100	22		1,151,066
Lake Drummond Branch	do	Lake Drummond—Main Canal	5.00		16	$2\frac{1}{4}$					
Albemarle and Chesapeake	Virginia	Southwest Branch of Elizabeth River—North Landing River	8.50		60	8					*250,000
Albemarle and Chesapeake	North Carolina	Coinjock Bay—North River	5.50		60	8					
Weldon	do	(Roanoke River Improvement)	12.00							100	
Clubfoot and Harlow	do	Clubfoot Creek—Harlow Creek	1.50								
Santee	South Carolina	Charleston Harbor—Santee River	22.00		32	4	13	60	10	103	720,000
Winyaw	do	Winyaw Bay—Kinlock Creek	7.40								
Catawba	do	(Several short canals)	6.50								
Wateree Canal	do	Jones' Mills—Ellicott's	4.00								
Saluda	do	Head of Saluda Shoals—Granby Ferry (Congaree river)	6.20							36	
Drehr's	do	(Round Falls in Saluda river)	1.50							120	
Lorick's	do	(On Broad river, above Columbia)	1.00								
Lockhart's	do	(Around Lockhart's Fall in Broad river)	2.72								
Brunswick	Georgia	Brunswick Harbor—Altamaha River	12.00								500,000

Ogeechee	....do	Savannah—Ogeechee River	16.00								165,000
Muscle Shoals	Alabama	(Along Muscle Shoals of Tennessee river)	35.76		60	6	16	120	32	96	1,400,000
Huntsville	....do	Huntsville—Triana (Tennessee river)	16.00								
Orleans Bank	Louisiana		4.25								
Barataria Navigation	....do		22.00	63							
Carondelet	....do	New Orleans—Bayou St. John	2.00								
Lake Veret	....do	Lafourche Bayou—Lake Veret	8.00								
Louisville and Portland	Kentucky	Louisville—Portland	2.50		50	10	4			22	
Kentucky River Navigation	....do	Mouth of Kentucky—Junction of North Fork		260			17	175	38	216	2,500,000
Licking River Navigation	....do	Mouth of Licking—West Liberty		231			21	130	25	310	2,000,000
Green River Navigation	....do	Mouth of Green—Bowling Green		175				160	36		500,000
Barren River Navigation	....do			100							
Ohio and Erie	Ohio	Portsmouth, Ohio river—Cleveland (Lake Erie)	307.00		40	4	152			1,085	
Columbus Branch	....do	Main Canal—Columbus	10.00								
Lancaster Branch	....do	Main Canal—Lancaster	9.00								
Zanesville Branch	....do	Main Canal—Zanesville	14.00								
Athens Branch	....do	Lancaster—Athens	56.00								
Granville Branch	....do	Main Canal—Granville	6.00								
Walhonding Branch	....do	Main Canal—Coshocton	23.00								
Eastport Branch	....do	Main Canal—Eastport	4.00								
Dresden Branch	....do	Main Canal—Dresden (Muskingum river)	2.00								
Miami and Erie	....do	Cincinnati—Defiance	178.00								
Lebanon Branch	....do	Main Canal—Lebanon	20.00								
Wabash and Erie	....do	Toledo—State Line of Indiana	90.00								
Sandy and Beaver	....do	Bolivar—Liverpool	86.00								
Canton Branch	....do	Main Canal—Canton	14.00								
Mahcning	....do	Akron—State Line of Pennsylvania	87.00								
Muskingum Improvement	....do	Dresden—Marietta (Ohio river)		91							
Wabash and Erie	Indiana	Evansville (Ohio river)—State Line of Ohio	379.00								
Whitewater	....do	Lawrenceburg (Ohio river)—Cambridge City	74.00								
Illinois and Michigan	Illinois	Chicago (Lake Michigan)—La Salle (Illinois river)	102.00								
Fox and Wisconsin	Wisconsin	Green Bay—Mississippi River †									
Sault St. Marie	Michigan	Lake Michigan—Lake Superior	‡0.75								
Des Moines River Improvem't.	Iowa	Keokuk—Des Moines City §									

* Completed in1861. † Not yet completed through. ‡ Completed in 1856. § Not yet completed.

Table No. 40.

Table showing the population of the principal cities and towns in the United States, according to the Seventh Census (1850) and the Eighth Census (1860,) respectively; also the numerical increase and increase per cent.

Cities and towns.	Counties.	States.	Population in 1850.	Population in 1860.	Increase.	Increase per cent.
Albany	Albany	New York	50,763	62,367	11,604	22.86
Alleghany City	Alleghany	Pennsylvania	21,261	28,702	7,441	35.00
Augusta	Richmond	Georgia	11,753	12,493	740	6.30
Augusta	Kennebec	Maine	8,225	7,609	....	*l.* 7.49
Auburn	Cayuga	New York	9,548	10,986	1,438	15.06
Alexandria	Alexandria	Virginia	8,734	12,652	3,918	44.86
Ann Arbor	Washtenaw	Michigan	4,868	4,483	....	*l.* 7.91
Annapolis	Anne Arundel	Maryland	3,011	4,529	1,518	50.42
Alton	Madison	Illinois	3,585	7,338	3,753	104.69
Baltimore	Baltimore	Maryland	169,054	212,418	43,364	25.65
Buffalo	Erie	New York	42,261	81,129	38,868	91.97
Boston	Suffolk	Massachusetts	136,881	177,812	40,931	29.90
Bangor	Penobscot	Maine	14,432	16,407	1,975	13.68
Bath	Sagadahoc	Maine	8,020	8,076	56	0.70
Burlington	Chittenden	Vermont	6,110	7,713	1,603	26.24
Burlington	Burlington	New Jersey	4,536	5,193	657	14.48
Burlington	Des Moines	Iowa	4,082	6,706	2,624	64.28
Brooklyn	Kings	New York	96,838	266,661	169,823	175.37
Charleston	Charleston	South Carolina	42,985	40,578	....	*l.* 5.60
Cincinnati	Hamilton	Ohio	115,436	161,044	45,608	39.51
Columbus	Franklin	Ohio	17,882	18,554	672	3.76
Cleveland	Cuyahoga	Ohio	17,034	43,417	26,383	154.88
Chicago	Cook	Illinois	29,963	109,260	79,297	264.65
Cambridge	Middlesex	Massachusetts	15,215	26,060	10,845	71.28
Canandaigua	Ontario	New York	6,143	7,075	932	15.17
Columbia	Richland	South Carolina	6,060	8,059	1,999	32.98
Columbus	Muscogee	Georgia	5,942	9,621	3,679	61.91
Chilicothe	Ross	Ohio	7,100	7,626	526	7.40
Detroit	Wayne	Michigan	21,019	45,619	24,600	117.03
Dover	Strafford	New Hampshire	8,196	8,502	306	3.73
Dayton	Montgomery	Ohio	10,970	20,081	9,111	83.05
Davenport	Scott	Iowa	1,848	11,267	9,419	509.68
Dubuque	Dubuque	Iowa	3,108	13,000	9,892	318.27
Des Moines	Polk	Iowa	986	3,965	2,979	302.12
Fall River	Bristol	Massachusetts	11,524	14,026	2,502	21.71
Frederick	Frederick	Maryland	6,028	8,143	2,115	35.08
Fayetteville	Cumberland	North Carolina	4,646	4,790	144	3.09
Fredericksburg	Spottsylvania	Virginia	4,061	5,022	961	23.66
Freeport	Stephenson	Illinois	1,436	3,529	2,093	145.75
Fort Wayne	Allen	Indiana	4,282	10,388	6,106	142.59
Gardiner	Kennebec	Maine	6,486	4,487	....	*l.* 30.82
Gloucester	Essex	Massachusetts	7,786	10,904	3,118	40.04

TABLE No. 40.—*Population of the principal cities and towns, &c.*—Continued.

Cities and towns.	Counties.	States.	Population in 1850.	Population in 1860.	Increase.	Increase per cent.
Georgetown	Washington	Dist. of Columbia	8,366	8,733	367	4.38
Galveston	Galveston	Texas	4,177	7,307	3,130	74.93
Galena	Jo Daviess	Illinois	6,004	8,193	2,189	36.45
Hartford	Hartford	Connecticut	13,555	29,154	15,599	115.08
Hudson	Columbia	New York	6,286	7,187	901	14.33
Harrisburg	Dauphin	Pennsylvania	7,834	13,405	5,571	71.11
Ithaca	Tompkins	New York	6,909	6,843	....	*l.* 0.95
Indianapolis	Marion	Indiana	8,034	18,611	10,577	131.65
Iowa City	Johnson	Iowa	1,582	5,214	3,632	229.58
Jersey City	Hudson	New Jersey	6,856	29,226	22,370	326 28
Keokuk	Lee	Iowa	2,478	8,136	5,658	228.32
Lowell	Middlesex	Massachusetts	33,383	36,827	3,444	10.31
Louisville	Jefferson	Kentucky	43,194	68,033	24,839	57.50
Lynn	Essex	Massachusetts	14,257	19,083	4,826	33.85
Lockport	Niagara	New York	12,323	13,523	1,200	9.73
Lancaster	Lancaster	Pennsylvania	12,369	17,603	5,234	42.31
Lynchburg	Campbell	Virginia	8,071	6,853	....	*l.* 15.09
Lexington	Fayette	Kentucky	9,180	9,321	171	1.53
La Fayette	Tippecanoe	Indiana	1,215	9,387	8,172	672.59
Lansing	Ingham	Michigan	1,229	3,074	1,845	150.12
La Porte	La Porte	Indiana	1,824	5,028	3,204	175.65
Manchester	Hillsboro'	New Hampshire	13,932	20,109	6,177	44.33
Mobile	Mobile	Alabama	20,515	29,258	8,743	42.61
Montgomery	Montgomery	Alabama	4,935	35,902	30,967	627.49
Milwaukie	Milwaukie	Wisconsin	20,061	45,246	25,185	125.54
Marblehead	Essex	Massachusetts	6,167	7,647	1,480	23.99
Middleboro'	Plymouth	Massachusetts	5,336	6,272	936	17.54
Memphis	Shelby	Tennessee	8,839	22,623	13,784	155.94
Muscatine	Muscatine	Iowa	2,540	5,324	2,784	109.60
Madison	Jefferson	Indiana	8,012	8,130	118	1.47
New Haven	New Haven	Connecticut	20,345	39,267	18,922	93.00
New York	New York	New York	515,547	805,651	290,104	56.27
Newark	Essex	New Jersey	38,894	71,914	33,020	84.89
Norfolk	Norfolk	Virginia	14,326	15,611	1,285	8.96
Nashville	Davidson	Tennessee	10,478	16,988	6,510	62.13
New Orleans	Orleans	Louisiana	116,375	168,675	52,300	44.94
Nashua	Hillsboro'	New Hampshire	5,820	10,065	4,245	72.93
Nantucket	Nantucket	Massachusetts	8,452	6,094	....	*l.* 27.89
Newburyport	Essex	Massachusetts	9,572	13,401	3,829	40.00
Newport	Newport	Rhode Island	9,563	10,508	945	9.88
New London	New London	Connecticut	8,991	10,115	1,124	12.50
Newburg	Orange	New York	11,415	15,196	3,781	33 12
Newbern	Craven	North Carolina	4,681	5,432	751	16.04
Natchez	Adams	Mississippi	4,434	6,612	2,178	49.12
Pekin	Tazewell	Illinois	1,678	3,467	1,789	106.61

TABLE No. 40.—*Population of the principal cities and towns, &c.*—Continued.

Cities and towns.	Counties.	States.	Population in 1850.	Population in 1860.	Increase.	Increase per cent.
Portland	Cumberland	Maine	20,815	26,341	5,526	26.54
Portsmouth	Rockingham	New Hampshire	9,738	9,335	....	*l.* 4.13
Portsmouth	Norfolk	Virginia	8,122	9,502	1,380	16.99
Providence	Providence	Rhode Island	41,513	50,666	9,153	22.04
Philadelphia	Philadelphia	Pennsylvania	340,045	562,529	222,484	65.43
Pittsburg	Alleghany	Pennsylvania	46,601	49,217	2,616	5.61
Petersburg	Dinwiddie	Virginia	14,010	18,266	4,256	30.38
Plymouth	Plymouth	Massachusetts	6,024	6,272	248	4.12
Poughkeepsie	Dutchess	New York	13,944	14,726	782	5.61
Paterson	Passaic	New Jersey	11,334	19,588	8,254	72.83
Peoria	Peoria	Illinois	5,095	14,045	8,950	175.66
Quincy	Adams	Illinois	6,902	13,632	6,730	97.51
Rochester	Monroe	New York	36,403	48,204	11,801	32.42
Richmond	Henrico	Virginia	27,570	37,910	10,340	37.50
Roxbury	Norfolk	Massachusetts	18,364	25,137	6,773	36.88
Reading	Berks	Pennsylvania	15,743	23,161	7,418	47.12
Raleigh	Wake	North Carolina	4,518	4,780	262	5.80
Richmond	Wayne	Indiana	1,443	6,603	5,160	357.51
Rock Island	Rock Island	Illinois	1,711	5,130	3,419	199.82
Springfield	Hampden	Massachusetts	11,766	15,199	3,433	29.18
Salem	Essex	Massachusetts	20,264	22,252	1,988	9.81
Syracuse	Onondaga	New York	22,271	28,119	5,848	26.26
Savannah	Chatham	Georgia	15,312	22,292	6,980	45.59
St. Louis	St. Louis	Missouri	77,860	160,773	82,913	106.49
San Francisco	San Francisco	California	34,776	56,802	22,026	63.34
Schenectady	Schenectady	New York	8,921	9,579	658	7 38
Steubenville	Jefferson	Ohio	6,140	6,154	10	0.16
Thomaston	Knox	Maine	2,723	3,218	495	18.18
Troy	Rensselaer	New York	28,785	39,232	10,447	36.29
Taunton	Bristol	Massachusetts	10,441	15,376	4,935	47.27
Utica	Oneida	New York	17,565	22,529	4,964	28.26
Vicksburg	Warren	Mississippi	3,678	4,591	913	24.82
Washington	Washington	Dist. of Columbia	40,001	61,122	21,121	52.78
Wilmington	New Hanover	North Carolina	7,264	9,552	2,288	31.50
Worcester	Worcester	Massachusetts	17,049	24,960	7,911	46.40
West Troy	Albany	New York	7,564	8,820	1,256	16.60
Wilmington	New Castle	Delaware	13,979	21,508	7,529	53.86
Wheeling	Ohio	Virginia	11,435	14,083	2,648	23.16
Zanesville	Muskingum	Ohio	10,355	9,229	....	*l.* 10.87

l indicates loss.

TABLE NO. 41.

Population of the United States by Counties, Census 1860.

STATE OF ALABAMA.

COUNTIES.	WHITES.			FREE COLORED.			Total free.	SLAVES.			Agg'te population.
	Male.	Female.	Total.	Male.	Fem.	Total.		Male.	Female.	Total.	
Autauga..........	3,616	3,502	7,118	7	7	14	7,132	4,677	4,930	9,607	16,739
Baldwin..........	2,105	1,571	3,676	67	73	140	3,816	2,266	1,448	3,714	7,530
Barbour..........	7,490	7,139	14,629	20	13	33	14,662	7,996	8,154	16,150	30,812
Bibb..............	4,045	3,982	8,027	9	16	25	8,052	1,899	1,943	3,842	11,894
Blount............	5,165	5,028	10,193	3	3	6	10,199	295	371	666	10,865
Butler............	5,881	5,379	11,260	26	18	44	11,304	3,411	3,407	6,818	18,122
Calhoun..........	8,624	8,545	17,169	11	17	28	17,197	2,107	2,235	4,342	21,539
Chambers.........	5,764	5,551	11,315	25	25	50	11,365	5,908	5,941	11,849	23,214
Cherokee.........	7,665	7,656	15,321	16	21	37	15,358	1,479	1,523	3,002	18,360
Choctaw..........	3,539	3,228	6,767	9	7	16	6,783	3,552	3,542	7,094	13,877
Clarke............	3,987	3,612	7,599	7	7	14	7,613	3,617	3,819	7,436	15,049
Coffee............	4,275	3,925	8,200	4	2	6	8,206	673	744	1,417	9,623
Conecuh..........	3,318	3,101	6,419	4	6	10	6,429	2,463	2,419	4,882	11,311
Coosa............	7,314	6,736	14,050	7	4	11	14,061	2,530	2,682	5,212	19,273
Covington........	2,863	2,768	5,631	8	9	17	5,648	396	425	821	6,469
Dale..............	5,264	5,117	10,381	6	1	7	10,388	870	939	1,809	12,195
Dallas............	4,025	3,760	7,785	28	52	80	7,865	12,907	12,853	25,760	33,625
DeKalb...........	4,866	4,987	9,853	2	2	4	9,857	430	418	848	10,705
Fayette..........	5,735	5,410	11,145	.....	2	2	11,147	815	888	1,703	12,850
Franklin..........	5,259	4,860	10,119	5	8	13	10,132	4,136	4,359	8,495	18,627
Green............	3,887	3,364	7,251	6	4	10	7,261	11,981	11,617	23,598	30,859
Henry............	5,343	5,121	10,464	10	11	21	10,485	2,213	2,220	4,433	14,918
Jackson..........	7,582	7,229	14,811	26	41	67	14,878	1,724	1,681	3,405	18,283
Jefferson........	4,573	4,505	9,078	6	13	19	9,097	1,298	1,351	2,649	11,746
Lawrence.........	3,627	3,546	7,173	9	5	14	7,187	3,311	3,477	6,788	13,975
Lauderdale........	5,312	5,327	10,639	19	25	44	10,683	3,666	3,371	6,737	17,420
Limestone.........	3,615	3,600	7,215	3	3	6	7,221	3,970	4,115	8,085	15,306
Lowndes..........	4,299	4,063	8,362	9	5	14	8,376	9,650	9,690	19,340	27,716
Madison..........	5,969	5,717	11,686	105	87	192	11,878	7,237	7,336	14,573	26,451
Marengo..........	3,527	3,234	6,761	1	......	1	6,762	12,313	12,096	24,409	31,171
Marion...........	4,921	4,973	9,894	4	1	5	9,899	648	635	1,283	11,182
Marshall..........	4,868	4,732	9,600	22	29	51	9,651	896	925	1,821	11,472
Macon............	4,425	4,200	8,625	......	1	1	8,626	9,014	9,162	18,176	26,802
Mobile...........	15,730	12,830	28,560	543	652	1,195	29,755	5,912	5,464	11,376	41,131
Montgomery.......	6,473	5,651	12,124	27	43	70	12,194	11,908	11,802	23,710	35,904
Monroe...........	3,560	3,356	6,916	15	31	46	6,962	4,293	4,412	8,705	15,667
Morgan...........	3,781	3,811	7,592	18	19	37	7,629	1,817	1,889	3,706	11,335
Perry............	4,866	4,613	9,479	27	12	39	9,518	9,275	8,931	18,206	27,724
Pickens..........	5,152	4,965	10,117	4	4	8	10,125	5,976	6,215	12,191	22,316
Pike..............	8,068	7,578	15,646	3	1	4	15,650	4,433	4,352	8,785	24,435
Randolph.........	9,134	8,998	18,132	10	13	23	18,155	896	1,008	1,904	20,059
Russell...........	5,543	5,393	10,936	12	6	18	10,954	7,823	7,815	15,638	26,592
Shelby............	4,623	4,347	8,970	7	19	26	8,996	1,851	1,771	3,622	12,618
St. Clair..........	4,703	4,533	9,236	5	4	9	9,245	867	901	1,768	11,013
Sumter...........	3,095	2,824	5,919	13	12	25	5,944	9,402	8,689	18,091	24,035
Tallapoosa........	8,718	8,436	17,154	1	......	1	17,155	3,220	3,452	6,672	23,827
Talladega.........	7,305	7,329	14,634	11	10	21	14,655	4,430	4,435	8,865	23,520
Tuscaloosa........	6,582	6,389	12,971	35	49	84	13,055	5,196	4,949	10,145	23,200
Walker...........	3,777	3,684	7,461	......	.....	......	7,461	246	273	519	7,980
Washington.......	1,093	1,026	2,119	24	32	56	2,175	1,296	1,198	2,494	4,669
Wilcox...........	3,578	3,217	6,795	15	11	26	6,821	8,816	8,981	17,797	24,618
Winston..........	1,742	1,712	3,454	......	......	......	3,454	61	61	122	3,576
Total.......	270,271	256,160	526,431	1,254	1,436	2,690	529,121	217,766	217,314	435,080	964,201

NOTE—160 Indians included in white population.

TABLE No. 41—*Population of the United States by Counties, &c.*—Continued.

STATE OF ARKANSAS.

COUNTIES.	WHITES.			FREE COLORED.			Total free.	SLAVES.			Agg'te population.
	Male.	Female.	Total.	Male.	Fem.	Total.		Male.	Female.	Total.	
Arkansas	2,094	1,829	3,923	......	......	......	3,923	2,603	2,318	4,921	8,844
Ashley	2,592	2,237	4,829	......	......	......	4,829	1,818	1,943	3,761	8,590
Benton	4,534	4,387	8,921	1	......	1	8,922	190	194	384	9,306
Bradley	3,026	2,672	5,698	......	......	......	5,698	1,263	1,427	2,690	8,388
Calhoun	1,660	1,462	3,122	......	......	......	3,122	492	489	981	4,103
Carroll	4,641	4,412	9,053	......	......	......	9,053	152	178	330	9,383
Chicot	1,011	711	1,722	......	......	......	1,722	3,888	3,624	7,512	9,234
Clark	3,990	3,526	7,516	2	3	5	7,521	1,083	1,131	2,214	9,735
Columbia	4,682	4,163	8,845	3	2	5	8,850	1,814	1,785	3,599	12,449
Conway	3,104	2,791	5,895	......	......	......	5,895	377	425	802	6,697
Crawford	3,597	3,389	6,986	......	6	6	6,992	403	455	858	7,850
Crittenden	1,522	1,051	2,573	......	......	......	2,573	1,231	1,116	2,347	4,920
Craighead	1,564	1,414	2,978	......	1	1	2,979	44	43	87	3,066
Dallas	2,508	2,280	4,788	......	1	1	4,789	1,865	1,629	3,494	8,283
Desha	1,532	1,123	2,655	8	12	20	2,675	1,955	1,829	3,784	6,459
Drew	2,955	2,626	5,581	......	......	......	5,581	1,725	1,772	3,497	9,078
Franklin	3,319	3,011	6,330	4	2	6	6,336	493	469	962	7,298
Fulton	2,086	1,850	3,936	......	......	......	3,936	33	55	88	4,024
Green	2,934	2,720	5,654	......	......	......	5,654	82	107	189	5,843
Hempstead	4,618	3,971	8,589	2	......	2	8,591	2,733	2,665	5,398	13,989
Hot Spring	2,632	2,387	5,019	2	1	3	5,022	298	315	613	5,635
Independence	6,793	6,177	12,970	......	......	......	12,970	647	690	1,337	14,307
Izard	3,487	3,346	6,833	......	......	......	6,833	181	201	382	7,215
Jefferson	4,271	3,542	7,813	3	9	12	7,825	3,667	3,479	7,146	14,971
Johnson	3,476	3,163	6,639	......	......	......	6,639	486	487	973	7,612
Jackson	4,234	3,723	7,957	......	1	1	7,958	1,254	1,281	2,535	10,493
Lafayette	2,263	1,883	4,146	4	3	7	4,153	2,294	2,017	4,311	8,464
Lawrence	4,654	4,221	8,875	3	......	3	8,878	247	247	494	9,372
Madison	3,793	3,651	7,444	......	......	......	7,444	134	162	296	7,740
Marion	3,108	2,815	5,923	2	6	8	5,931	118	143	261	6,192
Mississippi	1,276	1,158	2,434	......	......	......	2,434	746	715	1,461	3,895
Monroe	1,853	1,578	3,431	......	......	......	3,431	1,138	1,088	2,226	5,657
Montgomery	1,866	1,675	3,541	......	......	......	3,541	48	44	92	3,633
Newton	1,705	1,664	3,369	......	......	......	3,369	12	12	24	3,393
Ouachita	4,552	3,905	8,457	1	......	1	8,458	2,187	2,291	4,478	12,936
Perry	1,138	1,024	2,162	......	......	......	2,162	152	151	303	2,465
Phillips	3,363	2,569	5,932	1	3	4	5,936	4,675	4,266	8,941	14,876
Pike	2,017	1,781	3,798	......	......	......	3,798	114	113	227	4,025
Poinsett	1,368	1,167	2,535	......	......	......	2,535	522	564	1,086	3,621
Polk	2,109	1,981	4,090	......	......	......	4,090	77	95	172	4,262
Pope	3,600	3,305	6,905	......	......	......	6,905	488	490	978	7,883
Prairie	3,265	2,750	6,015	......	......	......	6,015	1,412	1,427	2,839	8,854
Pulaski	4,555	3,632	8,187	6	1	7	8,194	1,782	1,723	3,505	11,699
Randolph	3,079	2,823	5,902	......	......	......	5,902	175	184	359	6,261
St. Francis	3,272	2,779	6,051	......	......	......	6,051	1,324	1,297	2,621	8,672
Saline	3,096	2,795	5,891	......	......	......	5,891	361	388	749	6,640
Scott	2,578	2,352	4,930	......	......	......	4,930	109	106	215	5,145
Searcy	2,686	2,492	5,178	......	......	......	5,178	49	44	93	5,271
Sebastian	4,499	4,058	8,557	1	......	1	8,558	311	369	680	9,238
Sevier	3,768	3,382	7,150	......	......	......	7,150	1,717	1,649	3,366	10,516
Union	3,194	2,763	5,957	......	......	......	5,957	3,161	3,170	6,331	12,288
Van Buren	2,664	2,493	5,157	......	......	......	5,157	93	107	200	5,357
Washington	6,859	6,274	13,133	27	20	47	13,180	741	752	1,493	14,673
White	3,621	3,260	6,881	2	1	3	6,884	687	745	1,432	8,316
Yell	2,838	2,497	5,335	......	......	......	5,335	523	475	998	6,333
Total	171,501	152,690	324,191	72	72	144	324,335	56,174	54,941	111,115	435,450

NOTE.—48 Indians included in white population.

TABLE No. 41.—*Population of the United States by Counties, &c.*—Continued.

STATE OF CALIFORNIA.

COUNTIES.	WHITES.			FREE COLORED.			INDIANS.			HALF-BREEDS.			CHINESE.			Aggregate population.
	M.	F.	Total.	M.	F.	Tot'l	M.	F.	Total	M.	F.	Tot'l	M.	F.	Total	
Alameda	5,489	3,059	8,548	37	18	55	70	61	131	....	....	....	188	5	193	8,927
Amador	6,151	2,101	8,252	65	23	88	....	....	......	15	7	22	2,468	100	2,568	10,930
Butte	7,770	1,967	9,737	57	14	71	98	23	121	....	....	....	2,111	66	2,177	12,106
Calaveras	10,088	2,458	12,546	83	12	95	....	1	1	....	....	....	3,527	130	3,657	16,299
Colusi	1,543	622	2,165	18	7	25	48	20	68	4	3	7	9	....	9	2,274
Contra Costa	3,395	1,790	5,185	18	9	27	52	44	96	8	10	18	2	....	2	5,328
Del Norte	1,050	291	1,341	27	21	48	139	126	265	....	1	1	337	1	338	1,993
El Dorado	11,844	3,671	15,515	210	67	277	4	4	8	....	....	....	4,603	159	4,762	20,562
Fresno	774	225	999	3	....	3	1852	1442	3,294	....	....	...	304	5	309	4,605
Humboldt	1,721	777	2,498	5	1	6	59	69	128	17	8	25	24	13	37	2,694
Klamath	1,077	143	1,220	4	....	4	17	9	26	13	7	20	525	8	533	1,803
Los Angelos	5,712	3,509	9,221	59	28	87	1095	884	1,979	20	15	35	10	1	11	11,333
Mariposa	3,385	918	4,303	69	21	90	3	4	7	....	....	....	1,784	59	1,843	6,243
Marin	2,339	758	3,097	22	1	23	85	45	130	47	33	80	4	....	4	3,334
Mendocino	2,037	868	2,905	3	...	3	693	361	1,054	....	....	....	5	....	5	3,967
Merced	800	314	1,114	16	7	23	3	1	4	....	....	....	......	....	......	1,141
Monterey	2,708	1,597	4,305	15	2	17	248	163	411	....	....	....	6	....	6	4,739
Napa	3,445	2,003	5,448	33	22	55	....	1	1	....	....	....	17	....	17	5,521
Nevada	11,457	2,681	14,138	111	45	156	3	2	5	....	....	....	2,064	83	2,147	16,446
Placer	8,507	2,312	10,819	43	9	52	5	2	7	....	....	....	2,347	45	2,392	13,270
Plumas	3,284	567	3,851	5	...	5	84	24	108	....	....	....	399	....	399	4,363
Sacramento	14,738	6,954	21,692	308	160	468	186	65	251	....	....	....	1,527	204	1,731	24,142
Santa Barbara	1,816	1,362	3,178	....	...	....	220	145	365	....	....	....	......	....	......	3,543
San Bernardino	1,482	1,022	2,504	11	8	19	1689	1339	3,028	....	....	....	......	....	......	5,551
Santa Clara	7,426	4,399	11,825	52	35	87	....	....	......	....	....	....	......	....	......	11,912
Santa Cruz	3,148	1,764	4,912	22	10	32	....	....	......	....	....	....	......	....	......	4,944
San Diego	850	399	1,249	7	1	8	1616	1451	3,067	....	....	....	......	....	......	4,324
San Francisco	33,990	21,636	55,626	786	390	1176	....	....	......	....	....	....	......	....	......	56,802
San Joaquin	6,131	3,178	9,309	80	46	126	....	....	......	....	....	....	......	....	......	9,435
San Luis Obispo	1,098	672	1,770	9	3	12	....	....	......	....	....	....	......	....	......	1,782
San Mateo	2,211	935	3,146	44	24	68	....	....	......	....	....	....	......	....	......	3,214
Shasta	3,295	1,023	4,318	32	10	42	....	....	......	....	....	....	......	....	......	4,360
Sierra	9,793	1,537	11,330	40	17	57	....	....	......	....	....	....	......	....	......	11,387
Siskiyou	6,252	1,306	7,558	47	24	71	....	....	......	....	....	....	......	....	......	7,629
Solano	4,681	2,446	7,127	30	12	42	....	....	......	....	....	....	......	....	......	7,169
Sonoma	7,425	4,357	11,782	58	27	85	....	....	......	....	....	....	......	....	......	11,867
Stanislaus	1,606	594	2,200	24	21	45	....	....	......	....	....	....	......	....	......	2,245
Sutter	2,390	970	3,360	18	12	30	....	....	......	....	....	....	......	....	......	3,390
Tehama	2,997	1,005	4,002	31	11	42	....	....	......	....	....	....	......	....	......	4,044
Trinity	4,469	639	5,108	16	1	17	....	....	......	....	....	....	......	....	......	5,125
Tulare	3,456	1,159	4,615	12	11	23	....	....	......	....	....	....	......	....	......	4,638
Tuolumne	12,575	3,488	16,063	129	37	166	....	....	......	....	....	....	......	....	......	16,229
Yolo	3,196	1,493	4,689	18	9	27	....	....	......	....	....	....	......	....	......	4,716
Yuba	10,255	3,180	13,435	150	83	233	....	....	......	....	....	....	......	....	......	13,668
Total	239,856	98,149	338,005	2827	1259	4086	8269	6286	14,555	124	84	208	22,261	879	23,140	379,994

NOTE.—Included in white population, in the last twenty counties, excepting San Diego, there are 3,007 Indians, 28 half-breeds, and 11,779 Chinese.

TABLE No. 41.—*Population of the United States by Counties, &c.*—Continued.

STATE OF CONNECTICUT.

COUNTIES.	WHITES.			FREE COLORED.			Aggregate population.
	Male.	Female.	Total.	Male.	Female.	Total.	
Fairfield	36,614	39,186	75,800	790	886	1,676	77,476
Hartford	43,766	44,877	88,643	671	648	1,319	89,962
Litchfield	23,001	23,206	46,207	577	534	1,111	47,318
Middlesex	14,771	15,751	30,522	153	184	337	30,859
New Haven	46,881	48,351	95,232	942	1,171	2,113	97,345
New London	29,989	30,398	60,387	634	710	1,344	61,731
Tolland	10,105	10,348	20,453	137	119	256	20,709
Windham	16,731	17,545	34,276	232	239	471	34,747
Total	221,858	229,662	451,520	4,136	4,491	8,627	460,147

NOTE.—16 Indians included in white population.

STATE OF DELAWARE.

COUNTIES.	WHITES.			FREE COLORED.			Total free.	SLAVES.			Agg'te population.
	Male.	Female.	Total.	Male.	Female.	Total.		Male.	Fem.	Total.	
Kent	10,614	9,716	20,330	3,671	3,600	7,271	27,601	89	114	203	27,804
Newcastle	23,035	23,320	46,355	4,068	4,120	8,188	54,543	121	133	254	54,797
Sussex	12,291	11,613	23,904	2,150	2,220	4,370	28,274	650	691	1,341	29,615
Total	45,940	44,649	90,589	9,889	9,940	19,829	110,418	860	938	1,798	112,216

STATE OF FLORIDA.

COUNTIES.	WHITES.			FREE COLORED.			Total free.	SLAVES.			Agg'te population.
	Male.	Female.	Total.	Male.	Fem.	Total.		Male.	Female.	Total.	
Alachua	2,034	1,733	3,767	4	4	8	3,775	2,263	2,194	4,457	8,232
Brevard	136	88	224	1	......	1	225	8	13	21	246
Calhoun	442	453	895	17	10	27	922	254	270	524	1,446
Clay	716	672	1,388	4	3	7	1,395	268	251	519	1,914
Columbia	1,367	1,215	2,582	1	......	1	2,583	1,058	1,005	2,063	4,646
Dade	54	26	80	1	......	1	81	1	1	2	83
Duval	1,561	1,364	2,925	71	91	162	3,087	1,050	937	1,987	5,074
Escambia	2,034	1,620	3,654	77	76	153	3,807	1,076	885	1,961	5,768
Franklin	730	648	1,378	3	3	6	1,384	271	249	520	1,904
Gadsden	2,085	1,896	3,981	2	4	6	3,987	2,809	2,600	5,409	9,396
Hamilton	1,505	1,229	2,734	12	11	23	2,757	697	700	1,397	4,154
Hernando*	500	500	1,000	......	......	......	1,000	100	100	200	1,200
Hillsborough	1,291	1,124	2,415	2	......	2	2,417	264	300	564	2,981
Holmes	619	652	1,271	2	1	3	1,274	49	63	112	1,386
Jackson	2,757	2,506	5,263	26	17	43	5,306	2,442	2,461	4,903	10,209
Jefferson	1,764	1,734	3,498	1	3	4	3,502	3,075	3,299	6,374	9,876

* Estimated; no schedule returned.

TABLE No. 41.—*Population of the United States by Counties, &c.*—Continued.

STATE OF FLORIDA.

COUNTIES.	WHITES.			FREE COLORED.			Total free.	SLAVES.			Agg'te popula-tion.
	Male.	Female.	Total.	Male.	Fem.	Total.		Male.	Female.	Total.	
Lafayette........	761	729	1,490	1	......	1	1,491	294	583	877	2,068
Leon.............	1,687	1,507	3,194	26	34	60	3,254	4,599	4,490	9,089	12,343
Levy	696	635	1,331	.....	......	......	1,331	203	247	450	1,781
Liberty..........	490	445	935	.....	1	1	936	266	255	521	1,457
Madison..........	1,823	1,698	3,521	8	1	9	3,530	2,131	2,118	4,249	7,779
Manatee	323	278	601	......	......	......	601	132	121	253	854
Marion	1,796	1,498	3,294	1	......	1	3,295	2,689	2,625	5,314	8,609
Monroe	1,276	1,026	2,302	73	87	160	2,462	257	194	451	2,913
Nassau	1,108	870	1,978	23	31	54	2,032	840	772	1,612	3,644
New River........	1,622	1,453	3,075	1	......	1	3,076	392	352	744	3,820
Orange	452	371	823	1	......	1	824	88	75	163	987
Putnam	914	720	1,634	12	19	31	1,665	543	504	1,047	2,712
Santa Rosa	2,117	1,931	4,048	36	25	61	4,109	825	546	1,371	5,480
St. John's	975	978	1,953	33	49	82	2,035	448	555	1,003	3,038
Suwanne.........	796	671	1,467	......	1	1	1,468	428	407	835	2,303
Sumter...........	534	466	1,000	......	.....	......	1,000	275	274	549	1,549
Taylor	673	586	1,259	......	......	......	1,259	60	65	125	1,384
Volusicr	467	394	861	......	......	......	861	158	139	297	1,158
Wakalla..........	868	804	1,672	.....	......	......	1,672	573	594	1,167	2,839
Walton	1,314	1,270	2,584	7	5	12	2,596	224	217	441	3,037
Washington	841	829	1,670	8	2	10	1,680	238	236	474	2,154
Total........	41,128	36,619	77,747	454	478	932	78,679	31,348	30,397	61,745	140,424

STATE OF GEORGIA.

COUNTIES.	WHITE.			FREE COLORED.			Total free.	SLAVES.			Agg'te popula-tion.
	Male.	Female.	Total.	Male.	Fem.	Total.		Male.	Female.	Total.	
Appling	1,770	1,672	3,442	2	1	3	3,445	364	381	745	4,190
Baker	824	669	1,493	......	......	......	1,493	1,739	1,753	3,492	4,985
Baldwin	2,143	1,914	4,057	46	46	92	4,149	2,500	2,429	4,929	9,078
Banks............	1,768	1,842	3,610	7	4	11	3,621	552	534	1,086	4,707
Berrien...........	1,567	1,474	3,041	2	.....	2	3,043	195	237	432	3,475
Bibb	4,940	4,520	9,460	18	23	41	9,501	3,241	3,549	6,790	16,291
Brooks	1,639	1,433	3,072	1	1	2	3,074	1,609	1,673	3,282	6,356
Bryan	831	805	1,636	.. ...	......	......	1,636	1,163	1,216	2,379	4,015
Bullock	1,815	1,691	3,506	......	......	......	3,506	1,046	1,116	2,162	5,668
Burke............	2,552	2,461	5,013	47	53	100	5,113	5,950	6,102	12,052	17,165
Butts	1,674	1,699	3,373	7	8	15	3,388	1,512	1,555	3,067	6,455
Calhoun	1,107	1,067	2,174	3	5	8	2,182	1,364	1,367	2,731	4,913
Camden	660	616	1,276	......	1	1	1,277	2,047	2,096	4,143	5,420
Campbell.........	3,178	3,111	6,289	5	3	8	6,297	942	1,062	2,004	8,301
Carroll	5,169	4,947	10,116	7	6	13	10,129	884	978	1,862	11,991
Cass..............	5,786	5,647	11,433	4	5	9	11,442	2,202	2,080	4,282	15,724
Catoosa	2,210	2,158	4,368	3	1	4	4,372	352	358	710	5,082
Chattahoochie	1,544	1,490	3,034	2	3	5	3,039	1,344	1,414	2,758	5,797

TABLE No. 41.—*Population of the United States by Counties, &c.*—Continued.

STATE OF GEORGIA.

COUNTIES.	WHITES.			FREE COLORED.			Total free.	SLAVES.			Agg'te population.
	Male.	Female.	Total.	Male.	Fem.	Total.		Male.	Female.	Total.	
Charlton	634	589	1,223	......	......	......	1,223	376	181	557	1,780
Chattooga	2,551	2,556	5,107	2	2	4	5,111	1,044	1,010	2,054	7,165
Chatham	8,489	7,022	15,511	334	391	725	16,236	7,190	7,617	14,807	31,043
Cherokee	5,040	5,007	10,047	26	19	45	10,092	569	630	1,199	11,291
Clark	2,660	2,879	5,539	10	9	19	5,558	2,722	2,938	5,660	11,218
Clay	1,365	1,261	2,626	9	5	14	2,640	1,096	1,157	2,253	4,893
Clayton	1,642	1,598	3,240	......	......	......	3,240	567	659	1,226	4,466
Clinch	1,394	1,215	2,609	3	2	5	2,614	211	238	449	3,063
Cobb	5,172	5,238	10,410	4	9	13	10,423	1,898	1,921	3,819	14,242
Colquitt	614	581	1,195	8	3	11	1,206	52	58	110	1,316
Columbus	1,785	1,726	3,511	28	28	56	3,567	4,144	4,149	8,293	11,860
Coffee	1,110	1,096	2,206	6	4	10	2,216	319	344	663	2,879
Coweta	3,770	3,663	7,433	7	15	22	7,455	3,471	3,777	7,248	14,703
Crawford	1,771	1,636	3,407	10	6	16	3,423	2,170	2,100	4,270	7,693
Dade	1,419	1,346	2,765	3	1	4	2,769	157	143	300	3,069
Dawson	1,698	1,828	3,526	2	2	4	3,530	164	162	326	3,856
Decatur	3,126	2,859	5,985	5	8	13	5,998	2,946	2,978	5,924	11,922
De Kalb	2,884	2,914	5,798	6	2	8	5,806	982	1,018	2,000	7,806
Dooly	2,457	2,388	4,845	2	......	2	4,847	1,982	2,088	4,070	8,917
Dougherty	1,190	1,017	2,207	8	1	9	2,216	3,135	2,944	6,079	8,295
Early	1,092	1,000	2,092	......	......	......	2,092	2,101	1,956	4,057	6,149
Echolls	613	564	1,177	......	......	......	1,177	161	153	314	1,491
Effingham	1,261	1,311	2,572	11	7	18	2,590	1,121	1,044	2,165	4,755
Elbert	2,409	2,288	4,697	11	14	25	4,722	2,875	2,836	5,711	10,433
Emanuel	1,913	1,835	3,748	20	19	39	3,787	632	662	1,294	5,081
Fannin	2,483	2,512	4,995	......	1	1	4,996	76	67	143	5,139
Fayette	2,560	2,462	5,022	2	4	6	5,028	964	1,055	2,019	7,047
Floyd	4,812	4,457	9,269	7	6	13	9,282	2,923	2,990	5,913	15,195
Forsyth	3,443	3,408	6,851	5	3	8	6,859	430	460	890	7,749
Franklin	3,043	2,995	6,038	19	23	42	6,080	604	709	1,313	7,393
Fulton	5,897	5,544	11,441	12	19	31	11,472	1,397	1,558	2,955	14,427
Gilmer	3,261	3,293	6,554	......	3	3	6,557	86	81	167	6,724
Glasscock	827	827	1,654	13	12	25	1,679	389	369	758	2,437
Glynn	521	527	1,048	2	......	2	1,050	1,346	1,493	2,839	3,889
Gordon	4,074	3,927	8,001	25	14	39	8,040	1,021	1,085	2,106	10,146
Greene	2,153	2,076	4,229	12	13	25	4,254	4,177	4,221	8,398	12,652
Gwinnett	5,107	5,251	10,358	13	18	31	10,389	1,254	1,297	2,551	12,940
Habersham	2,563	2,573	5,136	24	19	43	5,179	345	442	787	5,966
Hall	4,032	4,059	8,091	9	5	14	8,105	596	665	1,261	9,366
Hancock	1,919	1,952	3,871	19	17	36	3,907	4,242	3,895	8,137	12,044
Haralson	1,427	1,383	2,810	......	......	......	2,810	115	114	229	3,039
Hart	2,324	2,279	4,603	3	3	6	4,609	732	796	1,528	6,137
Harris	3,001	2,978	5,979	9	12	21	6,000	3,753	3,983	7,736	13,736
Heard	2,550	2,429	4,979	10	5	15	4,994	1,393	1,418	2,811	7,805
Henry	3,117	3,058	6,175	7	5	12	6,187	2,209	2,306	4,515	10,702
Houston	2,462	2,366	4,828	10	18	28	4,856	5,428	5,327	10,755	15,611
Irwin	764	689	1,453	......	......	......	1,453	124	122	246	1,690
Jackson	3,647	3,602	7,249	13	14	27	7,276	1,595	1,734	3,329	10,605
Jasper	1,966	1,805	3,771	5	13	18	3,789	3,505	3,449	6,954	10,743
Jefferson	2,077	2,056	4,133	20	21	41	4,174	3,115	2,930	6,045	10,219
Johnson	1,045	1,018	2,063	4	3	7	2,070	437	412	849	2,919

TABLE No. 41.—*Population of the United States by Counties, &c.*—Continued.

STATE OF GEORGIA.

COUNTIES.	WHITES.			FREE COLORED.			Total free.	SLAVES.			Agg'te popula-tion.
	Male.	Female.	Total.	Male.	Fem.	Total.		Male.	Female.	Total.	
Jones	1,566	1,518	3,084	15	19	34	3,118	3,053	2,936	5,989	9,107
Laurens	1,901	1,822	3,723	3	3	6	3,729	1,669	1,600	3,269	6,998
Lee	1,147	1,095	2,242	3	4	7	2,249	2,514	2,433	4,947	7,196
Liberty	1,145	1,139	2,284	......	......	......	2,284	2,997	3,086	6,083	8,367
Lincoln	833	842	1,675	10	13	23	1,698	1,868	1,900	3,768	5,466
Lowndes	1,565	1,285	2,850	....	......	......	2,850	1,232	1,167	2,399	5,249
Lumpkin	2,053	2,103	4,156	21	17	38	4,194	210	222	432	4,626
Macon	1,851	1,724	3,575	3	6	9	3,584	2,350	2,515	4,865	8,449
Madison	1,911	2,013	3,924	4	13	17	3,941	967	1,025	1,992	5,933
Marion	1,912	1,942	3,854	4	3	7	3,861	1,780	1,749	3,529	7,390
McIntosh	740	689	1,429	34	20	54	1,483	1,971	2,092	4,063	5,546
Meriwether	3,367	3,211	6,578	1	3	4	6,582	4,392	4,356	8,748	15,330
Miller	599	552	1,151	......	......	......	1,151	291	349	640	1,791
Milton	1,987	1,997	3,984	......	1	1	3,985	302	315	617	4,602
Mitchell	1,425	1,291	2,716	3	......	3	2,719	750	839	1,589	4,308
Monroe	2,940	2,813	5,753	14	9	23	5,776	5,078	5,099	10,177	15,953
Montgomery	1,041	973	2,014	3	3	6	2,020	479	498	977	2,997
Morgan	1,536	1,448	2,984	7	......	7	2,991	3,463	3,543	7,006	9,997
Murray	2,791	2,848	5,639	1	1	2	5,641	693	749	1,442	7,083
Muscogee	4,508	4,458	8,966	72	101	173	9,139	3,781	3,664	7,445	16,584
Newton	3,916	3,906	7,822	22	18	40	7,862	3,202	3,256	6,458	14,320
Oglethorpe	2,025	1,989	4,014	13	8	21	4,035	3,685	3,829	7,514	11,549
Paulding	3,216	3,244	6,460	1	5	6	6,466	274	298	572	7,038
Pickens	2,353	2,352	4,705	......	......	......	4,705	114	132	246	4,951
Pierce	909	831	1,740	......	......	......	1,740	109	124	233	1,973
Pike	2,719	2,613	5,332	10	14	24	5,356	2,373	2,349	4,722	10,078
Polk	1,962	1,891	3,853	2	......	2	3,855	1,183	1,257	2,440	6,295
Pulaski	2,396	2,211	4,607	13	18	31	4,638	2,105	2,001	4,106	8,744
Putnam	1,518	1,438	2,956	15	16	31	2,987	3,599	3,539	7,138	10,125
Quitman	975	895	1,870	4	......	4	1,874	791	834	1,625	3,499
Rabun	1,556	1,505	3,061	1	3	4	3,065	96	110	206	3,271
Randolph	2,650	2,453	5,103	1	......	1	5,104	2,161	2,306	4,467	9,571
Richmond	6,229	6,176	12,405	200	290	490	12,895	3,983	4,406	8,389	21,284
Schley	1,184	1,090	2,274	7	4	11	2,285	1,123	1,225	2,348	4,633
Scriven	1,939	1,803	3,742	1	1	2	3,744	2,277	2,253	4,530	8,274
Spalding	2,462	2,364	4,826	21	33	54	4,880	1,856	1,963	3,819	8,699
Stewart	2,860	2,674	5,534	1	3	4	5,538	3,912	3,972	7,884	13,422
Sumter	2,345	2,191	4,536	1	1	2	4,538	2,460	2,430	4,890	9,428
Talbot	2,535	2,459	4,994	7	12	19	5,013	4,335	4,268	8,603	13,616
Taliaferro	828	865	1,693	19	22	41	1,734	1,391	1,458	2,849	4,583
Tatnall	1,664	1,527	3,191	2	2	4	3,195	574	583	1,157	4,352
Taylor	1,795	1,806	3,601	......	......	......	3,601	1,238	1,159	2,397	5,998
Telfair	966	911	1,877	......	......	......	1,877	389	447	836	2,713
Terrell	1,750	1,593	3,343	1	......	1	3,344	1,442	1,446	2,888	6,232
Thomas	2,338	2,150	4,488	18	16	34	4,522	3,110	3,134	6,244	10,766
Towns	1,201	1,145	2,346	3	2	5	2,351	49	59	108	2,459
Troup	3,267	2,956	6,223	16	21	37	6,260	5,001	5,001	10,002	16,262
Twiggs	1,480	1,450	2,930	34	38	72	3,002	2,670	2,648	5,318	8,320
Union	2,183	2,112	4,295	2	......	2	4,297	52	64	116	4,413
Upson	2,481	2,534	5,015	5	2	7	5,022	2,433	2,455	4,888	9,910
Walker	4,344	4,173	8,517	16	14	30	8,547	729	806	1,535	10,082

TABLE No. 41.—*Population of the United States by Counties, &c.*—Continued.

STATE OF GEORGIA.

COUNTIES.	WHITES.			FREE COLORED.			Total free.	SLAVES.			Agg'te popula-tion.
	Male.	Female.	Total.	Male.	Fem.	Total.		Male.	Female.	Total.	
Walton	3,205	3,242	6,447	1	5	6	6,453	2,254	2,367	4,621	11,074
Warren	2,137	2,210	4,347	52	42	94	4,441	2,676	2,703	5,379	9,820
Ware	944	874	1,818	5	......	5	1,823	226	151	377	2,200
Washington	3,168	2,975	6,143	13	10	23	6,166	3,309	3,223	6,532	12,698
Wayne	819	798	1,617	14	16	30	1,647	326	295	621	2,268
Webster	1,420	1,321	2,741	2	......	2	2,743	1,138	1,149	2,287	5,030
White	1,523	1,518	3,041	2	9	11	3,052	129	134	263	3,315
Whitefield	4,202	4,112	8,314	1	......	1	8,315	868	864	1,732	10,047
Wilcox	884	808	1,692	2	......	2	1,694	205	216	421	2,115
Wilkes	1,750	1,684	3,434	18	15	33	3,467	3,901	4,052	7,953	11,420
Wilkinson	2,780	2,692	5,472	7	10	17	5,489	1,950	1,937	3,887	9,376
Worth	1,076	1,042	2,118	6	7	13	2,131	308	324	632	2,763
	301,083	290,505	591,588	1,669	1,831	3,500	595,088	229,193	233,005	462,198	1,057,286

NOTE.—38 Indians included in white population.

STATE OF ILLINOIS.

COUNTIES.	WHITE.			FREE COLORED.			Aggregate popula-tion.
	Male.	Female.	Total.	Male.	Female.	Total.	
Adams	21,204	19,940	41,144	74	105	179	41,323
Alexander	2,593	2,059	4,652	30	25	55	4,707
Bond	5,255	4,512	9,767	23	25	48	9,815
Boon	6,036	5,634	11,670	5	3	8	11,678
Brown	5,258	4,661	9,919	6	13	19	9,938
Bureau	14,197	12,218	26,415	5	6	11	26,426
Calhoun	2,883	2,260	5,143	1	....	1	5,144
Carroll	6,266	5,452	11,718	8	7	15	11,733
Cass	6,105	5,208	11,313	9	3	12	11,325
Champaign	7,872	6,709	14,581	26	22	48	14,629
Christian	5,649	4,826	10,475	10	7	17	10,492
Clark	7,716	7,232	14,948	22	17	39	14,987
Clay	4,857	4,452	9,309	16	11	27	9,336
Clinton	5,999	4,730	10,729	114	98	212	10,941
Coles	7,468	6,706	14,174	14	15	29	14,203
Cook	74,162	69,785	143,947	521	486	1,007	144,954
Crawford	5,943	5,586	11,529	10	12	22	11,551
Cumberland	4,245	4,064	8,309	1	1	2	8,311
De Kalb	10,107	8,972	19,079	4	3	7	19,086
De Witt	5,746	5,068	10,814	2	4	6	10,820
Douglas	3,977	3,132	7,109	9	22	31	7,140
Du Page	7,719	6,977	14,696	4	1	5	14,701
Edgar	8,746	8,142	16,888	19	18	37	16,925
Edwards	2,812	2,567	5,379	38	37	75	5,454
Effingham	4,190	3,615	7,805	6	5	11	7,816
Fayette	5,842	5,304	11,146	19	24	43	11,189
Ford	1,077	902	1,979	....	....	....	1,979

TABLE NO. 41.—*Population of the United States by Counties, &c.*—Continued.

STATE OF ILLINOIS.

COUNTIES.	WHITE.			FREE COLORED.			Aggregate population.
	Male.	Female.	Total.	Male.	Female.	Total.	
Franklin	4,807	4,560	9,367	14	12	26	9,393
Fulton	17,250	16,039	33,289	26	23	49	33,338
Gallatin	3,897	3,732	7,629	200	226	426	8,055
Green	8,500	7,567	16,067	14	12	26	16,093
Grundy	5,608	4,764	10,372	5	2	7	10,379
Hamilton	5,049	4,800	9,849	33	33	66	9,915
Hancock	15,272	13,769	29,041	10	10	20	29,061
Hardin	1,897	1,807	3,704	27	28	55	3,759
Henderson	5,062	4,437	9,499	2	....	2	9,501
Henry	10,966	9,692	20,658	2	....	2	20,660
Iroquois	6,549	5,736	12,285	24	16	40	12,325
Jackson	5,061	4,499	9,560	18	11	29	9,589
Jasper	4,346	4,004	8,350	9	5	14	8,364
Jefferson	6,661	6,270	12,931	18	16	34	12,965
Jersey	6,401	5,541	11,942	52	57	109	12,051
Jo Daviess	14,091	13,056	27,147	95	83	178	27,325
Johnson	4,849	4,457	9,306	16	20	36	9,342
Kane	15,638	14,386	30,024	20	18	38	30,062
Kankakee	8,120	7,273	15,393	14	5	19	15,412
Kendall	6,922	6,151	13,073	....	1	1	13,074
Knox	14,904	13,608	28,512	70	81	151	28,663
Lake	9,447	8,801	18,248	4	5	9	18,257
La Salle	25,585	22,687	48,272	25	35	60	48,332
Lawrence	4,752	4,224	8,976	132	106	238	9,214
Lee	9,259	8,384	17,643	4	4	8	17,651
Livingston	6,350	5,282	11,632	2	3	5	11,637
Logan	7,864	6,383	14,247	10	15	25	14,272
McDonough	10,610	9,451	20,061	4	4	8	20,069
McHenry	11,460	10,625	22,085	3	1	4	22,089
McLean	15,096	13,484	28,580	87	105	192	28,772
Macon	7,288	6,367	13,655	39	44	83	13,738
Macoupin	13,032	11,472	24,504	46	52	98	24,602
Madison	16,521	14,168	30,689	262	300	562	31,251
Marion	6,585	6,145	12,730	3	6	9	12,739
Marshall	7,206	6,231	13,437	....	....	....	13,437
Mason	6,026	4,903	10,929	2	....	2	10,931
Massac	3,219	2,882	6,101	63	49	112	6,213
Menard	5,117	4,460	9,577	4	3	7	9,584
Mercer	8,107	6,930	15,037	2	3	5	15,042
Monroe	7,046	5,769	12,815	8	9	17	12,832
Montgomery	7,439	6,442	13,881	47	51	98	13,979
Morgan	11,520	10,417	21,937	82	93	175	22,112
Moultrie	3,404	2,980	6,384	1	....	1	6,385
Ogle	12,229	10,634	22,863	10	15	25	22,888
Peoria	19,038	17,437	36,475	58	68	126	36,601
Perry	5,038	4,470	9,508	20	24	44	9,552
Piatt	3,449	2,675	6,124	3	....	3	6,127
Pike	14,103	13,079	27,182	45	22	67	27,249
Pope	3,397	3,149	6,546	85	111	196	6,742
Pulaski	2,148	1,756	3,904	19	20	39	3,943
Putnam	2,973	2,606	5,579	5	3	8	5,587

TABLE No. 41.—*Population of the United States by Counties, &c.*—Continued.

STATE OF ILLINOIS.

COUNTIES.	WHITE.			FREE COLORED.			Aggregate population.
	Male.	Female.	Total.	Male.	Female.	Total.	
Randolph	8,941	7,825	16,766	220	219	439	17,205
Richland	5,073	4,636	9,709	....	2	2	9,711
Rock Island	10,908	10,073	20,981	13	11	24	21,005
St. Clair	20,355	16,814	37,169	270	255	525	37,694
Saline	4,673	4,488	9,161	89	81	170	9,331
Sangamon	16,956	15,007	31,963	135	176	311	32,274
Schuyler	7,669	7,001	14,670	5	9	14	14,684
Scott	4,769	4,278	9,047	15	7	22	9,069
Shelby	7,711	6,879	14,590	12	11	23	14,613
Stark	4,819	4,184	9,003	1	....	1	9,004
Stephenson	13,115	11,997	25,112	....	....	....	25,112
Tazewell	11,450	9,977	21,427	22	21	43	21,470
Union	5,794	5,351	11,145	19	17	36	11,181
Vermillion	10,489	9,290	19,779	12	9	21	19,800
Wabash	3,652	3,581	7,233	40	40	80	7,313
Warren	9,753	8,540	18,293	23	20	43	18,336
Washington	7,354	6,371	13,725	4	2	6	13,731
Wayne	6,234	5,988	12,222	....	1	1	12,223
White	6,315	5,959	12,274	72	57	129	12,403
Whitesides	10,053	8,676	18,729	4	4	8	18,737
Will	15,794	13,470	29,264	38	19	57	29,321
Williamson	6,216	5,871	12,087	55	63	118	12,205
Winnebago	12,554	11,903	24,457	19	15	34	24,491
Woodford	7,223	6,058	13,281	1	....	1	13,282
Total	898,952	805,371	1,704,323	3,809	3,819	7,628	1,711,951

NOTE.—32 Indians included in white population.

STATE OF INDIANA.

COUNTIES.	WHITES.			FREE COLORED.			Aggregate population.
	Male.	Female.	Total.	Male.	Female.	Total.	
Adams	4,837	4,409	9,246	4	2	6	9,252
Allen	15,349	13,916	29,265	33	30	63	29,328
Bartholomew	9,175	8,683	17,858	4	3	7	17,865
Benton	1,575	1,234	2,809	....	....	....	2,809
Blackford	2,153	1,969	4,122	....	....	....	4,122
Boone	8,641	8,022	16,663	43	47	90	16,753
Brown	3,376	3,131	6,507	....	....	....	6,507
Carroll	7,040	6,436	13,476	8	5	13	13,489
Cass	8,814	7,964	16,778	30	35	65	16,843
Clark	10,398	9,584	19,982	274	246	520	20,502
Clay	6,337	5,802	12,139	11	11	22	12,161
Clinton	7,465	7,020	14,485	9	11	20	14,505
Crawford	4,355	3,871	8,226	....	....	....	8,226
Daviess	6,777	6,472	13,249	38	36	74	13,323

TABLE NO. 41.—*Population of the United States by Counties, &c.*—Continued.

STATE OF INDIANA.

COUNTIES.	WHITES.			FREE COLORED.			Aggregate population.
	Male.	Female.	Total.	Male.	Female.	Total.	
Dearborn	12,639	11,693	24,332	36	38	74	24,406
Decatur	8,813	8,457	17,270	11	13	24	17,294
De Kalb	7,156	6,709	13,865	7	8	15	13,880
Delaware	8,173	7,564	15,737	8	8	16	15,753
Dubois	5,333	5,049	10,382	4	8	12	10,394
Elkhart	11,020	9,946	20,966	8	12	20	20,986
Fayette	5,152	4,986	10,138	40	47	87	10,225
Floyd	9,811	9,615	19,426	336	421	757	20,183
Fountain	8,074	7,419	15,493	35	38	73	15,566
Franklin	9,965	9,481	19,446	53	50	103	19,549
Fulton	4,987	4,429	9,416	3	3	6	9,422
Gibson	7,435	6,823	14,258	144	130	274	14,532
Grant	7,974	7,439	15,413	190	194	384	15,797
Green	8,162	7,800	15,962	42	37	79	16,041
Hamilton	8,611	8,349	16,960	181	169	350	17,310
Hancock	6,489	6,220	12,709	49	44	93	12,802
Harrison	9,471	8,936	18,407	64	50	114	18,521
Hendricks	8,671	8,237	16,908	26	19	45	16,953
Henry	10,092	9,744	19,836	149	134	283	20,119
Howard	6,405	5,954	12,359	80	85	165	12,524
Huntington	7,762	7,103	14,865	1	1	2	14,867
Jackson	8,399	7,708	16,107	91	88	179	16,286
Jasper	2,228	2,058	4,286	3	2	5	4,291
Jay	5,917	5,461	11,378	11	10	21	11,399
Jefferson	12,386	12,138	24,524	243	269	512	25,036
Jennings	7,605	6,993	14,598	82	69	151	14,749
Johnson	7,690	7,145	14,835	10	9	19	14,854
Knox	8,334	7,273	15,607	224	225	449	16,056
Kosciusko	8,941	8,475	17,416	2	....	2	17,418
La Grange	5,886	5,464	11,350	7	9	16	11,366
Lake	4,911	4,229	9,140	3	2	5	9,145
Laporte	11,944	10,840	22,784	73	62	135	22,919
Lawrence	7,074	6,500	13,574	64	54	118	13,692
Madison	8,503	7,955	16,458	29	31	60	16,518
Marion	20,048	18,982	39,030	412	413	825	39,855
Marshall	6,701	6,018	12,719	2	1	3	12,722
Martin	4,586	4,337	8,923	32	20	52	8,975
Miami	8,726	8,078	16,804	26	21	47	16,851
Monroe	6,537	6,285	12,822	10	15	25	12,847
Montgomery	10,732	10,006	20,738	72	78	150	20,888
Morgan	8,143	7,860	16,003	57	50	107	16,110
Newton	1,257	1,103	2,360	....	....	....	2,360
Noble	7,683	7,224	14,907	3	5	8	14,915
Ohio	2,778	2,661	5,439	13	10	23	5,462
Orange	6,006	5,810	11,816	142	118	260	12,076
Owen	7,273	7,018	14,291	41	44	85	14,376
Parke	7,974	7,368	15,342	109	87	196	15,538
Perry	6,106	5,738	11,844	1	2	3	11,847
Pike	5,236	4,828	10,064	11	3	14	10,078
Porter	5,431	4,865	10,296	9	8	17	10,313
Posey	8,580	7,451	16,031	61	75	136	16,167

TABLE No. 41.—*Population of the United States by Counties, &c.*—Continued.

STATE OF INDIANA.

COUNTIES.	WHITES.			FREE COLORED.			Aggregate population.
	Male.	Female.	Total.	Male.	Female.	Total.	
Pulaski	2,998	2,713	5,711	....	....	....	5,711
Putnam	10,669	9,993	20,662	10	9	19	20,681
Randolph	9,399	8,773	18,172	431	394	825	18,997
Ripley	9,808	9,159	18,967	38	49	87	19,054
Rush	8,111	7,663	15,774	209	210	419	16,193
St. Joseph	9,555	8,812	18,367	47	41	88	18,455
Scott	3,753	3,548	7,301	1	1	2	7,303
Shelby	10,047	9,501	19,548	10	11	21	19,569
Spencer	7,673	6,881	14,554	1	1	2	14,556
Stark	1,214	980	2,194	....	1	1	2,195
Steuben	5,405	4,967	10,372	1	1	2	10,374
Sullivan	7,730	7,214	14,944	56	64	120	15,064
Switzerland	6,450	6,206	12,656	22	20	42	12,698
Tippecanoe	13,542	12,041	25,583	77	66	143	25,726
Tipton	4,118	4,017	8,135	21	14	35	8,170
Union	3,642	3,427	7,069	20	20	40	7,109
Vanderberg	10,797	9,628	20,425	64	63	127	20,552
Vermillion	4,922	4,470	9,392	18	12	30	9,422
Vigo	11,099	10,712	21,811	363	343	706	22,517
Wabash	9,034	8,480	17,514	20	13	33	17,547
Warren	5,335	4,705	10,040	12	5	17	10,057
Warrick	6,827	6,415	13,242	5	14	19	13,261
Washington	9,109	8,613	17,722	79	108	187	17,909
Wayne	14,646	14,042	28,688	461	409	870	29,558
Wells	5,616	5,227	10,843	1	....	1	10,844
White	4,354	3,883	8,237	13	8	21	8,258
Whitely	5,514	5,124	10,638	47	45	92	10,730
Total	693,469	645,531	1,339,000	5,791	5,637	11,428	1,350,428

NOTE.—290 Indians included in white population.

STATE OF IOWA.

COUNTIES.	WHITES.			FREE COLORED.			Aggregate population.
	Male.	Female.	Total.	Male.	Female.	Total.	
Adair	536	448	984	....	....	....	984
Adams	822	711	1,533	....	....	....	1,533
Allamakee	6,408	5,823	12,231	3	3	6	12,237
Appanoose	6,236	5,682	11,918	6	7	13	11,931
Audubon	239	215	454	....	....	....	454
Benton	4,481	4,014	8,495	1	....	1	8,496
Black Hawk	4,282	3,944	8,226	9	9	18	8,244
Boone	2,233	1,999	4,232	....	....	....	4,232
Bremer	2,620	2,290	4,910	3	2	5	4,915
Buchanan	4,164	3,740	7,904	2	....	2	7,906
Buena Vista	36	21	57	....	....	....	57

TABLE No. 41.—*Population of the United States by Counties, &c.*—Continued.

STATE OF IOWA.

COUNTIES.	WHITES.			FREE COLORED.			Aggregate population.
	Male.	Female.	Total.	Male.	Female.	Total.	
Buncombe							
Butler	1,977	1,746	3,723	1		1	3,724
Calhoun	84	63	147				147
Carroll	142	139	281				281
Cass	913	699	1,612				1,612
Cedar	6,892	6,045	12,937	10	2	12	12,949
Cerro Gordo	505	435	940				940
Cherokee	35	23	58				58
Chickasaw	2,260	2,071	4,331	3	2	5	4,336
Clarke	2,818	2,609	5,427				5,427
Clayton	11,072	9,631	20,703	12	13	25	20,728
Clay	31	21	52				52
Clinton	10,037	8,888	18,925	7	6	13	18,938
Crawford	201	182	383				383
Dallas	2,776	2,468	5,244				5,244
Davis	7,114	6,648	13,762	2		2	13,764
Decatur	4,506	4,164	8,670	3	4	7	8,677
Delaware	5,787	5,236	11,023	1		1	11,024
Des Moines	10,223	9,360	19,583	16	12	28	19,611
Dickinson	113	67	180				180
Dubuque	16,170	14,913	31,083	36	45	81	31,164
Emmett	60	45	105				105
Fayette	6,360	5,659	12,019	29	25	54	12,073
Franklin	716	593	1,309				1,309
Fremont	2,779	2,290	5,069	1	4	5	5,074
Floyd	1,987	1,757	3,744				3,744
Greene	736	638	1,374				1,374
Grundy	428	365	793				793
Guthrie	1,626	1,432	3,058				3,058
Hamilton	906	793	1,699				1,699
Hancock	95	84	179				179
Hardin	2,830	2,610	5,440				5,440
Harrison	1,974	1,646	3,620		1	1	3,621
Henry	9,590	9,087	18,677	11	13	24	18,701
Howard	1,689	1,478	3,167	1		1	3,168
Humbolt	188	144	332				332
Ida	25	18	43				43
Iowa	4,304	3,725	8,029				8,029
Jackson	9,626	8,856	18,482	7	4	11	18,493
Jasper	5,270	4,612	9,882		1	1	9,883
Jefferson	7,783	7,247	15,030	3	5	8	15,038
Johnson	9,054	8,481	17,535	17	21	38	17,573
Jones	7,064	6,235	13,299	2	5	7	13,306
Keokuk	6,948	6,323	13,271				13,271
Kossuth	232	184	416				416
Lee	14,987	14,000	28,987	138	107	245	29,232
Lynn	9,954	8,982	18,936	6	5	11	18,947
Louisa	5,398	4,878	10,276	56	38	94	10,370
Lucas	3,044	2,720	5,764	1	1	2	5,766
Madison	3,771	3,568	7,339				7,339
Mahaska	7,669	7,131	14,800	9	7	16	14,816

TABLE No. 41.—*Population of the United States by Counties, &c.*—Continued.

STATE OF IOWA.

COUNTIES.	WHITES.			FREE COLORED.			Aggregate population.
	Male.	Female.	Total.	Male.	Female.	Total.	
Manona	453	378	831	1	....	1	832
Marion	8,701	8,079	16,780	20	13	33	16,813
Marshall	3,169	2,846	6,015	....	....	....	6,015
Mills	2,441	2,024	4,465	10	6	16	4,481
Mitchell	1,858	1,551	3,409	....	....	....	3,409
Monroe	4,422	4,188	8,610	1	1	2	8,612
Montgomery	660	596	1,256	....	....	....	1,256
Muscatine	8,558	7,774	16,332	47	65	112	16,444
Osceola	....	....	....	....	....	....	....
O'Brien	4	4	8	....	....	....	8
Page	2,384	2,034	4,418	....	1	1	4,419
Pocahontas	51	52	103	....	....	....	103
Palo Alto	75	57	132	....	....	....	132
Plymouth	82	66	148	....	....	....	148
Polk	6,058	5,554	11,612	6	7	13	11,625
Pottawatomie	2,645	2,314	4,959	6	3	9	4,968
Poweshiek	2,990	2,671	5,661	5	2	7	5,668
Ringgold	1,538	1,384	2,922	1	....	1	2,923
Sac	136	110	246	....	....	....	246
Scott	13,579	12,341	25,920	21	18	39	25,959
Shelby	442	375	817	1	....	1	818
Sioux	9	1	10	....	....	....	10
Story	2,096	1,955	4,051	....	....	....	4,051
Tama	2,796	2,489	5,285	....	....	....	5,285
Taylor	1,903	1,687	3,590	....	....	....	3,590
Union	1,072	940	2,012	....	....	....	2,012
Van Buren	9,068	8,009	17,077	1	3	4	17,081
Wappello	7,546	6,925	14,471	26	21	47	14,518
Warren	5,271	4,996	10,267	8	6	14	10,281
Washington	7,491	6,731	14,222	7	6	13	14,235
Wayne	3,395	3,003	6,398	4	7	11	6,409
Webster	1,316	1,184	2,500	3	1	4	2,504
Winnebago	93	75	168	....	....	....	168
Winneshiek	7,470	6,472	13,942	....	....	....	13,942
Woodbury	604	512	1,116	2	1	3	1,119
Worth	395	361	756	....	....	....	756
Wright	350	303	653	....	....	....	653
Total	353,927	319,917	673,844	566	503	1,069	674,913

NOTE.—65 Indians included in white population.

TABLE No. 41.—*Population of the United States by Counties, &c.*—Continued.

STATE OF KANSAS.

COUNTIES.	WHITES.			FREE COLORED.			SLAVES.			Aggregate population.
	Male.	Female.	Total.	Male.	Female	Total.	Male.	Fem.	Total.	
Allen	1,720	1,359	3,079	....	3	3	....	....	....	3,082
Anderson	1,331	1,067	2,398	....	....	....	....	2	2	2,400
Atchison	4,283	3,410	7,693	19	17	36	....	....	....	7,729
Bourbon	3,305	2,731	6,036	32	33	65	....	....	....	6,101
Breckenridge	1,805	1,392	3,197	....	....	....	....	....	....	3,197
Brown	1,482	1,125	2,607	....	....	....	....	....	....	2,607
Butler	239	193	432	3	2	5	....	....	....	437
Chase	470	338	808	....	....	....	....	....	....	808
Clay	97	66	163	....	....	....	....	....	....	163
Coffee	1,607	1,235	2,842	....	....	....	....	....	....	2,842
Davis	680	482	1,162	....	1	1	....	....	....	1,163
Dickinson	236	142	378	....	....	....	....	....	....	378
Doniphan	4,408	3,634	8,042	19	22	41	....	....	....	8,083
Dorn	46	42	88	....	....	....	....	....	....	88
Douglas	4,844	3,789	8,633	4	....	4	....	....	....	8,637
Franklin	1,673	1,357	3,030	....	....	....	....	....	....	3,030
Godfrey	14	5	19	....	....	....	....	....	....	19
Greenwood	428	331	759	....	....	....	....	....	....	759
Hunter	84	66	150	4	4	8	....	....	....	158
Jackson	1,030	906	1,936	....	....	....	....	....	....	1,936
Jefferson	2,487	1,952	4,439	9	11	20	....	....	....	4,459
Johnson	2,397	1,967	4,364	....	....	....	....	....	....	4,364
Leavenworth	6,696	5,615	12,311	128	167	295	....	....	....	12,606
Linn	3,385	2,950	6,335	1	....	1	....	....	....	6,336
Lykins	2,695	2,285	4,980	....	....	....	....	....	....	4,980
Madison	356	280	636	....	....	....	....	....	....	636
Marion	45	29	74	....	....	....	....	....	....	74
Marshall	1,267	1,013	2,280	....	....	....	....	....	....	2,280
McGhee	785	650	1,435	30	36	66	....	....	....	1,501
Morris	438	332	770	....	....	....	....	....	....	770
Nemeha	1,321	1,115	2,436	....	....	....	....	....	....	2,436
Osage	613	500	1,113	....	....	....	....	....	....	1,113
Otoe	127	87	214	9	15	24	....	....	....	238
Pottawatomie	830	699	1,529	....	....	....	....	....	....	1,529
Riley	720	504	1,224	....	....	....	....	....	....	1,224
Shawnee	1,911	1,594	3,505	4	4	8	....	....	....	3,513
Wabaunsee	590	433	1,023	....	....	....	....	....	....	1,023
Washington	229	154	383	....	....	....	....	....	....	383
Wilson	16	11	27	....	....	....	....	....	....	27
Woodson	834	654	1,488	....	....	....	....	....	....	1,488
Wyandott	1,368	1,193	2,561	24	24	48	....	....	....	2,609
Total	58,892	47,687	106,579	286	339	625	....	2	2	107,206

NOTE.—189 Indians included in white population.

TABLE No. 41.—*Population of the United States by Counties, &c.*—Continued.

STATE OF KENTUCKY.

COUNTIES.	WHITES.			FREE COLORED.			Total free.	SLAVES.			Agg'te popula-tion.
	Male.	Female.	Total.	Male.	Fem.	Total.		Male.	Female.	Total.	
Adair	3,968	3,879	7,847	29	31	60	7,907	751	851	1,602	9,509
Allen	3,811	3,814	7,625	20	20	40	7,665	743	779	1,522	9,187
Anderson	3,101	2,932	6,033	6	8	14	6,047	688	669	1,357	7,404
Ballard	3,652	3,291	6,943	18	13	31	6,974	817	901	1,718	8,692
Barren	6,406	6,133	12,539	19	29	48	12,587	2,020	2,058	4,078	16,665
Bath	4,874	4,598	9,472	69	72	141	9,613	1,241	1,259	2,500	12,113
Boone	4,961	4,442	9,403	27	21	48	9,451	810	935	1,745	11,196
Bourbon	4,225	3,568	7,793	129	171	300	8,093	3,447	3,320	6,767	14,860
Boyd	3,003	2,868	5,871	10	7	17	5,888	66	90	156	6,044
Boyle	2,921	2,669	5,590	215	220	435	6,025	1,674	1,605	3,279	9,304
Bracken	5,256	4,932	10,188	44	39	83	10,271	343	407	750	11,021
Breathitt	2,420	2,345	4,765	12	13	25	4,790	91	99	190	4,980
Breckenridge	5,565	5,314	10,879	9	8	17	10,896	1,130	1,210	2,340	13,236
Bullitt	3,012	2,803	5,815	6	10	16	5,831	708	750	1,458	7,289
Butler	3,673	3,459	7,132	15	10	25	7,157	371	399	770	7,927
Caldwell	3,575	3,298	6,873	22	17	39	6,912	1,213	1,193	2,406	9,318
Calloway	4,359	4,050	8,409	8	6	14	8,423	702	790	1,492	9,915
Campbell	10,535	10,170	20,705	45	43	88	20,793	41	75	116	20,909
Carroll	2,839	2,652	5,491	25	17	42	5,533	489	556	1,045	6,578
Carter	4,326	3,844	8,170	19	18	37	8,207	152	157	309	8,516
Casey	2,870	2,873	5,743	27	30	57	5,800	325	341	666	6,466
Christian	6,189	5,430	11,619	29	28	57	11,676	5,119	4,832	9,951	21,627
Clark	3,421	3,177	6,598	64	60	124	6,722	2,449	2,313	4,762	11,484
Clay	3,038	3,003	6,041	117	145	262	6,303	169	180	349	6,652
Clinton	2,762	2,741	5,503	8	12	20	5,523	118	140	258	5,781
Crittenden	4,092	3,746	7,838	11	8	19	7,857	453	486	939	8,796
Cumberland	2,972	2,902	5,874	29	24	53	5,927	714	699	1,413	7,340
Daviess	6,408	5,550	11,958	40	36	76	12,034	1,784	1,731	3,515	15,549
Edmondson	2,215	2,146	4,361	7	4	11	4,372	131	142	273	4,645
Estill	3,265	3,098	6,363	8	8	16	6,379	243	264	507	6,886
Fayette	6,097	5,802	11,899	289	396	685	12,584	5,194	4,821	10,015	22,599
Fleming	5,342	5,017	10,359	45	67	112	10,471	960	1,058	2,018	12,489
Floyd	3,175	2,993	6,168	39	34	73	6,241	76	71	147	6,388
Franklin	4,749	4,111	8,860	209	241	450	9,310	1,703	1,681	3,384	12,694
Fulton	2,189	2,031	4,220	9	10	19	4,239	527	551	1,078	5,317
Gallatin	2,226	2,108	4,334	9	5	14	4,348	342	366	708	5,056
Garrard	3,514	3,343	6,857	51	45	96	6,953	1,858	1,720	3,578	10,531
Grant	3,929	3,701	7,630	13	17	30	7,660	319	377	696	8,356
Graves	7,010	6,376	13,386	1	1	2	13,388	1,434	1,411	2,845	16,233
Grayson	3,782	3,846	7,628	1	2	3	7,631	187	164	351	7,982
Green	3,160	3,163	6,323	47	64	111	6,434	1,208	1,164	2,372	8,806
Greenup	4,337	4,013	8,350	26	21	47	8,397	176	187	363	8,760
Hancock	2,802	2,580	5,382	7	6	13	5,395	409	409	818	6,213
Hardin	6,557	6,069	12,626	16	17	33	12,659	1,212	1,318	2,530	15,189
Harlan	2,692	2,660	5,352	8	7	15	5,367	65	62	127	5,494
Harrison	5,398	4,943	10,341	89	60	149	10,490	1,663	1,626	3,289	13,779
Hart	4,584	4,294	8,878	40	35	75	8,953	694	701	1,395	10,348
Henderson	4,523	3,895	8,418	39	38	77	8,495	3,046	2,721	5,767	14,262
Henry	4,526	4,076	8,602	23	13	36	8,638	1,657	1,654	3,311	11,949
Hickman	3,068	2,671	5,739	14	6	20	5,759	581	668	1,249	7,008
Hopkins	5,037	4,799	9,836	12	18	30	9,866	968	1,041	2,009	11,875
Jackson	1,568	1,491	3,059	15	6	21	3,080	4	3	7	3,087
Jefferson	39,751	37,342	77,093	904	1,103	2,007	79,100	4,703	5,601	10,304	89,404
Jessamine	2,974	2,697	5,671	49	47	96	5,767	1,933	1,765	3,698	9,465
Johnson	2,695	2,565	5,260	10	9	19	5,279	13	14	27	5,306
Kenton	12,520	12,295	24,815	44	41	85	24,900	230	337	567	25,467
Knox	3,545	3,489	7,034	90	94	184	7,218	251	238	489	7,707
LaRue	3,064	2,923	5,987	3	1	4	5,991	468	432	900	6,891

TABLE No. 41.—*Population of the United States by Counties, &c.*—Continued.

STATE OF KENTUCKY.

COUNTIES.	WHITE.			FREE COLORED.			Total free.	SLAVES.			Agg'te population.
	Male.	Female.	Total.	Male.	Fem.	Total.		Male.	Female.	Total.	
Laurel	2,640	2,661	5,301	1	......	1	5,302	90	96	186	5,488
Lawrence	3,872	3,571	7,443	1	11	12	7,455	73	73	146	7,601
Letcher	1,934	1,853	3,787	5	4	9	3,796	55	53	108	3,904
Lewis	4,156	3,958	8,114	8	9	17	8,131	88	142	230	8,361
Lincoln	3,609	3,450	7,059	73	85	158	7,217	1,788	1,642	3,430	10,647
Livingston	3,090	2,865	5,955	14	22	36	5,991	625	597	1,222	7,213
Logan	6,321	5,974	12,295	177	193	370	12,665	3,217	3,139	6,356	19,021
Lyon	2,197	1,970	4,167	25	21	46	4,213	635	459	1,094	5,307
McCracken	4,561	3,993	8,554	35	33	68	8,622	831	907	1,738	10,360
McLean	2,720	2,507	5,227	14	15	29	5,256	434	454	888	6,144
Madison	5,812	5,213	11,025	70	78	148	11,173	3,005	3,029	6,034	17,207
Magoffin	1,718	1,620	3,338	41	35	76	3,414	43	28	71	3,485
Marion	4,578	4,426	9,004	51	59	110	9,114	1,705	1,774	3,479	12,593
Marshall	3,451	3,145	6,596	17	18	35	6,631	170	181	351	6,982
Mason	7,015	7,050	14,065	170	215	385	14,450	1,831	1,941	3,772	18,222
Meade	3,616	3,328	6,944	11	11	22	6,966	942	990	1,932	8,898
Mercer	5,134	5,015	10,149	125	153	278	10,427	1,662	1,612	3,274	13,701
Metcalfe	2,979	2,935	5,914	26	24	50	5,964	395	386	781	6,745
Monroe	3,773	3,839	7,612	9	8	17	7,629	457	465	922	8,551
Montgomery	2,577	2,390	4,967	69	71	140	5,107	1,399	1,353	2,752	7,859
Morgan	4,616	4,370	8,986	41	40	81	9,067	81	89	170	9,237
Muhlenburg	4,645	4,456	9,101	22	18	40	9,141	789	795	1,584	10,725
Nelson	5,100	5,060	10,160	59	50	109	10,269	2,741	2,789	5,530	15,799
Nicholas	4,797	4,464	9,231	69	86	155	9,416	789	825	1,614	11,030
Ohio	5,671	5,217	10,888	16	13	29	10,917	661	631	1,292	12,209
Oldham	2,453	2,362	4,815	22	15	37	4,852	1,213	1,218	2,431	7,283
Owen	5,702	5,287	10,989	35	35	70	11,059	812	848	1,660	12,719
Owsley	2,683	2,522	5,205	11	7	18	5,223	59	53	112	5,335
Pendleton	5,181	4,796	9,977	21	21	42	10,019	208	216	424	10,443
Perry	2,031	1,832	3,863	8	6	14	3,877	35	38	73	3,950
Pike	3,688	3,559	7,247	23	17	40	7,287	44	53	97	7,384
Powell	1,036	1,072	2,108	14	10	24	2,132	61	64	125	2,257
Pulaski	8,019	7,800	15,819	22	30	52	15,871	642	688	1,330	17,201
Rock Castle	2,527	2,419	4,946	28	12	40	4,986	154	203	357	5,343
Rowan	1,057	1,082	2,1 9	1	.....	1	2,140	82	60	142	2,282
Russell	2,762	2,691	5,453	4	8	12	5,465	245	314	559	6,024
Scott	4,439	4,002	8,441	109	123	232	8,673	2,942	2,802	5,744	14,417
Shelby	5,042	4,592	9,634	79	86	165	9,799	3,440	3,194	6,634	16,433
Simpson	2,951	2,792	5,743	50	46	96	5,839	1,128	1,179	2,307	8,146
Spencer	2,099	1,875	3,974	4	5	9	3,983	1,094	1,111	2,205	6,188
Taylor	2,879	2,876	5,755	60	69	129	5,884	785	812	1,597	7,481
Todd	3,434	3,247	6,681	25	20	45	6,726	2,452	2,397	4,849	11,575
Trigg	3,936	3,626	7,562	22	19	41	7,603	1,806	1,642	3,448	11,051
Trimble	2,582	2,462	5,044	3	2	5	5,049	388	443	831	5,880
Union	5,272	4,394	9,666	10	10	20	9,686	1,590	1,515	3,105	12,791
Warren	6,257	5,542	11,799	93	110	203	12,002	2,707	2,611	5,318	17,320
Washington	4,482	4,225	8,707	25	21	46	8,753	1,471	1,351	2,822	11,575
Wayne	4,676	4,568	9,244	15	13	28	9,272	491	496	987	10,259
Webster	3,364	3,053	6,417	11	22	33	6,450	523	560	1,083	7,533
Whiteley	3,824	3,729	7,553	13	13	26	7,579	87	96	183	7,762
Woodford	2,725	2,551	5,276	55	59	114	5,390	3,161	2,668	5,829	11,219
Total	474,211	445,306	919,517	5,101	5,583	10684	930,201	113,009	112,474	225,483	1,155,684

NOTE—33 Indians included in white population.

TABLE NO. 41.—*Population of the United States by Counties, &c.*—Continued.

STATE OF LOUISIANA.

PARISHES.	WHITES.			FREE COLORED.			Total free.	SLAVES.			Agg'te popula-tion.
	Male.	Female.	Total.	Male.	Fem.	Total		Male.	Female.	Total.	
Ascension	1,977	1,963	3,940	77	91	168	4,108	4,003	3,373	7,376	11,484
Assumption	3,781	3,408	7,189	47	47	94	7,283	4,484	3,612	8,096	15,379
Avoyelles	3,173	2,735	5,908	41	33	74	5,982	4,081	3,104	7,185	13,167
Baton Rouge, E	3,727	3,217	6,944	277	255	532	7,476	4,383	4,187	8,570	16,046
Baton Rouge, W	973	886	1,859	59	54	113	1,972	2,801	2,539	5,340	7,312
Bienville	3,170	2,730	5,900	51	49	100	6,000	2,881	2,119	5,000	11,000
Bossier	1,803	1,545	3,348	......	......	......	3,348	4,188	3,812	8,000	11,348
Caddo	2,806	1,927	4,733	35	34	69	4,802	3,682	3,656	7,338	12,140
Calcasieu	2,361	2,091	4,452	150	155	305	4,757	606	565	1,171	5,928
Caldwell	1,542	1,346	2,888	......	......	......	2,888	910	1,035	1,945	4,833
Carroll	2,307	1,817	4,124	9	11	20	4,144	7,062	6,846	13,908	18,052
Catahoula	2,965	2,527	5,492	23	23	46	5,538	3,086	3,027	6,113	11,651
Claiborne	4,821	4,175	8,996	4	......	4	9,000	3,785	4,063	7,848	16,848
Concordia	724	518	1,242	8	13	21	1,263	6,445	6,097	12,542	13,805
De Soto	2,545	2,232	4,777	6	8	14	4,791	4,273	4,234	8,507	13,298
Feliciana, E	2,140	1,941	4,081	10	13	23	4,104	5,162	5,431	10,593	14,697
Feliciana, W.	1,111	925	2,036	35	29	64	2,100	4,852	4,719	9,571	11,671
Franklin	1,526	1,232	2,758	1	1	2	2,760	1,654	1,748	3,402	6,162
Iberville	2,030	1,763	3,793	94	94	188	3,981	5,990	4,690	10,680	14,661
Jackson	2,862	2,505	5,367	......	......	......	5,367	2,035	2,063	4,098	9,465
Jefferson	5,151	4,814	9,965	129	158	287	10,252	2,941	2,179	5,120	15,372
Lafayette	2,252	2,057	4,309	96	135	231	4,540	2,210	2,253	4,463	9,003
Lafourche	3,985	3,515	7,500	61	88	149	7,649	3,492	2,903	6,395	14,044
Livingston	1,642	1,478	3,120	......	......	......	3,120	659	652	1,311	4,431
Madison	964	676	1,640	11	5	16	1,656	6,434	6,043	12,477	14,133
Morehouse	2,115	1,669	3,784	2	2	4	3,788	3,283	3,286	6,569	10,357
Natchitoches	3,329	2,977	6,306	467	492	959	7,265	4,794	4,640	9,434	16,699
Orleans	77,735	71,333	149,068	4,583	6,356	10,939	160,007	6,007	8,477	14,484	174,491
Ouichita	1,028	859	1,887	......	......	......	1,887	1,395	1,445	2,840	4,727
Opelousas	5,488	5,215	10,703	459	506	965	11,668	5,866	5,570	11,436	23,104
Plaquemines	1,486	1,109	2,595	257	257	514	3,109	2,948	2,437	5,385	8,494
Point Coupee	2,243	1,851	4,094	341	380	721	4,815	6,753	6,150	12,903	17,718
Rapides	5,390	4,321	9,711	128	163	291	10,002	7,968	7,390	15,358	25,360
Sabine	2,161	1,954	4,115	......	......	......	4,115	895	818	1,713	5,828
St. Bernard	1,077	694	1,771	32	33	65	1,836	1,378	862	2,240	4,076
St. Charles	506	432	938	79	98	177	1,115	2,407	1,775	4,182	5,297
St. Helena	1,807	1,606	3,413	2	4	6	3,419	1,906	1,805	3,711	7,130
St. James	1,738	1,610	3,348	29	32	61	3,409	4,536	3,554	8,090	11,499
St. John the Baptist	1,637	1,400	3,037	118	181	299	3,336	2,619	1,975	4,594	7,930
St. Martin's	2,760	2,245	5,005	142	169	311	5,316	3,817	3,541	7,358	12,674
St. Mary's	1,973	1,535	3,508	121	130	251	3,759	7,212	5,845	13,057	16,816
St. Tammany	1,685	1,468	3,153	217	195	412	3,565	989	852	1,841	5,406
Tensas	840	639	1,479	1	6	7	1,486	7,544	7,048	14,592	16,078
Terre Bonne	2,835	2,399	5,234	35	37	72	5,306	3,571	3,214	6,785	12,091
Union	3,505	3,136	6,641	2	1	3	6,644	1,827	1,918	3,745	10,389
Vermillion	1,559	1,442	3,001	4	3	7	3,008	657	659	1,316	4,324
Washington	1,560	1,436	2,996	11	11	22	3,018	845	845	1,690	4,708
Winn	2,943	2,538	5,481	25	16	41	5,522	661	693	1,354	6,876
Total	189,738	167,891	357,629	8,279	10,368	18,647	376,276	171,977	159,749	331,726	708,002

NOTE.—173 Indians included in white population.

TABLE No. 41.—*Population of the United States by Counties, &c.*—Continued.

STATE OF MAINE.

COUNTIES.	WHITES.			FREE COLORED.			Aggregate population.
	Male.	Female.	Total.	Male.	Female.	Total.	
Androscoggin	14,610	15,105	29,715	7	4	11	29,726
Aroostook	12,207	10,246	22,453	14	12	26	22,479
Cumberland	36,950	38,166	75,116	212	263	475	75,591
Franklin	10,409	9,989	20,398	3	2	5	20,403
Hancock	19,310	18,407	37,717	21	19	40	37,757
Kennebec	27,497	28,014	55,511	74	70	144	55,655
Knox	16,390	16,196	32,586	69	61	130	32,716
Lincoln	14,191	13,623	27,814	23	23	46	27,860
Oxford	18,800	17,896	36,696	1	1	2	36,698
Penobscot	37,675	34,957	72,632	56	43	99	72,731
Piscataquis	7,809	7,223	15,032	....	....	....	15,032
Sagadahoc	10,845	10,862	21,707	37	46	83	21,790
Somerset	18,911	17,827	36,738	10	5	15	36,753
Waldo	19,720	18,703	38,423	10	14	24	38,447
Washington	21,550	20,810	42,360	95	79	174	42,534
York	29,656	32,398	62,054	27	26	53	62,107
Total	316,530	310,422	626,952	659	668	1,327	628,279

NOTE.—5 Indians included in white population.

STATE OF MARYLAND.

COUNTIES.	WHITES.			FREE COLORED.			Total free.	SLAVES.			Agg'te population.
	Male.	Female	Total.	Male.	Fem.	Total		Male.	Female.	Total.	
Alleghany	13,890	13,325	27,215	224	243	467	27,682	290	376	666	28,348
Anne Arundel	6,258	5,446	11,704	2,501	2,363	4,864	16,568	3,937	3,395	7,332	23,900
Baltimore City	88,613	95,907	184,520	10,346	15,334	25,680	210,200	677	1,541	2,218	212,418
Baltimore County	23,970	22,752	46,722	2,153	2,078	4,231	50,953	1,617	1,565	3,182	54,135
Calvert	2,044	1,953	3,997	908	933	1,841	5,838	2,329	2,280	4,609	10,447
Caroline	3,914	3,690	7,604	1,381	1,405	2,786	10,390	377	362	739	11,129
Carroll	11,353	11,172	22,525	589	636	1,225	23,750	405	378	783	24,533
Cecil	10,235	9,759	19,994	1,498	1,420	2,918	22,912	467	483	950	23,862
Charles	2,929	2,867	5,796	518	550	1,068	6,864	4,950	4,703	9,653	16,517
Dorchester	5,933	5,721	11,654	2,373	2,311	4,684	16,338	2,105	2,018	4,123	20,461
Frederick	18,929	19,462	38,391	2,527	2,430	4,957	43,348	1,628	1,615	3,243	46,591
Harford	9,105	8,866	17,971	1,822	1,822	3,644	21,615	876	924	1,800	23,415
Howard	4,550	4,531	9,081	663	732	1,395	10,476	1,470	1,392	2,862	13,338
Kent	3,914	3,433	7,347	1,839	1,572	3,411	10,758	1,285	1,224	2,509	13,267
Montgomery	5,804	5,545	11,349	790	762	1,552	12,901	2,798	2,623	5,421	18,322
Prince George	4,853	4,797	9,650	601	597	1,198	10,848	6,513	5,966	12,479	23,327
Queen Anne	4,420	3,995	8,415	1,650	1,722	3,372	11,787	2,189	1,985	4,174	15,961
Saint Mary's	3,472	3,326	6,798	932	934	1,866	8,664	3,315	3,234	6,549	15,213
Somerset	7,801	7,531	15,332	2,306	2,265	4,571	19,903	2,688	2,401	5,089	24,992
Talbot	4,065	4,041	8,106	1,505	1,459	2,964	11,070	1,887	1,838	3,725	14,795
Washington	13,981	14,324	28,305	803	874	1,677	29,982	684	751	1,435	31,417
Worcester	6,806	6,636	13,442	1,817	1,754	3,571	17,013	1,826	1,822	3,648	20,661
Total	256,839	259,079	515,918	39,746	44,196	83,942	599,860	44,313	42,876	87,189	687,049

TABLE No. 41.—*Population of the United States by Counties, &c.*—Continued.

STATE OF MASSACHUSETTS.

COUNTIES.	WHITES.			FREE COLORED.			Aggregate population.
	Male.	Female.	Total.	Male.	Female.	Total.	
Barnstable	17,745	18,145	35,890	55	45	100	35,990
Berkshire	26,606	27,304	53,910	579	631	1,210	55,120
Bristol	44,410	47,448	91,858	863	1,073	1,936	93,794
Dukes	2,357	2,028	4,385	5	13	18	4,403
Essex	79,565	85,387	164,952	301	358	659	165,611
Franklin	15,791	15,579	31,370	29	35	64	31,434
Hampden	27,007	29,876	56,883	214	269	483	57,366
Hampshire	18,470	19,099	37,569	125	129	254	37,823
Middlesex	102,703	112,755	215,458	432	464	896	216,354
Nantucket	2,737	3,229	5,966	55	73	128	6,094
Norfolk	52,667	57,035	109,702	123	125	248	109,950
Plymouth	31,982	32,347	64,329	225	214	439	64,768
Suffolk	91,055	99,247	190,302	1,086	1,312	2,398	192,700
Worcester	79,149	79,741	158,890	377	392	769	159,659
	592,244	629,220	1,221,464	4,469	5,133	9,602	1,231,066

NOTE.—32 Indians included in white population.

STATE OF MICHIGAN.

COUNTIES.	WHITES.			FREE COLORED.			INDIANS.			Aggregate population.
	Male.	Female.	Total.	Male.	Fem.	Total.	Male.	Female.	Total.	
Alcona	123	62	185	......	......	......	......	......	......	185
Allegan	8,575	7,454	16,029	34	24	58	......	......	......	16,087
Alpena	188	102	290	......	......	......	......	......	......	290
Antrim	101	78	179	......	......	......	......	......	......	179
Barry	7,247	6,553	13,800	36	22	58	......	......	......	13,858
Bay	1,825	1,333	3,158	4	2	6	......	......	......	3,164
Berrien	11,548	10,420	21,968	215	195	410	......	......	......	22,378
Branch	10,820	10,128	20,948	18	15	33	......	......	......	20,981
Calhoun	15,235	13,953	29,188	202	174	376	......	......	......	29,564
Cass	8,614	7,739	16,353	717	651	1,368	......	......	......	17,721
Cheboygan	291	226	517	......	......	......	......	......	......	517
Chippewa	847	748	1,595	4	4	8	......	......	......	1,603
Clinton	7,301	6,601	13,902	12	2	14	......	......	......	13,916
Delta	742	430	1,172	......	......	......	......	......	......	1,172
Eaton	8,572	7,888	16,460	9	7	16	......	......	......	16,476
Emmet	604	545	1,149	......	......	......	......	......	......	1,149
Genesee	11,650	10,804	22,454	23	21	44	......	......	......	22,498
Gladwin	11	3	14	......	......	......	......	......	......	14
Grand Traverse	779	507	1,286	......	......	......	......	......	......	1,286
Gratiot	2,147	1,886	4,033	5	4	9	......	......	......	4,042
Hillsdale	13,323	12,319	25,642	18	15	33	......	......	......	25,675
Houghton	6,160	2,733	8,893	37	25	62	103	176	279	9,234
Huron	1,859	1,305	3,164	1	......	1	......	......	......	3,165
Ingham	9,220	8,178	17,398	25	12	37	......	......	......	17,435
Ionia	8,662	7,950	16,612	17	13	30	23	17	40	16,682

TABLE No. 41.—*Population of the United States by Counties, &c.*—Continued.

STATE OF MICHIGAN.

COUNTIES.	WHITES.			FREE COLORED.			INDIANS.			Aggregate population.
	Male.	Female.	Total.	Male.	Fem.	Total.	Male.	Female.	Total.	
Isabella	767	676	1,443	......	......	......	....	....	....	1,443
Jackson	14,101	12,385	26,486	107	78	185	....	....	....	26,671
Josco	112	63	175	......	......	......	....	....	....	175
Kalamazoo	12,781	11,546	24,327	151	168	319	....	....	....	24,646
Kent	16,026	14,564	30,590	60	65	125	....	1	1	30,716
Lapeer	7,770	6,915	14,685	26	26	52	8	9	17	14,754
Leelenau	873	654	1,527	2	1	3	313	315	628	2,158
Lenawee	19,514	18,347	37,861	137	106	243	4	4	8	38,112
Livingston	8,866	7,959	16,825	15	11	26	....	....	....	16,851
Macomb	11,738	11,042	22,780	32	31	63	....	....	....	22,843
Manato	488	374	862	......	......	......	90	90	180	1,042
Manistee	610	361	971	4	......	4	....	....	....	975
Marquette	1,735	999	2,734	34	26	60	13	14	27	2,821
Mason	284	135	419	......	1	1	206	205	411	831
Michilimackinac	1,029	889	1,918	9	11	20	....	....	....	1,938
Midland	413	373	786	1	......	1	....	....	....	787
Monroe	11,112	10,452	21,564	19	10	29	....	....	....	21,593
Montcalm	2,087	1,870	3,957	5	6	11	....	....	....	3,968
Muskegon	2,335	1,588	3,923	18	6	24	....	....	....	3,947
Nicosta	549	416	965	4	1	5	....	....	....	970
Newago	1,508	1,153	2,661	26	24	50	25	24	49	2,760
Oakland	19,645	18,307	37,952	175	134	309	....	....	....	38,261
Oceana	757	479	1,236	4	6	10	283	287	570	1,816
Osceola	18	9	27	......	......	......	....	....	....	27
Ontonagon	3,011	1,533	4,544	10	14	24	....	....	....	4,568
Ottawa	7,126	6,041	13,167	29	14	43	1	4	5	13,215
Presque Isle	16	10	26	......	......	......	....	....	....	26
Saginaw	6,764	5,793	12,557	18	20	38	43	55	98	12,693
Saint Clair	14,014	12,537	26,551	27	26	53	....	....	....	26,604
Sanilac	4,211	3,388	7,599	......	......	......	....	....	....	7,599
Schoolcraft	28	24	52	2	2	4	10	12	22	78
Shiawassee	6,354	5,980	12,334	4	10	14	1	....	1	12,349
St. Joseph's	11,087	10,113	21,200	31	31	62	....	....	....	21,262
Tuscola	2,627	2,255	4,882	......	......	......	1	3	4	4,886
Van Buren	7,842	7,059	14,901	88	63	151	82	90	172	15,224
Washtenaw	18,067	16,982	35,049	350	284	634	2	1	3	35,686
Wayne	37,210	36,664	73,874	802	871	1,673	....	....	....	75,547
Total	389,919	349,880	739,799	3,567	3,232	6,799	1,208	1,307	2,515	749,113

TABLE No. 41.—*Population of the United States by Counties, &c.*—Continued.

STATE OF MINNESOTA.

COUNTIES.	WHITES.			FREE COLORED.			INDIANS.			Aggregate population.
	Male.	Female.	Total.	Male.	Fem.	Total.	Male.	Female.	Total.	
Aitken	2	......	2	......	......	......	......	......	......	2
Anoka	1,141	965	2,106	......	......	......	......	......	......	2,106
Becker	48	29	77	......	......	......	177	132	309	386
Benton	341	285	626	......	......	......	......	1	1	627
Blue Earth	2,563	2,239	4,802	......	1	1	......	......	......	4,803
Breckenridge	44	28	72	......	......	......	3	4	7	79
Brown	1,287	971	2,258	......	......	......	44	37	81	2,339
Buchanan	17	9	26	......	......	......	......	......	......	26
Carlton	36	15	51	......	......	......	......	......	......	51
Carver	2,795	2,311	5,106	......	......	......	......	......	......	5,106
Cass	39	23	62	6	7	13	38	37	75	150
Chisago	969	760	1,729	5	7	12	1	1	2	1,743
Cottonwood	6	6	12	......	......	......	......	......	......	12
Crow Wing	122	67	189	......	......	......	39	41	80	269
Dakota	4,867	4,185	9,052	21	18	39	......	2	2	9,093
Dodge	2,074	1,723	3,797	......	......	......	......	......	......	3,797
Douglas	122	73	195	......	......	......	......	......	......	195
Faribault	746	589	1,335	......	......	......	......	......	......	1,335
Fillmore	7,294	6,248	13,542	......	......	......	......	......	......	13,542
Freeborn	1,811	1,556	3,367	......	......	......	......	......	......	3,367
Goodhue	4,812	4,159	8,971	3	3	6	......	......	......	8,977
Hennepin	6,882	5,953	12,835	6	7	13	......	1	1	12,849
Houston	3,505	3,140	6,645	......	......	......	......	......	......	6,645
Isanto	174	110	284	......	......	......	......	......	......	284
Itasca	5	2	7	......	1	1	24	19	43	51
Jackson	107	74	181	......	......	......	......	......	......	181
Kandiyohi	46	30	76	......	......	......	......	......	......	76
Kennebeck	23	7	30	......	......	......	......	......	......	30
Lake	130	118	248	......	......	......	......	......	......	248
Le Sueur	2,870	2,408	5,278	10	10	20	10	10	20	5,318
Manomin	85	50	135	......	1	1	......	......	......	136
Martin	80	71	151	......	......	......	......	......	......	151
McLeod	707	579	1,286	......	......	......	......	......	......	1,286
Meeker	518	410	928	......	......	......	......	......	......	928
Mille Lac	40	30	70	2	......	2	......	1	1	73
Monongalia	203	147	350	......	......	......	......	......	......	350
Morrison	333	254	587	......	1	1	17	13	30	618
Mower	1,662	1,554	3,216	......	1	1	......	......	......	3,217
Murray	14	15	29	......	......	......	......	......	......	29
Nicollet	2,098	1,614	3,712	1	......	1	29	31	60	3,773
Noble	21	14	35	......	......	......	......	......	......	35
Olmstead	5,047	4,477	9,524	......	......	......	......	......	......	9,524
Otter Tail	125	53	178	......	......	......	28	34	62	240
Pembina	225	113	338	......	......	......	670	604	1,274	1,612
Pierce	6	4	10	......	......	......	......	1	1	11
Pine	45	30	75	11	5	16	1	......	1	92
Pipestone	18	5	23	......	......	......	......	......	......	23
Polk	94	52	146	......	......	......	46	48	94	240
Ramsey	6,230	5,850	12,080	30	40	70	......	......	......	12,150
Renville	138	102	240	......	......	......	5	......	5	245
Rice	4,042	3,490	7,532	4	7	11	......	......	......	7,543

TABLE No. 41.—*Population of the United States by Counties, &c.*—Continued.

STATE OF MINNESOTA.

COUNTIES.	WHITES.			FREE COLORED.			INDIANS.			Aggregate population.
	Male.	Female.	Total.	Male.	Fem.	Total.	Male.	Female.	Total.	
St. Louis	164	98	262	....	....	....	79	65	144	406
Scott	2,454	2,140	4,594	....	....	....	1	....	1	4,595
Sherburne	406	317	723	....	....	....	....	....	....	723
Sibley	1,984	1,625	3,609	....	....	....	....	....	....	3,609
Stearns	2,442	2,060	4,502	1	2	3	....	....	....	4,505
Steele	1,539	1,324	2,863	....	....	....	....	....	....	2,863
Todd	293	137	430	....	....	....	....	....	....	430
Toombs	29	11	40	....	....	....	....	....	....	40
Wabasha	3,976	3,238	7,214	7	7	14	....	....	....	7,228
Waseca	1,370	1,228	2,598	1	....	1	....	2	2	2,601
Washington	3,436	2,607	6,043	3	4	7	42	31	73	6,123
Winona	4,921	4,268	9,189	10	9	19	....	....	....	9,208
Wright	2,081	1,641	3,722	5	2	7	....	....	....	3,729
Total	91,804	77,691	169,495	126	133	259	1,254	1,115	2,369	172,123

STATE OF MISSISSIPPI.

COUNTIES.	WHITES.			FREE COLORED.			Total free.	SLAVES.			Agg'te population.
	Male.	Female.	Total.	Male.	Fem.	Total.		Male.	Female.	Total.	
Adams	2,966	2,682	5,648	103	122	225	5,873	7,023	7,269	14,292	20,165
Amite	2,299	2,128	4,427	5	4	9	4,436	3,972	3,928	7,900	12,336
Attala	4,727	4,417	9,144	3	7	10	9,154	2,469	2,546	5,015	14,169
Bolivar	810	583	1,393	....	....	....	1,393	4,634	4,444	9,078	10.471
Clark	2,986	2,706	5,692	2	1	3	5,695	2,494	2,582	5,076	10,[illegible]
Covington	1,493	1,352	2,845	....	....	....	2,845	756	807	1,563	4,408
Carroll	4,308	3,906	8,214	7	6	13	8,227	6,852	6,956	13,808	22,035
Calhoun	3,994	3,701	7,695	....	....	....	7,695	893	930	1,823	9,518
Chickasaw	3,868	3,470	7,338	1	....	1	7,339	4,617	4,470	9,087	16,426
Choctaw	6,014	5,511	11,525	....	....	....	11,525	2,011	2,186	4,197	15,722
Claiborne	1,822	1,517	3,339	22	22	44	3,383	6,111	6,185	12,296	15,679
Coahoma	851	670	1,521	....	....	....	1,521	2,665	2,420	5,085	6,606
Copiah	3,900	3,532	7,432	1	....	1	7,433	3,949	4,016	7,965	15,398
De Soto	5,089	4,260	9,349	....	....	....	9,349	6,996	6,991	13,987	23,336
Franklin	1,839	1,659	3,498	6	9	15	3,513	2,300	2,452	4,752	8,265
Green	785	741	1,526	1	....	1	1,527	322	383	705	2,232
Hancock	1,282	1,000	2,282	....	....	....	2,282	457	400	857	3,139
Harrison	1,993	1,758	3,751	25	28	53	3,804	520	495	1,015	4,819
Hinds	4,844	4,096	8,940	19	17	36	8,976	11,254	11,109	22,363	31,339
Holmes	3,064	2,742	5,806	7	3	10	5,816	5,902	6,073	11,975	17,791
Issaquina	343	244	587	....	....	....	587	3,671	3,573	7,244	7,831
Itawamba	7,413	6,743	14,156	6	5	11	14,167	1,725	1,803	3,528	17,695
Jackson	1,500	1,455	2,955	40	40	80	3,035	594	493	1,087	4,122
Jasper	3,442	3,011	6,453	3	2	5	6,458	2,228	2,321	4,549	11,007
Jefferson	1,562	1,356	2,918	17	18	35	2,953	6,187	6,209	12,396	15,349
Jones	1,492	1,424	2,916	....	....	....	2,916	199	208	407	3,323
Kemper	3,137	2,799	5,936	5	....	5	5,941	2,953	2,788	5,741	11,682

TABLE No. 41.—*Population of the United States by Counties, &c.*—Continued.

STATE OF MISSISSIPPI.

COUNTIES.	WHITES.			FREE COLORED.			Total free.	SLAVES.			Agg'te population.
	Male.	Female.	Total.	Male.	Fem.	Total.		Male.	Female.	Total.	
Lafayette	4,812	4,177	8,989	5	2	7	8,996	3,609	3,520	7,129	16,125
Lauderdale	4,306	3,918	8,224	1	......	1	8,225	2,516	2,572	5,088	13,313
Lawrence	2,889	2,624	5,513	2	2	4	5,517	1,834	1,862	3,696	9,213
Leake	3,266	3,000	6,266	1	1	2	6,268	1,491	1,565	3,056	9,324
Lowndes	3,648	3,243	6,891	1	3	4	6,895	8,404	8,326	16,730	23,625
Madison	2,889	2,371	5,260	2	2	4	5,264	9,018	9,100	18,118	23,382
Marion	1,274	1,226	2,500	......	1	1	2,501	1,104	1,081	2,185	4,686
Marshall	6,037	5,339	11,376	5	3	8	11,384	8,785	8,654	17,439	28,823
Monroe	4,377	4,168	8,545	3	6	9	8,554	6,415	6,314	12,729	21,283
Neshoba	3,166	2,965	6,131	......	......	......	6,131	1,097	1,115	2,212	8,343
Newton	3,293	2,986	6,279	1	2	3	6,282	1,630	1,749	3,379	9,661
Noxubee	2,721	2,450	5,171	......	....	.....	5,171	7,759	7,737	15,496	20,667
Oktibbeha	2,782	2,546	5,328	6	12	18	5,346	3,980	3,651	7,631	12,977
Panola	2,820	2,417	5,237	......	......	.....	5,237	4,404	4,153	8,557	13,794
Perry	948	910	1,858	4	6	10	1,868	358	380	738	2,606
Pike	3,286	2,888	6,174	15	11	26	6,200	2,441	2,494	4,935	11,135
Pontotoc	7,491	7,022	14,513	4	......	4	14,517	3,796	3,800	7,596	22,113
Rankin	3,412	3,118	6,530	1	1	2	6,532	3,446	3,657	7,103	13,635
Scott	2,713	2,467	5,180	......	......	......	5,180	1,520	1,439	2,959	8,139
Simpson	1,915	1,829	3,744	7	5	12	3,756	1,141	1,183	2,324	6,080
Smith	2,817	2,618	5,435	3	5	8	5,443	1,036	1,159	2,195	7,638
Sunflower	602	500	1,102	......	......	......	1,102	2,000	1,917	3,917	5,019
Tallahatchie	1,532	1,303	2,835	1	......	1	2,836	2,553	2,501	5,054	7,890
Tippah	8,328	7,878	16,206	5	8	13	16,219	3,074	3,257	6,331	22,550
Tishomingo	9,914	9,245	19,159	6	3	9	19,168	2,404	2,577	4,981	24,149
Tunica	515	368	883	......	......	......	883	1,851	1,632	3,483	4,366
Warren	3,764	3,132	6,896	15	22	37	6,933	7,791	5,972	13,763	20,696
Washington	612	600	1,212	......	......	......	1,212	7,467	7,000	14,467	15,679
Wayne	924	820	1,744	......	......	......	1,744	927	1,020	1,947	3,691
Wilkinson	1,461	1,318	2,779	5	17	22	2,801	6,541	6,591	13,132	15,933
Winston	2,895	2,688	5,583	2	3	5	5,588	2,054	2,169	4,223	9,811
Yalabusha	3,968	3,447	7,415	4	2	6	7,421	4,685	4,846	9,531	16,952
Yazoo	3,075	2,582	5,657	......	......	......	5,657	8,416	8,300	16,716	22,373
Total	186,275	167,626	353,901	372	401	773	354,674	219,301	217,330	436,631	791,305

NOTE.—2 Indians included in white population.

STATE OF MISSOURI.

COUNTIES.	WHITES.			FREE COLORED.			Total free.	SLAVES.			Agg'te population.
	Male.	Female.	Total.	Male.	Fem.	Total.		Male.	Female.	Total.	
Adair	4,442	3,994	8,436	4	5	9	8,445	35	51	86	8,531
Andrew	5,884	5,065	10,949	10	11	21	10,970	414	466	880	11,850
Atchison	2,554	2,024	4,578	4	8	12	4,590	25	34	59	4,649
Audrain	3,655	3,254	6,909	......	......	......	6,909	576	590	1,166	8,075
Barry	3,950	3,788	7,738	6	4	10	7,748	113	134	247	7,995
Barton	975	821	1,796	......	......	......	1,796	4	17	21	1,817

TABLE No. 41.—*Population of the United States by Counties, &c.*—Continued.

STATE OF MISSOURI.

COUNTIES.	WHITES.			FREE COLORED.			Total free.	SLAVES.			Agg'te population.
	Male.	Female.	Total.	Male.	Fem.	Total.		Male.	Female.	Total.	
Bates	3,635	3,130	6,765	4	4	8	6,773	224	218	442	7,215
Benton	4,416	4,044	8,460	8	5	13	8,473	286	313	599	9,072
Bollinger	3,604	3,522	7,126	......	......	......	7,126	129	116	245	7,371
Boone	7,577	6,822	14,399	24	29	53	14,452	2,529	2,505	5,034	19,486
Buchanan	11,883	9,916	21,799	30	21	51	21,850	970	1,041	2,011	23,861
Butler	1,506	1,331	2,837	1	1	2	2,839	26	26	52	2,891
Caldwell	2,563	2,247	4,810	1	1	2	4,812	106	116	222	5,034
Callaway	6,814	6,081	12,895	18	13	31	12,926	2,252	2,271	4,523	17,449
Camden	2,460	2,309	4,769	......	......	......	4,769	99	107	206	4,975
Cape Girardeau	7,312	6,649	13,961	22	31	53	14,014	743	790	1,533	15,547
Carroll	4,606	4,086	8,692	2	1	3	8,695	514	554	1,068	9,763
Cass	4,699	4,082	8,781	2	1	3	8,784	472	538	1,010	9,794
Carter	625	575	1,200	7	8	15	1,215	9	11	20	1,235
Cedar	3,279	3,141	6,420	4	2	6	6,426	104	107	211	6,637
Chariton	5,153	4,519	9,672	25	26	51	9,723	1,440	1,399	2,839	12,562
Christian	2,656	2,606	5,262	......	......	......	5,262	107	122	229	5,491
Clark	5,948	5,268	11,216	7	6	13	11,229	219	236	455	11,684
Clay	5,044	4,481	9,525	26	17	43	9,568	1,763	1,692	3,455	13,023
Clinton	3,610	3,075	6,685	11	8	19	6,704	578	566	1,144	7,848
Cole	4,805	3,840	8,645	43	22	65	8,710	482	505	987	9,697
Cooper	7,138	6,390	13,528	13	15	28	13,556	1,906	1,894	3,800	17,356
Crawford	2,928	2,712	5,640	1	......	1	5,641	88	94	182	5,823
Dade	3,464	3,257	6,721	2	3	5	6,726	171	175	346	7,072
Dallas	2,936	2,841	5,777	......	1	1	5,778	50	64	114	5,892
Daviess	4,920	4,328	9,248	......	......	......	9,248	170	188	358	9,606
De Kalb	2,666	2,415	5,081	2	4	6	5,087	65	72	137	5,224
Dent	2,850	2,648	5,498	......	......	......	5,498	80	76	156	5,654
Douglass	1,251	1,163	2,414	......	......	......	2,414	......	......	......	2,414
Dunklin	2,490	2,365	4,855	......	......	......	4,855	85	86	171	5,026
Franklin	8,854	7,611	16,465	6	13	19	16,484	824	777	1,601	18,085
Gasconade	4,572	4,070	8,642	2	7	9	8,651	39	37	76	8,727
Gentry	6,248	5,614	11,862	......	......	......	11,862	52	66	118	11,980
Green	5,964	5,545	11,509	5	4	9	11,518	834	834	1,668	13,186
Grundy	3,936	3,660	7,596	4	2	6	7,602	126	159	285	7,887
Harrison	5,549	5,052	10,601	......	......	......	10,601	9	16	25	10,626
Henry	4,581	4,039	8,620	1	......	1	8,621	601	644	1,245	9,866
Hickory	2,382	2,121	4,503	4	3	7	4,510	101	94	195	4,705
Holt	3,311	2,930	6,241	......	......	......	6,241	143	166	309	6,550
Howard	5,244	4,742	9,986	31	43	74	10,060	3,104	2,782	5,886	15,946
Howell	1,610	1,523	3,133	......	......	......	3,133	12	24	36	3,169
Iron	2,970	2,559	5,529	......	......	......	5,529	138	175	313	5,842
Jackson	10,292	8,607	18,899	36	34	70	18,969	1,963	1,981	3,944	22,896
Jasper	3,480	3,053	6,533	7	8	15	6,548	145	190	335	6,883
Jefferson	5,218	4,545	9,763	10	7	17	9,780	297	267	564	10,344
Johnson	6,837	5,906	12,743	3	2	5	12,748	910	986	1,896	14,644
Knox	4,461	3,975	8,436	6	1	7	8,443	132	152	284	8,727
Laclede	2,477	2,398	4,875	1	1	2	4,877	154	151	305	5,182
Lafayette	7,431	6,257	13,688	15	21	36	13,724	3,379	2,995	6,374	20,098
Lawrence	4,343	4,216	8,559	1	2	3	8,562	132	152	284	8,846
Lewis	5,887	5,096	10,983	12	12	24	11,007	630	649	1,279	12,286
Lincoln	6,003	5,344	11,347	13	10	23	11,370	1,450	1,390	2,840	14,210

TABLE NO. 41.—*Population of the United States by Counties, &c.*—Continued.

STATE OF MISSOURI.

COUNTIES.	WHITES.			FREE COLORED.			Total free.	SLAVES.			Agg'te popula-tion.
	Male.	Female.	Total.	Male.	Fem.	Total.		Male.	Female.	Total.	
Linn	4,501	4,008	8,509	15	11	26	8,535	276	301	577	9,112
Livingston	3,674	3,138	6,812	......	......	....	6,812	278	327	605	7,417
Macon	7,180	6,493	13,673	5	8	13	13,686	314	346	660	14,346
Madison	2,717	2,462	5,179	9	9	18	5,197	231	236	467	5,664
Maries	2,495	2,335	4,830	3	4	7	4,837	30	34	64	4,901
Marion	8,402	7,330	15,732	44	45	89	15,821	1,406	1,611	3,017	18,838
McDonald	2,091	1,866	3,957	3	6	9	3,966	25	47	72	4,038
Mercer	4,831	4,443	9,274	1	1	2	9,276	11	13	24	9,300
Miller	3,374	3,198	6,572	2	......	2	6,574	106	132	238	6,812
Mississippi	2,178	1,671	3,849	......	......	......	3,849	514	496	1,010	4,859
Moniteau	4,918	4,457	9,375	1	3	4	9,379	359	386	745	10,124
Monroe	6,201	5,521	11,722	18	24	42	11,764	1,528	1,493	3,021	14,785
Montgomery	4,186	3,875	8,061	5	5	10	8,071	805	842	1,647	9,718
Morgan	3,996	3,549	7,545	4	4	8	7,553	320	329	649	8,202
New Madrid	2,167	1,696	3,863	6	8	14	3,877	939	838	1,777	5,654
Newton	4,560	4,282	8,842	19	32	51	8,893	220	206	426	9,319
Nodaway	2,725	2,398	5,123	......	2	2	5,125	65	62	127	5,252
Oregon	1,569	1,414	2,983	......	......	......	2,983	16	10	26	3,009
Osage	4,057	3,566	7,623	......	......	......	7,623	113	143	256	7,879
Ozark	1,203	1,158	2,361	23	20	43	2,404	21	22	43	2,447
Peniscot	1,420	1,262	2,682	5	7	12	2,694	135	133	268	2,962
Perry	4,441	3,925	8,366	9	14	23	8,389	358	381	739	9,128
Pettis	3,969	3,535	7,504	4	2	6	7,510	994	888	1,882	9,392
Phelps	3,257	2,371	5,628	......	2	2	5,630	44	40	84	5,714
Pike	7,406	6,896	14,302	26	34	60	14,362	2,025	2,030	4,055	18,417
Platte	8,145	6,836	14,981	26	30	56	15,037	1,671	1,642	3,313	18,350
Polk	4,800	4,668	9,468	7	8	15	9,483	239	273	512	9,995
Pulaski	2,001	1,778	3,779	......	......	......	3,779	24	32	56	3,835
Putnam	4,812	4,364	9,176	......	......	......	9,176	10	21	31	9,207
Ralls	3,630	3,158	6,788	8	5	13	6,801	896	895	1,791	8,592
Randolph	4,660	4,117	8,777	9	2	11	8,788	1,301	1,318	2,619	11,407
Ray	6,431	5,607	12,038	6	1	7	12,045	1,050	997	2,047	14,092
Reynolds	1,586	1,549	3,135	......	......	......	3,135	12	26	38	3,173
Ripley	1,886	1,780	3,666	1	2	3	3,669	40	38	78	3,747
St. Charles	7,786	6,527	14,313	13	16	29	14,342	1,103	1,078	2,181	16,523
St. Clair	3,310	2,919	6,229	5	4	9	6,238	272	302	574	6,812
St. François	3,274	3,018	6,292	38	42	80	6,372	449	428	877	7,249
St. Genevieve	3,861	3,462	7,323	46	43	89	7,412	299	318	617	8,029
St. Louis	98,460	85,853	184,313	847	1,018	1,865	186,178	1,944	2,402	4,346	190,524
Saline	5,294	4,506	9,800	12	11	23	9,823	2,583	2,293	4,876	14,699
Schuyler	3,427	3,231	6,658	......	......	......	6,658	19	20	39	6,697
Scotland	4,627	4,115	8,742	......	......	......	8,742	71	60	131	8,873
Scott	2,509	2,221	4,730	9	5	14	4,744	256	247	503	5,247
Shannon	1,180	1,091	2,271	......	......	......	2,271	7	6	13	2,284
Shelby	3,502	3,063	6,565	5	7	12	6,577	380	344	724	7,301
Stoddard	3,944	3,715	7,659	3	......	3	7,662	104	111	215	7,877
Stone	1,261	1,123	2,384	......	......	......	2,384	7	9	16	2,400
Sullivan	4,674	4,421	9,095	1	......	1	9,096	50	52	102	9,198
Taney	1,738	1,751	3,489	2	3	5	3,494	33	49	82	3,576
Texas	3,164	2,845	6,009	2	......	2	6,011	28	28	56	6,067
Vernon	2,508	2,204	4,712	......	2	2	4,714	66	70	136	4,850

TABLE No. 41.—*Population of the United States by Counties, &c.*—Continued.

STATE OF MISSOURI.

COUNTIES.	WHITES.			FREE COLORED.			Total free.	SLAVES.			Agg'te popula-tion.
	Male.	Female.	Total.	Male.	Fem.	Total.		Male.	Female.	Total.	
Warren	4,234	3,564	7,798	5	2	7	7,805	520	514	1,034	8,839
Washington	4,550	4,120	8,670	12	13	25	8,695	528	500	1,028	9,723
Wayne...........	2,687	2,674	5,361	4	3	7	5,368	124	137	261	5,629
Webster	3,476	3,403	6,879	.....	.....	.....	6,879	103	117	220	7,099
Wright	2,261	2,181	4,442	.....	.....	.....	4,442	29	37	66	4,508
Total.......	563,144	500,365	1,063,509	1,697	1,875	3,572	1,067,081	57,360	57,571	114,931	1,182,012

NOTE.—20 Indians included in white population.

STATE OF NEW HAMPSHIRE.

COUNTIES.	WHITES.			FREE COLORED.			Aggregate popula-tion.
	Male.	Female.	Total.	Male.	Female.	Total.	
Belknap	9,134	9,376	18,510	18	21	39	18,549
Carroll	10,276	10,189	20,465	....	....	....	20,465
Cheshire	13,703	13,696	27,399	16	19	35	27,434
Coos	7,030	6,124	13,154	2	5	7	13,161
Grafton	21,401	20,836	42,237	13	10	23	42,260
Hillsboro'	28,926	33,107	62,033	59	48	107	62,140
Merrimack	20,306	20,980	41,286	67	55	122	41,408
Rockingham	24,589	25,436	50,025	46	51	97	50,122
Strafford	14,814	16,648	31,462	14	17	31	31,493
Sullivan	9,384	9,624	19,008	18	15	33	19,041
Total................. ...	159,563	166,016	325,579	253	241	494	326,073

STATE OF NEW JERSEY.

COUNTIES.	WHITES.			FREE COLORED.			Total free.	SLAVES.			Agg'te popula-tion.
	Male.	Female.	Total.	Male.	Female.	Total.		Male.	Fem.	Total.	
Atlantic..........	6,048	5,544	11,592	104	90	194	11,786	......	......	......	11,786
Bergen	10,323	9,632	19,955	869	794	1,663	21,618	......	......	......	21,618
Burlington	23,429	24,077	47,506	1,046	1,178	2,224	49,730	......	......	......	49,730
Camden	15,743	16,140	31,883	1,176	1,398	2,574	34,457	......	......	......	34,457
Cape May.........	3,411	3,446	6,857	124	149	273	7,130	......	......	......	7,130
Cumberland.......	10,851	10,459	21,310	670	625	1,295	22,605	......	......	......	22,605
Essex.	47,385	49,735	97,120	787	970	1,757	98,877	......	......	......	98,877
Gloucester	9,152	8,585	17,737	352	355	707	18,444	......	......	......	18,444
Hudson...........	30,717	31,347	62,064	289	364	653	62,717	......	......	......	62,717
Hunterdon........	16,519	16,335	32,854	402	394	796	33,650	1	3	4	33,654
Mercer.	17,503	17,691	35,194	1,049	1,176	2,225	37,419	......	......	......	37,419
Middlesex	16,641	16,863	33,504	632	675	1,307	34,811	......	1	1	34,812
Monmouth........	18,501	18,187	36,688	1,325	1,333	2,658	39,346	......	......	......	39,346
Morris	17,026	16,964	33,990	335	351	686	34,676	......	1	1	34,677

TABLE No. 41.—*Population of the United States by Counties, &c.*—Continued.

STATE OF NEW JERSEY.

COUNTIES.	WHITES.			FREE COLORED.			Total free.	SLAVES.			Agg'te popula- tion.
	Male.	Female.	Total.	Male.	Female.	Total.		Male.	Fem.	Total	
Ocean	5,634	5,418	11,052	66	58	124	11,176	......	......	......	11,176
Passaic	13,938	14,516	28,454	252	305	557	29,011	......	2	2	29,013
Salem	10,256	9,740	19,996	1,237	1,225	2,462	22,458	......	......	......	22,458
Somerset	10,242	10,218	20,460	823	765	1,588	22,048	5	4	9	22,057
Sussex	11,922	11,600	23,522	165	159	324	23,846	......	......	......	23,846
Union	13,061	13,854	26,915	402	463	865	27,780	......	......	......	27,780
Warren	14,431	13,615	28,046	207	179	386	28,432	......	1	1	28,433
Total	322,733	323,966	646,699	12,312	13,006	25,318	672,017	6	12	18	672,035

STATE OF NEW YORK.

COUNTIES.	WHITES.			FREE COLORED.			Aggregate popula- tion.
	Male.	Female.	Total.	Male.	Female.	Total.	
Alleghany	21,210	20,407	41,617	132	132	264	41,881
Albany	55,516	57,463	112,979	450	488	938	113,917
Broome	17,862	17,580	35,442	222	242	464	35,906
Cattaraugus	22,677	21,058	43,735	79	72	151	43,886
Cayuga	28,017	27,299	55,316	238	213	451	55,767
Chautauqua	29,672	28,545	58,217	99	106	205	58,422
Chemung	13,243	13,102	26,345	294	278	572	26,917
Chenango	20,251	20,420	40,671	125	138	263	40,934
Clinton	23,335	22,272	45,607	90	38	128	45,735
Columbia	22,450	23,342	45,792	639	741	1,380	47,172
Cortland	13,108	13,170	26,278	13	3	16	26,294
Delaware	21,455	20,824	42,279	95	91	186	42,465
Dutchess	31,069	31,821	62,890	969	1,082	2,051	64,941
Erie	71,091	70,002	141,093	458	420	878	141,971
Essex	14,478	13,613	28,091	62	61	123	28,214
Franklin	15,670	15,148	30,818	11	8	19	30,837
Fulton	11,826	12,151	23,977	97	88	185	24,162
Green	15,440	15,671	31,111	396	423	819	31,930
Genesee	16,204	15,901	32,105	45	39	84	32,189
Hamilton	1,662	1,359	3,021	2	1	3	3,024
Herkimer	20,374	19,936	40,310	128	123	251	40,561
Jefferson	34,900	34,716	69,616	102	107	209	69,825
Kings	131,359	142,764	274,123	2,253	2,746	4,999	279,122
Lewis	14,886	13,655	28,541	22	17	39	28,580
Livingston	19,809	19,553	39,362	93	91	184	39,546
Madison	21,616	21,629	43,245	135	165	300	43,545
Monroe	49,861	50,220	100,081	288	279	567	100,648
Montgomery	15,483	15,026	30,509	168	189	357	30,866
New York	391,522	409,573	801,095	5,468	7,106	12,574	813,669
Niagara	24,954	24,928	49,882	303	214	517	50,399
Oneida	51,816	52,748	104,564	305	333	638	105,202
Onondaga	45,445	44,686	90,131	276	279	555	90,686
Ontario	22,077	21,847	43,924	283	356	639	44,563

TABLE No. 41.—*Population of the United States by Counties, &c.*—Continued.

STATE OF NEW YORK.

COUNTIES.	WHITES.			FREE COLORED.			Aggregate population.
	Male.	Female.	Total.	Male.	Female.	Total.	
Orange	30,645	31,055	61,700	1,028	1,084	2,112	63,812
Orleans	14,542	14,044	28,586	62	69	131	28,717
Oswego	39,059	36,564	75,623	175	160	335	75,958
Otsego	24,911	25,039	49,950	113	94	207	50,157
Putnam	6,852	6,967	13,819	97	86	183	14,002
Queens	27,488	26,516	54,004	1,682	1,705	3,387	57,391
Rensselaer	41,870	43,400	85,270	511	547	1,058	86,328
Richmond	12,236	12,597	24,833	312	347	659	25,492
Rockland	11,583	10,360	21,943	269	280	549	22,492
Saratoga	25,233	25,805	51,038	312	379	691	51,729
Schenectady	9,899	9,862	19,761	107	134	241	20,002
Schoharie	17,024	16,961	33,985	248	236	484	34,469
Schuyler	9,464	9,276	18,740	52	48	100	18,840
Seneca	14,155	13,770	27,925	96	117	213	28,138
Steuben	33,832	32,383	66,215	233	242	475	66,690
Saint Lawrence	42,426	41,204	83,630	28	31	59	83,689
Suffolk	20,694	20,783	41,477	882	916	1,798	43,275
Sullivan	16,819	15,472	32,291	47	47	94	32,385
Tioga	14,352	14,148	28,500	130	118	248	28,748
Tompkins	15,433	15,679	31,112	142	155	297	31,409
Ulster	38,160	36,612	74,772	771	838	1,609	76,381
Washington	22,999	22,646	45,645	136	123	259	45,904
Warren	11,033	10,343	21,376	29	29	58	21,434
Wayne	24,139	23,353	47,492	135	135	270	47,762
Wyoming	16,033	15,883	31,916	25	27	52	31,968
Westchester	48,978	48,249	97,227	1,142	1,128	2,270	99,497
Yates	10,157	9,976	20,133	74	83	157	20,290
Total	1,910,354	1,921,376	3,831,730	23,178	25,827	49,005	3,880,735

NOTE.—140 Indians included in white population.

STATE OF NORTH CAROLINA.

COUNTIES.	WHITES.			FREE COLORED.			Total free.	SLAVES.			Agg'te population.
	Male.	Female.	Total.	Male.	Fem.	Total.		Male.	Female.	Total.	
Alamance	3,872	4,113	7,985	214	208	422	8,407	1,720	1,725	3,445	11,852
Alexander	2,680	2,707	5,387	12	12	24	5,411	292	319	611	6,022
Alleghany	1,712	1,639	3,351	18	15	33	3,384	96	110	206	3,590
Anson	3,279	3,282	6,561	73	79	152	6,713	3,396	3,555	6,951	13,664
Ashe	3,738	3,685	7,423	75	67	142	7,565	185	206	391	7,956
Beaufort	4,061	4,099	8,160	377	351	728	8,888	3,066	2,812	5,878	14,766
Bertie	2,826	2,980	5,806	147	172	319	6,125	4,067	4,118	8,185	14,310
Bladen	3,176	3,057	6,233	215	220	435	6,668	2,785	2,542	5,327	11,995
Brunswick	2,281	2,234	4,515	129	131	260	4,775	2,024	1,607	3,631	8,406
Buncombe	5,342	5,268	10,610	59	52	111	10,721	991	942	1,933	12,654
Burke	3,307	3,338	6,645	106	115	221	6,866	1,200	1,171	2,371	9,237
Cabarras	3,708	3,683	7,391	65	50	115	7,506	1,522	1,518	3,040	10,546

TABLE No. 41.—*Population of the United States by Counties, &c.*—Continued.

STATE OF NORTH CAROLINA.

COUNTIES.	WHITES.			FREE COLORED.			Total free.	SLAVES.			Agg'te population.
	Male.	Female.	Total.	Male.	Fem.	Total.		Male.	Female.	Total.	
Caldwell	3,116	3,179	6,295	51	63	114	6,409	489	599	1,088	7,497
Camden	1,526	1,416	2,942	150	124	274	3,216	1,147	980	2,127	5,343
Carteret	3,001	3,063	6,064	60	93	153	6,217	984	985	1,969	8,186
Caswell	3,252	3,326	6,578	126	156	282	6,860	4,841	4,514	9,355	16,215
Catawba	4,330	4,703	9,033	14	18	32	9,065	806	858	1,664	10,729
Chatham	6,129	6,420	12,549	138	168	306	12,855	3,109	3,137	6,246	19,101
Cherokee	4,471	4,138	8,609	24	14	38	8,647	244	275	519	9,166
Chowan	1,416	1,563	2,979	67	83	150	3,129	1,876	1,837	3,713	6,842
Cleveland	5,007	5,101	10,108	59	50	109	10,217	1,045	1,086	2,131	12,348
Columbus	3,016	2,763	5,779	193	162	355	6,134	1,231	1,232	2,463	8,597
Craven	4,314	4,433	8,747	598	734	1,332	10,079	3,058	3,131	6,189	16,268
Cumberland	4,670	4,884	9,554	461	524	985	10,539	3,022	2,808	5,830	16,369
Currituck	2,294	2,375	4,669	103	120	223	4,892	1,373	1,150	2,523	7,415
Davidson	6,714	6,662	13,376	73	76	149	13,525	1,482	1,594	3,076	16,601
Davie	3,019	2,982	6,001	55	46	101	6,102	1,168	1,224	2,392	8,494
Duplin	4,118	4,171	8,289	175	196	371	8,660	3,535	3,589	7,124	15,784
Edgecombe	3,395	3,484	6,879	184	205	389	7,268	5,238	4,870	10,108	17,376
Forsyth	5,261	5,449	10,710	93	125	218	10,928	915	849	1,764	12,692
Franklin	3,224	3,241	6,465	280	286	566	7,031	3,534	3,542	7,076	14,107
Gaston	3,418	3,579	6,997	53	58	111	7,108	1,077	1,122	2,199	9,307
Gates	2,078	2,103	4,181	166	195	361	4,542	1,898	2,003	3,901	8,443
Granville	5,567	5,620	11,187	540	583	1,123	12,310	5,507	5,579	11,086	23,396
Greene	1,889	1,935	3,824	75	79	154	3,978	2,007	1,940	3,947	7,925
Guilford	7,961	7,777	15,738	355	338	693	16,431	1,792	1,833	3,625	20,056
Halifax	3,316	3,325	6,641	1,209	1,243	2,452	9,093	5,144	5,205	10,349	19,442
Harnett	2,704	2,648	5,352	61	42	103	5,455	1,292	1,292	2,584	8,039
Haywood	2,686	2,788	5,474	7	7	14	5,488	158	155	313	5,801
Henderson	4,524	4,457	8,981	46	39	85	9,066	711	671	1,382	10,448
Hertford	1,954	1,993	3,947	529	583	1,112	5,059	2,282	2,163	4,445	9,504
Hyde	2,420	2,264	4,684	136	121	257	4,941	1,504	1,287	2,791	7,732
Iredell	5,354	5,787	11,141	13	16	29	11,170	2,112	2,065	4,177	15,347
Jackson	2,704	2,537	5,241	3	3	6	5,247	135	133	268	5,515
Johnson	5,269	5,276	10,545	100	95	195	10,740	2,504	2,412	4,916	15,656
Jones	1,126	1,078	2,204	61	52	113	2,317	1,734	1,679	3,413	5,730
Lenoir	2,465	2,437	4,902	95	83	178	5,080	2,549	2,591	5,140	10,220
Lillington	1,476	1,457	2,933	60	65	125	3,058	1,623	1,605	3,228	6,286
Lincoln	2,971	3,028	5,999	41	40	81	6,080	1,089	1,026	2,115	8,195
Macon	2,734	2,636	5,370	64	51	115	5,485	262	257	519	6,004
Madison	2,885	2,793	5,678	12	5	17	5,695	102	111	213	5,908
Martin	2,676	2,759	5,435	216	235	451	5,886	2,151	2,158	4,309	10,195
McDowell	2,767	2,775	5,542	133	140	273	5,815	660	645	1,305	7,120
Mecklenburg	5,358	5,182	10,540	132	161	293	10,833	3,190	3,351	6,541	17,374
Montgomery	2,875	2,905	5,780	24	22	46	5,826	873	950	1,823	7,649
Moore	4,312	4,413	8,725	91	93	184	8,909	1,237	1,281	2,518	11,427
Nash	3,129	3,191	6,320	326	361	687	7,007	2,271	2,409	4,680	11,687
New Hanover	4,053	3,631	7,684	283	359	642	8,326	3,552	3,551	7,103	15,429
Northampton	2,931	2,978	5,909	333	326	659	6,568	3,539	3,265	6,804	13,372
Onslow	2,618	2,577	5,195	80	82	162	5,357	1,672	1,827	3,499	8,856
Orange	5,529	5,782	11,311	258	270	528	11,839	2,529	2,579	5,108	16,947
Pasquotank	2,207	2,243	4,450	732	775	1,507	5,957	1,604	1,379	2,983	8,940
Perquimans	1,635	1,650	3,285	193	202	395	3,680	1,893	1,665	3,558	7,238

TABLE No. 41.—*Population of the United States by Counties, &c.*—Continued.

STATE OF NORTH CAROLINA.

COUNTIES.	WHITES.			FREE COLORED.			Total free.	SLAVES.			Aggt'e population.
	Male.	Female.	Total.	Male.	Fem.	Total.		Male.	Female	Total.	
Person	2,797	2,911	5,708	150	168	318	6,026	2,599	2,596	5,195	11,221
Pitt	3,733	3,747	7,480	71	56	127	7,607	4,334	4,139	8,473	16,080
Polk	1,639	1,678	3,317	38	68	106	3,423	295	325	620	4,043
Randolph	7,284	7,432	14,716	214	218	432	15,148	793	852	1,645	16,793
Richmond	2,567	2,644	5,211	184	161	345	5,556	2,791	2,662	5,453	11,009
Robeson	4,330	4,242	8,572	708	754	1,462	10,034	2,755	2,700	5,455	15,489
Rockingham	4,927	5,092	10,019	200	209	409	10,428	3,084	3,234	6,318	16,746
Rowan	5,184	5,339	10,523	68	68	136	10,659	1,958	1,972	3,930	14,589
Rutherford	4,537	4,522	9,059	53	70	123	9,182	1,158	1,233	2,391	11,573
Sampson	4,566	4,542	9,108	261	227	488	9,596	3,535	3,493	7,028	16,624
Stanly	3,314	3,273	6,587	23	22	45	6,632	579	590	1,169	7,801
Stokes	3,937	3,910	7,847	45	41	86	7,933	1,221	1,248	2,469	10,402
Surry	4,500	4,450	8,950	97	87	184	9,134	605	641	1,246	10,380
Tyrrel	1,621	1,583	3,204	73	70	143	3,347	827	770	1,597	4,944
Union	4,449	4,454	8,903	27	26	53	8,956	1,106	1,140	2,246	11,202
Wake	7,963	8,485	16,448	706	740	1,446	17,894	5,296	5,437	10,733	28,627
Warren	2,467	2,456	4,923	198	204	402	5,325	5,254	5,147	10,401	15,726
Washington	1,734	1,859	3,593	150	149	299	3,892	1,206	1,259	2,465	6,357
Watauga	2,436	2,336	4,772	37	44	81	4,853	52	52	104	4,957
Wayne	4,352	4,365	8,717	367	370	737	9,454	2,747	2,704	5,451	14,905
Wilkes	6,519	6,761	13,280	131	130	261	13,541	570	638	1,208	14,749
Wilson	2,910	3,033	5,943	144	137	281	6,224	1,762	1,734	3,496	9,720
Yadkin	4,430	4,676	9,106	84	88	172	9,278	692	744	1,436	10,714
Yancey	4,225	4,001	8,226	30	37	67	8,293	156	206	362	8,655
Total	314,267	316,833	631,100	14,880	15,583	30,463	661,563	166,469	164,590	331,059	992,622

NOTE.—1,158 Indians included in white population.

STATE OF OHIO.

COUNTIES.	WHITES.			FREE COLORED.			Aggregate population.
	Male.	Female.	Total.	Male.	Female.	Total.	
Adams	10,326	9,878	20,204	50	55	105	20,309
Allen	9,830	9,285	19,115	33	37	70	19,185
Ashland	11,461	11,474	22,935	7	9	16	22,951
Ashtabula	15,929	15,860	31,789	16	9	25	31,814
Athens	10,680	10,298	20,978	190	196	386	21,364
Auglaise	8,927	8,196	17,123	33	31	64	17,187
Belmont	17,817	17,584	35,401	479	518	997	36,398
Brown	14,660	14,182	28,842	571	545	1,116	29,958
Butler	18,166	16,945	35,111	357	372	729	35,840
Carroll	7,898	7,799	15,697	25	16	41	15,738
Champaign	11,123	10,787	21,910	393	395	788	22,698
Clark	12,573	12,235	24,808	259	233	492	25,300
Clermont	16,306	15,895	32,201	402	431	833	33,034
Clinton	10,580	10,058	20,638	429	394	823	21,461
Columbiana	16,214	16,342	32,556	154	126	280	32,836

TABLE No. 41.—*Population of the United States by Counties, &c.*—Continued.

STATE OF OHIO.

COUNTIES.	WHITES.			FREE COLORED.			Aggregate population.
	Male.	Female.	Total.	Male.	Female.	Total.	
Coshocton	12,596	12,412	25,008	13	11	24	25,032
Crawford	12,255	11,586	23,841	20	20	40	23,881
Cuyahoga	38,485	38,654	77,139	461	433	894	78,033
Darke	13,165	12,363	25,528	247	234	481	26,009
Defiance	6,069	5,739	11,808	43	35	78	11,886
Delaware	12,210	11,561	23,771	61	70	131	23,902
Erie	12,413	11,912	24,325	63	86	149	24,474
Fairfield	15,301	14,980	30,281	120	137	257	30,538
Fayette	7,920	7,326	15,246	368	321	689	15,935
Franklin	25,298	23,485	48,783	814	764	1,578	50,361
Fulton	7,315	6,727	14,042	1	....	1	14,043
Gallia	10,398	10,055	20,453	800	790	1,590	22,043
Geauga	8,013	7,797	15,810	2	5	7	15,817
Green	12,503	12,219	24,722	686	789	1,475	26,197
Guernsey	12,159	12,038	24,197	137	140	277	24,474
Hamilton	108,702	103,100	211,802	2,268	2,340	4,608	216,410
Hancock	11,662	11,174	22,836	23	27	50	22,886
Hardin	6,922	6,538	13,460	58	52	110	13,570
Harrison	9,480	9,473	18,953	76	81	157	19,110
Henry	4,690	4,210	8,900	....	1	1	8,901
Highland	13,591	13,224	26,815	476	482	958	27,773
Hocking	8,531	8,307	16,838	109	110	219	17,057
Holmes	10,327	10,257	20,584	5	....	5	20,589
Huron	15,216	14,321	29,537	45	34	79	29,616
Jackson	8,907	8,338	17,245	350	346	696	17,941
Jefferson	12,587	12,821	25,408	351	356	707	26,115
Knox	14,014	13,662	27,676	23	36	59	27,735
Lake	7,750	7,790	15,540	22	14	36	15,576
Lawrence	11,634	10,930	22,564	349	336	685	23,249
Licking	18,560	18,308	36,868	80	63	143	37,011
Logan	10,255	10,086	20,341	333	322	655	20,996
Loraine	14,779	14,416	29,195	267	282	549	29,744
Lucas	13,278	12,275	25,553	164	114	278	25,831
Madison	6,714	6,025	12,739	155	121	276	13,015
Mahoning	13,089	12,744	25,833	31	30	61	25,894
Marion	8,064	7,380	15,444	23	23	46	15,490
Medina	11,404	11,075	22,479	23	15	38	22,517
Meigs	13,394	12,849	26,243	145	146	291	26,534
Mercer	6,971	6,527	13,498	323	283	606	14,104
Miami	14,776	14,383	29,159	411	389	800	29,959
Monroe	13,130	12,527	25,657	44	40	84	25,741
Montgomery	26,208	25,627	51,835	198	197	395	52,230
Morgan	11,120	10,856	21,976	75	68	143	22,119
Morrow	10,257	10,099	20,356	52	37	89	20,445
Muskingum	21,373	21,953	43,326	537	553	1,090	44,416
Noble	10,557	10,172	20,729	13	9	22	20,751
Ottawa	3,731	3,285	7,016	....	....	....	7,016
Paulding	2,492	2,319	4,811	70	64	134	4,945
Perry	9,755	9,874	19,629	27	22	49	19,678
Pickaway	11,638	10,892	22,530	492	447	939	23,469
Pike	6,533	6,268	12,801	434	408	842	13,643

TABLE No. 41.—*Population of the United States by Counties, &c.*—Continued.

STATE OF OHIO.

COUNTIES.	WHITES.			FREE COLORED.			Aggregate population.
	Male.	Female.	Total.	Male.	Female.	Total.	
Portage	12,245	11,887	24,132	33	43	76	24,208
Preble	10,982	10,714	21,696	65	59	124	21,820
Putnam	6,670	6,132	12,802	3	3	6	12,808
Richland	15,541	15,599	31,140	12	6	18	31,158
Ross	16,331	15,959	32,290	1,379	1,402	2,781	35,071
Sandusky	11,092	10,282	21,374	38	17	55	21,429
Scioto	12,342	11,632	23,974	164	159	323	24,297
Seneca	15,758	14,987	30,745	51	72	123	30,868
Shelby	8,666	8,247	16,913	294	286	580	17,493
Stark	21,531	21,275	42,806	84	88	172	42,978
Summit	13,635	13,621	27,256	39	49	88	27,344
Trumbull	15,315	15,261	30,576	45	35	80	30,656
Tuscarawas	16,342	16,051	32,393	38	32	70	32,463
Union	8,361	7,923	16,284	113	110	223	16,507
Van Wirt	5,283	4,887	10,170	31	37	68	10,238
Vinton	6,903	6,575	13,478	70	83	153	13,631
Warren	13,314	12,912	26,226	340	336	676	26,902
Washington	18,152	17,468	35,620	313	335	648	36,268
Wayne	16,318	16,138	32,456	15	12	27	32,483
Williams	8,752	7,880	16,632	1	....	1	16,633
Wood	9,412	8,471	17,883	2	1	3	17,886
Wyandott	8,094	7,460	15,554	26	16	42	15,596
Total	1,171,720	1,131,118	2,302,838	18,442	18,231	36,673	2,339,511

NOTE.—30 Indians included in white population.

STATE OF OREGON.

COUNTIES.	WHITES.			FREE COLORED.			INDIANS.			Aggregate population.
	Male.	Female.	Total.	Male.	Fem.	Total	Male.	Female.	Total.	
Benton	1,806	1,253	3,059	5	5	10	5	......	5	3,074
Coos	305	116	421	......	......	......	5	19	24	445
Clackamas	1,980	1,484	3,464	......	1	1	1	......	1	3,466
Clatsop	307	189	496	2	......	2	......	......	......	498
Columbia	334	198	532	......	......	......	......	......	......	532
Curry	287	89	376	......	......	......	6	11	17	393
Douglas	1,957	1,210	3,167	4	5	9	15	12	27	3,203
Jackson	2,789	900	3,689	26	16	42	2	3	5	3,736
Josephine	1,288	321	1,609	3	1	4	3	7	10	1,623
Lane	2,735	2,044	4,779	1	......	1	......	......	......	4,780
Linn	3,787	2,976	6,763	2	5	7	1	1	2	6,772
Marion	4,004	3,018	7,022	12	8	20	14	32	46	7,088
Multnomah	2,446	1,680	4,126	10	7	17	2	5	7	4,150
Polk	2,104	1,519	3,623	2	......	2	......	......	......	3,625

TABLE No. 41.—*Population of the United States by Counties, &c.*—Continued.

STATE OF OREGON.

COUNTIES.	WHITES.			FREE COLORED.			INDIANS.			Aggregate population.
	Male.	Female.	Total.	Male.	Fem.	Total.	Male.	Female.	Total.	
Tillamook	61	34	95	......	......	......	....	....	....	95
Umpqua	745	497	1,242	1	2	3	1	4	5	1,250
Wasco	1,160	513	1,673	7	2	9	....	7	7	1,689
Washington	1,554	1,226	2,780	......	......	......	9	12	21	2,801
Yam Hill	1,802	1,442	3,244	1	......	1	....	....	....	3,245
Total	31,451	20,709	52,160	76	52	128	64	113	177	52,465

STATE OF PENNSYLVANIA.

COUNTIES.	WHITES.			FREE COLORED.			Aggregate population.
	Male.	Female.	Total.	Male.	Female.	Total.	
Adams	13,708	13,824	27,532	228	246	474	28,006
Allegheny	88,555	87,551	176,106	1,202	1,423	2,625	178,731
Armstrong	18,069	17,550	35,619	90	88	178	35,797
Beaver	14,404	14,462	28,866	137	137	274	29,140
Bedford	13,310	12,932	26,242	270	224	494	26,736
Berks	46,530	46,791	93,321	248	249	497	93,818
Blair	13,958	13,588	27,546	141	142	283	27,829
Bradford	24,888	23,643	48,531	104	99	203	48,734
Bucks	31,316	30,644	61,960	795	823	1,618	63,578
Butler	18,022	17,516	35,538	27	29	56	35,594
Cambria	14,902	14,138	29,040	67	48	115	29,155
Carbon	11,070	9,954	21,024	5	4	9	21,033
Centre	13,613	13,126	26,739	132	129	261	27,000
Chester	34,342	34,329	68,671	2,995	2,912	5,907	74,578
Clarion	12,657	12,268	24,925	33	30	63	24,988
Clearfield	9,907	8,771	18,678	39	42	81	18,759
Clinton	9,210	8,376	17,586	71	66	137	17,723
Columbia	12,667	12,295	24,962	47	56	103	25,065
Crawford	24,662	23,911	48,573	94	88	182	48,755
Cumberland	19,299	19,459	38,758	638	702	1,340	40,098
Dauphin	22,452	22,595	45,047	814	895	1,709	46,756
Delaware	14,250	14,698	28,948	817	832	1,649	30,597
Elk	3,234	2,670	5,904	5	6	11	5,915
Erie	24,906	24,345	49,251	97	84	181	49,432
Fayette	18,907	19,453	38,360	722	827	1,549	39,909
Forest	505	393	898	....	....	....	898
Franklin	20,102	20,225	40,327	866	933	1,799	42,126
Fulton	4,587	4,443	9,030	56	45	101	9,131
Green	12,079	11,738	23,817	258	268	526	24,343
Huntingdon	14,184	13,626	27,810	142	148	290	28,100
Indiana	16,815	16,686	33,501	100	86	186	33,687
Jefferson	9,450	8,739	18,189	49	32	81	18,270
Juniata	8,552	8,173	16,725	139	122	261	16,986
Lancaster	56,250	56,605	112,855	1,760	1,699	3,459	116,314
Lawrence	11,334	11,563	22,897	49	53	102	22,999

TABLE No. 41.—*Population of the United States by Counties, &c.*—Continued.

STATE OF PENNSYLVANIA.

COUNTIES.	WHITES.			FREE COLORED.			Aggregate population.
	Male.	Female.	Total.	Male.	Female.	Total.	
Lebanon	15,862	15,886	31,748	46	37	83	31,831
Lehigh	22,316	21,380	43,696	35	22	57	43,753
Luzerne	46,540	43,254	89,794	228	222	450	90,244
Lycoming	18,953	18,047	37,000	197	202	399	37,399
McKean	4,728	4,131	8,859	....	....	....	8,859
Mercer	18,252	18,323	36,575	148	133	281	36,856
Mifflin	8,009	7,916	15,925	187	228	415	16,340
Monroe	8,613	8,018	16,631	60	67	127	16,758
Montgomery	34,975	34,621	69,596	440	464	904	70,500
Montour	6,581	6,358	12,939	59	55	114	13,053
Northampton	23,976	23,787	47,763	67	74	141	47,904
Northumberland	14,600	14,207	28,807	61	54	115	28,922
Perry	11,589	11,085	22,674	65	54	119	22,793
Philadelphia	260,156	283,188	543,344	9,177	13,008	22,185	565,529
Pike	3,668	3,350	7,018	68	69	137	7,155
Potter	6,051	5,404	11,455	9	6	15	11,470
Schuylkill	45,667	43,486	89,153	188	169	357	89,510
Snyder	7,516	7,484	15,000	20	15	35	15,035
Somerset	13,442	13,289	26,731	25	22	47	26,778
Sullivan	2,980	2,648	5,628	3	6	9	5,637
Susquehanna	18,465	17,593	36,058	113	96	209	36,267
Tioga	16,101	14,841	30,942	47	55	102	31,044
Union	7,010	7,080	14,090	28	27	55	14,145
Venango	13,084	11,890	24,974	37	32	69	25,043
Warren	10,101	9,038	19,139	31	20	51	19,190
Washington	22,328	22,751	45,079	844	882	1,726	46,805
Wayne	16,919	15,280	32,199	17	23	40	32,239
Westmoreland	26,691	26,613	53,304	229	203	432	53,736
Wyoming	6,512	6,023	12,535	4	1	5	12,540
York	33,565	33,269	66,834	703	663	1,366	68,200
Total	1,427,946	1,421,320	2,849,266	26,373	30,476	56,849	2,906,115

NOTE.—7 Indians included in white population.

STATE OF RHODE ISLAND.

COUNTIES.	WHITES.			FREE COLORED.			Aggregate population.
	Male.	Female.	Total.	Male.	Female.	Total.	
Bristol	4,130	4,469	8,599	153	155	308	8,907
Kent	8,038	9,006	17,044	134	125	259	17,303
Newport	10,196	10,878	21,074	360	462	822	21,896
Providence	51,007	54,815	105,822	898	1,079	1,977	107,799
Washington	8,931	9,198	18,129	286	300	586	18,715
Total	82,302	88,366	170,668	1,831	2,121	3,952	174,620

NOTE.—19 Indians included in white population.

TABLE No. 41.—*Population of the United States by Counties, &c.*—Continued.

STATE OF SOUTH CAROLINA.

DISTRICTS.	WHITES.			FREE COLORED.			Total free.	SLAVES.			Agg'te popula-tion.
	Male.	Female.	Total.	Male.	Fem.	Total.		Male.	Female.	Total.	
Abbeville	5,786	5,730	11,516	184	183	367	11,883	9,909	10,593	20,502	32,385
Anderson	7,138	7,148	14,286	81	81	162	14,448	3,956	4,469	8,425	22,873
Barnwell	6,396	6,306	12,702	325	315	640	13,342	8,522	8,879	17,401	30,743
Beaufort	3,385	3,329	6,714	410	399	809	7,523	15,484	17,046	32,530	40,053
Charleston	14,761	14,427	29,188	1,455	2,167	3,622	32,810	17,957	19,333	37,290	70,100
Chester	3,486	3,612	7,098	82	74	156	7,254	5,294	5,574	10,868	18,122
Chesterfield	3,614	3,740	7,354	60	72	132	7,486	2,210	2,138	4,348	11,834
Clarendon	2,249	2,129	4,378	73	78	151	4,529	4,154	4,412	8,566	13,095
Colleton	4,780	4,475	9,255	174	180	354	9,609	15,334	16,973	32,307	41,916
Darlington	4,328	4,104	8,432	30	22	52	8,484	5,779	6,098	11,877	20,361
Edgefield	7,802	7,852	15,654	83	90	173	15,827	12,040	12,020	24,060	39,887
Fairfield	3,241	3,132	6,373	111	93	204	6,577	7,543	7,991	15,534	22,111
Georgetown	1,589	1,424	3,013	91	92	183	3,196	9,143	8,966	18,109	21,305
Greenville	7,280	7,351	14,631	112	100	212	14,843	3,390	3,659	7,049	21,892
Horry	2,866	2,698	5,564	21	18	39	5,603	1,212	1,147	2,359	7,962
Kershaw	2,503	2,545	5,048	89	108	197	5,245	3,668	4,173	7,841	13,086
Lancaster	3,055	2,999	6,054	47	46	93	6,147	2,795	2,855	5,650	11,797
Laurens	5,165	5,364	10,529	61	68	129	10,658	6,633	6,567	13,200	23,858
Lexington	4,630	4,703	9,333	25	19	44	9,377	3,174	3,028	6,202	15,579
Marion	5,504	5,503	11,007	112	120	232	11,239	4,807	5,144	9,951	21,190
Marlborough	2,682	2,691	5,373	74	94	168	5,541	3,370	3,523	6,893	12,434
Newberry	3,601	3,399	7,000	81	103	184	7,184	6,801	6,894	13,695	20,879
Orangeburg	4,097	4,011	8,108	117	88	205	8,313	8,162	8,421	16,583	24,896
Pickens	7,593	7,742	15,335	47	62	109	15,444	2,064	2,131	4,195	19,639
Richland	3,477	3,386	6,863	182	257	439	7,302	5,445	5,560	11,005	18,307
Spartanburg	9,147	9,390	18,537	65	77	142	18,679	4,017	4,223	8,240	26,919
Sumter	3,429	3,428	6,857	159	161	320	7,177	8,233	8,449	16,682	23,859
Union	4,379	4,291	8,670	98	66	164	8,834	5,378	5,423	10,801	19,635
Williamsburg	2,712	2,475	5,187	18	25	43	5,230	5,153	5,106	10,259	15,489
York	5,526	5,803	11,329	81	108	189	11,518	4,944	5,040	9,984	21,502
Total	146,201	145,187	291,388	4,548	5,366	9,914	301,302	196,571	205,835	402,406	703,708

NOTE.—88 Indians included in the white population.

STATE OF TENNESSEE.

COUNTIES.	WHITES.			FREE COLORED.			Total free.	SLAVES.			Agg'te popula-tion.
	Male.	Female.	Total.	Male.	Fem.	Total.		Male.	Female.	Total.	
Anderson	3,269	3,208	6,477	4	4	8	6,485	302	281	583	7,068
Bedford	7,578	7,210	14,788	27	25	52	14,840	3,447	3,297	6,744	21,584
Benton	4,193	3,725	7,918	4	7	11	7,929	253	281	534	8,463
Bledsoe	1,886	1,757	3,643	63	64	127	3,770	361	328	689	4,459
Blount	5,901	5,810	11,711	105	91	196	11,907	672	691	1,363	13,270
Bradley	5,299	5,171	10,470	25	33	58	10,528	559	614	1,173	11,701
Campbell	3,211	3,070	6,281	34	31	65	6,346	183	183	366	6,712
Cannon	4,269	4,261	8,530	......	5	5	8,535	496	478	974	9,509
Carroll	6,733	6,606	13,339	18	16	34	13,373	1,990	2,074	4,064	17,437

TABLE NO. 41.—*Population of the United States by Counties, &c.*—Continued.

STATE OF TENNESSEE.

COUNTIES.	WHITES.			FREE COLORED.			Total free.	SLAVES.			Agg'te population.
	Male.	Female.	Total.	Male.	Fem.	Total.		Male.	Female.	Total.	
Carter	3,377	3,351	6,728	10	12	22	6,750	181	193	374	7,124
Cheatham	2,829	2,547	5,376	......	......	......	5,376	951	931	1,882	7,258
Claiborne	4,444	4,280	8,724	78	98	176	8,900	408	335	743	9,643
Cocke	4,734	4,748	9,482	33	44	77	9,559	434	415	849	10,408
Coffee	4,108	4,042	8,150	6	4	10	8,160	745	784	1,529	9,689
Cumberland	1,650	1,671	3,321	11	7	18	3,339	57	64	121	3,460
Davidson	16,597	14,459	31,056	544	665	1,209	32,265	7,214	7,576	14,790	47,055
Decatur	2,803	2,674	5,477	8	7	15	5,492	354	430	784	6,276
DeKalb	4,749	4,784	9,533	7	8	15	9,548	471	554	1,025	10,573
Dickson	4,027	3,747	7,774	4	3	7	7,781	1,126	1,075	2,201	9,982
Dyer	4,078	3,811	7,889	4	2	6	7,895	1,297	1,344	2,641	10,536
Fayette	4,639	4,187	8,826	12	16	28	8,854	7,690	7,783	15,473	24,327
Fentress	2,459	2,406	4,865	.....	2	2	4,867	84	103	187	5,054
Franklin	5,213	5,036	10,249	20	28	48	10,297	1,765	1,786	3,551	13,848
Gibson	8,038	7,507	15,545	42	49	91	15,636	2,935	3,206	6,141	21,777
Giles	7,898	7,397	15,295	8	15	23	15,318	5,262	5,586	10,848	26,166
Grainger	4,867	4,860	9,727	81	89	170	9,897	521	544	1,065	10,962
Greene	8,735	8,750	17,485	119	103	222	17,707	604	693	1,297	19,004
Grundy	1,404	1,409	2,813	6	8	14	2,827	137	129	266	3,093
Hamilton	5,937	5,710	11,647	90	102	192	11,839	699	720	1,419	13,258
Hancock	3,322	3,384	6,706	35	33	68	6,774	123	123	246	7,020
Hardeman	5,401	5,104	10,505	16	12	28	10,533	3,598	3,638	7,236	17,769
Hardin	4,812	4,742	9,554	19	18	37	9,591	767	856	1,623	11,214
Hawkins	6,988	7,055	14,043	101	93	194	14,237	969	956	1,925	16,162
Haywood	4,241	3,924	8,165	19	22	41	8,206	5,495	5,531	11,026	19,232
Henderson	5,612	5,577	11,189	9	10	19	11,208	1,552	1,731	3,283	14,491
Henry	6,946	6,646	13,592	7	4	11	13,603	2,698	2,832	5,530	19,133
Hickman	3,725	3,807	7,532	18	9	27	7,559	880	873	1,753	9,312
Humphrey	4,081	3,538	7,619	6	8	14	7,633	728	735	1,463	9,096
Jackson	5,220	5,247	10,467	25	21	46	10,513	588	624	1,212	11,725
Jefferson	6,878	6,899	13,777	79	91	170	13,947	1,035	1,061	2,096	16,043
Johnson	2,393	2,364	4,757	11	17	28	4,785	114	119	233	5,018
Knox	10,196	9,824	20,020	199	224	423	20,443	1,194	1,176	2,370	22,813
Lauderdale	2,453	2,231	4,684	11	10	21	4,705	1,456	1,398	2,854	7,559
Lawrence	4,035	4,101	8,136	12	12	24	8,160	564	596	1,160	9,320
Lewis	998	994	1,992	2	......	2	1,994	112	135	247	2,241
Lincoln	8,058	7,868	15,926	26	29	55	15,981	3,382	3,465	6,847	22,828
McNary	6,497	6,313	12,810	12	10	22	12,832	885	1,015	1,900	14,732
Macon	3,105	3,139	6,244	55	62	117	6,361	485	444	929	7,290
McMinn	5,830	5,720	11,550	48	48	96	11,646	911	998	1,909	13,555
Madison	6,002	5,438	11,440	40	43	83	11,523	4,971	5,041	10,012	21,535
Marion	2,837	2,650	5,487	15	10	25	5,512	340	338	678	6,190
Marshall	5,107	4,957	10,064	17	31	48	10,112	2,170	2,310	4,480	14,592
Maury	8,893	8,808	17,701	68	75	143	17,844	7,145	7,509	14,654	32,498
Meigs	2,038	1,984	4,021	3	4	7	4,029	326	312	638	4,667
Monroe	5,450	5,449	10 899	52	56	108	11,007	779	821	1,600	12,607
Montgomery	5,864	5,371	11,235	59	47	106	11,341	4,887	4,667	9,554	20,895
Morgan	1,630	1,562	3,192	22	19	41	3,233	57	63	120	3,353
Obion	5,474	4,906	10,380	25	13	38	10,418	1,182	1,217	2,399	12,817
Overton	5,727	5,725	11,452	45	53	98	11,550	504	583	1,087	12,637
Perry	2,797	2,689	5,486	2	6	8	5,494	278	270	548	6,042

TABLE No. 41.—*Population of the United States by Counties, &c.*—Continued.

STATE OF TENNESSEE.

COUNTIES.	WHITES.			FREE COLORED.			Total free.	SLAVES.			Agg'te popula-tion.
	Male.	Female.	Total.	Male.	Fem.	Total.		Male.	Female.	Total.	
Polk	4,234	4,027	8,261	16	15	31	8,292	224	210	434	8,726
Putnum	3,904	3,936	7,840	18	18	36	7,876	321	361	682	8,558
Rhea	2,176	2,170	4,346	17	13	30	4,376	311	304	615	4,991
Roane	5,870	5,860	11,730	57	48	105	11,835	918	830	1,748	13,583
Robertson	5,278	5,097	10,375	14	15	29	10,404	2,419	2,442	4,861	15,265
Rutherford	7,542	7,202	14,744	93	97	190	14,934	6,417	6,567	12,984	27,918
Scott	1,704	1,742	3,446	5	9	14	3,460	32	27	59	3,519
Sevier	4,268	4,252	8,520	36	28	64	8,584	245	293	538	9,122
Sequatchie	957	961	1,918	1	......	1	1,919	108	93	201	2,120
Shelby	17,656	13,207	30,863	120	156	276	31,139	8,297	8,656	16,953	48,092
Smith	6,124	5,891	12,015	54	60	114	12,129	2,147	2,081	4,228	16,357
Stewart	3,864	3,541	7,405	47	29	76	7,481	1,378	1,037	2,415	9,896
Sullivan	6,084	6,225	12,309	85	84	169	12,478	562	512	1,074	13,552
Sumner	7,252	6,975	14,227	53	50	103	14,330	3,810	3,890	7,700	22,030
Tipton	2,860	2,548	5,408	8	1	9	5,417	2,706	2,582	5,288	10,705
Union	2,910	2,943	5,853	42	40	82	5,935	98	84	182	6,117
Van Buren	1,149	1,185	2,334	3	5	8	2,342	125	114	239	2,581
Warren	4,438	4,323	8,761	33	33	66	8,827	1,158	1,162	2,320	11,147
Washington	6,760	6,820	13,580	132	165	297	13,877	456	496	952	14,829
Wayne	4,003	3,838	7,841	3	2	5	7,846	642	627	1,269	9,115
Weakly	7,361	6,624	13,985	6	12	18	14,003	2,042	2,171	4,213	18,216
White	4,099	3,975	8,074	81	81	162	8,236	543	602	1,145	9,381
Williamson	5,791	5,624	11,415	22	23	45	11,460	6,088	6,279	12,367	23,827
Wilson	8,991	8,796	17,787	171	150	321	18,108	3,950	4,014	7,964	26,072
Total	422,810	403,972	826,782	3,538	3,762	7,300	834,082	136,370	139,349	275,719	1,109,801

NOTE.—60 Indians included in white population.

STATE OF TEXAS.

COUNTIES.	WHITES.			FREE COLORED.			Total free.	SLAVES.			Agg'te popula-tion.
	Male.	Female.	Total.	Male.	Fem.	Total.		Male.	Female	Total.	
Anderson	3,595	3,135	6,730	......	......	......	6,730	1,774	1,894	3,668	10,398
Angelina	1,841	1,734	3,575	6	4	10	3,585	336	350	686	4,271
Atascosa	832	639	1,471	......	......	......	1,471	50	57	107	1,578
Austin	3,387	2,838	6,225	......	......	......	6,225	2,011	1,903	3,914	10,139
Banderah	218	169	387	......	......	......	387	4	8	12	399
Bastrop	2,392	2,023	4,415	......	......	......	4,415	1,381	1,210	2,591	7,006
Baylor	......	......	......	......	......	......	......	......	......	......	......
Bee	465	366	831	......	......	......	831	42	37	79	910
Bell	2,061	1,733	3,794	......	......	......	3,794	529	476	1,005	4,799
Bexar	7,013	6,044	13,057	......	2	2	13,059	670	725	1,395	14,454
Blanco	643	540	1,183	......	......	......	1,183	46	52	98	1,281
Bowie	1,332	1,069	2,401	......	......	......	2,401	1,303	1,348	2,651	5,052
Bosque	916	796	1,712	......	......	......	1,712	138	155	293	2,005
Brazoria	1,190	837	2,027	6	......	6	2,033	2,659	2,451	5,110	7,143
Brazos	941	772	1,713	......	......	......	1,713	526	537	1,063	2,776

TABLE No. 41.—*Population of the United States by Counties, &c.*—Continued.

STATE OF TEXAS.

COUNTIES.	WHITES.			FREE COLORED.			Total free.	SLAVES.			Agg'te population.
	Male.	Female.	Total.	Male.	Fem.	Total.		Male.	Female.	Total.	
Brown	133	111	244	......	......	......	244	......	......	......	244
Buchanan	109	89	198	......	......	......	198	15	17	32	230
Burleson	2,003	1,677	3,680	......	......	......	3,680	1,034	969	2,003	5,683
Burnet	1,268	984	2,252	......	......	......	2,252	108	127	235	2,487
Caldwell	1,540	1,330	2,870	1	......	1	2,871	800	810	1,610	4,481
Calhoun	1,258	970	2,228	......	......	......	2,228	184	230	414	2,642
Camanche	350	298	648	......	......	......	648	28	33	61	709
Cameron	3,334	2,621	5,955	28	38	66	6,021	2	5	7	6,028
Cass	2,671	2,265	4,936	......	......	......	4,936	1,703	1,772	3,475	8,411
Chambers	532	463	995	......	......	......	995	254	259	513	1,508
Cherokee	4,628	4,221	8,849	2	1	3	8,852	1,583	1,663	3,246	12,098
Clay	85	22	107	1	1	2	109	......	......	......	109
Collehan	......	......	......	......	......	......	......	......	......	......	......
Collin	4,376	3,841	8,217	......	......	......	8,217	491	556	1,047	9,264
Coleman	......	......	......	......	......	......	......	......	......	......	......
Colorado	2,398	1,928	4,326	......	......	......	4,326	1,819	1,740	3,559	7,885
Comal	2,072	1,765	3,837	......	......	......	3,837	88	105	193	4,030
Concho	......	......	......	......	......	......	......	......	......	......	......
Cook	1,799	1,592	3,391	......	......	......	3,391	175	194	369	3,760
Coryell	1,274	1,086	2,360	......	......	......	2,360	145	161	306	2,666
Dallas	4,135	3,456	7,591	......	......	......	7,591	513	561	1,074	8,665
Dawson	185	96	281	......	......	......	281	......	......	......	281
Denton	2,525	2,255	4,780	......	......	......	4,780	115	136	251	5,031
De Witt	1,888	1,577	3,465	......	......	......	3,465	788	855	1,643	5,108
Demmit	......	......	......	......	......	......	......	......	......	......	......
Duval	......	......	......	......	......	......	......	......	......	......	......
Eastland	56	43	99	......	......	......	99	......	......	......	99
Edwards	......	......	......	......	......	......	......	......	......	......	......
Ellis	2,265	1,877	4,142	......	......	......	4,142	545	559	1,104	5,246
El Paso	2,390	1,632	4,022	6	8	14	4,036	7	8	15	4,051
Ensinal	28	15	43	......	......	......	43	......	......	......	43
Erath	1,222	1,085	2,307	......	......	......	2,307	52	66	118	2,425
Falls	1,051	845	1,896	2	......	2	1,898	879	837	1,716	3,614
Fannin	4,012	3,484	7,496	......	......	......	7,496	834	887	1,721	9,217
Fayette	4,232	3,576	7,808	4	6	10	7,818	1,822	1,964	3,786	11,604
Fort Bend	1,143	864	2,007	7	2	9	2,016	2,133	1,994	4,127	6,143
Free Stone	1,748	1,520	3,268	......	......	......	3,268	1,739	1,874	3,613	6,881
Frio	25	15	40	......	......	......	40	2	......	2	42
Galveston	3,756	2,951	6,707	1	1	2	6,709	693	827	1,520	8,229
Guadalupe	1,930	1,759	3,689	5	2	7	3,696	850	898	1,748	5,444
Gillespie	1,477	1,226	2,703	......	......	......	2,703	17	16	33	2,736
Goliad	1,387	1,154	2,541	......	......	......	2,541	369	474	843	3,384
Gonzales	2,759	2,132	4,891	......	......	......	4,891	1,605	1,563	3,168	8,059
Grayson	3,732	3,160	6,892	......	......	......	6,892	648	644	1,292	8,184
Grimes	2,724	2,114	4,838	1	......	1	4,839	2,841	2,627	5,468	10,307
Hamilton	245	218	463	......	......	......	463	11	15	26	489
Hardeman	......	......	......	......	......	......	......	......	......	......	......
Hardin	646	516	1,162	......	......	......	1,162	88	103	191	1,353
Harris	3,976	3,032	7,008	2	7	9	7,017	1,011	1,042	2,053	9,070
Harrison	3,304	2,913	6,217	......	......	......	6,217	4,462	4,322	8,784	15,001
Hays	728	601	1,329	......	......	......	1,329	381	416	797	2,126

TABLE No. 41.—*Population of the United States by Counties, &c.*—Continued.

STATE OF TEXAS.

COUNTIES.	WHITES.			FREE COLORED.			Total free.	SLAVES.			Agg'te population.
	Male.	Female.	Total.	Male.	Fem.	Total.		Male.	Female.	Total.	
Haskell	......	......	......	......	......	......	......	......	......	......	......
Henderson	1,864	1,614	3,478	1	......	1	3,479	530	586	1,116	4,595
Hidalgo	657	500	1,157	19	15	34	1,191	......	1	1	1,192
Hill	1,629	1,374	3,003	......	......	......	3,003	320	330	650	3,653
Hopkins	3,520	3,235	6,755	......	......	......	6,755	461	529	990	7,745
Houston	2,805	2,434	5,239	......	......	......	5,239	1,414	1,405	2,819	8,058
Hunt	3,227	2,826	6,053	......	......	......	6,053	279	298	577	6,630
Jack	527	423	950	......	......	......	950	18	32	50	1,000
Jackson	795	601	1,396	10	12	22	1,418	607	587	1,194	2,612
Jasper	1,315	1,111	2,426	......	......	......	2,426	790	821	1,611	4,037
Jefferson	981	703	1,684	1	1	2	1,686	158	151	309	1,995
Johnson	2,028	1,764	3,792	......	......	......	3,792	252	261	513	4,305
Jones	......	......	......	......	......	......	......	......	......	......	......
Karnes	1,058	786	1,844	......	......	......	1,844	163	164	327	2,171
Kaufman	1,802	1,601	3,403	......	......	......	3,403	246	287	533	3,936
Kerr	345	240	585	......	......	......	585	27	22	49	634
Kimble	......	......	......	......	......	......	......	......	......	......	......
Kinney	30	16	46	7	8	15	61	......	......	......	61
Knox	......	......	......	......	......	......	......	......	......	......	......
Lamar	3,865	3,429	7,294	5	4	9	7,303	1,448	1,385	2,833	10,136
Lanpassus	486	388	874	1	......	1	875	73	80	153	1,028
Lasalle	......	......	......	......	......	......	......	......	......	......	......
Lavaca	2,341	1,897	4,238	......	......	......	4,238	916	791	1,707	5,945
Leon	2,273	1,888	4,161	......	......	......	4,161	1,345	1,275	2,620	6,781
Liberty	1,155	947	2,102	3	5	8	2,110	571	508	1,079	3,189
Limestone	1,861	1,603	3,464	......	1	1	3,465	510	562	1,072	4,537
Live Oak	294	214	508	......	......	......	508	46	39	85	593
Llano	561	486	1,047	......	......	......	1,047	23	31	54	1,101
McCulloch	......	......	......	......	......	......	......	......	......	......	......
McLennan	2,137	1,665	3,802	7	2	9	3,811	1,224	1,171	2,395	6,206
McMullen	......	......	......	......	......	......	......	......	......	......	......
Madison	822	741	1,563	......	......	......	1,563	326	349	675	2,238
Marion	1,109	851	1,960	......	......	......	1,960	971	1,046	2,017	3,977
Mason	359	247	606	3	3	6	612	4	14	18	630
Matagorda	756	591	1,347	......	......	......	1,347	1,085	1,022	2,107	3,454
Maveric	434	270	704	9	12	21	725	......	1	1	726
Medina	928	804	1,732	......	......	......	1,732	53	53	106	1,838
Menora	......	......	......	......	......	......	......	......	......	......	......
Milam	1,952	1,680	3,632	1	......	1	3,633	744	798	1,542	5,175
Montague	424	390	814	......	......	......	814	15	20	35	849
Montgomery	1,443	1,225	2,668	......	......	......	2,668	1,440	1,371	2,811	5,479
Nacogdoches	3,233	2,697	5,930	1	2	3	5,933	1,181	1,178	2,359	8,292
Navarro	2,233	1,872	4,105	......	1	1	4,106	951	939	1,890	5,996
Newton	1,095	1,011	2,106	......	......	......	2,106	510	503	1,013	3,119
Nueces	1,521	1,168	2,689	......	1	1	2,690	88	128	216	2,906
Orange	869	626	1,495	15	14	29	1,524	201	191	392	1,916
Palo Pinto	750	644	1,394	......	......	......	1,394	62	68	130	1,524
Panola	2,899	2,518	5,417	......	......	......	5,417	1,492	1,566	3,058	8,475
Parker	2,134	1,857	3,991	......	......	......	3,991	101	121	222	4,213
Polk	2,178	1,920	4,098	1	3	4	4,102	2,091	2,107	4,198	8,300
Presidio	436	138	574	......	2	2	576	1	3	4	580

TABLE No. 41.—*Population of the United States by Counties, &c.*—Continued.

STATE OF TEXAS.

COUNTIES.	WHITES.			FREE COLORED.			Total free.	SLAVES.			Agg'te population.
	Male.	Female.	Total.	Male.	Fem.	Total.		Male.	Female.	Total.	
Red River	2,929	2,562	5,491	2	3	5	5,496	1,508	1,531	3,039	8,535
Refugio	763	597	1,360	3	3	6	1,366	119	115	234	1,600
Robertson	1,490	1,249	2,739	.....	.....	......	2,739	1,150	1,108	2,258	4,997
Runnels	....	....	....	......	......	......	....	....	....	....	....
Rusk.............	5,198	4,472	9,670	1	......	1	9,671	3,086	3,046	6,132	15,803
Sabine	841	759	1,600	......	......	......	1,600	584	566	1,150	2,750
San Augustine....	1,255	1,122	2,377	......	......	......	2,377	830	887	1,717	4,094
San Patricio	295	230	525	......	......	......	525	45	50	95	620
San Saba.........	427	397	824	......	......	......	824	44	45	89	913
Shackleford	15	20	35	.....	......	......	35	2	7	9	44
Shelby	2,061	1,824	3,885	1	......	1	3,886	727	749	1,476	5,362
Smith	4,459	3,949	8,408	2	......	2	8,410	2,433	2,549	4,982	13,392
Starr..............	1,380	1,016	2,396	2	2	4	2,400	....	6	6	2,406
Tarrant	2,772	2,398	5,170	......	......	......	5,170	410	440	850	6,020
Taylor	....	....	....	......	......	......	....	....	....	....	....
Throckmorton	65	59	124	......	......	......	124	....	....	....	124
Titus.............	3,889	3,320	7,209	1	......	1	7,210	1,207	1,231	2,438	9,648
Travis	2,670	2,261	4,931	8	5	13	4,944	1,572	1,564	3,136	8,080
Trinity...........	1,823	1,609	3,432	1	......	1	3,433	491	468	959	4,392
Tyler	1,791	1,586	3,377	......	......	......	3,377	577	571	1,148	4,525
Upshur...........	3,713	3,138	6,851	......	......	......	6,851	1,891	1,903	3,794	10,645
Uvalde...........	290	189	479	......	......	......	479	13	14	27	506
Van Zandt	1,797	1,656	3,453	1	1	2	3,455	164	158	322	3,777
Victoria	1,490	1,267	2,757	1	......	1	2,758	716	697	1,413	4,171
Walker...........	2,302	1,754	4,056	......	......	......	4,056	2,107	2,028	4,135	8,191
Washington.......	3,992	3,279	7,271	2	1	3	7,274	4,019	3,922	7,941	15,215
Webb............	762	635	1,397	.....	......	.. ...	1,397	....	....	....	1,397
Wharton	369	277	646	......	......	......	646	1,406	1,328	2,734	3,380
Williamson.......	1,955	1,683	3,638	......	.....	......	3,638	440	451	891	4,529
Wise	1,599	1,432	3,031	......	1	1	3,032	57	71	128	3,160
Wood	2,098	1,865	3,963	......	......	......	3,963	502	503	1,005	4,968
Young	270	230	500	......	......	......	500	49	43	92	592
Zapata	665	583	1,248	......	.....	......	1,248	....	....	....	1,248
Zavola	16	10	26	......	......	......	26	....	....	....	26
Total........	228,797	192,497	421,294	181	174	355	421,649	91,189	91,377	182,566	604,215

NOTE.—403 Indians included in white population.

TABLE NO. 41.—*Population of the United States by Counties, &c.*—Continued.

STATE OF VERMONT.

COUNTIES.	WHITE.			FREE COLORED.			Aggregate population.
	Male.	Female.	Total.	Male.	Female.	Total.	
Addison	11,943	11,978	23,921	41	48	89	24,010
Bennington	9,795	9,550	19,345	50	41	91	19,436
Caledonia	10,866	10,818	21,684	12	12	24	21,708
Chittenden	13,948	14,124	28,072	54	45	99	28,171
Essex	3,088	2,698	5,786	....	....	....	5,786
Franklin	13,669	13,524	27,193	17	21	38	27,231
Grand Isle	2,175	2,096	4,271	3	2	5	4,276
Lamoille	6,201	6,109	12,310	....	1	1	12,311
Orange	12,755	12,676	25,431	11	13	24	25,455
Orleans	9,615	9,346	18,961	12	8	20	18,981
Rutland	18,267	17,539	35,806	78	62	140	35,946
Washington	14,028	13,567	27,595	10	7	17	27,612
Windham	13,573	13,376	26,949	21	12	33	26,982
Windsor	18,492	18,573	37,065	62	66	128	37,193
Total	158,415	155,974	314,389	371	338	709	315,098

NOTE—20 Indians included in white population.

STATE OF VIRGINIA.

COUNTIES.	WHITES.			FREE COLORED.			Total free.	SLAVES.			Agg'te population.
	Male.	Female.	Total.	Male.	Fem.	Total.		Male.	Female.	Total.	
Accomack	5,314	5,347	10,661	1,629	1,789	3,418	14,079	2,252	2,255	4,507	18,586
Albemarle	6,147	5,956	12,103	270	336	606	12,709	7,128	6,788	13,916	26,625
Alexandria	4,732	5,119	9,851	583	832	1,415	11,266	498	888	1,386	12,652
Alleghany	3,225	2,418	5,643	90	42	132	5,775	636	354	990	6,765
Amelia	1,461	1,436	2,897	90	99	189	3,086	3,808	3,847	7,655	10,741
Amherst	3,697	3,470	7,167	165	132	297	7,464	3,240	3,038	6,278	13,742
Appomattox	2,079	2,039	4,118	84	87	171	4,289	2,310	2,290	4,600	8,889
Augusta	10,880	10,667	21,547	276	310	586	22,133	2,851	2,765	5,616	27,749
Barbour	4,454	4,274	8,728	74	61	135	8,863	41	54	95	8,958
Bath	1,381	1,271	2,652	54	24	78	2,730	510	436	946	3,676
Bedford	7,236	7,152	14,388	264	240	504	14,892	5,245	4,931	10,176	25,068
Berkeley	5,299	5,290	10,589	134	152	286	10,875	766	884	1,650	12,525
Boone	2,448	2,233	4,681	......	1	1	4,682	69	89	158	4,840
Botetourt	4,117	4,324	8,441	144	162	306	8,747	1,414	1,355	2,769	11,516
Braxton	2,533	2,352	4,885	3	......	3	4,888	50	54	104	4,992
Brooke	2,707	2,718	5,425	24	27	51	5,476	6	12	18	5,494
Brunswick	2,459	2,533	4,992	333	338	671	5,663	4,576	4,570	9,146	14,809
Buchanan	1,439	1,323	2,762	1	......	1	2,763	11	19	30	2,793
Buckingham	2,985	3,056	6,041	183	177	360	6,401	4,499	4,312	8,811	15,212
Cabell	3,901	3,790	7,691	9	15	24	7,715	137	168	305	8,020
Calhoun	1,323	1,169	2,492	......	1	1	2,493	6	3	9	2,502
Campbell	6,967	6,621	13,588	487	542	1,029	14,617	6,055	5,525	11,580	26,197
Caroline	3,340	3,608	6,948	420	424	844	7,792	5,124	5,548	10,672	18,464
Carroll	3,858	3,861	7,719	15	16	31	7,750	119	143	262	8,012

TABLE No. 41.—*Population of the United States by Counties, &c.*—Continued.

STATE OF VIRGINIA.

COUNTIES.	WHITES.			FREE COLORED.			Total free.	SLAVES.			Agg'te popula-tion.
	Male.	Female.	Total.	Male.	Fem.	Total.		Male.	Female.	Total.	
Clay	924	837	1,761	3	2	5	1,766	10	11	21	1,787
Charles City....	931	875	1,806	417	439	856	2,662	1,549	1,398	2,947	5,609
Charlotte	2,524	2,457	4,981	128	124	252	5,233	4,746	4,492	9,238	14,471
Chesterfield	4,913	5,106	10,019	311	332	643	10,662	4,456	3,898	8,354	19,016
Clarke	1,851	1,856	3,707	37	27	64	3,771	1,803	1,572	3,375	7,146
Craig...........	1,564	1,539	3,103	15	15	30	3,133	217	203	420	3,553
Culpeper	2,410	2,549	4,959	210	219	429	5,388	3,396	3,279	6,675	12,063
Cumberland	1,508	1,438	2,946	142	168	310	3,256	3,522	3,183	6,705	9,961
Dinwiddie......	6,837	6,841	13,678	1,681	2,065	3,746	17,424	6,499	6,275	12,774	30,198
Doddridge	2,641	2,527	5,168	1	......	1	5,169	10	24	34	5,203
Elizabeth City..	1,755	1,425	3,180	100	101	201	3,381	1,236	1,181	2,417	5,798
Essex	1,626	1,670	3,296	234	243	477	3,773	3,346	3,350	6,696	10,469
Fairfax.........	4,167	3,879	8,046	354	318	672	8,718	1,516	1,600	3,116	11,834
Fauquier	5,125	5,305	10,430	409	412	821	11,251	5,180	5,275	10,455	21,706
Fayette	2,995	2,721	5,716	4	6	10	5,726	133	138	271	5,997
Floyd	3,821	3,924	7,745	9	7	16	7,761	223	252	475	8,236
Fluvanna.......	2,507	2,586	5,093	131	135	266	5,359	2,509	2,485	4,994	10,353
Franklin	6,791	6,851	13,642	50	55	105	13,747	3,082	3,269	6,351	20,098
Frederick	6,550	6,529	13,079	572	636	1,208	14,287	1,104	1,155	2,259	16,546
Gilmer	1,858	1,827	3,685	10	12	22	3,707	25	27	52	3,759
Giles...........	3,014	3,024	6,038	33	34	67	6,105	396	382	778	6,883
Gloucester......	2,301	2,216	4,517	356	347	703	5,220	2,834	2,902	5,736	10,956
Goochland......	1,870	1,944	3,814	334	369	703	4,517	3,200	2,939	6,139	10,656
Grayson........	3,823	3,830	7,653	20	32	52	7,705	263	284	547	8,252
Greenbrier......	5,509	4,991	10,500	117	69	186	10,686	783	742	1,525	12,211
Greenville......	972	1,002	1,974	120	113	233	2,207	2,082	2,085	4,167	6,374
Green	1,493	1,522	3,015	6	17	23	3,038	990	994	1,984	5,022
Halifax.........	5,498	5,562	11,060	271	292	563	11,623	7,582	7,315	14,897	26,520
Hampshire......	6,344	6,134	12,478	109	113	222	12,700	595	618	1,213	13,913
Hancock.......	2,253	2,189	4,442	......	1	1	4,443	....	2	2	4,445
Hardy..........	4,304	4,217	8,521	137	133	270	8,791	547	526	1,073	9,864
Hanover.......	3,724	3,758	7,482	131	126	257	7,739	4,702	4,781	9,483	17,222
Harrison.......	6,671	6,505	13,176	11	21	32	13,208	259	323	582	13,790
Henrico........	19,596	18,389	37,985	1,598	1,992	3,590	41,575	10,942	9,099	20,041	61,616
Henry...........	3,379	3,394	6,773	160	154	314	7,087	2,535	2,483	5,018	12,105
Highland.......	2,024	1,866	3,890	13	14	27	3,917	199	203	402	4,319
Isle of Wight....	2,510	2,527	5,037	640	730	1,370	6,407	1,780	1,790	3,570	9,977
Jackson	4,237	4,003	8,240	10	1	11	8,251	23	32	55	8,306
James City.....	1,088	1,079	2,167	479	566	1,045	3,212	1,318	1,268	2,586	5,798
Jefferson.......	5,061	5,003	10,064	236	275	511	10,575	2,049	1,911	3,960	14,535
Kanawha.......	7,084	6,701	13,785	91	90	181	13,966	1,234	950	2,184	16,150
King George....	1,161	1,349	2,510	193	195	388	2,898	1,810	1,863	3,673	6,571
King and Queen.	1,842	1,959	3,801	181	207	388	4,189	3,068	3,071	6,139	10,328
King William...	1,284	1,305	2,589	202	214	416	3,005	2,688	2,837	5,525	8,530
Lancaster	1,009	972	1,981	141	160	301	2,282	1,424	1,445	2,869	5,151
Lee............	5,051	5,144	10,195	8	5	13	10,208	392	432	824	11,032
Lewis..........	3,977	3,759	7,736	19	14	33	7,769	94	136	230	7,999
Logan..........	2,501	2,288	4,789	......	1	1	4,790	85	63	148	4,938
Loudon	7,426	7,595	15,021	592	660	1,252	16,273	2,770	2,731	5,501	21,774
Louisa.........	3,027	3,156	6,183	155	169	324	6,507	5,284	4,910	10,194	16,701
Lunenberg.	2,237	2,184	4,421	133	124	257	4,678	3,711	3,594	7,305	11,983

TABLE No. 41.—*Population of the United States by Counties, &c.*—Continued.

STATE OF VIRGINIA.

COUNTIES.	WHITES.			FREE COLORED.			Total free.	SLAVES.			Agg'te popula-tion.
	Male.	Female.	Total.	Male.	Fem.	Total.		Male.	Female.	Total.	
Madison	2,112	2,248	4,360	50	47	97	4,457	2,243	2,154	4,397	8,854
Marshall	6,641	6,270	12,911	21	36	57	12,968	15	14	29	12,997
Marion	6,350	6,306	12,656	1	2	3	12,659	28	35	63	12,722
Mason	4,556	4,194	8,750	26	21	47	8,797	159	217	376	9,173
Matthews	1,831	2,034	3,865	93	125	218	4,083	1,502	1,506	3,008	7,091
McDowell	774	761	1,535	......	......	......	1,535	......	......	......	1,535
Mecklenburg	3,384	3,394	6,778	456	442	898	7,676	6,417	6,003	12,420	20,096
Mercer	3,315	3,113	6,428	15	14	29	6,457	182	180	352	6,819
Middlesex	969	894	1,863	58	68	126	1,989	1,189	1,186	2,375	4,364
Montgomery	4,193	4,058	8,251	80	67	147	8,398	1,141	1,078	2,219	10,617
Monongalia	6,385	6,516	12,901	26	20	46	12,947	42	59	101	13,048
Monroe	4,826	4,710	9,536	44	63	107	9,643	573	541	1,114	10,757
Morgan	1,847	1,767	3,614	10	14	24	3,638	46	48	94	3,732
Nansemond	2,838	2,894	5,732	1,166	1,314	2,480	8,212	2,765	2,716	5,481	13,693
Nelson	3,360	3,289	6,649	60	68	128	6,777	3,200	3,038	6,238	13,015
New Kent	1,093	1,053	2,146	170	194	364	2,510	1,649	1,725	3,374	5,884
Nicholas	2,349	2,122	4,471	2	......	2	4,473	82	72	154	4,627
Norfolk	12,091	12,329	24,420	1,222	1,581	2,803	27,223	4,346	4,658	9,004	36,227
Northampton	1,493	1,505	2,998	472	490	962	3,960	1,980	1,892	3,872	7,832
Northumberland	1,873	1,997	3,870	115	107	222	4,092	1,664	1,775	3,439	7,531
Nottoway	1,156	1,114	2,270	47	51	98	2,368	3,242	3,226	6,468	8,836
Ohio	10,990	11,206	22,196	59	67	126	22,322	42	58	100	22,422
Orange	2,299	2,254	4,553	107	80	187	4,740	3,095	3,016	6,111	10,851
Page	3,424	3,451	6,875	186	198	384	7,259	400	450	850	8,109
Patrick	3,603	3,555	7,158	59	72	131	7,289	969	1,101	2,070	9,359
Pendleton	2,957	2,913	5,870	20	30	50	5,920	119	125	244	6,164
Pittsylvania	8,619	8,486	17,105	324	335	659	17,764	7,403	6,937	14,340	32,104
Pleasants	1,503	1,422	2,925	3	2	5	2,930	8	7	15	2,945
Pocahontas	1,887	1,799	3,686	14	6	20	3,706	137	115	252	3,958
Powhatan	1,272	1,308	2,580	204	205	409	2,989	2,815	2,588	5,403	8,392
Preston	6,787	6,413	13,200	28	17	45	13,245	31	36	67	13,312
Prince Edward	2,055	1,982	4,037	233	233	466	4,503	3,869	3,472	7,341	11,844
Prince George	1,463	1,436	2,899	268	247	515	3,414	2,652	2,345	4,997	8,411
Prince William	2,826	2,864	5,690	254	265	519	6,209	1,163	1,193	2,356	8,565
Princess Anne	2,226	2,107	4,333	103	92	195	4,528	1,646	1,540	3,186	7,714
Pulaski	1,907	1,907	3,814	11	2	13	3,827	806	783	1,589	5,416
Putnam	2,875	2,833	5,708	5	8	13	5,721	281	299	580	6,301
Raleigh	1,672	1,619	3,291	13	6	19	3,310	28	29	57	3,367
Randolph	2,498	2,295	4,793	7	7	14	4,807	88	95	183	4,990
Rappahannock	2,547	2,471	5,018	150	162	312	5,330	1,769	1,751	3,520	8,850
Richmond	1,833	1,737	3,570	410	410	820	4,390	1,237	1,229	2,466	6,856
Rockingham	10,299	10,190	20,489	254	278	532	21,021	1,143	1,244	2,387	23,408
Ritchie	3,528	3,281	6,809	......	......	......	6,809	13	25	38	6,847
Roane	2,722	2,585	5,307	......	2	2	5,309	34	38	72	5,381
Roanoke	2,717	2,533	5,250	78	77	155	5,405	1,378	1,265	2,643	8,048
Rockbridge	6,640	6,201	12,841	241	181	422	13,263	2,142	1,843	3,985	17,248
Russell	4,616	4,514	9,130	20	31	51	9,181	550	549	1,099	10,280
Scott	5,748	5,782	11,530	28	24	52	11,582	252	238	490	12,072
Shenandoah	6,394	6,433	12,827	157	159	316	13,143	378	375	753	13,896
Smyth	3,913	3,819	7,732	85	98	183	7,915	556	481	1,037	8,952
Southampton	2,790	2,923	5,713	836	958	1,794	7,507	2,821	2,587	5,408	12,915

TABLE No. 41.—*Population of the United States by Counties, &c.*—Continued.

STATE OF VIRGINIA.

COUNTIES.	WHITES.			FREE COLORED.			Total free.	SLAVES.			Agg'te popula-tion.
	Male.	Female.	Total.	Male.	Fem.	Total.		Male.	Female.	Total.	
Spottsylvania...	3,725	3,991	7,716	244	330	574	8,290	3,713	4,073	7,786	16,076
Stafford	2,423	2,494	4,922	152	167	319	5,241	1,649	1,665	3,314	8,555
Sussex.........	1,542	1,576	3,118	368	305	673	3,791	3,279	3,105	6,384	10,175
Surrey.........	1,151	1,183	2,334	608	676	1,284	3,618	1,365	1,150	2,515	6,133
Taylor.........	3,717	3,583	7,300	31	20	51	7,351	47	65	112	7,463
Tazewell.......	4,355	4,270	8,625	55	38	93	8,718	612	590	1,202	9,920
Tucker.........	718	674	1,392	8	8	16	1,408	10	10	20	1,428
Tyler	3,334	3,154	6,488	4	7	11	6,499	7	11	18	6,517
Upshur.........	3,637	3,427	7,064	9	7	16	7,080	103	109	212	7,292
Warwick........	340	322	662	31	28	59	721	577	442	1,019	1,740
Warren.........	2,297	2,286	4,583	144	140	284	4,867	795	780	1,575	6,442
Washington.....	7,104	6,992	14,096	126	123	249	14,345	1,331	1,216	2,547	16,891
Wayne..........	3,521	3,083	6,604	......	......	......	6,604	58	85	143	6,747
Webster........	833	719	1,552	......	......	......	1,552	1	2	3	1,555
Westmoreland...	1,721	1,666	3,387	524	667	1,191	4,578	1,822	1,882	3,704	8,282
Wetzel.........	3,408	3,283	6,691	1	1	2	6,693	3	7	10	6,703
Wood	5,624	5,167	10,791	36	43	79	10,870	85	91	176	11,046
Wirt...........	1,921	1,807	3,728	......	......	......	3,728	9	14	23	3,751
Wise...........	2,224	2,192	4,416	16	10	26	4,442	30	36	66	4,508
Wyoming........	1,446	1,349	2,795	1	1	2	2,797	35	29	64	2,861
Wythe..........	5,045	4,941	9,986	76	81	157	10,143	1,104	1,058	2,162	12,305
York...........	1,210	1,132	2,342	350	332	682	3,024	1,006	919	1,925	4,949
Total........	528,897	518,514	1,047,411	27,721	30,321	58,042	1,105,453	249,483	241,382	490,865	1,596,318

NOTE.—112 Indians included in white population.

STATE OF WISCONSIN.

COUNTIES.	WHITES.			FREE COLORED.			Aggregate popula-tion.
	Male.	Female.	Total.	Male.	Female.	Total.	
Adams	3,402	3,070	6,472	11	9	20	6,492
Ashland	273	242	515	....	....	....	515
Bad Ax................	5,815	5,153	10,968	24	15	39	11,007
Brown	6,149	5,626	11,775	10	10	20	11,795
Buffalo	2,157	1,707	3,864	....	....	....	3,864
Burnette	7	5	12	....	....	....	12
Calumet	4,096	3,799	7,895	....	....	....	7,895
Chippewa	1,172	723	1,895	....	....	....	1,895
Clark	471	318	789	....	....	....	789
Columbia..............	12,772	11,649	24,421	12	8	20	24,441
Crawford	4,236	3,804	8,040	14	14	28	8,068
Dallas	8	5	13	....	....	....	13
Dane	23,151	20,699	43,850	34	38	72	43,922
Dodge	22,534	20,265	42,799	14	5	19	42,818
Door	1,659	1,288	2,947	1	....	1	2,948
Douglas	431	377	808	2	2	4	812
Dunn..................	1,678	1,008	2,686	9	9	18	2,704

TABLE No. 41.—*Population of the United States by Counties, &c.*—Continued.

STATE OF WISCONSIN.

COUNTIES.	WHITES.			FREE COLORED.			Aggregate population.
	Male.	Female.	Total.	Male.	Female.	Total.	
Eau Claire	1,834	1,319	3,153	6	3	9	3,162
Fond du Lac	17,843	16,252	34,095	28	31	59	34,154
Grant	16,548	14,606	31,154	21	14	35	31,189
Green	10,397	9,411	19,808	....	....	....	19,808
Green Lake	6,531	6,101	12,632	23	8	31	12,663
Iowa	9,919	9,025	18,944	14	9	23	18,967
Jackson	2,301	1,865	4,166	3	1	4	4,170
Jefferson	15,621	14,812	30,433	3	2	5	30,438
Juneau	4,605	4,164	8,769	1	....	1	8,770
Kenosha	7,305	6,567	13,872	17	11	28	13,900
Kewaunee	2,993	2,537	5,530	....	....	....	5,530
Lacrosse	6,599	5,550	12,149	19	18	37	12,186
Lafayette	9,617	8,491	18,108	13	13	26	18,134
La Pointe	203	149	352	1	....	1	353
Manitowoc	11,631	10,781	22,412	2	2	4	22,416
Marathon	1,624	1,258	2,892	....	....	....	2,892
Marquette	4,381	3,852	8,233	....	....	....	8,233
Milwaukie	31,452	30,959	62,411	54	53	107	62,518
Monroe	4,496	3,911	8,407	2	1	3	8,410
Oconto	2,221	1,344	3,565	18	9	27	3,592
Outagamie	5,036	4,541	9,577	6	4	10	9,587
Ozaukee	8,119	7,563	15,682	....	....	....	15,682
Pepin	1,341	1,051	2,392	....	....	....	2,392
Pierce	2,572	2,067	4,639	16	17	33	4,672
Polk	767	633	1,400	....	....	....	1,400
Portage	4,017	3,483	7,500	2	5	7	7,507
Racine	11,069	10,156	21,225	88	47	135	21,360
Richland	5,118	4,605	9,723	5	4	9	9,732
Rock	19,133	17,464	36,597	57	36	93	36,690
Saint Croix	2,893	2,497	5,390	....	2	2	5,392
Sauk	9,830	9,097	18,927	20	16	36	18,963
Shawano	441	341	782	22	25	47	829
Sheboygan	13,849	13,021	26,870	2	3	5	26,875
Trempeleau	1,397	1,162	2,559	....	1	1	2,560
Walworth	13,629	12,807	26,436	29	31	60	26,496
Washington	12,401	11,221	23,622	....	....	....	23,622
Waukesha	14,035	12,762	26,797	19	15	34	26,831
Waupaca	4,659	4,191	8,850	1	....	1	8,851
Waushara	4,555	4,211	8,766	1	3	4	8,770
Winnebago	12,368	11,350	23,718	28	24	52	23,770
Wood	1,425	999	2,424	1	....	1	2,425
Total	406,796	367,914	774,710	653	518	1,171	775,881

NOTE.—613 Indians included in white population.

TABLE No. 41.—*Population of the United States by Counties, &c.*—Continued.

TERRITORY OF COLORADO.

	WHITES.			FREE COLORED.			Aggregate population.
	Male.	Female.	Total.	Male.	Female.	Total.	
Total in Territory	32,654	1,577	34,231	37	9	46	34,277

TERRITORY OF DAKOTA.

	WHITES.			INDIANS.			Aggregate population.
	Male.	Female.	Total.	Male.	Female.	Total.	
Total in Territory	1,592	984	2,576	1,205	1,056	2,261	4,837

DISTRICT OF COLUMBIA.

SUBDIVISIONS.	WHITES.			FREE COLORED.			Total free.	SLAVES.			Agg'te population.
	Male.	Female.	Total.	Male.	Female.	Total.		Male.	Fem.	Total.	
Georgetown	3,234	3,564	6,798	554	804	1,358	8,156	199	378	577	8,733
Washington city	24,323	25,816	50,139	3,858	5,351	9,209	59,348	574	1,200	1,774	61,122
Remainder of Dist.	2,028	1,799	3,827	290	274	564	4,391	439	395	834	5,225
Total	29,585	31,179	60,764	4,702	6,429	11,131	71,895	1,212	1,973	3,185	75,080

NOTE.—1 Indian included in white population.

TERRITORY OF NEVADA.

COUNTIES.	WHITES.			FREE COLORED.			Aggregate population.
	Male.	Female.	Total.	Male.	Female.	Total.	
Carson	5,957	710	6,667	35	10	45	6,712
Humboldt	40	....	40	....	....	....	40
Saint Mary's	105	....	105	....	....	....	105
Total	6,102	710	6,812	35	10	45	6,857

TABLE No. 41.—*Population of the United States by Counties, &c.*—Continued.

TERRITORY OF NEBRASKA.

COUNTIES.	WHITES.			FREE COLORED.			INDIANS.			Total free.	SLAVES.			Aggregate population.
	Male.	Fem.	Total.	M.	F.	Tot'l	M.	F.	Tot'l		M.	F.	Tot'l	
Buffalo	66	48	114	....	....	....	....	....	....	114	....	....	....	114
Burt	215	173	388	....	....	....	....	....	....	388	....	....	....	388
Butler	19	8	27	....	....	....	....	....	....	27	....	..	....	27
Calhoun	24	17	41	..	....	....	....	....	....	41	....	....	....	41
Cass	1,839	1,530	3,369	...	....	....	....	....	....	3,369	....	....	....	3,369
Cedar	142	101	243	2	1	3	....	....	....	246	....	....	....	246
Clay	99	66	165	....	....	....	....	....	....	165	....	....	....	165
Cuming	40	27	67	....	....	....	....	....	....	67	....	....	....	67
Dakota	464	342	806	6	7	13	....	....	....	819	....	....	....	819
Dawson	14	2	16	....	....	....	....	....	....	16	....	....	....	16
Dixon	134	113	247	....	....	....	....	....	....	247	....	....	....	247
Dodge	184	125	309	....	....	....	....	....	....	309	....	....	....	309
Douglas	2,252	2,053	4,305	13	8	21	1	1	2	4,328	....	....	....	4,328
Fort Randall	298	53	351	1	1	2	....	....	....	353	....	....	....	353
Gage	258	163	421	....	....	....	....	....	....	421	....	....	....	421
Green	6	10	16	....	....	....	....	....	....	16	....	....	....	16
Hall	73	43	116	....	....	....	....	....	....	116	....	....	....	116
Johnson	282	246	528	....	....	....	....	....	....	528	....	....	....	528
Jones	77	45	122	....	....	....	....	....	...	122	....	....	....	122
Kerney	372	93	465	2	2	4	....	....	....	469	2	3	5	474
Lancaster	85	68	153	....	....	....	....	....	....	153	...	....	....	153
L'Eau Qui Court	104	31	135	7	7	14	....	3	3	152	....	....	....	152
Merick	79	28	107	....	..	....	2	....	2	109	....	....	....	109
Nemeha	1,704	1,393	3,097	1	4	5	20	17	37	3,139	....	....	....	3,139
Nucolls	15	7	22	....	....	....	....	....	....	22	....	....	....	22
Otoe	2,402	1,792	4,194	2	2	4	2	1	3	4,201	4	6	10	4,211
Pawnee	470	412	882	....	....	....	....	....	....	882	....	....	....	882
Platte } Madison }	441	334	775	....	....	....	3	4	7	782	....	....	....	782
Polk	15	4	19	....	....	....	....	....	....	19	....	....	....	19
Richardson	1,560	1,274	2,834	1	...	1	....	....	....	2,835	..	....	....	2,835
Salino	26	13	39	....	....	....	....	....	....	39	....	....	....	39
Sarpy	677	522	1,199	....	....	....	1	1	2	1,201	....	....	....	1,201
Shorter	97	17	114	....	....	....	....	3	3	117	....	....	....	117
Washington	688	561	1,249	....	....	....	....	....	...	1,249	....	...	...	1,249
All that portion north of latitude 40° and west of longitude 103°; also, that portion bounded north by latitude 42°, east by longitude 101° 30′, south by latitude 40°, and west by longitude 103°	1,468	293	1,761	...	....	...	1	3	4	1,765	....	....	....	1,765
Total	16,689	12,007	28,696	35	32	67	30	33	63	28,826	6	9	15	28,841

TABLE No. 41.—*Population of the United States by Counties, &c.*—Continued.

TERRITORY OF NEW MEXICO.

COUNTIES.	WHITES.			FREE COLORED.			INDIANS.			Aggregate population.
	Male.	Female.	Total.	Male.	Fem.	Total.	Male.	Female.	Total.	
Arizona	1,678	743	2,421	15	6	21	2,102	1,938	4,040	6,482
Bernalillo	4,716	3,858	8,574	6	3	9	50	136	186	8,769
Dona Anna	3,481	2,758	6,239	......	......	......	....	....	....	6,239
Mora	2,846	2,678	5,524	8	6	14	12	16	28	5,566
Rio Ariba	4,738	4,591	9,329	......	......	......	279	241	520	9,849
Santa Ana	793	712	1,505	......	......	......	1,103	964	2,067	3,572
Santa Fé	4,068	3,964	8,032	13	14	27	15	40	55	8,114
San Miguel	7,355	6,315	13,670	1	......	1	13	30	43	13,714
Socorro	2,947	2,759	5,706	......	6	6	25	50	75	5,787
Taos	6,765	6,714	13,479	2	5	7	293	324	617	14,103
Valencia	4,312	4,188	8,500	......	......	......	1,455	1,366	2,821	11,321
Total	43,699	39,280	82,979	45	40	85	5,347	5,105	10,452	93,516

TERRITORY OF UTAH.

COUNTIES.	WHITES.			FREE COLORED.			INDIANS.			Total free.	SLAVES.			Agg'te population.
	Male.	Fem.	Total.	M.	F.	Tot'l.	M.	F.	Tot'l.		M.	F.	Tot'l.	
Beaver	408	377	785	....	....	.....	....	....	.....	785	....	....	.....	785
Box Elder	809	799	1,608	....	....	.....	....	....	.....	1,608	....	....	.....	1,608
Cache	1,308	1,293	2,601	....	...	.....	4	....	4	2,605	....	....	.....	2,605
Cedar	387	351	741	....	....	.....	....	....	.....	741	....	....	.....	741
Davis	1,425	1,461	2,886	....	....	.....	4	4	8	2,894	6	4	10	2,904
Desert	......	......	......	....	....	.....	....	...	.....	......	....	....	.....	......
Greasewood	......	......	......	....	....	.....	....	....	.....	......	....	....	.....	......
Green River	94	39	133	....	....	.....	....	8	8	141	....	....	.....	141
Iron	513	497	1,010	....	....	.....	....	....	.....	1,010	....	....	.....	1,010
Juab	330	342	672	....	....	.....	....	....	.....	672	....	....	.....	672
Millard	386	329	715	....	....	.....	....	....	.....	715	....	....	.....	715
Salt Lake	5,467	5,733	11,200	12	14	26	27	23	50	11,276	12	7	19	11,295
Sampeto	1,965	1,841	3,806	...	....	.....	5	4	9	3,815	....	....	.....	3,815
Shambip	91	71	162	....	....	.....	....	....	.....	162	....	....	.....	162
Summit	102	96	198	...	....	.....	....	....	.....	198	.. .	....	.....	198
Tooele	518	482	1,000	....	....	.....	5	3	8	1,008	....	....	.....	1,008
Utah	4,208	4,035	8,243	1	3	4	1	....	1	8,248	....	....	.....	8,248
Walade	......	......	......	....	....	.....	....	...	.....	......	....	....	.....	......
Washington	360	331	691	....	....	.....	....	....	.....	691	....	....	.....	691
Weber	1,807	1,867	3,674	....	....	.....	....	1	1	3,675	....	....	.....	3,675
County east Wasatch mountains	......	......	......	....	.. .	.....	....	....	.....	......	....	....	.....	......
Total	20,178	19,947	40,125	13	17	30	46	43	89	40,244	18	11	29	40,273

TABLE No. 41.—*Population of the United States by Counties, &c.*—Continued.

TERRITORY OF WASHINGTON.

COUNTIES.	WHITES.			FREE COLORED.			INDIANS.			Agg'te population.
	Male.	Female.	Total.	Male.	Fem.	Total.	Male.	Female.	Total.	
Chihalis	201	82	283				1	1	2	285
Clallam	132	17	149							149
Clark	1,625	742	2,367	1		1	4	12	16	2,384
Cowlitz	256	149	405					1	1	406
Island	212	80	292				2		2	294
Jefferson	430	93	523	7	1	8				531
King	221	80	301	1		1				302
Kitsap	474	66	540	4		4				544
Klikatat	155	75	230							230
Lewis	219	117	336	1		1	25	22	47	384
Pacific	265	141	406				1	13	14	420
Pierce	806	308	1,114					1	1	1,115
Suwamish	123	39	162							162
Sukamania	108	63	171					2	2	173
Spokane	643	31	674	1	1	2	162	158	320	996
Thurston	976	519	1,495	10	2	12				1,507
Walla-Walla	1,028	269	1,297	1		1		20	20	1,318
Wahkiakum	33	8	41					1	1	42
Whatcom	318	34	352							352
Total	8,225	2,913	11,138	26	4	30	195	231	426	11,594

NOTE.

The suggestion of any supposed error in figures or in the orthography of places, will be thankfully received by the Superintendent of Census, who may be addressed through the mail free of postage.

www.ingramcontent.com/pod-product-compliance
Lightning Source LLC
LaVergne TN
LVHW020239110826
845151LV00003B/972

* 9 7 8 1 4 2 5 5 3 0 3 7 2 *